DELINQUENCY AND JUSTICE

SECOND EDITION

William E. Thornton, Jr.
LOYOLA UNIVERSITY

Lydia Voigt
LOYOLA UNIVERSITY

William G. Doerner
FLORIDA STATE UNIVERSITY

RANDOM HOUSE
NEW YORK

Acknowledgments for copyrighted material and credits for the photographs are included in the Acknowledgments section on pp. 503–504. These pages are an extension of the copyright page.

Library of Congress Cataloging-in-Publication Data

Thornton, William E., 1946–
 Delinquency and justice.

 Bibliography: p.
 Includes index.
 1. Juvenile delinquency—United States.   2. Juvenile justice, Administration of—United States.   3. Juvenile corrections—United States.   I. Voigt, Lydia.   1946–
 II. Doerner, William G., 1949–   .   III. Title.
 HV9104.T48   1987   364.3'6'0973   86-15448
 ISBN 0-394-34741-2

Manufactured in the United States of America

Cover photo: Charles Harbutt/Archive
Book Design: Glen M. Edelstein
Cover Design: Marsha Cohen

To Tanya, Karl, Baxter, and Koshka

PREFACE

Delinquency and Justice is an introductory text designed to provide students with an overview of the extent, causes, nature, and control of juvenile delinquency in the United States. However, the text is intended to furnish more than just a survey of the theory and research in the field of delinquency. Critical analysis of the major theories of delinquency and delinquency control programs is intended to provoke thought, discussion, and debate among students, academics, and those who work with delinquents. The second edition of the book, we think, reflects the "state of the art" in the study of juvenile delinquency. Several new chapters have been added, reflecting areas usually neglected in introductory delinquency texts: (1) adolescence and delinquency, (2) cross-cultural delinquency, (3) conflict and radical theories and delinquency, (4) and media and delinquency.

This book is unique because it takes a sociological perspective on the nature and causes of delinquency; yet it provides an in-depth account of the actual operation of the juvenile justice system. The backgrounds of the authors yield the book's orientation toward both sociological and criminal justice perspectives on delinquency. Although formally trained as sociologists, each of the authors has had practical experience with the day-to-day workings of the juvenile justice system. This experience includes work with police, correctional, and diversionary agencies. Two of the authors engage in family counseling and continue to work closely with juvenile justice agents.

Although primarily sociological in orientation, the book views delinquency as a complex and multifaceted phenomenon. It discusses theories about the causes of delinquency from biological and psychological as well as sociological points of view. It also examines a diverse range of proposed solutions to the problem of delinquency.

The book is intended for use at the undergraduate level. It therefore presents delinquency theory and research in a clear, precise fashion. To help students understand the material, the text makes use of several teaching aids. Each chapter begins with an outline and includes numerous examples, case histories, charts, and other visual aids. And each chapter concludes with a detailed summary, and review questions. Included at the end of the book are abstracts of leading cases that affect juvenile law and procedure and an extensive glossary of key terms used throughout the book. An instructor's manual is also available.

Part 1 of the text explores the origin of the concept of delinquency and discusses how the term is defined and applied today. The special period of youth called *adolescence* is examined in a separate chapter as a period between childhood and adulthood, in which the individual experiences rapid physical and psychological growth. These changes have often been linked with various aspects of juvenile delinquency. Part One also examines the extent of delinquency in the United States. It uses a concise historical review to explain the development of the concept of delinquency in the United States. Official, self-report, and victimization studies are included, and the strengths and weaknesses of each of the measures are critically evaluated. A new section is devoted to cohort analyses in an effort to understand career delinquency patterns.

Part 2 discusses theories of delinquency causation. Separate chapters are devoted to biological, psychological, and sociological theories of delinquency. Relevant historical and contemporary research in each of these disciplines is presented and criticized. Sociological theories of delinquency are treated in three separate chapters. The classical chapter examines and evaluates early explanations for the causes of delinquency. The contemporary chapter discusses social control, labeling, and phenomenological theories of delinquent behavior. The third chapter in this section is devoted to conflict and radical explanations of crime and delinquency.

Part 3 focuses on the social institutions of the family and school as dynamic entities that are undergoing vast changes which have implications for delinquency prevention and control. Individual chapters are devoted to each of these social institutions. A separate chapter is devoted to the influence of peers on delinquent behaviors. A new chapter examines the role of the mass media and its relationship to juvenile delinquency. The final chapter in this section examines the drugs and delinquency connection, concentrating on the parameters of adolescent drug use with special emphasis on the drug subculture.

Part 4 focuses on four components of the juvenile justice system: the police, juvenile law, the juvenile court, and juvenile corrections. The implications of police decision making, the importance of police discretion, and juvenile police procedures are explored in detail in the chapter on the police. Current juvenile law is given special attention in the following chapter. Since case law relating to the actions of the juvenile court is a relatively new area, special attention has been devoted to those laws pertaining to the constitutional rights of juveniles coming into contact with the juvenile justice system.

Both traditional juvenile corrections and the new field of community corrections are reviewed in Part 4. Given the current disenchantment with long-term incarceration, it is especially important to have a firm grasp of the issues involved in attempting to rehabilitate juvenile offenders through confinement. Therefore, Part 4 examines the types of juvenile correctional facilities, their goals, and the characterisitics of inmates. A critical review of treatment strategies employed in these facilities provides a multidisciplinary view of juvenile corrections. The current state of community corrections is also presented. Juvenile diversionary programs and community-based correctional programs are described.

The final section of the book explores the cross-cultural dynamics of youth crime in other countries and also attempts to chart the course of American delinquency in the future. American criminologists have recently become interested in the cross-cultural dynamics of youth crime. The research methods employed in the study of cross-cultural delinquency are examined and applied to several countries. The summary chapter of the book relates changes in the position of children in the United States to likely changes in the nature of delinquency. It also reviews current themes in delinquency prevention and control that are especially likely to influence juvenile justice. Finally, it examines the future direction of the juvenile justice system within the framework of past and future federal policy and the work of juvenile justice standards committees.

The completion of a text involves the efforts of many people. The authors would like to note the support given by Random House in the production of this second edition. Special thanks go to Bertrand Lummus and Lisa Moore for their advice and guidance on the project. We also wish to thank Professor Benedict Alper for his excellent foreword to the book. Professor Alper is indeed an influential scholar and practitioner in the field of juvenile delinquency. A note of thanks is also due Karen Reddinger and Daisy Galon for their skills in editing and word processing which made the book both readable and correct. Our thanks also extend to the many reviewers for their criticisms and suggestions.

William E. Thornton, Jr.
Lydia Voigt
William G. Doerner

CONTENTS

INTRODUCTION

Benedict S. Alper
Visiting Professor of Criminology
Boston College

Young people and their problems had long been an area of personal and professional interest for me. Adolescents have never found it easy to mature to adulthood—the process is especially troublesome in Western societies; the tumult and confusion of today makes the progression more difficult, even hazardous, now. I had personal testimony of the truth of this, having long suspected that my interest in delinquency stemmed from my own troubled teens and the help and guidance I received from a special mentor at a critical period during those years.

Deciphered Sumerian tablets (only recently has a dictionary of that ancient language been compiled) record the rebuke of a father to his son: "Where have you been?" "Why do you not respect your teachers and your parents?" Socrates went to his death partly because of his interventions in behalf of youth who plagued their elders. The moons of Saturn defied their father so that in the end he consumed them; Oedipus slew his father and sired his own half-brother.

So this is no new phenomenon that is treated in this book. The historic response, which has not changed basically in all these millennia, springs from the very simple notion that children are the property of their parents—particularly of their fathers—and, like women and domestic animals, are common chattels. So it is completely understandable that until very recently, the idea of childrens' rights—like women's rights—simply did not exist.

The result has been, and still is, that when children do not toe the mark or when they seek to work out their destinies according to their own lights, they are met with opposition which, when it is deemed necessary, in the last resort is all too often expressed in physical terms and by means of the application of force. Those children who fall into the juvenile justice net are, by and large, the result of the failure of society—the education system, the welfare system, the health system, the work system—to deal adequately with them.

Measures for dealing with these young people are extensively and clearly set out in the text. The contributors have wisely decided to enhance the original edition with several new chapters, three of which I have chosen to comment upon, by reason of their special relevance.

"Adolescence and Delinquency" (Chapter 2) sets forth a faithful view of the history of the development of the concept of adolescence itself. Its relevance lies in the fact, one of the few indisputable postulates that criminology has developed, that the earlier the onset of criminal behavior, the greater the likelihood of its continuance into adulthood. The significance of this finding can only be disregarded at our peril. The staggering increase in delinquency rates, doubling in fifteen years—despite some minor decreases (as Chapter 3 points out), can only imply a subsequent increase in adult offenses as the juvenile delinquents of today mature into the adult offenders of tomorrow.

Another noteworthy finding with regard to the volume of juvenile offenders is that self-report surveys indicate that delinquent acts are by no means the monopoly or even the characteristic of any single class, sex, ethnic group, or residential area. No more striking evidence of the basic lawlessness of contemporary life can be adduced than that the overwhelming majority of our young people admit to having committed offenses for which they could have been arrested had a police officer been present. College students in my classes freely maintain in anonymous questionnaires that same high percentage of antisocial conduct. If this be so, then who is deviant?

What happens to these young people who so readily admit to lawlessness depends, as this text describes, on the race and class of the offender. The well-to-do white teenage shoplifter who steals for "kicks" is more likely to be brought home by the police to be rebuked by parents. Seldom does such good fortune await fatherless black children from a housing project. The result for them, all too often, is the affixing of a label on the apprehended offender that is not easily sloughed off. It is in this sense that much of today's "delinquency" may be said to be a "legal creation as a deviant role for children," in the words of a recent article by Professor John Sutton of Princeton.

Two characteristic attributes of youth are their vulnerability and their enormous potential for growth and development. The first makes them dependent on others for material and emotional support; the second can—at its best—challenge the world to provide the appropriate trellis on which to cling and flower.

The word "suffer" has always appealed to me as one peculiarly applicable to children and youth because of its many different significances. When Christ said "Suffer little children to come unto me" he meant, I believe, that children were a precious asset to be nurtured and loved. Children can also be "suffered" in the sense of being endured, which is the least damaging course of treatment to which they can be subjected. And then there is the third meaning—the passive form, the kind of cruelty and abuse young people are forced to suffer literally and most painfully. In the chapter on the institutional setting, the authors correctly point out that current institutions for juveniles are, in Goffman's term, total. Inmates are treated with regimentation, isolation, and brutality all largely undiminished since the first places of confinement for children—apart from adults— were introduced into the United States 150 years ago. Anyone seeking a true and detailed description of the conditions under which committed children suffer today has only to dip into Kenneth Wooden's "Weeping in the Playtime of Others" to be shocked into the realization that child abuse is not merely a one-to-one experience between parents and other adults and their young victims.

It is, in fact, not going too far to say that at this moment in this country our young are experiencing a national campaign of child abuse. It is not enough that we are the only country in the world that has no system of children's allowances paid, regardless of need, to families for their support. Of 130 countries reporting to the International Labor Organisation, we hold that singular honor.

This is only the negative aspect. For the rest, the statistics of what is being done or not done to and for our oncoming generation abound with frightening consistency: high school dropout rates of close to 50 percent in some of our large cities; a million or so teenage pregnancies; runaways in excess of a million annually; lost and kidnapped children in such numbers that our Department of Justice has just created a special agency to deal with this tragic problem. The exploitation of children for pornography has become a national scandal.

Funds for education, for maternal nutrition, for health care for the poor, for aid to dependent children, for school lunches, for vaccination against preventable childhood diseases fall under the axe in favor of escalating appropriations for even more deadly weapons to be launched from land, sea, and now—the sky. The net effect of this misappropriation of our common wealth is not lost on the young. They pay for it not only in their physical well-being and their lack of preparation for their future as functioning and productive adults, but—and perhaps more important—in their emotional life.

Erik Erikson has said that hope is the basic attribute of being alive. Our young freely express their concern that they may yet be the last generation upon this green earth. A precise causal connection cannot, of course, be postulated between what Harvard psychiatrist Dr. Margaret Brenham-Gibson has described as "despair— from the French 'loss of hope,' which springs from the knowledge that life is bounded at the beginning and the end by non-life." If college students in conversations can articulate their profound concern for their individual futures because they cannot see clearly the future of their world, it is no wonder that they find difficulty establishing significant relationships with the adult world, and so turn increasingly to their peers for support and understanding to help them find some antidote to offset their "lack of security about whether there will be a future," again in the words of Dr. Brenham-Gibson.

In the early years of the antiwar and antinuclear movements in this country, a group on the West Coast originated the slogan "War is unhealthy for children and other living things." Today the effects of the threat of war can be said to be no less unhealthy for their emotional and moral development.

Chapter 12, "Mass Media and Delinquency," sets forth the influences of print, radio, and television on the attitudes and actions of the young. The office of the Surgeon General of the United States issued its monumental report on television eleven years ago. This past year a new study by the National Institute of Mental Health comes to the same conclusion: that violence on television leads to aggressive behavior by youths. The evidence is overwhelming, states the NIH report, that children's programs are "dominated by action, power and danger . . . there is an average of five violent acts per hour on prime time and 18 acts per hour on children's weekend programs."

It is difficult to counter the argument that if advertisers consider the TV screen to be an effective persuader of the viewing audience to purchase their goods or services, and are willing to pay enormous sums for fractions of a minute to promote these, the messages of violence and brutality contained in the nonadvertising portions of a television broadcast can be expected to be equally persuasive influences—especially on young, impressionable audiences.

Most recently (March 1984) the Surgeon General's office warns that watching rock and roll videocassettes may cause difficulty in establishing satisfactory relations with the opposite sex: "Many rock programs have a dangerous combination of pornography and violence." A veteran radio critic, journalist, and commentator stated in a speech before a university audience (April 1984): "The pop culture strikes the young at their most impressionable years, when their potential for learning, for appreciation, for discrimination should be developed."

I cannot recall who it was who said, "Let me write a country's music and I do not care who writes its laws." This takes on real significance for anyone who can subject himself to the deafening decibels of the music young people flock to listen to. The themes conduce to license, to preoccupation with self, to violence. Which of the popular rock stars is it who bites off the heads of live birds during his public performances? Whence comes this unfeeling attitude toward living things; what has happened to what was called, once upon a time, "the sanctity of life"? I submit that it is the quite natural and even inevitably resulting effect of the example set in the conduct of affairs at both the domestic and the international level.

When, for whatever reason, national leadership cannot—or will not—set out to resolve the basic social and economic problems which beset its citizens, it turns to force and to violence as alternative measures. How did the State of New York come to grips with the complaint of the prisoners in Attica that they be permitted more than one shower a week; how did it react to their plea that they "be treated like human beings"? The response was to mow down two score of them with National Guard bullets, since which time it is reported that conditions in Attica have worsened. Demands for equal rights and opportunities by minority group members are confronted by the forces of law and order in the kind of riots that have made Watts memorable in Los Angeles and that continue to plague the ghettos of our larger cities from New York south to Florida and back to California.

On the international level, the process is little different: Regimes which we find repugnant because their political-economic systems differ from our own are subjected to invasion and assault, direct or covert, while our tax dollars go to support the arms of dictators and associated bully boys around the world.

The announced intention of our government to refuse to be bound by any decision of the World Court at the Hague with regard to our open intervention in the internal affairs of the government of Nicaragua sound a clear and unmistakable note that might is right; that the powerful can defy any decision of a tribunal with which they were not in accord. The message is clearly not lost on those who contemplate violence against others, for which they might expect to be called to account by a court of law.

The totality of these policies, national and international, has a no less real and profound effect on our own body politics by reason of the distance between those who govern and those who are governed. If delinquency and crime haunt us, it is all of a piece with the example set by corrupt politicians, multinational corporations, and a national administration that sets a higher priority on the means of destroying life than on its preservation and enhancement.

The international implications of these policies points up the universality of the problem of youthful delinquency itself. The authors of this book are to be commended for including a new chapter ("Cross-Cultural Delinquency," Chapter 18) which takes us to other parts of the world for a cross-cultural review. As they point out, American criminology has been, by and large, myopic in its view of the challenge presented by delinquency of the young. Left to ourselves, we tend to believe that we are more sorely bedevilled by delinquency than are other societies, that we possess a more profound and accurate explanation for its causes as well as the most advanced programs for coping with it.

In the first year of its establishment, the United Nations created the Section of Social Defence to assume responsibility for crime prevention and treatment—a responsibility inherited from the League of Nations and the International Penal and Penitentiary Commission. One of the first acts of the newly created Section was to send questionnaires to all the member nations inquiring as to the problem of crime after World War II as compared with the years immediately prior to the war. A high percentage of returns brought the following interesting responses: the rate of crime was up; more young people were involved than previously; the average age of children complained of to the courts had dropped; more females were now involved in delinquent acts; a higher level of violence accompanied many of those acts. Everything that has happened in the almost forty years since the survey has largely confirmed those early findings, so that they may be said to have been prophetic of what was later to happen.

With very few exceptions, all countries report an increase in delinquency by young people. Even the socialist countries, which in previous years prided themselves on their low rates, now more freely report concern with the problem in the international crime conferences in which they participate.

We have Durkheim to thank for cautioning us that a rising crime rate indicates that changes are taking place in a society. We can deduce, therefore, that when the crime rate escalates fairly steadily over a period of years, the societies which experience it must be undergoing truly profound changes in their structure and life styles and in the shifts in values and standards which accompany such changes. Durkheim's dictum that a certain amount of crime is healthy for society in that it helps the majority to reassert their adherence to a moral standard stirs an interesting concern: as long as the majority of the population is law-abiding, the society can presumably continue to function. But what will happen when less than 50 percent abstain from criminal acts? When our young people freely admit to involvement in illegal acts in a percentage that comes dangerously close to 100, what can we say of the security of our daily lives and the soundness of our social fabric? When homicide is the leading cause of death among young blacks; when one home in ten is burglarized in the course of any recent year; when some 25,000 murders by handguns take place annually and almost half a million men, women, and children are in confinement

for criminal acts, is it too much to ask whether the pathology of the society may well be taking over? To employ a medical term to describe the crime picture (which I acknowledge may not be good sociology) is, I submit, an effective way to dramatize what is happening in our streets and in the lives of all whose manner of living has been drastically altered by the fear of attack on their persons or property.

The growing impersonality and facelessness of much criminal behavior—juvenile as well as adult—should tell us something about what is happening in our midst. It is no longer the victim's usual lot to be robbed or mugged or burglarized; nor is the loss of property the sole result of such assaults. All too often they are accompanied by senseless, brutal, personal attacks which can deprive the victim not only of property, but of health, and even life, into the bargain.

Burglary is all too often accompanied by a destructive vandalism that seems as pointless as it is indecent. The theories sociologists have advanced over the years seem inadequate at this juncture to explain satisfactorily what is happening. The concept of alienation conceived by Karl Marx, the *anomie* which Durkheim has given us, expanded as it was by Merton and others, falls somehow short these days in helping us make sense of what we see and read in the daily accounts of criminal attacks upon our citizens.

It may well be time now to reexamine some of the theoretical explanations that have been brought forward in the past to help explain criminal behavior among the young as well as among adults. It is not unlikely, for example, that a higher standard of living, a greater abundance of things, an unending campaign to persuade us to obtain those things (preferably by purchase) bears some relationship to the increase in robberies, thefts, and burglaries. What is the relationship between the numbers of registered motor vehicles on the road and the auto theft rate?

The late Professor Willem Nagel of Leiden, in a study of juvenile delinquency commissioned by the government of Thailand, reports that before World War II, the "unauthorized use" of water buffaloes was one of the most frequent offenses of teenage youngsters in that country. With rising prosperity during that war, bicycle thefts exceeded water buffalo thefts. And after Korea and Vietnam, stealing automobiles topped the juvenile crime list simply as a result of their sudden availability.

Here at home, the stealing of civilian band radios became the theft most frequently reported to the police when they were first introduced. The rate dropped drastically when the distinctive antenna which had been mounted on the exterior of the car was concealed inside. Burglarizing of well-to-do dwellings has declined perceptibly with the sharp drop in the price of silver. A home that mounts a TV antenna on its roof announces to every passerby that there is a property within which has an assured black market demand.

The rapid spread of self-service in retail establishments has been followed by a level of shoplifting which has increased the cost of goods by 3 to 5 percent. Does each upturn in the tide of affluence lap at a higher threshold of resistance to temptation? Deprived of the means of lawful access, are the young particularly vulnerable to the lures of the market?

Profound social and economic changes may move some to look to the basic inequities in the distribution of wealth in our society as a likely source of antisocial acts, as the inequities and inequalities among nations may well be the provocation for the forty wars which the eighties have already experienced. Such considerations do not lie outside the scope of this text. It is to be hoped that it will inspire its readers—whether students, practitioners in the field, ordinary citizens, or concerned legislators—to assess the present state of the art of dealing with the individual young offender as well as with the conditions that seem to give rise to his or her behavior.

We spend enormous sums each year trying juveniles in our courts, subjecting them to a wide diversity of treatment modalities in an attempt to straighten out bent twigs while they are still green and amenable. But this cannot and should not detract from the responsibility to seek out the source of the winds that blow down those young shoots and to resolve to expend some efforts in attempting to temper them.

By the time this book appears in print, International Youth Year of 1985 will be over. The secretary-general of the United Nations has issued a preliminary report whose closing words have immediate significance for all concerned not only with delinquents, but with all young people everywhere:

> Preparation for the International Youth Year provides the opportunity for increasing the realization of the seriousness of the problems that will be confronting youth and society at large in the 1980's.

Delinquency and Justice can help to enlighten us all as to how we deal with these problems, how we may improve our procedures, and how we can and should move to prevent those problems from overwhelming our social structures in the second half of this decade.

PART 1

THE CONCEPT OF DELINQUENCY

Delinquency as an idea is relatively new; only in the past century has the misbehavior of juveniles come to be viewed as something distinct from adult crime. Contemporary society has reacted to the transgressions of children in unique ways. In this part we will discuss how and why the concept of delinquency was created (Chapter 1). One area of special concern involves adolescence, the period between childhood and adulthood in which children undergo physical, psychological, and social changes. We review the physical and social aspects of adolescence in depth in Chapter 2. We will also look at the extent and nature of juvenile delinquency in the United States by exploring current statistics (Chapter 3).

The creation of juvenile delinquency as a special category for child offenders can be understood only in relation to the discovery of childhood as a separate stage of life and to social currents in the eighteenth and nineteenth centuries. During the eighteenth century, childhood came to be thought of as a unique phase of life, and children were seen as special creatures who needed both protection and education. As American cities grew during the nineteenth century, urban reformers became distressed over the large numbers of children who were thought to commit criminal acts and lead idle lives. The creation of the concept of childhood and concern with the supposedly corrupting influences of the urban environment set the stage for what has been called the invention of delinquency. Children who did not submit to close supervision, adult authority, and strict discipline were seen as needing special care to prepare

them for normal roles within society. Guidance could be given by the controlled environment of an institution if it was not supplied in the family. The first court especially for children was created in Chicago in 1899. The juvenile court idea spread rapidly, bringing with it new legal rules and procedures for handling juveniles. The jurisdiction of these early juvenile courts forms the basis for our present legal definition of delinquency.

To understand juvenile delinquency better, we need to examine some broader issues relating to youth and culture. Reports from other countries, especially those experiencing rapid social change, indicate that problems affecting youth are not exclusively an American concern. In Chapter 2 we explore a number of historical, cultural, and theoretical studies that have examined the adolescent period of life. While all individuals must pass from childhood to adulthood, the meaning and significance of the experience is largely determined by the social and historical context in which maturation takes place. The forces of modernization and the processes of industrialization, urbanization, and nuclearization have, according to many experts, affected the current generation of youth more than at any other time in history. A wide spectrum of problems affecting today's adolescents has been linked to delinquent activity. The search for identity, self-actualization, and meaning are but a few of these problems.

Measuring the extent and nature of juvenile delinquency remains an elusive goal. Researchers suggest that most juveniles engage in behaviors for which they could be formally charged. However, very few adolescents are officially processed by the juvenile justice system.

The three major sources of data on the extent and nature of juvenile delinquency in the United States are official statistics (those collected by law enforcement agencies and the courts), self-report statistics (those collected voluntarily from juvenile perpetrators of delinquent acts), and victimization statistics (those collected voluntarily from victims of delinquent and criminal acts). Another source of data, cohort analysis, is being used to trace the career patterns of juvenile offenders over time. Each of these sources of information on delinquency has its own inherent weaknesses. Each source therefore presents a somewhat inaccurate picture of delinquents and the extent of delinquency within American society. But as we will see in Chapter 3, when different types of statistics are analyzed, a more reliable picture of patterns of delinquency is possible.

CHAPTER 1

DEFINING DELINQUENCY

THE SOCIAL HISTORY OF
ADOLESCENCE AND DELINQUENCY

PERCEPTIONS OF YOUTH IN
AMERICA

THE INVENTION OF DELINQUENCY

THE DEFINITION OF DELINQUENCY
TODAY

Our earth is degenerate . . .
Children no longer obey their parents . . .

This complaint, etched in stone six thousand years ago by an Egyptian priest, could easily be printed out on a computer today. All indications suggest that just as adults have always been known to violate their social norms, children too have engaged in norm-violating or forbidden behaviors since the beginning of human history (Kett, 1977). But for most of human history, very little distinction was made between adult and youthful deviance. Punishment or treatment was not age-specific. In the last two hundred years, the misbehavior of the young has come to be viewed in Western society as something distinct from adult crime. The distinction, signified by the emergence of a new concept, that of juvenile delinquency, both reflected and initiated far-reaching social change.

The concept of delinquency is suggestive of a new way of assessing, classifying, and treating youthful misbehavior. It represents a historically new view of youth in society, including a qualitatively different approach to the study of youth's problems. From its inception the concept of delinquency has been associated with a vast array of social mechanisms, institutions, and experts all dealing with different facets of the problems of youth.

Before exploring the contemporary meaning of delinquency with all its complexities, we will trace the social conditions and intellectual climate that gave rise to the development of the juvenile court. Since the ideal expectations of adolescence comprise the flip side of delinquency, we will also examine the history and significance of the concept of adolescence in Western Europe and the United States.

This chapter will provide the broad historical, social, and legal foundation for the further study of delinquency and thus set the stage for the following chapters. Many of the historical issues raised in this introductory section continue to be relevant in the present context of juvenile justice and will be explored in greater detail throughout the book.

THE SOCIAL HISTORY OF ADOLESCENCE AND DELINQUENCY

The American concepts of deliquency and youth have been shaped by a number of social and historical factors. Chief among these were attitudes toward children and adolescence derived from Western European philosophical and religious traditions, and certain legal concepts derived from English common law. American ideas about delinquency were also influenced by the vast social changes that occurred in the United States during the nineteenth century as a result of industrialization, urbanization, and immigration.

Ancient and Premodern Views of Adolescence

Concern with children and the history of childhood and youth represent a history of rediscovery. "With remarkable regularity, the same themes appear, are elaborated for a while, then fade" (Kessen, 1965: 1). While the terms **adolescence** and **delinquency** are relatively new, awareness of the special nature of youth and its problems goes back to time immemorial. Even Aristotle's ancient characterization of youth rings with familiarity:

> The young are in character prone to desire and ready to carry any desire they may have formed into action. Of bodily desires it is the sexual to which they are most disposed to give way, and in regard to sexual desire they exercise no self-restraint; for their wishes are keen without being permanent, like a sick man's fits of hunger and thirst. They are passionate, irascible and apt to be carried away by their impulses. . . . Youth is the age when people are most devoted to their friends or relations or companions, as they are then extremely fond of social intercourse and have not yet learned to judge their friends, or indeed anything else, by the rule of expediency. If the young commit a fault, it is always on the side of excess and exaggeration . . . ; for they carry everything too far, whether it be their love

or hatred or anything else. They regard themselves as omniscient and are positive in their assertions, this is, in fact, the reason of their carrying everything too far. Also their offenses take the line of insolence and not of meanness. (cited in Hall, 1905: 523)

Aristotle's depiction is rather sympathetic; it implicitly asks for adult understanding even of youthful misbehaviors, which appear to be causally connected to this stage of development. Plato also devotes considerable attention to adolescence. His dialogues may be viewed as "sources for the study of the pedagogy of adolescence" (Hall, 1905: 513), and many of the characters in the dialogues are adolescents.

We cannot fully account for why the contributions of the Greeks faded. But there is evidence that the awareness of youth, with the emphasis on specialness, required rediscovery later in Western history. This is not to say that awareness of adolescence disappeared entirely. Certainly it was maintained in the concept of the ages of life, which originated in the Byzantine Empire in the sixth century. The ages of life included seven stages beginning with infancy and ending with old age. The third stage was adolescence. The concept was a theme for literature throughout the succeeding centuries. As late as the sixteenth century, Shakespeare refers to the seven stages of life in his famous passage:

> All the world's a stage
> And all the men and women merely players:
> They have their exits and their entrances;
> And one man in his time plays many parts;
> His acts being seven ages. . . .
> (As You Like It, II, vii, 139)

After the "whining school-boy," we come to the "lover," "Sighing like a furnace, with a woeful ballad made to his mistress's eyebrow," which signifies the stage of adolescence. Shakespeare provides many insights into adolescence, since many of his characters are adolescents—Romeo and Juliet, and Hamlet. But even in Shakespeare we can sense confusion: Adolescence is confused on the one hand with childhood, on the other with young adulthood.

From a practical stance, the ages of life for the most part were three: childhood, youth, and old age. Philippe Ariès, in his book *Centuries of Childhood* (1962: 29), notes that until the eighteenth century

> an ambiguity remained between childhood and adolescence on the one hand and the category known as youth on the other. People had no idea of what we called adolescence, and the idea was a long time taking shape.

Perhaps what appears to be confusion is partially a reflection of the fact that human beings living in preindustrial society matured physiologically at a later age than is true today in Western industrial nations (see Chapter 2). What this suggests is that many individuals probably experienced bodily changes at an age closer to what we now commonly call young adulthood.

Ariès (1962) argues convincingly that for centuries children were believed to be miniature versions of adults. Adults paid relatively little attention to the qualitative difference of childhood and almost ignored adolescence. Even artists failed to differentiate children from adults. Except for the ancient Greeks, early painters and sculptors represented children as shrunken adults. Not until the thirteenth century were children portrayed as children, and not as little adults.

Medieval European attitudes toward children may have been shaped by certain grim demographic facts; many children died in infancy and early childhood. Given the extremely high death rates, adults may have been forced to regard the young with indifference. Children generally experienced infrequent contact with their parents. They were typically wetnursed, apprenticed, and abandoned. Often they were ignored and exploited in large numbers.

Until the end of the sixteenth century, childhood was considered to last only until the age of 4 or 5. During the seventeenth century, noticeable differences in attitudes toward childhood and adolescence began to appear. For instance, a special type of dress for children appeared. Moreover, it was not until the sixteenth and seventeenth centuries that fables, fairy stories, and nursery rhymes became the property of children.[1]

Church leaders, moralists, and teachers promoted the idea that children were weak and innocent creatures who needed the protection, guidance, and especially the instruction of adults. As Ariès has observed: "The moralists and pedagogues of the seventeenth century . . . succeeded in imposing their considered concept of a long childhood thanks to the success of the educational institutions and practices which they guided and supervised" (1962: 329). Childhood now extended beyond age 5, and a new life stage, the period of schooling, was recognized.

As childhood became a time of life characterized by careful protection and strict control, along with segregation from adult life, certain **norms** or rules specifying appropriate behavior for youngsters began to emerge. According to Empey (1978):

> Based on the precepts of the new morality, many treatises and manuals were written in the seventeenth and eighteenth centuries to guide parents. The principles they set forth were important because implicit in them was the image of the ideal child. Such an image became the standard by which not only conformity but deviance among children was judged. (p. 54)

In 1693 John Locke wrote *Some Thoughts Concerning Education,* which went through 26 editions before 1800; this was one of the best-known books on the philosophy of childrearing. It was devoted entirely to the rearing of boys. Locke took exception to the somewhat exalted view of children that characterized seventeenth century philosophy; he claimed children are nonmoral creatures that may be molded according to one's desires. He advocated obedience so that children would not grow up to be "defiant" adolescents. The best method of correction was the use of shame or guilt, because this allowed the child to internalize the parent's judgment (1699, 4th ed.: 54–66).

Parents were warned to treat their offspring as friends in their late teens and to be careful not to break their spirits. On the basis of the standards that were being introduced by such writings, the young were expected to submit to close supervision, adult authority, strict discipline, and vocational education. Those who did not conform to these standards were believed to need firm control and restraint.

Jean Jacques Rousseau's *Emile* (1762/1977) represents a clear departure from some of the earlier depictions of children by providing the first real consideration of the different levels of development and by emphasizing the specialness of each stage. While many preceding writers generally believed that human institutions were indispensable to social order and functioned primarily to counterbalance the insufficiencies of human nature, Rousseau began with the assumption that human nature was essentially good and that human institutions were the cause of problems in society. His educational plan centered on learning in and through the goodness of nature.

In contrast to Locke's program of discipline, Rousseau advocated permissiveness in childrearing. More important, Rousseau argued that different developmental levels should be taken into account in the learning process. He claimed that religious training, which required more advanced levels of reasoning, should not be started at age 7, as was the common practice, but should be delayed until age 15, when children are more intellectually mature.

Rousseau's depiction of adolescence may be captured in the following statement:[2]

> He leaves childhood behind him at the time ordained by nature; and this critical moment, short enough in itself, has far-reaching consequences. . . . As the roaring of the waves precedes the tempest, so the murmur of using passions announces this tumultuous change; a suppressed excitement warns us of the approaching danger. A change of temper, frequent outbreaks of anger, a perpetual stirring of the mind, make the child almost ungovernable. He becomes deaf to the voice he used to obey; he is a lion in a fever; he distrusts his keeper and refuses to be controlled.
>
> With the moral symptoms of a changing temper there are perceptible changes in appearance. . . . He is neither a child nor a man and cannot speak like either of them. His eyes, those organs of the soul which till now were dumb, find speech and meaning; a kindling fire illuminates them, there is still a sacred innocence in their ever brightening

glance, but they have lost their first meaningless expression; he is beginning to learn to lower his eyes and blush, he is becoming sensitive, though he does not know what it is that he feels; he is uneasy without knowing why. . . .

> This period when education is usually finished, is just the time to begin. . . . (Rousseau, 1762/1977: 172–173)

Rousseau, like Locke, also devoted most of his attention to males; however, in Rousseau's work there is a section on females entitled "Sophy, or Woman." Rousseau reasoned that the perfect man should have a perfect woman for a mate. But this perfect woman "is specially made for man's delight" (322). He concludes that "they [girls] should learn many things but only such things that are suitable" (327). Rousseau's views were not enlightened when it came to the rearing of females, but his work did serve to draw attention to the unique status and place of youngsters in society.

These first books of advice for parents on the rearing of their children did not rely on any scientific investigation; they largely reflected the pet theories of the authors. Paradoxically, as childhood increasingly became the subject of philosophical and literary exaltation, there was growing evidence that children themselves did not conform to some of the lofty and unrealistic images and further that they were not treated as angels by adults. Indeed, there was growing awareness of extensive inhumane exploitation of the young.

Early Views of Childhood Crimes: Legal Precedents in England

Many social attitudes are expressed in legal codes. By the eighteenth century, English common law had recognized a distinct set of rules regarding the criminal intent of children. Under that law, children under the age of 7 were assumed to be incapable of criminal intent and thus unable to commit actions regarded as crimes. Children from the ages of 7 to 14 were similarly presumed innocent of criminal intent unless it could be proved that they possessed knowledge of right and wrong. And the evidence of such knowledge was required to be strong and irresistible.[3] After they reached 14, children were held accountable for their crimes, and children in custody received the same treatment as adults. Separate jails and courts were not provided for children; children were detained, tried, and punished with adults (Dunham, 1972; Vedder, 1963).

There is some evidence, however, that under the rule of common law children were often treated leniently. Knell (1965) studied the use of capital punishment for juvenile offenses in the eighteenth and nineteenth centuries in England, and concluded: "The law . . . was for all intents and purposes, a dead letter" (p. 206). Most children were accused of minor offenses, and there was reluctance to condemn children to death for relatively insignificant crimes. Between 1801 and 1863, 103 children were sentenced to death, but none was executed. Platt (1969) studied fourteen leading cases of criminal responsibility between 1806 and 1882 in the United States and found that only two of the fourteen cases resulted in execution. And in both the defendants were black slaves, a reflection of discrimination on the basis of race.

Other legal distinctions between children and adults were made in English **equity** courts and through the philosophy of **parens patriae.** According to Caldwell (1972), "the principle of equity . . . originated because of the rigidity of the common law and its failure to provide adequate remedies in deserving cases" (pp. 399–400). The English equity or chancery court, granted the power to act as representative of the monarch, was charged with the protection of children. This protective function is called *parens patriae,* which literally means "the parent of the country." Children in general, but especially children who owned property, were regarded as wards of the state. "The essential idea of chancery is welfare or balancing of interest. It stands for flexibility, guardianship, and protection rather than rigidity and punishment" (Lou, 1927, p. 4). In principle, then, the court was to exercise the power of the English crown in guarding the young and their property (see, for example, Caldwell, 1972; Dunham, 1972; Hawkes, 1971; Rosenheim, 1962; Rubin, 1976).

Standardization of Youth: The Industrial Revolution

The Industrial Revolution of the nineteenth century brought great changes that altered many values and beliefs and affected the fundamental relationships between children and family and between children and society. First, new medical and biological innovations, especially the discovery of germs, assured that more children survived. Lower mortality rates along with low fertility rates, perhaps more than any other factors, led to the present concepts of childhood and adolescence (Kessen, 1965).

Second, changes in the family and the movement away from the extended or clanlike family pattern toward the nuclear family served to intensify parents' relations with their offspring.[4] Increasingly, children were raised by their own parents rather than by strangers (wetnursing, apprenticeships, and foundling homes were on the decline). Because of this, the child's personality became more visible to parents and there came a greater need for parents to understand their children.

Before industrialization, parents mainly determined the occupations of their children. Training for handicraft skills took many years, and most youths were apprenticed away from home. Industrialization caused the decline of the crafts, and so apprenticeship and training programs began to disappear. After 1800 the laws of apprenticeship were repealed. Employers were free to hire youths to do work for low wages, but without having a commitment to train them. Most youths now lived at home while working. Their low wages and the fact that they resided with their parents placed them in a particularly dependent role. It was also becoming more difficult to practice a profession— more and more emphasis was placed on public education. Getting jobs now depended more on skill than on family background. The ideal childhood now meant that children spent a significant portion of their time in school and in specifically childhood activities.

Religious reformers, notably the Puritans, stressed self-reliance and individual responsibility. The survival of the relatively new Protestant religions appeared more and more dependent upon the indoctrination of the young. So greater attention was given to the "proper" education of children. Concern for the survival of religious beliefs, along with the development of the democratic spirit, made parents particularly conscious of the proper techniques or methods of education.

The combination of scientific, religious, economic, and legal trends during the nineteenth century provided the impetus for the development of the study of the child. As scientists became embroiled in controversy over the relative importance of heredity and environment, they became more interested in the study of children. Numerous experts, including psychologists and sociologists, were beginning to focus upon youth.

People were also becoming aware of the plight of children and adolescents. Much of this awareness was tied to the development of the concept of the ideal childhood. Many of the problems of children were believed to stem from improper or inadequate socialization. The new sympathizers with the problems of children began to concern themselves with child labor laws and universal education, and with ensuring parental and societal control over children. Inadvertently, ideal childhood increasingly emphasized a dependent, subordinate role in society. Of course, interest in ideal childhood, normal development, proper socialization, and education quickly raised the issue of abnormal development and juvenile delinquency. Historically, the concepts of adolescence and delinquency were "dialectically inseparable," with regard to both origin and development (Gillis, 1981: 137).

Youth Movements and Rebellion against Conformity

The stress on conformity and youth's loss of independence did not go unchallenged, however; youthful uprisings appeared early in the nineteenth century (Sommerville, 1982: 183) when some German university students began openly to protest certain social policies. Even though these early uprisings involved mainly university students, the defiance represented a growing aversion by youth to the pressures of conformity and dependence.

Opposing the expectation of docility, obedience, and authority, radical students advocated the abolition of traditional institutions and demanded more freedom for all. They symbolized their protest by "wearing their hair loose, rather than powdered and pigtailed" (Sommerville, 1982: 183). Although the revolt was not successful in any immediate sense, the idea that change can come only from youthful radicalism gained prominence (p. 184).

Another type of youth movement emerged in France in 1830. Reponding to the aftermath of a political revolution in Paris, disappointed students began to seek greater changes. They formed one of the first youth "counterculture" movements, which was called the Bohemians. The Bohemians broke with tradition by dressing in strange attire, participating in "bizarre" religious observances such as satanism, and generally leading hedonistic lives (Sommerville, 1982: 184). For most youths, the unconventional life style did not last long, since the majority of Bohemians returned to "straight society" within five years (p. 185). A few of the artists and playwrights who were contemporaries of the Bohemians (Hugo, Dumas, and Delacroix) preserved their memory by including rebellious youths among their characters.

The revolutionary writers to come (such as Karl Marx and Friedrich Engels) did not make any special appeals to the young, nor did they look for support from the young. Marx and Engels never envisioned that they would contribute to another type of class demarcation—the one along generational lines—in their pursuit of harmony among the economic classes (p. 185). For example, young radicals in Russia in the late nineteenth century were inspired by the writings of Marx and Engels. By 1860 in Russia there was a large radical movement battling the czarist regime. The young radicals considered themselves "nihilists" and "atheists." From their point of view, the only Russian institution worth retaining was the peasant commune. Despite this idealistic affirmation of their life, the peasants did not support the revolution. The movement culminated with the assassination of Czar Alexander II, and among those involved in the assassination was Lenin's older brother. All these students were executed. But the peasants mourned the czar's death, not the execution of the assassins. The event left a lasting impression on Lenin, who was then 17 years old (Sommerville, 1982: 187).

Student revolts have long been documented in the United States. Even in the early nineteenth century, students mounted movements against the injustices of their society. Students protested against slavery and spearheaded the abolition movement. One of the results was the founding in 1833 of Oberlin College, the first institution of higher education to accept women and blacks. The youth movement of the 1960s was reminiscent of that of the Bohemians. The radical underpinnings of the antiwar and civil rights outcries included some Marxist overtones. The demonstrations of the 1960s involved the largest number of youths in history.

Radicalism on the part of youth in some measure may have stemmed from adolescents finding themselves more and more confined and less and less potent in the economic and political spheres of society. To a certain degree, youthful rebelliousness represents an attempt by young people to adjust to a rapidly changing social world. Young people (especially students, because they are organized) of every subsequent generation have found social evils to protest. However, if the protests threaten the formal social order, they are not tolerated, and the protesters become subject to harsh forms of punishment or control.

During the nineteenth century, institutions to contain and control restless youth were emerging at a rate almost proportional to the rate of youthful revolt. These institutions included compulsory schools, youth groups (the YMCA was founded in 1844), welfare agencies, and juvenile detention facilities. The growth of these control agencies and the growth of industrialization, with the emphasis on uniformity, increasingly forced the standardization of youth and childhood. For example, "Uniforms, whether athletic or military, underlined the growing intolerance of individuality that characterized late nineteenth century schooling in both England and Germany" (Gillis, 1981: 111). The consequence of greater conformity, of course, was greater delinquency.

The social definition of adolescence, however, had a distinctly middle class bias, since conformity meant conformity largely to middle class standards.[5] "Ideal" adolescents were mostly middle class youngsters, and the typical delinquent came from the laboring classes. Gillis (1981:134) states:

> The imposition of adolescence provoked a strong resistance from a sizeable part of the population, particularly the laboring poor, with the result that for most of the period 1900–1950 the lines drawn between conformity and delinquency were drawn along what were essentially class divisions.

The application of statistics and the increased emphasis on recordkeeping, resulting in the development of the "new" criminology, offered confirmation of the correlation between poverty and criminality. The new statistics indicated that low intelligence and alcoholism were also associated with criminality and that a significant number of criminals were young. Moreover, the statistics suggested that crime rates were on the rise. Such evidence had noticeable effects, particularly on the development of the juvenile justice systems.

The first welfare agencies and houses of refuge were primarily philanthropic efforts to help poor children who were victimized by society and by parents. The new statistical evidence, however, introduced a new function, lowering the rate of crime. As a result, the "potential criminal" and ways to "prevent" the behavior became major concerns. However, when the main objectives became prevention, all of the young suddenly became targets of suspicion (Sommerville, 1982: 201).

The growing number of professionals for whom the images of youth were a matter of concern found themselves in a dilemma. Public support of institutions dealing with the problems of youth depended on an old image of youth as noble and worth saving. Yet, fearing their jobs might appear too easy and fearing their roles might become obsolete, the professionals needed to maintain the troubled image of adolescence. So institutions dealing with the problems of youth encouraged the idea that youth was a growing problem. Despite the discovery of mitigating circumstances affecting the rising trends in crime statistics, the emphasis was on the increasing rate of crime among adolescents, especially those coming from poor urban environments.

PERCEPTIONS OF YOUTH IN AMERICA

Besides bringing English legal precedents to the colonies in America, the immigrants brought Western European attitudes toward youth to the New World. These ideas, coupled with the realities of day-to-day life in a harsh wilderness, helped shape the existence of colonial American children.

Youth in Colonial America

In the American colonies, the family was the basic social and economic unit. Living primarily in small towns and rural areas, families were forced to be largely self-sufficient. Children were especially valued for the labor they provided (Kephart, 1977; Leslie, 1979).

Colonial American children were not, however, pampered. Central to the religious beliefs of most colonists were ideas about original sin. Children were believed to be flawed from the moment of conception because they were conceived in an act of lust through which "Adam's sin was considered to have been transferred to all mankind" (Kephart, 1977: 86). The key task of the colonial parent was to reform and harness the child's inherent "willfulness." Discipline was therefore strict. Children were taught to call their parents "sir," "ma'am," or even "esteemed parent." When children refused to work willingly or defied their parents, punishment was severe. Caning was common. If the family could not control the errant child, community leaders would often place the child in another family (Kephart, 1977; Empey, 1978).

The control of the family, church, and community over colonial American children was so complete that, to a large extent, "elaborate legal machinery for children was unnecessary" (Empey, 1978, p. 76). For the most part, misbehavior was a matter for parents, church leaders, and neighbors to handle informally. However, children over the age of 7 were subject to the criminal law. Only the New England colonies had special punishments for children. Whippings were given for minor offenses, and parents were fined when their children were found to be thieves. In some colonies, children who disobeyed their parents could be put to death. But, as in England, children under the age of 16 were rarely executed. The American colonists had some ideas about how children should be trained and how juvenile offenders should be punished, but the concept of juvenile delinquency as a special category of rule-breaking behavior had not yet been invented (Empey, 1978; Griffin and Griffin, 1978).

Nineteenth-century American Constructions of the Problems of Youth

Life in the United States underwent vast transformations in the nineteenth century. Heretofore sparsely populated, with an ethnically similar collection of small towns and rural areas, the young country experienced a metamorphosis. In the nineteenth century, the cities grew with an influx of foreign immigrants and rural migrants. From 1850 to 1900, the urban population increased sevenfold (Hawkes, 1971: 160; see also Dunham, 1972; Platt, 1969). Initially most cities were not prepared for such rapid growth, and housing and employment were lacking. To many native-born Americans, the twin forces of urbanization and immigration represented a threat to the social order and explained the cause of social problems: "Many penal and education reformers considered that human nature operated in a radically different way in the city as compared with the country." City conditions, especially in slum areas, were thought to breed crime and all sorts of "depravity and corruption" (Platt, 1969: 36–38).

The child welfare movement developed in response to these conditions. Child welfare agencies "concentrated their attack on protecting young people," particularly in the cities (Carr, 1949: 32). Special attention was paid to the effects on children of the transition from city to country life. Cities, considered "no place for the innocence of a young child," were said to have "debilitized, corrupted, misled, and tarnished youth," producing "intellectual dwarfs" and "physical and moral wrecks" (Platt, 1969: 40). Country family life was recommended as a model for reform schools and juvenile institutions. Children "destitute of proper parental care, wandering about the streets, committing mischief, and growing up in mendicancy, ignorance, idleness, and vice" were placed in such institutions, which tried to replicate traditional rural family life (Fox, 1970: 1208). The goal was to assimilate them and thus to restore the stability and preserve the identity of earlier American life (Fox, 1970; Hawkes, 1971).

Immigrant children were regarded as particularly likely to be "warped" by the urban environment. In the 1890s, a large percentage of juveniles arrested in Chicago and other large cities were the offspring of immigrants. Besides living in poverty, immigrant children and the offspring of immigrant parents faced the problem of adjusting to a strange culture. The children of immigrant parents were characterized as being caught in a "cultural conflict" which was assumed to exist as old immigrant and new American norms and expectations clashed (Hawkes, 1971; Mennel, 1973; Platt, 1969). Early programs for the rehabilitation of native and immigrant juvenile offenders emphasized the teaching of middle class rural values and standards of behavior.

THE INVENTION OF DELINQUENCY

The invention of delinquency as a special category of illegal behavior developed in response to the changes in social life and concepts about children that occurred in the United States in the nineteenth century. In 1899 the first court designed to hear the cases of children opened its doors in Chicago. For the first time, the criminal acts of children were regarded as different and separate from those of adults.

Early Innovations in Juvenile Justice

The juvenile court movement "was started principally as a protest against the inhumane attitudes of the criminal law, and the court that administered it, towards offending children" (Lou, 1927:13). The punishment, treatment, and handling of the criminal, especially the young criminal, met with growing criticism. Many juvenile justice reforms preceded the founding of the juvenile court. Separate institutions for juveniles, probationary supervision of the "redeemable" offenders, and separate trials and court records for children predate the establishment of the juvenile court. However, prior to the court act, they were not integrated or part of a coherent system for dealing with youthful offenders.

Before the establishment of the juvenile court, the typical case of a young offender resembled the following pattern. Let's take a youngster who was caught stealing apples from a grocer as an example. In this case, the youth would be apprehended and taken to the neighborhood police court, where the magistrate would set **bail.** If neither the youngster nor his parents could pay the bail, he would be confined in a cell with adult criminals to await trial. He would then be tried in the same court with adults, usually facing a small fine or period of imprisonment, again in institutions with adults. He might even be let go with a warning, especially if the judge felt compassion for the youth's age or considered the offense minor.

In the case of more serious offenses, detention would have occurred while the grand jury decided whether or not an indictment was appropriate. Imprisonment was a distinct possibility. During these periods of confinement, the child would have opportunities to learn skills and attitudes from adult criminals. After release, the child could teach these skills and attitudes "to his companions, thus spreading the infection and starting other youths on the same path of crime in which he had several footprints" (Hawkes, 1971: 161–162).

These practices were widespread throughout the United States. The first official change in the handling of juvenile offenders came in 1824 with the establishment of the New York House of Refuge. Fox (1970) traces the history of this reform:

An 1823 report by the Society for the Prevention of Pauperism in the City of New York called for the rescue of children from a future of crime and degradation. . . . The 1822 Report on the Penitentiary System in the United States, submitted by the same group of reformers, called public attention to the corruptive results of locking up children with mature criminals, citing this contamination of innocence as one of major evils that had resulted from the prison reform. In 1824 the New York legislature responded by granting a charter and authority to erect a House of Refuge to be the successor of the Society for the Prevention of Pauperism, the Society for the Reformation of Juvenile Delinquents. (pp. 1189–1190)

The House of Refuge was designed to accept criminal and vagrant children deemed "proper objects" for separate institutionalization. This provision meant that children considered beyond rescue from a life of crime were to be excluded. Although most commentators emphasize the humanitarian motives underlying the creation of institutions for children, these reforms were, according to Fox, instituted to prevent and control the delinquency of lower class youth:

Whether a child's deviant conduct was primarily seen as offensive to legal rules or as an improper demand on the charity of the wealthier classes made little difference. Protection of society against crime and vicious pauperism by means of a more severe and more efficient institutionalization provided the rationale for the county poorhouse system and for the House of Refuge. (p. 1201)

Separate institutions reflecting similar desires to control poor and neglected youth and perhaps similar acceptance of public responsibility for the protection and care of youth were opened in Boston in 1826 and Philadelphia in 1828 and gradually spread to other parts of the country. The founding of separate institutions in New York and other states led to the establishment of reform schools throughout the country in the middle and late nineteenth century (Caldwell, 1972; Fox, 1970).

Another innovation influencing the development of the juvenile court was probation, a practice based on the common law power of the courts to suspend or defer sentences. Probation is thought to have originated in 1841 in Massachusetts, when John Augustus by chance met a drunkard in court. Augustus persuaded the judge in the case to postpone sentencing of the drunkard while attempts were made at reformation. Later, Augustus became the first official probation officer and worked with several judges to establish a plan to extend probation services to juvenile offenders. By 1852 Augustus had supervised the probation of 116 boys, 80 percent of whom, Augustus maintained, were totally reformed by the experience (Chute, 1949; Hawkes, 1971; Lou, 1927).

In 1869 a statute was enacted requiring an agent of the state board to attend all trials of children and to protect the interests of the children. These duties were soon specifically assigned to a probation officer. From 1878 to 1898, Massachusetts created a system of probation for adults and juveniles. The practice appeared to be successful, and representatives of the juvenile justice reform movement in Illinois visited Massachusetts to study probation practices there (Caldwell, 1972; Schultz, 1974). Massachusetts was also in the forefront of juvenile justice reform with the establishment of separate court trials for juveniles in 1872 and separate juvenile calendars in 1877. Apparently agreeing that children should not be contaminated by adult criminals before as well as during institutionalization, New York and Rhode Island also enacted early statutes that segregated the trials, arraignments, detention, dockets, and records of children from those of adults (Lou, 1927; Schultz, 1974).

The Chicago Juvenile Court

Throughout the nineteenth century, various reforms in the handling of juvenile offenders were attempted. But it was not until the end of the century that these practices were consolidated in the creation of a new institution, the Chicago juvenile court. Reformers in Illinois were at work long before their efforts produced the first juvenile court law.

Following the lead of other states in founding separate institutions for juvenile offenders, the Chicago City Council established the Chicago

Reform School in the 1850s. The professed goal of the school was to impose discipline on delinquent, dependent, and neglected youth in a family setting and to encourage young people to walk the straight and narrow path of law-abiding behavior. By the 1860s, the Chicago Reform School "was falling on bad times. The courts seemed to be turning against the institution" (Fox, 1970: 1215). Some judges preferred to send first offenders to jail rather than to the reform school because the reform school became associated with even worse conditions than the adult jail, and had the reputation of being a junior penitentiary and school for crime.

In 1870 the Supreme Court of Illinois ruled, in the case of *People ex rel. O'Connell v. Turner,* that a boy who committed no criminal offense could not be sent to the Chicago Reform School but must be released, because to do otherwise was tantamount to a conviction without **due process** of law. This court decision raised questions about the state's power of *parens patriae* and its jurisdiction over children who had committed no crime other than being poor or neglected: "Destitution of proper parental care, ignorance, idleness and vice are misfortunes, not crimes. . . . This boy is deprived of a father's care, benefit of home influences, has no freedom of action, is committed for an uncertain time; is branded as a prisoner" (Mennel, 1973: 125). This decision and other circumstances, including the burning of the school in the Chicago fire of 1871, resulted in the closing of the Chicago Reform School in 1872 (Fox, 1970).

Child welfare reformers viewed the demise of the Chicago Reform School with great distress because, to a large extent, children were now thrown back into jails and prisons with adult offenders or into privately organized industrial schools. In 1888 the power to commit dependent and delinquent children to these industrial schools was challenged by other court decisions. By 1890 the Illinois system for handling delinquent children had virtually disappeared (Mennel, 1973).

In 1892 the Chicago Women's Club recommended the creation of a totally separate juvenile court, but no real attempt was made to start one at that time. In 1893 the club did establish both

a school for young offenders detained in the city jail and a separate police station limited to women and juveniles. Two years later, the club again advocated the passage of a law to set up a court for minors, but legal advisors cautioned club members that such a law was unconstitutional. The women tabled their proposal, but concern for the plight of juvenile offenders continued. The 1898 convention of the Illinois State Conference of Charities devoted its entire program to the children of the state, especially "those in trouble" (Hawkes, 1971; Mennel, 1973; Platt, 1969).

Shortly after the convention, the State Board of Charities asked the Chicago Bar Association to study the situation and draft a juvenile court bill. After the initial bill was drawn up and revised, it was endorsed by a variety of organizations and sent to the state legislature in 1899. Passing on the last day of the legislative session, the Juvenile Court Act legitimized the opening of the first juvenile court in Chicago on July 1, 1899.[6]

After the Chicago court opened its doors, juvenile courts proliferated in the United States. By 1904, ten states had juvenile courts; by 1909, the number had grown to twenty. The District of Columbia and every state except Maine and Wyoming had passed juvenile court laws by 1923. Concurrently, the juvenile court idea was adopted in many other countries besides the United States[7] (Dunham, 1972; Hawkes, 1971; President's Commission on Law Enforcement and the Administration of Justice, 1967c).

These early courts integrated previous reforms in juvenile justice, including probation, separate hearings, and provisions for separate treatment facilities or institutions.[8] The Illinois Juvenile Court Act (1899), which served as a model for other states, made explicit what was already implicit in the handling and institutionalization of juvenile offenders. Based on the philosophy of *parens patriae*, it was "an act to regulate the treatment and control of dependent, neglected, and delinquent children" (Illinois Juvenile Court Act, 1899). The act ended with the following often quoted and widely criticized section:

> This act shall be liberally construed to the end that its purpose may be carried out, to wit: That

the care, custody and discipline of a child shall approximate as nearly may be that which should be given by its parents, and in all cases where it can properly be done the child placed in an improved family home and become a member of the family by legal adoption or otherwise. (Hawkes, 1971: 170)

The basic idea underlying the juvenile court was that children were to receive parental care from the court. The problems of each child were to be individually diagnosed and treated. Applying this philosophy to dependent and neglected children (who, along with delinquents under the age of 16, were included in juvenile court jurisdiction) was not new. But requiring the application of parentlike concern in the court proceedings was (Schramm, 1949; Vedder, 1963). The juvenile court thus became one of the earliest examples of "personalized justice," because it applied the principles of *parens patriae* to dependent, neglected, and delinquent children.

The ultimate goal of the juvenile court was to rehabilitate, not to mete out punishment or retribution. The rehabilitation plan or treatment prescribed by the court was supposed to be suited to the individual. Chute (1949), commenting on this facet of the Illinois court legislation, has written that the act was

the embodiment of a new principle: that law violators, the anti-social, and maladjusted, especially among children, should be treated individually through social and protective processes, for their own protection and that of society, instead of by the punitive and retaliatory methods of the criminal laws, which have always failed to repress crime. The juvenile court was the first legal tribunal in which law and the sciences, especially those which deal with human behavior, were brought into close working relationship. (p. 3)

The focus on rehabilitation created a climate in which the court and its clients were compared to doctors and their patients: evaluation, diagnosis, treatment, and prevention soon became key elements of the court proceeding. As a result, numerous experts were immediately introduced into the proceedings (see Chapters 5 and 15 for discussions of the role of psychiatrists and psychologists in courts and treatment, respectively).

Juvenile Court Procedure

In addition to offering personalized justice, the Illinois Court Act provided for a special children's court judge, selected by circuit judges from among their number; separate court records, dockets, and hearings; informal court procedures; the use of probation as a dispositional alternative; and detention apart from adults. The law drafted in Illinois was the basis for most juvenile court legislation in the United States. For sixty years, most of these statutes were unrevised; until recently, most juvenile court laws contained the provisions of the original Illinois Act (Caldwell, 1972; President's Commission, 1967c).

Of the original provisions of the Illinois Juvenile Court Act, perhaps the one establishing informal procedures was the most controversial. Informal procedures in the juvenile court have been defended on the basis of the principles of *parens patriae* and the responsibility of equity courts to hear the cases of dependent and neglected minors. There were basic differences, however, in equity courts and juvenile courts, since equity courts were bound by certain legal procedures and rules of evidence. Juvenile courts, on the other hand, "were not to be encumbered by official indictments, prosecutors, defense lawyers, a jury and a sticky set of procedures" (Empey, 1978: 102). Formal procedures were considered anathema to the goals of individually diagnosing, treating, and reforming wayward children (Empey, 1978; Handler, 1965; Lemert, 1967; President's Commission, 1967c).

It is clear that the drafters of juvenile court bills viewed the juvenile court as unique in terms of procedures. Although informality in children's trials was common before the beginning of juvenile courts, informality had never before been legislatively mandated. Change was even recommended in the vocabulary used to describe the various stages of juvenile justice. Children who broke laws or violated more general conceptions of the ideal child were not to be stigmatized and labeled "criminals" but to be called "delinquents." When the decision to bring a child to court was made, a "petition," not a "warrant for arrest," was filed. The juvenile was "taken into custody," not "arrested." While in custody, the minor was "detained," not "imprisoned"; "committed," not "sentenced"; and "trained," not "punished." The shift in terminology emphasized that the juvenile court was not a criminal court.

To underscore the noncriminal nature of the court, its setting was to resemble a library or a committee room. Loevinger (1949) summarized the juvenile court procedure thought to be most effective in achieving the goal of protecting and rehabilitating:

> It is now almost universally recognized that juvenile court hearings should not be held in the conventional courtroom with the judge sitting on a high bench, with the witnesses in the witness chair, and with the juvenile and his parents standing in front of the bench as in criminal arrangements. It is quite generally recommended that the hearing should be held in a place more like a committeeroom. . . . Everyone is seated except that sometimes witnesses stand while telling their story. It may often happen that the judge may send everyone out of the room while he talks alone with the child or a parent. Clerks, bailiffs, and courthouse attaches generally should not be around. (p. 68)

Both court provisions and procedures were designed to emphasize the uniqueness of delinquency and the delinquent. It was clear that juveniles who broke rules were to be treated in a fashion very different from the way adults who broke the same rules were to be handled.

THE DEFINITION OF DELINQUENCY TODAY

Today, the delinquent child continues to hold a distinct status conferred by court adjudication,

and legislation continues to define behaviors that bring a juvenile before the juvenile court. There is, however, no single definition of delinquency or the delinquent. According to one criminologist:

> The designation of a child as delinquent is likely to mean anything from the loose employment of a value judgement in the description of the child to the official judgment of a court about [the child's] behavior. A look at the literature on delinquency indicates that a great many different approaches have been applied to the task of defining delinquency. (Teele, 1970: 1)

Legal Definitions

Legally, the delinquent is an individual who has committed a prohibited behavior, an individual who has been picked up by the police for an alleged violation, or an individual who has been referred to the court created for children and officially **adjudicated** delinquent.

All fifty states, the District of Columbia, and Puerto Rico have laws delimiting delinquency. Legal definitions describe behaviors that are considered delinquent. However, the specific behaviors that are prohibited vary from state to state. Thus, the legal definition of delinquency varies from state to state. Criminal acts are, of course, legislatively forbidden, but so are a variety of acts that would not be illegal if committed by an adult.

Prohibited Behaviors.   The number of behaviors that can result in adjudication in the juvenile court was and still is extensive. Moreover, descriptions of these behaviors are vague enough that almost any child could be considered to have committed a delinquent act. In the report of the President's Commission on Law Enforcement and the Administration of Justice, juvenile court laws were said to amount "virtually to a manual of undesirable youthful behavior. A precocious tobacco user or a youngster with [a] shady friend or foul speech could be brought to court, adjudicated a delinquent and sentenced to a plan of treatment, as well as the grade-school housebreaker or strong-arming teenager" (1967c: 22). A delinquent child has been defined as one who does any of the following:

- Violates any law or ordinance
- Engages in immoral or indecent conduct
- Behaves immorally around a school
- Engages in an illegal occupation
- Associates with vicious or immoral persons
- Grows up in idleness or crime
- Enters or visits a house of ill repute
- Patronizes, visits a policy shop or a gaming place
- Patronizes a place where intoxicating liquor is sold
- Patronizes public pool rooms
- Wanders the street at night, not on lawful business (breaking curfew)
- Wanders about railroad yards or tracks
- Jumps a train or enters a train without authority
- Is habitually truant from school
- Is incorrigible
- Uses vile, obscene, or vulgar language (in a public place)
- Absents self from home without consent of parent or guardian
- Loiters, sleeps in alleys
- Refuses to obey parent or guardian
- Uses intoxicating liquors
- Deports self so as to injure self or others
- Smokes cigarettes (around a public place)
- Is in occupation or situation dangerous to self or others
- Begs or receives alms (or is in the street for that purpose). (Levin and Sarri, 1974; President's Commission, 1967c; Rubin, 1961, 1976; Sussman, 1950; Tappan, 1976)

Behaviors that are forbidden by law for juveniles but permissible for adults are called **status offenses** (truancy, running away, smoking, drinking, violating curfew). In 1961 Rubin observed that "no juvenile court law confines its definitions of delinquency to violations of laws and ordinances" (p. 49). In 1974 Levin and Sarri reported that "all 51 Juvenile Codes bring within the purview of the juvenile court conduct that is illegal only because of the child's age" (p. 11). Despite efforts to remove status offenses from the juvenile court, most state codes continue to include references to such vague behaviors as "incorrigibility," "immorality," "idleness," "beyond control," or "wayward."

In recent years, there has been a movement to designate and handle noncriminal acts or conditions of children as something other than delinquency. Today, legislation commonly refers to children who commit status offenses as "persons (or children or minors) in need of supervision." In twenty-five states, status offenders are no longer called delinquent, but are instead given special labels. This change in terminology has been accompanied by innovations in the handling of status offenders in eighteen states. Some states prohibit the housing of criminal juveniles with noncriminal ones, and others allow institutionalization of status offenders only as a last resort. It has been suggested by many experts that processing and arrest of noncriminal children may have the unintended consequence of producing criminal conduct among juveniles who were originally involved only in noncriminal offenses (Handler, 1965). According to sociologist Edwin Lemert (1967):

The net conclusion is that incorrigibility, truancy, and running away should not in themselves be causes for assuming juvenile court jurisdiction over children. There is much reason to believe that the bulk of such problems can be handled successfully by referrals, demonstrated by an inquiry in the District of Columbia where it was found that non-court agencies took responsibility for 98 percent of the total identifiable reported runaways, 95 percent of truancies, 76 percent of sex offenses, and 46 percent of youth termed ungovernable. (p. 99)

Many reformers have called for the elimination of juvenile court jurisdiction over noncriminal offenses (**jurisdiction** refers to the types of cases a court is empowered to hear). This recommendation was endorsed by the 1967 President's Commission and in a 1974 statement of the National Council on Crime and Delinquency. The proposal has been opposed by some juvenile court judges, who view it as an indicator of diminishing court jurisdiction and symbolic of the erosion of the juvenile court philosophy (Handler, 1965; Lemert, 1967; Rubin, 1976).

The problem of jurisdiction is further complicated by the fact that the juvenile court considers two other "nondelinquent" types of cases in addition to status offenses: **dependent** and **neglected** youths. **Dependency** is generally considered to occur when parents cannot care for their children, **neglect** when they will not care for them or are found to be abusive. Since late nineteenth-century reformers believed that poverty and crime were closely related, they thought it natural for the juvenile court to process dependent and neglected youth in the same court as delinquents. Juvenile courts also traditionally have jurisdiction over adults involved in "contributing to the delinquency, dependency and neglect of a juvenile" (Handler, 1965; Platt, 1969; President's Commission, 1967c).

Removing cases of dependency from the juvenile court has been advocated on the grounds that cases involving parents who cannot take care of their children are more appropriately handled by social welfare agencies. Moreover, there is evidence that the stigma of juvenile court processing extends to those adjudicated dependent or neglected as well as those termed delinquent. Once the label "delinquent" is applied, for whatever reason, it is difficult to shed.

In the past, when few services were available, the juvenile court may have filled a gap by supplying social services to children in need. Advocates for limiting the jurisdiction of the court claim that since today there are many social welfare agencies, there seems to be little reason to continue handling neglected and dependent youth in juvenile court. While acknowledging the tremendous growth that has taken place in the area of social services, proponents of traditional court jurisdiction argue that the need for the coordination of services and an established system of referrals is greater now than ever and properly falls to the court. Supporters of the traditional model also claim that social agencies by themselves lack the power to ensure the maximum support and cooperation of all concerned, especially in cases where voluntary compliance may not be assumed.

Paulsen and Whitebread (1974) summarized the jurisdiction of the juvenile court and explained how a legal definition of delinquency relates to that jurisdiction:

> Generally speaking, the jurisdiction of juvenile courts over children extends to four kinds of cases: (a) those in which a youth has committed an act which if done by an adult would be a crime; (b) those in which a child is beyond the control of his [or her] parents or is engaging in noncriminal conduct thought to be harmful . . . ; (c) those in which parents (or other custodian) of the person fail to offer proper care and guidance to a child though they are able to do so; or (d) those in which a child's parents (or other custodian) are unable to care for him [or her]. Again, speaking generally (a) and (b) above define a "delinquent" child (in some cases (b) is labeled differently such as "a person in need of supervision" or an "unruly child"), (c) a "neglected" child and (d) a "dependent" child. Some statutes do not employ specifically labeled categories to describe the youngsters subject to adjudication in juvenile court. (p. 32)

The issue of jurisdiction is not confined to nondelinquency cases; it is also raised in cases involving serious or capital criminal offenses. Most states have provisions for transfer or **waiver** to the criminal court of any juvenile over a certain age thought to have committed a serious crime, usually a felony (see Chapter 15). While statutory provisions regarding waiver to the adult criminal court vary greatly from state to state, making comparisons difficult, they usually hinge upon factors such as the age of the juvenile offender and/or the seriousness of the offense.[9] The most frequent age in most states for transfer to criminal court has been 16 years, although recent changes in many state juvenile codes allow transfer at 14 or 15 years of age for the commission of particularly serious crimes. This change generally reflects the more conservative trend in juvenile justice as a possible reaction to the public's demand for a tougher stance on crime (Kluegel, 1983).

Some states may specify two or three minimum age criteria for transfer to the adult court or specify no age criteria, making the decision dependent upon the nature of the offense. For example, in South Carolina waiver is permitted when a child of any age is charged with murder or sexual assault; waiver is also permitted where a child 14 or 15 has two prior adjudications for assault, assault and battery with intent to kill, aggravated assault and battery, arson, housebreaking, burglary, kidnapping, attempted criminal sexual conduct, or robbery and is charged with a third or subsequent offense [S.C. Code 20-7-430(4)-(6) (Supp.1982)].

The decision to transfer a juvenile to an adult court generally lies with the juvenile court judge, but several factors may mitigate this. Nine states allow *concurrent jurisdiction* between the juvenile court and the criminal court contingent upon either the age of the offender, the type of offense, or a combination of both factors.[10] The commission of serious offenses, especially capital or life sentence offenses such as murder, armed robbery, rape, and kidnapping, may also be classified as *excluded offenses* and are automatically excluded from juvenile court jurisdiction. Thirty states make provisions for such offenses (Davis, 1984). In most states a *waiver hearing* is guaranteed by statute and legal representation is required. However, in some states the hearing may be circumvented by the prosecutor, bypassing the juvenile court judge; in these cases it is the prosecutor who makes the decision of whether to handle the case in juvenile or criminal court (Davis, 1984).

Age Limits.   All juvenile codes observe two chronological age references: the maximum and the minimum age of jurisdiction. *Minimum age of jurisdiction* refers to the earliest age at which a juvenile is held responsible for his or her actions. Under English common law, children under 7 years of age were thought to be incapable of forming criminal intent and thus improper subjects for criminal liability. Many state juvenile statutes incorporate the English common law assumption and do not specify a lower age limit for the delinquent adjudication. The few states that do establish a specific minimum statutory age limit for delinquency usually set the lower age limit at 10 or 12 years. (Two states, Massachusetts and New York, set the minimum at 7, while North Carolina begins jurisdiction at age 6.) Of course, the juvenile court retains immediate jurisdiction in situations involving the welfare of neglected or abused children.

The *maximum age of jurisdiction* is the upper limit for original jurisdiction by the juvenile court. As Table 1.1 shows, the majority of states commonly define a delinquent child as any person under the age of 18 who commits a delinquent act. Under common law, a child over the age of 13 was considered an adult and was held criminally responsible. At one time, 21 was commonly the maximum age of juvenile court jurisdiction; now the maximum age in most states is 18. Until recently, some states set different limits for males and females. Males were usually considered suitable for adjudication in adult courts at a younger age than females. But these age distinctions have been declared unconstitutional because they deny equal protection to boys and girls. In 1973 Texas became the last state to abolish age distinctions in juvenile court jurisdiction (Fox, 1977; Levin and Sarri, 1974).

Although age demarcations in legal definitions of delinquency may seem relatively clear, there has been some confusion over the exact date at which age is measured for purposes of determining

TABLE 1.1   Statutory Age at Which Adult Court Holds Jurisdiction by State

16	17	18	18	19
Connecticut	Georgia	Alabama	Montana	Wyoming
New York	Louisiana	Alaska	Nebraska	
North Carolina	Michigan	Arizona	Nevada	
Vermont	Missouri	Arkansas	North Dakota	
	South Carolina	California	New Hampshire	
	Texas	Colorado	New Jersey	
	Illinois	Delaware	New Mexico	
	Massachusetts	D.C.	Ohio	
		Florida	Oklahoma	
		Hawaii	Oregon	
		Idaho	Pennsylvania	
		Indiana	Rhode Island	
		Iowa	South Dakota	
		Kansas	Tennessee	
		Kentucky	Utah	
		Maine	Virginia	
		Maryland	Washington	
		Minnesota	West Virginia	
		Mississippi	Wisconsin	

court jurisdiction. **Attachment time** refers to whether the juvenile court receives jurisdiction at the time the offense is committed or when the suspect is apprehended. The answer to the question of attachment, as can be seen from Table 1.2, depends upon the particular state.

Most often, attachment is governed by the age at which the offense was allegedly committed (Davis, 1984: 2–7). A person who was a juvenile when the offense occurred but an adult when he or she was apprehended must be returned to the juvenile court for adjudication. Fox (1977) comments that there "would be obvious objection to a juvenile court trial for [people] in [their] thirties, or older, even if the offense with which [they] were charged was committed while [they] were young adolescent[s] within the upper age limits of the age jurisdiction" (p. 34).

Of course, attachment can be superseded by various statutes of limitations; for example, the case must be brought to trial within a set period of time after which it is dropped. However, a different set of problems is presented by the age limits inherent in the definition of status offenses,

acts, or conditions illegal only for those under a certain age. Should a person who ran away at age 15 be referred to the juvenile court when he or she is apprehended at age 19? Several states have passed legislation setting such individuals free from juvenile court jurisdiction. There is no prosecution in adult courts for status offenses, so the runaway or other noncriminal offender who attains the upper age limit of juvenile court jurisdiction is released from the threat of legal sanction.

Another controversy over age revolves around the question of how long an adjudicated child can he held by the court. In thirty-one states, a child who has been placed under the supervision of the juvenile court remains subject to court jurisdiction until he or she reaches the age of 21 (King, 1980: 19–21). Other states set the age limits of 18 or 19 or set no limits at all on continuing juvenile court jurisdiction. **Continuing jurisdiction** means the juvenile court can retain the child in an institution or on probation. If an offender over the age of original jurisdiction commits another offense while on juvenile court probation, the case will be handled in the adult system. Often legis-

TABLE 1.2 **Attachment Time by State**

Offense		Apprehension
Alabama	Nebraska	Alaska
California	Nevada	Arizona
District of	New Hampshire	Askansas
Columbia	New York	Colorado
Florida	North Dakota	Connecticut
Georgia	Ohio	Delaware
Hawaii	Pennsylvania	Iowa
Idaho	South Carolina	Kansas
Illinois	South Dakota	Michigan
Indiana	Texas	Mississippi
Kentucky	Utah	New Jersey
Louisiana	Vermont	New Mexico
Maine	Virginia	North Carolina
Maryland	West Virginia	Oklahoma
Massachusetts	Wyoming	Oregon
Minnesota		Rhode Island
Missouri		Tennessee
Montana		Washington
		Wisconsin

lation establishes the upper boundaries of continuing court jurisdiction in terms of the age of majority, the age set by law at which "a person is entitled to the management of his or her own affairs and to the enjoyment of civic rights" (*Black's Law Dictionary*, 1979). As that age is legislatively lowered, the extent of the juvenile court's continuing jurisdiction is diminished.

Who Is the Juvenile Delinquent?   A legal definition of delinquency may lead to several definitions of the delinquent. The answer to the question of who is delinquent is not as obvious as it first appears. A **juvenile delinquent** is variously identified as a child (1) who commits a criminal act or a status offense, (2) who is apprehended by the police for commission of a criminal act or a status offense, or (3) who is referred to the juvenile court and adjudicated "delinquent." These legal conceptions of delinquency and the delinquent are employed by law enforcement officials, correctional personnel, and social scientists. For the sake of clarity it is important to establish which definition is being used.

In the first instance, a youngster who has committed one or more delinquent behaviors even though the behaviors never come to the attention of any authorities is defined as a delinquent. According to some surveys, more than 90 percent of juveniles have admitted to committing acts prohibited by juvenile delinquency law, especially those which fall in the category of status offenses. Although this definition of delinquency leads to a more accurate estimate of the actual amount of delinquent behavior in a society, it seems somewhat unrealistic and impractical to call almost all children juvenile delinquents. For example, few people would define the child who occasionally disobeys his or her parents or drinks a beer as a juvenile delinquent, even though the law codes of most states encompass such behaviors.

A narrower definition of the juvenile delinquent is the child who is picked up by the police for allegedly committing a criminal act or, in many states, a status offense. Given this definition, about 20 percent of all juveniles are delinquents. Here, the behavior of the child is not the only criterion, and the role of officials in the definitional process cannot be overemphasized. Judgments pertaining to the seriousness and frequency of the offenses, considerations of personal and family characteristics of the child, and community attitudes and pressures are all essential elements in identifying those who are likely to be labeled delinquent.

The most restricted definition of the delinquent includes only those youths who have committed delinquent acts and have been adjudicated delinquent by the juvenile court. This definition is probably the most correct in strictly legal terms. In other words, a delinquent is the child who has been ruled to be a delinquent by the juvenile court. Based on this definition, about 5 percent of all juveniles are delinquents. Once again, the likelihood of being officially defined delinquent by the court depends not only on a particular youngster's behavior, but on the judgments of various officials about that individual and the behavior (Cavan and Ferdinand, 1975; Griffin and Griffin, 1978).

Nonlegal Definitions

We have shown that legal definitions of delinquency include not only behaviors that are criminal in nature, such as murder, rape, and theft, but also behaviors that are forbidden only for children. The vagueness of such terms as "wayward," "beyond control," or "ungovernable" means that a child may be found legally delinquent for a wide range of behaviors. The legal definition of delinquency is so broad that a child can be picked up by the police or referred to the court for just about any behavior. Again, juvenile self-report inventories of delinquency reveal that more than 90 percent of juveniles have engaged in behaviors that are included in juvenile codes as delinquent. Often, "the legal status of 'delinquent' tends to depend more on attitudes of parents, the police, the community, and juvenile courts than on any specific behavior of the child" (Haskell and Yablonsky, 1978: 3). One author, Ruth Cavan (1961), has pointed out an important problem with legal definitions of delinquency:

In defining juvenile delinquency, laws are of little use. Usually laws are specific only in relation to serious adult offenses, such as murder, assault, robbery, burglary, and so forth. Children are delinquent if they are found guilty in court of breaking any of the federal, state, or local laws designed to control adult behavior. Delinquency statistics, however, indicate that these serious offenses account only for a small proportion of the delinquencies of children. Most of the behavior that gets a child into trouble with the police and courts comes under a much less definite part of the law on juvenile delinquency. . . . In these laws, there is no definition of such words or phrases as incorrigible, habitual, indecent conduct. . . . How much disobedience constitutes incorrigibility? How often may a child perform an act before it is considered habitual? (p. 23)

In an attempt to overcome the shortcomings of legal definitions of delinquency, Cavan and Ferdinand reconceptualized delinquency as part of a continuum of behavior that ranges from "extremely antisocial actions to extremely conforming behavior which elicits a variety of public responses ranging from outraged condemnation through mild disapproval to strong approval" (Cavan and Ferdinand, 1975: 28). Cavan and Ferdi-

nand summarized their ideas in a model with seven stages, depicted in Figure 1.1. The mid-stage, stage D, represents the average expected behavior of juveniles. At this stage, there may be some deviation from social rules and values, but the divergences are perceived as being minor. The researchers suggest that certain behaviors—an occasional truancy, mischief on Halloween, slight deviations from parental curfews, and the like—will be tolerated by the community and may even find mild approval, since they are viewed as "indicative of ingenuity, competitiveness or aggressiveness" (Cavan and Ferdinand, 1975: 28).

Two stages, C and E, are variations of stage D, but community response to the behavior represented by these stages may be somewhat strained. Penalties are not serious, yet there will be some efforts by parents and school personnel to transform the behavior into more accepted patterns. The child who exhibits stage E behaviors may be urged to "show more spirit and less docility," while the stage C child may be encouraged to be more restrained.

Stage B behavior brings more serious reaction from the community, as parents and school personnel come to feel ineffective in handling the juvenile's behavior. The police are involved in efforts to change the extremely underconforming behavior, but the child is not yet thought to be or called a "real delinquent." Accordingly, the police may release the child to parents or send him or her to a social service agency. Females and status offenders are especially likely to be handled in this way. Disapproval is also clearly manifested to stage F behavior, or overly conforming actions, but the negative reaction is likely to come from peers rather than officials.

The so-called real delinquent is the child who consistently underconforms to rules and values, a child who is represented in the scheme by stage A. The child whose behavior falls into this stage "tends to make delinquency a central and important part of his [or her] life" and "has a juvenile court hearing, followed by probation or commitment to a correctional school" (Cavan and Ferdinand, 1975: 31). Cavan and Ferdinand assert that the child rejects and is rejected by the community and often forms part of a "contraculture,"

FIGURE 1.1   Hypothetical Formulation of a Behavior Continuum

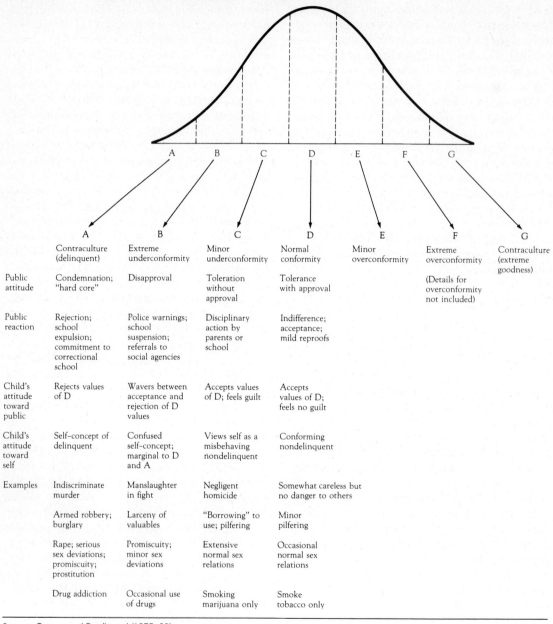

	A	B	C	D	E	F	G
	Contraculture (delinquent)	Extreme underconformity	Minor underconformity	Normal conformity	Minor overconformity	Extreme overconformity	Contraculture (extreme goodness)
Public attitude	Condemnation; "hard core"	Disapproval	Toleration without approval	Tolerance with approval		(Details for overconformity not included)	
Public reaction	Rejection; school expulsion; commitment to correctional school	Police warnings; school suspension; referrals to social agencies	Disciplinary action by parents or school	Indifference; acceptance; mild reproofs			
Child's attitude toward public	Rejects values of D	Wavers between acceptance and rejection of D values	Accepts values of D; feels guilt	Accepts values of D; feels no guilt			
Child's attitude toward self	Self-concept of delinquent	Confused self-concept; marginal to D and A	Views self as a misbehaving nondelinquent	Conforming nondelinquent			
Examples	Indiscriminate murder	Manslaughter in fight	Negligent homicide	Somewhat careless but no danger to others			
	Armed robbery; burglary	Larceny of valuables	"Borrowing" to use; pilfering	Minor pilfering			
	Rape; serious sex deviations; promiscuity; prostitution	Promiscuity; minor sex deviations	Extensive normal sex relations	Occasional normal sex relations			
	Drug addiction	Occasional use of drugs	Smoking marijuana only	Smoke tobacco only			

Source: Cavan and Ferdinand (1975: 29).

a part of society with values and modes of behavior in opposition to those of the dominant culture. Also rejected by society are extremely overconforming youth, represented by stage F and characterized as "saintly" and "too good to be true."

Cavan and Ferdinand's scheme is useful because it points out that many children engage in acts that are legally delinquent without being thought of as delinquent. The "misbehaving nondelinquent" generally accepts social values, associates with conforming groups, and feels guilty when he or she misbehaves. The scheme is unique because it attempts to account for overconformity as well as underconformity. According to Cavan and Ferdinand, a legal definition of delinquency and the delinquent is more helpful in understanding the workings of the police, courts, and juvenile institutions. Nonlegal definitions are appropriate when studying more general social reaction to delinquency and the delinquent, the development of delinquency, and delinquency prevention.

SUMMARY

Even though youthful misbehavior has long been noted, the process of the legalization, formalization, or institutionalization of the problems of youth is a recent event in history. Prior to the invention of delinquency, youthful misbehaviors were treated informally by families and communities.

The emergence of the concept of delinquency is directly related to the emergence of the concept of adolescence. As adolescents increasingly became defined as a subordinate dependent segment of the population, and as their behaviors became legislated, thereby bringing greater social control over young people, the concept of delinquency simultaneously evolved.

The concept of delinquency is a relatively recent one that can be traced to developments in ways of viewing children, in the nature of American life, in expectations about the behavior of children and the causes of their misbehavior, and in the official processing of juvenile rule-breakers.

During the eighteenth and nineteenth centu-

ries, youth came to be thought of as a special phase of life, and youngsters came to be seen as special creatures in need of protection and education. The Western European idea that the young needed guidance and discipline, as well as English principles of jurisprudence, were brought to the American colonies by English settlers. These European ideas strongly influenced the way in which youngsters were treated in the American colonies.

During the late nineteenth century, immigration and urbanization created vast changes in American life. American cities grew rapidly, and within them poverty and crime appeared to be rampant. Child welfare workers viewed youthful crime as the result of social conditions and attempted to reform youthful offenders through innovations in court handling and institutionalization. In 1899 the first court especially for children was created in Chicago. The idea of juvenile courts spread rapidly, and the Illinois Juvenile Court Act became the model for similar legislation throughout the United States. The laws mandating a court for children established new legal rules and proceedings. Juvenile courts operated on the principles of personalized justice and through informal procedures, with the goal of reforming and treating minors rather than punishing them.

The jurisdiction of early juvenile courts forms the basis for our present legal definition of delinquency. Delinquent acts are defined legally as criminal acts committed by juveniles and offenses prohibited for children but not for adults. Laws, which detail proscribed behaviors, outline the ages at which children are subject to delinquent jurisdiction and the procedures for transferring juveniles to adult courts. Criminologists and criminal justice officials, using a legal definition of delinquency, may variously identify juvenile delinquents as youngsters who have committed a criminal act or status offense (behavior illegal only for minors), youngsters picked up by the police, or youngsters referred to the juvenile court and adjudicated delinquent.

Different estimates of the amount of delinquency and other considerations depend on the definition employed. In recent years, there has been a tendency to give children who commit noncriminal offenses a label other than "delinquent." Still, half of the states continue to include status offenders under the classification of delinquent. Delinquency and delinquents are also defined in nonlegal terms. According to sociologist Ruth Cavan, minor deviations from rules are tolerated by the community, but the child who consistently and extremely "underconforms" will be looked at as a "real" delinquent and will probably be adjudicated as such by the juvenile court.

PROGRESS CHECK

1. After the seventeenth century, moralists and pedagogues saw childhood as extending beyond ages 5 to 7. (p. 5)
   a. True
   b. False

2. Discuss some of the changes which altered values and beliefs and affected the fundamental relationships between children and their families after the Industrial Revolution. (pp. 7–8)

3. Under English common law, children under the age of _____ were assumed to be incapable of criminal intent. (p. 6)

4. What is meant by the assertion that the philosophy of *parens patriae* and the principle of equity helped shape American concepts about delinquency? (p. 7)

5. When was the first juvenile court in the United States founded?
   a. 1749
   b. 1869
   c. 1899
   d. 1909 (p. 11)

6. When, where, and by whom is probation thought to have originated in this country? (p. 12)

7. What role did the Illinois courts play in developing an American approach to juvenile justice and a definition of delinquency? (p. 14)

8. Who is the juvenile delinquent? (pp. 15–20)

9. Briefly discuss the following terms: (1) transfer or waiver; (b) minimum age of jurisdiction; (3) continuing jurisdiction. (pp. 17–19)

10. Utilizing the contributions of sociologist Ruth Cavan, distinguish between legal and nonlegal definitions of delinquency. (p. 21)

NOTES

1. It is interesting to note that almost immediately following the designation of a children's literature, there were fears about the possible effects the stories may have on children. Children's books on chivalry were criticized for glamorizing idleness, violence, adultery, and militarism (Sommerville, 1982: 137).
2. Rousseau's observations are very close to our contemporary construction or understanding of adolescence; see Chapter 2.
3. In 1776 the famous English jurist and legal scholar Sir William Blackstone explained that a boy of 10 was considered liable for the murder of a companion because the boy tried to hide the body—an action, according to the court, that showed a knowledge of good and evil (Bruce, 1933; Platt, 1969).
4. Murdock's (1949) definition of the nuclear and extended family is generally accepted and most often cited: (1) the nuclear family consists of husband, wife, and offspring; and (2) the extended family consists of one or more nuclear families living with additional relatives (two or more) in a household joined together by multiple marriage (p. 1). Some consider the single parent and remarried families so common today to be derivatives of the nuclear and extended families (Coleman, 1984: 7). The definition of the family, however, is not resolved. The problem of including long-term cohabiting couples and homosexual relationships as well as childless married couples is highly controversial (Skolnick, 1981). We discuss some of the changes in the traditional American family in Chapter 9.
5. See Chapter 8, which reviews the history of youth and delinquency within the conflict and radical perspectives.
6. The Australian juvenile court in Adelaide actually predates the Chicago court.

7. Although the first juvenile court act contained provisions for probation and forbade detention of minors under 12 in jails, no money was provided by the legislature for probation officers or detention facilities. Early amendments to the Illinois Act did provide funding for probation and separate detention, but until then private funding replaced some of the "missing public funding" (see Schultz, 1974: 246–248).

8. See Chapter 3 and the Glossary for definitions of specific types of crimes.

9. Several excellent sources offer relatively current comparisons of selected state statutes. See Davis, 1984; Hamparian et al., 1982; King, 1980.

10. As Davis (1984) notes, "confronted with what appears to be a jurisdictional conflict, some courts have concluded that statutory grants of exclusive jurisdiction to the juvenile court are in violation of constitutional grants of jurisdiction to another court to try criminal cases; consequently, the juvenile court and criminal court have concurrent jurisdiction in certain criminal cases" (pp. 2–26). Some legal critics have frowned upon concurrent jurisdiction between juvenile and criminal courts for several reasons. Often the criminal courts tend to take the more sensational cases which elicit public reaction. Also, there may be an implied basic mistrust of the juvenile courts' ability to deal with serious offenders. However, with most states having a statutory scheme that allows waiver to the adult court, concurrent jurisdiction may be unnecessary.

CHAPTER 2

ADOLESCENCE AND DELINQUENCY

DEFINITION OF ADOLESCENCE

RITES OF PASSAGE

STATUS DISCONTINUITY

SOCIAL STEREOTYPES

THE ADOLESCENT SUBCULTURE

THE SCIENTIFIC STUDY OF ADOLESCENCE: THEORY AND RESEARCH

DEVELOPING AN UNDERSTANDING OF ADOLESCENCE

Some day a Dr. Salk will probably come along with a vaccine for adolescence. If so, the only question will be which Nobel Prize he should get—the one for medicine or the one for peace. (Richard Armour, 1978: 131)[1]

No treatment of delinquency can be complete without a discussion of adolescence. Not only are the concepts of adolescence and delinquency historically and definitionally interrelated, but they are also causally intertwined. Some have proposed adolescence itself as a cause of delinquency (see Gillis, 1981).

The purpose of this chapter is to review historical, theoretical, and cultural studies of adolescence. Special attention will be given to the social

scientific research on adolescence that has implications for our understanding of delinquency.

DEFINITION OF ADOLESCENCE

The term **adolescence** is derived from the Latin verb *adolescere* meaning "to grow" or "to mature." Adolescence commonly refers to the period of time between childhood and adulthood, a period of rapid growth. The adolescent, who is the individual in this interim stage, experiences tremendous changes both physically and socially. While references to this transitional period date far back in history, adolescence in the contemporary sense is relatively new.[2] G. Stanley Hall was one of the first social scientists officially to recognize the stage of adolescence as requiring special attention. His two-volume book, *Adolescence* (1905), is the first major work devoted entirely to the stage of adolescence.

There is general cultural disagreement about when adolescence begins and ends. In Western society today, the period of adolescence begins at approximately 11 or 12 and ends in the late teens or early twenties.[3] Biologically, the period of maturational and hormonal changes inducing rapid physiological growth and the development of sexual characteristics, which is called **pubescence,** usually marks the onset of adolescence. During pubescence, changes in the primary and secondary sex characteristics occur. Changes in the primary sex characteristics refer to the development of the reproductive sex organs. Changes in the secondary sex characteristics include other signs of physiological maturity (enlargement of the breasts in females, broadening of the shoulders and voice changes in males, skin and hair changes in both). The period of rapid physical growth and sexual development lasts about two years and terminates with **puberty,** which means that the individual is able to reproduce.

Individuals mature earlier physically in modern industrial societies. There is evidence that people today reach sexual maturity sooner and generally grow larger and live longer. This has been called the secular trend (Muuss, 1970). Social and technical advancements that have led to a higher living standard (including better health and nutrition) may in part explain this trend. The acceleration of physical maturity has also been linked to the discovery and use of electricity. The pituitary gland, which is the master gland governing growth in the body, is photo sensitive. Due to the invention of electricity and its widespread use in industrialized nations, people are in lighted areas for greater periods of time, which stimulates the pituitary gland and accelerates maturation. For example, today the average age for onset of menstruation in girls is significantly earlier than it was a century ago (Tanner, 1978). The secular trend began about a century ago and now seems to have

stabilized in Western industrial nations (Bakwin and McLaughlin, 1964).

Almost paradoxically, the technological and social changes that have influenced earlier physical maturation toward adulthood are the same changes that have led to the adolescent's prolonged dependence on parents and schools, because it now takes longer to prepare for independent adult status (Gordon, 1978: 133; Garbarino, 1985). An incongruity between biological and social maturity has evolved.

In the modern context, the concept of maturity has come to entail many dimensions. The major elements that signal the termination of adolescence are these:

1. Sociologically, the termination of status discontinuity

2. Psychologically, completing a number of developmental tasks and achieving a modicum of consistent identity

3. Biologically, achieving physiological maturity

4. Legally, reaching the age limit specified by law

5. Economically, becoming self-supporting and maintaining a balance between production and consumption

6. Traditionally, when informal customs lift the restrictions on adult privileges (Sebald, 1977: 7, 8)

Maturity is that age, state, or condition of life at which a person is considered fully developed physically, emotionally, socially, intellectually, and spiritually. But the achievement of all these characteristics is not always simultaneous.

RITES OF PASSAGE

While our society offers a series of different life crisis ceremonies that involve rites of passage (birth, marriage, graduation, and death ceremonies), there are no commonly held rites of passage to enable adolescents to mark the specific life experiences of the stage. Nor are adolescents provided with a social structure that accommodates change in an ordered process.

Arnold Van Gennep's classic study *Rites of Passage* (1908/1960) introduces a descriptive model that may be applied to all forms of life crisis ceremonies. Any rites of passage are fundamentally composed of three major phases: separation, transition, and incorporation. Each phase marks the performance of rituals connected with a person's passage between the secular and sacred areas or activities, admission to a group, and entry into a new social position. While these rituals vary in degrees of explicitness and elaboration, they are part of an ordered sequence: Each rite of passage moves the individual from separation through transition to incorporation. Behaviors and activities are prescribed by certain rules or norms specified by each phase. Certain taboos may restrict certain ordinary activities. These norms and taboos may define the preparation and consumption of food, the wearing of clothes, the assumption of body postures, and the adoption of various modes of interaction, including a special vocabulary or set of mannerisms.

Some cultures define maturity mainly in biological terms. Puberty, in these types of societies, is often a natural end point in adolescent development. In such societies, movement from childhood to adulthood (separation from family), transition from one status to another, and incorporation into the adult community are usually connected with various puberty rites. Societies that stress biological maturity often rely on physical tests in their rites of passage (tests of endurance, ear piercing, tattooing, scarring, circumcision, or other bodily mutilations) (Young, 1965). The rites also include symbolic ceremonies that socially confirm the passage to a new stage.

Western societies such as our own, which emphasize social and intellectual maturity (for which concrete signs are much more difficult to determine), offer no distinct common rites of passage signifying adulthood. Religious confirmation, graduation from school, getting a driver's license, being inducted into the military, getting

a job, voting, or having permission to marry are among the signs people use to mark the onset of adulthood. However, the different signs are associated with different minimum ages, and there is little consensus over their meaning or accompanying set of expectations. The result is that the stage of "adolescence refers to the crisis of status discontinuity" (Sebald, 1977: 37).

Moreover, these various signs of adulthood are not equally available to all classes of people. Saul Bernstein (1964) in his book *Youth on the Streets,* addressed this point. Speaking of lower class youth, he said:

> While he experiences some aspects of adolescence and even of adulthood (independence of parents) earlier than his middle class confrere, other dimensions of adulthood are confused and uncertain. Marriage and a regular income via a job are central goals and yet, increasingly, the route to them has become more education, a prerequisite for a satisfactory job. If he is a school dropout—and many are—the only road may be blocked. After repeated failures in school and much negative feelings about it, he is apt to regard it as hopeless to try to return. Where does this leave him with adulthood? Yet he wants the outlets of grown-ups, such as sexual activity, becoming a parent, drinking and spending generously on his pleasures. (1964: 23)

In many lower class communities, gangs have taken over the role of conferring adult status. Gang ceremonies often include physical type rites of passage that closely resemble those in societies stressing biological maturity. This may be because the physical signs are more tangible and easier to mark. Among many less affluent youth, the physical signs are the only signs available—opportunities for graduating from school, getting a job, owning a car or a house are not equally distributed across the society.

A collective response to status discontinuity is not just a lower class phenomenon. The general lack of consensus within our society over the attributes and onset of adulthood have resulted in a complicated and uneven movement from adolescence to adulthood for all youth. Sebald (1977:

37) suggested that the crisis of discontinuity, "since shared with peers, has evolved into collective compensations: youth subcultures."

However, adolescence as a collective phenomenon is not exclusively the property of American culture; it is associated with certain worldwide social cultural conditions, especially urban-industrial development (Sebald, 1977: 37–38). The collectivization of adolescence is both a by-product and a response to the complex changes in society. The variety or types of youth subcultures, however, vary even within a society and usually reflect social class differences (see Schwendinger and Schwendinger, 1976a; Greenberg, 1981).

STATUS DISCONTINUITY

The problem of status discontinuity or role confusion is very complex and may manifest itself in many different ways. It may result in prolonging the time to reach adulthood. Adolescents may express their confusion by regressing into childishness or by avoiding conflicts or by acting impulsively or by committing themselves to ill-formed courses of action. The cliquishness of adolescents or the intolerance of differences so characteristic of this age group has been described by Erik Erikson (1968) as a defense against role confusion. Erikson argued that the cirsis of role confusion in adolescence takes place because our society offers little to help adolescents mark status changes or validate status. He described adolescence ideally as a socially designated period of "psychosocial moratorium," suggesting that it serve as an official delay of adult commitment. However, he pointed out that in reality the psychosocial moratorium is a period full of contradictions. It is characterized by a "combination of prolonged immaturity and provoked precocity" (1968: 156).

Along these same lines, Paul Goodman (1960) in his book *Growing Up Absurd* claimed that the main problem facing young people is their sense of uselessness. While on the one hand adolescents are expected to act more like adults than children, they are not allowed to participate in adult activities. He noted that the emphasis on nonproduc-

tivity has had demoralizing effects. Adolescent sexual activity is still frowned upon. Adolescents are not allowed to work or have political power. Unable to make contributions that really count, adolescents feel a sense of uselessness. Families usually offer few constructive activities for young people. Taking out the garbage hardly constitutes a worthwhile, productive contribution. Much of juvenile delinquency, especially in its organized form, may be an attempt to cope with the indeterminate place of adolescence in our society.

Some experts today believe that the problem of role confusion during adolescence has become worse. Elkind (1984) described today's youth as "unplaced" (p. 5). The luxury of a psychosocial moratorium for most youth today does not exist. Instead, "they have had a premature adulthood thrust upon them" (p. 3). Elkind further noted:

> In a rapidly changing society, when adults are struggling to adapt to a new social order, few adults are genuinely committed to helping teenagers attain a healthy adulthood. Young people are thus denied the special recognition and protection that society previously accorded their age group. The special stage belonging to teenagers has been excised from the life cycle, and teenagers have been given proforma adulthood, an adulthood with all of the responsibilities but few of the prerogatives. Young people today are quite literally all grown up with no place to go. (1984, p. 5)

The premature adulthood that has been imposed upon the young impairs their construction of identity and leaves them particularly vulnerable to stress (Elkind, 1984: 6). Unprepared to cope with that stress, they are relying heavily on alcohol and drugs and are exhibiting other self-destructive behaviors. As a result, they are less prepared than ever before to assume responsible adult roles in society.

SOCIAL STEREOTYPES

Much of the adolescent role confusion, of course, stems from adult confusion. A review of the stereotypic images of adolescents demonstrates this confusion and the contradictory attitudes surrounding adolescence. Rice (1981), who summarized the presently held stereotypes, asserts: "Adolescents are admired, praised, and almost worshipped; they are criticized, belittled, and rejected" (p. 4).

Our society is frequently described as a youth-oriented society. In the span of the last eighty years, there has been more written about childhood and adolescence than the total in all of the preceding centuries of human history. Benjamin Spock's *Baby and Child Care* remains next to the Bible as one of the all-time best sellers (Sommerville, 1982: 12).

More and more professionals from all fields of interest and life are specializing in children and adolescence (producers of goods and services including physicians, lawyers, merchants, advertisers, and teachers, as well as academicians, including historians, economists, political scientists, psychologists, sociologists, biologists, and criminologists). Philippe Ariès accentuated this point in his book *Centuries of Childhood*, which he begins by describing a society that is seemingly unaware of childhood and adolescence, and which he ends by commenting on a society that has become obsessed by youth. He summed it up with the following:

New sciences such as psychoanalysis, pediatrics and psychology devote themselves to the problems of childhood, and their findings are transmitted to parents by way of a mass of popular literature. Our world is obsessed by the physical, moral and sexual problems of childhood. (1962: 411)

Despite the demonstrated increase in our quest for knowledge of childhood and adolescence, and despite the increases in professional concern and study of youth, there appear to be signs that youngsters are of less value in our society. For example, more and more people are choosing not to have children. There is evidence that youngsters from all classes are suffering neglect and abuse (Burgdorf, 1981; Giovannoni and Becerra, 1979; Justice and Justice, 1976). There is a noted decline

in the relationship between parents and children (Sommerville, 1982). Parents again seem to be delegating the responsibility of childrearing to strangers; day care centers, schools, peer groups, and television are increasingly part of children's daily experiences. Even though absence of contact with parents has been found to correlate with problem behavior, young people continue to be excluded from adult activities and social events. Not much has changed since James Coleman (1961), a sociologist, declared: "Our adolescents today are cut off more than ever from adult society" (p. 9).

Concern over the problems posed by adolescents and the ambivalent attitudes of adults toward adolescents seems to be on the rise. Rates of accidents, suicides, teenage pregnancies, and delinquency are alarmingly high. Today, despite the allegations that our society is youth-oriented, there is evidence that most problems of youth (especially emotional and adjustment problems) still go unattended, and there is reason to believe that the rates of maladjustment for adolescent populations have increased in recent years (Dohrenwent et al., 1980).

Negative stereotypes include allegations that today's adolescents are spoiled and pampered, lazy, irresponsible, hedonistic, immoral, cynical, and rebellious. These images often lead to the conclusion that adolescence is a time for parent-youth conflict. Kaplan in *The Farewell to Childhood* (1984) described adolescence as a unique, tumultuous transitional period. Drugs, fast cars, pranks, wild parties, wild music, and bizarre fashions are frequently associated with youth.

But are these various stereotypes accurate? There are several reasons why they may be misleading. First, these stereotypes assume that youth constitutes a single homogeneous group. Obviously not all young people are the same (see Simpson and Yinger, 1972). Second, the evidence does not support the stereotypes. For example, for very large numbers of youngsters, particularly those who are poor, fun, parties, and fast cars are not typical. The fact that adolescents have the highest rate of unemployment of any age group cannot be taken as an indicator that they do not want to work

(Gordon, 1978). The majority want jobs and believe that work is among the main goals of adult life (Yankelovich, 1974).

Finally, the labels or negative descriptions applied to youth lack clarity of meaning. For instance, there is a general lack of consensus over what youthful rebellion actually entails. The typical use of the term *rebellion* to describe youthful behavior is vague and overextended. Everything from disobedience or adherence to certain styles to protest marching or juvenile delinquency has been subsumed under the term. All considered, rebelliousness is still far less characteristic of youth than conformity. Indeed, it is youthful cliquishness that is erroneously mistaken for rebellion. Many of the negative images are associated with the youth subculture, which is itself a widely debated topic.

THE ADOLESCENT SUBCULTURE

There are even disagreement and inconsistent attitudes about the existence of an adolescent subculture. Because adolescents exhibit certain characteristics that serve to identify them with a unique clothing style, vocabulary, and gestures; with special tastes in food, music, and art; with a critical philosophy or world view; and because they as a group are given minority status in the larger society, many researchers have proposed studying adolescence as a subcultural phenomenon (Friedenberg, 1965; 1967). The subculture approach to adolescence became popular with the publication of James Coleman's *The Adolescent Society* in 1961. This view tends to highlight youth alienation from the adult world and promotes the stormy and stressful idea of youth.

Other writers have questioned the stereotype of youthful rebelliousness by deemphasizing the evidence of stress and underscoring the sources of agreement between adolescents and their parents (Matteson, 1975: 92, 95). Such writers as Matteson (1975), Elkin and Westly (1955), and Bealer et al. (1965) argue that the adolescent culture is a myth on these grounds: (1) That adolescence is

too brief in duration; (2) that adolescents lack intergenerational continuity; and (3) that most of the behavior of adolescents is not deviant but actually conformist.

While the adolescent subculture does not clearly comprise a fully developed cultural system, there are elements of one (Yinger, 1960). The Hippie movement or the alternative life style movement of the 1960s represents an example of an adolescent subculture.

Lewis Yablonsky in his *The Hippie Trip* (1973) described the phenomenon in the following manner:

> The new youth life-style developed in that decade [1960s] encompassed among other characteristics: an extremist approach to "love"; greater sexual freedom; and a concept of work that defied the Protestant ethic. Drugs were used as a vehicle for pleasure, new levels of consciousness, and internal social change. The movement was essentially a counterattack against formalism, bureaucracy, and robot behavior. The hippie phenomenon involved disaffiliation from existing society, and at its peak around 1967–68, several million people dropped out. (p. 5)

Youthful dissent, which "constituted a nearly global stirring of youth demanding recognition of new ideas and instant reform of traditional ways of doing things," involved a total of 500 million worldwide during the 1960s and 1970s (Sebald, 1977: 501). These various youth movements, while historically documented, have also received mixed reviews. Some observers have assessed youthful rebellion in positive terms—as creative, catalytic, renovating, inspiring, hopeful, visionary (Goodman, 1960; Friedenberg, 1965; Slater, 1970; Reich, 1970; Roszak, 1968). Others have given more negative interpretations, calling youthful dissent immature, narcissistic, dysfunctional, wasteful, unrealistic, deviant, and pathological (Bettelheim, 1969; Feuer, 1969; Aldridge, 1970).

Despite the lack of consensus over the extent and interpretation of these youthful activities, many of these ideas served to identify all youth of the period. Though such large numbers were involved, the activities that received greatest media coverage included only select groups. For example, in the United States coverage of the youth movement focused primarily on college students and leading activists who came from such schools as Berkeley, Harvard, and the University of Michigan (Lipsett, 1972; Kahn and Bowers, 1970). Very little information was given on the nature and level of dissent among noncollege youth (Levinson, 1973). The 1960s have gone down in history as a decade of youthful rebellion despite the fact that most youths did not participate in the movement or in demonstrations (Lipsett, 1972; Yablonsky, 1973).

The adult and societal responses to the events of the sixties were also varied. The rising rates of juvenile delinquency, the violent outbreak at the 1968 Democratic national convention (Walker, 1968), and the 1970 shooting of students at Kent State and Jackson State Universities (Scranton, 1970) suggest that negative reactions were present. On the other hand, the fact that the sixties were also associated with the children's rights movement (Zimring, 1982), the lowering of the voting age, and other civil rights for youth suggests adult accommodation (Gordon, 1978).

Young people today do not seem to exhibit the level of organization of the 1960s, yet cliquish behavior and elements of a youth subculture continue to be evident. And while society frequently appears intolerant of the cliquishness of the young (they are ridiculed and punished for it), there continue to be inordinate social pressures to standardize adolescence (via television and schools). Indeed, the cliquish behavior may be a response to adult ambivalence and inconsistent attitudes toward adolescence. Cliquish behavior may serve as a medium for the adolescent desire to merge with others while at the same time trying to differentiate themselves.

Few will dispute the fact that there is confusion in our society over what is expected of youth. Many contradictory images of youth have been proposed. They are described as alienated and as having a sense of solidarity; as confused and as having common norms; as rebellious and as being conformist. In large part the confusion reflects the increasing complexity and pluralism of contemporary society. The traditional developmental tasks of adolescence, especially role identity, may be increasingly difficult to accomplish in a standardized fashion. Standard role expectations are made tenuous due to the heterogeneity of youth; there are differences among young people depending on age, socioeconomic level, racial and ethnic background, gender, residential location, and so on.

Moreover, due to the tremendous advances in telecommunications, computerization, and transportation, people are exposed to many different groups of people, to varying behavior patterns, and to a kaleidoscope of shifting and conflicting values. Traditional behavioral expectations and reference groups have become more diffused. Perhaps the challenge of the future is to destandardize youth by emphasizing the development of interpersonal communication skills and tolerance of human and social variations during adolescence. Despite the controversy and confusion surrounding the place, role, and significance of adolescence in society, there is some consensus among social scientists that the stage represents a very special phase of the life cycle that requires our attention and understanding.

THE SCIENTIFIC STUDY OF ADOLESCENCE: THEORY AND RESEARCH

In some respects, the professional attention given to adolescence has been helpful in developing an appreciation of the specialness of the stage and has perhaps even led to some adult accommodation, such as the development of special services. In other respects, however, the process of identifying this stage as unique has also been associated with some negative consequences. After all, development or maturation is a continuous process, not one neatly broken up into stages based on limited criteria of demarcation. The arbitrary definition and special treatment of various stages have resulted in many subtle forms of discrimination and segregation of the young in families, schools, and society.

As we have seen, the social construction of adolescence is full of contradictions. Adolescents represent many different kinds of individuals and different experiences, making generalizations difficult. However, theoretically and as subjects of research, they increasingly occupy a special place in the life cycle. For a fuller understanding of the contemporary meaning of adolescence and its relationship to delinquency, we must look at the scientific knowledge of adolescence that has accumulated during this century.

The idea that childhood and adolescence are phenomena unto themselves, requiring special study and analysis, has been supported by philosophers, biologists, psychologists, and sociologists of the late nineteenth and early twentieth centuries who, perhaps after observing their own children, offered insights into the development of human nature. In the words of Kessen (1965):

> The study of child behavior began anew, fresh and enthusiastic, with the birth of Doddy Darwin, Armande Binet, Polly Watson, Helen Baldwin, Jacqueline Piaget, Axel Preyer, and Friedrich Tiedemann. Each father saw his own child—that is, the child that his prejudice or theory would predict—but sharing a common object of observation bound these men of divergent times and opinions to a set of common problems about human development. (p. 12)

The first ten years of the twentieth century ushered in tremendous changes for the public and academic treatment of childhood and adolescence:

> The invention of mental tests, rise of behaviorism, and, most of all the foundation of psychoanalysis changed the child as much as all earlier history had; he had become valuable, meaningful and intricate in ways unknown before the twentieth century. (Kessen, 1965: 6)

The theories of the stage of adolescence and supporting research are presented under three separate headings: physical and sexual development, intellectual and moral characteristics, and the forming of the self-concept. In reality these topics are difficult to consider independently, since they are all related.

Physical and Sexual Development

The physical changes experienced in adolescence are very important. The changes in the endocrine, pituitary, and sex glands trigger the secretion of hormones that stimulate and regulate not only growth, but motivational and emotional reactions. Until the changes stabilize or become balanced, the adolescent may exhibit moodiness, emotional outbursts, extreme irritability, sensitivity, and fluctuation between periods of great elation and happiness and periods of deep depression and crying spells (Doering et al., 1975; Garrison, 1976; Schonfeld, 1961; Thomas, 1979). These changes in personality and behaviors have a physiological basis and must be taken into account, along with family and social factors that affect adolescent behavior or in some cases delinquent behavior. The emotional reactions of adolescents to the physical transformation and the reactions of society to these changes are as important as the physical changes themselves.

Physiology.   Most of the early theories of adolescence emphasized physical and sexual changes. For example, G. Stanley Hall (1905) claimed that hormonal changes and the accompanying growth spurts caused a wide range of emotional fluctuations in youth, including the oscillation between depression and happiness, egoism and insecurity, love and hate, motivation and indifference. Physical changes were considered to be at the root of the moody and unpredictable nature of adolescents and at the root of misbehavior, including delinquency. These conditions, he reasoned, affect the quality of social and interpersonal relations. Hall was led to characterize the stage of adolescence universally as a time of "storm and stress."

Based on her observations of Samoan adolescents, Margaret Mead (1950, 1953) argued that Hall's typification of the "storm and stress" of adolescence is not universal, but largely a creation of Western culture. She found that among Samoan youth, there was significantly less storm and stress than in more advanced societies. Infancy, childhood, adolescence, and adulthood were more smoothly connected and continuous rather than being discrete, independent stages. One progresses, Mead surmised, from one stage to another with less contradiction and in a less abrupt manner.

In contrast to the United States, where the youngsters are assumed to be irresponsible, sexless, and subordinate, youngsters' roles in other cultures are relatively more consistent with adult roles. The children of Samoa, for example, assumed roles of responsibility and domination and were permitted sexual expression throughout childhood.[4] Mead (1950, 1953) suggested that the hardships associated with the Western concept of adolescence are linked to the discontinuity between the stages of development. Adolescents have to unlearn the taboos and attitudes of childhood in order to become adults.

Similarly, Ruth Benedict concluded that cultures which stress discontinuity between childhood and adult roles may be described as "age-grade societies" (1938: 161–167). The universality or inevitability of "storm and stress" have been challenged by these anthropologists by understressing the physiological aspects of development and by emphasizing cultural attitudes. According to this view, whether adolescence is perceived as a period of stress and strain or as a period of smooth, continuous progression to adulthood depends largely on the cultural interpretations of pubescent physical changes.

It is interesting to note that in those societies in which adolescence is perceived as a continuous stage of development, there is relatively little concern over delinquency. Such societies are less likely to view adolescence as any kind of special problem. So while certain aspects of development (such as physical change) are universally present, it is very important to consider the social and cultural factors that influence and define experiences (Brown, 1969; Muuss, 1970).

Sexuality. Sigmund Freud (1953a) focused his attention on the physical and sexual development of individuals living in Western industrial cultures. Freud described five fundamental stages: oral (birth–1 year); anal (1–3 years); phallic (3–6 years); latency (6–puberty); genital (from puberty on). For Freud, adolescence represented a reawakening of the sexual urges of the phallic stage he described with reference to the Oedipus complex.[5] He suggested that sexual urges during the phallic stage are repressed and that the child enters a period of latency until puberty, at which point the natural biological sexual urges reemerge. They are so strong that continued repression at this stage is impossible.

Freud claimed that the sexuality during adolescence (genital stage) is distinct from sexuality during childhood (phallic stage). First, the child experiences sexual pleasure through bodily contact and the stimulation of the erotogenic zones. During adolescence, sexual pleasure and satisfaction depend not only on the stimulation of the erotogenic zones, but on obtaining an orgasm in intercourse. Moreover, adolescent sexual curiosity, as contrasted with sexual curiosity during the phallic stage, is primarily directed toward developing heterosexual relations with nonfamily members. The focus upon nonfamily members for sexual expression serves to break the dependence of the adolescent on the family (p. 227). Freud went on to say that the affection formerly directed toward parents is transferred to peers. Moreover, the hostility for the same-sex parent manifest during the phallic stage is transferred to the community during the genital stage.

In Western society, adolescent sexuality and aggression are usually denied and diverted into other socially approved channels. In other words, because the society particularly limits sexual activity and aggressiveness among adolescents, it becomes necessary for individuals to **sublimate** their natural drives (find diversionary or alternate acceptable behaviors). Since sexual expression is delayed, the adolescent's dependence on family (on a psychological level) is prolonged. When the natural sexual and aggressive urges (and it is important to note here that Freud linked sex and aggression, suggesting they are inseparable) are not satisfied through sublimation, the individual may adapt in socially disapproved ways. Delinquent behavior may be one outcome. While each stage represents a unique psychosexual context, repression and sublimation of natural, instinctive behavior are requirements of each level and together constitute the prerequisite for civilization. In other words, for the sake of civilization, natural expressions of aggression and sex must be controlled and channeled into socially acceptable forms.

The individual's general renunciation of instinctive gratification of sex and aggression creates inner psychological antagonism and conflict, accounting, according to Freud (1930), for the turmoil and unhappiness of today's civilization. But while repression and social control may be related to certain problems in the development of adult personalities, Freud does not suggest that the solution lies in lifting the social limitations on behavior (especially sexual inhibitions). Since sex and aggression are inseparable, the loosening up of either would, according to Freud, result in disorder, which cannot be tolerated by civilized society. He argues that as civilization advances, the natural sexual and aggressive urges must be progressively checked and socially defined (1930). Psychoanalysis is intended by Freud to help people cope with the social controls that increasingly inhibit the expression of natural urges.

Most of Freud's theories cannot easily be tested. Yet it is interesting to note the almost prophetic character of some of his assertions. Using Freud's theoretical reasoning, one would expect that more permissive sexual attitudes would result in more aggressive behavior. In American society today, adolescents appear more free to express their sexual urges. It may be more than coincidence that the incidence of violence among adolescents is also alarmingly high. Of course, the problems associated with defining and measuring such concepts as violence and "acceptable sexual practices" within our complex society make any attempt to explain their relationship extremely difficult.

Even though many of Freud's propositions are hard to document empirically and are debatable, they have inspired nearly all the researchers who have studied normal and deviant development (see Chapter 5 for a discussion of the psychoanalytic perspective on deliquency).

Intellectual and Moral Capabilities

Along with the unique physiological characteristics of adolescence, differences in intellectual and moral development have been noted throughout history. But it was not until the monumental work of Piaget and his collaborator, Barbara Inhelder, that the stages of intellectual maturity became more fully understood and appreciated.

Cognition. According to Inhelder and Piaget (1958), puberty is not the distinctive characteristic of adolescence; they claimed that adolescence represents a new stage in thinking and that this affects the introduction into adult society more than puberty. During adolescence mental capacities expand, the social milieu widens, and greater opportunities present themselves. Social and environmental factors interact with physical and neurological maturation.

Piaget (1971) noted that as children develop physically, they exhibit certain regularities in thinking or *schemata*. He introduced four broad stages of development associated with specific schemata. The four are summarized in Table 2.1.

During the formal operational or adolescent stage, the formation of values (social justice, rational esthetic values, and other social ideals) is no longer bound by concrete reality; rather, values begin to encompass all sorts of social and interpersonal possibilities (1969: 149). Piaget and Inhelder wrote:

> As a result of the acquisition of such values, decisions, whether in opposition to or in agreement with the adult, have an altogether different significance than they do in a small social group of younger children. The possibilities opened up by these new values are obvious in the adolescent, who differs from the child in that he is not only capable of forming theories but is also concerned with choosing a career that will permit him to satisfy his need for social reform and for new ideas. (1969: 151)

Piaget and Inhelder maintained that when youngsters are presented with new information, they use their mental capacities to process that information. Each stage of development has a unique schema or system for making sense of the data. *Assimilation* and *accommodation* are two ways

TABLE 2.1 **A Summary of Piaget's Stages of Cognitive Development**

Sensorimotor (birth to 2 years)	*Preoperational* (2–7 years)	*Concrete Operational* (7–11 years)	*Formal Operational* (12–15 years)
Emphasis is on the development of all the sense modalities, and at first the motto is out of sight out of mind. The infant begins as a passive responder and then becomes an initiator. The infant learns to observe and to reconstruct. The child is very egocentric but realizes self limitations and by the end of the stage is able to engage others to help. Generally the child, at this stage, is unable to comprehend any external rules imposed by family or society. Elkind (1966) suggests that the chief cognitive task during this period is *conquest of objects*.	Emphasis is on language development. By the end of this stage symbols are clearly understood and manipulated. Elkind suggests that the main task during this stage is the *conquest of symbols* (1966). Emotions such as anger or happiness are expressed through overt actions and not imaginatively. Conceptions of equality or justice are based on quantifiable measures and "tit for tat" reasoning. The stage is generally marked by a perspective called *moral realism* (i.e., children have the ability to learn rules but they perceive them as entities not to be questioned although not always followed). Moral realism involves the insistence upon obeying the letter of the law, not the spirit of the law. Moral realism is connected with the attitude of *unilateral respect*, which suggests that the child who has respect for adults does not expect the adult to reciprocate with equal respect. Children at this level are still very conscious of self limitations and their inferior status.	This stage is marked by a more sophisticated level of reasoning. The child performs imaginatively or mentally what previously would have been acted out; and the child distinguishes among logical classes of things. Elkind labels the primary cognitive tasks of this stage *mastering classes, relations, and quantities* (1966). The level of reasoning about rules and obligations is called the *morality of cooperation*. Rules are rationally established by argument and by mutual satisfaction; they are no longer fixed absolute principles. There is concern now for the "spirit of the law" and the views of reciprocity and equality are no longer based on quantity. Children now expect mutual respect from adults. They become highly indignant when denied respect or consideration. (Also check description by Muuss, 1975).	This stage is marked by advanced symbolizing. Elkind refers to this stage as the *conquest of thought* (1966). At this point of development, the individual is able to understand probability, analogies, hypothetical problems, abstract ideals, theories and principles, and even ideas contrary to facts. While in the concrete operational stage the individual deals mainly with present reality, in the operational thought stage one is able to grasp "the possible transformations and assimilates reality only in terms of imagined or deduced events" (Piaget and Inhelder, 1969: 149). During this stage the adolescent is capable of scientific reasoning because he/she is able to develop and check various theories (see Okun and Sasfy, 1977).

This summary is based on the synthesis of many different works, including Piaget (1971); Piaget and Inhelder (1969); Elkind (1966); Muuss (1975); Okun and Sasfy (1977).

in which individuals process data. When individuals interpret new information with reference to what they already know, they are using assimilation. When individuals change their thinking to take into account the new information, they are using accommodation. In other words, individuals try to make sense of new information by using old assumptions, and they alter those assumptions when the new information no longer fits.

The physical and sexual changes experienced by adolescents and the new social reactions associated with these changes force the adolescent toward accommodation. The changes force adolescents to alter their thinking about themselves and others. But despite adolescents' greater conceptual capabilities, they still have to overcome a lingering egocentrism before the more sophisticated thought processes begin to manifest themselves. While they are more advanced than children because they recognize the thoughts of others, they are not like adults because they are still largely preoccupied with themselves. Elkind (1967) noted that adolescents believe their appearance and behavior are the focal concern of others. This egocentrism must be overcome before the sophisticated level of abstract, hypothetical, and theoretical reasoning occurs with regularity.

Elkind and Bowen (1979) described two forms of egocentrism: imaginary audience and the personal fable. Many adolescents feel that others are as pleased or as critical of their behavior as they themselves are. The *imaginary audience* is described as the belief "that others in our immediate vicinity are as concerned with our thoughts or behaviors as we ourselves are" (Elkind and Bowen, 1979: 38). The *personal fable* refers to the adolescent's feeling of specialness or uniqueness and the feeling that others are especially interested in him or her. The feeling of specialness often leads to a belief that one is an exception to the general rule or that one is magically protected from the consequences which beset others. The personal fable phenomenon accounts for the assumption "it won't happen to me" and explains why some adolescents take undue risks, including delinquent behaviors such as shoplifting.

By age 15 or 16, egocentrism begins to lessen as the individual increasingly appreciates the difference between one's own priorities and preoccupations and those of others. Elkind (1967) suggests that the imaginary audience is replaced by the real audience and the personal fable eventually fades with the realization that one is subject to the same consequences as everyone else. As adolescents' egocentrism is overcome, they are better able to formulate their own identities, to relate to others, and to consider their role in society (Looft, 1972).

By age 16, an individual's cognitive structures are almost fully formed. Piaget (1971) suggests that by this point the adolescent is capable of coping with most intellectual problems and may be said to be in an advanced state of equilibrium. However, if sociocultural and educational experiences have not encouraged the development of hypothetical deductive reasoning, individuals may not attain this level of thinking despite innate intelligence or neurological readiness (Piaget, 1971).

Berzensky (1978) argued that the first three Piagetian stages are universally sequential. However, achievement of the formal operational level is especially dependent on appropriate stimulation. Various cultures differ with respect to average level of abstract thinking. Those cultures which stimulate and facilitate the acquisition of cognitive skills necessary for abstract thought usually demonstrate higher norms of thinking in the population. Miller et al. (1978) cite Piaget's comparison of Martinique (a Caribbean island) and Montreal, Canada: Children in Montreal advanced to the higher cognitive levels at an earlier age. Dasen (1972) and Dulit (1972) suggest that underdeveloped societies are less likely to stimulate and reinforce advanced levels of thinking. A higher degree of literacy, a higher level of education (Gallagher and Moppe, 1976), and a greater degree of urbanization (Youniss and Dean, 1974) are correlated with the achievement of the formal operational level of thinking.

Internal cultural differences have also been noted. Disadvantaged social environments appear to discourage the more advanced levels of thinking (Piaget, 1972). Kohlberg and Gilligan (1971) have found that nearly half of American adults never advance to the formal operational level of thinking. Using different levels of language as an example of varying environmental stimuli, the linguist Basil Bernstein (1975) argued that level of language expression may have an impact on cognitive development. He claimed that opportunities for language learning are not equally distributed across a culture and that different levels of language stimulate different levels of cognition. Bernstein described two patterns of language expression: public language and formal language.

While no particular vocabulary characterizes public languages, there are certain identifying features: Sentences are simple, short, and often unfinished or poorly constructed. Use of adjectives and adverbs is limited; impersonal pronouns are rarely used ("I think" instead of "one thinks that"); and simple conjunctions ("so," "then," "and," "because") are repetitively employed. Public language is a "restricted code," since it permits only a simple expression of ideas and simple reasoning. It inhibits complicated analysis, hypothetical reasoning, and discourages abstract thought. Moreover, public language generally lacks emotional and descriptive elements by omitting shades of meaning and intonation. The presumption of a common context is one reason why many sentences are left incomplete. Consequently, public speech requires the listener to be familiar with the background of the speaker. The omission of the critical elements forces the listener to be more conscious of who is speaking than of what is spoken.

In contrast, formal language allows more subtle and complex distinctions to be made and has greater possibilities. Bernstein (1975) argues that individuals trained to use formal language develop more advanced intellectual capabilities, while those trained to use public language are more limited. Because language use is determined largely along class lines, the lower classes are therefore more restricted in opportunities for intellectual development.

Morality.   Lawrence Kohlberg's (1963, 1964) three levels of moral maturity, the preconventional, conventional, and postconventional, are closely associated with Piaget's stages of cognition. The preconventional level corresponds roughly to Piaget's concrete operational stage. The basis for evaluating behavior as good or bad during this

stage does not include concern for others, but concern mainly for oneself. Behavior is generally evaluated not in terms of intent, but in terms of consequences.

Kohlberg's conventional stage corresponds to Piaget's formal operational stage, which occurs during adolescence. Kohlberg (1971) argues that early adolescents generally think that moral behavior is behavior others approve. This is often expressed in the need to conform. The more mature level of the conventional stage includes a "law and order" mentality. Individuals test the extent to which ideals, objectives, or rules are consistent with actions and the extent to which these ideals, objectives, and rules are functional. Often the rules adolescents accept are justified as operative or functional in maintaining the well-being of the group.

The postconventional stage is reached only by those who develop through the formal operational stage, who have been exposed to the cultural relativity of norms, and who understand the concept of relativity. The postconventional level of morality, however, usually manifests itself in young adulthood, and especially among college graduates.[6] Many people never attain this level of sophistication.[7] Abstract values such as justice, equality, fairness, and human dignity, become important concepts in the postconventional stage. Individuals at this stage understand value relativism and the importance of critically evaluating standards, rights of individuals, and the role of social agreement in the determination of what is right or wrong.[8]

Jennings, Kilkenny, and Kohlberg (1983) reported that studies which focus on the stages of moral development and their link to criminal behavior provide empirical data which support the conclusion that the juvenile delinquent's stage of moral judgment is not as advanced at that of nondelinquent control groups (also see Sagi and Eisikovits, 1981). While the authors do not intend to imply causal connections, they do suggest that increased maturity provides "an insulating effect against delinquency" (Jennings, Kilkenny, Kohlberg, 1983: 311).

This conclusion appears evident, especially given the fact that most delinquents grow out of their delinquency. Jennings, Kilkenny, and Kohlberg conclude:

> Higher reasoning makes one a more reliable moral agent and thus better able to withstand some incentive to illegal conduct postulated by a variety of sociological and psychological theories of the etiology of delinquency. The preconventional thinker is not more delinquent by nature, but simply feels less obligated to conform to any conventions, whether of the larger society or of a subcultural group. (1983: 311)

The significance of this research depends on how the delinquent is defined (are we referring to the self-reported delinquent, a court-adjudicated delinquent; and is the person a status offender or a violent offender?). According to official statistics, most adolescents *do not* become adjudicated delinquents. However, self-report inventories on national samples indicate that most adolescents have committed delinquent acts, especially nonviolent and status offenses. Since many juveniles who are not considered delinquent are in the preconventional reasoning stage, this is not enough to explain delinquent behavior. Thus, "moral reasoning is not a necessary and sufficient cause of delinquency" (Jennings, Kilkenny, and Kohlberg, 1983: 317).

Both Piaget and Kohlberg stipulated that cognitive and moral development are not only dependent on physical maturation or innate intelligence, but also require environmental or educational stimulation. Since different types of cognitive and social experiences are prerequisites for moral development, there may be important implications for educational programs. This approach may be significant in models of educational prevention and treatment of delinquents (Jennings, Kilkenny, Kohlberg, 1983: 346). To provide the optimal opportunity in the moral stages, other aspects of development (including cognitive, social, ego) may be stimulated.

The California Treatment Studies of Interpersonal Maturity Levels (I levels) (Jesness, 1974; Palmer, 1974, 1978; Warren, 1976, 1983) comprise a body of research that integrates cognitive, moral, and ego development. This research is especially relevant to our discussion because a great

deal of effort has been made to relate the dimension of maturity (made up of cognitive, moral, and ego components) to delinquency. Seven broad stages characterize the interpersonal maturity scale, ranging from infancy (I_1) to the ideal maturity level of adulthood (I_7). This scheme indicates that the progress of integrative cognitive abilities along the scale depends not only on physical and mental age, but also on social stimulation. Most institutions that include the participation of youth assume and require at least an I_4 level of functioning (taking others into account and assuming responsibility for one's own behavior). While deviations from this expectation may be tolerated more in younger children, older children (particularly older adolescents) who function at an I_2 or I_3 level are not well received or tolerated by society.

The delinquents who were studied ranged from the I_2 to I_4 levels. Special delinquent subcategories have been designed to provide greater depth of understanding (see Chapter 5). Most of the work relating the I levels to delinquency has been produced with the express purpose of developing treatment models appropriate for delinquents at different levels of functioning (see Warren, 1983, 1976; Palmer, 1967, 1971, 1972, 1974, 1978).

There is agreement among the models of cognition, morality, and maturity described above. Higher levels of functioning in all three models depend on the quality of interpersonal interactions and social stimulation. Higher levels of achievement are manifest in the development of greater self-understanding, social consciousness, and an appreciation or acceptance of individual and cultural differences. Without a fundamental understanding of the relationship between self and society, the levels the individual achieves may be limited.

Forming the Self-Concept

The adolescent struggle for identity stems from the physical, cognitive, and social changes associated with the stage (Jones, 1969). The development of a stable self-concept is perhaps the primary task of adolescence (Erikson, 1963; Havighurst, 1951). It is not until adolescence that theoretical reasoning becomes apparent (Piaget, 1971). Forming a self-concept requires the same creative and abstract process involved in forming a theory. Elkind (1984) noted that "the task of forming an identity is a difficult and complex one. . . . And it is not unreasonable to characterize identity as a theory of oneself" (pp. 8–9). The self-concept is sociologically significant because it highlights the fact that what individuals come to think of themselves largely determines their behavior.

The Looking Glass Self. By watching his own youngsters mature, Charles Horton Cooley, a social psychologist, became interested in how the self-image forms and how social experiences affect it. Cooley (1909/1964) concluded that individuals acquire their self-image by imagining how they appear to other people. Cooley referred to this process as the *looking glass self*. This self is composed of three elements:

> the imagination of our appearance to the other person, the imagination of his judgment of that appearance, and some sort of self-feeling such as pride or mortification. (Cooley, 1964: 184)

During the course of daily interactions, people accumulate sets of evaluations and expectations about themselves and about who and what they are and what that means in a particular social context. What this suggests is that an individual is not simply born knowing the meaning of being delinquent or nondelinquent or being white, or Anglo-Saxon, or Protestant or male, or anything else. Rather, an individual develops an identity by interacting with others and by attaching socially constructed meanings to certain attributes and behaviors.

George Herbert Mead (1934: 154), another social psychologist, suggested that people are influenced mainly by the reactions of **significant others** (parents, siblings, and others who are close). Additional significant others beyond the family include teachers, employers, ministers, even television personalities. The general appraisals of the main others with whom an individual identifies

will largely determine how that individual will feel about him or herself. The extent to which the significant others like or dislike, accept or reject, consider one to be bright or dull, attractive or homely, mature or immature, has bearing on the development of the self-concept, which in turn may affect behavior.

It is important to underscore that the self-concept is essentially subjective, since it depends on one's self perceptions or one's own interpretation of the reactions of others (Kaplan, 1975). The significance of this is that the self-concept is vulnerable to error. Errors may result because the reactions of others are not always consistent and because we may misinterpret those reactions. Moreover, individuals themselves often exhibit inconsistent behavior (sometimes unconsciously) so that the variable responses, even though accurate reflections of behavior, may appear inconsistent. Finally, the assessment by another may be biased or incorrect. For example, Alice Miller (1981) claimed that the failure of a mother to accept a child's "reality" may affect a child's ability to develop his or her own "true self."

Self-Fulfilling Prophecy. W. I. Thomas argued that the development of the self-concept irrespective of whether or not it is based on reality leads to a **self-fulfilling prophecy** (forecasts which create the conditions for their own fulfillment) (1931: 189). There are two types of self-fulfilling prophecies. The first is the kind one brings upon oneself. If a person believes that he or she is inadequate or that he or she cannot do something, then that person is likely to find confirming evidence. Indeed, an individual's own expectations may even create the type of response he or she will receive. This type of self-fulfilling prophecy is especially familiar to psychiatrists.

The second type is the kind others impose upon individuals. Another name for this second type is the *Pygmalion effect*. In other words, the expectations others hold of an individual may produce confirming behavior. This second type is particularly familiar to sociologists and educators. In his study of Polish immigrants in Chicago, Thomas (1918–1920; 1928) attributed the poor school performance of Polish youngsters to the low expectations held by their teachers. It was from this observation that Thomas first coined the phrase "self-fulfilling prophecy." Rosenthal and Jacobson (1968) in their book *Pygmalion in the Classroom*, and Charles Silberman in *Crisis in the Classroom* (1970) also found that children for whom teachers had greater expectations performed better in school and vice versa.

People may learn to be (or "play") stupid, crazy, or bad to conform to others' expectations. This, of course, often serves to reinforce the others' original beliefs. The process is thus self-confirming and circular. Bandura (1964) noted that one reason why American adolescents have presented a problem to society is that the "storm and stress" so widely associated with adolescence may often be a case of self-fulfilling prophecy. He summarized his position in the following statement:

> If a society labels its adolescents as "teen-agers," and expects them to be rebellious, unpredictable, sloppy, and wild in their behavior, and if this picture is repeatedly reinforced by the mass media, such cultural expectations may very well force adolescents into the role of rebel. In this way, a false expectation may serve to instigate and maintain certain role behaviors, which, in turn, then reinforce the originally false belief. (Bandura, 1964: 230)

The Search for Identity

So much of what youths think of themselves depends on how they are perceived and received in society. In order to understand the nature of the search for identity, we must take a closer look at the adolescent desire to be accepted, to have a place or role and purpose or meaning in the adult world.

Physical Attractiveness: Search for Self-Acceptance. Paramount to a conception of self are a number of biological or physical factors that might affect the self-concept of adolescents (Elkind, 1971; McCandless, 1970; Simmons and Rosen-

berg, 1975). Concern over physical appearance is a central interest of the adolescent (Jersild, 1952; Simmons and Rosenberg, 1975). Erikson (1968: 128) described adolescent concern over physical appearance in the following passage:

> They [adolescents] are sometimes morbidly, often curiously preoccupied with what they appear to be in the eyes of others as compared with what they feel they are, and with the question of how to connect the roles and skills cultivated earlier with the ideal prototypes of the day.

With the great emphasis placed on physical appearance in our society, it is little wonder that the self-concepts of adolescents are often related to perceptions of physical attractiveness. In a study by Rosenbaum (1979), approximately one-third of early adolescent boys and one-half of early adolescent girls were dissatisfied with their physical appearance. Berscheid, Walster, and Bohrnstedt (1973) reported that adults who perceived themselves as more attractive during adolescence indicated more positive self-assessments and reported being happier than those whose self-perceived attractiveness was less. Some delinquency research has reported that youths who regard themselves as unattractive are disproportionately represented in certain types of delinquency (Cavior and Howard, 1973; Agnew, 1984a).

During adolescence, attractiveness is frequently related to the timing of maturation. Generally boys and girls want to look like their peers, and they feel uncomfortable when they mature earlier or later than their peers. The timing of maturation has also been linked with delinquency. The Gluecks (1974), who studied the effects of physical maturation on delinquency, found that the adjudicated delinquents in this study lagged significantly in maturity up to about the age of 14. But this finding does not explain why delinquency rates are lower at age 14 and do not peak until the age of 16 or 17, after which they again decline.

Although the timing of maturation is not directly a cause of delinquency, it does seem to affect not only the self-concept, but performance and behavior generally, which may in turn be related to delinquency. Tanner (1978) concluded that the early maturer on average scores higher on most tests of intellectual and moral ability. Tanner submits that this edge is usually retained in adulthood. In a national health and behavioral survey conducted by Gross and Duke (1980), the results suggest that late maturity is correlated with educational disadvantages and lower self-esteem and misbehavior in school, all of which have also been associated with delinquency.

Substantial evidence, for example, suggests that the self-concept may be an underlying component in delinquent or antisocial conduct (Ansbacher and Ansbacher, 1956; Dinitz and Pfau-Vincent, 1982; Goldfried, 1963; Kaplan, 1980; Reckless and Dinitz, 1972; Reckless, Dinitz, and Murray, 1957; Carl Rogers, 1951; Voss, 1969). It has been argued that likelihood of experiencing difficulty with the law may depend on the extent to which an adolescent's self-concept is socially acceptable. Jensen (1973) found a relationship between self-concept and "inner containment." According to Jensen, self-esteem, self-control, and level of conventional belief were all related, and he claimed that all three are parts of the self-concept. Moreover, he concluded that they were inversely related to delinquency. Hall (1966), however, found that delinquents with a weaker delinquency orientation were considerably more inclined to demonstrate low self-assessments than nondelinquents. But when he compared delinquents with a strong orientation and commitment to delinquency with nondelinquents, there were no significant differences in self-esteem.

It is difficult to determine whether delinquency (however it is defined) is a coping strategy to counteract a poor self-evaluation, or the cause of a poor self-evaluation. In view of the fact that most youths are involved in various forms of antisocial behavior, and further that most seem to grow out of their so-called antisocial tendencies (particularly if they are not apprehended), a question is raised about the effects of the delinquent label itself. Once the label "delinquent" is successfully applied to an individual, it is difficult to shed. The label is suggestive of a whole host of behavioral and personal expectations and response sets (see Chapter 7). The self-fulfilling prophecy may very well explain why those who have been labeled bad or delinquent devalue themselves and are less likely to outgrow their delinquencies.

Vocational Aspirations: Search for Role.   The adolescent quest for identity can be related to vocational aspirations. The questions "What will I be?" and "What will I do?" are closely linked. Erikson (1968) considers the first to be an abstract version and the second a more concrete version of the fundamental question of "What is my occupational identity?" (p. 129). Historically this is a relatively new problem, since in the past most children followed the occupational patterns of their parents. In urban postindustrial nations, most young people enter occupations different from their parents'. Increasingly, parents themselves find they have to retrain in order to stay employable. Today there are thousands of vocations or job roles, making the choice of one a particularly difficult decision. Furthermore, the limited range of part-time or summer jobs available for young people does not permit experimenting or trying out different roles. And traditional sex-role orientations frequently discourage young people, particularly females, from even considering certain options.

Due to the vast technological expansion currently under way, greater pressures and demands are being placed on the young to compete for jobs and positions in a high-tech society and to succeed. These pressures are now felt even during childhood; in school, increasingly one must succeed or be left behind (Elkind, 1981; Packard, 1983). For those who fall behind, technological expansion means fewer jobs and fewer opportunities to find a place in society. For many, the fear of failure or not finding a meaningful role has become overwhelming. According to Erikson, the inability to settle on an occupational identity is especially disturbing to the young (1968: 262). Most young people recognize the fact that work is central to adulthood and that work defines who one is (Yankelovich, 1974). Young people coming from the lower strata of society who have far fewer and less desirable options may find the search for occupational identity even more stressful. Delinquency in this context may be viewed as a rebellion or perhaps even an attempt to put off the inevitable. Opportunity and delinquency have been studied by a number of sociologists, such as Cloward and Ohlin (1960).

Idealism: Search for Worthwhile Goals.   The search for identity may also appear in explicit ideological terms. The search for an "inspiring unification of tradition" is ultimately a search for operative ideas or ideals (Erikson, 1968: 130). The more advanced cognitive abilities of adolescents permit the development of a world view or philosophy of life, including a set of guiding morals and values. Erikson believed that when adolescents meet obstacles in the pursuit of goals or encounter discrepancies between the stated ideals and the realities of society, they may react "with the wild strength encountered in animals who are suddenly forced to defend their lives" (p. 130).

Merton (1938) referred to the incongruity between the ideal and the real in his famous work "Social Structure and Anomie," in which he argued that in the United States there is generally an inconsistency between the cultural ideals and the available institutional means of achievement. Merton claimed that the lack of consistency leads to widespread anomie, which may result in any one of the nonconventional modes of response: innovation, retreatism, ritualism, and rebellion. Mertons's model has been used to explain various types of delinquency (see Chapter 6).

Our society today continues to be full of contradictions which certainly complicate the value-sorting process for the adolescent. Great technological advances have brought with them such nagging realities as growing unemployement, internal social problems, and the threat of nuclear war. In our atomic, highly technical, urban society, young people are confronted more than ever with inexperience, limited power, and uncertain status.

Some people have even come to lament the passing of the dissent and idealism manifest in the 1960s over the environment, civil rights, and peace. They fear that social idealism may have turned into a personalized and selfish "me" orientation. Even though social conditions and the cohort of young people are constantly changing, there is little evidence that the stated values of

today's cohort of youth differ significantly from those of the past (Jennings and Niemi, 1975; Kohn, 1977). Young people continue to be influenced most by their parents' values and hopes for the future (McKinney and Moore, 1982). While the search for worthwhile goals and values is extremely difficult for many young people due to the enormous contradictions and the plurality of values in our society, there is no evidence that the search has been abandoned.

DEVELOPING AN UNDERSTANDING OF ADOLESCENCE

It is now widely accepted that because childhood and adolescence are periods of unique physical, mental, and social characteristics, the emotional or behavior problems of each age group may be better understood in light of the specific stage of development. An appreciation for the stage of adolescence may also be helpful in evaluating the significance of antisocial or delinquent behavior. Behavior that appears psychotic or criminal may not have the "same fatal significance" in adolescence as it may at other ages (Erikson, 1968: 132).

Many adolescent problems may be due to the individuals' limited cognitive, emotional, and social perspectives. They have less understanding of themselves and others. Their perceptions of reality—past and future—and their values are less stable and in the process of formation. As a result they may experience difficulty in dealing with stress. Some events become disproportionately important, and the threat of some things is more acutely felt. Adolescents tend to be more easily upset over things that may seem trivial to adults. Indeed, frequently they can elicit very little help and may actually be verbally "put down" by adults who dismiss or deny the importance of their problems or their insights. Overall, adolescent emotional problems have been found to be shorter in duration, less systemized, more undifferentiated, and more transient (Elkind and Weiner, 1978; Coleman, Butcher, and Carson, 1984: 536).

This limited perspective suggests limited understanding or interpretation of their own behavior and the behavior of others. For example, acts of suicide or violence against another may be committed by a youngster who does not fully realize the finality of death or the consequences of certain actions.

Another aspect of the limited perspective of juveniles is associated with their almost total dependence on adults. While the dependency certainly shields them against some problems, it also makes them more vulnerable to rejection and disappointment. For this reason, in the case of childhood and adolescent misbehavior or disorders, one must pay close attention to environmental factors. The meaning or significance of behavior depends very much on the type of interpretation the behavior receives in a particular family or social setting. Since adolescents are vulnerable and subject to the specific definitions of the surrounding adults on whom they depend, behaviors or symptoms must be judged in the context of their social environment.

Finally, judging adults frequently forget that different behaviors are appropriate for different age levels. Sometimes a youngster's behavior may stand out and appear unacceptable to judging adults when the behavior is actually appropriate for that youngster's age level. Often, the incongruity of physical appearance and cognitive development results in negative sanctioning by judging adults. For example, an adolescent may look like a fully mature adult and thus be expected to act and think as one. The "normal" inability of 15-year-olds to act and think like adults irrespective of how they appear physically does not prevent many adults from labeling normal behavior as immature or delinquent.

By developing an appreciation of this special stage in the life cycle, we can come to a better understanding of some of the problems associated with the search for self and coming of age in our society. Erikson described the optimal sense of identity as a sense of psychosocial well-being:

> Its most obvious concomitants are a feeling of being at home in one's body, a sense of "knowing where one is going," and an inner assuredness of anticipated recognition from those who count. (1968: 165)

If the contrary exists—feeling uncomfortable with one's body, lacking a sense of direction or purpose, and not getting recognition or support from those who count (parents, teachers, community)—this may lead to an endless search, or in some cases to an unconventional fulfillment of self.

In 1970 the Presidential Task Force report, *Emergence of Identity*, prepared for the White House Conference on Children, described seven major obstacles to the development of healthy self-concepts:

1. Deprivation (economic, psychological, social, cultural)

2. Sex discrimination and overemphasis on socially determined sex differences unrelated to sexuality

3. Ethnic, racial, and religious prejudices and discriminations

4. Taboos against acceptance of biological identity

5. Taboos against acceptance and expression of affection

6. Failure to learn skills of mastery and competence

7. Overemphasis on conformity and uniformity with a resultant discrepancy between a healthy identity and a functional identity

These obstacles affect all members of society, but especially adolescents whose self-concepts are in the process of emerging. If delinquency is an indicator of failure, then the obstacles may be viewed as the sources of failure. Indeed, many of the causative theories of delinquency we shall discuss in Part II of this book reflect this list of obstacles.

SUMMARY

Juvenile delinquency by definition is an adolescent phenomenon. Most delinquents leaving their adolescent years also leave behind their delinquencies, suggesting that the stage of adolescence itself may be implicated as a contributing factor. Since adult expectations for adolescence affect attempts to control deviations or definitions of delinquency, it is important for us as students of delinquency to take a closer look at what it means to be an adolescent in American society. The fact that delinquency is such a widespread problem in the United States may be an indication that adolescence is especially difficult in this society, particularly for the poor or disadvantaged.

During the course of maturation, all people must pass from childhood to adulthood. The length of the course, and the meaning and significance of the experience associated with that course, are largely determined by the cultural context. The forces of modernization and industrialization, urbanization and nuclearization have affected every aspect of contemporary life, including adolescence. Young people have been affected not only socially, but physically as well.

Maturity has become a very complicated process involving sociological, psychological, biological, economic, legal, and traditional dimensions. The criteria, however, are vague and the opportunities for experiencing different forms of rites of passage (religious confirmation, graduation from school) are not consistent, nor are they equally available to all in society. Adolescents are expected to behave as adults, but they are denied the privileges and rights of adulthood. Adult confusion, uncertainty, and ambivalence toward youth are frequently reflected in contradictory sets of stereotypes.

Since the beginning of the twentieth century, interest in adolescence has grown. Many studies dealing with all facets of adolescent development and social experiences have been conducted. Social scientists generally agree that the stage of adolescence is unique and requires special attention. In our society, the physical and sexual changes of adolescence have typically been associated with "storm and stress."

Along with the physical changes comes the onset of a new schema of thought. Adolescents experience new ways of thinking. They are able to think more abstractly, to hypothesize and theorize, and they are able to accommodate new information and experiences. The ability to theorize permits one to begin developing a theory of oneself. Adolescence has thus been described in terms of a search for identity. There is some evidence suggesting that a poor self-concept is associated with delinquency, although it is not certain whether a poor self-evaluation is a cause or a consequence.

The challenge of coming of age in this society necessitates overcoming problems associated with various forms of discrimination (age, gender, race, religion, ethnicity, residence); the national obsession with physical appearance; and inadequate educational systems that annually leave millions of youngsters without mastery over skills which are vital for participation in a high-tech society.

Neither the problems of the young nor their solutions are simple; nor are they independent of more general problems such as poverty, racism, and war. The future of adolescence and our ability to cope with adolescent problems, especially delinquency, depend heavily on our capacity to deal with these issues.

PROGRESS CHECK

1. Why is *adolescence* a difficult concept to define? (pp. 26–27)

2. Note six major elements signaling the termination of adolescence. (pp. 27)

3. Discuss the physical and sexual changes that occur during adolescence. How do these changes affect the behavior of adolescents? To what extent do these changes explain delinquency? (pp. 33–35)

4. Discuss Piaget's steps of cognitive development. What insights does Piaget offer for our understanding of delinquency? (pp. 35–38)

5. How can such concepts as Elkind's *personal fable* and *imaginary audience* relate to cognitive development and possibly some problems during adolescence? (p. 37)

6. According to Lawrence Kohlberg, there are three levels of moral maturity. What are these? (pp. 38–39)

7. Explain the process of the development of the self-concept. (pp. 39–41)

8. How might the self-fulfilling prophecy explain the high rate of delinquency among adolescents? (p. 41)

9. What significance do cross-cultural comparisons of adolescence have for our own understanding of adolescence and the problems of adolescence? (pp. 33–34)

10. Discuss how different social classes within the same society experience adolescence. (pp. 28–29)

11. Discuss the impact of the social stereotype of adolescence on the development of a healthy self image. (pp. 39–44)

NOTES

1. Cited in Gordon, 1978: 131.
2. *The New English Dictionary on Historical Principles* cites references to the term *adolescence* dating back to 1430; to *adolesceny* dating back to 1398; and to *adolescent* dating back to 1482 (J. Murray, ed., 1888, Vol. 1, p. 123).
3. *The New English Dictionary on Historical Principles* (1888) defines adolescence as "the period which extends from childhood to adulthood; youth; ordinarily considered as extending from 14 to 25 in males and from 12 to 21 in females" (J. Murray, ed., Vol. 1, p. 123).
4. Mead's observations about Samoa have recently been challenged by an Australian anthropoligist, Derek Freeman (1983), who claims Mead was misled by Samoan youth and that they too were sexually repressed and perfect candidates to support a storm and stress typification. Obviously this issue is still far from being resolved.
5. According to Freud, male children are sexually attracted to their mothers and females to their fathers (called Oedipus and Electra complexes, respectively). Since direct expression of sexual desires is usually denied, the child may exhibit hostility toward the same-sex parent. If all goes well, the sexual urges are repressed, the hostility turns into competition, and the child identifies with the parent of the same sex in order to be accepted and to maintain a loving relationship with both parents.
6. Kohlberg's emphasis on college learning has been criticized as being elitist.
7. Carol Gilligan's book, *In a Different Voice: Psychological Theory and Women's Development* (1982), successfully demonstrates the male gender bias inherent in Kohlberg's model of moral development and makes a persuasive case for more encompassing theories taking women into account.
8. Note that moral maturity as defined by Kohlberg has a social scientific bias (especially because of the emphasis on cultural relativity).

CHAPTER 3

MEASURING JUVENILE DELINQUENCY

OFFICIAL STATISTICS

SELF-REPORT STATISTICS

VICTIMIZATION SURVEYS

COHORT ANALYSIS

Tim is a 14-year-old boy who was caught by his parents on several occasions drinking alcohol and smoking marijuana. Tim's parents felt increasingly unable to control him. He rarely came home, and when he did he disrupted the life of the entire family. His parents tried to send Tim for psychological counseling, but he refused to attend the sessions. Tim's parents even had the local police talk to him. Eventually, the parents referred Tim to the juvenile court and he was adjudicated delinquent.

Before Tim's contact with the police, his delinquency would have been reported only if measures of the actual number of prohibited behaviors—that is, the number of times he drank, used illegal drugs, or refused to obey his parents—had been taken. This type of measurement has been attempted in self-report techniques, in which children are questioned about their delinquency. The police encounter initiated by Tim's parents meant that his delinquency might have been measured as some form of police-juvenile contact. But since Tim was never formally taken into custody, it is unlikely he was included in arrest statistics. When the referral to the juvenile court and subsequent hearings resulted in application of the "delinquent" category to Tim, however, there arose a strong possibility that he would be counted in juvenile court statistics. A researcher examining the record might find Tim's delinquency reported in several ways—or not at all.

Similar problems occur in measuring more serious delinquency offenses. Look at the case of Sarah, a 16-year-old girl who "borrowed" a car one evening. Before that incident, Sarah had engaged in only minor status offenses, drinking once in a while and occasionally coming home past the curfew set by her parents. Prior to her arrest for auto theft, if Sarah had been part of a self-report study she would have been included in the "no delinquency" or "slight delinquency" category. When Sarah impulsively took a car and was apprehended for it, she became part of police arrest statistics. When her case was referred to the juvenile court and she was held "delinquent,"

47

Sarah was probably counted in court statistics. Further, Sarah's act and her characteristics could be reported by the owners of the stolen car if they were part of the sample of crime victims. Again, one individual's delinquency can be measured in several ways.

The last chapter made the point that legal definitions of delinquency led to various definitions of the term **juvenile delinquent**. To some researchers and theorists, the child is delinquent if he or she has committed an act that is legally prohibited. To others, a delinquent is a juvenile who has been "caught" in an illegal act or condition by the police. The delinquent has also been defined as a child referred to the court and adjudicated as delinquent. These three definitions of the term form the basis for methods of measuring the amount and nature of delinquency.

Until recently, the numbers of delinquent acts and the characteristics of delinquents were reported through the use of police and juvenile court statistics. Statistics based on police-juvenile contacts, including those found in the *Uniform Crime Reports* of the Federal Bureau of Investigation (FBI), are premised on a definition of delinquency as police action involving a juvenile. Studies that measure juvenile court referral and adjudication employ a definition of the delinquent as a child processed by the court and found delinquent. Although police and court data are still used to study delinquents, other techniques of measuring delinquency have attained a degree of popularity and support. Self-report studies measure delinquency defined as both criminal and status offenses committed by youth.

Accurately measuring the extent and nature of juvenile delinquency has been a pervasive problem for criminologists. Although most juveniles engage in behaviors for which they could be formally adjudicated, very few become enmeshed in the juvenile justice system, and fewer still are formally adjudicated as delinquent offenders. Official reports of delinquency found in court and arrest statistics represent only crimes that are reported and have come to the attention of authorities.

Even crimes that come to the attention of the police may not be included in official crime statistics. Because the police are allowed wide discretion in handling juvenile offenders, individuals may be warned and released or placed in the custody of their parents. Furthermore, many factors, including the age, sex, and race of the adolescent, may affect how he or she is handled by police and courts. The results of self-report studies outlining the extent of hidden delinquency among adolescents differ widely from the conclusions of studies using official data. When self-reported measures of delinquency are used, the amount of delinquency and the characteristics of the typical delinquent are very unlike figures about the extent and nature of delinquency derived from official statistics.

In this chapter, we will explore the major sources of data on the extent of delinquency in the United States. These sources include official crime statistics and self-report delinquency studies. In addition, surveys in which respondents are asked to report their experiences as crime victims, a relatively new source of crime data, are examined. These victimization data shed additional light on the amount of unreported crime and on characteristics of youthful offenders and their victims. Cohort analysis, measuring the delinquency of a group of individuals over time, is also reviewed as an important way of providing information about the long-term dynamics of delinquency and criminal careers of juveniles.

Only a general picture of juvenile crime can be given by the crime sources we discuss in this chapter. Each source is hampered by definitional problems—for example, official versus unofficial definitions of delinquency—as well as by methodological (measurement) weaknesses. Each data source used separately presents a biased account of juvenile crime. When used together, however, the sources can present a more reliable picture of patterns of delinquency.

OFFICIAL STATISTICS

One broad category of data about delinquency and delinquents is called *official* because the information is collected from reports of the law enforcement and court agencies that do officially react to delinquent behavior (see Chilton, 1980). At one time, sociologists employed official measures of delinquency almost exclusively. Even though these official measures have been criticized and serious shortcomings revealed, juvenile delinquency is still most often measured by juvenile court statistics and the reports of police agencies.

Juvenile Court Statistics

Juvenile Court Statistics (1975), originally published by the Children's Bureau of the U.S. Department of Labor, is an attempt to "furnish an index of the general nature and extent of the problems brought before the juvenile courts" (p. 1). Estimates of the number of delinquency, neglect, and dependency cases handled by juvenile courts throughout the country are compiled from the voluntary reports of the various juvenile courts.

Responsibility for publishing juvenile court statistics shifted to the Office of Youth Development (U.S. Department of Health, Education, and Welfare) in the 1960s (under the Law Enforcement Assistance Administration—LEAA). In 1974, the National Center for Juvenile Justice (NCJJ) submitted a proposal to LEAA to assume HEW's juvenile court statistical reporting function. Since that time, NCJJ has been authorized to collect and prepare juvenile court statistical information. Since NCJJ has had full responsibility for compiling juvenile court statistics, the data have been very comprehensive. Inconsistencies in earlier data collection, however, cause some problems in comparing past with more current years. One inconsistency that hampers the comparability of statistics before and after 1970 concerns the number of courts included in the count. Between 1957 and 1970, juvenile court statistics were drawn from a randomly selected representative sample of juvenile courts (U.S. Department of Health, Education and Welfare, Office of Youth Development, 1970). Now, however, all juvenile courts supplying data are used to calculate nationwide statistics on juvenile court handling of youths. The most current juvenile court statistics (1985), reporting through the year 1982, are based on court data from some 1,695 counties in the United States (see Table 3.1).

TABLE 3.1   Estimated Number and Rate of Delinquency Case Dispositions, 1957–1982

Year	Estimated Number of Delinquency Cases*	Child Population 10–17 Years of Age†	Rate‡
1957	440,000	22,173,000	19.8
1958	470,000	23,433,000	20.0
1959	483,000	24,607,000	19.6
1960	510,000	25,368,000	20.1
1961	503,000	26,056,000	19.3
1962	555,000	26,989,000	20.6
1963	601,000	28,056,000	21.4
1964	686,000	29,244,000	23.5
1965	697,000	29,536,000	23.6
1966	745,000	30,124,000	24.7
1967	811,000	30,837,000	26.3
1968	900,000	31,566,000	28.5
1969	988,500	32,157,000	30.7
1970	1,052,000	33,141,000	31.7
1971	1,125,000	33,643,000	33.4
1972	1,112,500	33,954,000	32.8
1973	1,143,700	34,126,000	33.5
1974	1,252,700	34,195,000	36.6
1975	1,317,000	33,960,000	38.8
1976	1,432,000	33,482,000	42.3
1977	1,389,000	32,896,000	42.2
1978	1,359,000	32,276,000	42.1
1979	1,374,500	31,643,000	43.4
1980	1,445,400	31,171,000	46.4
1981	1,350,500	30,725,000	44.0
1982	1,292,500	29,914,000	43.2

* Estimates for 1957–1969 were based on data from a national sample of juvenile courts. Estimates for 1970–1981 were based on data from all units reporting consistently for two consecutive years.
† Based on estimates from Bureau of the Census, U.S. Department of Commerce (Current Resident Population Reports, Population Estimates and Projections, Series P-25, No. 949, Issued May 1984). Also included are population figures for Puerto Rico and the Virgin Islands.
‡ Rate was based on the number of delinquency cases per 1,000 children 10 through 17 years of age.
Source: National Center for Juvenile Justice, 1984.

According to the statistics for 1982, 1,292,500 juvenile delinquency cases, excluding traffic offenses, were handled by courts having juvenile jurisdiction in the United States. This figure represents approximately a 3 percent increase over the 1974 estimate of 1,252,700 cases. Although the overall increase in the number of delinquency cases was an estimated 3 percent, the child population aged

10 through 17 actually decreased by about 14 percent. In Table 3.1, we see that from 1960 until 1982, the number of delinquency cases more than doubled, but there was only about a 17 percent increase in the number of children aged 10 through 17. Table 3.1 also presents rates of referral to the juvenile court from 1957 through 1982. A **rate**, in this case a delinquency rate, relates the number of events during a specified time against some population base. In 1957 the rate of referral to the juvenile court per 1,000 child population aged 10 through 17 was 19.8. By 1982, that rate had increased to about 43.0. The **volume** of crime, as opposed to the rate, refers to the absolute number of events committed in a particular locale during a specified period of time. For 1982, the volume of estimated delinquency cases from a national sample of courts was 1,292,500, compared to 440,000 in 1957.

Just as in the past, more males than females were referred to the juvenile court in 1982. However, the gap between the number of male and female court referrals was narrowing. Until about 1968, juvenile courts disposed of almost four times as many boys' cases. Since 1970, this ratio has decreased to approximately 3 to 1. In 1982, 23 percent of the total cases involved females, and 77 percent of the delinquency cases involved males. Although males were still more likely to be reported in court statistics, the rate of female involvement increased more rapidly than the rate of male involvement. Between 1964 and 1974, girls' delinquency cases increased by 129 percent; boys' cases increased by 67 percent.[1]

In addition to delinquency cases, *Juvenile Court Statistics* reports the estimated number and rate of dependency and neglect cases disposed of by juvenile courts in the United States. When juvenile court jurisdiction over such cases is deemed appropriate, dependency may be defined in terms of denoting (1) destitution or failure to provide necessities; (2) parental physical or mental incapacity; or perhaps (3) lack of parents or guardians (U.S. Department of Justice, Law Enforcement Assistance Administration, *Abuse and Neglect*, Vol. 6, 1977a). *Juvenile Court Statistics*, however, makes no attempt to distinguish between cases of neglect and cases of dependency. An estimated 172,500 dependency/neglect cases were disposed of by courts with juvenile jurisdiction in 1982.

Unlike the generally steady increase in delinquency cases since 1957, the annual volume of dependency/neglect cases has fluctuated during the same period, producing a total increase of about 60 percent, compared to a more than 200 percent increase in delinquency cases. Like delinquency, some of this increase may be due to the increase in the child population over this time. However, controlling for the population difference between years reveals that the processing of dependency/neglect cases is becoming a smaller and smaller portion of the workload of juvenile courts. This may reflect the growing practice of handling dependency/neglect cases through social service agencies outside the court, or it may mean that delinquency is increasing at a faster rate.

Juvenile Court Statistics is one source of data about the extent of juvenile delinquency, but there are several problems with these statistics. First, information collected by the NCJJ is only an estimate of the total volume of juvenile crimes that come to the attention of authorities. Many crimes are never reported, and many juvenile offenders are channeled to other agencies—for example, youth service bureaus or mental health clinics—and are never formally processed by the court. Second, *Juvenile Court Statistics* has not, until recently, been published on a regular basis. There is often a time lag in the completion of the final statistics. Third, *Juvenile Court Statistics* provides very little information about the type of juvenile offender who is formally adjudicated by the court. To encourage more courts to report, detailed information about the age, offense, prior record, and race of the juvenile offender is not included in juvenile court data.[2]

Uniform Crime Reports

Other official sources of data present a more detailed picture of juvenile delinquency and the juvenile delinquent. The FBI's annual *Uniform Crime Reports* (UCR), in particular, supplies additional information on national crime trends among the young. The data have flaws, however, and cannot be used alone to illustrate the extent and nature of juvenile delinquency (Sellin and Wolfgang, 1964). Nevertheless, the UCR does supply valuable information about certain aspects of adolescent crime.

Since 1930, the FBI has published "crimes known to the police" and arrest statistics in the UCR. The data are voluntarily submitted by more than 10,000 law enforcement agencies representing 98 percent of the United States population living in Metropolitan Statistical Areas (MSAs), 94 percent of the population in other cities, and 90 percent of the rural population (FBI, 1985).

The FBI classifies eight of the most serious crimes into Crime Index Offenses (also known as Part I offenses):

1. **Criminal homicide:** Murder and manslaughter—the willful (negligent) killing of one human being by another.

2. **Forcible rape:** Rapes by force or attempts to rape.

3. **Robbery:** Taking or attempting to take anything of value by force or threat.

4. **Aggravated assault:** An unlawful attack by one person upon another with the intent to kill or do bodily harm.

5. **Burglary:** Breaking and entering a structure to commit a felony, usually theft. (A **felony** is any offense punishable by death or imprisonment.)

6. **Larceny-theft:** The unlawful taking, carrying, leading, or riding away of property from the possession of another.

7. **Motor vehicle theft:** The theft or attempted theft of a motor vehicle.

8. **Arson:** Willful or malicious burning or attempt to burn . . . a dwelling house, public building, etc. (FBI, 1985, p. 328)

A *crime index total* is computed by adding "crimes known to the police" for violent crimes, including murder, forcible rape, robbery, and aggravated assault; and property crimes, which include burglary, larceny-theft, motor vehicle theft, and arson.

In addition to the eight index offenses reported by the FBI, several other types of crimes are listed and offer arrest information. These nonindex offenses include such diverse acts as running away, embezzlement, gambling, vagrancy, and curfew and loitering violations. Many of these offenses are infrequently committed by youth (for example, embezzlement and fraud). It should be noted that while many minor status offenses are not included in the UCR, running away and violating curfew are included.

Age and Official Delinquency.   Law enforcement agencies in the United States made an estimated 11.7 million arrests in 1984, excluding traffic offenses. As Figure 3.1 indicates, a large proportion of those arrested were young people. Further, in relation to their proportion of the total population, juveniles in some age categories are overrepresented in arrest statistics. In the nation, 5 percent of all persons arrested were under the age of 15; 17 percent were under 18; 32 percent were under 21; and 51 percent were under 25. After the age interval of 25 through 29, numbers of arrests drop substantially.

Although these figures indicate that many youths engage in criminal acts, the reports obviously underestimate the number of offenses committed by juveniles. Not all youths are arrested when they come into contact with the police, and many crimes "known to the police" are never cleared by arrest (FBI, 1985).

The FBI reports that juveniles under the age of 18 account for 31.3 percent of such index crime arrests (see Table 3.2). Among the serious index offenses, 36.1 percent of all those arrested for auto theft were under 18; 38.1 percent of all those arrested for burglary were under 18; and 26.3 percent of all those arrested for robbery were under 18.

Juveniles under age 18 account for all runaway and curfew and loitering violations (see Table 3.3). With the exception of local statutory prohibitions against adult loitering, runaway and curfew crimes are both status offenses and thus

FIGURE 3.1 **Persons Arrested in Relation to Total Population, by Age**

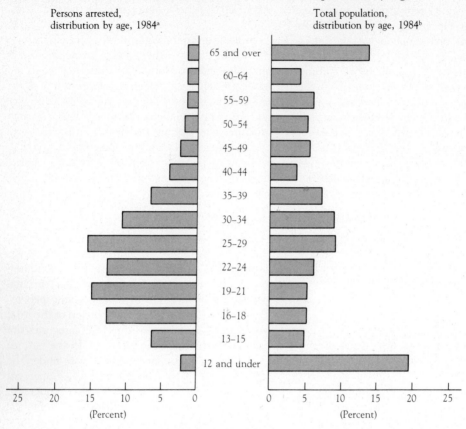

Persons arrested,
distribution by age, 1984[a]

Total population,
distribution by age, 1984[b]

[a] Persons arrested is based on reports received representing 179,871,000 population
[b] The total population is 237,622,000 for the U.S., based on Bureau of Census provisional estimates, July 1, 1984
Source: FBI (1985)

applicable only to children. Vandalism (47 percent), liquor law violations (27 percent), and dealing in stolen property (24 percent) are also crimes for which juveniles have high arrest rates. There were more than 15,000 reported arrests of juveniles for "driving under the influence" in the United States in 1984. Reported arrests for drunkenness surpassed 18,000 cases (FBI, 1985).

Sex and Official Delinquency.   Males under 18 are arrested for index offenses more than four times

as often as females (374,713 versus 90,750, as can be seen in Table 3.2). Males were arrested for 35.3 percent of all burglaries. Females, on the other hand, were arrested for only 2.8 percent of all burglaries. Similarly, males accounted for 36.1 percent of all motor vehicle thefts; females accounted for only 4.0 percent. Approximately 24 percent of arrests for larceny-thefts involved juvenile males, whereas only about 9 percent of larceny-thefts involved juvenile females.

Juvenile offenders as a whole are more often taken into custody for property offenses than for

TABLE 3.2   **Juvenile Arrests for Index Crimes, 1984**

Offense	All Ages Total Arrests	Juveniles under 18	Males under 18	Females under 18
Number	1,486,784	465,463	374,713	90,750
Percent	100	31.3	25.2	6.1
		Percent of All Arrests		
Murder and nonnegligent manslaughter	11,230	7.3%	6.5%	0.8%
Forcible rape	23,091	15.8	15.6	0.2
Robbery	94,415	26.3	24.7	1.6
Aggravated assault	187,751	13.5	11.3	2.2
Burglary	272,241	38.1	35.3	2.8
Larceny-theft	809,698	34.0	24.8	9.1
Motor vehicle theft	76,511	36.1	32.1	4.0
Arson	11,847	43.3	41.0	3.7
Violent crimes	316,487	17.3	16.0	1.8
Property crimes	1,170,297	35.1	28.0	7.3

Based on 6,134 agencies; 1984 estimated population 141,692,000.
Source: FBI (1985; pp 169–170).

TABLE 3.3   **Juvenile Arrests for Selected Crimes, 1984**

		Percent of All Arrests		
Offense	All Ages	Juveniles under 18	Males under 18	Females under 18
Running away	88,159	100.0%	42.0%	58.0%
Drug abuse violations	460,356	12.0	10.0	2.0
Disorderly conduct	410,180	15.0	12.0	3.0
Vandalism	152,702	47.0	43.0	4.0
Liquor laws	301,288	27.0	20.0	7.0
Curfew and loitering	57,666	100.0	77.0	23.0
Sex offenses (except forcible rape and prostitution)	61,001	18.0	17.0	1.0
Stolen property; buying, receiving, possessing	82,645	24.0	22.0	2.0

Based on 6,134 agencies; 1984 estimated population 141,692,000.
Source: FBI (1985; pp 169–170).

violent crimes. In 1984, juveniles accounted for about 17 percent of the total number of arrests for violent crimes, but for approximately 35 percent of the total arrests for crimes against property. Males under 18 were arrested for about 16 percent of all violent crimes; minor females were arrested for only about 2 percent of these offenses.[3] Overall, the crime index totals from 1983 to 1984 show arrests of males under 18 to be decreasing (2.1 percent) while female arrests have increased slightly (1.0 percent).

When male and female juvenile arrests are reported as proportions of all male and female index arrests, arrests of juveniles are still greatest for property crimes (see Table 3.4). Males under age 18 account for 45 percent of all male arrests

TABLE 3.4 Juvenile Arrest Rates of Males and Females as Proportions of All Male and Female Index Arrests, 1984

Offense	Males under Age 18		Females under Age 18	
	Number Arrested	Percent of All Male Arrests	Number Arrested	Percent of All Female Arrests
Murder and nonnegligent manslaughter	734	7.5%	85	6.0%
Forcible rape	3,605	15.8	49	2.0
Robbery	23,322	27.0	1,539	23.0
Aggravated assault	21,277	13.0	4,129	17.0
Burglary	96,132	38.0	7,568	37.0
Larceny-theft	200,379	36.0	73,882	30.0
Motor vehicle theft	24,575	35.0	3,061	44.0
Arson	4,689	45.0	437	31.0

Based on 6,134 agencies; 1984 estimated population 141,692,000.
Source: FBI (1985; pp 169–170).

for arson and for about 38 percent of all male arrests for burglary. Motor vehicle thefts (35 percent) and larceny-thefts (36 percent) are also high arrest crimes for juvenile males in proportion to all male arrests. Females under age 18 are arrested for 44 percent of the total female arrests for motor vehicle thefts and for about 37 percent of burglaries. Juvenile females also have high arrest rates for arson (31 percent) and larceny-theft (30 percent). Among violent crimes, the greatest proportion of male and female juvenile arrests is for robbery. Juvenile males are arrested for 27 percent of robberies committed by all males, and juvenile females are arrested for 23 percent of all female robberies.

When male and female arrests for selected nonindex crimes are compared, as in Table 3.3, males surpass females in all categories except runaways. Girls comprise approximately 58 percent of all juvenile arrests for running away. The difference in arrests of males and females for running away may be explained by the emphasis on control and protection of females. Formal arrest allows police to hold a girl until her parents or guardians are contacted. Parents may be more likely to report runaway daughters than runaway sons. Arrest rates for males are high for curfew and loitering (77 percent), vandalism (43 percent), and stolen property (22 percent).

The extent and distribution of female delin-

quency have become a growing concern. Some criminologists have suggested that female involvement in criminal and deliquent behavior has shown a marked increase during recent years (F. Adler, 1975; Simon, 1975; Datesman, Scarpitti, and Stephenson, 1975). They contend that feminist political theory and application have been indirectly responsible for increased female criminality and delinquency (Deming, 1977; Austin, 1982). In other words, changing gender roles are thought to have freed females from traditional cultural restraints, presenting them with increased opportunities to engage in hitherto restricted activities. Other criminologists, analyzing official data, maintain that much of the female increase in criminal behavior has been trivial (Steffensmier, 1978, 1980; Steffensmier and Steffensmier, 1980).

An examination of Table 3.5 presents the national distribution of juvenile arrests by sex for 1975 and 1984. As previously noted, the actual number of female juveniles arrested for index offenses is small in comparison to their male counterparts. The percent change figures, however, show some interesting results over the decade. Although both sexes showed a reduction in index offense arrests, the female figures are slightly lower than the male statistics. Females exhibited less decline for murder and nonnegligent manslaughter, aggravated assault, burglary, and motor vehicle theft. The index offense figures, when

TABLE 3.5   **National Juvenile Arrest Trends by Sex, 1975–1984**

Index Offenses	Males			Females		
	1975	1984	Percent Change	1975	1984	Percent Change
Murder and nonnegligent manslaughter	870	620	−28.7%	90	77	−14.4%
Forcible rape	2,657	2,898	+9.1	31	35	+12.9
Robbery	28,404	18,770	−33.9	2,419	1,340	−44.6
Aggravated assault	20,393	18,908	−7.3	3,505	3,739	+6.7
Burglary	161,273	88,638	−46.3	9,140	6,937	−24.1
Larceny-theft	228,189	188,755	−17.3	92,000	70,655	−23.2
Motor vehicle theft	44,263	22,238	−49.8	3,548	2,881	−18.8
Arson	5,134	4,318	−15.9	510	399	−21.8
Violent crimes	55,324	41,196	−23.3	6,045	5,191	−14.1
Property crimes	438,859	301,949	−31.2	105,198	80,872	−23.1

Based on 5,097 agencies; 1984 estimated population 132,927,000.
Source: FBI (1985: 167).

taken as a whole, however, seem to indicate that female juveniles have not been that much more involved in serious crimes in the past ten years. A similar picture emerges for the less serious nonindex offenses (not included in Table 3.5).

Summarizing the conclusions drawn about youth crime in the *Uniform Crime Reports,* we find that juveniles under 18 commit a large share of serious crimes in proportion to their numbers in the population. UCR information about less serious nonindex offenses reveals that juveniles are arrested for both status offenses and adult crimes. Males are arrested more frequently than females for both index and nonindex crimes. Generally the past decade has shown a decrease in arrest rates for both males and females.

Race and Official Delinquency.   Besides reporting the age and sex differences in the commission of index and nonindex crimes, the UCR gives detailed information on the racial and ethnic backgrounds of arrested juveniles. The UCR compares the arrest rates of several racial and ethnic groups: White, Black, American Indian or Alaskan Native, and Asian or Pacific Islander. Although social scientists have questioned the validity and utility of racial designation, these broad categories are used to measure racial and ethnic differences in delinquency.[4]

We will limit our examination of the relationship between race and delinquency to arrest data on whites and blacks. As reported in Table 3.6, white and black juveniles under age 18 account for about 99 percent of reported index arrests for juveniles. One percent of juvenile index arrests under age 18 are distributed among other racial and national categories.

The data in Table 3.6 indicate that approximately 75 percent of all juvenile arrestees were white and 24 percent were black. Black juveniles were arrested most frequently for robbery (69 percent), forcible rape (54 percent), homicide (45 percent), and aggravated assault (39 percent). These trends are similar to total index arrests for black adult offenders. Since blacks make up only about 14 percent of the United States population (U.S. Department of Commerce, 1984), their arrests are disproportionately high, especially for violent offenses. White juveniles are frequently arrested for various types of property crime, such as motor vehicle theft (72 percent), burglary (77 percent), and larceny-theft (71 percent). Generally, black youth tend to be arrested more fre-

TABLE 3.6   **Juvenile Arrests by Race for Index Crimes, 1984**

Offense	Total Juvenile Arrests	White Juveniles under 18	Black Juveniles under 18
Number	1,534,372	1,153,612	354,038
Percent	100*	75.2	23.8
		Percent Committed by Whites and Blacks	
Murder and nonnegligent manslaughter	1,004	54.0%	45.0%
Forcible rape	4,394	45.0	54.0
Robbery	27,788	30.3	69.0
Aggravated assault	31,126	60.0	39.0
Burglary	127,521	77.0	22.0
Larceny-theft	338,235	71.0	27.0
Motor vehicle theft	33,795	72.0	26.0
Arson	6,235	85.0	14.0
Violent crimes	64,312	46.0	53.0
Property crimes	505,786	73.0	25.0

Based on 9,851 agencies; 1984 estimated population 179,374,000.
* Figures do not add to 100 percent due to the small influences of "other races" in the arrest statistics.
Source: FBI (1985; p 181).

quently for violent crimes (53 percent), whereas the arrests of white youth are highest for the commission of property crimes (73 percent).

For nonindex offenses, black juvenile arrests surpass white arrests in only two offense categories: sex offenses and gambling. When compared to white juveniles, black juveniles are infrequently arrested for drug abuse violations (20 percent), including alcohol-related arrests. Vandalism also appears to be a more common white juvenile offense. The most frequent nonindex arrests for blacks are disorderly conduct (24 percent), other assaults (31 percent), and curfew and loitering (28 percent).

In summary, the *Uniform Crime Reports* indicates that black juveniles are disproportionately likely to be arrested. Blacks make up a small percentage of the total population, but black juveniles under age 18 account for about 24 percent of all juveniles arrested. Blacks tend to be arrested more frequently than whites for violent personal crimes, such as rape and robbery, and as frequently for homicide. Common index arrests for white juveniles are property offenses, such as burglary,

larceny-theft, and motor vehicle theft. Arrests of white juveniles for less serious offenses often involve drug abuse violations, vandalism, liquor law violations, driving under the influence, and drunkenness. Black youths are more likely to be arrested for the nonindex offenses of disorderly conduct, other assaults, and curfew and loitering.

Other official data sources support the trends in black and white arrest rates reported in the UCR. Mulvihill, Tumin, and Curtis (1968), for example, investigated the relationship between race and crime in a study published by the President's Commission on the Causes and Prevention of Violence in 1968. Using police arrest reports from seventeen major American cities, they found that the race of the offender was black in 72 percent of the criminal homicides, in 74 percent of the aggravated assaults, in 70 percent of the forcible rapes, in 85 percent of the armed robberies, and in 81 percent of the unarmed robberies.

In a study specifically looking at delinquent crime, Marvin Wolfgang and his associates at the Center for Studies in Criminology and Criminal Law of the University of Pennsylvania studied the police records of 9,946 juvenile males born in Philadelphia in 1945. About 35 percent of the birth cohort—that is, children born in the same year—who numbered 3,475 had police records before they reached the age of 18. Defining delinquency as any police contact, including minor infractions and traffic offenses, they reported that slightly over half (50.2 percent) of nonwhite juveniles had police records, but that only 28.6 percent of white juveniles had records (Wolfgang, Figlio, and Sellin, 1972).

Looking only at males who had police records, Wolfgang et al. reported that whites were involved in 4,458 (44 percent) offenses and blacks in 5,756 (56 percent) offenses. Nonwhites were more often arrested than whites in nearly all the twenty-eight offense categories. The only exceptions to greater black arrests were in the categories of fraud, embezzlement, and prostitution, offenses with very low juvenile involvement. All the criminal homicides (fourteen in number) recorded for the entire cohort were allegedly committed by nonwhites. These findings match closely those reported in the UCR. Racial differentials are most pronounced in the serious offenses.

Residence and Official Delinquency.   Sociologists have studied the effects of residence, more formally called *spatial patterning,* on juvenile delinquency for many years. Working at the University of Chicago in the 1920s, sociologists Clifford Shaw and Henry McKay used court and arrest data to analyze the rates of delinquency in Chicago. They noted that the highest rates of delinquency were generally concentrated in the central city, where ethnic and racial minorities resided in low-rent housing. As the distance from the central city increased, delinquency rates decreased, reaching the lowest levels on the outskirts of the city. Shaw and McKay's findings were verified in several other U.S. cities (Shaw and McKay, 1942), but critics of their research have argued that other factors, such as substandard housing, social class, education, race, differential enforcement of the law, and the like may be more important than spatial patterning in explaining delinquency.

Still, sociologists look with interest at the UCR arrest data for city, suburban, and rural residential areas in the United States for evidence of trends.[5] Since the population bases are different for each of these categories, the volume of juvenile crime must be interpreted in relation to the total population of the area. By comparing percentages of the total number of juvenile arrests for specific offenses in each residential area, we can make general statements about differences in the types of juvenile crimes likely to occur in city, suburban, and rural areas.

More total arrests, as well as index arrests, occur in urban areas than in any other areas, but youth in all areas are arrested for similar types of offenses. Juveniles living in all areas have relatively low arrests for homicide and forcible rape. In each location, youth are arrested most frequently for larceny-theft and burglary. About 12 percent of urban juvenile arrestees, 11 percent of suburban offenders, 9 percent of suburban area arrestees, and 8 percent of rural county juvenile arrestees were accused of violent offenses. Property offenses were involved in 88 percent of urban arrests, 89 percent of suburban county youth arrests, 91 percent of suburban area arrests, and 92 percent of rural county arrests. Overall, then, the percentages of arrests for different types of index crimes are similar in urban, suburban, and rural areas.

The trends in juvenile arrests for selected nonindex offenses in the various residential areas are similar to arrest trends for index offenses. Youth in all three areas are arrested for nearly the same types of nonindex offenses. According to number of arrests, the greatest differences between the offense patterns of city and rural locales are found in curfew violations, loitering, and disorderly conduct. There may be less opportunity for youth to commit these offenses in less populated rural areas, and the offenses may not draw the attention of authorities as much as in cities.

To summarize, the UCR data on delinquency in city, suburban, and rural areas reveal that more delinquency is committed in cities, but the types of delinquency offenses committed in the city do not differ significantly from those committed in suburban and rural areas.[6] Property arrests account for the majority of juvenile index arrests in each locale. Arrests for violent juvenile offenses are only slightly higher in the cities than in suburban and rural areas (FBI, 1985).[7]

Limitations of Official Statistics

Official statistics such as the UCR offer valuable information about crime within the United States. However, criticisms of the UCR range from the mild to the very serious.[8] As Michael Hindelang has observed, "Recognition of the problems involved in using the UCR is one of the few areas of general agreement in the field of criminal justice" (Hindelang, 1974: 1).

One of the more serious charges is that much crime is never discovered and that many discovered crimes are not reported to the police. Various factors, such as level of professionalism of the police, size of the police agency, and local political considerations, may influence the accurate reporting and presentation of crimes (DeFleur, 1975; Harries, 1974). Further, changes in reporting procedures may have a profound effect on crime rates. For example, Kansas City, Missouri, experienced an increase of more than 200 percent in index crimes between 1959 and 1961 because of an improvement in police reporting practices (Black, 1970; President's Commission, 1967a). Another limitation of UCR statistics is that it is impossible to determine from the volume of offenses (the absolute number of crimes committed in a particular locale during a specified period of time) the number of offenders who committed these crimes.[9] The arrest of one person may clear several crimes, or the arrest of a gang may solve one crime. Thus, if 100 crimes are committed in a community, 100 or more separate criminals or only 1 very energetic criminal may be responsible.

Furthermore, the UCR is sometimes a source of inaccurate estimates of actual crime because some offenses are more likely to be discovered than others. Victimless crimes, such as gambling or prostitution, are less likely than theft or murder to come to the attention of the authorities (DeFleur, 1975; Sellin and Wolfgang, 1964). Also, the

offense categories used by the FBI, index and nonindex crimes, are very broad and thus allow dissimilar events to fall in the same category. Since the definitions of offense categories vary so much from state to state, some critics charge that in spite of the FBI's efforts to standardize the categories, police agencies in different states invariably miscategorize certain crimes or utilize categories in different ways (Hindelang, 1974). In the case of auto theft, one police department may classify a missing car in the "motor vehicle theft" category today, but another may not do so until the car has been missing for several days. Addressing this dilemma, Harries (1974) has cautioned: "Clearly, the statistics become less meaningful as the geographic area in which the offense was committed becomes more remote from the [police agency] actually reporting the offense" (pp. 4–5).[10]

Other serious measurement flaws are found in the UCR. Tabulation of data "using different aggregates of geographic areas for different tables often makes exact comparisons of data from table to table and year to year impossible" (Hindelang, 1974: 2). Also, the use of crude rates, rather than rates where age, sex, and race are held constant, may result in distorted time comparisons about increases or decreases among these individuals as a group.[11] Perhaps most damaging is the criticism that arrest statistics and the detailed characteristics of those arrested, such as race, sex, and age, are no more than descriptions of the person who, for any number of reasons, comes to the attention of the police. Finally, it is charged that valuable information about a particular offense—circumstances of the offense, the extent of injury to the victim, the victim-offender relationship, and so forth—is ignored in the UCR format (Hindelang, 1974).

Although there are many other criticisms of the UCR (and other official statistics), we have listed the major ones. These criticisms of validity and reliability make important points about the limitations and shortcomings of finding the total number of crimes committed in any society. We are most likely looking at the tip of the iceberg and observing only broad trends that come to the attention of the authorities. Certain individuals, such as members of some minority groups, may be overrepresented in official statistics. Other individuals, such as middle and upper class juveniles, may be underrepresented (or not represented at all).

SELF-REPORT STATISTICS

Some social scientists, in an attempt to overcome the limitations of official measures of crime, use self-report measures to gauge the incidence and types of delinquency. When self-report studies are examined, the frequency of delinquent behavior and the characteristics of offenders look very different from those reported in official data, although some criminologists have recently argued that some of these differences are largely illusory. Self-report measures of delinquency are based on youths' responses to questions about their delinquency involvement and are thought to eliminate the biases produced in official crime statistics. There is, however, no consensus among researchers that self-reports provide a clearer picture of juvenile delinquency than official statistics. Unofficial measures of crime also have limitations, including inconsistent results from study to study.

The Methodology of Self-Reports

Several versions of the self-report technique are employed by criminologists measuring delinquency. The most frequently employed technique involves asking juveniles to indicate the number of times they have engaged in each of a number of violations during a specific time period. Then the total number of delinquent acts and the seriousness of these are computed. The effects of other factors, such as sex, race, socioeconomic status, and residence, are considered in order to determine their influence. According to Nettler (1984: 81), the variations of the self-report technique include these:

1. Asking people to complete anonymous questionnaires

2. Asking people to confess to criminal acts on signed questionnaires, later validated against police records

3. Having people complete anonymous questionnaires identified by number and validated against follow-up interviews

4. Interviewing respondents

5. Interviewing respondents and validating their responses against official records[12]

In general, the conclusions of self-report studies indicate that (1) most juveniles admit to committing delinquent (and criminal) offenses; (2) the volume of hidden delinquency (and crime) is considerable; and (3) juveniles are not simply "delinquent" or "nondelinquent"—their involvement in offenses is best described as a continuum ranging from more to less delinquency (Nettler, 1978). Although most self-report studies concur in these findings, there are also conflicting results. The relationship between **social class** and delinquency is an example. Some studies report few significant differences in the reported delinquency of juveniles of varying social classes, but others reveal that extent and seriousness of delinquency vary among social classes (Gold, 1970; Elliott and Ageton, 1980).

Self-report data have been used to answer the following questions:

1. What is the extent of reported juvenile crime?

2. What types of offenses are most often reported by juveniles?

3. How do the self-reported acts of official delinquents compare with those of nonofficial delinquents?

4. How does reported juvenile crime vary based on such variables as sex, age, social class, race, and residence?

5. What are the limitations of self-report studies?

The Extent of Self-Reported Delinquency

Some of the most important findings of self-report studies concern the extent of delinquent behavior. Most self-report research indicates that an extremely large amount of juvenile crime is never officially recorded (Gold, 1966, 1970; Illinois Institute for Juvenile Research, 1972; Short and Nye, 1958; Wallerstein and Wyle, 1947; Williams and Gold, 1972; Hindelang, Hirschi, and Weis, 1981).[13] Although there are no definite figures, estimates are that 90 percent of all juveniles commit delinquent and criminal acts for which they could be formally adjudicated (President's Commission on Law Enforcement and the Administration of Justice, 1967c). Erickson and Empey, for example, studied the self-reported delinquency of 15- to 17-year-olds and found that, in nine out of ten cases, minor offenses (for example, traffic violations, minor thefts, liquor law violations, and destroying property) go "undetected and unacted upon" (1963: 462). When offenses are serious, probabilities of detection and official reaction are greater. Even in more serious cases, however, "eight out of ten [youth] reported that their violations went undetected, and nine out of ten did not result in court action" (p. 462).

Self-report research has produced one particularly startling finding: Many youths in correctional institutions have committed fewer crimes than many juveniles who are at large in the community. Short (1955) reported that 22 percent of the boys in a Washington State correctional facility were no more delinquent than 90 percent of a sample of public high school youths. Similarly, Gough (1945) compared institutionalized delinquents, high school disciplinary problem youths, and a sample of nondelinquents and found "44 percent of the nondelinquents fell above the [number of delinquent acts] on his scale, which supposedly divided delinquents from nondelinquents; 12 percent of the so-called delinquents fell below the 'cutting point' " (Erickson, 1972: 389). The results of these studies suggest that many who are officially labeled delinquent are no more (or less) delinquent than those not officially "delinquent." Other studies, however, reveal that formally adjudicated delin-

quents do commit more frequent and serious delinquencies than their nonofficial counterparts.

Types of Self-Reported Juvenile Crime

Another goal of self-report research has been to identify the most and least frequent varieties of delinquency. Over a thirty-year period and in different regions of the country, self-report researchers have consistently found that juveniles engage in a multitude of offenses. Reported delinquent behaviors range from less serious status offenses, behaviors prohibited only for children, to more serious personal and property crimes, behaviors illegal for anyone. Drug use, especially marijuana consumption, is also a frequent juvenile offense (Thornton, 1981).

Earlier self-report studies are criticized because their inventories or checklists give more attention to minor offenses than to more serious offenses (Ageton, 1983). Apparently, researchers have assumed that there are either too few cases of serious offenses in an average-sized population to draw meaningful conclusions, or that too many juveniles will be reluctant to admit such offenses. Thus, trivial and less serious types of offenses were overrepresented, while serious violations of the criminal codes such as burglary, robbery, and assault were omitted. More recent self-report research has, however, included a broader span of serious offenses and found that some youth do indeed report such occurrences (Elliott and Huizinga, 1983; Elliott and Ageton, 1980; Higgins and Albrecht, 1981; Hindelang, Hirschi, and Weis, 1981).

We have included an inventory from one of the larger self-report research projects, the National Youth Survey (NYS), which shows the wide range of offenses and misbehaviors now utilized in current self-report studies (see Elliott and Huizinga, 1983).[14] Juveniles were asked how many times they engaged in a certain behavior during a set period of time (such as the last year). The offenses in Table 3.7 have been collapsed into various scales that can easily be analyzed to give prevalence or incidence rates for the particular samples of juveniles employed in the survey. A *prevalence rate*

TABLE 3.7 **Delinquency Scales—National Youth Survey**

Offense-Specific Scales	Offense-Category Scales	Summary Scales	

Offense-Specific Scales

Felony assault
(1) Aggravated assault
(2) Sexual assault
(3) Gang fights

Minor assault
(1) Hit teacher
(2) Hit parent
(3) Hit students

Robbery
(1) Strongarmed students
(2) Strongarmed teachers
(3) Strongarmed others

Felony theft
(1) Stole motor vehicle
(2) Stole something GT$50
(3) Broke into bldg/vehicle
(4) Bought stolen goods

Minor theft
(1) Stole something LT$5
(2) Stole something $5–50
(3) Joyriding

*Damaged property**
(1) Damaged family property
(2) Damaged school property
(3) Damaged other property

Drug use
(1) Hallucinogens
(2) Amphetamines
(3) Barbiturates
(4) Heroin
(5) Cocaine

Offense-Category Scales

Illegal services
(1) Prostitution
(2) Sold marijuana
(3) Sold hard drugs

*Public disorder**
(1) Hitchhiked illegally
(2) Disorderly conduct
(3) Public drunkenness
(4) Panhandled
(5) Obscene calls

*Status offenses**
(1) Runaway
(2) Skipped classes
(3) Lied about age
(4) Sexual intercourse

Crimes against persons
(1) Aggravated assault
(2) Gang fights
(3) Hit teacher
(4) Hit parent
(5) Hit students
(6) Sexual assault
(7) Strongarmed students
(8) Strongarmed teachers
(9) Strongarmed others

General theft
(1) Stole motor vehicle
(2) Stole something GT$50
(3) Bought stolen goods
(4) Stole something LT$5
(5) Stole something $5–50
(6) Broke into bldg/vehicle
(7) Joyriding

Summary Scales

*School delinquency**
(1) Damaged school property
(2) Cheated on school tests
(3) Hit teacher
(4) Hit students
(5) Strongarmed students
(6) Strongarmed teachers
(7) Stole at school
(8) Skipped classes

*Home delinquency**
(1) Damaged family property
(2) Runaway
(3) Stole from family
(4) Hit parent

Index offenses
(1) Aggravated assault
(2) Sexual assault
(3) Gang fights
(4) Stole motor vehicle
(5) Stole something GT$50
(6) Broke into bldg/vehicle
(7) Strongarmed students
(8) Strongarmed teachers
(9) Strongarmed others

*General delinquency A**
(1) Damaged family property
(2) Damaged school property
(3) Damaged other property
(4) Stole motor vehicle
(5) Stole something GT$50
(6) Bought stolen goods
(7) Runaway
(8) Lied about age
(9) Carried hidden weapon
(10) Stole something LT$5
(11) Aggravated assault
(12) Prostitution
(13) Sexual intercourse
(14) Gang fights
(15) Sold marijuana
(16) Hitchhiked illegally
(17) Hit teacher
(18) Hit parent
(19) Hit students
(20) Disorderly conduct
(21) Sold hard drugs
(22) Joyriding
(23) Bought liquor for minor
(24) Sexual assault
(25) Strongarmed students
(26) Strongarmed teachers
(27) Strongarmed others
(28) Evaded payment
(29) Public drunkenness
(30) Stole something $5–50
(31) Broke into bldg/vehicle
(32) Panhandled
(33) Skipped classes
(34) Didn't return change
(35) Obscene calls

* Not available for 1977.
Source: Elliott and Huizinga (1983: 156–157).

involves a calculation of the proportion of youth in the study population or in some subgroup who reported involvement in at least one of the offenses included in a given scale. An *incidence rate* refers to the frequency or number of times a given offense was reported by the study population or subgroup. Usually incidence rates are obtained by summing or adding up the number of reported offenses for separate items included in a particular scale.

Researchers in the NYS, in addition to having offense-specific scales in their design, devised certain summary scales (school delinquency, home delinquency, index offenses, and general delinquency) for which they could calculate incidence scores. The offense items employed in the inventory include all but one of the UCR Part I offenses (homicide was excluded), 60 percent of Part II offenses, and a wide range of UCR "other" offenses. An extensive selection of status and minor offenses is also included in the instrument.

Status and Minor Offenses. According to self-report findings, both males and females engage in numerous status offenses as well as other minor offenses. In an early study, Short and Nye (1958) found that common status offenses committed by juveniles include truancy, drinking, defying parents, and sexual violations. When compared to a training school sample, high school samples of boys and girls reported the commission of lesser numbers of juvenile offenses. Short and Nye's results also revealed that several other minor offenses, such as petty theft and the lesser traffic violations, are committed by large numbers of males and females. Dentler and Monroe (1961) extended the work of Short and Nye by concentrating on juvenile theft and discovered large amounts of minor theft among males and females in three Kansas communities.

More recent self-report investigations have also disclosed that status and minor offenses are committed frequently by juveniles (Clark and Wenninger, 1962; Gold, 1966, 1970; Hirschi, 1969; Hirschi, Hindelang, and Weis, 1981; Elliott and Huizinga, 1983). Studying a sample of 950 rural high school males and females, Hindelang (1971) found that a large percentage of youth engaged in

both status offenses (for example, cutting school, cheating, getting drunk) and minor thefts. Females in Hindelang's sample reported fewer incidences of each offense.

Thornton and James (1977) collected self-report data on the delinquency of ninth- through twelfth-graders in two southern cities and a northeastern city and found that a large proportion of all samples admitted frequent alcohol consumption and minor theft. Truancy, which is usually a common offense, was reported infrequently by both boys and girls. Johnstone (1978) conducted a self-report study in Chicago and reported that juveniles admitted minor thefts, drinking violations, and truancy. Hindelang, Hirschi, and Weis (1981) found relatively high levels of self-reported truancy and runaways in their samples of youth from the Seattle Youth Survey. From the NYS, Elliott and Huizinga (1983) report on a full range of minor and status offenses committed by both males and females from several social class categories. Incidence rates reported in Table 3.8 indicate fluctuations for certain types of offenses (minor theft, public disorder) over a five-year period.

Serious Juvenile Offenses. Self-report research indicates that serious juvenile crimes, some of which are crimes for adults as well as children, are committed by youth, particularly males. Serious offenses have, however, been reported less often than less serious offenses. This may be explained in part because earlier self-report studies have not included many serious offenses in their inventories. However, even more sophisticated self-report studies reveal that serious crimes against property are far more frequent than serious crimes against persons.

Serious offenses also generally remain low in frequency when compared with lesser offenses. Short and Nye, for example, reported high incidences of property damage, fistfights, and gang fighting in their high school samples. Similarly, Hindelang reported large amounts of property destruction and fighting, primarily among boys. Results from the Seattle Youth Survey indicate that a number of major crimes were reported by males, including auto theft, armed robbery, breaking and entering, and carrying weapons. Data from the National Youth Survey (Table 3.8) also show that both serious personal and property crimes (though in lesser incidence) are reported by males and to a lesser extent by females.

Thus, self-report surveys lead to the conclusion that more serious types of offenses are committed by certain youths and that many of the juveniles committing these offenses are never formally sanctioned. Generally, however, less serious types of offenses predominate among adolescents.

Official Compared to Nonofficial Delinquents

Several researchers have compared samples of adjudicated delinquents with samples of nonofficial delinquents—that is, youth in the community who commit "hidden delinquency." As we stated previously, research evidence does suggest that some youths in correctional facilities have committed fewer offenses than some adolescents at large in the community. Other research, however, finds significant differences in the frequency of offenses admitted by official and nonofficial delinquents.

Comparing samples of high school boys and girls with a sample of training school boys and girls, Short and Nye concluded that "significantly higher proportions of the 'official' delinquents [committed] virtually all of the offenses, and [committed] them more often than [did] the high school students" (1958: 299). Exceptions were found only in the categories of homosexual relations among boys, operating a car unlawfully among girls, and game (hunting and fishing) violations among both sexes. These findings were confirmed by Erickson and Empey's research (1963), conducted with a sample of high school boys and three samples of officially designated delinquents (boys who had been to court once, repeat offenders on probation, and incarcerated offenders).

According to Erickson and Empey's findings, high school boys and boys referred to the court differed significantly in the commission of only one offense—destruction of property.[15] Official delinquents were more likely to engage in this

activity. Although high school boys and boys once referred to the court reported delinquency, both differed significantly from serious offenders placed on probation or incarcerated in a correctional facility. Serious offenders reported much greater amounts of delinquency (for example, theft, property violations, offenses against the person, open defiance of authority) than the other boys. In fact, the violations of the serious offenders exceeded the offenses of the other two groups by thousands. Two other studies that have examined the connection between self-reports of official contacts and self-reported delinquency likewise show "official" delinquents as being more involved in delinquency. Elmhorn (1965) found that among a sample of Scandinavian juveniles, those who had admitted contact with the police had an average delinquency score substantially higher than "nonofficial" delinquents. Christie et al. (1965) reported similar results.

The research of Short and Nye, Erickson and Empey, and others does not support the conclusion that nondelinquents (that is, unofficial delinquents) commit as many offenses as official delinquents. It probably follows, then, that most juveniles who receive harsh sanctions such as incarceration have committed offenses commensurate with their sentences.

Characteristics of Self-Reported Delinquents

Studies of self-reported delinquency have sought to identify the personal and social characteristics of juveniles who report delinquent behavior. To achieve this aim, questionnaires often include questions about the age, sex, socioeconomic status, race, and residence of the respondent. Because these factors are measured differently from study to study and because how juveniles are selected to participate in studies varies, comparisons about the characteristics of delinquents are often misleading. Added to these problems are those brought about by the ever-changing nature of the youth subculture. Certain activities, some of which are delinquent, are popular at one time and not at other times. Thus, when marijuana use was in-

TABLE 3.8   Incidence of Delinquent Behavior: 1976–1980 Self-Reported Delinquency Scales by Social Class and Sex, Rate Per 100 Youth

	1976			1977			1978			1979			1980		
(N)	(196)	(266)	(399)	(194)	(256)	(376)	(190)	(253)	(370)	(176)	(233)	(348)	(175)	(228)	(334)
Males	Middle	Working	Lower	Middle	Working	Lower	Middle	Working	Lower	Middle	Working	Lower	Middle	Working	Lower
Offense-specific scales															
1. Felony assault	28	76	103	10	246	142	20	60	53	23	82	96	18	54	56
2. Minor assault	333	1259	1524	187	514	534	190	378	487	118	440	280	116	134	286
3. Robbery	8	52	69	26	44	161	30	75	49	6	45	28	29	20	8
4. Felony theft	54	182	65	28	139	293	15	162	91	15	99	169	14	97	82
5. Minor theft	107	220	345	94	415	137	55	246	126	99	209	152	75	130	111
6. Damaged property*	162	435	598	529	215	316	98	182	172	79	159	95	79	110	96
7. Hard drug use†	5.16	5.24	5.11	5.24	5.41	5.28	5.43	5.85	5.40	5.71	6.20	5.84	5.87	6.38	5.77
8. Fraud	—	—	—	—	—	—	—	—	—	14	43	82	6	117	67
Offense-category scales															
9. Illegal services	36	124	248	51	175	441	65	489	641	94	524	833	156	1143	999
10. Public disorder*	494	1339	880	446	1508	583	1408	1313	851	1163	1709	1007	1896	1533	1123
11. Crimes against persons	370	1386	1693	224	808	839	241	514	590	147	567	406	162	208	350
12. General theft	161	402	410	122	554	432	70	408	217	114	308	321	90	228	193
13. Status offenses*	704	1031	1249	498	1774	760	761	1708	1558	728	1897	1930	1215	2780	1899
Summary scales															
14. School delinquency	1097	1907	2636	1250	1934	1450	1003	1462	1558	946	1435	953	1159	1161	915
15. Home delinquency	114	407	489	128	130	128	73	95	115	59	115	51	42	63	43
16. Index offenses	52	199	195	42	371	486	54	177	127	39	180	200	53	122	103
17. General delinquency B	945	2982	3399	948	3611	2870	2030	3439	2945	1667	3794	3955	2880	5019	4495
18. General delinquency A*	2278	5217	6058	2159	6701	3710	4418	6175	5402	4155	6881	6097	6167	7892	6655

Females (N)	(195)	(242)	(321)	(195)	(235)	(307)	(192)	(228)	(306)	(184)	(222)	(298)	(171)	(223)	(285)
Offense-specific scales															
1. Felony assault	10	14	32	6	17	23	4	6	15	64	8	27	4	11	18
2. Minor assault	247	150	543	62	166	154	204	79	219	584	50	274	27	43	45
3. Robbery	3	4	11	4	1	5	2	1	3	1	10	1	7	6	1
4. Felony theft	14	25	52	9	27	15	4	7	13	11	7	53	19	12	20
5. Minor theft	72	57	91	35	34	60	41	40	82	226	29	85	108	165	70
6. Damaged property*	63	93	93	216	125	49	58	71	48	46	36	63	31	17	38
7. Hard drug use†	5.15	5.18	5.14	5.13	5.28	5.23	5.21	5.22	5.21	5.55	5.58	5.54	5.83	5.53	5.57
8. Fraud	—	—	—	—	—	—	—	—	—	10	6	8	20	17	6
Offense-category scales															
9. Illegal services	83	21	10	191	143	28	31	19	132	25	30	105	15	35	131
10. Public disorder*	336	401	287	489	737	297	404	586	451	1053	606	463	951	714	461
11. Crimes against persons	261	167	586	73	185	184	210	86	237	648	69	302	39	59	64
12. General theft	86	83	143	44	61	75	45	47	94	238	36	138	127	177	99
13. Status offenses*	506	661	941	495	803	733	793	635	962	1801	1124	1624	1506	1537	1905
Summary scales															
14. School delinquency	984	736	992	985	999	745	967	611	808	1660	860	1011	934	744	544
15. Home delinquency	162	93	234	55	405	43	346	129	80	180	64	67	240	59	35
16. Index offenses	17	21	48	13	44	33	8	10	22	68	21	68	25	21	31
17. General delinquency B	769	643	1140	683	1112	1086	1058	846	1497	2262	1939	2688	2067	1623	2643
18. General delinquency A*	1498	1586	2395	1715	2190	1795	2203	1844	2496	4398	3455	3946	4050	3222	3890

* 1977 estimates are based upon NIMH sample only.
† Mean categorical score: Never = 1; once or twice = 2; once every 2–3 months = 3; once a month = 4; once every 2–3 weeks = 5; once a week = 7; once a day = 8; 2–3 times a day = 9.
Source: Elliott and Huizinga (1983: 166–167).

cluded on earlier self-reports, infrequent consumption of the drug was reported. Later self-report studies revealed substantially different patterns of marijuana use. Keep in mind the difficulty of comparing findings from study to study as you read the results of self-report research on the characteristics of delinquents.

Age and Self-Reported Delinquency. As you will recall from Figure 3.1, estimates derived from official statistics indicate that roughly 17 percent of all arrests take place among youth under the age of 18. Arrest rates are particularly high for those between the ages of 13 and 18. In particular, the results of self-report studies also show high involvement of those from 13 to 18 in delinquent behaviors. Using grade as an indicator of age (a tenth-grader would be 15 to 16 years old), Hirschi (1969) found that in a sample of males, middle adolescence (approximately 14 to 16) is the period of maximum delinquent activity. Looking only at self-reported theft, Dentler and Monroe (1961) also concluded that males and females 14 years of age or older were more frequently involved in theft than younger children. Similarly, Williams and Gold's classic study (1972) reported that older boys and girls were more frequently and more seriously delinquent than younger adolescents.

Ageton and Elliott (1979) report on the self-reported delinquencies of the 1976 phase of the National Youth Survey. Their data suggest that for some forty offenses, older juveniles 15 to 17 generally appear more involved in more serious crimes (carrying a hidden weapon, major theft, and damaging property) than younger juveniles aged 11 to 14. Some younger adolescents, however, do report engaging in rather serious offenses (destroying property, hitting parents and teachers). Analyzing a panel of females from the NYS, Ageton noted that as of 1980 there was a decline in more general types of self-reported delinquency for girls. She suggests that as these juveniles get older, they decrease some of their earlier delinquency involvement (Ageton, 1983).

Sex and Self-Reported Delinquency. Some official statistics on delinquency suggest that the

gap between male and female delinquency has been narrowing. The ratio of male to female juvenile court referrals prior to 1965 was 4 to 1. As of 1980, this ratio had declined to about 3 to 1. While interpretations of official crime statistics vary regarding the actual increase in the crimes that females commit, evidence does suggest that the nature of female crime has changed considerably over the last decade.

Self-report studies also reveal that the nature of female delinquency has been changing. Self-report ratios of male to female delinquency, depending on the study, range from 2.7 to 1 to 1.7 to 1 (Clark and Haurek, 1966; Gold, 1970; Hindelang, 1971; Short and Nye, 1958; Wise, 1967; Cernkovich and Giordano, 1978a; Jessor and Jessor, 1977). Studies that have calculated male to female ratios for offense-specific crimes indicate that for more serious types of crimes, ratios may be extremely disproportionate. Canter (1982a) found a 7 to 1 ratio for robbery and a 5.1 to 1 ratio for property damage.

Generally speaking, however, most self-report studies indicate that the female pattern is beginning to resemble the male pattern, though not necessarily in increased female crime rates (Steffensmier and Steffensmier, 1980). Most self-reports disclose that patterns of male and female delinquency are now very similar, even though female involvement is much less frequent.[16] Males and females both engage in offenses such as theft, drinking, drug use, truancy, property destruction, and fighting (see Table 3.8).

Some self-report data do suggest, however, that females may be less delinquent in the 1980s than in the immediate past. More recent analysis of NYS data through 1980 (Ageton, 1983; Canter, 1982a) show a leveling off, and in some instances decline, in female delinquency.

Socioeconomic Status and Self-Reported Delinquency. Self-report studies have also explored the relationship between social class and delinquent behavior. Traditionally, sociologists thought that juveniles from the lower social classes engaged in a disproportionate amount of delinquency compared to youth from the middle and upper classes. A generation of sociologists oriented their explanations of delinquency and their research toward the study of the lower class delinquent offender.[17]

Unlike research using official statistics, some self-report studies have found that the relationship between social class and delinquency is slight, if it exists at all.[18] Although there are variations, social class is usually measured by fathers' occupations or some other factor indicative of family income. Hindelang, Hirschi, and Weis (1981), employing such a definition, do not find even a moderate relationship between social class and self-reported delinquency. Hirschi (1969), basing his measure of social class on fathers' occupation, also found little evidence of a relationship between the number of self-reported delinquent acts and social class. While his research shows youth who come from families in which the fathers are professionals and executives to be least likely to have engaged in many delinquent acts, it also indicates that sons of white collar workers are more delinquent than sons of unskilled laborers. Also examining social class as measured by fathers' occupations, Williams and Gold (1972) found only a negligible relationship between social class and delinquency. The only reliable relationship reported was that higher-status boys are the most seriously delinquent. Other studies have noted that high-status juveniles report more extensive involvement in delinquent activities than do other respondents (Voss, 1966). The findings of these studies have, however, been the exception rather than the rule.

Although the Hirschi and the Williams and Gold studies suggest there is little correlation between social class and self-reported delinquency, several self-report studies reach different conclusions and report finding such a relationship. Clark and Wenninger (1962), for example, reported that juveniles from all social classes engaged in delinquent offenses at almost equal rates, but "serious offenses [were] much more likely to have been committed by lower-class urban youngsters" (p. 883). Reiss and Rhodes (1961) also discovered more frequent and serious self-reported delinquency in the lower than in the middle social class, but the strength of the relationship between social class and delinquency in that study is weak.

In 1977 Elliott and Ageton began their National Youth Survey with 1,726 adolescents aged 11 to 17. The two researchers found a significant relationship between social class and self-reported delinquency. Lower class youth (those with semi-skilled parents with little education) reported greater numbers of offenses than working class youth (those with parents who had some job skill or who owned a small business) or middle class youth (those with college-educated, professional parents). When self-reported predatory crimes against persons, assaults, and robberies, were examined, the researchers found that lower class juveniles reported almost four times as many offenses as working class juveniles (Elliott and Ageton, 1980).

Similar conclusions were reached by Elliott and Huizinga (1983) in their examination of the full panel data for the NYS for the years 1976–1980 (see Table 3.8). They reported that while there are a few specific offenses for which middle class juveniles have higher prevalence rates (cheating on tests, skipping classes, public drunkenness), there are no offenses for which middle class youth (males and females) report higher incidence rates than working or lower class youth. Lower class males report, for example, greater involvement in serious assaults and felony thefts than middle class males. In fact, "Middle-class males report substantially lower prevalence and incidence rates on most serious offenses and scales, lower incidence rates on a number of nonserious offenses and scales, and lower incidence rates on global [delinquency] scales" (1983: 169).

The issue of the connection between social class and delinquency is far from resolved. In a recent study, Johnstone (1978) found that lower class youth did commit serious offenses—for example, stealing—because they wanted and could not afford an item, more often than middle class youth. This was the case only when lower class youth lived in middle or upper middle class communities, however. So it appears that the important factor is the sharp contrast in the life styles of lower and middle class adolescents, rather than social class itself.

Race and Self-Reported Delinquency.   Self-report studies have also investigated the relationship between race and crime. The conclusions reached, for the most part, are quite different from findings based on official statistics. Self-report research, which concentrates almost exclusively on black and white differences, reveals marked similarities in the reported crimes of black and white juveniles. Although these findings have been consistent, the results of the studies must be interpreted cautiously. Very few self-report studies have exclusively focused on racial distinctions; racial factors are generally just one variable out of many. Further, samples of black respondents tend to be quite small in most self-report studies (Pope, 1979).

Several self-report studies are representative of the research in the area. Chambliss and Nagasawa (1969) compared the self-reported delinquent behaviors of high school boys living in a lower class urban community with official juvenile court records in the area. The youth were black, white, and Japanese. The official statistics indicated that black juveniles had the highest arrest rate and Japanese juveniles the lowest. Conversely, when the researchers examined self-reported delinquency, they found that white juveniles had a slightly higher self-reported rate of delinquency than black juveniles. But again, Japanese youth reported the least delinquency.

Gould (1969) examined the self-reported and official delinquency of seventh-grade boys in Seattle and noticed that race was related to official delinquency (juvenile court, police, and school misconduct records), but was virtually unrelated to self-reported delinquency. Black juveniles committed four offenses at higher rates than white juveniles: threatening other children for money, beating them up, skipping school, and driving without a license. White boys did the most larceny, destruction of property, drinking, and running away. So there was a slight tendency for black boys to commit more violent offenses, but overall the delinquency of black respondents was very similar to that of the white respondents (Gould, 1969).

After questioning more than 800 black and 1,300 white males in California high schools, Travis Hirschi (1969) wrote that "42 percent of the Negro and 18 percent of the white boys in the analyzed sample had police records in the two

years prior to the administration of the questionnaire" (p. 75). When the self-reported delinquency of the boys was examined, the differences between the percentages of black and white involvement were almost reversed. About 19 percent of the black and 44 percent of the white boys admitted one or more delinquent acts during the past year. Once again, we see that official reports of delinquency estimate racial differences in delinquency as much greater than is indicated by self-report data.

Research by Williams and Gold (1972) also compared the self-reported delinquency of black and white boys and girls. White girls were found to be neither more nor less frequently or seriously involved in delinquency than black girls. White boys were less frequently delinquent than black boys, but white boys were no less seriously delinquent than black boys. Supporting results were reached in a 1972 study, published in 1975, conducted by Gold and Reimer.

The frequency of the delinquency of blacks and whites, males and females, was similar. Black males, however, admitted slightly more serious offenses than did white males. Other researchers have also found that racial differences in self-reported delinquency increase with the severity of the offense (Gold and Reimer, 1975; Hindelang, 1978; Hindelang, Hirschi, and Weis, 1981).

Hindelang, Hirschi, and Weis (1981) employed a newer, comprehensive self-report inventory in their samples of Seattle youth, which included black males and females. They found considerable variation in magnitude of black to white ratios from offense to offense. However, black males in their sample "disproportionately and consistently reported being involved in what could be characterized as face-to-face violent offenses often involving theft: used club, knife, or gun to get something; threatened to beat someone up if he didn't give you money; used physical force to get money; carried a razor, switchblade, or gun; pulled a knife; hit a teacher; beat up someone so badly they probably needed a doctor; and jumped or helped jump somebody" (p. 170).

The National Youth Survey reported findings on black-white self-report delinquency at variance with the results of most previous self-report studies.

At least in the first phase of that study, Elliott and Ageton observed a greater consistency between self-reported and official data with respect to race. Black youth reported greater numbers of delinquencies on all measures, which ranged from status to serious delinquent offenses. For total delinquency offenses—that is, all offenses—black youths reported three offenses for every two reported by whites. For predatory crimes against property such as vandalism, burglary, and auto theft, blacks reported more than two offenses for every offense reported by whites.

Elliott and Ageton claimed their findings differed from past self-report studies because of differences in the self-reported delinquency measures. They noted that earlier measures failed to distinguish between the range of self-reported delinquency; that is, they did not offer a wide selection of nonserious and serious offenses, and failed to analyze the self-reported delinquencies of those who reported having committed many delinquent acts, especially serious delinquencies.

Although recent evidence suggests that black-white differences in self-reported delinquency may be greater than previously thought, most self-report research indicates that there appears to be a minimal difference in the frequency of self-reported delinquent activities. Some evidence, especially from new self-report inventories, does suggest that adolescent black males commit more serious delinquent offenses than white males. At least one study shows the same for black females (Hindelang, Hirschi, and Weis, 1981). Generally, however, the findings of self-report studies contradict official data which show that blacks commit a disproportionate share of delinquency.

We have stated that one criticism of self-report methodologies has been the lack of attention given to more serious delinquent offenses. More extensive research must be undertaken utilizing the newer, more comprehensive self-report measures with diverse samples before any definite conclusions can be reached.

Residence and Self-Reported Delinquency. Few self-report studies have specifically looked at the relationship between residence and self-reported delinquency. Even though self-report researchers have selected samples from many residential locales, most have studied urban or metropolitan areas. Because comparisons across localities are rare, it is difficult to assess variations in self-reported delinquency among residential areas.

When self-reports examine delinquency differences among residential areas, the findings of official statistics are generally supported. Few differences have been found in the delinquencies of juveniles from different residential locations.

Concentrating on self-reported theft, Dentler and Monroe (1961) observed no significant differences in the offenses of youth from suburban, urban, and small communities. Frequency and seriousness of admitted thefts were very similar from locale to locale. Short and Nye (1958) also found little variation in the frequency of self-reported delinquency between respondents from different residential locales. Hindelang (1976) employed a sample of males and females from both urban and rural areas in a self-report study. He found that although urban juveniles generally report greater numbers of delinquent acts, with some exceptions the types of offenses engaged in by rural and urban youths are quite similar. The offenses range from status and drug offenses to more serious adult crimes.

Clark and Wenninger (1962) did one of the few studies that included samples of juveniles from diverse communities, including one rural farm area and three urban areas. After comparing youths from these different environments on thirty-eight self-reported offenses, they concluded that rural adolescents differed very little from urban youths in the commission of offenses such as minor theft, telling lies, loitering, beating up other youngsters, using narcotics, and arson. Rural farm youth, however, engaged in fewer offenses involving major thefts, consumption of alcohol, taking money on the pretense of paying it back, and skipping school. Generally, rural and urban adolescents engaged in similar amounts of delinquent acts, but the rural delinquents involved themselves in less serious types of delinquency, with the obvious exception of arson.

Other studies, among them those of Clinard (1942, 1944), report that rural youth are less sophisticated in their delinquencies than urban youth. However, most of these studies are now out of date. Ageton (1983) reports some rather dramatic shifts in mean incidence rates of female self-reported delinquency by residence from 1976 to 1980. While her urban and suburban groups display an overall increase from 1976 to 1980 in the incidence of general delinquency, the rural females show a declining incidence rate until 1980, when the rate rises to its 1976 level. No explanation is offered for this shift in rural female delinquency. Ageton concluded that basically her data do not show strong or consistent differences in the incidence of general delinquency based on where a juvenile lives.

Residential area, a variable once thought essential in explaining delinquency, has become less important as the population in the United States has migrated from the central cities. Also, self-report studies that use diverse residential samples are for the most part outdated, and any differences in residential rates of delinquency have more than likely changed substantially.

Limitations of Self-Reports

Any method of data collection that relies on respondents to answer questions truthfully and accurately is subject to errors and distortions. Self-report questionnaires and interviews depend on the accurate reporting of juveniles. But some may not wish to disclose their past deeds, even if anonymity is assured; or they may simply not recall the number and types of offenses they have committed. Efforts to validate self-reported acts by comparisons with official court records and police records and even polygraph examinations have been conducted. Official data have generally verified self-reports.

Another problem of self-reports is that the more serious types of offenses, such as rape, assault, and burglary, are often not included in self-report inventories. Researchers have withheld questions about serious offenses either because of the sensitivity of inquiring about the offense or on the assumption that most juveniles have not engaged

in these acts. More recent self-report studies, however, have begun to correct this deficiency.

Self-report studies are further limited because they are conducted at one point in time and are usually not given annually. Self-reports thus fail to show trends in delinquency rates. Additionally, little effort has been given to national self-report data collection. Most self-report research is conducted in local areas, usually the researchers' home territories. The results from these limited samples may not apply to the larger national population. Several large-scale national self-report studies, such as the National Youth Survey, the Seattle Youth Survey, and the Richmond Youth Survey, have overcome some of these problems.

Many self-report studies attempt to measure delinquency by summing the reported number of incidents and then obtaining a total delinquency score without weighting items as to seriousness. Since nonserious offenses tend to be high-frequency offenses and serious offenses tend to be low-frequency offenses, a scale with an excessive number of nonserious offenses can be very misleading. The use of a wide range of delinquency scales categorized by serious or nonserious level can correct for some of the measurement problems encountered in self-report research.

Self-report studies should, then, be interpreted cautiously. Although earlier measurement problems have to some extent been solved, self-reports are still plagued by the lack of comparability in the questions and design of different studies.

VICTIMIZATION SURVEYS

A third approach to crime measurement is victim survey research. Beginning in the mid-1960s, **representative samples** of citizens in major cities (that is, a sample of citizens having characteristics similar to those of the United States population as a whole) were asked to report the crimes committed against them during the preceding year. *Victimization studies*, as they are called, have revealed that many crimes are underreported. The volume of crime as indicated in the UCR substantially underestimates the incidence of crime in the United States. The conclusion of a national crime survey in which 136,000 people were questioned about their victimization was that many crimes were not reported to the police. The rate at which victims report crime to the police varies widely, depending upon the type or seriousness of the crime. Personal crimes such as rape, robbery, and personal larceny are greatly underreported. With the possible exception of motor vehicle theft, household crimes follow the same pattern. Commercial crimes, such as burglary and robbery of business establishments, are the most reported (U.S. Department of Justice, 1985).

The first nationwide victimization surveys in the United States were sponsored by the President's Commission on Law Enforcement and Administration of Justice and published in 1967 (Biderman, Johnson, McIntyre, and Weir, 1967; Ennis, 1967; Reiss, 1967a). Of the three surveys sponsored by the president's commission, the most widely known is the national survey conducted by the National Opinion Research Center (NORC) (Ennis, 1967). In the 1967 NORC survey, interviews were held in 10,000 households (containing 33,000 eligible persons) in the continental United States. A knowledgeable respondent from each household was asked a series of questions about victimizations of members of the household. This national study indicated that the estimated rate of victimization for index crimes—homicide, rape, robbery, aggravated assault, burglary, larceny, and auto theft—was more than twice the rate indicated by the *Uniform Crime Reports* (Garofalo and Hindelang, 1977).

Victimization surveys are used to supplement and verify official statistics about the incidence of crime and the types of individuals who are most victimized. Data on the age, race, sex, income, and residential locality of victims and nonvictims are collected. Because they deal with only one dimension of delinquent behavior—criminal offenses—criminal victim surveys do not provide a complete picture of delinquency. Nevertheless, these surveys do offer information about the extent of serious victimization. Since the surveys are self-reports of individual victimizations, they are largely uncontaminated by the biases that plague official statistics.

Beginning with the early NORC study and continuing with later surveys, victimization research demonstrates that rates for personal crimes of violence, such as rape, robbery, and assault, are relatively higher for males, younger persons, blacks, the poor, and the urban.[19] When we look at the victimization rates of various segments of the population, some important trends emerge.

Victim Characteristics: Age, Sex, and Race

According to the data presented in Table 3.9, the young face the greatest risk. Young persons aged 12 to 24 have the highest victimization rates for personal crimes of violence and theft. Beyond age 24, the rates generally decline. Both black and white females have lower victimization rates for all personal crimes than males do. Young females up to age 24 of both races report lower victimization rates than males of the same age. On the other hand, black females aged 25 and over have somewhat higher victimization rates than older white females. Black males aged 16 to 19 have the highest victimization rates for crimes of violence; 12- to 15-year-old black males have the next highest victimization rates for personal crimes of violence, followed by 16- to 19-year-old white males. Black and white males over age 35 have similar victimization rates for all personal crimes (U.S. Department of Justice, 1985).

Hindelang (1979) conducted extensive analyses of the National Crime Survey data and issued a report that dealt with offender characteristics as identified by victims. In particular, he examined the percentage of female offenders involved in various offenses for the period 1972 to 1976. Although these data do not differentiate juveniles from adult female offenders, the findings are relevant to our previous discussion about the crime involvement of females. First, female involvement in criminal activity was low. Second, the figures were rather stable, meaning that there was no large increase in female criminality during the

TABLE 3.9   **Personal Crimes, 1983: Victimization Rates for Persons Age 12 and over, by Race, Sex, and Age of Victims and Type of Crime**

(Rate per 1,000 population in each age group)

Race, Sex and Age	Crimes of Violence	Crimes of Theft
White		
Male		
12–15 (6,174,780)	62.5	135.6
16–19 (6,343,310)	84.6	140.4
20–24 (8,796,570)	79.6	128.1
25–34 (16,934,290)	50.1	92.1
35–49 (17,553,790)	23.5	74.5
50–64 (13,960,840)	11.8	45.0
65 and over (9,645,310)	7.0	25.8
Female		
12–15 (5,896,400)	34.2	123.5
16–19 (6,218,220)	41.7	114.4
20–24 (8,952,200)	39.0	120.2
25–34 (17,017,100)	32.5	84.6
35–49 (17,949,950)	16.7	71.9
50–64 (15,461,440)	5.7	40.5
65 and over (13,973,350)	4.7	20.5
Black		
Male		
12–15 (1,064,350)	85.1	101.8
16–19 (1,095,240)	99.0	89.7
20–24 (1,278,880)	93.1	90.0
25–34 (2,167,010)	40.1	107.2
35–49 (1,903,570)	27.3	78.7
50–64 (1,329,080)	13.5	60.6
65 and over (864,420)	a11.7	29.8
Female		
12–15 (1,058,700)	59.3	132.5
16–19 (1,128,640)	52.6	71.2
20–24 (1,494,160)	48.7	95.5
25–34 (2,575,420)	43.2	88.0
35–49 (2,346,050)	22.5	70.5
50–64 (1,707,120)	12.2	49.8
65 and over (1,314,120)	a0.9	19.4

a Estimate, based on zero or on about 10 or fewer sample cases, is statistically unreliable.
NOTE: Numbers in parentheses refer to population in the group.
Source: U.S. Department of Justice (1985: 20).

1972–1976 period. A review of more current victimization survey results indicates continued stability of female involvement in victimization episodes, according to the National Crime Survey data for the reporting years 1979, 1981, and 1982. Women were the offenders in 13 percent of the single-offender violent crimes and in 7 percent of the multiple-offender violent cases (U.S. Department of Justice, 1981, 1983, 1984).

Victim Characteristics: Income Level

When the victimization rates at various income levels are compared for the year 1983, the incidence of violent crime appears generally highest among members of families with the lowest incomes. Moreover, there is a tendency for the overall rate of victimization to decline with increased income. Crimes of theft, however, are a different story. Family members in the most affluent group examined had the highest victimization rate for personal crimes of theft.

When the victimization rates of black and white families at various income levels are compared, these patterns remain generally the same. The rate of victimization for crimes of violence is, however, generally greater for blacks at all income levels. One striking difference involves a comparison of white and black families earning $50,000 or more; the victimization rate for violent crimes in affluent families is almost twice as high. Crimes of theft are also much more frequent among affluent black families earning $50,000 or more a year than among similarly affluent white families (U.S. Department of Justice, 1985).

Victim Characteristics: Residence

Victimization rates for three residential areas (central cities, suburbs, and nonmetropolitan areas) indicate that the risk of personal victimization generally was highest for central city residents and lowest for nonmetropolitan populations, with suburbanites ranking in between. Although similar crimes were committed in each locale, the volume of crime in the more urban areas was substantially greater. The victimization rate of residents of central cities was roughly twice that of the non-metropolitan population. The UCR also reports a higher rate of urban crime (U.S. Department of Justice: 1985).

Limitations of Victimization Surveys

Basically, the results of victimization surveys reveal two important facts. The first is that many crimes are not reported to the police. Personal crimes such as rape, robbery, and assault are greatly underreported. When questioned, crime victims who fail to report their losses or injuries to the police give many reasons. Chief among these are the feelings that nothing can be done or that the offense was not very important. Other reasons include the notions that the police do not want to be bothered or simply that reporting the victimization is too inconvenient or time-consuming. Some victims feared reprisal if they reported the offense.

The second important fact revealed by victimization research is that there is a much greater risk of victimization among the young. After age 24, the risk of being victimized for a personal crime of violence or theft is substantially reduced. But other factors, such as sex, race, and residence, alter this trend. Males, particularly black males, stand a greater chance of being victimized than females of either race. Further, income level and location of residence influence the probability of victimization. Poorer people are more vulnerable to violent personal crimes than are the affluent. An individual living in the central city, as opposed to a suburban or rural area, also has an increased risk of personal victimization. The typical victim of a violent crime, then, is a young male, probably black, who comes from a poor family living in a central city.

Like official and self-report measures of delinquency, victimization surveys are also limited. First, victim surveys deal with only one aspect of juvenile delinquency: criminal offenses. Status and other minor offenses are not included on most victim questionnaires.

Second, victim surveys exclude information on several other types of offenses, such as murders,

kidnapping, drug use, gambling, and prostitution. White collar crimes, such as embezzlement, bribery, fraud, income tax evasion, and the like, are similarly omitted. The emphasis is generally given to lower class and youthful criminal activities. It is assumed that most individuals would not incriminate themselves by confessing to various offenses where the offender is also the victim—for example, prostitution, drug use, and status offenses.

Third, problems arise whenever a **sample** of individuals is used to represent the attitudes and experiences of the larger **population**. Most of the national victimization surveys have scientifically drawn samples of more than 100,000 people, so results can be generalized to others with similar characteristics who were not actually questioned. This same technique is used by various public opinion polls, which have an impressive record of predictability based on relatively small, well-selected samples.

Fourth, a more serious problem than sampling involves the accuracy of respondents' statements. People are often unwilling or unable to recall details about traumatic incidents that occurred even a short time ago. Also, since many people are unwilling to report their victimizations to the police, some researchers feel they may be even less inclined to tell an interviewer.[20]

COHORT ANALYSIS

One recent innovation in the study of juvenile delinquency has been the introduction of **cohort analysis**. Cohort analysis is not a new technique in the social sciences. Demographers commonly apply cohort techniques to study changes and trends in mortality, morbidity (sickness), and fertility. In fact, insurance companies derive their actuarial tables from this brand of research. The application of cohort analysis to the area of juvenile delinquency represents a simple transfer of methodology from an allied field.

The term **cohort** refers to a group of individuals who share the same event during some common point in time (Glenn, 1977: 8). A **birth cohort** consists of all persons born in the same year in a particular geographical area. Suppose, for example, that a criminologist is interested in studying all the delinquent activity juveniles engage in prior to age 18 in a particular city. If the researcher identified all the children born in that city in 1960 and traced all their police and juvenile court records up until the end of 1978, that researcher would be conducting a birth cohort analysis of delinquency.

Cohort analysis can be used to address a variety of key policy issues (see Maxim, 1985). For example, do status offenders go on to commit progressively more serious offenses, or do they cease delinquent activity after official detection and reaction? Here a cohort analysis could prove very appropriate. If status offenders do progress to more serious offenses, cohort analysis can indicate the typical line of progression. These results can be used to justify intervention at an appropriate point. In the absence of any progression, the results call into question the need for system intervention.

Another area of application concerns the chronic delinquent and the decision to waive a juvenile to adult court. Do older juveniles who commit more serious crimes continue to engage in more serious crimes, or do these juveniles cease their illegal activities as part of the normal life cycle? Should juveniles typically mature out of illegal activity, the propriety of waiver becomes questionable. So cohort analysis is a powerful analytical tool with tremendous policy implications. In order to appreciate this technique better, we will consider several studies utilizing cohort analysis and focus on three concepts: desistance, age of onset, and escalation.

Wolfgang, Figlio, and Sellin: Delinquency in a Birth Cohort

One of the premier juvenile delinquency cohort studies was reported by Marvin E. Wolfgang, Robert M. Figlio, and Thorsten Sellin (1972) in the book *Delinquency in a Birth Cohort*. Wolfgang and his colleagues monitored the police records of almost 10,000 boys born in Philadelphia during 1945. This comprehensive data collection effort allowed the researchers to analyze the nature and

extent of delinquency perpetrated by cohort members, as well as to trace the criminal histories or career patterns of delinquents.

The research team reported that 35 percent of the male juveniles emerged from adolescence with a police record. In terms of race, half the nonwhites and 29 percent of the whites were known offenders (p. 245). While approximately 54 percent of the cohort members with police records committed more than one offense, the corresponding recidivism proportions were 65 percent for nonwhites and 45 percent for whites (p. 67).

In terms of offenses, recidivists committed nine times as many index crimes as one-time delinquents. A much smaller group of juveniles, called chronic offenders, were responsible for the bulk of offenses known to the police. These 627 youths accounted for over half the offenses recorded in the cohort. Black youths figured prominently in the chronic delinquent category.

Wolfgang, Figlio, and Sellin also examined three other aspects of delinquency: desistance, age of onset, and escalation. *Desistance* occurs when a delinquent stops committing any further offenses. *Age of onset* refers to the expectation that the younger the child at the time of first offense, the more likely it is for that juvenile to commit a greater volume of offenses before attaining adulthood.[21] *Escalation* generally means that as a youth commits more and more offenses, the offenses increase in terms of seriousness.

Desistance occurs when an individual who has committed one or more delinquent acts subsequently refrains from further delinquency. Wolfgang and his research team found that 55 percent of the white males committed one offense and then stopped their delinquent activity; the corresponding figure was 35 percent for nonwhites (p. 74). For the cohort as a whole, an additional 35 percent of the boys committing a second offense desisted from further recidivism (p. 254). Only 18 percent of the cohort participated in five or more delinquent acts. Thus, a small group of juveniles did not desist, and this group was responsible for a large number of offenses.

The age analysis indicated that offender rates gradually increased from age 7 to 11, then boomed until age 16 before registering a dramatic decline.

Thus, if a juvenile did not have a police dossier by age 16, the odds were that he would enter adulthood without ever having been arrested for a juvenile offense. The results further showed that black youth committed their first offense at a much earlier age than their white counterparts. However, contrary to expectation, an early age of onset did not automatically produce an extensive juvenile history. Juveniles who recorded extensive delinquency histories exhibited a flurry of delinquent activity at ages 15 through 16.

The escalation hypothesis did not fare well either. In general, offense severity did not increase with the commission of additional offenses; offense seriousness remained relatively constant (p. 248). The researchers did find that chronic offenders registered the highest seriousness scores, followed by nonchronic recidivists, and then by one-time offenders in descending order. However, once a juvenile had perpetrated an index crime, the odds favored another index violation in the future. Interestingly, the researchers found no evidence of offense specialization among offenders.

Although the Wolfgang, Figlio, and Sellin cohort study was an ambitious and provocative undertaking, other criminologists have voiced some concerns. First, the delinquency histories are derived from official sources and are subject to the usual distortions associated with this data base. Second, the selection of a single cohort in a single location at a single point in time may not produce generalizable findings (Erickson, 1973c: 362–363). Third, cohort membership was restricted to males. No female delinquents were included in the study. Fourth, status offenders were eliminated from the analysis, thus not allowing a complete test of the escalation hypothesis (Rojek and Erickson, 1982: 8). Fifth, there are some indications that the statistical techniques chosen restricted the type of results the researchers could uncover (Bursik, 1980).

Bursik: Another Look at Offense Specialization

Dissatisfied with some of the statistical shortcomings in the cohort study by Wolfgang and associates, Bursik (1980) decided to analyze the police and juvenile court histories of 750 delinquent Chicago boys. When applying the same technique utilized by Wolfgang and his team, Bursik found that "although there is some evidence of specialization, it is not very convincing" (p. 856). Application of different statistical techniques overlooked by Wolfgang et al. produced some interesting results. First, most delinquents did not specialize; they tended to engage in random delinquent activities. Second, the only evidence of specialization concerned white juveniles. Those white boys who had already committed a personal injury crime (murder, rape, assault) were subsequently more prone to commit a personal property crime (robbery and strong-arm robbery). Third, the number of white boys completing the discovered personal injury–personal property crime sequence was tiny. Thus, while the results here generally agreed with the findings obtained from the Philadelphia study, more refined techniques were able to isolate some discrepancies.

Rojek and Erickson: Another Look at Career Escalation

Objecting to the elimination of female delinquents and status offenses in earlier studies, Rojek and Erickson (1982) examined the offense histories of 1,619 Arizona children referred to juvenile court. The researchers found that 26 percent of the juveniles were one-time offenders, and most had committed a status offense. Multiple offenders were more likely to be processed for criminal offenses than one-time offenders. But if the multiple offender happened to be a female, the charge was most likely a status offense.

In terms of the escalation hypothesis, the researchers found no evidence of a trend toward more serious offenses with an increased volume of arrests. Males tended to remain within the property category, while females were absorbed into the running away or other status violations categories. Similarly, age of onset showed no impact upon career histories.

According to the researchers, these findings undermined the juvenile justice system's preoccupation with status offenders and emphasis on diversion programs. Rojek and Erickson conclude: "There is no evidence that juvenile programs predicated on the notion of official offense escalation will have any significant impact on delinquency rates. What emerges is a picture of adolescents who are extremely versatile in their delinquent activities" (p. 26).

Lab: Multiple Cohorts

One of the tidy features of cohort analysis is that it permits the comparative analysis of age, period, and cohort effects when the researcher is studying more than one cohort. **Age effects** refer to changes that can be attributed solely to developmental or maturational processes. **Period effects** reflect the life experiences of a particular group, and **cohort effects** may be thought of as generational differences. Because he was examining more than one cohort, Lab (1982) was able to determine whether these effects had an impact on delinquency. The three cohorts were the 1942, 1949, and 1955 birth cohorts in Racine, Wisconsin, and utilized the official information collected originally by Professor Lyle Shannon (1978). Thus, in addition to the usual age of onset and escalation analyses, Lab was able to compare the experiences of three different deliquent groups.

Like other researchers, Lab found that there was very little support for the escalation hypothesis. Very few juveniles showed a progression to more serious kinds of offenses, hardly any juveniles exhibited specialization, and approximately two-thirds of the offenders desisted by the fourth offense. In addition, age of onset was not related to increased commission of delinquent acts throughout one's career. However, Lab did note that the initial age of onset moved downward to earlier ages with each successive cohort.

Age, period, and cohort effects were subjected to scrutiny in Lab's study. The age effect means that the odds of system contact increase as juveniles become older. This result is quite consistent with the Wolfgang study. Period effects appear in almost every instance. Although the study was capable of locating period effects, the exact attribution of

impending forces is mostly speculative. The increasing delinquency rates could have been the product of altered police policies, civil and racial unrest, unemployment, and radical life style changes, among other things. Finally, there was no evidence of any cohort effect. It would seem that the increasing delinquency rates associated with each cohort reflected societal changes and moods over the past few decades.

By way of summary, cohort analysis has proved to be quite useful in delinquency research. In general, the literature lends no support to the expectations underlying age of onset, escalation, and offense specialization. Instead, it appears that the vast number of juvenile offenses are minor and that virtually all juveniles desist from further recidivism after a short career. However, chronic delinquents do appear to be a troublesome group. It would seem that both future researchers and system personnel could maximize their returns by concentrating their resources on this active offender group.

SUMMARY

Measuring the extent and nature of delinquency within American society is a difficult task. Three major types of statistics are used to measure delinquency: official statistics, collected by police and the courts; self-report statistics, obtained through the voluntary cooperation of perpetrators of delinquent acts; and victimization statistics, obtained from victims of delinquent acts and crimes who are willing to respond to questioning. Official statistics on delinquency, collected by police and courts, present a picture of delinquency far different from self-report accounts. Victimization surveys confirm suspicions that much crime, both juvenile and adult, is underreported—or not reported at all.

Despite the differences among the diverse measures of delinquency and crime, some similarities can be found. Juvenile court statistics, self-report, and victim survey statistics all suggest that delinquency, whether officially detected or self-reported, is widespread among the youth population.

Court records indicate that, between 1960 and 1974, delinquency cases more than doubled in comparison to the percentage of increase in the number of children aged 10 through 17. According to self-report studies, some 90 percent of illegal acts by youth go undetected. Similarly, victim accounts of crime suggest that the young stand a much greater chance of being victims of personal crimes. Even official arrest statistics such as the UCR, which have been criticized as grossly underestimating the extent of actual juvenile law violation, indicate that juvenile crime, especially that of females, has been on the increase over the last decade. In addition, all three data sources—official, self-report, and victim surveys—show that juveniles commit a variety of offenses ranging from status and minor offenses to more serious adult crimes. Cohort analysis shows, however, that most juveniles who engage in delinquency have rather short-lived careers and generally do not go on to more serious types of crimes.

Although there is agreement that juvenile crime is widespread, the social characteristics of juvenile offenders vary, depending on the data source. Perhaps the most serious discrepancy is in the nature and extent of black delinquency. Official sources such as the UCR indicate that black youth are disproportionately represented in juvenile crimes, especially those of a violent nature. Self-report studies, however, suggest that the extent of differences in white and black delinquent behavior is minimal. Black juveniles may be slightly more involved than whites in violent offenses, but the difference is not great. Victim accounts show that young white and black males have high rates of victimization up to about age 24, at which point vulnerability decreases for each race.

Self-report measures show that the assumed differences between male and female involvement in delinquency are not accurately reported in official accounts, which overreport the differences. Although boys generally commit greater numbers of delinquent acts, with some exceptions girls report engaging in similar types of offenses, including serious violations. Similarly, the relationship between social class and the commission of delinquent activities has been found to be less important than previously thought. Self-report studies present conflicting evidence about the relationship between social class and delinquency. These studies do, however, raise questions about the assumption that lower class youngsters are more frequently and seriously delinquent than middle and upper class youth. Victimization accounts of income and crime show that members of the lower classes are victimized for violent crimes substantially more often than members of the middle and upper classes; the opposite is true for crimes of theft.

All three sources of data on delinquency report similar findings about the relationship between residential locale and juvenile crime. Each measure of juvenile crime shows that, although urban and suburban locales report a greater volume of juvenile crime, the rate of the offenses committed in each area does not vary significantly. Despite traditional arguments stating that rural and suburban areas are relatively crime-free in relation to more urbanized areas, recent evidence disputes these findings. As population continues to migrate from the central cities, rural and suburban locales will more than likely experience the same problems, including crime, that cities have long experienced.

PROGRESS CHECK

1. Based on the *Uniform Crime Reports* data supplied in the chapter, give a brief summary of the types of major crimes (Part I offenses) that juveniles are most often arrested for. (pp. 51–58)

2. Which of the following is *not* ordinarily embraced by the term *dependence*? (p. 50)
   a. Destitution
   b. Parental incapacitation
   c. Lack of parents
   d. Intentional neglect

3. Utilizing the data from Juvenile Court Statistics, indicate recent trends in juvenile court referrals in relation to earlier trends. (p. 49–50)

4. Cite several problems associated with the use of official data such as the *Uniform Crime Reports* in making statements regarding the increase or decrease in juvenile delinquency in the United States from year to year. (pp. 58–59)

5. What conclusions would you reach about the relationship between race and official delinquency based on data from the *Uniform Crime Reports?* (pp. 55–56)

6. Utilizing both official and self-report studies, portray what seems to be happening in the United States in respect to correlates of (a) sex and (b) residence as they relate to juvenile delinquency. (a: pp. 53–58; b: pp. 66–70)

7. Earlier self-reported delinquency studies are said to differ from more recent self-reports in terms of one particular factor. What is this factor? Explain how this might call into question the results of earlier studies. (p. 70)

8. According to victimization studies, which of the following is the most reported offense? (pp. 70–71)
   a. Rape
   b. Assault
   c. Commercial robbery
   d. Household crime

9. Explain what is meant by the term *cohort analysis* and briefly respond to the following statement based on cohort analysis findings: Most juvenile offenses are major; most juvenile offenders continue their crimes in adulthood. (pp. 73–76)

10. Victimization is presented in terms of
    a. Age
    b. Sex
    c. Race
    d. Income level
    e. Residence
    Evaluate the extent of victimization in terms of any three categories. (pp. 70–73)

NOTES

1. According to the FBI's 1976 *Uniform Crime Reports* (FBI, pp. 182–183), between 1960 and 1975 index arrests of girls under 18 years of age increased by 425 percent for violent crimes; for boys, the increase was 117 percent.

2. We note that the National Center for Juvenile Justice published in June 1985 a report, "Delinquency in the United States," which gives detailed information about age, race, and type of offense for which juveniles were referred to the juvenile court (Snyder, Hutzler, and Finnegan, 1985).

3. Violent crimes include murder, forcible rape, robbery, and aggravated assault; property crimes include burglary, larceny-theft, motor vehicle theft, and arson. Percentages computed from FBI (1985).

4. For example, see Geis (1965), Hindelang (1978), Pope (1979), Radzinowicz and King (1977), and Wolfgang and Cohen (1970).

5. UCR data are often presented using three community-type aggregations. These are MSAs, other cities, and rural areas. The concept of the MSA as used in the 1985 UCR made up approximately 76 percent of the total U.S. population. A suburban area includes cities with fewer than 50,000 inhabitants in addition to counties (unincorporated areas) within the MSA. Suburban areas can therefore be subdivided into suburban cities and suburban counties. Other cities are those outside MSAs. Most of these places are incorporated; they comprised 10 percent of the 1985 population of the United States.

   A rural county is that portion of a county outside the MSA excluding areas covered by city police agencies. For crime reporting purposes, rural areas are made up of unincorporated portions of counties outside urban places and MSAs. They comprised 14 percent of the 1984 population (FBI, 1985: 330).

6. A national study on juvenile delinquency done by the University of Michigan similarly found that differences in crimes by place of residence (city, suburban, small town, and rural area) were not significant (Doleschal, 1979). Several other studies indicating that suburban and rural areas have experienced crime and delinquency problems similar to those found in the cities can be cited. See, for instance, Ball (1977), Ball and Lilly (1976), Hardman (1969), Loth (1967), Poveda (1972), Shotland, Hayward, Young, Signorella, Mindingall Kennedy, Robine, and Danowitz (1979), and Tobias (1970).

7. Some interesting studies on the relationship between population density and crime have recently been published. See Shichor, Decker, and O'Brien (1979).

8. For examples, see Beattie (1960), Cressey (1957), Doleschal and Wilkins (1972), Kitsuse and Cicourel (1963), Sellin and Wolfgang (1964), and Zeisel (1971).

9. It is important in dealing with the UCR statistics to distinguish between the volume of crime and a crime rate. **Volume** simply refers to the absolute number of crimes committed in a particular locale during a specified time interval. A **crime rate**, however, relates the number of crimes to the number of inhabitants.

10. See also Biderman and Reiss (1967: 4): "In general, it may be said that the value of a crime rate for index purposes is in inverse ratio to the procedural distance between the commission of the crime and the recording of it as a statistical unit."
11. See also Chilton and Spielberger (1971).
12. For examples of the variations of the self-report technique, see Akers (1964); Belson (1970); Christie, Andenaes, and Skerbaekk (1965); Clark and Tifft (1966); Clark and Wenninger (1962); Dentler and Monroe (1961); Erickson (1971); Erickson and Empey (1963); Gold (1966); Hardt and Hardt (1977); Hirschi (1969); McCandless, Persons, and Roberts (1972); McDonald (1969); Nettler (1959); Nye and Short (1957); Porterfield (1946); Reiss and Rhodes (1961); Voss (1963); Waldo and Chiricos (1972); Wallerstein and Wyle (1947); Ageton and Elliott (1979); Huizinga (1978); Elliott and Huizinga (1983); Hindelang, Hirschi, and Weis (1981); Thornton (1982); Thornton and Voigt (1984); Higgins and Albrecht (1981). Several works also offer reviews and summaries of past self-report delinquency studies examining numerous variables in relation to a broad range of offenses (e.g., Hindelang, Hirschi, and Weis, 1981; Braithwaite, 1981).
13. Studies of adults indicate the same picture. Wallerstein and Wyle (1947) found that 91 percent of a sample of New York adults admitted having committed felonies and misdemeanors (see also Marguis and Ebener, 1981).
14. The National Youth Survey (NYS) was conducted by a group of researchers (Delbert Elliott, Suzanne Ageton, Frian Knowles, Tim Brennan, Rachelle Canter, and David Huizinga) at the Behavioral Research Institute in Boulder, Colorado. The NYS employed a probability sample of households and contained approximately 2,360 eligible youth aged 11–17 at the time of the initial interview in 1976. Of this number, 1,725 agreed to participate in the survey and completed interviews in the initial 1977 survey. Since the NYS was a panel study and the same respondents were measured at several points in time, four other interviews have been conducted, the fifth being completed in 1981. For a detailed description of the NYS sample and results, see Elliott, Ageton, Huizinga, Knowles, and Canter, 1983.
15. Actually, three articles have been published from these data; see Empey and Erickson (1966) and Erickson and Empey (1963, 1965).
16. See Thornton and James (1979) for a review of the literature suggesting that females are becoming more involved in traditionally masculine offenses.
17. For example, see Cloward and Ohlin (1960), Cohen (1955), Miller (1958), and Wattenberg and Balistrieri (1950).
18. See Akers (1964), Dentler and Monroe (1961), Empey and Erickson (1966), Hirschi (1969), Illinois Institute for Juvenile Research (1972), Johnson (1979), Short and Nye (1958), Tittle, Villemez, and Smith (1978), Voss (1966), and Williams and Gold (1972).
19. The bulk of statistics suggests that the typical characteristics of various kinds of personal and property offenders closely parallel the characteristics associated with the victims. Research demonstrates that personal crimes of violence are high for the young, the urban, the poor, the black, and males. Correspondingly, the statistics indicate that typical victims of crime are likely to be among the young, the urban, the poor, the black and males (e.g., Laub and Hindelang, 1981; McDermott and Hindelang, 1981; Danser and Laub, 1981; Hindelang and McDermott, 1981). There is relatively little research on the relationship of juveniles who are delinquent and their proneness to be victims of crimes. Juvenile delinquents are automatically associated with the offender role (as in official statistics) and rarely with the victim role. Some work is now being done in this area (e.g., Savitz, Lalli, and Rosen, 1977; Voigt and Thornton, 1982).
20. For more information on victimization surveys, including methodological problems, see Drapin and Viano (1974), Schafer (1977), and Sparks, Ginn, and Dodd (1977).
21. Two researchers, Hirschi and Gottfredson (1983), have recently argued that "although age is correlated with crime, [it] is not useful in predicting involvement in crime over the life cycle of offenders" (p. 581). The implications of their argument call into question many traditional arguments regarding prevention and treatment efforts for youths who begin their delinquent careers early in life.

PART 2

THEORIES OF DELINQUENCY

Each generation of social scientists has sought explanations for the causes of delinquent and criminal behavior. These explanations have been tied to the knowledge and techniques available at the time of their origins. Some explanations of delinquent and criminal behavior are called theories. Although there are many definitions of **theory**, we can generally call it a speculation, usually stated in some logical framework, about why and how certain behaviors or events occur.

In this section we will examine both historical and contemporary theories of delinquency from three disciplines: biology, psychology, and sociology. Each discipline has a particular perception of social reality, so each may produce explanations that conflict with those of other disciplines. Moreover, different theories even within the same discipline may attempt to explain different aspects of reality. When one is comparing theories, it is important to establish exactly what it is that the theories are seeking to explain. For example, when evaluating theories, one must consider where the sample of delinquents came from and how delinquency is **operationally defined**. Is the theorist using high schoolers' self-reports, or officially adjudicated delinquents, or a subset of institutionalized delinquents? How inclusive is the term? Is delinquency a catch-all concept, or are distinctions made among violent, nonviolent, criminal acts and status offenses? The type of method used to obtain evidence in support of theories can affect the results. For instance, are case studies, interviews, self-administered inventories, court records, local, state or national statistics, or observations used by the researcher?

Chapter 4 presents biological explanations of delinquency and crime. Central to these approaches is the assumption that biological phenomena either cause or contribute to delinquent and other antisocial behavior. Early biological proponents, though not directing their efforts specifically at delinquents, believed that criminals formed a separate biological category, easily distinguishable from noncriminals. Later researchers have sought to explain delinquent behavior in terms of physiology, morphology, heredity, endocrine abnormalities, or genetic abnormalities.

Psychological theories of delinquency are presented in Chapter 5. Four separate theoretical orientations are distinguishable. First is the psychiatric approach, which explains present behavior in terms of early childhood experiences; second is the psychoanalytic approach, which explains delinquent behavior as the product of unconscious drives or instincts not directly perceived or understood by the individual; third is the personality approach, which attributes delinquency to certain personality characteristics of individuals; and fourth is learning or reinforcement theory, which explains delinquent behavior in terms of past learning experiences.

Chapters 6, 7, and 8 present sociological explanations of delinquency. These theories differ from psychological explanations by concentrating less on the individual and more on rates and how the social environment influences fluctuations in rates.

The emphasis in Chapter 6 is on classic sociological theories of delinquency. Early ecological theories tried to explain delinquency in relation to population concentrations in the city. Social learning theories explained delinquency as the product of social interaction. Anomie theories attributed delinquency to a disparity between cultural goals and cultural means for achieving those goals. Subcultural theories viewed delinquent behavior as an expression of the standards espoused by an individual's referent or peer group.

Chapter 7 concentrates on contemporary sociological theories of delinquency. These theories differ from classic sociological theories by emphasizing, for the most part, social groups and social institutions as causes of delinquency. According to social control theorists, delinquency is at a minimum when children have strong bonds to society. Labeling theorists, on the other hand, point to the role of societal reaction in formulating definitions and future patterns of delinquency. Phenomenologists extend the labeling theory by exploring the subjective meaning an individual applies to his or her delinquent behavior.

Separate coverage is given to conflict and radical theories of delinquency and crime (Chapter 8). Unlike theories of delinquency based on a consensual view of society, conflict and radical theoreticians see crime and delinquency as products of the conflict that emerges when groups or classes with differing power and interests come into contact. Conflict theorists, by definition, view dissension and conflict as ubiquitous. They argue that some societal members have economic and political control over other members. Those groups having the most power are able to determine existing definitions of deviance and enforce adherence to such definitions.

In this part we will present numerous theories about delinquency and criminality that have evolved over the decades. Some of these theories have become outdated with the accumulation of new knowledge; some have remained as competitors to newer theories. Although the goal of these theories has been to find a way to eliminate or reduce delinquency, most of them have failed at the task. The causes and treatment of delinquency remain elusive. Yet each theory, however limited and fallible, represents a step forward in our understanding. Each new theory has been built upon the limitations associated with earlier traditions. In this sense, criminological knowledge is a cumulative enterprise. The theorist explains a perspective and researchers begin investigating that particular viewpoint. Through this scientific process, theory becomes clarified, and the conditions under which the theory holds true become specified. Taken together, the theories all contribute to an understanding of the multifaceted problem of delinquency. No evidence, no matter how persuasive, can prove a theory to be true. Supporting evidence assures only that the search will continue. Disconfirming evidence, however, can make a theory obsolete. Controversy among the theories/theorists is not to be taken as an indictment of the scientific enterprise but as an inherent element of progress.

CHAPTER 4

BIOLOGICAL THEORIES

EARLY BIOLOGICAL THEORIES OF DELINQUENCY AND CRIME

VARIATIONS ON CONTEMPORARY BIOMEDICAL AND BIOSOCIAL THEORIES OF DELINQUENCY AND CRIME

Commenting on the physical characteristics of young male delinquents housed in a reformatory in Pontiac, Michigan, at the end of the nineteenth century, a physician wrote:

> First—coarse features. Second—high cheek bones. Third—thick, heavy and drooping eyebrows. Fourth—flat forehead. Fifth—coarse straight hair (among whites only). These are about the first things a person notices about these boys, except the expressions of guilt which [are] upon their faces. Next, by looking at them from behind, the very thick, large and heavy neck is very noticeable; the sterno-cleidmastoid and trapezius muscles seem to be abnormally well developed in nearly every one. Then, from a side view of the neck and head, it will be noticed that the occipital bone seldom, if ever, projects very far past a line let fall parallel with the posterior surface of the neck, thus giving the head and neck a very straight and peculiar appearance, which is invariably the case among young criminals. (Fink, 1938: 129)

This doctor was so certain these physical differences were real and apparent that he claimed he could distinguish offenders and nonoffenders in 98 out of 100 cases.

One has only to look over the "wanted" posters displayed in any Post Office around the country to be reminded that in even today's highly technical and scientific society, the idea that certain physical traits are indicative of antisocial tendencies lingers in us all. The posters seem to symbolize a "type" of individual whose menacing physiognomy identifies that person as a dangerous deviant, one who becomes even more stigmatized with the increase of listed offenses.

The social need for the criminal or delinquent to look guilty or to otherwise demonstrate some recognizable physical trait goes far back in history. In the Bible, God put a mark on Cain for the murder of his brother Abel, and King Solomon proclaimed that "the heart alters the face of the evil man." Masks symbolizing good and evil were worn in early Greek drama to facilitate the identification of character types. Shakespeare's Julius Caesar alludes to the relationship between body and soul when he contemplates:

> Let me have men about me that are fat,
>   sleek headed men, and such as sleep
>   o'nights.
> Yon Cassius has a lean and hungry look.
> He thinks too much.
> Such men are dangerous.

Even in the works of the great philosopher Aristotle, and in the works of sociologist Auguste Comte and psychologist William James, references to physical characteristics may be found.

A long list can be drawn of the many fertile minds throughout history that have considered certain physical traits to be predictive of criminal or antisocial tendencies. Indeed, the idea that individual constitution and criminal behavior are linked has endured throughout history with amazing regularity and tenacity. Just what accounts for the persistence or the recurrence of this theme is difficult to ascertain.

The history and development of the biological perspective are especially important because it exposes the roots of criminological thought. The biological legacy predates the scientific study of crime and was the first to be submitted to scientific investigation and tests. Even though some of the early theories are now merely historical curiosities, they are links in the development of various causative models of delinquency.

Few American criminologists have been serious adherents of biological determinism. Perhaps the early methodological inadequacies, the lack of consistency among the different lists of physical traits which correlate with criminality, and the possible association of this orientation with genetic engineering and the World War II Nazi experiments, exterminations, and other racist ideologies have produced an unfavorable climate for the biological study of crime in this country. But there are examples of several comprehensive studies of biological influences on delinquency conducted by American scholars. The works of William Sheldon (1940) and Sheldon and Eleanor Glueck (1956) on delinquent body types and the more recent biomedical research on chromosomal abnormalities (Brown, 1968; Kessler and Moos, 1970; U.S. Department of Health, Education and Welfare, National Institute of Mental Health, 1970) are examples of biological explanations proposed by American researchers.

The interactive relationship between the internal and external environments of the individual is extremely complex. No single set of variables explains deviance or criminality adequately. Studies attempting to factor out the influence of heredity or physiology and of the environment have produced conflicting results (Shoemaker, 1984: 24). Noting the general aversion of American criminologists to the study of biological determinants of crime, Rosenthal (1984: 22) writes:

> As scientists, however, we are obliged to make a reasonable effort not to put blinders on ourselves, but rather to examine this troublesome issue thoroughly, to question its validity, and judge its implications.

Let's turn now to the individual or biological approach to delinquency and consider its implications.

EARLY BIOLOGICAL THEORIES OF DELINQUENCY AND CRIME

Although other types of biological research such as phrenology (Caldwell, 1824; Spurzheim, 1832) were in existence, our exploration will begin with the Italian school of positivism, led by Cesare Lombroso and continued by Enrico Ferri. Variations of Lombroso's theme found in the works of American theorists Ernest Hooten, William Sheldon, Sheldon and Eleanor Glueck, and Juan Cortes and Florence Gatti will also be explored.

The remainder of the chapter will focus on other types of contemporary biological theories of crime, including the genetic and endocrinal abnormalities that have recently become part of biomedical explanations of violent crime. We will also discuss the effects of tumors, epileptic seizures, and neurological or brain dysfunctions. The effects of drugs on behavior, especially delinquent behavior, while certainly in line with some of the ideas about the biochemical determinants of antisocial behavior, will be discussed in Chapter 13, which is devoted solely to this theme.

Italian Positivism

The positivist school of criminology was founded by Cesare Lombroso, an Italian physician. It stressed experimental and inductive methodology, which emphasizes observable facts, rather than the juristic or deductive methods or philosophical inquiry. This school of criminology was a reaction to the existing classical school, whose major theorist was Cesare Beccaria (1764) and which had a dominant influence on criminological thought until the 1930s. Classical criminologists thought that all individuals, including criminals, determined their own destiny through calculated choices. Because they viewed criminals as exercising free will, classical criminologists proposed that individuals could be taught to abstain from criminal acts through a rational system of control and punishment.

However, with the advent of Charles Darwin's theory of evolution, signaled by the publication of *The Origin of Species* in 1859, scientists began to doubt that humans were radically different from other members of the animal kingdom (Halleck, 1967). Even though the evolutionary paradigm accentuated the human propensity for building impressive and complex civilizations which justify the human position at the apex of the evolutionary schema, there were hints that the path traveled by the human species has not been so smooth. For all the marvelous manifestations of civilization, there are the unpleasant and undesirable realities such as crime, war, intolerance, and cruelty. To explain these phenomena, the thesis emerged that the evolutionary process implies not only progress, but the possibility of regression as well. Here are Darwin's own words:

> With mankind some of the worst dispositions which occasionally, without any assignable cause, make their appearance in families, may perhaps be reversion to a savage state from which we are not removed by very many generations. This view seems indeed recognized in the common expressions that such are the black sheep of the family. (1897: 137)

The position developed that perhaps aberrant behavior could be better described biologically, particularly with reference to the evolutionary process, than by free will or legal doctrine or philosophical precepts.

Early biological criminologists and anthropological criminologists, working in the period beginning about 1850 and extending to the late 1930s, thought that criminals formed a separate biological category. Claiming that certain criminals were biological throwbacks to "primitive man," some of these early researchers, especially the Italian criminologist Cesare Lombroso, believed that criminals were easily recognizable on the basis of various physical features, such as large ears; small, beady eyes; and large foreheads. According to these researchers, the fate of criminal individuals was biologically determined; environmental influences were insignificant.

Accepting the evolutionist notions, certain criminologists advocated the study of criminals from a scientific or postivistic perspective. Implicit in this position was the idea that biological defects were in some way capable of producing criminal behavior. Further, the positivists thought that "criminal man" (females were rarely given attention in the early crime literature) could be identified and isolated.[1] They also argued that crime should be viewed as a medical or scientific problem rather than as a political, social, moral, economic, or ethical problem, and that crime could be controlled and treated by experts through biological analysis.

The goal of the positivist criminologists was, for the most part, to identify biologically deviant types and to discover the forces that produced them. Since crime was attributed to physical factors, the positivists viewed the regulation of crime through punishment or sanctions as ineffective. They proposed instead that crime be handled on an individual basis; each individual case must be diagnosed by experts, and then appropriate treatment must be prescribed. The extreme cases of "born" offenders could be treated only by permanent incarceration or annihilation. Our study of the positivist theories will begin with the work of Cesare Lombroso.[2]

Cesare Lombroso.   Although his later work took many factors other than the biological or the physical into account, Cesare Lombroso is best known for his early views on the "born criminal."

Trained as a psychiatrist, Lombroso came upon the idea of the "atavistic man" as a special type of criminal while dissecting cadavers in the prisons and asylums of Pavia, Italy, in 1870:

> Suddenly, one morning, on a gloomy day in December I found in the skull of a brigand a very long series of atavistic abnormalities . . . analagous to those that are found in inferior vertebrates. At the sight of these strange abnormalities—as an extensive plain is lit up by a glowing horizon I realized that the problem of the nature and generation of criminals was resolved for me. (1876: 1)

Lombroso (1911) thought most deviant individuals were biologically inferior types resembling earlier and more primitive human beings. Possessing unrefined instincts, the atavistic man—the most extreme of the biological misfits—was, Lombroso believed, predestined to engage in criminal activities. Using physical stigmata and physical deviations found through anthropomorphic measurements as criteria, Lombroso and his students attempted to categorize anatomically atavistic types (Roebuck, 1967).

In the first edition of *The Criminal Man*, Lombroso painstakingly labeled criminals on the basis of physical characteristics, such as thickness of the bones of the skull, pigmentation of the skin, hair type, ear size, dentition, arm length, and a host of other traits. In addition, he recorded other characteristics of born criminals, including tattooing, laziness, lack of foresight, and moral insensibility. Comparing Italian criminals and noncriminal Italian soldiers, Lombroso later concluded that only about a third of all criminals were "born," or atavistic, criminals. Lombroso's typology included other classes of criminals, among them the insane or the "criminaloids," who might today be called psychopaths. "Criminaloids" were not thought to possess the physical characteristics of the born criminal, but they nevertheless were expected to demonstrate vicious behaviors (Vold, 1979).

Lombroso, besides altering his theory to include types of criminals other than atavistic man, acknowledged in his *Crime, Its Causes and Remedies* (1911), that a multitude of other factors were related to crime. These factors ranged from climate and the economy to sex and marriage customs. Although it remained an important part of his thought, Lombroso relegated the concept of atavism to a single chapter of his later book. By the time of Lombroso's death in 1909, his theories were already on the decline in both Europe and the United States, despite the efforts of many, including his daughter, to keep them alive (Schafer and Knudten, 1970).

The most devastating blow to Lombroso's work came from another physician, Charles B. Goring, an Englishman, who tested Lombroso's hypothesis that physical stigmata play a dominate role in crime. Goring engaged in a meticulous biological examination of 3,000 English convicts. The physical measurements of convicts (for example, skull size, arm length, height, and weight) were compared with those of control groups of university students, hospital patients, and soldiers. Goring's research began in 1901, spanned a period of eight years, and involved the efforts of many medical, correctional, scientific, and academic personnel. Statistical expert Karl Pearson was one of Goring's team. The research was unprecedented in criminological literature.

Goring and his colleagues were unable to find significant morphological differences between the criminal and noncriminal samples, thus repudiating Lombroso's notion of a distinct physical type. Goring bluntly stated in his work, *The English Convict: A Statistical Study*, published in 1913, that "there is no such thing as a physical criminal type." But although Goring's study did not find any absolute difference that distinguished criminals from noncriminals, he did suggest relative differences were present. For example, Goring did report that criminals, with the exception of those convicted of fraud, tended to be smaller in stature and weight than noncriminals. Violent offenders were somewhat stronger and healthier than thieves, burglars, and the general noncriminal population (Mannheim, 1972).

Goring concluded that the relative differentiation of criminals from the population mean can be attributed to the fact that individuals who become incarcerated are generally selected from the physically weaker and mentally less able portion of the general population. Goring asserted that captive criminals do not constitute random samples either physically or mentally of the general population or even the criminal population (which includes those who never get caught).

Lombroso's supporters were quick to seize upon this finding and take it not as a repudiation of the biological origin of crime, but as a confirmation of it (DeSanctis, 1914–1915; Lombroso-Ferrero, 1914–1915; Garofalo, 1914). In particular, Enrico Ferri, an Italian criminologist, came to the defense of Lombroso, his deceased mentor. In an early critique of Goring's *English Convict*, Ferri argued that Goring's findings offered "impressive and positive confirmation" of an organic anatomic type of criminal (Ferri, 1914–1915: 226).

Enrico Ferri.   Although Ferri was a student of Lombrosian positivism, he differed somewhat in his approach to criminal anthropology. Ferri thought that Lombroso gave undue importance to craniology, measurement of the skull, and anthropometry, measurement of other parts of the body (Rennie, 1978). In his 1892 work, *Criminal Sociology*, Ferri suggested that social, political, and economic factors also played a part in causing crime. His classification included five types of criminals: criminal lunatics; born criminals (incorrigibles); habitual criminals; occasional criminals; and emotional criminals. Ferri used examples from art and literature to demonstrate his types and to prove the universality of his schema. For instance, he cited Macbeth, Hamlet, and Othello from Shakespeare as perfect representatives of the born criminal, the criminal lunatic, and the emotional criminal, respectively.

Even though they can be subdivided into numerous categories, Ferri argued that all criminals comprise a distinct physical type, possessing aberrant organic and psychological characteristics. In his opinion, the offender could never be considered normal. But Ferri also firmly believed that although the constitutional makeup of the criminal caused the consequent antisocial behavior, the offender, including the child offender, must be held responsible. He argued that gradations of responsibility based on any typological differences

would be impossible to combine in any practical legal formulas. Ferri claimed that the law must be based not on the issue of responsibility or free will, but on society's need.

As the years passed, explanations of crime shifted from biological to psychological and sociological analyses. The later works of Rafael Garofalo (1914), one of the founders of the Italian positivist school, reflected this change. Although not discounting Lombroso's notion of a distinct anthropological type, Garofalo focused on psychological factors. He claimed the true criminal lacked proper development of altruistic sensibilities—concern for others—and that this moral anomaly had some physical basis (Mannheim, 1972).

Critique of Italian Positivism.   The biological approach to crime advocated by Lombroso now has only historical importance. It is generally accepted that biological variations in no way account for variations in crime rates. Crime has been recognized as a social phenomenon that differs from time to time and place to place. Lombrosians did not address the question of how and why certain behaviors became illegal. Further, they failed to see that harm could result from labeling certain individuals as distinct criminal types when the labeling was based on unfounded and unsubstantiated assumptions about the biological nature of crime.

Given the obvious flaws in **biological determinism**, one may ask why such a theory gained the popularity it had during the early twentieth century. According to Thomas Kuhn (1973), the process of paradigm shifting occurs regularly in the history of scientific thought. Obviously, the intellectual currents stirred by the nineteenth- and early twentieth-century theories of evolution and the impressive advances of the biological sciences convinced many people that the mysteries of human social behavior would soon unfold. The influence of biology on human beings' past and present appeared indisputable. However, in the early twentieth century new **paradigms** for explaining behavior began to appear and to compete with existing ways of explaining reality.

Biological explanations for crime were especially attractive because they directed attention away from the role of a malfunctioning society and social inequality. The blame could be placed on specific individuals or groups, instead of on the structure of the society as a whole (Taylor, Walton, and Young, 1973). Some criminologists have observed that it is precisely this aspect of positivistic theory that lends itself to abuse. Both Ferri and Garofalo easily adapted their views to Mussolini's Fascist regime in Italy during the 1920s (Vold, 1979). Similarly, Nazi Germany altered its criminal law so that criminality became defined on the basis of biological (and psychological) traits, rather than acts. Jews and other "non-Aryan" people, by virtue of their physical (and cultural) heritage, were labeled physically or mentally unfit and sent to extermination centers.

We should add, however, that not all aspects of early positivism were negative. Lombroso's scientific methodology, though unsound and crude by today's standards, paved the way for contemporary scientific criminology, including international criminological conferences. Ironically, his techniques of comparing criminal and noncriminal samples, measurements, and statistics made possible the repudiation of his own claims (Roebuck, 1967).

American Positivism

In the United States, Charles Goring's critique of Lombroso came to be accepted by most criminologists. In light of Goring's extensive research, the notion of criminals being somehow physically different or inferior from noncriminals was pretty well laid to rest. The weight of opinion in American criminology was against the idea of a physical criminal type. This is not to suggest, however, that there was no interest in the idea. Arthur Fink's 1938 *Causes of Crime: Biological Theories in the United States, 1800–1915* reveals that in certain circles (for example, among prison physicians and criminal anthropologists), a strong concern with the physiology of the criminal existed. One American anthropologist in particular, Ernest Hooten, attempted through physical anthropology to prove that criminals have inferior physical characteris-

tics. His work rekindled an interest in biological explanations of crime in America.

Ernest Hooten.   Although he dismissed Lombroso's notions of atavism, Ernest Hooten believed that criminals are organically inferior and that this inferiority is genetically inheritable. In his 1931 work, *Crime and the Man,* he advocated eugenic programs of sterilization to solve the problem of crime.[3] Hooten based his views on a twelve-year study of more than 17,000 individuals, including college students, firemen, convicts, policemen, and mental patients. Taking elaborate measurements of these individuals, he concluded that in nineteen out of thirty-five measurements there were significant differences between offenders and nonoffenders. Criminals, he said, had low foreheads, high, pinched nasal roots, crooked noses, compressed faces, and narrow jaws (Rennie, 1978). In addition, they possessed small ears, long necks, and stooped shoulders. Mental inferiority was also thought to be directly related to physical inferiority, making the problem of crime all the more serious.

Hooten's work met with numerous criticisms from all academic camps. Sociologists and criminologists pointed to such blatant deficiencies in his methodology as inadequate control groups and unrepresentative criminal samples. Biologists and anthropologists criticized his work for failing to show that physical deviations are in any way indicative of inferiority (Vold, 1979). As in the case of earlier efforts to explain crime and delinquency through physical characteristics, Hooten's research is now of only historical importance.

William Sheldon.   Another important American positivist was William Sheldon, who was inspired by the work of Ernst Kretschmer, a German psychiatrist. Sheldon's 1949 study of delinquents in *Varieties of Delinquent Youth* was one of the first American efforts at somatotype or body type research. Sheldon set out to quantify Kretschmer's (1925) classification of body types and to test its relationship to delinquency. Sheldon renamed Kretschmer's three types. Thin types were *ectomorphs,* athletic types were *mesomorphs,* and obese types were *endomorphs.* A quantitative scale, based on one used to grade poultry and dogs, was devised to classify people into the three types.

Sheldon (1949) thought a basic temperament accompanied each body type. Ectomorphs, said Sheldon, were "cerebrotonic": restrained, self-conscious, and hypersensitive. Endomorphs were "viscerotonic": relaxed, food-oriented, and even-tempered. Mesomorphs, however, were "soma-tonic": dominating, assertive, competitive, and unrestrained. Although the temperaments in themselves were not viewed as criminal, the me-somorphic physique with corresponding tempera-ment, in combination with certain social factors, was considered to be a precursor to crime or delinquency.

To test his ideas, Sheldon compared 200 delin-quent boys committed to the Hayden Goodwill Inn in Boston with a control group of 200 non-delinquent youths. From extensive measurements taken from detailed photographs of each youth, he concluded that boys classified as mesomorphs possessed the physical and psychological charac-teristics most suitable for delinquency. The me-somorph's love of adventure, crime, and physical prowess, coupled with an insensitivity to other people, "tend to produce a predatory person" (Cohen, 1966: 52). Although Sheldon realized that it was possible in some instances for these energies to be directed toward legitimate pursuits, he chose what he considered a biological "solution" to the crime problem and advocated selective breeding as the only sure means of reducing criminality. This so-called solution was not sup-ported by Sheldon's own data.

Sheldon's work came under intense criticism shortly after its publication in 1949. Criminologist Edwin Sutherland (1951) pointed to numerous flaws in the research. Perhaps most damaging was Sheldon's definition of delinquency. Delinquency was vaguely defined as "disappointingness." There-fore, its measurement was virtually impossible. Sheldon's scheme of measuring delinquency re-sulted in some children who never actually engaged in aberrant behavior being classified as delinquent. Cohen (1966) notes: "From the very outset, there-fore, any conclusion he might draw about the

cases of delinquency are destined to be worthless" (p. 52). Other problems affecting the validity of the study included sampling defects and lack of reliability in the assignment of youth to the three physique types.

In a follow-up review, Hartl, Monnelly, and Elderkind (1982) attempted to trace the biological and experiential characteristics of the 200 indi-viduals whose adolescent biographies and soma-totyping provided the materials for Sheldon's work in 1949. The 200 male subjects had been followed from the late 1930s to 1970. The follow-up review was begun in 1958 under the direction of Sheldon, who worked on the project until his death in 1977.

Of the original 200 males, 14 (7 percent) were classified as criminals. In five other cases, crimi-nality was listed as a secondary diagnosis. The strongest discriminatory variable between the crim-inal and normal groups was mesomorphy, which by the suggestion of the authors supposedly reaf-firms Sheldon's finding in 1949. Given that as youths 60 percent of this sample were characterized as mesomorphs, one may ask what types of changes in body structures occurred over the years and what relationship this has to behavior. Neither of these questions is adequately addressed. The num-ber of cases in the criminal category is so small that no conclusions can be drawn. The book emphasizes the psychopathic descriptions, which are highly speculative at best.

Sheldon and Eleanor Glueck.   Undaunted by Sheldon's critics, two criminologists, the husband and wife team of Sheldon and Eleanor Glueck (1956), employed Sheldon's typology in their attempts to prove a relationship between physical or constitutional type and delinquency. The Gluecks (1956) compared 500 delinquents with 500 non-delinquent controls and claimed support for Shel-don's thesis. They found that 60.1 percent of a delinquent sample was mesomorphic, but only 30.7 percent of the nondelinquent sample was mesomorphic. The two researchers also reported a correspondence between body build and tem-perament traits. Extending Sheldon's work, the Gluecks contrasted the personality and social and environmental characteristics of delinquents and nondelinquents.

Rather than couching their claims in causal terms, the Gluecks mainly referred to body type as a predisposing factor. The potential for delinquency was greater among mesomorphic boys living in environments amenable to criminal activities. The Gluecks, however, did not consider the likelihood that mesomorphs might have been overrepresented in delinquent activities for purely social reasons. Past research suggests that organized delinquent subcultures recruit youths who have some physical prowess. Today, with the burgeoning use of weapons, there may be little correspondence between recruitment into a delinquent group and physique; it takes very little physical strength to pull the trigger of a gun.

The Gluecks' research also met with little support in the United States. Critics pointed to serious methodological weaknesses in the study, which included selection and matching of delinquent and nondelinquent subjects and uncontrolled subjectivity in somatotyping procedure (Clinard, 1968; Cohen, 1966; Shah and Roth, 1974). Besides these technical criticisms, there were contentions that the theory failed to address key issues. The Gluecks never explained precisely how they determined that anatomical characteristics produced delinquency. When considered at all, socioeconomic factors were given only a minor role in their explanations of delinquent behavior.

Juan B. Cortes and Florence M. Gatti. Attempting to overcome some of the methodological problems associated with the research of Sheldon and the Gluecks, Cortes and Gatti (1972) in a biophysical approach to the causes of crime included a consideration of the relationship between somatotypes and delinquency. They used Parnell's (1958) system of somatotyping. Their sets of comparative measurements included variations in structure, skin folds, muscular development, and body weight and height. These measurements were based on actual observations, rather than observations from photographs. Information about the personality or temperament characteristics was based on self-report inventories. The subjects

classified themselves into personality types, rather than being classified by an observer. Delinquency, however, was *not* determined from the self-report data but from official records, which of course affects the generalizability of the research. The researchers compared 100 delinquents with 100 nondelinquents. The results are shown in Table 4.1.

Mesomorphy does seem to be significantly related to delinquency. Despite the fact that Cortes and Gatti used a different method than the Gluecks or Sheldon, the results are remarkably similar; mesomorphy is significantly more prevalent among delinquents. Cortes and Gatti, however, suggest that after looking at all the factors, both biological and environmental variables interact to produce antisocial behavior. But no distinct causal relationship can be deduced from their research.

Critique of American Positivism. The works of American positivists have spanned years and encompassed both hereditary and body-type explanations of delinquency and crime. Although some theorists have postulated that hereditary differences produce anatomical differences between criminals and noncriminals, we know today that physical deviations have not been proved to indicate criminality. What might have begun as a simple route to explaining delinquent behavior has turned into a complex "biopsychosocial" problem. Ironically, with increased sophistication in measurement techniques, "the biological connection has become less distinct, less powerful and less imbued with moral and evolutionary characteristics" (Shoemaker, 1984: 19).

Somatotype research such as that of Sheldon and the Gluecks has not been popular in the United States. While there is some evidence suggestive of a relationship between mesomorphy and officially registered delinquents, the interpretation of these results is still highly questionable. Self-report studies which indicate that delinquency is very prevalent and widespread in all segments of society complicate the meaning and significance of the biological correlates of official delinquency. To date no objective basis for categorizing certain traits as acceptable or unacceptable exists. The

TABLE 4.1 Delinquent and Nondelinquent Classified According to Somatotype

	Endomorph	Mesomorph	Ectomorph	Behavioral	Mean Somatotype
Nondeliquent (N = 100)	37%	19%	33%	11%	3.9–3.5–3.5
Delinquent (N = 100)	14	57	16	13	3.5–4.4–3.1

Source: Cortes and Gatti (1972: Table 1.3, p. 26).

only continuity among the proposed typologies or lists of characteristics that has emerged is more a reflection of white, male, Western industrial bias than a result of converging objective research findings (Empey, 1982).

Commenting on somatotyping, Sutherland and Cressey (1978) have argued that Sheldon and the Gluecks "adopted a system characterized by a noted physical anthropologist as a 'new phrenology [study of skull contours] in which the bumps of the buttocks take the place of the bumps on the skull' " (p. 124). This statement illustrates the rather low opinion of somatotype and eugenic studies held by criminologists in the United States, most of whom were sociologically trained.

VARIATIONS ON CONTEMPORARY BIOMEDICAL AND BIOSOCIAL THEORIES OF DELINQUENCY AND CRIME

Most contemporary biological theories of delinquency and crime are not likely to claim that delinquency is solely a product of internal forces, but they do at least assume that certain internal or physical properties predispose individuals to antisocial behavior.[4] A number of predisposing factors have been proposed, including heredity, genetic and endocrine gland abnormalities, conditionability, nutritional deficiencies, hyperactivity, and brain dysfunctions. We will examine each of these areas as they have been related to violent crime.

Heredity and Delinquency

The issue of nature versus nurture, or the question of what has the greatest effect on individuals, heredity or environment, has been debated for hundreds of years. In the early part of the twentieth century, the consensus was in favor of heredity (Fink, 1938). Richard Dugdale's study of the Jukes (a family that included a large number of criminals, prostitutes, and paupers) living in New York in the latter part of the nineteenth century seemed to reaffirm the idea that criminality can be inherited (Dugdale, 1877). Other studies of "family trees" followed (H. H. Goddard, 1912, 1914). Over the years, studies that looked at the relationship between parental and offspring criminality (often as part of larger research projects) have reported significant associations between them (Glueck and Glueck, 1974; Ferguson, 1952; McCord and McCord, 1958; Wooton, 1959; Robins, 1966; Scanlon and Harville, 1966; Jonsson, 1967; Cloninger and Guze, 1970; Ahlstrom and Havinghurst, 1971; West and Farrington, 1973; Roberts, 1978). It has been estimated that 30 to 45 percent of the offspring with official criminal records had parents with recorded offenses (Ellis, 1982). This evidence, however, has been insufficient to suggest the existence of an inheritance factor.

The major difficulty with establishing a causal relationship has been the control and the factoring out of the social labeling, social learning, and genetic influences. When parents manifest disturbed or antisocial behavior themselves, it is practically impossible to ascertain from the usual family studies how much of the antisocial behavior is attributed to social forces or to inheritance.

Even Dugdale (1877) conceded that one does not have to stretch the imagination to appreciate the difficulty that a "Juke" boy coming from a noted family of criminals and the feebleminded would encounter in attempting to prove to his local community that he was intelligent, moral, and respectable (Shoemaker, 1984: 21).

Two types of research strategies attempt to control for the methodological drawbacks of family studies: twin and adoption studies (Rosenthal, 1984). The key concept of such studies is **concordance rate**, which refers to the similarity of behavioral outcome among pairs of individuals (Shoemaker, 1984: 20). When the pair is dissimilar, they are **discordant**. The difference in the concordance rate between identical twins (monozygotic, MZ) and fraternal twins (dizygotic, DZ) is assumed to demonstrate the influence of heredity. If heredity is a significant influence, the rate of concordance will be greater among identical twins than among fraternal twins or siblings. The other side of this question is approached by adoption or separation studies in which the concordance or discordance is noted not only for twins and siblings, but for the parents as well.

Since the 1930s, many studies on the criminality of twins and siblings have been done all over the world (Rennie, 1978).[5] These studies have found that the concordance rate among identical twins is higher than for fraternal twins or siblings (see Rosanoff et al., 1934; Kranz, 1936; Yoshimasu, 1961; Christiansen, 1968, 1977a; Cortes and Gatti, 1972; Reid, 1979; Vold, 1979).

One of the main problems inherent in such research projects is uncertainty in the classification of monozygotic and dizygotic twins (see Rowe, 1983). This uncertainty has forced some researchers to clarify their findings. For example, some researchers suggest that adult criminality is largely inherited, but that juvenile delinquency, especially among females, is subject more to environmental influences (Rosanoff et al., 1934). Rosanoff and associates argued that at the onset of life both males and females tend to have similar propensity for antisocial behavior, but as males and females get older, the rate of antisocial behavior declines sharply for females but remains stable for males.[6] According to Rosanoff, part of this may be explained by the social milieu exerting a stronger role in inhibiting aggressive and overt acting out in females than in males.

The other methodological problems that make the results of twin studies tenuous include: (1) concern over the representativeness of twin studies, since they hardly represent a random sample of the population as a whole; (2) concern over the statistical validity of the comparison, since the number of twins in such studies usually tends to be very small; (3) concern over the exclusive use of official definitions of delinquency and crime, since the selectivity factor restricts the generalizability of the results, and in addition these similarities of societal responses and expectations may be what is reflected in the concordance of official records rather than likeness of behavior; (4) concern over the inability of any researchers to specify exactly what elements are being transmitted genetically to cause antisocial behavior; (5) concern over the effect of the environmental influences, since the mitigating effects of the environment are still inadequately controlled (Shoemaker, 1984; Reid, 1979; Sutherland and Cressey, 1978). The environmental effects are especially difficult to control now that it is believed environmental influences begin before birth (Shah and Roth, 1974).

Christiansen (1977a, 1977b) in Denmark and Dalgard and Kringlen (1978) in Norway have tried to overcome some of the methodological concerns leveled against twin studies. Results of their studies, for example, were based on a register of all twins, not just those twins found in institutions during the span of investigation. These studies also tend to be a great deal more comprehensive and include extensive background studies on all the sets of twins. Generally, the conclusions tend to confirm that a higher concordance rate exists for monozygote twins. However, when environmental influences are taken into account, the concordance rate among twins, even monozygotic twins, is no longer significant. Dalgard and Kringlen (1978) conclude that heredity alone cannot predict criminality.

A recent twin study by Rowe and Osgood (1984) arrived at a similar conclusion. While they report a phenotypic correlation between self-reported delinquency and delinquency of peers, they do not attribute the relationship specifically to genetic factors. They indicate that in addition to genetic variation, common environmental influences that affect family members equally, and specific environmental influences that affect each individual uniquely, also are viable explanatory factors for differences in the delinquency of twins.

Conditioning and Delinquency

Another series of biological studies of delinquency focuses on conditioning (learning by association). Hans Eysenck, a British criminologist, writes:

It is conscience which is, in the main, instrumental in making us behave in a moral and socially acceptable manner; . . . this conscience is a combination and culmination of a long process of conditioning; and . . . failure on the part of the person to become conditioned is likely to be a prominent cause of his running afoul of the law and of the social mores generally. (1964: 120)

While Eysenck credits the mitigating influence of environment on the process of conditioning, his theory holds that conditionability (ability to learn by association and reinforcement) is genetically and physiologically determined. Varying degrees of conditionability are associated with inherited personality traits, depending largely on whether a person is born introverted (shy, inward) or extroverted (outgoing). According to this theory, extroverts are less inhibited, less restrained, more difficult to condition, and usually need more stimulation in order to be aroused. Consequently, extroverts are more prone to antisocial or criminal behavior.

Eysenck (1964, 1977) cites many studies on conditioning as well as the studies on somatotypes (Sheldon, 1949; Hooten, 1931; Glueck and Glueck, 1956) in support of his hypothesis that prisoners and delinquents respond poorly to conditioning and are more often extroverts. Eysenck's general hypothesis is that delinquents and criminals are more often extroverted and that the more serious

offenders are psychopathic (1977), suggesting that criminals can be classified according to degrees. He believes that the psychopathic personality is caused primarily by a malfunction of the autonomic nervous system (ANS).[7] The ANS controls or affects emotions and reflexes, and the ability of the individual to be conditioned. Eysenck argues that it is the conditionability of the individual which ultimately determines the success of social learning and the degree to which individuals will comply with social mores. The ultimate root of crime, according to Eysenck, is the inability of an individual to be conditioned to sanctioned behavior.

Research on ANS psychological response patterns and their association with antisocial behavior is growing. Some researchers have proposed alternative definitions of psychopathy (Reid, 1978; Hare and Schalling, 1978), and not all the research is consistent. At this time, no substantial evidence exists on the relationship between ANS and criminality; all the evidence to date is still tentative and inconclusive and must be interpreted with great caution. Methodological problems, especially small sample sizes, prohibit our drawing any conclusions at this time.

Chromosomal Abnormalities: The XYY and XXY Syndromes

It was not until 1956 that research established the normal number of chromosomes in human beings. **Chromosomes** are the parts of cells that contain genes, the biological structures responsible for the transmission, development, and determination of inherited characteristics. Before the development of the bucall mucosa smear technique, in which cells are scraped from the inside of the cheek, humans were believed to possess forty-eight chromosomes. Through the new technique, the correct number was discovered to be forty-six. Other new laboratory techniques, arresting cell growth at various stages of development, revealed that some people have an extra sex chromosome. Normal females carry two X (female) chromosomes, one from each parent. The normal male carries one X chromosome, inherited from his mother, and one Y (male) chromosome, inherited from his father. It was found that some males possess three sex chromosomes. Called the **XYY chromosome** syndrome, this discovery received great attention from scientists and the public (Rennie, 1978).

In 1965 a British research team headed by Patricia Jacobs (1965) reported that 7 out of 197 mentally abnormal males in a prison hospital had an extra Y chromosome. All seven inmates had a history of extreme violence, and the proportion of inmates possessing the XYY syndrome was more than twice as great as that occurring in the general population per 1,000 live births (Moran, 1978). The Jacobs study also reported that XYY males were, on the average, quite tall—that is, over 6 feet.

After publication of the Jacobs report in the British journal *Nature* (1965), dozens of other studies were conducted in penal and mental institutions (Baker, Telfer, Richardson, and Clark, 1970; Nielsen, Tsuboi, Sturup, and Romano, 1968; Price, Whatmore, and McClemont, 1966). Over 400 articles and books have been generated on the topic of the XYY karyotype implication in criminality (Ellis, 1982). Some of the interest was stimulated by the discovery of an extra Y chromosome in some of the more famous rapist-murderers (Jarvik, Klodin, and Matsuyama, 1984).

Some scientists hailed this new research as the long-sought link between biology and crime. It was thought that there would soon be a way scientifically to identify potential violent offenders in the population. The results of these studies, however, have been far from conclusive. Disagreement over the incidence of XYY males in the general population and the assumed physical and psychological characteristics of these individuals caused the Center for Studies of Crime and Delinquency of the National Institute of Mental Health to conclude in 1970 that the XYY theory of criminal behavior is "not proven" (U.S. Department of Health, Education and Welfare, NIMN, 1970). The American Psychiatric Association also questioned the claim that the extra Y chromosome leads to aggressive behavior. An official statement in 1969 read as follows: "It appears that the XYY males in general have been falsely stigmatized . . .

most XYY men are solid citizens" (cited in Jarvik, Klodin, and Matsuyama, 1984: 78). Several major studies (Canada, Scotland, and the United States in Boston and New Haven), which totaled over 10,000 cases, found only 13 newborn males with an extra Y chromosome and 14 newborn males with an extra X chromosome. From most of the studies, it is estimated that approximately one or two per 1,000 males will have an extra Y or X chromosome (Jarvik, Klodin, and Matsuyama, 1984).

The XXY karyotype has been associated with a symptomatology referred to as Klinefelter's syndrome. Males possessing an extra X chromosome are typically sterile, since their testicular tissue tends to be underdeveloped. There is a higher rate of retardation which, however, does not preclude the possibility of superior intelligence; this, of course, also holds true for the XYY syndrome.

Since antisocial behavior in the general sense has been the target of most of the karyotype studies, surveys of mental patients as well as criminals have been conducted. Among mental patients (Akesson et al., 1968; Marinello et al., 1969; Noel et al., 1969), an extra X chromosome is as common as an extra Y chromosome. However, among prison inmates (Jacobs et al., 1968; Court-Brown and Smith, 1969; Baker et al., 1970; Noel et al., 1969; Melnuk et al., 1969), an extra Y chromosome seems to have a significantly higher probability of occurring (Jarvik, Klodin, and Matsuyama, 1984). Since the general incidence of an extra Y or X chromosome is slight, all the studies are based on extremely small samples. Moreover, since those individuals possessing an extra Y or X chromosome who lead normal lives have not been considered in the studies, the interpretations of the results are severely limited. It is also important to remember that most violent crimes are committed by "normal" individuals and that even if the relationship between an extra Y chromosome and crime could be established, it would account for only an insignificant proportion of violent crimes.

At this time, however, there is no evidence to support a cause and effect relationship between the XYY chromosome syndrome and criminal behavior. Certain chromosomal abnormalities can and obviously do affect the physical and mental functioning of humans, but no definite connection has been drawn from the XYY abnormality to a tendency to commit deviant acts (Shah and Roth, 1974). Much of the research conducted in the area has been plagued with methodological problems (Amir and Berman, 1970; Figlio, 1977). Very few studies adequately address the question of the extent or range of chromosomal deviations in the general population. Inferences about criminal and delinquent behavior have been based totally on institutionalized samples, rendering most results highly questionable. Studies of imprisoned individuals do not constitute accurate depictions of the general population—or even of delinquents and criminals, for much juvenile (and adult) crime goes undetected and the perpetrators unapprehended.

Some researchers also argue that the increased frequency of XYY cases among institutionalized delinquents may not relate to the extra Y chromosome itself, but to physical traits of XYY males. XYY males have several distinct physical characteristics, including extremely tall stature, long limbs with strikingly long arm spans, and facial acne. In addition, some are mentally retarded. Physical anomalies may make individuals with an extra Y chromosome more vulnerable to social responses leading to incarceration. Extremely tall, badly complexioned, and less alert individuals may find it difficult to adapt to normal life styles. We are not suggesting that these individuals automatically pursue criminal and delinquent careers. However, their potential for criminality and for identification as criminals may be greater than that of males who attract less attention.[8] On the basis of physical appearance, XYY males may be singled out by the criminal justice system as being especially dangerous individuals (Amir and Berman, 1970). The social labeling, rather than biological determinism, may account for the relationship between the XYY syndrome and crime.

Despite inconclusive evidence about the relationship of the XYY phenomenon and criminal behavior, efforts have begun to incorporate the theory into correctional practices. For example, in 1968 psychiatrist Stanley Walzer of the Harvard Medical School began typing the sex chromosomes of all newborn male infants. His research team continued to type all newborn males until 1975, when public pressure from concerned citizen groups, including the Science for the People and Children's Defense Fund, forced a shutdown of the screening portion of the study. However, the research team will continue for the next twenty years to visit the homes of the "affected" males, particularly XYYs, in order to record descriptions of the children's behavior. School personnel will also be contacted and asked to note their observations of any sexual and aggressive behavior in the XYY males (Moran, 1978; Roblin, 1975).

The ethical implications of singling out youth at birth based on an unproved hypothesis about the relationship of the XYY syndrome to delinquency and crime are staggering. By creating expectations of deviant behavior among parents and teachers of XYY boys, the researchers expose the children to the effects of a self-fulfilling prophecy. Further, it may be impossible for the researchers to determine the effect, if any, of chromosome abnormalities on behavior in light of the social consequences of singling out particular XYYs for study.

More frightening than Walzer's research is a suggestion made in 1971 by Arnold Hutschnecker, one of President Richard Nixon's personal medical advisors. Hutschnecker, a physician, proposed a massive program of chromosomal screening for every 6-year-old in the country. He suggested that "hard-core" 6-year-olds showing evidence of criminal potential be sent to "therapeutic" camps where they could learn to be "good social animals." This particular plan was sent to Elliot Richardson, secretary of health, education and welfare, for consideration. Richardson turned down the plan "because it was not feasible to implement on a national scale, at that time" (Hunt, 1973; Moran, 1978: 347).

Scientifically, legally, and ethically, there is not enough evidence to condone attempts to control crime through genetic or chromosome tracking. In this case, as in many others, a little knowledge can most definitely be a dangerous thing. Even if a direct causal link between genetic abnormalities and crime is found, a highly unlikely event in view of the present data, the decision to employ this knowledge in delinquency and crime prevention programs must be well thought out. More than likely, new constitutional interpretations will be necessary to ensure that those singled out as "potential" offenders are protected under the law. Interestingly enough, several defendants in the late 1960s employed the XYY chromosome defect as a defense in criminal cases. In most of these cases, the court was not favorably impressed by the defense.

Disorders of the Limbic System

Some scientists have long pursued the idea that the criminal possesses a brain distinct from the "normal" brain. A growing body of research, beginning in the 1940s, produced evidence of functional, as compared to structural, defects in the brains of individuals with patterns of aggressive behaviors. These studies by no means offer proof of a relationship between brain dysfunctions and crime. What these studies have shown, though, is that certain portions of the limbic area of the brain have considerable importance "in the regulation and control of emotional, aggressive, sexual, and other behaviors" (Shah and Roth, 1974: 115).[9]

Tumors and various lesions or inflammations of the limbic system have resulted in marked behavioral abnormalities. Antisocial behavior has also been attributed to head injuries, viral infections, and brain damage resulting from lack of oxygen in the limbic region. Several cases have been reported where tumors or lesions in portions of the human limbic system were thought to bring about assaults, murder, and other types of abnormal and explosive behaviors. Other manifestations of brain disease—for example, seizures—were in many instances preceded by the abnormal behaviors. Often the malady was diagnosed only after autopsy.

Other limbic-based disorders, such as subcortical **epilepsy**, have been found among violent criminals, motiveless criminals, and children referred to clinics for displaying "disturbed conduct" (for example, stealing, temper tantrums, and impulsive disorders). Such violent or antisocial behaviors as assaults and setting fires have been reported to occur at the time of the seizure, shortly after the seizure (ictal disturbances), and between seizures (interictal disturbances). Some researchers

have observed that aggressiveness on the part of people who have just had seizures may be attributed to their confused efforts to fight off attempts at restraint. These theories must be considered with caution. It is important to underscore that there are many types of epilepsy, and most epileptics are not violent and do not engage in criminality (Shah and Roth, 1974).

Electroencephalographs, devices that record brain waves, are often used to distinguish between individuals who have epilepsy-related disorders and those who do not. Psychosurgeons attempting to treat cerebral disorders, including violent seizures and acting-out behaviors, have removed or destroyed portions of the temporal lobe or the amygdala. (The temporal lobe is that portion of the brain, including the amygdala, which controls the discrimination of sound and the language function.) The surgery has had limited success. Mark and Erwin (1970), for instance, report favorable outcomes in about 50 percent of cases where uncontrolled violence and aggression were apparent.

In sum, there is some evidence suggesting that certain disorders of the limbic brain find expression in aggressive or violent behaviors (Monroe, 1978). The results are, however, too inconclusive to derive a relationship between the disorders and crime and delinquency. Brain disorders may be contributory factors in maladaptive behaviors, but we simply do not know their full effects on antisocial or criminal behavior. The prevalence of these brain diseases in the general population is rather low, and their incidence among delinquent and criminal populations also appears quite low (Shah and Roth, 1974). Additionally, some research indicates that aggression is not a unitary, or single, phenomenon. Instead, there are different kinds of aggression, ranging from predatory (that is, attack aggression) to fear-induced. Efforts to pinpoint a single physiological basis for aggression might well lead to confusing and contradictory results (Mayer, 1968; Yaryura-Tobias, 1978).

Endocrine Abnormalities

Another contemporary biological approach that has received a considerable amount of attention centers on the functioning of the **endocrine glands.**

These glands, through the secretion of hormones, regulate body activities such as growth, the shape of the body, and the way in which the body uses food.

One of the first attempts to explain delinquency and criminality in endocrinological terms took place in 1928. Max G. Schlapp and Edward Smith suggested that crime results from emotional disturbances arising from hormonal imbalances. Schlapp and Smith proposed a "new criminology," in which criminals would be depicted and treated as criminal types within the framework of glandular malfunctioning. Their work was based purely on speculation and never acquired any support among criminologists.

A great deal of scientific research on the relationship of glandular secretions to crime has followed Schlapp and Smith's speculative work, but the results are not conclusive. The endocrine glands, including the pituitary, thyroid, adrenals, and gonads, secrete hormones that affect such body functions as metabolism and nervous, emotional, and sexual processes. Glandular abnormalities can cause structural defects such as gigantism or dwarfism or diseases such as diabetes and hypertension (high blood pressure). Researchers have recognized that endocrine gland secretions greatly affect emotions and behaviors and have searched for a connection between endocrine abnormalities and criminal behavior. But no direct connection has yet been found.

In an early study (1938), Louis Berman compared a group of criminals with a control group and reported that the criminals had two or three times as many glandular defects and disturbances as the noncriminals. A group of delinquents also tested was said to exhibit the same proportion of glandular disturbances as the adult offenders. Berman did not, however, report how his comparisons were made or how his controls were selected. He also did not make any statistical findings available; later and more rigorous research has not supported his findings.

Animal research has shown that the male of the species is usually more aggressive than the female, a finding that has been attributed to the male hormone androgen. Researchers have utilized this knowledge in attempts to curb aggression among humans. It has been found that adminis-

tering the female hormone estrogen to sex offenders serves to inhibit their sexual drive, possibly curbing the commission of aggressive sexual assaults (Shah and Roth, 1974). However, this finding is by no means conclusive, and more controlled research is needed.

Research on female crime has linked involvement of women in criminal and delinquent activities to their premenstrual and menstrual cycles, which are controlled by the endocrine glands. Morton, Addison, Addison, Hunt, and Sullivan (1953), for example, found that among fifty-eight women who had committed crimes of violence (murder, manslaughter, and assault), 62 percent had committed their crimes during the premenstrual cycle and 17 percent had committed them during the menstrual cycle. Other studies have reported similar results (Dalton, 1961, 1964). Although research of this type does not mean that variations in hormone levels cause crime, it does indicate that, for a number of women, premenstrual and menstrual symptoms cause irritability, tension, and nervousness which may contribute to the commission of certain crimes.

It is likely that endocrine imbalance in itself is an incomplete explanation of criminal activity in either of the sexes. We have already urged caution in relying on any single factor to explain crime. Discussing the relationship of crime to endocrinology, biologist Ashley Montague noted: "We are still almost completely in a world of the unknown, and to resort to that system for an explanation of criminality is merely an attempt to explain the known by the unknown" (1941, p. 55).

Orthomolecular Imbalances

Another type of biological disorder that has been related to crime is chemical imbalances in the body. Biochemists point to orthomolecular research demonstrating that some deviant behavior can be attributed to chemical deficiencies or imbalances in the body or to brain toxicity. Biochemical research of this nature appears highly speculative; it is also quite different from the modes of research and thought most criminologists are accustomed to. At the heart of orthomolecular theory is the belief that the functioning of the brain is affected by molecular concentrations of many substances that are normally present in the brain. A person's optimum or normal concentrations of these substances vary, depending on diet and/or genetic deficiencies.

Abnormal deficits or excesses in molecular brain concentrations are thought to lead to a variety of pathological mental and behavior patterns, some of which may be construed as antisocial (Hippchen, 1978; Kelly, 1979; Schauss, 1981). According to Abraham Hoffer (1975, 1978), a founder of the orthomolecular medicine movement, two major groups of symptoms accompany biochemical abnormalities in the body and lead to possible deviant behavior. The first group involves changes in perception induced by nutritional disorders and by brain allergies. The second group includes hyperactivity brought about by nutritional deficiencies or by hypoglycemia (low blood sugar).

In the first group are several diseases, stemming primarily from vitamin deficiencies or dependencies, that lead to disorders in seeing, hearing, and the other senses. People suffering from these symptoms may become violent at times and engage in antisocial behavior. Some studies indicate that alcoholics and drug addicts, people overrepresented among criminals, have vitamin deficiencies. Similarly, many delinquents with learning and behavior disorders have been found to be deficient in vitamin B (Pawlak, 1972).

Research indicates that allergies to a large number of substances can also cause perceptual changes that trigger violent behavior. Wheat, corn, and milk have been linked with perceptual disorders ("Bad Child or Bad Diet," 1979). One study of prison inmates, for instance, concluded that at least one-third of the offenders suffered serious perceptual disorders affecting sight and the other senses as a result of allergies to certain foods. Erratic behaviors brought about by these perceptual disorders were usually classified as psychopathic (Newbolt, Philpot, and Mandell, 1972).

Hyperactivity is frequently seen as a form of antisocial or delinquent behavior among children. Hyperactivity is a syndrome that causes overactivity, distractability, and often aggressiveness. Some researchers think hyperactivity results from nutri-

tional deficiencies or a condition of low blood sugar (hypoglycemia) (Philpot, 1978; Yaryura-Tobias, 1978). This problem relates to a high consumption of sugar and starches and to toxic food additives. The junk foods consumed by American children are extremely high in sugar and starch and may produce major fluctuations in blood sugar levels. These fluctuations can cause symptoms of lethargy and depression as well as irritability, suspiciousness, bizarre thoughts, hallucinations, extreme mania, anxiety, and violent behavior.[10]

Children who are hyperactive often become labeled as problem cases by parents and teachers. Unable to concentrate and learn, they can grow into adulthood lacking a wide variety of knowledge and skills. Thus, they are prime candidates for truancy and dropping out of school, activities conducive to delinquent behavior (Solomon, 1972). Individuals, both children and adults, exhibiting the symptoms of low blood sugar are thought by orthomolecular experts to be capable of acts such as stealing, rape, arson, assault, and homicide (Geary, 1983). One orthomolecular researcher estimates that 90 percent of inmates imprisoned for criminal homicide are actually suffering from hypoglycemia or vitamin deficiency (Hippchen, 1978).

Present evidence provides little support for orthomolecular arguments about the causes of crime and delinquency. Although there is evidence suggesting that nutrition and vitamin deficiencies affect physical and mental well-being, it is going too far to attribute a large proportion of crime and delinquency to orthomolecular imbalances. It is, however, undeniable that a syndrome like hyperactivity can lead to the labeling of a child as a troublemaker, suggesting that social reactions to biological conditions, not purely biological malfunctioning, must be considered. Further, these disorders are not prevalent enough to explain, even indirectly, today's large volume of criminal and delinquent activity. Support for these theories is usually in the form of anecdotal materials based on relatively few cases. At the present time, the statements of orthomolecular theorists that vitamin therapy and changes in diet can "cure" crime and delinquency simply cannot be supported.[11]

Critique of Contemporary Biological Theories

Modern biological theorists appear to be more willing to consider the influence of environmental factors on crime than were their predecessors. Discussing the relationship between heredity and environment on antisocial behavior, David Baker, a medical doctor, writes (1972: 92):

In recent years . . . there has been increased acceptance of the concept of a continuum of relationships between these polar factors [of heredity and environment], resulting in a spectrum of variation with, on the one hand, those situations in which the outcome may be determined by purely genetic factors, and, on the other hand, those situations which depend entirely on the environment. In between, however, are many clinical examples of combined genetic and environmental interaction.

We must add that the more zealous advocates of biological explanations, the sociobiologists, boldly claim that all human behavior is biologically determined. Though varying in specific beliefs, sociobiologists generally argue that without the consideration of biology, the study of human culture makes no sense. Carried to its extreme, sociobiology "holds that all forms of life exist solely to serve the purpose of DNA, the coded master molecule that determines the nature of all organisms and is the stuff of genes" ("Why You Do What You Do," 1977, p. 54; Wilson, 1975).[12] Some sociobiologists suggest that there may be human genes for such behaviors as altruism, conformity, homosexuality, and aggressiveness. These claims have made sociobiology one of the most controversial theoretical trends in decades. The legitimacy of all biological explanations of behavior has suffered in the eyes of many social scientists, who reject the rigid biological determinism of sociobiology.

Criminologists, in particular, have been reluctant to accept biological theories of deviant behavior, and they generally do not support genetically based arguments. Criminologists are wary of these explanations for several reasons. First, no

one has shown the physical processes through which behavior can be inherited (Shah, 1972). Since the conclusive links between genetic abnormalities and criminal behavior have not been scientifically demonstrated, thought on the subject remains speculative. Second, the official labeling of an individual as criminal or delinquent is usually based on only one or a few incidents, yet the label is applied to the whole person. While the specific offense may represent aberrant behavior, other behaviors and actions are probably "normal." The genetic explanation of crime more or less explains a particular type of behavior, but the same theories cannot account for the normal behavior.

Third, even if we were to add up all the probabilities of the various biologically caused crimes, this would still explain only an insignificant portion of the total crimes committed. Along these lines, Soviet criminologists claim that biological aberrations tend to be random and rare; therefore, biological models at best can explain only infrequent, sporadic occurrences of crime. Furthermore, they suggest that it is social forces, not biological aberrations, which contribute to systematic fluctuations in crime rates. It is social factors that govern trends or differences in rates of crime over time and in different cultures (Voigt and Thornton, 1985). The biological theories take the social order for granted, never questioning why some behaviors are considered criminal and others are not.

Finally, there is some apprehension on the part of social scientists that the moral and legal concepts of individual responsibility and free will might be seriously eroded once heredity is linked to personal conduct, especially criminal behavior. C. Ray Jeffery's (1978, 1979) biosociological approach to the study of criminal and delinquent behavior, for example, falls prey to the general criticisms of biological determinism. As Platt and Takagi noted, "Since there are no criminals, only criminogenic conditions, people are not accountable or responsible for their actions" (1979: 184).

Limiting his views to street crime, Jeffery attributes crime to both genetic and environmental factors. Crime can be controlled, he says, by regulating the environment through the "science and technology of behavior," especially physiology and psychopharmacology (the study of the action of drugs on the mind) (1971: 184). To accomplish his aims, Jeffery proposes establishing a private biomedical research system to parallel the present criminal justice system. These centers would have at their disposal techniques to control genetic defects thought to produce crime (Jeffery, 1978). Jeffery, unable to explain the prevalence of organized and white collar crime from a biosocial perspective, dismisses these crimes as problems of politics and economics rather than problems of criminology.

Jeffery has been severely criticized for his obvious double standard concerning lower class and white collar criminals (see Platt and Takagi, 1979). Historically, biological explanations of crime and delinquency have aimed at explaining lower class crime. There has been a conspicuous lack of attention to white collar, or upper class, offenders.[13] As we have already noted, the transformation of crime into a medical or biochemical problem has opened up new possibilities for abuses under the guise of treatment or prevention. Many criminologists see, as a very real possibility, the danger of a therapeutic or scientific tyranny that would circumvent the legal rights of individuals (see Endell, 1983; Katz and Abel, 1984).

SUMMARY

Central to both historical and contemporary biological explanations for delinquency and crime is the notion that biological characteristics, such as morphology, phenotype, physiology, endocrine abnormalities, genetic disorders, and the like, either cause or contribute to delinquent and antisocial behaviors. Early biological proponents stressed what they considered the unchanging and fixed nature of these aspects of the offender. Contemporary biological researchers, in varying degrees, see the potential to alter or control deviant behaviors through vitamin intake, changes in diet, and genetic screening.

Critics attack biological explanations of crime for ignoring social and environmental influences on behavior and for relying too heavily on spec-

ulation about single biological variables. These same critics point to past and present abuses of offenders' and preoffenders' rights (early phenotyping is an example), under the banner of scientific objectivity. They also point to potential political abuses of unverified theorizing on the biological causes of antisocial behavior like those that took place in Nazi Germany in the 1930s. Certain types of offenders, mainly from the lower classes, invariably are singled out for what is often called treatment. Sociologically trained criminologists, although not discounting the possible relationship of some forms of antisocial behavior to the various biological influences on people's behavior, emphasize that crime and delinquency are socially defined. They note that the defining and sanctioning of any behavior as criminal in any culture is a social process. While biological variables may contribute to the commission of certain acts, they are not the only causes of such behaviors. Historical accounts of attempts to explain crime and delinquency biologically have, if nothing else, revealed the futility of the search for any single variable to account for all crime and delinquency.

Cesare Lombroso's depiction of his "atavistic man" as a distinct criminal type fueled the imagination of later biological researchers seeking physical and constitutional causes of criminality. Although disproved many times throughout the decades, vestiges of Lombrosian theory can be found in the works of Ernest Hooten, William Sheldon, and Sheldon and Eleanor Glueck. These researchers have received little support from the criminology community.

Recent biocriminological investigations continue to depend on limited clinical and laboratory samples. While the laboratory techniques in some cases are technologically advanced, the explanatory models remain too simplistic and are unable to account for numerous compounding and intervening variables.

One biological explanation that has received a great deal of publicity since 1965 is the XYY syndrome. With the discovery that some violent institutionalized male offenders possessed an extra Y chromosome, researchers have tried to account for crime through genetic abnormalities. Disagreement over the incidence of XYY males in the general population and the physical and psychological characteristics of XYY individuals render the theory virtually untestable and inconclusive at the present time. Despite this fact, some practitioners have genetically typed male infants in an effort to prevent and offset their future criminality. Given the inconclusive nature of the available evidence, this type of activity is unethical, illegal, and grossly premature.

Limbic-based disorders of the brain, including subcortical epilepsy, have also been associated with antisocial and criminal types of behavior. Several cases have been reported where tumors or lesions in portions of the human limbic system were thought to result in murder, assault, and other types of abnormal and explosive behaviors. These studies suffer from lack of clarity and contradictory findings. Since the prevalence of these brain diseases is rather low, the incidence of these disorders among delinquent and criminal populations also appears to be quite low.

Endocrine abnormalities have also received attention, especially in relation to female crime. Research suggests that some involvement of women in cases of violent outbursts corresponds to their premenstrual and menstrual cycles, which are controlled by the endocrine glands. This finding is by no means definitive, but it does point to the fact that variations in hormonal levels influence irritability, tension, and other factors that may be conducive to certain forms of antisocial behavior. Numerous other social and psychological variables have been found to be of equal or greater importance.

Orthomolecular research, a relatively new biological approach to crime, attributes deviance to chemical or vitamin deficiencies or imbalances in the brain. For example, alterations in diet and prescribed vitamin supplements are the suggested means of treating orthomolecular disorders. Although there is evidence suggesting that nutrition and vitamin deficiencies affect mental and physical health, at the present time it is premature and unfounded to attribute the commission of crimes to these disorders.

While conclusive statements relating biological factors to delinquent or criminal behavior are at this time either unwarranted or premature, continued research in this area is greatly needed. Merely giving lip service to the biopsychological complexities is just not enough.

PROGRESS CHECK

1. What were some of the principal perceptions of criminals held by the early criminal biologists and anthropologists during the period between 1850 and 1930? (p. 85)

2. Giving particular emphasis to the contributions of Cesare Lombroso, outline and discuss the school of criminological thought known as Italian positivism. (pp. 85–86)

3. Which of the following physicians is credited with delivering the most devastating blow to Lombroso's work? (p. 86)
   a. Charles B. Goring
   b. Enrico Ferri
   c. Ernest Hooten
   d. Author Fink

4. Which of the following best incorporates such terms as endomorphs, ectomorphs, and mesomorphs? (p. 88)
   a. Endocrinology
   b. Genetics
   c. Atavism
   d. Somatotyping

5. Explain why biological explanations for crime attained popularity in the nineteenth and early twentieth centuries. Might the same reasons apply today? (pp. 87–88)

6. Define a *concordance rate* and relate it to the explanation of delinquency. (p. 92)

7. Outline and evaluate the XYY chromosome syndrome, in terms of (pp. 93–96)
   a. Basic position
   b. Research findings
   c. Research methodology

8. Explain in your own words Hans Eysenck's explanation of conditioning and delinquency. Do you see any merit to this position? Why or why not? (p. 93)

9. According to the text, there is now convincing research showing a relationship between limbic brain disorders and delinquency. (p. 96)
   a. True
   b. False

10. Debate the major contemporary biological explanations of crime and delinquency, providing at least five arguments for and five arguments against. (pp. 99–100)

NOTES

1. Lombroso (1899/1958) devoted a book to the female offender in which he argued that female deviations are usually sexual in nature; they are more apt to express their antisocial tendencies through prostitution. Moreover, he argued that in the unusual case where the female is involved in crime, she will likely be in possession of distinct masculine traits. Women were not typically criminal, he believed, because they were less intelligent and also because their jealous and cruel temperaments were mitigated by maternalism.

2. Although the positive school of criminology is generally recognized as having its origin in late nineteenth-century Italy, Lindesmith and Levin (1937) have argued that this point of origin is arbitrary. They suggest that an extensive literature on juvenile delinquency, professional crime, crime causation, the use of official statistics, and other aspects of criminology was already in existence when Lombroso began his work.

3. McCaghy (1976) has found that between 1907 and 1937, 31 states passed laws which permitted the sterilization of certain individuals (the feebleminded, mentally ill, and epileptics). Twenty-one states still maintained such laws in 1973. McCaghy cites 70,000 cases of sterilization as a result of the eugenics movement in the United States (pp. 20–21).

4. Criminologist James Q. Wilson and psychologist Richard J. Hernstein recently published a controversial book, *Crime and Human Nature* (1985), which attempts to present a comprehensive theory of crime. Included in their work is a chapter on constitutional factors in criminal behavior. The researchers argue that criminals may be born with "constitutional factors," such as mesomorphic body type, low intelligence, and aggressive personality, that predispose them to criminal behavior.

5. For a listing of studies noting the necessity for careful observation in twin identification, see Mednick and Christiansen (1977).

6. It is important to point out that the number of female twins who have been involved in delinquency studies is exceedingly small—too small for any reasonable conclusion to be drawn.

7. The psychopathic personality is discussed in more detail in Chapter 6.

8. Von Hentig (1948/1979) refers to the relationship between ugliness, physical defects, deformities, and crime and suggests that they play their main role in courts and district attorneys' offices (p. 64). However, Agnew (1984a) finds that unattractive individuals are more delinquent. Appearance is associated more with school-related than family-related delinquency, suggesting that situations where stereotypes and discrimination are more prevalent may affect the relationship (Agnew, 1984a: 435).

9. The limbic portion of the brain is that structure surrounding the brain stem (the nerve tissue connecting the brain to the spinal column). The limbic region communicates with the highly developed neocortex, the part of the brain that controls sensations and memory. The limbic brain, as it is often called, encompasses portions of the thalamus and the hypothalamus, upper parts of the brain stem and the other structures bordering the inner surfaces of the cerebral hemisphere. Also included is the amygdala, portions of the frontal lobes, and the temporal cortex.

10. There is evidence to suggest that even without treatment, most hyperactivity-related symptoms usually diminish or disappear by the late teen years (Coleman, Butcher, and Carson, 1984: p. 546).

11. Glow (1981) warns that pharmacological treatment of hyperactivity is not without hazards or long-term effects. He argues that the drugs can only arrest the symptoms, not cure the disorder.

12. General discussions of the role of biology in explaining human behavior can be found in Mazur and Robertson (1972) and in Sahlins (1979).

13. We should add that this preoccupation with lower class crime was, until very recently, shared by sociologists.

CHAPTER 5

PSYCHIATRIC AND PSYCHOLOGICAL THEORIES

HISTORICAL RELATIONSHIPS BETWEEN CRIME AND INSANITY

PSYCHIATRIC THEORIES OF CRIMINAL AND DELINQUENT BEHAVIOR

PSYCHOANALYTIC EXPLANATIONS OF CRIME AND DELINQUENCY

PERSONALITY TRAITS COMMONLY ASSOCIATED WITH CRIME AND DELINQUENCY

LEARNING–REINFORCEMENT THEORIES OF CRIME AND DELINQUENCY

Clarence was practically a model child at fifteen, never having been in any kind of trouble. A few weeks earlier, another boy had enlisted his aid in burglarizing a home, where they had found some rifles. They secreted the rifles on a hill near a high school. After an evening basketball game, Clarence and his friend climbed the hill and recovered the rifles. Clarence loaded one of the weapons and fired almost blindly into the school's parking lot. One of the persons there was a woman who had come to see her son play in the game. The shot hit her head, killing her immediately. Clarence and the woman had never seen each other, and Clarence could give no reason whatsoever for having fired into the crowd. (Sorrells, 1977: 313)

W‌hy did Clarence, a normal child from all outward appearances, commit such a terrible crime? Chapter 4 asked whether or not delinquents are physically or physiologically different from nondelinquents. In this chapter we will seek to answer the question of whether or not the psychic

103

or emotional condition or personality structure of delinquents differs from that of nondelinquents.[1]

Psychiatrists, psychoanalysts, and psychologists would look at Clarence's behavior quite differently. Clinical psychiatrists and psychologists would probably begin by looking at Clarence's early childhood experiences, parental relationships, and the development of his ego and superego. They might diagnose him as having a character disorder due to improper socialization and inadequate ego development.

Psychoanalysts would argue that conflicts between elements of Clarence's personality and his social environment, or perhaps his inadequate "psychosexual development," or his "masculinity-femininity conflicts," or some hidden motives such as a desire for punishment caused this manifestation of symptomatic behavior.

Research psychologists and psychiatrists who support **personality trait theories** would search for certain personality traits and characteristics—indicators of extreme aggressiveness or lack of conscience—that might explain Clarence's deviant act. Perhaps they would administer a series of personality inventories and attempt to determine the presence of psychopathic or sociopathic traits.

Psychologists and psychiatrists who support **learning or reinforcement theories** of behavior would view Clarence's act as an outgrowth of past learning experiences. They would ask this question: Did Clarence derive any approval or "beneficial" outcomes from engaging in deviant behavior in the past, and as a consequence was he somehow socially "conditioned" to engage in such behavior?

We will begin with the mental and emotional elements that have been associated with delinquent behavior. After a brief historical sketch of psychiatry and psychoanalysis as they have been employed in crime explanations, we will give a more detailed description of the specific psychological research that has examined juvenile delinquency.

While psychological theories of crime and delinquency are not as popular today as they once were, they continue to be very relevant, since they presuppose many treatment models.

HISTORICAL RELATIONSHIPS BETWEEN CRIME AND INSANITY

It is often difficult to mark the differences between the biological and the psychological causes of antisocial behavior. Even among the many characteristics Lombroso (1911) associated with his "born" criminal were several references to mental disorders. His later typology included the "criminaloid," whose characteristics closely resemble contemporary descriptions of the psychopathic personality. This should come as no surprise, given that the common practice in Lombroso's day was to incarcerate the insane and the criminal in the same facility.

Indeed, for most of history criminality and insanity have not always been distinct. Both the insane and the criminal have been subject to similar physical and social treatment. Comparable theoretical paradigms, especially the medical models, have been employed in the explanation of both crime and mental illness. The history of the relationship between criminality and insanity is important for our understanding of the psychiatric role in criminology.

Psychiatry may be defined as the study and treatment of various forms of maladaptive behavior, including signs of disturbances in thinking, emotion, motivation, perception, learning, memory, maturation, and interpersonal or social relations (Gaze, 1976). From the very beginning of medical history, psychiatry has constituted an important division of medical knowledge. In ancient Greece we find in the notes of Pythagoras (580–510 B.C.) and Hippocrates (460–377 B.C.) definitions of mental illness as a disorder of the brain, with references to different kinds of mental disorders and ways of controlling mentally impaired individuals (Inglis, 1965; Rosen, 1968).

Perhaps due to the invisibility of the mind and accompanying uncertainty of treatment, the clinical emphasis has been on control rather than treatment. Even in the earliest accounts, psychiatry has been different than other medical speciality areas because control, not treatment, has been the focal concern of the profession. Because of this emphasis, psychiatrists have become deeply involved in the legal and social processes of controlling mentally ill people in society (Halleck, 1967). The "treatability of the mentally ill" as a function of psychiatry was not seriously recognized until relatively recently—not until Freud's use of psychoanalytic insights for treatment, which has been a topic of much debate.

Thus, in order to understand the psychiatrist's role in criminology, we must begin in the courtroom, with the question of criminal responsibility (Halleck, 1967).

The Role of Psychiatry in Criminal Court

Presumably the most important reason for the psychiatrist's presence in the adult courtroom is to mitigate the harshness of punishment. The presumption of psychiatric mitigation of harshness is not without some ironic overtones, however.

The issue of responsibility places psychiatrists in an incongruous position. Without the presumption of responsibility, therapy, according to most psychiatric models, is considered impossible. The paradox lies in a fundamental contradiction of roles. In order to have the occasion to "help," the psychiatrist must declare the "defendant" incompetent or mentally not responsible. Yet without the presumption of responsibility the emphasis remains on control rather than treatment.

Since maximum security facilities in both the mental health and the correctional fields are primarily total control institutions, the separation of the insane from the criminal is more symbolic than factual. The evidence suggests that experiences in mental institutions are not any less harsh than in prisons (Goffman, 1961).

The role of the psychiatrist in the courtroom is complicated further by the controversy that has surrounded the criteria governing the determination of insanity and criminality. The insanity defense—"innocent by means of insanity"—has been at the center of this controversy, especially in capital offenses (Goldstein, 1970). Some people

fear that criminals will resort to this plea to escape legal responsibility. This objection was heard, for example, when President Reagan's attempted assassin (John Hinkley) was deemed "insane" at the time of the offense. Even with the noted increase in the use of the insanity defense over the last twenty-five years, an incredibly small percentage of cases are resolved using that plea (less than 2 percent) (Fersch, 1980). Some psychiatrists are troubled that use of the insanity plea occurs in such a small fraction of cases where emotional factors are indicated (Halleck, 1967: 218).

Public concern largely stems from the difficulty in defining insanity. The noted legal precedents delineating insanity are these (for more details, see Fersch, 1980):

1. *The M'Naghten rule* (1843): Applies to individuals whose reasoning capabilities can be proved to have been defective due to a disease of the mind which prevented the actor having knowledge of the nature or quality of the act.

2. *The irresistible impulse* (1887): Applies to individuals who may be cognizant of the wrongfulness of the act but who were unable to choose between right and wrong.

3. *The Durham rule* (1954): Applies to individuals whose "unlawful act was the product of mental disease or mental defect."[2]

4. *Diminished capacity* (1978): Focuses on the mental capability necessary to demonstrate the level of intent or knowledge associated with certain offenses. Individuals are not made innocent by reason of insanity; they are still guilty, but of a lesser charge. For example, the charge of first degree murder may be reduced to negligent homicide if the defendant was mentally incapable of intent. Some states have changed the defense to "guilty but mentally ill."

One of the main practical consequences of these rules has been the separation of criminal and noncriminal offenders. Defendants who are found nonculpable are treated in mental hospitals. The criminally liable, however, are sentenced to prison. Depending on the seriousness of the offense, those found guilty may be sentenced to execution. Thus, the psychiatrist's role may actually be to determine the question of life or death. This role has made many people uneasy about the validity of the indicators or tests of insanity. Although the various rules of the insanity defense imply the existence of clear definitions of mental illness, there is still much debate over these definitions, even among psychiatrists. To date, no set of indicators or criteria or tests differentiating the sane from the insane or criminal, especially the violent type, have been found to be both valid and reliable.

The Role of Psychiatry in Juvenile Court

In cases of delinquency, where the question of guilt or innocence has been philosophically excluded, where simple involvement is considered, the question of culpability or intent has been deemed inappropriate. In cases where involvement has been found, the focus is on the proximate cause, which is used as an indicator determining type of treatment. Historically, the purpose of the juvenile court was to prescribe not punishment, but treatment and protection.[3] The emphasis on treatment has provided the major justification for handling juveniles differently from adults.

In the absence of clear mental and psychological diagnostic materials, most juvenile court decisions reflect the court's assessment of the youth's home environment, including school and community. Investigation is geared primarily to answering the question of the parents' ability to control the youth. Youths whose parents appear less able to control them, thereby increasing the possibility of the recurrence of antisocial acts, are prime candidates for official handling. Rarely are psychiatrists used in the casework process, although psychiatric theories and testimonies of the negative effects of home life on children are frequently used to justify the separation of the child from the "improper" environment.

In relatively few instances does the question of "dangerousness" come up in juvenile cases. Psychiatrists and psychologists may be involved in such assessments, even though no one has yet demonstrated a basis for predicting dangerousness or violence.[4] Dangerousness, however, is supposed to underlie the type of handling—treatment—the youth will receive. Cases involving more dangerous youngsters are usually approached more formally or intrusively; the youngster is more likely to be placed in a detention center and is more likely to be institutionalized rather than placed on probation. The less dangerous cases are more likely to receive informal dispositions, such as probation or parental supervision.

If psychiatrists or clinical psychologists are involved in the proceedings, they may be consulted over the suitability and appropriateness of placement in a mental health facility. Again, few cases are disposed in this manner. A significant but still small number who are transferred to a mental health facility come from families who were more able to afford the full range of diagnostic tests and psychiatric services (see Chapter 16).

There are no diagnostic standards or rules governing the various dispositions to detain or to treat juveniles comparable to the adult rules. Moreover, no objective predictive tests of dangerousness or violence-prone behavior exist. Therefore, a wide variety of indicators, evaluations, and diagnostic tests (anything from the recidivism rate, teacher rating, case history produced by a probation officer, to a full psychiatric exam) are considered in the decision-making process.

Psychiatric Classifications of Crime and Delinquency

The psychiatrist's role in the courtroom has forced the profession to pay major attention to the categorization of mental illness and the distinctions between "normal" and "insane" (see Tancredi, Lieb, and Slaby, 1975; Brakel and Rock, 1971). Questions of reliability and validity tend to expose the controversy surrounding the role of psychiatry not only in criminology, but in society generally.

Even within the field of psychiatry, there is conflicting opinion about the definition of mental illness. More radical psychiatrists such as Thomas Szasz (1970a) have asserted that the concept of mental illness is arbitrarily defined using mainly middle and upper middle class criteria of "normal behavior." Szasz has suggested that the expression "mental illness" is a metaphor that society has come to mistake for a fact:

> We call people physically ill when their body functioning violates certain anatomical and physiological norms; similarly we call people mentally ill when their personal conduct violates certain ethical, political and social norms. This explains why many historical figures, from Jesus to Castro, and from Job to Hitler, have been diagnosed as suffering from this or that psychiatric malady. (p. 23)

According to Szasz, behaviors psychiatrists classify as mental illness are actually "problems of living." The concept of mental illness "serves mainly to obscure the everyday fact that life for most people is a continuous struggle, not for biological survival, but for a 'place in the sun,' 'peace of mind,' or some other meaning or value" (p. 23). Although recognizing that personal unhappiness and deviant behavior exist, Szasz has criticized the characterization of these feelings and behaviors as symptoms of disease. Not many psychiatrists, however, agree with Szasz's views.

Mental illnesses are typically regarded by psychiatrists as being basically similar to other diseases that can be diagnosed and treated. Certain behaviors, including violent acts, are thought to be symptomatic of a particular personality type related to some mental or emotional disorder. The **medical model** attributes mental disorders to causes within the individual personality structure. In more serious cases at least, the individual is considered both out of control and out of touch with reality, as in psychoses (McCaghy, 1976).

Some theorists do dispute the idea of a stable personality type, including different classifications of the mentally ill, by arguing that personality formation is a constantly changing process occurring throughout life and therefore impossible to classify. Others are convinced that stable personality types exist in concrete terms and that categories of "sick" and "normal," and especially the maladaptive and antisocial personality types, have been scientifically and clinically validated (Hakeem, 1958a; Mischel, 1968; Jones et al., 1971; Hogan and Jones, 1983).

Neuroses and Psychoses.   Psychiatrists broadly classify mental disorders as either **neuroses** or **psychoses**. Deriving from excessive anxiety or the inability to endure anxiety, neurotic disorders are generally considered less serious than psychoses. Neurotics who commit crimes are thought to be expressing unconscious guilt feelings that follow deeply embedded hostility. The criminal acts of neurotic offenders are said to range from kleptomania and pyromania to gambling and vagrancy (Roebuck, 1967). Frequently these crimes are motivated by an unconscious wish to be punished, and the offender often leaves obvious clues at the scene of the crime.

Psychoses, on the other hand, involve more severe and complete personality disruptions. Although neurotics are aware of their irrationality and deviance, psychotics are said to have lost contact with reality and rarely to acknowledge the irrationality and abnormality of their acts. Psychoses are divided into two types, organic and functional. *Organic psychoses* are physiological in nature and result from brain damage, tumors, and the like. *Functional psychoses* are psychological in origin. **Paranoia** and **schizophrenia** are both functional psychoses, as is psychopathic behavior (Coleman, Butcher, and Carson, 1984; Gazzaniga, 1973). The delinquent and criminal acts of psychotics tend to be more serious than those committed by neurotics. Frequently, the criminal acts of psychotics appear motiveless and are bizarre in nature.

Mental Illness and Delinquency.   Until very recently, psychiatric interest in youth was not to describe or explain youthful problems and misbehavior, as much as it was to shed light on adult behavior. Indeed, early childhood experiences were primary variables addressed by psychiatrists attempting to provide explanations for adult antisocial behavior. Even when emotional problems of the young were uncovered, they were generally viewed within the framework of adult problems.

No childhood or adolescent disorders were described or even suggested in the famous classical categorization of psychiatric disorders proposed by Kraepelin (1883). In the first attempt by the American Psychiatric Association (APA) to establish a formal nomenclature and classification system which resulted in the publication of the *Diagnostic and Statistical Manual of Mental Disorders* in 1952 (DSM-I), only two disorders specific to juveniles were included: inadequate adjustment reactions of childhood, and childhood schizophrenia. Several more categories appeared in the second revised edition, published in 1968 (DSM-II). This second edition reflected growing concern for a special juvenile diagnostic system. The third, the most recent of the series, released in 1980 (DSM-III), has further expanded the classification system to include a wider range of childhood and adolescent behavior problems.[5]

As students of the problem of delinquency, we may be concerned with the relative placement or approach to delinquency in the psychiatric classification systems. Of special interest are the distinctions between delinquents and adult criminals and psychopaths. There are two general approaches to the classification of juvenile behavior problems: the clinical-nosological strategy and the multivariate strategy. Each has its strengths and weaknesses (Quay, 1979).

Clinical-Nosological Strategy.   The clinical-nosological strategy underlies the DSM-III classification system. This strategy is based on case descriptions produced by clinicians who through their own observations identify certain conditions and associative symptoms that cover a wide range of behaviors, including some very rare types.[6] The diagnosis comes first; the commonalities between diagnoses are pulled together later.

Since crime and delinquency are both legal and not psychiatric terms, they are covered by general categories. Adult criminal behavior is covered

under the general category of personality disorders. The DSM-III personality disorders are grouped into three clusters based on symptomatic similarities. Cluster II includes histrionic, narcissistic, antisocial (psychopathic or sociopathic), and passive-aggressive personality disorders. Individuals who are classified under this cluster commonly exhibit dramatic, emotional, and impulsive behavior, and often law-violating behavior (Coleman, Butcher, Carson, 1984: 237). This list of common symptoms makes these individuals more likely to come to the attention of mental health and legal authorities. But while some of these individuals are criminals, not all of them are necessarily so. And note that even though psychopathy and delinquency have been studied by many researchers, psychopathy is regarded as an adult category in the DSM-III system. The official diagnosis applies only to individuals who are 18 years and older.

The following criteria are specified by the DSM-III psychopath classification (cited in Coleman, Butcher, and Carson, 1984: 248):

> (a) if there have been at least three instances of deviant behavior such as theft, vandalism, or unusually aggressive behavior before age 15;
> (b) if there have been at least four behavior problems such as financial irresponsibility, illegal occupation, ineffective functioning as a parent, or poor work history since age 15 and no period longer than five years without such a problem;
> (c) if the antisocial behavior endures, with no "remission" lasting longer than five years (unless the person is incapacitated or imprisoned);
> (d) if the antisocial behavior is not a symptom of another mental disorder.

The American Psychiatric Association (1980) has estimated that approximately 3 percent of males and 1 percent of females in the American population would fit the clinical description and criteria of the **psychopathic personality**. The character traits associated with the psychopathic personality, including inability to trust others, to empathize with others, to love others, and to learn from experience, make them very poor candidates for treatment (Charney, 1979). But despite the low rate of success in treatment, a substantial number of psychopaths improve even without any treatment by age 40 ("burned-out psychopaths") (Coleman, Butcher, and Carson, 1984: 258).

Juvenile delinquent behaviors are broadly classified under the general category of childhood conduct disorders, which may or may not include legal violations.

The DSM-III symptomatic behavior description of conduct disorders includes persistent, repetitive violation of rules and a disregard for the rights of others. Juveniles whose behavior falls under the category of conduct disorders usually manifest hostility (overt and covert), disobedience, and physical and verbal aggression. They are typically assessed as destructive, vengeful, and quarrelsome. Associated behaviors may include temper tantrums, deception and stealing, sexual promiscuity, sexual aggression, vandalism, and arson (Stewart et al., 1980; Coleman, Butcher, and Carson, 1984).

Most researchers agree that it is impossible behaviorally to differentiate conduct disorders, predelinquent behavior, and early signs of antisocial personality types (Coleman, Butcher, and Carson, 1984). The behavioral indicators are comparable for each of the different types. It is also difficult to tell "normal" children's pranks and misbehaviors from conduct disorders, except that the latter appear to be more persistent. Conduct disorders are difficult to distinguish from other childhood disorders except that onset is usually earlier (Behar and Steward, 1982). Early onset of troublesome behavior also serves to distinguish conduct disorders from "normal" delinquency (Behar and Steward, 1982).

Multivariate Strategy. The multivariate method of classification, which is preferred by empirically oriented researchers, uses a research model and involves advanced statistical procedures such as factor analysis and multiple regression.[7] Different data bases and rating methods may be employed for the development of classifications. Control groups and "normal" samples are used for comparative purposes in the development of typologies.

One of the early systems using the multivariate

strategy was developed by Hewitt and Jenkins (1947). Using their own rating system, they statistically analyzed 500 case records of children examined at the Michigan Child Guidance Institute. On the basis of their research, Hewitt and Jenkins concluded that maladjusted youth are of three major types: (1) the "over-inhibited neurotic," (2) the "unsocialized aggressive delinquent," and (3) the "socialized delinquent."

According to the researchers, overinhibited neurotic youths become delinquent because of internal conflict between impulses and repressive forces and an inadequate personality. These individuals are unable to mobilize their troublesome feelings into action and therefore keep their feelings within. Neurotic youths are thought to come from families where parents are repressive, cold, and unsocial. The child, continually trying to maintain the love of the parents, experiences insecurity and humiliation "which typically produce a powerful, unconscious desire for vengeance and counter aggression" (Ferdinand, 1966: 189). These feelings foster guilt. Although neurotic delinquents rarely act out their hostilities against their tormentors, they do engage in "more devious and less hazardous forms of agression, e.g., vandalism and theft" (Ferdinand, 1966: 190).

Unsocialized aggressive delinquents are cruel, defiant, remorseless, hostile, and bitter; their delinquent acts are directed against property as well as people. According to Hewitt and Jenkins, they come from families with a history of violence and abuse. Other psychiatrists (Alexander and Staub, 1956; Abrahamsen, 1960; Weinberg, 1952) have described delinquents with similar mental or emotional disorders.

Socialized delinquents are also defiant toward authority and unable to accept responsibility. They differ from unsocialized aggressive delinquents because they do express guilt for violating the code of the peer group (for example, the gang), but advocate attack on outsiders.

Although such classification schemes and their many variants seem to suggest that most delinquent youth are "maladjusted" or "emotionally disturbed," there is evidence that most delinquents are, in fact, psychiatrically "normal" (Schilder, 1940; Lewis, 1952; Bromberg, 1961, 1965; Gibbons, 1981).[8] It is, of course, very important that the base sample (the individuals who provide the data for the classification system) be considered. One of the limitations of this type of research is that most of the individuals whose characteristics are used for the different classification systems are institutionalized, thus representing only a biased population.

Because the multivariate strategy depends on a standard set of evaluations applied to many cases, it is also important to consider who the evaluators are. Are the results based on teacher ratings (Peterson, 1961), parental reports (Dreger et al., 1964), or clinicians' evaluations (Achenbach, 1966)? Differences in classifications may actually reflect differences in the orientation of the evaluators. When compared to the nosological method, the multivariate system, which depends on factor loading and statistical significance levels, requires many more cases and higher incidence of symptoms for patterns to emerge. Hence the system produces fewer categories (Quay, 1979).

PSYCHIATRIC THEORIES OF CRIMINAL AND DELINQUENT BEHAVIOR

The psychiatric theory of delinquency ascribes most present behavior, especially delinquency, to early childhood experiences. The relationship between children and their parents is believed to be particularly important. Clinard (1974a) expresses a common view—that "childhood is the arena in which personality traits toward or away from deviance are developed, and a person's behavior after the childhood years is fundamentally the acting out of tendencies formed at that time" (p. 197).

Early Childhood Experiences and Delinquency

Blocked Needs.   Central to this argument is the assumption that all people at birth have certain basic needs. After the fulfillment of the primary, physiological needs, such as food and elimination, secondary or psychological needs, such as emotional security, nurturance, affection, and feelings of self-worth, must be met, or the individual will develop abnormal symptoms.[9] Personality impairment in later life is thought to vary directly with the degree of early deprivation of these universal needs. Accordingly, delinquency is hypothesized to develop from deprivations early in life.

Healy and Bronner (1936), whose work is a classic in this area, thought that delinquents sought substitute satisfactions from the thrill of delinquent adventure and the gratification of recognition or attention as a delinquent. According to the psychiatric perspective, the delinquent is rarely consciously aware that delinquent acts are ways of satisfying basic needs. "Usually the act is engaged in by the delinquent without verbalizing to himself [or herself] that he [or she] is engaging in an evasive, substitutive, or compensatory form of behavior" (p. 135).

More recent studies also deal with the psychodynamic aspects of aggression and suggest that the psychiatric notion of need deprivation has not diminished in popularity over the years. For example, Solomon (1970) suggested that paranoia, a psychological state in which people feel victimized, threatened, or persecuted, originates from feelings of helplessness or powerlessness and from lack of basic trust in the predictable, reliable meeting of basic needs. An infant or child whose requests (or signals) for needs go unattended and whose care is based primarily on parental desires (for example, feeding when the mother, rather than the child, feels like it) is likely to develop a reactive rage. Solomon finds the potential for later violent behavior greater when others, especially significant others such as parents and teachers, are perceived as unresponsive.

Since the family is the child's primary socializing agent, early family experiences are viewed as exerting a major influence on personality and eventual behavior patterns.

Parental Deprivation and Rejection.   According to psychiatrists, parental, especially maternal, deprivation, separation, and neglect are typically found in the histories of violence-prone and antisocial people. Psychiatrists assume that children, males and females, must have a warm, intimate, and continous relationship with their mothers or mother substitutes if they are to develop normally. The child who experiences separation or rejection faces an increased chance of involvement in serious delinquency (Feldman, 1977). Emotional need deprivations are believed to lead to delinquency by damaging the ability of the child to form affectionate relationships with others.

Research on the relationship between early maternal deprivation and delinquent behavior has been criticized as being methodologically biased, so caution should be exercised when interpreting these studies. There is evidence suggesting that the father's behavior toward the child is just as important as the actions of the mother. Bandura and Walters (1958, 1963), as well as the Gluecks (1968), found a direct relationship between rejecting or hostile fathers and delinquency. The fathers of delinquent youth spent much less time with their children than did the fathers of the nondelinquent youth. Similarly, Andry (1957) reported that the role of the father is at least equally important as the role of the mother in explaining delinquency. Boys in mother-headed homes have been found to be more antisocial and impulsive, less self-controlled, and more rebellious. In fact, boys generally appear to be affected more negatively than girls by single parenthood.

Regardless of which parental source of affection is the more critical, a high quality of parent-child interaction appears to be an essential element in the prevention of delinquency.

Faulty Discipline.   Much of the research using case studies indicates that poor family relations typically characterize the delinquent's background. Harsh and inconsistent discipline, particularly in combination with parental rejection, has been associated with antisocial and aggressive behavior patterns (Langner et al., 1974; Lefkowitz et al., 1977; McCord and McCord, 1962; Pemberton and Benady, 1973). Parental psychopathology, which is suggestive of inconsistent discipline and communication of expectations and values, rejecting

and negligent parenting, and frequently harsh, unpredictable treatment, has been found in the case histories of some delinquents (Bandura, 1973; Glueck and Glueck, 1969; Ulmar, 1971; Elkind, 1967; Scharfman and Clark, 1967).

Psychopathic parents exercise greater influence when other models of behavior are not available. Parental relationships outside the family seem to be related to a youth's behavior (Griest and Wells, 1983; Wahler, 1980). Wahler found an inverse relationship between friendly parental contacts outside the home and the youths' misbehavior. Parents who are experiencing negative relationships or who are isolated are less able to monitor their youngsters' activities (Wahler et al., 1981).

PSYCHOANALYTIC EXPLANATIONS OF CRIME AND DELINQUENCY

As we have already seen, the psychiatric perspective has a long and varied history. The psychoanalytic school of thought is an offshoot of the psychiatric perspective that deserves special attention. It is important because it has had a tremendous impact on the field of psychiatry and on the thinking of ordinary citizens. The **psychoanalytic perspective** has also served as a springboard for the criticism of psychiatry and of the mental concepts or constructs many of us take for granted.

Psychoanalysis is a relatively new development and is associated with the insights of Sigmund Freud, who was a practicing psychiatrist in Vienna from the 1880s through the 1930s. Psychoanalysts are not as inclined to view mental problems as diseases. They see most mental problems as stemming from the conflict between the forces of society and the instinctive forces within human beings. The conflict is between the basic urges within human beings (called the libido) and the requirements for conformity by the community. Since the ultimate seeds of the problem lie not in the malfunction of the brain but in the inhibiting forces of civilization, a whole new approach to treatment is implied. In fact, as mentioned earlier, the emphasis on treatment is perhaps one of the greatest contributions of psychoanalysis.

Freud did not consider just criminal behavior as a problem; for him, conventional behavior was equally so. Freud's theory attempted to provide an inclusive explanation of human behavior generally, with crime as only one form. Thus, most of what constitutes the psychoanalytical view of crime and delinquency comes not from Freud, but from individuals applying his insights (Carl Jung, 1940; Karen Horney, 1937; Otto Rank, 1936; Alfred Adler, 1959; Erik Erikson, 1963).

Sigmund Freud's Principal Concepts

Freud began by explaining the process of socialization from infancy through adulthood and hypothesizing that there are **psychosexual stages** of development through which all normal children pass. According to Freud, the **oral**, the **anal**, and the **phallic stages** of development are critical in the fashioning of personality. Freud thought that adult neurosis stemmed from infantile frustrations or overindulgence. In the oral stage, for example, the child's feelings center around food and nursing. It is through activities such as sucking (breast or bottle) that the child derives pleasure. If the oral stage is cut short—for example, by too early weaning—or unduly prolonged, psychoanalysts argue that the child will not progress normally to the next developmental stage. "Mishandling of the oral drive," remarked Abrahamsen (1960), "lays the foundation for dependency and passivity and excessive passivity is often behind antisocial and criminal aggressions" (p. 71). From the Freudian viewpoint, delinquent activities, particularly stealing (to satisfy oral impulses) and the acting out of oral-sadistic fantasies, are associated with oral stage deficiencies.

The child's "normal" progression through the psychosexual stages—oral, anal, phallic, latency, and genital—is viewed as determining whether or not a healthy adult will develop. Each stage brings increased socialization demands and affects the way the child must deal with basic, innate drives. These drives, sexual and aggressive in nature, are said to create tensions that must be gratified

(Dunbar, 1977). When the tensions are not alleviated through socially acceptable behavior, criminal adaptations may occur.

Two drives in particular, the sexual and the aggressive, are thought to be most related to criminality. These drives derive from one of the basic units of the personality, the **id**. The id contains a primitive reservoir of instincts and seeks immediate gratification. To handle these hedonistic drives, the **ego** functions as "that part of the id which has been modified by the direct influence of the external world" (Rennie, 1978: 154). As the ego develops, it becomes the part of the personality that is in touch with reality; it operates in concert with the pleasure principle to guide behavior. The ego selectively determines how to satisfy the pleasure-seeking drives originating in the id. A product of the socialization process, the **superego** evolves as the final component of personality. Often called the conscience, the superego represents the individual's regulation of his or her own conduct. By internalizing the moral values of his or her parents, the maturing child learns to distinguish socially acceptable from socially unacceptable behavior.

Freudian theorists thus hypothesize a constant struggle within the individual between the need to satisfy drives and the demands of the larger society; the struggle can be consciously perceived or unconsciously assimilated. These struggles involve conflicts between the ego and the id, as well as between the ego and the superego. When the id seeks to satisfy particular needs and the superego represses these drives, anxiety builds within the individual. In an effort to reduce anxiety, the ego devises defense mechanisms such as rationalizations or reaction formations.

Applications of Psychoanalytic Views to Delinquency

Contemporary psychoanalysts who have studied criminality view it as an adaptation to tension states. Since each person, according to psychoanalysts, is born with sexual and aggressive drives, everyone is a *potential* criminal. However, *actual* criminal behavior "is a manifestation of a weakness in the internal control system (ego or superego)" found only in certain individuals (Dunbar, 1977: 87). Psychoanalysts further indicate that many males and females engage in delinquency because they unconsciously want to be punished, but they fail to explain why so many delinquents and criminals are successful in avoiding apprehension and punishment (Dunbar, 1977). Of the more popular works relating psychoanalytic principles to criminal behavior we will discuss two, the first by Franz Alexander and Hugo Staub, and the second by Kate Friedlander.

Franz Alexander and Hugo Staub.   In their book *The Criminal, the Judge and the Public* (1956), Alexander and Staub work within a classic Freudian framework and propose that all human beings enter the world as criminals who are not socially adjusted. This criminality lasts throughout the latency period of development, until the Oedipal conflict is resolved. According to Freudian psychology, the **Oedipus complex** is the phase in a normal young boy's life when he hates his father, viewing the father as a competitor for the mother's sexual love. Young girls are thought to go through similar torments (the **Electra complex**), except that their love centers on the father, with the mother as competitor.

Alexander and Staub, limiting their concern to males, write that unless the guilt or anxiety aroused by these feelings is resolved in the latency phase, later antisocial or ciminal behavior is probable. The normal individual progresses through this period by repressing "genuine criminal instinctual drives" and then transforms the drives into socially acceptable behaviors. The criminal "carries out in his actions his natural unbridled instinctual drives; he acts as the child would act if it only could" (p. 30).

Kate Friedlander.   Kate Friedlander (1947), a psychiatrist, provided another psychoanalytic approach to juvenile delinquency. Friedlander's theory, like the psychoanalytic interpretations of crime, is based on a standard set of psychological concepts. At the heart of her explanation is the idea that anticharacter formation (for example, selfishness, impulsiveness, and irresponsibility) results from disturbed ego development in early childhood. The coupling of neurotic symptoms, by themselves relatively harmless, with anticharacter formation can lead to delinquent behavior. In these cases, delinquency is often an alternative way of fulfilling desires the child dares not express directly.

Critique of the Psychiatric and Psychoanalytic Perspectives

Psychiatric classifications and explanations of crime and delinquency have been open to numerous criticisms and difficulties. Psychiatric practitioners employing the medical analogy equate antisocial behavior with certain types of mental and emotional disorders. Social or environmental factors, though recognized, are given a minimal amount of attention. Although psychiatrists claim they can distinguish among various types of mental aberrations, psychiatric diagnoses are extremely unreliable in differentiating between "mentally healthy" and "mentally unhealthy" individuals. Often psychiatrists will point to criminal or delinquent behavior as an indication of mental illness and then argue that the mental illness caused delinquent behavior. This kind of circular reasoning has brought psychiatry, as an effective force in defining and treating delinquency, under attack.

Another criticism of the psychiatric approach centers on its overemphasis on childhood experiences. Early family and childhood experiences, though certainly important, do not exclusively or consistently determine adult behavior. According to social psychologists, current social interactions have a strong influence on the human organism. It has been suggested, for instance, that individuals continually assess themselves in light of how they perceive others perceive them. This process continues throughout the life span of the individual.

Generally, psychiatric hypotheses have not been rigorously tested. Often relying on individual case histories or unrepresentative samples such as institutionalized groups or people under treatment, psychiatrists have generalized their findings to the population at large. As a result, highly subjective rather than scientifically verified findings are accepted by psychiatrists and by the public.

Because psychoanalysis is a subfield of psychiatry, many of the general criticisms of psychiatry apply also to psychoanalysis. Additional questions, however, may be raised about the effectiveness and soundness of psychoanalytic explanations. The concept of the personality as a compartmentalized vessel made up of such nebulous units as the id, ego, and superego is impossible to document empirically. Although it is probable that the internal dynamics of the personality influence human behavior, we can only guess the extent and direction of the effect (Cohen, 1966).

There is evidence that the nature and quality of our social interactions and relationships play a major role in determining the form behavior takes and the subsequent interpretation of that behavior. According to social psychologists, human behavior and the meanings given to it can be understood only in the context of social interaction. The notion that instincts and uncontrollable sexual and aggressive desires coming from the id are culturally and socially bound would make no sense if the social context were ignored. Many social scientists question the relevance of instincts in understanding human behavior. If instincts do exist, there is no apparent clear-cut link between them and deviant behavior. Many psychoanalytic interpretations explain behavior in terms of early life experiences, without attention to later socialization experiences. Despite some emphasis on social-environmental factors by psychoanalysts such as Adler (1959) and Horney (1937), psychoanalysts generally explain behavior almost exclusively in terms of early life experiences.

The family dynamics most psychoanalysts hold to be universal are also considered by many to be historically and culturally specific, severely limiting their usefulness in explaining all human behavior, particularly antisocial behavior. The "standard" family triangle is composed of a dominant, authoritarian father, subordinate mother, and subordinate child living in a capitalistic, urban, male-dominated, middle class, conservative society. As a treatment model, it is generally geared for the more affluent and educated classes. Several an-

thropologists have successfully demonstrated the Western European specificity of Freudian theories (Malinowski, 1953; Mead, 1950).

Yet even as a Western model, its usefulness in explaining behavior may be outmoded by recent changes in attitudes and definitions of "normal" family patterns and roles. For example, high divorce rates and accompanying remarriage rates have resulted in significant numbers of individuals experiencing two or more marriages during their lifetimes. The increased adoption of joint custody even of the very young and the emphasis on shared parenting after divorce suggest that individuals may actually grow up in several families simultaneously. At the same time, the number of single-parent households is also on the rise (see Chapter 9).

Changes in sex roles, including the influx of women into the labor force and professional sectors, the development of dual career families, and the greater emphasis on the democratization of domestic and occupational roles, also have profound implications for family dynamics. These facts, taken together, raise serious questions about a number of key Freudian concepts, such as the role of the Oedipus and Electra complexes in the development of both sex-role identity and deviations.

There is research suggesting that psychoanalysts place too much emphasis on psychological factors, such as the intake of nourishment (oral gratification), or the process of elimination (anal gratification), or sexual development, when explaining social (and antisocial) behavior (Clinard and Meier, 1979). Freud has also been criticized for too little attention to organic causes. For example, Freud's emphasis on fantasy, wish fulfillment, and unconscious motivation may have led him to misdiagnose organic problems as psychoanalytic problems (Elizabeth Thornton, 1984). Moreover, there are no data supporting the assertion that sexuality lies at the root of most mental conflict. Similarly, the relationship of criminal and delinquent acts to unfulfilled sexual desires has not been tested (Cohen, 1966).

Psychoanalysts, employing therapy such as dream analysis, transference, and free association, are depending on profoundly subjective treatment techniques. Psychoanalysts rely on their ability to impose meanings on their patients' behaviors in light of recalled childhood experiences. Even if analysts can interpret and diagnose behavioral difficulties, reliance on subjects' memories for accurate data is a highly questionable practice.

Of even greater concern, however, is the problem of deducing cause from prior experiences. Retroactive analysis runs the risk of selectively taking certain past experiences and arbitrarily linking them with certain other experiences for the purpose of creating an explanation of a particular behavior. It is alleged that this process somehow helps alleviate the problem. But besides relying on a faulty method of fact-finding, there is no evidence that the mere uncovering of certain details will be helpful. Glasser (1965: 63) noted: "Knowledge of cause has nothing to do with therapy." Indeed, the effectiveness of psychoanalytic therapy has not yet been proved scientifically. There is some evidence which suggests that the psychotherapeutic prognosis is very poor, especially for psychopaths (Charney, 1979).

Psychoanalysis has undergone many cycles of attack, and the attacks have not gone unnoticed. More radical adherents have countercharged with claims that conservative factions of the professional organization of psychiatrists (the APA), as well as conservative elements of society who take the social order for granted, stand in opposition because they are threatened by the critical insights of psychoanalysis. It is no coincidence that some of the most critical social thinkers in modern history have attempted to reconcile the Marxian and Freudian differences (see Marcuse, 1974; Kovel, 1981).[10]

This should come as no surprise, since psychoanalysis assumes that advanced civilization (including the forces of capitalism) is at the root of human suffering—see Freud's *Civilization and Its Discontents*, 1961, for example. The forces of civilization are believed to have transformed natural, unspecified inequalities and injustices into arbitrary social ones. The arbitrary distinctions among human beings are reinforced and confirmed by causing individual rebellion in the form of crime and mental illness, which are further used to justify inequitable treatment and subsequent control of these people by society. Thus, the radical psychoanalytic countercharges suggest that criticisms against psychoanalysis are largely political in nature.[11]

PERSONALITY TRAITS COMMONLY ASSOCIATED WITH CRIME AND DELINQUENCY

Studies too numerous to mention have attempted to identify specific traits of delinquency, and a wide variety of personality factors have been associated with delinquency.[12] For example, one of the most common factors in the psychological literature on delinquency is maturity level (see Conger and Miller, 1966; Hindelang, 1972; Baker and Spielberg, 1970; Sullivan, Grant, and Grant, 1957; Warren, 1976; Jesness, 1974). Porteous (1973) and Randolph (1973) have found that delinquents are less abstract in their ability to conceptualize. Delinquents have also been found to be deficient in ability to assume different roles, which suggests they are less able to be empathetic toward others (Kurtines and Hogan, 1972). Still other researchers have noted that delinquents are less future-oriented (Stein and Sarbin, 1968; Landau, 1975), less trusting (Austrin and Boenen, 1977), and more anxious and impulsive (Eysenck and Eysenck, 1971; Gough, 1971). A large body of both psychologists and sociologists conclude that delinquents are less attached to their families (see Sumpter, 1972; Hirschi, 1969). Many researchers have also found delinquents to be less compliant and less able to accept authority figures (Hindelang, 1972; Stein, Gough, and Sarbin, 1966).

Much of this research has focused on identifying the differences in the characteristics of offenders and nonoffenders. At one time or another, for instance, delinquents have been classified as retarded, overly aggressive, extroverted, rebellious, paranoid, hostile, and withdrawn. Particularly violent juvenile (and adult) offenders have been diagnosed as sociopaths or psychopaths, the most extreme type of disturbed personalities.

Seeking to identify delinquency-prone or particularly violence-prone individuals, psychologists as well as some psychiatrists and sociologists have tried to develop diagnostic instruments to select potential delinquents and criminals. Although there are indications of convergence among psychologists and sociologists in their lists of certain associative characteristics of delinquent personalities, there is still no agreement over the instruments or methods used to measure the traits (see McAuliffe and Handal, 1984).

Mental Deficiency and Delinquency

Hereditary degeneracy, including feeblemindedness, was once thought to limit the ability to understand and obey societal norms and thus to produce high involvement in crime. Offspring of mental degenerates were viewed as inheriting from their "criminogenic" parents both the physical and mental capabilities for committing crimes. Wrote Goddard (1921):

> There are two million people in the United States who because of their weak minds or their diseased minds are making our country a dangerous place to live. The two million is increasing both by heredity and by training. We are breeding defectives. We are making criminals. (p. iv)

At the heart of early hereditary studies was the belief that intellectual inferiority or low intelligence was a basic cause of crime. With the development of Alfred Binet and Theodore Simon's Scale of Intelligence in 1905, numerous studies conducted on prison inmates tested the hypothesized relationship between low intelligence, especially feeblemindedness, and crime. For example, Goddard in *Feeblemindedness: Its Causes and Consequences* (1914), found 89 percent of one inmate population to be feebleminded, but only 28 percent in another comparable institution. Using such data, Goddard arrived at a median estimate that 20 percent of all prisoners were feebleminded (Vold, 1979).

Intelligence testing during World War I showed that previous intelligence tests grossly underestimated the intelligence of law violators and over-

estimated the intelligence of the general population. During the 1920s and 1930s, there were more than 350 studies testing the intelligence of delinquents and criminals (Sutherland and Cressey, 1978). None of the early studies had control group comparisons or even a comparison to the average mental age of nonoffenders, making it very difficult to draw conclusions about the relationship between IQ and delinquency.

Travis Hirschi and Michael Hindelang (1977), who have reviewed more recent studies of the relationship between IQ and delinquency, found the evidence suggestive of an association between the two variables. They have concluded that on the average, an 8-point differential in IQ exists between the delinquents and nondelinquents who have been studied. They admit that while IQ is not as good a predictor as social class or race among official delinquents, it is more clearly established as a predictor among self-report delinquents. However, relatively few studies of IQ using self-report data are available; most of the studies in this area are based on official delinquents.

The evidence also suggests that where low intelligence does have an effect, it is usually indirect. For example, retardation may result in poor school performance, which has been found to affect delinquent behavior.[13] Moffit, Gabrielli, and Mednick (1980) found IQ to be of causal significance in delinquency, suggesting that low-IQ delinquents did not have a full appreciation of the consequences of their acts; they are also more vulnerable to falling under the control of brighter delinquents.

As a direct cause of delinquency, however, retardation is estimated to account for less than 1 percent of the cases (Caputo and Mendell, 1970; Kiester, 1974). Thus, as intelligence tests and methods of testing have improved, only negligible differences have been found between the average intelligence of delinquents and that of the general population. Today it is generally held that low intelligence is not a significant cause of crime and delinquency.

Personality Inventories of Delinquency

In an early study entitled *Unraveling Juvenile Delinquency* (1950), criminologists Sheldon and

Eleanor Glueck explored differences in the character and personality structure of delinquents and nondelinquents. Examining a sample of 500 juvenile offenders and 500 nonoffenders, the Gluecks claimed to find significant distinctions in the personality traits of the two groups. Basing their conclusions on the Rorschach test (analysis of a subject's responses to inkblots), the Gluecks argued that the delinquents were more defiant, extroverted, ambivalent about authority, fearful of failure, resentful, hostile, suspicious, and defensive than the nondelinquents. These results, however, have come under severe attack because the Rorschach test itself has been criticized for being statistically unreliable and invalid (see Hakeem, 1958b: 666).

Another psychological measuring instrument, the Minnesota Multiphasic Personality Inventory (MMPI), has also been employed in dozens of studies purporting to differentiate the personality characteristics of delinquents and nondelinquents. The MMPI is composed of several scales that refer to the more common syndromes or symptoms observed by clinicians. Each scale measures the similarity of the scores of tested individuals to the scores of persons clinically diagnosed as disordered in emotions or personality (see Caditz, 1959; Hathaway and McKinley, 1970; Hathaway and Monachesi, 1952, 1963; Jackson and Clark, 1958; Megargee and Bohn, 1979; Volkman, 1958–59; Widon, Katlin, Steward, and Fondacard, 1983).

However, these various studies using the MMPI have been criticized on methodological grounds. Hathaway and Monachesi, for instance, reported that MMPI scores in their study varied by age, place of residence, education, socioeconomic status, and many other key variables. Since these factors have traditionally been associated with delinquency, scores on various MMPI scales may not directly relate to delinquency; instead they may result from social factors that are associated with delinquency. Further, there is some question of the ability (or desire) of certain types of youths (for example, poor readers) to respond accurately to the 556 questions in the MMPI (Venezia, 1971).

Hindelang (1972) has criticized these studies of personality differences because they usually compare institutionalized and noninstitutionalized youth. Suggesting that the MMPI measures reflect the effects of institutional life, he questions whether personality tests of institutionalized youth before incarceration and those of noninstitutionalized youth would show similar differences. Rathus and Siegel (1980) explored the relationship of certain MMPI personality measures (for example, paranoia) and self-reported delinquency. They found that uncontrolled response sets (that is, exaggeration of aberrant behaviors or "faking bad") in the MMPI may produce false relationships between personality variables and delinquency.

After examining 94 studies, Waldo and Dinitz (1967) reported that in 81 percent there was a statistical difference between a criminal or delinquent group and matched controls. They caution, however, that their findings do not offer conclusive support for personality explanations of crime and delinquency. In particular, they criticize the studies included in their research for the following weaknesses:

1. Failure to control for other variables that might influence crime and delinquency

2. Failure to select random samples of delinquents and nondelinquents

3. Failure to define exactly what is measured by various personality tests

4. Failure to note that the differences *within* delinquent and nondelinquent populations are often greater than the differences *between* the two groups

5. Failure to specify whether criminal behavior is the result of a certain personality trait or whether the trait is the result of criminal experience (pp. 185–202)

More recently, Tennenbaum (1977) reviewed personality studies from 1966 to 1975 and presented results markedly similar to those of Waldo and Dinitz. He noted: "Personality tests, per se, are no better predictors of criminal personalities now than were those of ten years ago." "The data," he added, "do not reveal any significant differences between criminal and noncriminal psychology because most results are based on tautological [circular] argument" (p. 228). His reference here is to Waldo and Dinitz's fifth criticism of personality studies, the failure to distinguish between the causes and effects of personality traits.

Maturity and Ego Development of Delinquents

A significant portion of the psychological literature deals with the relationship between immature ego development and delinquency. The Interpersonal Maturity Level (I level) theory of ego development was introduced by Sullivan, Grant, and Grant in 1957 in an article in *Psychiatry*. I level theory, which is based on psychoanalytic principles, is one of the major applications of the psychoanalytic approach to delinquency. The theory is presented here in the psychological section because it has attracted the attention of numerous psychological investigators. I level theory underlies the famous California Community treatment program, which is the longest, most comprehensive study of delinquency personality factors in American correctional history (Palmer, 1974).

The I level theory of personality suggests that the development of social and interpersonal skills may be gauged in terms of seven progressive stages or levels along a continuum of maturity. Each level is associated with a distinct, relatively stable, and consistent set of interpersonal social skills and indicators of self-awareness. The continuum, which focuses primarily on the capacity to view interpersonal relationships in a complex and abstract manner, ranges from the least mature, represented by infancy (I_1), to an ideal or advanced level of maturity which is considered rare (I_7).[14]

In an Eriksonian fashion, the stages are defined in terms of a crucial interpersonal crisis or problem that must be resolved before movement forward is possible.[15] Not all individuals move successfully along the continuum. The hypothesis underlying the studies relating delinquency and I levels is that delinquents are less mature than nondelinquents.

These studies make the assumption that individuals are delinquent because they are immature. Moreover, since each level represents a distinct degree of social awareness and skills accompanied by a specific approach to interpersonal relationships, the levels are assumed to provide certain relevant indicators for treatment (Warren, 1983, 1976; Jesness, 1975; Palmer, 1967, 1971, 1972, 1974, 1978).

Much research has been done using the I levels and the I level subtypes. The most delinquency-prone subtypes include Cfc (cultural conformist), Mp (antisocial manipulator), and Na (neurotic acting out) (Harris, 1983). The causes or reasons behind each, however, are variable. The Cfc delinquent is conforming to the expectations of peer groups. The Mp delinquent is frustrated and trying to get back or get rid of those who are frustrating him or her. The Na delinquent is acting out as a result of internal conflicts. Warren and Hindelang (1979) have suggested that the I level model is actually a multiple-explanatory model that includes psychological as well as sociological explanations.

Psychopathy and Delinquency

Despite attempts by the American Psychiatric Association to standardize the meaning of the term **psychopath** or **sociopath**, it continues to have multiple meanings. Early researchers equated the term with a type of individual who was outwardly normal, but inwardly egocentric, insensitive to others, and prone to hostility. As many as 202 labels have been used to describe psychopathic behavioral symptoms. Two general approaches to the concept of psychopathy are currently used. In the first usage, psychopathy is viewed as a personality disorder that can be diagnosed and treated (Cleckley, 1955; McCords, 1956). A second usage of the term describes the phenomenon as "a hypothetical rather than an absolute condition. . . . Psychiatrists who support this position argue that one does not see real psychopaths, only individuals who are more or less psychopathic" (Halleck, 1967: 101). Thus, individuals who exhibit psychopathic traits fit the category as "a special type of person."

Whether or not psychopathic behavior can be diagnosed is perhaps one of the most controversial topics in modern psychiatry. Opinions about the meaning and validity of the psychopathic personality take almost every conceivable form. Some psychiatrists view psychopathy as a mental disease; others see it as only a personality disorder. Hakeem's (1958b) statement still seems to ring true in summing up the state of the art: "Psychiatrists are in disagreement on whether they are in agreement or in disagreement on the subject" (p. 669). In light of this confusion, it is impossible to conclude that psychopathy does or does not contribute to criminality.

Critique of the IQ and Personality Correlates of Delinquency

Two of the more serious weaknesses of the various studies of IQ and personality correlates of delinquency are the use of nonrandom samples of deviants and nondeviants and lack of consideration of other variables that may influence the relationship between various traits and delinquency.

Another particularly important criticism, originally voiced by Schuessler and Cressey (1950), centers on the causal sequence of personality variables and criminality. Thus far it has not been determined whether "criminal behavior is the result of a certain personality trait or whether the trait is the result of criminal experiences" (p. 483). There is no proof that personality predisposes an individual to engage in deviant activities. It may be, however, that involvement in illegal activities and subsequent official processing produce certain personality characteristics.

Moreover, the validity of personality inventories is questioned on several grounds: Do these inventories actually measure intellectual or personality components? For example, given the existing evidence, it appears unlikely that personality scales do measure personality traits or characteristics of individuals. Explains Vold (1979): "Few personality scales lend themselves well to interpretations in terms of a single numerical score to be taken by itself and independent of scores in related test areas . . . the nature of the performance

in some one area of the test usually affects and changes the significance of the score performance in another area" (p. 139). Clear-cut distinctions between delinquent and normal personalities tend, therefore, to be blurred by the problem of interrelatedness of scores in different areas of personality.

Hogan and Jones (1983), two psychologists who have considered the question of a criminal or delinquent personality type, conclude:

> Within the population of persons who have opted for a criminal identity, there is the same status hierarchy found in any human group: some will be better at it than others. Those who are good at it (high-status criminals) are indistinguishable from nondelinquents along many dimensions such as intelligence, self-confidence, and self-control. Incompetent criminals will differ from competent ones along these same dimensions; thus, low-status criminals will be less intelligent, anxious, and impulsive. (p. 13)

Assuming that those delinquents who have been caught are more likely to be incompetent and less intelligent and so would not be representative of the entire delinquent population, we are still left wondering: If we control for status (social class, intelligence, and so on), is there any substance to the idea that delinquents have personality traits different from those of nondelinquents?

LEARNING–REINFORCEMENT THEORIES OF CRIME AND DELINQUENCY

Learning theorists state that deviant behavior can be learned, just like any other response, through the principles of learning theory. According to this perspective, habits of violence are acquired largely through direct rewarding or modeling of destructive aggressive behavior (Ilfeld, 1970). Although learning theory proponents agree on the basic tenets of the theory, there is some disagreement over the importance of intrapsychic factors, such as the id, the superego, and defense mechanisms. Some learning theorists, probably in the minority, deemphasize the importance of environmental psychologies (Dunbar, 1977). Others, such as Bandura and Walters (1963), claim that an understanding of the learning principles of **conditioning, extinction, reinforcement,** and **modeling** adequately explains behavior.

It is argued that Freudian "translations are unnecessary and have served to further entrench psychoanalytic assumptions and concepts that have not been tested under controlled conditions" (Dunbar, 1977: 90). Learning theorists, rather than attributing delinquency to parental rejection, as many psychiatrists do, stress the role of specific training in determining behavior. The specific training delinquent youth receive includes rewards (or reinforcement) for engaging in delinquent behavior and/or exposure to delinquent role models.

Reinforcement of Behavior

Reinforcement principles have been applied in various ways to the study of delinquent behavior. For instance, researchers have found that parents of aggressive youth are more inclined to encourage and condone aggression in the home than the parents of nonagressive youth. The reinforcement of aggression toward siblings or other children at home can cause the child to be aggressive outside the home, at school and in the community. When aggression is rewarded rather than punished, chances for aggressive delinquency increase (Bandura and Walters, 1963).

The availability of conventional reinforcers also explains other types of delinquent behaviors. Adolescents raised in such culturally deprived areas of cities as slums or ghettos may be deprived of opportunities to learn socially acceptable values and behaviors, and they may substitute another set of values, conducive to deviant behavior. For example, youths who are constantly exposed to drugs, drug dealing, addicts, and pushers may be provided with a set of reinforcers overtly condoning

such activities. In short, "conditions are set for the emergence of a specifically drug-oriented **subculture** which is not only tolerant of drugs but also provides social reinforcers such as approval, recognition, and prestige for experimentation with drugs" (Akers, 1973: 81).

Obviously, all those living in slum areas do not become drug addicts, but there is greater potential for individuals who live in slum areas to develop values necessary for drug use and other illicit behaviors. Although attention generally focuses on the relationship of reinforcing values to delinquency in slum areas, it is equally likely that values favorable to more acceptable drug use, such as drinking, serve as reinforcers for drinking among middle class youth.

Modeling of Behavior

Reinforcement of behavior is one way individuals learn how to act. **Modeling** or imitation is another. Without actually receiving direct reinforcement, the individual can learn new behaviors through vicarious participation—for example, by watching other people engage in certain activities. The observation can be direct (watching others personally) or indirect (watching films and television). Learning theorists emphasize the importance of parental models in the child's learning of responses such as self-control. Children who witness parental aggression, even if they are not the direct object of that aggression, tend to be more aggressive themselves. Later, the adolescent's peer group provides role models for behavior. A child who sees a friend steal from the local five and dime and not get caught may later imitate the other child's behavior.

Since the late 1960s, a great deal of attention has been directed toward the effects of visual media, especially television, on behavior. Research shows that much of the programming on the major networks involves aggression and violent episodes. Evidence from hundreds of studies indicates that, at least in some instances, aggressive behaviors can be vicariously learned from viewing a violent scene or program (see Chapter 12).

Critique of Learning Theory

Although programs based on reinforcement theory appear promising, the theory has not escaped criticism. One of the more persistent criticisms concerns the dangers inherent when "behavior modifiers" apply behavioral contingencies in controlling and altering behavior (Shover, 1979). There is a legitimate question: Should certain individuals be able to manipulate others to bring about behavioral changes, even if it is for the "good" of society? This question remains unanswered, yet behavior modification programs have gained in popularity in both adult and juvenile institutions during the past few years, and their acceptance shows no signs of decline. Answering their critics, proponents of learning theory assert that these techniques work and should be used to alter nonconforming behavior. Some learning theory advocates, including B. F. Skinner (1971), go so far as to say that behavior should be controlled to the fullest extent for the good of society. They argue that since we are all controlled anyway, why not do it as efficiently as possible?

Obviously, we cannot solve these difficult issues in a brief discussion. It should suffice to say that serious ethical questions have been raised about the potential of learning theory to violate individual rights, and the solution to the problem is far in the future.

SUMMARY

The psychiatrist's role in the courtroom has resulted in a search for psychological indicators of crime, the separation of the criminal and the insane, and the development of alternative treatment models. The psychiatric approach to delinquency closely connects present behavior, especially delinquency, to early childhood experiences. Relationships between the child and his or her parents are thought to be particularly important in explaining later mental disturbance. When primary or secondary needs remain unfulfilled during infancy and childhood, feelings of mistrust and hostility, aggressiveness, and other forms of mental debilitation presumably develop during adolescent and adult years.

The psychoanalytic approach to delinquency holds that deviant behavior is largely the product of unconscious drives or instincts not directly perceived or understood by the individual. Behavioral disorders and maladjustments develop from conflicts related to these basic drives. Contemporary psychoanalytic thought, based to a large extent on original Freudian theory, emphasizes the individual unconscious, the inability to control drives, or inadequate ego-superego development. Criticisms of psychoanalytic interpretations of deviant behavior, however, are numerous. Psychoanalysts have been attacked for their reliance on case histories to document hypotheses and for their overemphasis on psychological and physical influences on behavior to the virtual exclusion of social effects.

The personality trait approach to delinquency focuses on personality and intellectual differences between offenders and nonoffenders. Delinquents, for instance, have at one time or another been classified as immature, overly aggressive, extroverted, rebellious, paranoid, hostile, and psychopathic. Overall, however, there is little evidence that deviants and nondeviants have distinct core personalities. Most personality studies suffer from methodological flaws, especially the failure to specify whether delinquent behavior is the result of a certain personality trait, or whether the trait is the result of the criminal experience. This criticism is particularly important, since the deviant samples in many studies are drawn from institutional populations, and the experience of institutionalization is known to alter inmates' behaviors and attitudes (for example, prisoners adopt the values of the inmate culture).

Within the personality trait approach, special attention has been given to the relationship of the psychopathic personality type to delinquency. There is, of course, a problem in the connection of psychopathy with delinquency, since psychopathy is generally an adult classification. Early signs of psychopathy and normal misbehavior and rebelliousness of adolescence are frequently difficult to distinguish. Despite the special clinical criteria used to distinguish psychopaths, the classification has been broadly applied even to juvenile cases. Psychopaths are generally described as socially aggressive, highly impulsive, and lacking feelings of guilt. Possessing neither clinical proof nor agreement about diagnosis, psychiatrists have nevertheless assumed a causal relationship between psychopathy and crime, with the implication that psychopathy and delinquency are also related. Generally little support has been found for the proposition that there is a distinct psychopathic personality type or that there is a relationship between the psychopathic personality and deviant behavior.

Lack of social awareness and interpersonal communication skills have been singled out as possible contributions to delinquency. Based on several degrees of social maturity, as measured by so-called I levels, some research has found a relationship between immaturity, such as lack of self-control, and juvenile delinquency.

The learning theory approach to delinquency postulates that such behavior is learned, just like any other type of behavior. According to learning theorists, youth can be reinforced by their parents to engage in aggressive behaviors, or they can acquire these behaviors vicariously from appropriate role models. Insights into the process of socialization are not only used to explain certain types of behavior (social or antisocial), but to modify or alter behavior. It is mainly the emphasis on modification that differentiates the learning theorist's and the psychiatrist's approach to socialization.

There are several psychological explanations of crime and delinquency. Proponents of the various perspectives, for the most part, disagree about the importance and definition of core concepts. With the possible exception of learning theory, much future work and clarification are needed before psychological approaches to the explanation of crime and delinquency are scientifically proved.

PROGRESS CHECK

1. Psychiatry is concerned with the study of various forms of _____; that is, disturbances of thinking, emotion, motivation, perception, learning, memory maturation, and behavior. (p. 104)

2. Discuss the different roles of psychiatry in criminology. Can you comment on some of the tensions or problems related to these roles? (p. 105)

3. Discuss the different classification systems used by psychiatrists. Consider the pros and cons of each strategy. (pp. 108–110)

4. Discuss the different rules of the insanity defense used in criminal cases. (pp. 105–106)

5. The psychiatric theory of delinquency ascribes most present behavior, especially delinquent, to (pp. 110–111):
   a. Early childhood experiences
   b. Late adolescent trauma
   c. Peer group influences
   d. Mental retardation

6. From among some of the psychiatric approaches, such as "blocked needs," "parental deprivation," and "faulty discipline," select the one you believe to make the most sense, then outline and defend your choice in terms of its relevance to delinquency. (pp. 110–111)

7. Psychoanalysts hold that behavior, including deviant behavior, is largely the product of certain drives or instincts that are mostly unconscious and not directly understood by the individual. (p. 111)
   a. True
   b. False

8. Outline and define the key personality components and developmental stages of Freud's psychoanalytic theory. (p. 112)

9. What are the major criticisms of the psychoanalytic approach? (pp. 113–115)

10. Summarize the strengths and weaknesses of learning-reinforcement explanations of crime and delinquency. (pp. 119–112)

NOTES

1. We thank Clinard (1974a: 196–224) for the taxonomy scheme used in this chapter.
2. The Durham rule is much broader in definition than M'Naghten. The Durham rule includes personality disorders, while the M'Naghten rule applies only to psychotics.
3. The emphasis in juvenile proceedings has undergone change. Serious offenders are again primarily punished, not treated; see Chapter 19.
4. Wenk, Robison, and Smith (1984), in a report entitled "Can Violence Be Predicted?", originally published in 1972, concluded: "The present state of the art holds little promise for the development of a prediction instrument that would warrant implementation in actual preventive or correctional programs" (p. 133).
5. There is some evidence that DSM-III has been more widely accepted by clinicians, and it is generally considered more reliable (Cantwell et al., 1979).
6. Garmezy (1978) has argued that this method is too inclusive, covering behaviors which should not require psychiatric attention.
7. For a review of the multivariate classification studies, see Quay (1979).
8. While not dealing with the explanation of crime and delinquency, Hollingshead and Redlich's (1958) study of the prevalence of mental illness in the general population suggests that many noncriminal individuals of all social classes experience symptoms related to neuroses. See also Gulevich and Bourne (1970).
9. See Maslow (1954) for a discussion of the hierarchy of basic physiological and psychosocial needs thought to influence personality development.
10. See Russell Jacoby's "The Repression of Psychoanalysis: The Lost Freudian Left" in *The Nation,* October 15, 1983, or Jacoby's book *The Repression of Psychoanalysis: Otto Fenichel and the Political Freudians* (New York: Basic Books, 1983).
11. Chapter 8 deals with a similar argument that has been developed by sociologists who have been referred to as radical criminologists.
12. For examples, see Baker and Spielberg (1970), Blackburn (1972), Conger and Miller (1966), Cowden and Monson (1969), Cross and Tracy (1970), Eysenck (1964), and Quay (1964).
13. See Chapter 10 for a discussion on the relationship between school performance and school attitudes and delinquency.
14. The model's emphasis on the capacity of abstraction is comparable to Kohlberg's (1969) approach to moral development.
15. Erik Erikson (1963) similarly describes the stages of life in terms of characteristic crises to be resolved.

CHAPTER **6**

CLASSICAL SOCIOLOGICAL THEORIES

ECOLOGICAL THEORIES

SOCIAL LEARNING THEORIES

ANOMIE THEORIES

SUBCULTURAL THEORIES

Fifteen-year-old Sammy whistled quietly to himself as he combed his hair in the mirror. Tonight was Friday night. Still whistling, he walked back into his bedroom and grabbed the jacket from the chair. It was a warm night, but Sammy decided to take his jacket anyway. The jacket made the gun less conspicuous. As he opened the door to leave, his mother yelled from the kitchen, "Where you going tonight, Sammy?" "Out with the guys. Nowheres special." "Be home early," warned his mother. "Yeah, yeah," came the usual response.

Sammy bounded down the two flights of stairs, pausing on the landing to hear Mr. and Mrs. Perez arguing again. "Hell, if he was any kind of a man, he'd thump her one and shut her mouth." As he raced down the last few stairs his eye caught some scrawling he'd written on the wall several months ago, "Sammy loves Joanna." "Might cruise on by and see Joanna tonight," he thought, though she was now Gary's girl. "Who knows, I might get lucky."

As Sammy stepped onto the porch, Morris and Ray were sitting there waiting. "Hey, cool, what's happening?" As they exchanged greetings, Sammy suggested what they should do. "Let's go down to the school yard. Suppose to be a big rumble tonight with the Dukes." Ray squirmed a bit. "I don't know, man. Dukes are mean!" Sammy just smiled and patted his jacket. "Not to worry, my man. We got some protection this time." "You got a piece?" exclaimed Morris. "Easy, man, not too loud. Course I do."

The three boys turned into the school yard and saw another group of friends sitting on the fire escape. "Hey, man, what's up?" "Hey, Sammy! Come on over. Want some beer, man?" While some of the girls danced to the blaring radio, the boys talked about the fight planned for the night. The boys agreed that the Dukes were tough, but they were reassured when Sammy showed them his gun. "Ain't going to be nobody pushing me and calling me a chump!"

Sammy looked around and spotted Joanna talking to some of the girls. Sammy sauntered over, talked with her a few minutes, and the two began to dance to the radio music. Sammy never saw the Dukes arrive. Suddenly, he felt a hand on his shoulder. "Hey, what you doing with my girl, little man Sam?" As Sammy wheeled around, he saw the voice belonged to Gary, one of the Dukes. "Get lost, man. Joanna's my honey tonight." As Sammy turned back toward Joanna to resume the dance, Gary slapped him lightly across the face. "Hey," yelled Sammy. "Who do you think you're touching?" As he scanned the school yard, Sammy realized that he and his friends were outnumbered. The odds were not good. "Hey, man," began Sammy, "you dance with her. It's cool." But Gary stepped up even closer. "That's my girl you're messing with, Sammy. Nobody plays with my woman." Sammy hesitated a moment and then backed up a step. "That's cool. She's all yours," conceded Sammy. But Gary had other ideas. "Sammy, I'm going to kick your tail so that you can remember that." Several of the girls giggled, and that made Sammy mad. "The hell you is," and with that Sammy punched Gary in the face. Gary jumped on Sammy, and two of Gary's friends grabbed at Sammy. Sammy reached for the gun he had tucked inside the jacket. "Get back, sucker, or I'll shoot." With that, Gary lunged at Sammy, grabbing at the gun. The next sound was a loud shot and Gary fell to this knees, clutching his stomach. Gary's hands were full of blood and his voice was raspy as he cursed Sammy and fell to the ground. Sammy backed away: "Everybody out of my way. Move!" As he raced away from the school yard, Sammy could hear Joanna wailing, "He's dead. Gary's dead!"

Although the view of delinquency presented by the story of Sammy seems outdated in the 1980s, during the first part of the twentieth century sociologists viewed delinquency as primarily the problem of youths like Sammy and Gary—that is, young, lower class males involved in inner city gangs. To the sociologists of this early, classical period of delinquency study, the story of Sammy and Gary was typical.

These early sociological theorists attempted to explain how the environment impinged upon individuals and produced a set of reactions. In this chapter, we will discuss some of the early twentieth-century sociological theories that attempted to explain delinquency through what we will call "classical theories." The theories presented in the chapter include the ecological, social learning, anomie, and subcultural theories. We will explain the basic ideas underlying each theoretical position, discuss some of the most important works written by sociologists, and provide a critique of each position.

At this point it is appropriate to return to Sammy's story. How do these theories explain Sammy's behavior? The ecologist would look at the neighborhood Sammy lived in to see what conditions prevailed. The ecologist would want to know whether the neighborhood was an urban slum area and whether it was socially disorganized. The social learning theorist would look at Sammy's companions and at his past behavior. The anomie theorist would be interested in Sammy's educational experiences, whether Sammy could get ahead in the world, and the presence of adult role models in his life. The subculturalist would pay attention to the fact that Sammy lived in a violent world, one in which an individual needed some type of personal, physical protection. In short, each theoretical perspective would focus on a slightly different aspect of Sammy's social life in an attempt to explain his delinquency.

ECOLOGICAL THEORIES

One important classical approach to the study of delinquency is the ecological approach, which has its roots in the field of human ecology. **Human ecology** is the study of how human beings adapt to their surrounding environments. Although all populations adapt in order to survive, not all adapt in the same way. Some, for example, may become industrialized; others may maintain a nonindustrial economic base. As a result, human ecologists are interested in two major questions. First, how does a society adapt itself to its environmental conditions? Second, what are the consequences of a society's adaptation to environmental conditions (Gibbs and Martin, 1959; Hawley, 1950)?

In order to answer the question of how societies have adapted, human ecologists have focused on the development of the community. Prior to the twentieth century, most of the world's people lived in very small communities, or what sociologists call Gemeinschaft societies (Toennies, 1957). A **Gemeinschaft society** is built around **primary relationships**, in which all parties know each other well and interact on a friendly, personal basis in everyday life. A community based on primary relationships is a small, close-knit society. Since all members know one another and treat one another in a friendly manner, there is no need for an elaborate set of formal social control devices such as laws. Informal social control techniques, such as gossip and ostracism, are effective. These informal techniques allow the members of a society to exert sufficient pressure to alert the deviant to his or her misbehavior. The threat of severing primary relationships in a Gemeinschaft society is usually enough to ensure conformity.

The hallmark of modern twentieth-century society, however, is the **Gesellschaft community**, which operates through **secondary relationships**, in which people interact on the basis of social roles rather than personal relationships. In other words, people in such a society know only their family and close friends; they do not know other members of the community very well. Family life and business life are separate. Since everyday living and social relationships are fragmented and primary relationships are not extensive, the informal social controls of gossip and ostracism have very little impact on the individual. Gesellschaft societies therefore resort to law as a formal social control technique.

Sociologists who study human ecology have concentrated on explaining why the transition from a Gemeinschaft to a Gesellschaft type of society occurred. Emile Durkheim, one of the founders of sociology, examined this transition in his 1893 book, *The Division of Labor in Society.* Durkheim isolated three important variables in the development of societies: population size,

population density, and the division of labor. In statements that would prove of great importance to American classicists, he argued that as societies became more populated and denser, there was a greater need for occupational specialization. Residents were no longer capable, for example, of growing all their own food, making all their own tools, and sewing all their own clothes. Workers began to specialize. One group provided agricultural products, and other groups supplied machinery and clothes. Each group exchanged its particular commodities for items other people had produced. This specialization, or **division of labor**, increased to the point where virtually every member was dependent on other people for basic goods. Such exchange and consumption fostered further specialization, with the net result that all members became interdependent in their bid for survival. Durkheim was very much aware that the transition from a Gemeinschaft to a Gesellschaft society carried several negative consequences, including relatively higher suicide and crime rates (1897, 1904).

Durkheim's ideas did not enjoy wide circulation in the United States until Louis Wirth, in a 1938 essay "Urbanism as a Way of Life," introduced American sociologists to Durkheim's ideas. Wirth, following Durkheim's general theory, argued that as cities became larger, denser, and more diversified, primary relationships gave way to secondary relationships. Instead of having warm and cordial personal relationships, people remained strangers. A direct result of this transition from a Gemeinschaft to a Gesellschaft society was that people were thrown into a state of **anomie**, meaning that people felt lost, abandoned, and unanchored, and in response began to display signs of nonconformity and lawlessness. As a result, Wirth expected urbanization to be accompanied by a rash of social problems that have come to be described as **social disorganization**. Thus cities undergoing the change from a Gemeinschaft to a Gesellschaft society would exhibit a variety of negative effects, such as higher divorce and suicide rates, increased incidence of mental illness, higher death rates, and higher delinquency rates.

In testing the Durkheim-Wirth hypothesis with regard to delinquency, sociologists noted that although growing urban areas had higher delinquency rates, these rates were distributed unevenly. Some urban neighborhoods had very high delinquency rates, and other neighborhoods had very low rates.

Taking their cue from Durkheim and Wirth, these sociologists attempted to explain the differential distribution of delinquency rates in terms of variations in the urban environment. They tried to determine whether specific urban characteristics were related to juvenile delinquency rates. If the Durkheim-Wirth perspective was correct, then such characteristics as substandard housing, poverty, migration, unemployment, overcrowded housing, and minority status should explain why delinquency rates were higher in some neighborhoods. This approach to understanding delinquency came to be known as the ecological approach.

The Chicago School: Founders of American Ecology

Much of the early ecological research on urban development was conducted by sociologists at the University of Chicago during the 1920s and 1930s. These sociologists knew there had been a transition from a Gemeinschaft to a Gesellschaft society. They also knew that the transition in urban areas did not simply happen overnight. Consequently, they asked a question that sounded very simple: How does a city grow?

Ernest W. Burgess: Urban Zones. Ernest W. Burgess studied various areas of Chicago and in 1925 developed what is known as the concentric zone theory of urban development (Park, Burgess, and McKenzie, 1925). The **concentric zone model** portrays the city as a series of rings or circles. The innermost circle, the nucleus, is zone I; it contains the main downtown area, where businesses and government buildings are located. Zone II is a transitional area of older houses that are being taken over by stores, factories, rooming houses, and tenant buildings. This zone contains typical ghetto areas. Zone III holds housing, usually

multiple-family structures, for people who work in zone II. Zone IV is also a residential area, except that it contains more expensive housing owned or occupied by middle class people. Beyond, in zone V, are the suburbs and commuter areas.

Not all cities follow the concentric zone model, and several other models exist that account for different patterns of urban growth. (The two other traditional models are the sector and the multiple nuclei models.) But the concentric zone model was particularly important in sociology because subsequent researchers borrowed it to analyze juvenile delinquency rates in Chicago (Harris and Ullman, 1945).

Clifford R. Shaw and Henry D. McKay: Delinquency in Chicago. Clifford R. Shaw and Henry D. McKay took the Burgess concentric zone model of Chicago and used it to analyze Chicago juvenile delinquency rates. After plotting juvenile delinquency rates for each zone on a city map, Shaw and McKay discovered several statistical regularities. In their book *Juvenile Delinquency and Urban Areas* (1942), they published their findings, some of which follow:

1. Delinquency rates varied throughout the city.

2. Delinquency rates were inversely related to distance from the center of town.

3. Zones with high delinquency rates tended to have high adult crime.

4. Zones with high delinquency rates generally maintained these rates over time.

5. High delinquency rates tended to occur in zones that were deteriorated and had declining populations.

6. **Recidivism** (offender rearrest) rates were inversely related to distance from the center of town.

The fact that zones closest to the center of town had the highest delinquency and recidivism rates, that delinquency and recidivism rates decreased as one moved away from the center of town to the suburbs, and that high delinquency zones also had high adult crime rates led Shaw and McKay to conclude that the root problem of delinquency was social disorganization. In other words, delinquency was highest in zones that had a great deal of substandard housing, a high concentration of nonwhite and immigrant populations, very few owner-occupied housing units, and in general, poor economic and social status. People in these zones were experiencing poor living conditions, and the outcome was a relatively higher rate of juvenile delinquency.

Delinquency in American Cities

Although researchers at the University of Chicago pioneered the way in the ecological approach to delinquency, the Chicago studies left other sociologists pondering two questions. First, was the theoretical perspective of the ecological Chicago school correct? Second, were delinquency rates similarly distributed in other American cities? Among those who attempted to answer these questions were Bernard Lander (1954), David Bordua (1958), and Roland J. Chilton (1964).

Bernard Lander: Delinquency in Baltimore. Lander conducted a study of Baltimore juvenile delinquency rates and published these results in 1954. Like other sociologists, Lander questioned Shaw and McKay's use of zones; he himself, in tracking his data, used smaller geographical areas called census tracts. A **census tract** is composed of several city blocks, and used as a unit by the federal government when it conducts a census of the population every ten years and gathers information concerning population characteristics, economic status, and living conditions. Lander's choice of census tracts as the unit of analysis made it possible for him to use detailed information compiled by the Bureau of the Census.

When analyzing the relationship between percentage of black population in a census tract and juvenile delinquency rates, Lander found an unanticipated result. Researchers over the years had

come to expect a simple positive correlation between percentage of black population and delinquency rates. In other words, *positive correlation* here meant that as the percentage of black population increased, delinquency rates increased, and as the percentage of black population decreased, delinquency rates also decreased. The delinquency rate of an area varied directly with the relative size of the black population. Lander, however, found some slightly different results. Delinquency rates increased in census tracts until the black population increased to 50 percent. Then, as the black population increased over 50 percent, census tract delinquency rates decreased. Thus, what Lander observed was a **curvilinear relationship**: an increase in delinquency rates up to a certain point, and then a decrease after that point. Lander concluded that delinquency rates would be higher in racially heterogeneous census tracts, but would decrease if the census tract was racially homogeneous.

Lander was also one of the earliest researchers to apply a statistical technique known as factor analysis to the ecology of delinquency. **Factor analysis** identifies clusters of variables that cling together in census tracts. Lander's analysis uncovered two prominent clusters of variables. The first contained a grouping of economic variables, and the second contained a grouping of anomie variables. Lander concluded that census tract delinquency rates increased as anomie increased and that delinquency rates increased with economic deterioration. Both conclusions supported the Durkheim-Wirth hypothesis that urbanization carries adverse social consequences.

David Bordua: Delinquency in Detroit, a Replication. Because Lander's stastistical techniques and findings were unique, there was some question about their **replicability**; that is, whether the same results would appear again if the study were repeated. David Bordua (1958) took up this issue of whether Lander's results were peculiar to Baltimore or whether the same results would be found in another location by examining 1940 census tract delinquency rates in Detroit.

Bordua combed the data quite carefully to see

if there was a curvilinear relationship between percentage of nonwhite population and census tract delinquency rates. Despite several procedures, Bordua could not replicate Lander's finding that, until they reached the 50 percent mark, as the percentage of nonwhite population increased, delinquency rates increased.

Like Lander, Bordua also conducted a factor analysis of the data. Three clusters of variables emerged, as opposed to Lander's two. The first isolated census tracts characterized by a high concentration of black population living in overcrowded and substandard housing. Quite clearly, this factor described slum or ghetto areas. The second, a socioeconomic cluster, contained census tracts that had a high educational level, more expensive housing, and higher income. As Shaw and McKay would have predicted, delinquency was not positively related to this factor. The final one, an anomie cluster, described census tracts with very little home ownership, a lot of substandard housing units, many unrelated persons living together, and very low income levels.

Although the results from the Detroit replication study were not exactly the same as what Lander found, Bordua reached the same conclusion. Anomie and economic deterioration figured prominently in the ecological distribution of Detroit census tract delinquency rates.

Roland J. Chilton: A Reanalysis and Replication. Although Bordua felt that his results matched Lander's theoretical conclusions, Roland J. Chilton (1964) was more concerned with the divergences between the two studies. Chilton chose a new strategy for analysis. He reexamined Lander's Baltimore data, Bordua's Detroit data, and added his own new data from Indianapolis. In order to ensure replicability, Chilton used exactly the same variables Lander and Bordua had used.

Chilton found that all the variables, with the exception of percentage nonwhite population, behaved similarly in all three cities. This minority population variable did exhibit a curvilinear relationship with Baltimore census tract delinquency rates, as reported by Lander. However, a similar curvilinear relationship was not present in the

Detroit or the Indianapolis data. Although there were important parallels in the three cities, Chilton did find some minor differences. For example, Chilton discovered that Lander made a mistake in his analysis, somehow assigning positive signs to numbers that should have had negative signs and negatve signs to numbers that should have had positive signs. Correcting for these sign reversals produced a similar result in all three cities. Anomie was an important predictor of census tract delinquency rates in all three cities.

Critique of Ecological Theories

Ecologically oriented sociologists have spent considerable time and energy trying to explain the differential distribution of urban delinquency rates. Although the studies presented in this section of the chapter are not the only ones conducted in the ecology of delinquency, they are representative of some of the problems in the field.[1] In general, the ecological approach has suffered from theoretical and methodological shortcomings (Hirschi and Selvin, 1967; Wilks, 1967; Bursik, 1984).

By far the most serious criticism of the ecological approach to the study of delinquency is that the field is theoretically stagnant and myopic. The dominant theme in this field is that urbanization, particularly the transition from a Gemeinschaft to a Gesellschaft society, results in the disintegration of primary relationships and the substitution of secondary relationships. However, several urban researchers have questioned the validity of this argument. Herbert Gans (1967), for example, studied the community development of Levittown, New York, and found many primary relationships. William Whyte, in his *Street Corner Society* (1943), discovered a flourishing network of primary relationships among inner city residents. Thus there is some evidence to suggest that the traditional Durkheim-Wirth depiction of urbanization as producing a deterioration in primary relationships is questionable.

Another serious problem that has hindered sound theoretical development in the ecology of delinquency concerns the error of **tautology**, or circular reasoning. Researchers generally make a distinction between two types of variables: dependent and independent. A **dependent variable** is the effect that one is trying to explain. Delinquency rate is an example of a dependent variable. **Independent variables** are the causes of the effect of the dependent variable. Some of the independent variables mentioned throughout this section include percentage nonwhite population, substandard housing, and poor education. The tautological problem appears when a researcher fails to keep the independent variables segregated from the dependent variables; mixed together, they can be meaningless or misleading. Typically, the researcher places the dependent variable with several independent variables when using factor analysis to identify clumps or clusters of variables. Then the researcher takes the clump or cluster containing the dependent variable and correlates that clump or cluster with the dependent variable. In such a procedure, the researcher is using delinquency rates simultaneously as both independent and dependent variables. This procedure is logically impossible, because something cannot be its own cause and effect at the same time.

Methodological problems have also hindered ecological research into delinquency. The advent of the computer, for example, has brought mixed blessings. The computer allows the researcher to conduct extremely complex mathematical analyses in the span of just a few seconds. However, some researchers use what is called the **shotgun approach**. Instead of logically deriving the variables from a theoretical perspective, the researcher simply collects as many variables as possible and lets the computer pick out the most important. Then the researcher attempts to make sense of the results by applying convenient theoretical concepts. Such a process reverses the logic of inquiry and can result in a potpourri of findings. Several researchers have criticized the exclusive use of factor analysis in ecological studies of crime and delinquency (Jackson and Borgotta, 1981). Berry and Kasarda (1977) argue that reliance on factor analysis "has given ecological studies an undeserved reputation as basically methodological exercises concerned with the analysis of spatial correlations and distributions" (Bursik, 1984: 393).

Another methodological deficiency occurs when the researcher misapplies a statistical technique. Many current statistical techniques are limited to linear relationships. If two variables do not share a linear relationship, then the researcher will underestimate the actual degree of relationship. In other words, a really strong relationship between an independent variable and delinquency rates can exist, but the researcher can mistakenly believe that the linear relationship is weak. This belief will distort the findings and can lead the researcher to a false conclusion and an erroneous theoretical statement (Beasley and Antunes, 1974; Doerner and Meade, 1978).

One other serious criticism of ecological studies involves the charge that various community dimensions often associated with delinquency variation are arrived at without regard for a particular historical setting or the urban dynamics at play within a community. For example, Bursik (1984) examines delinquency rates in Chicago communities for a thirty-year period. While he finds a basic pattern for 1940, 1960, and 1970, the 1950 data are very different. He reports, for instance, that one relatively stable community in the city showed a dramatic increase in delinquency rates during the 1950s. He attributes this to changes in black residential patterns, which began to infringe on this particular ethnic community (composed of Hungarians and Poles) during the 1950s. As a possible response to the threat, increased rates of delinquency occurred—often a common reaction in communities undergoing rapid social change (Berry and Kasarda, 1977). Failing to take this historical change in residential patterns into account would have resulted in a misinterpretation of the delinquency patterns in this community (Bursik and Webb, 1982).

SOCIAL LEARNING THEORIES

Another important approach to the study of delinquency is social learning theory. Several learning theories were presented in the previous chapter. The psychological brand of learning theories tends to convey the impression that the learner is isolated from other people during the learning experience. Instead of viewing learning as taking place within a social vacuum, the sociological approach emphasizes the social dynamics and interactions that occur during the learning process. For the sociologist, learning is a social process that takes place within a social environment. Among the major theorists who have made contributions in this area are Edwin Sutherland (1939) and Robert L. Burgess and Ronald L. Akers (1968).

Edwin Sutherland: Differential Association

Sutherland's theory of differential association was introduced in 1939. Differential association theory is the sociological successor to some of the earlier psychological theories and the behaviorist tradition. Sutherland's basic premise was that delinquency, like any other form of behavior, is the product of social interaction.

Nine formal theoretical propositions, when taken together, constitute **differential association theory:**

1. Criminal behavior is learned.

2. Criminal behavior is learned in interaction with other persons in a process of communication.

3. The principal part of the learning of criminal behavior occurs within an intimate personal group.

4. When criminal behavior is learned, the learning includes (a) techniques of committing the crime, which are sometimes very complicated, sometimes very simple; (b) the specification of motives, drives, rationalizations, and attitudes.

5. The specific direction of motives and drives is learned from definitions of the legal code as favorable or unfavorable.

6. A person becomes delinquent because of an excess of definitions favorable to violation of law over definitions unfavorable to violation of law.

7. Differential associations may vary in frequency, duration, priority, and intensity.

8. The process of learning criminal behavior by association with criminal and anticriminal patterns involves all of the mechanisms that are involved in any other learning.

9. While criminal behavior is an expression of general needs and values, it is not explained by those general needs and values since noncriminal behavior is an expression of the same needs and values. (Sutherland and Cressey, 1978: 80–82)

Sutherland stressed the importance of the belief that an individual would learn to become delinquent or criminal. In other words, delinquency was not an inherent trait. According to Sutherland, delinquency, like anything else, involved socialization. A person must be taught how to commit a delinquent act, either directly or vicariously. And mere possession of the techniques does not ensure participation. The individual must acquire the necessary attitudes, motives, and rationalizations conducive to the violation of legal norms. However, their acquisition depends on the degree to which a person is immersed in the differential associations. Sutherland recognized that differential associations varied in terms of frequency (number of contacts), duration (length of contact), priority (time and precedence of contact), and intensity (involvement in the contact). Thus, mere exposure to a criminal element is not a sufficient cause of delinquency. All these components taken together determine whether the individual develops definitions favorable or unfavorable to law violations.

Robert L. Burgess and Ronald L. Akers: Differential Reinforcement

Robert L. Burgess and Ronald L. Akers presented a reformulation of differential association in 1968. They contended that Sutherland's rendition of differential association needed elaboration and refinement. These two researchers proposed **operant conditioning** as a more appropriate mechanism for understanding how a juvenile learns delinquent behavior.

Burgess and Akers maintained that some criminal behavior can be learned in nonsocial settings as long as the learner is reinforced. However, much of the learning takes place in the group that provides the greatest amount of reinforcement. Through reinforcement, this group directs the learner to specific techniques, attitudes, and motives. Criminal behavior will become part of the individual's repertoire only if that individual has received ample positive reinforcement.

Critique of Social Learning Theories

Sutherland's idea of differential association did not pass by without criticism. A major criticism has been that the theory is virtually impossible to test empirically.[2] Short (1960), for example, suggested that the concept of "definitions favorable to violation of law over definitions unfavorable to violation of law" is elusive. Short contended that Sutherland simply failed to provide an adequate research definition. Another sociologist, C. Ray Jeffery (1959), observed that differential association theory failed to address the issue of why certain acts are regarded as delinquent. Furthermore, Jeffery contended that the theory ignored crimes of passion and negligence, bypassed any consideration of the "good boy in the bad environment," failed to consider motivation and differential responses, and also overlooked differential exposure to criminal associations.

Donald R. Cressey (1952, 1954), once a student of Sutherland, provided answers to a number of critical questions, but four general criticisms still remain. First, both the Sutherland and the Burgess and Akers theories viewed the individual learner as a passive recipient. Both theories portrayed the individual as a *tabula rasa*, reacting to a bombardment of external forces. The individual learner does not choose between behavioral alternatives;

nor can the individual learner reject the material being presented. Second, both theories overlooked the fact that delinquency can be reinforcing in and of itself. As Jeffery pointed out, delinquency can produce money, property, and the removal of aversive stimuli in the case of personal offenses. Third, both theories neglected the role of punishment in the acquisition and suppression of delinquent behavior. Finally, the two theories have ignored the question of how certain behaviors came to be defined as desirable or pursuable.

ANOMIE THEORIES

Anomie theories of delinquency, like ecological and social learning theories, are another important classical approach to the study of delinquency. They owe their intellectual heritage to the French sociologist Emile Durkheim. Durkheim wrote several seminal pieces during the late nineteenth century, when Western society was undergoing a tremendous transition from a Gemeinschaft to a Gesellschaft society. This transition was accompanied by an increase in anomie, or normlessness. Durkheim maintained that rapid social change promoted anomie. One result was that individuals lost their bond to conventional morality. The societal flux that led to a loosening of conventional bonds also caused an increase in deviant behavior. Thus, Durkheim perceived rapid social change as inducing aberrant behavior.

Because Durkhiem's work was published in French, sociologists in other countries remained for years unaware of his writings. One American sociologist, Robert K. Merton, had studied Durkheim's materials and recognized the applicability of several of his concepts to American society. After several years of study, Merton wrote an article connecting anomie and deviance in the United States. Merton's work, in turn, generated other American theoretical endeavors that elaborated on the genesis of delinquent behavior. In this section of the chapter, we present a discussion of Merton's ideas and then review the work of several other theorists who expanded upon his formulations.

Robert K. Merton: Social Structure and Anomie

Robert K. Merton published in 1938 an article called "Social Structure and Anomie." In it, he linked Durkheim's ideas to deviance in American society. Merton remained loyal to Durkheim's analysis by arguing that deviance results from forces external to the individual. Durkheim had argued that rapid social change in a society induces anomie; Merton elaborated on these concepts and arguments. He contended that people acquired higher aspirations when society progressed. However, the mere desire for bigger and better things is not the same as their actual achievement. Although society may present achievement as desirable to all members of the society, not all members can partake in the rewards. Some people are going to be thwarted by their inability to satisfy these aspirations and will become disillusioned. According to Merton, this disillusion promotes frustration and anxiety and eventually leads to norm violations or deviance.

Cultural Means and Cultural Goals. Merton took Durkheim's concept of anomie and tied it directly to the American way of life. According to his analysis, two major components in American society are responsible for the creation of a strain toward deviance. These are cultural goals and cultural means. A **cultural goal** is that which is held out to all members of society as a legitimate objective for which they should strive. The major cultural goal of contemporary American society is success, particularly in the form of money, since money is the most visible sign of success. Although the acquisition of money is a dominant concern, society also identifies the appropriate **cultural means** or ways to achieve success. One of the more acceptable cultural means to achieve success in the United States is education. The more education a person acquires, the better that person's chances of making money and being successful in life.

American society defines the acceptable cultural goal and the acceptable method for attaining it.

When people receive rewards in direct proportion to the energies they expend, society is at equilibrium; it is also said to be in harmony. Disequilibrium exists when the cultural means and goals are not in sync. When a large group of a society's members do not enjoy equitable returns or are systematically denied access to cultural means or goals, society encounters strain. In this situation, not all members of society enjoy the same opportunity or chance of achieving success. When the cultural means and goals are not completely accessible or are not in direct proportion to each other, *disjunction* exists. According to Merton, if a disjunction is apparent between cultural means and cultural goals, strain appears and, in turn, causes deviance. This is what Merton meant when he claimed that the social structure is responsible for the genesis of deviance.

Cultural Axioms. According to Merton, strain occurs because of the imbalance between cultural means and cultural goals. American society promotes the cultural goal of success by instilling three **cultural axioms** (beliefs) into all its members:

1. Everyone must strive for success, since success is equally available to all persons.

2. Failure is just a temporary detour to ultimate success.

3. The real failure is the person who reduces or withdraws his or her ambition for success.

Adherence to these axioms is important. Society inculcates its members with these axioms for at least three reasons. First, these axioms deflect criticism from the social structure and place the blame for failure on the individual. Second, they help maintain the status quo. Third, these axioms create pressures for conformity by defining failure to attain success as being un-American. As a result, the blame for failure is on the individual, and society is able to continue functioning without jeopardizing the entire social structure.

TABLE 6.1 Merton's Typology of Individual Adaptation to Anomie

Mode of Adaptation	Cultural Goal	Cultural Means
Conformity	+	+
Innovation	+	−
Ritualism	−	+
Retreatism	−	−
Rebellion	±	±

A plus sign (+) indicates acceptance; a minus sign (−) indicates rejection; a combined plus and minus sign (±) indicates rejection of existing value and substitution of new value.
Source: Adapted from Merton (1938, p. 676).

Modes of Adaptation.   Given the impact and force these cultural axioms carry, how do people react to an obstacle between cultural means and cultural goals? As Table 6.1 demonstrates, Merton suggested five potential reactions in everyday living: conformity, innovation, ritualism, retreatism, and rebellion.

Conformity is the most common adaptation. It means that people simply accept the cultural goal and pursue legitimate cultural means. This mode of adaptation ensures the smooth continuation of the existing social order. For example, a juvenile who decides not to drop out of high school so that he or she will have a diploma when searching for a job is a conformist.

Innovation is another adaptation. Innovators are those who accept the cultural goal but embrace nonstandard means for attaining it. This adaptation is a direct response to the heavy incentive for goal attainment and restricted access to legitimate means. An innovator is a person who has internalized the goal of acquiring wealth but does so in an unconventional way. The school-age juvenile who extorts lunch money from other students in return for not assaulting them would be a maladaptive example of the innovative thinker. Another example would be the juvenile who burglarizes residences and then fences the goods. In both examples, the juvenile concentrates on acquiring money, but does so in an illegitimate fashion.

Ritualism is an adaptation that involves abandonment of the cultural goal of success, but strict adherence to the cultural means. A person choosing ritualism, for example, stresses compliance with the rules of the game and becomes absorbed in playing the game. A good example of a ritualist would be the child who stresses observance of a game's rules, whatever the win-lose chances.

The fourth adaptation, **retreatism**, involves the rejection of both cultural means and goals. Although retreatists may be physically present in society, they are not true members of it. Some examples of this adaptation would be drug addicts, alcoholics, or youth who join religious cults that force them to leave "this world"—for example, the Guyana settlement led by the Reverend Jim Jones.

Rebellion is the final mode of adaptation. This adjustment entails the rejection of both means and goals. A person choosing this adaptation seeks to destroy the existing social structure and to substitute a new order. Quite clearly, people who fall into this category threaten the status quo, and the structure finds it necessary to keep them in check. Subversive and politically destructive groups would fall under this heading.

Albert Cohen: Reaction to a Middle Class Educational System

Albert Cohen was another anomie theorist. He attempted to explain juvenile delinquency by focusing on the educational system in his book *Delinquent Boys* (1955). Cohen's starting point was the fact that delinquency appeared to be concentrated among lower class males. Like Merton, Cohen recognized that denial of educational opportunities, the most acceptable means for attaining success, created frustration. Cohen contended that lower class juveniles felt that they could not compete with others in a school system geared toward middle class ideals.

According to Cohen, lower class parents did not socialize their children according to the middle class value system, especially with respect to ambition, responsibility, delayed gratification, and self-control. As a result, lower class children had great difficulty achieving success in an educational system dominated by middle class values. Teachers in particular sought out the so-called better-adjusted middle class children to work with and shunned the lower class youth. Lower class juveniles felt rejected and inferior.

These feelings inspired what Cohen called a **reaction formation**: Lower class youth, feeling unjustly deprived of attention in the educational system, formed groups with other rejected lower class youth in order to give meaning to their lives. The resulting subculture could serve as the resolution to rejection by the middle class educational system and offer its members social support and reinforcement.

This subculture, according to Cohen, did not represent a perfect solution; it represented a withdrawal from the middle class educational system and a complete rejection of middle class standards. As a result of the frustration and hatred experienced by these youth, the subculture assumed a negativistic, nonutilitarian, hedonistic, and malicious tone. Emphasis was on immediate gratification, destruction of property, rowdiness, and violent outbursts. The subculture became a vehicle for acting out frustrations stemming from rejection by representatives of the educational system. For Cohen, then, the lower class delinquent subculture represented a somewhat imperfect collective solution to the problem of thwarted aspirations.

Cohen's theoretical elaboration gained early acceptance among some sociologists because he located the cause of delinquency within the social structure. However, in 1959 John I. Kitsuse and David C. Dietrick published an article containing a detailed critique of the logic behind Cohen's work. Kitsuse and Dietrick criticized Cohen on three major points.

First, they contended that Cohen did not formulate a theory of delinquency—nor did he intend to. Instead, Kitsuse and Dietrick claimed that Cohen was attempting to account for the content and the distribution of the delinquent subculture as a response to a hostile environment. In other words, Cohen wanted to explain what values, attitudes, and beliefs delinquents acquired; how they acquired them; and what benefits accrued to the delinquents after their acquisition. Sociologists who invoked Cohen's framework as a theo-

retical explanation were mostly to blame for this misrepresentation of his work. However, Kitsuse and Dietrick admonished Cohen for allowing this erroneous interpretation to occur. They contended Cohen was so imprecise in his writing that even the most careful reader could not help but construe his material as a theory of delinquency instead of a theory of delinquent subculture formation.

Second, Kitsuse and Dietrick accused Cohen of a social class bias. Cohen argued that lower class boys aspired to middle class conventions but received setbacks from an educational system run by middle class teachers and administrators. Consequently, lower class boys reacted by forming negativistic, hedonistic, nonutilitarian, and destructive subcultures. Kitsuse and Dietrick pointed out several inconsistencies in Cohen's model. For example, Cohen assumed that lower class boys aspired to middle class norms, but he failed to produce any documentation that supported this assumption. In addition, Cohen failed to consider the case of the lower class boy who is not oriented toward the middle class philosophy of achievement. In Cohen's theory, such a juvenile did not exist. Furthermore, Cohen characterized lower class delinquents as being negativistic, malicious, and destructive. By doing so, Cohen implied that similar behavior, such as vandalism, never entered the repertoire of middle class youth. Yet middle class children do engage in vandalism and other destructive and malicious behavior.

Third, Kitsuse and Dietrick argued that Cohen's theory was largely untestable. It was a historical explanation for the shape and genesis of this lower class subculture. Members of this subculture did not have to be ambivalent about middle class conventions. They only had to have been ambivalent about middle class conventions prior to entrance into the subculture. Accurate testing of Cohen's theory, charged Kitsuse and Dietrick, required examination of psychological data from the delinquent's past. Cohen observed delinquent involvement and then assumed the existence of a reaction-formation process. A much better approach would have been to observe the reaction-formation process and then monitor the juveniles to see whether they chose delinquency as the best solution.

Richard Cloward and Lloyd E. Ohlin: Differential Opportunity

Merton maintained that anomie resulted from the gap between the cultural goal and the availability of access to legitimate means. Richard Cloward and Lloyd E. Ohlin had no quarrel with that formulation. However, Cloward and Ohlin did make two theoretical additions to Merton's perspective in their book *Delinquency and Opportunity* (1960).

First, they questioned Merton's assumption that blocked access to the legitimate means automatically created access to illegitimate means. Cloward and Ohlin argued instead that there was a differential access to the illegitimate opportunity structure. To be more concise, there was a differential opportunity structure. Just because a juvenile rejects or is denied access to the legitimate means does not mean the juvenile will become delinquent. For that to happen, the juvenile needs an opportunity to learn how to become delinquent.

Second, Cloward and Ohlin argued that access to illegitimate opportunities was determined through subcultural membership. In other words, the subculture promotes an atmosphere conducive to the learning of delinquent behavior. Thus, lack of access to cultural means by itself does not ensure delinquent participation.

According to Cloward and Ohlin's analysis, there were three distinct subcultures. They called them the conflict subculture, the criminal subculture, and the retreatist subculture.

The conflict subculture, Cloward and Ohlin's first type, is characterized by the use of violence and destructive assaults. Members of this subculture stress the value of a "tough" reputation and being "macho," exhibiting masculinity through violent victimization. This particular subcultural variant tends to develop in areas where there are no adult models who can channel juveniles into legitimate or illegitimate careers. In one sense, the conflict subculture is self-defeating. Adults will not settle in this area because of the emphasis upon violence, which subsequently attracts police attention. Thus, the emphasis on violence deters both legitimate and illegitimate role models from entering this neighborhood.

The criminal subculture, Cloward and Ohlin said, depends heavily on adult models for successful development. This pattern basically describes an apprenticeship system. Adults in this subculture teach juveniles the importance of criminal behavior as a mechanism for achieving success. The emphasis is on the transmission of skills necessary to acquire property illegally. Juveniles learn how to pick locks, what to steal, where to fence goods, and how to avoid detection. Should the juveniles in the criminal subculture become involved in violence or in the conflict subculture, the adults will simply vacate the area for fear of detection and apprehension. The emphasis of the criminal subculture is on learning nonviolent illegal opportunities to acquire property.

The third type, the retreatist subculture, represents a "lost" group. Members of this group focus intensely on pleasure, usually through drugs and alcohol. For the most part, retreatists reject violence and instead place a premium on hustling and conning people. This group, then, lives by its wits and street sense.

Critique of Anomie Theories

Proponents of the anomie perspective, Merton in particular, have been met with objections from several corners. First, Merton failed to recognize the cultural diversity within American society and assumed that all groups strive for the same goal. Second, Merton never answered the question of why people resort to one particular mode of adaptation over other available types. Third, Merton's typology was incomplete. For example, the case of the overconformer, the person who subscribes overzealously to the cultural means and cultural goals, received no consideration. Furthermore, the typology can be expanded by considering the context of a group's norms as they relate to cultural means and goals (Dubin, 1959).

Fourth, Merton's theory, as well as the versions offered by Cohen and later by Cloward and Ohlin, applies only to American society. The perspective is not able to account for delinquency in other countries (see McDonough, 1983). Finally, any application of the anomie perspective carries the assumption that juveniles have internalized the cultural goal of achievement and have experienced or are experiencing strain. The problem here is that of an appropriate time order. Anomie theorists contend that delinquency is the product of strain between cultural goals and cultural means. Thus goal discrepancy must occur prior to delinquency involvement.

At least one researcher, John C. Quicker (1974), suggested that delinquency may cause strain instead of strain causing delinquency. Quicker examined the effect of occupational goal discrepancy and educational goal discrepancy on both official and unofficial delinquency of 1,338 California high school boys. The results showed that occupational goal discrepancy was not related to delinquency involvement. However, those high school boys who experienced educational goal discrepancy were more likely to engage in delinquent behavior. Thus, it would appear that the anomie perspective is in need of greater empirical clarification before it can emerge as a sound and viable explanation for delinquency (see Bernard, 1984).

Another recent critique of anomie theory suggests that most youth are able to achieve some of their important goals. This in itself may be enough to prevent strain and strain-produced delinquency. Thus, the adolescent who does not do well in school may compensate by being a good athlete or having an active social life (Agnew, 1984b: 336). Agnew indicates that the low strain may be traced to the nature of the adolescent's environment. For example, Coleman (1961) argues that the isolation of adolescents from adult society has resulted in adolescents' developing a wide range of immediate goals (see Agnew, 1984b). The attainment of some of these goals makes strain unlikely.

One other problem with anomie theory is that is has been typically applied to male delinquency. Cohen, for example, saw his formulations as explaining the lower class male reaction to a middle class educational system. Cloward and Ohlin introduced the theoretical concept of differential access to the illegitimate opportunity structure as a viable explanation for lower class male delinquency. However, there is no compelling reason to assume that female juveniles are immune from strain. Freda Adler (1975), for instance, maintained that recent changes in the American sex-role structure have freed females from traditional cultural restraints. Although it is now more acceptable for females to seek access to legitimate means and goals, not every avenue is open to female participation. Thus, it would not be unreasonable to hypothesize that females who are denied access to the legitimate means and goals experience anomie or strain and may engage in delinquency in order to reduce that strain (see Cernkovich and Giordano, 1978; Simons et al., 1980).

SUBCULTURAL THEORIES

Subcultural theories of delinquency, along with ecological, social learning, and anomie theories, are another important classical approach to understanding delinquency. Subcultural theorists perceive delinquency to be simultaneously a reaction to the larger cultural value system and an adherence to group norms. Subculturalists maintain that delinquency is an expression of standards espoused by one's reference group—in this case, other members of the subculture. For the subculturalists, delinquency constitutes behavior consistent with a set of norms. Among the major proponents of subcultural theories have been Walter Miller, Marvin E. Wolfgang, and Franco Ferracuti.

Walter Miller: Focal Concerns

In 1958 Walter Miller published a paper titled "Lower-Class Culture as a Generating Milieu of Gang Delinquency." In this article Miller attributed delinquency to the lower class environment. Miller derived his theoretical ideas from a community research project involving an on-the-street study of delinquent gangs over a three-year period.

On the basis of his study, Miller suggested that the lower class possesses its own distinctive subcultural system, which is responsible for delinquency. The system differs from the larger society in terms of **focal concerns**, or value orientations. According to Miller, six major focal concerns characterize the lower class: trouble, toughness, smartness, excitement, fate, and autonomy.

Trouble, according to Miller's analysis, is a major point of concern among the lower class, especially when it involves intervention by law enforcement personnel or social agency workers. From the lower class male perspective, trouble often entails getting into fights, drinking, and the sexual conquest of women. The culture is most clearly distinguished from the middle class in the way it deals with trouble as a result of law-abiding or law-breaking behavior. In contrast to middle class people, who evaluate others in terms of achievement or success, lower class people regard getting into trouble as prestigious or normative.

The focal concern of *toughness* contains several elements, the least of which are physical strength, masculinity, and bravery. The ideal model of toughness would be the steely, cool character who never shows emotion and is hardened to the needs of others. Miller contended that the preoccupation with being tough stems from the domination of females in this class. Many households are headed by women in the absence of a male. According to Miller, this preoccupation with toughness or "being a man" represents an attempt to affirm a personal masculine identity.

Smartness as a focal concern of lower class culture does not refer to schooling or to intelligence; instead, it refers to cunning—outfoxing and outwitting others through mental agility. This trait is necessary for survival in a world permeated by gambling, hustling, prostitution, and the fast shuffle. This orientation creates two groups of persons: those who exploit and those who are exploited. Being the exploiter rather than the exploited is a desired status in lower class culture.

Excitement, or achieving a thrill, is a prized quest in the otherwise dull, repetitive world of the lower class culture. The thrill may consist of a night on the town, getting drunk, gambling, fighting, and finding women. Often all these elements are combined into a single adventurous evening. The activities all involve a certain degree of danger and represent escape from an otherwise tedious routine.

Fate, particularly being lucky, is highly related to the preceding focal concerns. Life is pretty much against the lower class person. Success depends on getting the right breaks or being in the right place at the appropriate time. Excitement, especially in terms of gambling or scoring with a woman, depends on how lucky one is. Thus, things just happen, as opposed to being planned in advance or part of a rational scheme.

Autonomy as a focal concern in lower class culture means being one's own man or being in control. There is almost an inherent tension in the area of dependence-independence. Although lower class males are quick to demonstrate that they will not take any guff, they also, Miller believed, exhibit a desire for external control. Thus, many members of the lower class will be overtly hostile to authority, but still search for dependency. An example of this phenomenon would be joining the Marines, a highly controlled environment, in order to become a tough and arrogant man at the same time.

According to Miller, these focal concerns propel lower class male youths to become obsessed with belonging to a group and with establishing a "rep" (reputation). One achieves both belongingness and a rep by acting in accordance with the focal concerns. These concerns, when placed within the context of group membership, promote delinquency as a behavioral alternative to status attainment. Delinquency, then, allows status achievement within one's reference group.

There are at least four general criticisms of Miller's theory. First, although Miller's orientation may adequately explain group involvement in delinquency, it neglects the lone delinquent acting by himself. Second, since he studied males, Miller's theory does not appear to explain female delinquency. Third, Miller's theory fails to shed any light on the issue of types of delinquency. In other words, Miller cannot account for why some delinquent groups resort to violence and why others choose to engage in property crimes. Fourth, it is difficult, with today's mass communication and transportation, to envision the lower class as forming a separate, distinct, and isolated subculture.

Marvin E. Wolfgang and Franco Ferracuti: Subculture of Violence

Two other subcultural theorists were Marvin E. Wolfgang and Franco Ferracuti. In their book *The Subculture of Violence* (1967), they attempted to account for the relatively higher incidence of violence among young, lower class, black males, both as offenders and as victims.

Wolfgang and Ferracuti argued that these black males possess a value system that deviates from that of the larger society in its emphasis upon violence as an acceptable form of behavior. Some of these youth may believe it is necessary to carry a knife for protection. Others (like Sammy at the beginning of the chapter) may believe that assaultive behavior is a proper and normal response to verbal insults. Wolfgang and Ferracuti contended that membership in this subculture produces higher rates of violence among young, black, lower class males.

Critique of Subcultural Theories

The major problem subcultural perspectives share is the question of subcultural identification. Although some theorists devote attention to the genesis of particular subcultures and to their distinguishing characteristics, scant attention has been paid to defining what constitutes a subculture. The result is that one would be hard-pressed to recognize a subculture, perhaps with the exception of a pronounced pattern like that of the Amish, as a distinct phenomenon.

The first criticism of subcultural theories is that they are tautological, or circular in argument. For example, although Wolfgang and Ferracuti point to elements such as machismo as responsible for subculture formation, they fail to document the existence of this subculture. Wolfgang and Ferracuti began with the observation that persistently higher violent crime rates appear among a certain population segment. During the search for a theoretical construct to explain this differential distribution, Wolfgang and Ferracuti invented the term *subculture of violence*. By definition, a subculture of violence manifests itself in relatively higher rates of interpersonal violence. Since young, black, lower class males exhibit a relatively higher violent crime rate, they must belong to this subculture. Consequently, a higher violent crime rate indicates the presence of a subculture of violence, which Wolfgang and Ferracuti claimed gives rise to greater violence.

A second criticism of subcultural theories is whether, as subculturalists assume, behavioral variations do in fact indicate the presence of a subculture. Wolfgang and Ferracuti, for example, argued that because blacks have a higher involvement in violence, they must possess a subculture of violence that accounts for this trait. Similarly, Gastil (1971) contended that since the southern portion of the United States is persistently high in homicide rates, the South must have a regional culture of violence. These three criminologists, however, do not present evidence that a subculture of violence exists among young black urban males or among southerners.

A third criticism of subcultural theories involves value differentiation—that is, how to distinguish supposed subcultural values from other values. A subculture may share many commonalities with the parent culture. Yet by definition a subculture has a certain set of divergences that do make it different from the parent culture. The question is one of identification criteria. How many values must be different from the parent culture before there is a subculture? Five? Seven? Sixteen? Twenty-three? Furthermore, some values are more important than others, and some are not significant or should be weighted less than other values. Subculturalists have been silent on these issues.

A fourth criticism of subcultural theories concerns the question of socialization. Subcultures are assumed by theorists to persist over lengthy periods of time. But in order for a subculture to persist, values must be transmitted from old to new members. Several questions then require attention. First, how are members recruited? Second, what sustains the subculture? Third, why does the subculture persist? Finally, which values, if any, change over time? Subculturalists have not yet dealt with these questions.

A fifth criticism of subcultural theories involves nonmember violators. It is entirely possible that people who are not members of the subculture violate the same norms as members of the subculture. In other words, subculture members are not the only violators. Although subculture members may be the most chronic and persistent violators, the subculturalist theorist needs to differentiate the same violations committed by subculture members and by nonmembers.

Subculturalists have contended that adherence to a different value system is responsible for delinquency. But several important issues remain unanswered. And without answers to these issues, the subcultural explanation remains questionable.

SUMMARY

The theories presented in this chapter, representing early sociological attempts to explain crime and delinquency, included ecological, social learning, anomie, and subcultural theories.

The ecological perspective came from the field of human ecology, the study of the relationship between humans and the environment. Scholars at the University of Chicago were particularly interested in assessing the impact of urbanization on delinquency. Borrowing Burgess's concentric zone model of urban development, Shaw and McKay found delinquency in Chicago to be concentrated in the inner city, decreasing as one moved toward the suburbs. Delinquency thus appeared related to poor economic and lower social status conditions.

Since there was some question whether Shaw and McKay's findings could be generalized, a series of studies were done in other American cities. Bernard Lander improved on the Shaw and McKay study by analyzing Baltimore census tract characteristics. The Lander study was important for two reasons. First, Lander found a curvilinear relationship between the percentage of nonwhite population and delinquency rates. Delinquency rates increased as racial heterogeneity increased and decreased as racial homogeneity increased. Second, Lander concluded that delinquency rates were

a function of anomie and of economic deterioration. David Bordua conducted a similar analysis of Detroit delinquency rates. Although there were some differences between the two studies, Bordua affirmed Lander's conclusion. Roland J. Chilton reexamined the Baltimore and Detroit data, adding some new data from Indianapolis. His study substantiated the earlier conclusions.

Although researchers have conducted a number of ecological analyses, the field is not immune from criticism. Some critics contend that the field is theoretically stagnant. For example, ecologists believed that the transition from a Gemeinschaft to a Gesellschaft society spelled the end of primary relationships. Herbert Gans and William Whyte showed that primary relationships persisted and flourished in urban areas. In addition to theoretical problems, the ecological perspective also suffers from logical and methodological problems, including tautological reasoning, the shotgun approach, and misapplication of statistical techniques.

The second theoretical family was social learning theories of delinquency. One of the most famous criminological theories, Edwin Sutherland's differential association theory, belongs to this group. Sutherland maintained that delinquency, like all other forms of behavior, was learned through social interaction. In other words, delinquency resulted when a juvenile learned more definitions favorable to violation of laws than unfavorable to violation of laws. However, Sutherland's theory was largely untestable. To lessen this deficiency, Burgess and Akers recast Sutherland's theoretical propositions in line with the principles of operant conditioning, contending that the greatest factor involved in delinquent behavior acquisition was the strength of reinforcement. Sociologists had some criticisms even with this new version of social learning. For example, the theory assumed a passive learner who could not selectively receive reinforcement. Much work remains to be done in this theoretical area.

The third theoretical family discussed in this chapter is that of anomie theories. *Anomie* is a term developed by the French sociologist Emile Durkheim. Robert K. Merton borrowed Durkheim's concept and related it to the American social structure. Merton argued that delinquency resulted from the disjunction between cultural means and cultural goals, but in fact this disjunction does not automatically produce delinquency. Instead, Merton suggests five possible modes of adaptation—conformity, innovation, ritualism, retreatism, and rebellion.

Merton's work stimulated Albert Cohen to advance a slightly different explanation of delinquency. Cohen felt delinquency stemmed from a reaction formation. Lower class youth realized that they could not compete in a middle class educational system. As a result, they became embittered toward the school system and formed their own subculture, which emphasized violence and destruction as means of protest. Cohen's formulation drew criticism from John I. Kitsuse and David C. Dietrick, sociologists who contended that Cohen did not offer a theory of delinquency, but simply a description of the subcultural response of lower class children. Cohen also viewed delinquency as a lower class phenomenon, ignoring the middle class youth engaged in similar activity. Finally, Kitsuse and Dietrick charged that Cohen's theory had not been tested adequately.

Merton's work stimulated another theoretical development: Richard Cloward's and Lloyd E. Ohlin's argument that anomie did not always result in delinquency. The missing ingredient in Merton's theory, according to Cloward and Ohlin, was differential opportunity. In other words, not all youth enjoy equal access to delinquent opportunities. To demonstrate their point, Cloward and Ohlin discussed the conflict, the criminal, and the retreatist subcultures. Their material emphasized that some youth are blocked in their bid to learn delinquency by their immediate social environment.

The fourth theoretical family discussed in this chapter was that of the subcultural theories. Walter Miller argued that lower class culture had a set of focal concerns that propelled youth toward delinquent activity. Miller felt that the lower class emphasis on trouble, toughness, smartness, excitement, fate, and autonomy promoted illegal activity. This value orientation, then, was presumed to be responsible for lower class involvement in delinquency.

Another subcultural theory, the "subculture of

violence" idea, was promoted by Marvin E. Wolfgang and Franco Ferracuti. These sociologists argued that young, lower class black males possessed a distinguishable subculture that emphasized the use of violence. This emphasis became apparent in relatively higher rates of violence, especially lethal violence, among this population segment. But the subcultural perspective is also open to criticism. In addition to the tautological logic—violence serving as an indicator of the presence of a subculture of violence—there are also questions concerning subculture identification, value differentiation, socialization, and similar violations by nonmembers.

PROGRESS CHECK

1. Differentiate between a *Gemeinschaft* and a *Gesellschaft* society, showing the relevance of these to the field of human ecology and delinquency. (pp. 126–127)

2. Which of the following contradicts the 1942 Chicago findings of Clifford Shaw and Henry D. McKay? (p. 127)
   a. Delinquency rates varied throughout the city.
   b. Delinquency rates were inversely related to distance from the center of town.
   c. Zones with high delinquency rates tended to have low adult crime rates.
   d. Zones with high delinquency rates generally maintained these high rates over time.

3. In his 1954 Baltimore study, Bernard Lander observed an increase in delinquency rates up to a certain point and then after that point, a decrease; in other words, Lander found a _____. (p. 128)

4. After outlining Edwin Sutherland's differential association theory, cite at least three general criticisms the text authors assert still remain. (pp. 131–132)

5. Robert Merton remained loyal to Emile Durkheim's psychological analysis by arguing that deviance results primarily from forces internal to the individual. (pp. 133–134)
   a. True
   b. False

6. Present Robert Merton's formulation of social structure and anomie, incorporating his crucial features: (pp. 133–134)
   a. Cultural means and goals
   b. Cultural axioms
   c. Modes of adaptation

7. Extending the ideas of Robert Merton, _____ attempted to explain juvenile delinquency by focusing on the educational system in the book *Delinquent Boys* (1955), which examined behavior among lower class males. (p. 134)
   a. David Bordua
   b. Albert Cohen
   c. Robert Burgess and Ronald Akers
   d. John Kitsuse and David Dietrick

8. Describe three distinctive subcultures identified by Richard Cloward and Lloyd Ohlin. (p. 136)

9. This chapter provides critiques of four major theories of delinquency:
   a. Ecological
   b. Social learning
   c. Anomie
   d. Subcultural
   Select the theory you consider to be strongest and defend it against its major criticism.

10. *Matching:* Match these persons to the concepts with which their names are most appropriately associated. Use each entry only once.

    ___ 1. Ernerst Burgess   a. concentric zone model

    ___ 2. Robert Burgess and Ronald Akers   b. focal concerns

    ___ 3. Albert Cohen   c. operant conditioning

    ___ 4. Walter Miller   d. reaction formation

    ___ 5. Marvin Wolfgang and Franco Ferracuti   e. subculture of violence

NOTES

1. For instance, see Voss and Petersen (1971) for a collection of works on the ecology of crime and delinquency.
2. Matsuda (1982) operationalizes one of the most critical variables in Sutherland's theory—the ratio of learned behavior variables favorable and unfavorable to the violation of legal codes. He finds support for differential association over social control theory.

CHAPTER 7

CONTEMPORARY SOCIOLOGICAL THEORIES

SOCIAL CONTROL THEORIES

LABELING THEORIES

PHENOMENOLOGICAL THEORIES

As he turned over in bed and noticed dawn peeking through the window, Michael groaned and knew the first pangs of dread. "Damn," he thought. "School today." His mind drew vivid pictures of Mrs. Princeton, the homeroom teacher—her angry face, her violent words. Would she shout today, "Michael, shut up, sit down, sign the roll, give me your excuse, straighten up in your chair, stop talking"? Would she send him to Mr. Brown's office to wait for more warnings, orders, and punishments? "Oh, Lord," he sighed. "Why do they always pick on me? I'm sick, sick, sick of school. Who needs English history? Who cares about algebra? Shakespeare—why can't he write something a normal person can understand?"

With these thoughts whirling in his head, his dread became more focused. "Report cards today. More Fs. Mama crying. Pop shouting." In his sleepy daze, he could hear his father's words: "Michael, I break my back to give you what I can. I work two jobs—for you. And what do you do? You flunk school. I'm dead tired, and I have to go to the police station every couple of weeks because you do some damn fool mischief. You threaten Mrs. Princeton. You steal from Mr. Razor's store. You're good for nothing. You'll never amount to anything."

Michael's father's face was lined with worry, overwork, and anger; and Michael had vowed that he would not kill himself working, unlike his father and his father before him. You wouldn't catch him driving a bus days and guarding apartments at night. Michael knew what he would do: "I'm gonna quit that lousy school and get me a job and make lots of money. Nobody can push me around then and tell me I'm no good—I'll show them."

Then he heard his mama's voice, "Michael, you get up now. Breakfast is almost ready." "Who cares?" he thought. "Maybe I'll just skip school today, meet the guys. Oh yeah, Dave had an idea about stealing some car parts from Tony's garage. We'll do that. Then, we can buy some joints, get high, and forget about report cards. Yeah, I'm gonna have a good time today. Let Mrs. Princeton yell at her fat self. Let Mr. Brown shake his fist at his own bald head. What's one more day missed when you're on the way to the world's record for skipping school?"

And so began a day in the life of Michael. Michael fits the average citizen's description of a delinquent. He disobeys his parents. He fails in school and disrupts his classes. His police record is extensive.

Why is Michael a delinquent? What is it about his personality, his background, or his environment that seems to be leading him down the path of crime? Classical sociological theorists would look for the answer in the neighborhood he came from, the friends he keeps, the bleakness of his expectations for the future. Contemporary sociologists and criminologists, however, might look for the answer in the degree of Michael's attachment to those who are or should be important to him or in the reaction of his parents or the school to his initial misbehavior.

In this chapter we examine contemporary explanations for delinquency. We will discuss three contemporary social theories: social control, labeling, and phenomenological theories. We will discuss major premises, major proponents, relevance to delinquency, and major criticisms of each.

SOCIAL CONTROL THEORIES

According to social control theorists, delinquent acts result basically from the weakening, breakdown, or absence of effective social controls. This perspective is so all-inclusive some theorists have argued that sociology has only a single theory of delinquent behavior. At least one delinquency theorist, for instance, has classified the classical theories of social disorganization and subcultural delinquency as types of social control theories (Weis, 1977).[1] Relying on a more common classification scheme, we will discuss works most sociologists consider representative of the control theory of juvenile delinquency.

Each of these authors' works, to some extent, owes its origins to the work of a French sociologist, Emile Durkheim. Durkheim's theory of suicide was first published in France in 1897. His chief concern

was to use the study of suicide to prove that sociological explanations of human behavior made sociology an independent science. Durkheim wished to show that one cannot explain variation in group rates in suicide—or any social problem—by analyzing individual motivation (psychology) or inspecting chromosomes and genes (biology).

Variations in suicide rates, according to Durkheim, could be explained by the social integration of the group. Durkheim suggested that the higher suicide rate among European Protestants, as compared with European Catholics, was due to less solidarity among Protestants. He called this **egoistic suicide**. High rates of suicide among the divorced, as compared with married persons, was the result of the **anomic** situation of being cut off from the social control of marriage and family. Durkheim felt a third type, **altruistic suicide**, occurred when the individual was tightly bound to the norms of a culture that regarded suicide as an honorable death in certain circumstances—for example, the Japanese. Anomic and egoistic suicides were conceptually similar, since they referred to disengagement from a social bond.

Durkheim argued that to the extent that a society is integrated—that is, to the extent that its members feel morally bound to each other, are committed to common societal goals, and share a "collective conscience" (culture)—deviant behavior will be controlled. It was his belief that society exerts social control over the individual through custom, tradition, laws, and religious codes. When members of a society accepted and internalized these guidelines for behavior, conformity would exist. Durkheim thus explained suicide through the bonding of the individual to the norms of society; some criminologists have similarly developed theories of juvenile delinquency from this model. The basic premise of social control theories of delinquency is that juveniles who accept societal goals and feel a moral tie to others will engage in less delinquency than those who are not committed to social goals and not attached to important others.

Control theorists drawing on Durkheim's early works ask, "If human beings by nature do *not* desire to conform, why, then, do they?" Rather than puzzling over why people are bad, they wonder, "Why is anyone good?" This approach assumes, as did many of the eighteenth-century philosophers, that the human mind is originally a *tabula rasa*, a clean slate. The mind of an infant is like a blackboard ready to be written on. In this system, humans are born neutral; they become moral or criminal through the socialization process. Delinquents are children who have not developed bonds to the society that spawned them. Unattached to society's norms, they are free to engage in a variety of deviant activities, including delinquency.

Put simply, control theorists say that delinquency occurs because it is not prevented (Nye, 1958). The prevention of delinquency rests on adequate social controls. These controls are of two types: personal, or inward; and societal, or external. For example, a youth may refrain from stealing an item from a store because what the child considers conscience forbids the breaking of laws (inner control). Lacking this personal commitment to law, a youth may have a healthy respect for the police authority that may be employed if he or she is caught (external control). Several sociologists, including Travis Hirschi, Albert Reiss, Ivan Nye, and Walter Reckless, have discussed the concept of social controls and their relationship to delinquency.

Albert Reiss: Personal and Social Controls

Albert Reiss, an early control theorist, used this approach to define delinquency, in an article written in 1951, as:

> the behavior consequent to the failure of personal and social controls to produce behavior in conformity with the norms of the social system to which legal penalties are attached. (p. 169)

Since socialization is the function of a child's primary group relationships—that is, a child's early intimate and close attachments—delinquency is seen as the failure of these groups to exercise social controls or to provide nondelinquent roles with

which the child may identify. Reiss found that delinquents on probation were more likely to fail to complete the terms of their probation in the following circumstances:

1. They came from a home supported by welfare.

2. The parents were divorced, or one parent was deceased.

3. There was an open breach or gross incompatibility with the natural parents.

4. Unfavorable moral ideas had been institutionalized. (pp. 197–200)

In Reiss's study, the family obviously played an important role in keeping youngsters from becoming further entangled with the juvenile justice system. For the family to be a source of social control, however, the child must identify with the parents and noncriminal roles, and the family is not, of course, the only source of social roles.

Peer groups, also called reference groups, may exert a controlling influence on adolescents when the groups engage in either legitimate or illegitimate activities. An adolescent who is a member of such a group, or one who aspires to membership, may base personal behavior on the norms of the group. A boy aspiring to be a member of the local Scout chapter is likely to engage in behaviors congruent with the philosophy of that organization—for example, doing good deeds. Deviant peer groups, on the other hand, do not ordinarily encourage conformity to dominant social norms and may actually serve to weaken existing inner controls on behaviors.[2]

Walter Reckless: Containment Theory

Walter Reckless (1961b, 1973) has attempted to account for delinquency as a character disorder on one hand and as a social pursuit or a way of life on the other. Reckless's approach represents a sociopsychological synthesis. According to Reckless, not everyone is susceptible to the "pull" of certain delinquent and criminal activities because some individuals are contained or restrained from these behaviors through various **outer** and **inner** **containments.**

Outer containments consist of social controls or constraints on individuals' behaviors that encourage conformity to group or community norms. Sanctions against aberrant behavior work as sources of social control, and restraints are those social pressures which encourage obedience to the norms of one's group. Through normal socialization within the family, youth learn the norms, goals, and expectations of the community and develop a sense of identity and belonging. They also learn what Reckless calls appropriate "safety valves" for legitimately working off their frustrations (1973: 56). Family or social disorganization, however, may prevent external controls from keeping individuals in check. Juvenile delinquency may be a consequence.

Inner containments are self-controls that develop in the socialization process. In Reckless's theory, inner control is a result of moral training. Five components of inner control indicate a high degree of self-control:

1. *A good self-concept.* Basically, the poorer the self-concept, the greater the probability that a youth will get into trouble with the law.

2. *Goal directedness.* Youth who have long-range legitimate goals are thought to be insulated against criminal activity.

3. *Realistic objectives.* Choosing realistic goals that can be fulfilled through normal channels is a deterrent to deviance. Unrealistic goals that cannot be met may cause a collapse of inner containment.

4. *Tolerance of frustration.* Being able to cope is an indicator of self-control. Juvenile offenders exhibit less tolerance for frustration than nonoffenders.

5. *Identification with lawfulness.* Attitudes or beliefs in support of law and its agents are another important indicator of self-control. (Nettler, 1978: 309–312)

It is these qualities that control the external and internal sources of delinquency. If a child is to refrain from delinquent acts, he or she must resist external pressures, including the lure of the values of a deviant subculture, and internally suppress urges to hostility and aggression. A child who has a positive self-concept, aspires realistically to a profession, and can handle the normal frustrations of life is protected against drift toward a life of delinquency and crime. Conversely, the child who does not have a positive self-concept, who has either no goals in life or unrealistic ones that guarantee disappointment, and who cannot handle frustrations is a prime candidate for being pushed or pulled into delinquent or criminal behaviors.

Another question addressed by Reckless and his colleagues concerns youth raised in "delinquency-prone" or "bad" neighborhoods. How do we explain conformity in the midst of pulls to nonconformity? Reckless and two colleagues studied sixth-grade white boys in a high delinquency area, asking this question: What insulates a young teenage boy against delinquency? They identified 125 boys who had good conduct records. In response to self-evaluation items on a questionnaire, the boys portrayed themselves as law-abiding and obedient. These positive self-images (a form of inner containment) did not develop in a vacuum, but within stable family backgrounds. A "good" child is therefore presumptive evidence of a good family background. The parents of these boys, without exception, knew the boys with whom their sons associated, and knew their whereabouts at almost all times. Further, the families were stable maritally, economically, and residentially (Reckless, Dinitz, and Murray, 1956).[3]

David Matza and Gresham Sykes: Delinquency and Drift

Control theories typically view delinquent behavior as the result of a complete break between the child and the conventional moral order. One exception is found in the position of Gresham

Sykes and David Matza. Sykes and Matza have viewed delinquency as "episodic," since delinquent acts occur at times when the child feels released from the moral constraints of the law.

David Matza's book *Delinquency and Drift* (1964) and Sykes and Matza's earlier article (1957) argue that delinquency cannot be explained simply as an absence of controls, that something else must provide a "will to delinquency." This will to delinquency grows out of the feelings of desperation that haunt lower class urban males. These boys attempt to solve the problems of despondent feelings by denying that they are passive victims of social processes through the positive activity of delinquency (Weis, 1977).

Although delinquency may occur on any of a number of occasions, the times it actually happens are comparatively few. During most of the delinquent's life, he is constrained by social convention. According to Matza, when a boy commits a delinquent act, he is not expressing a commitment to a delinquent subculture or a Freudian compulsion (a "devil in the mind"); instead, he has found himself in a situation where he has drifted into delinquency. This situation of "unregulated choice" tends to be episodic rather than constant and is akin to Durkheim's anomie. Matza prefers to define *drift* as episodic release from moral constraint. Sykes and Matza argue that rationalization, **techniques of neutralization**, occur prior to releases from moral constraint and enable youths to break the moral bind of law and engage in delinquency.

Important to the understanding of Matza's position is the view that delinquents are at least partially committed to the social order they offend. Delinquents learn to extend legitimate legal defenses to their crime and to distort these defenses to fit their own situation. Through a set of rationalizations, delinquents are able to protect themselves from self-blame. These justifications precede deviant behavior and make delinquency possible. Sykes and Matza isolate five principal techniques of neutralization: denial of responsibility, denial of injury, denial of the victim, condemnation of the condemners, and appeal to higher loyalties.

Denial of Responsibility.   Justice Oliver Wendell Holmes observed that even a dog distinguishes between being stumbled over and being kicked. Similarly, the law takes into consideration the *intent* of an act. Delinquents may attempt to rationalize delinquent acts by broadening the meaning of the term *accident.* The result is a widening of the conditions under which a child may behave wildly and excuse his or her behavior as not being intentional, but merely the action of a wild kid. Extensions of this denial of personal responsibility are the delinquent's eagerness to "give the problem away" to a slum environment, unloving parents, or bad companions. Delinquents may view themselves as the helpless victims of forces outside their control.

The law also "excuses" from responsibility those persons adjudged "insane." As in the case of an accident, delinquents may seek refuge from the requirement of the law by pleading extenuating circumstances: for example, "I was drunk out of my mind," or "I lost my head." As a consequence of anger or the influence of alcohol or drugs, delinquents may view themselves as seized by "momentary insanity" and thus excuse themselves from responsibility.

Denial of Injury.   The criminal law has long made a distinction between acts that are wrong in themselves (**mala in se**) and acts that are illegal but not immoral (**mala prohibita**). Similarly, if delinquents interpret their acts as clearly not hurting anyone, they can neutralize any guilt feelings. A stolen car is simply "borrowed" from someone who was not using it at the time, and a gang fight is a private quarrel entered into by consenting adolescents. Matza does not argue that these neutralizations represent a systematic ideology, but rather a hazy and somewhat Byzantine set of justifications. In this case, the link between the delinquent acts and their consequences is broken by the denial of injury, thus absolving the delinquent of any genuine wrongdoing.

Denial of the Victim.   Juvenile delinquents often draw a sharp line between those who can be victimized and those who cannot. The choice of victims tends to be a function of the social distance between the delinquents and their target. In this instance, delinquents admit that their behavior causes harm. They neutralize the guilt, however, by asserting that injury is a form of rightful retaliation. Vandalism may be seen as revenge on an "unfair" teacher, and thefts from a "crooked" store owner are merely an attempt by a ghetto Robin Hood to balance the scales of justice.

Condemnation of the Condemners.   Delinquents shift the focus of attention from their acts to the motives of their accusers, thereby denying authority figures the right to condemn the delinquent actions, since authorities are "hypocrites." Police are "corrupt, stupid, and brutal." Teachers "play favorites." Parents use delinquent children as "scapegoats." The effect is an attempt to shift attention away from the delinquent's own actions and to neutralize the normative sanctioning system these authority figures represent.

Appeal to Higher Loyalties.   In a conflict between the claims of friendship and the claims of the law, delinquents present themselves as acknowledging the claims of the larger society, but not able to "squeal on a friend." The law recognizes that self-defense justifies certain actions that might otherwise be deemed criminal. A man attacked in his own home has a legal right, and a moral duty, to stand his ground—as does a woman. Similarly, it is the expectation of the delinquent subculture that anyone who would not defend his or her turf (home) is a coward; thus repelling an aggressor (outsider) is justified. By borrowing this legal defense, delinquents justify their allegiance to the gang to which they belong (Sykes and Matza, 1957: 664–670).

Control theorists have criticized Sykes and Matza's views on neutralization and "will to delinquency" for two reasons: (1) "Many persons do not have an attitude of respect toward the rules of society." (2) "Many persons feel no moral obligation to conform regardless of personal ad-

vantage" (Hirschi, 1969: 25). Because of inadequate socialization, many adolescents' belief in the moral validity of law is weak. This serves to increase the probability that they will engage in delinquent activities. Further, control theory, in most of its versions, "proposes that if a youngster has established a moral bond to the conventional order, he or she will be less able to use techniques of neutralization" (Weis, 1977: 35).

Travis Hirschi: Social Bonds to Conventional Society

One of the most complete control theories of delinquency has been constructed by Travis Hirschi in his book *Causes of Delinquency* (1969). Hirschi called this general position on the causes of delinquency the "social control" perspective and argued that delinquent acts result when an individual's bond to the social order is weak or broken. There are four elements of that bond, according to Hirschi: attachment to **conventional others**, specifically, parents and peers, and the school; commitment to conventional action; involvement in conventional activities; and belief in obeying the rules of the society. Distinctive rates of delinquency for different social categories of individuals are explained on the basis of variations in the strength of the four bond variables. For instance, if girls commit fewer delinquent acts than boys, it is because the feminine gender role ensures (or did ensure) that females are more closely controlled and supervised and more strictly disciplined than males.[4] We will examine each of the four bonds more closely.

Attachment.   Hirschi explained that the attachment of an individual to significant others, such as parents and peers, and to a school provides constraints on delinquent behavior. It is possible to measure the extent to which an individual is attached to others independently of the person's behavior—deviant or otherwise. Most social control sources indicate that "affection for parents and other conforming individuals plays a major role in the control of deviant behavior" (Nye,

1958: 6). The individual's relationship with his or her parents and disciplinary actions by parents are significantly related to frequency of delinquent activities.

Hirschi noted that those individuals most closely attached to their parents are least likely to engage in delinquent activities.[5] The adolescent attached to parents may be less prone to get into situations where delinquent acts are possible because he or she spends more time under parental supervision. Although this could explain some delinquency prevention, the more probable reason that adolescents who are attached to their parents engage in less delinquency has to do with the acquisition of internal controls. Before acting, the child considers how his or her parents would react to any given behavior—especially a delinquent one. Nye has suggested that internal controls initially evolve from the parents' direct controls on the child's behavior. Direct controls, such as the supervision of leisure time, of companions, and of the type of activities children engage in, and the infliction of punishment for infractions of parental rules, are viewed as being enforced more strictly and consistently for nondelinquents than for delinquents.

When analyzing the importance of attachment to others, Hirschi also stressed the influence of the school on behavior. Those who do poorly in academic pursuits and who believe their teachers think of them as incompetent feel free to reject the authority of school personnel. Hirschi suggested that concern for the opinion of teachers is, in itself, related to delinquency. Furthermore, rejection can be generalized to other adult authorities and to conventional institutions, and the commission of delinquent acts may result. Numerous studies on delinquency indicate that a strong correlation exists between school failure and problems and rates of delinquency (Schafer and Polk, 1967; see also Chapter 10).

The final element of attachment concerns the bond to peers. *Causes of Delinquency* explores the attachment to peers from two perspectives: (1) the influence of actual attachment to peers on delinquency, and (2) the effects of the companionship factor of delinquent friends on delinquent behaviors. In dealing with the first matter, Hirschi

argued that delinquents are less attached to and respectful of their friends than are nondelinquents. It is even the case among boys who have delinquent friends that the more they are attached to these friends, the less is their delinquency. On the second matter, Hirschi wrote that the delinquency of companions is strongly related to rule-breaking behaviors in his sample of adolescent males. This finding has been substantiated in numerous other studies (Erickson, 1971; Hindelang, 1976).

Although Hirschi includes the delinquency of friends as part of the attachment to peers, it is unclear that the delinquency of friends acts as an inhibitor to delinquency. On the contrary, the delinquency of companions may serve as a resource that provides a push into delinquent behavior when controls are weakened. In a replication of Hirschi's study, Michael Hindelang (1973) found that, contrary to Hirschi, there is "a direct relationship between the extent of reported identification with friends and the extent of self-reported delinquency" (p. 479).

Commitment.   Hirschi stressed not only the importance of attachment to conventional others in the development of delinquent behavior, but also the commitment to conventional lines of action. The aspirations to achieve occupational and educational goals are interpreted as constraints on delinquent activities. An assessment of Hirschi's data supports the view that the higher the educational and occupational expectations, the lower the rate of delinquency.

Involvement.   Another social bond factor thought to inhibit delinquent behavior, according to Hirschi, is involvement in conventional activities. Some theorists have suggested that mere involvement in conventional activities restrains delinquency (A. K. Cohen, 1967). But Hirschi has taken the position that what the child is doing is more important in explaining differences in delinquency. Participation in conventional activities, such as doing homework and spending time with the family, generally means less delinquency apparently because the child conforms to ideas about appropriate behavior for children. Involvement by a child in working class adult activities, on the other hand, such as riding around in a car or sitting and talking with friends away from home, associates strongly with delinquency, possibly because the child rejects standards of behavior thought appropriate for children.

Belief.   In writing about the fourth and final element of the tie to the social order, Hirschi proposed that variation exists in the extent to which people believe social rules should be obeyed. Rather than assuming, as some theorists do, that delinquency is caused by beliefs requiring delinquency, the line of thought in control theory is that delinquency is made possible by the absence of beliefs forbidding delinquency. Hirschi tied lack of the belief that societal rules should be obeyed to the lack of attachment to parents and devaluation of concern for approval of persons in a position of authority. The adolescent who has little intimate communication with parents, the adolescent who feels little desire for success in conventional terms, is unlikely to feel that the demands of law are binding on his or her conduct.

Female Delinquency and Social Control Theory: A Special Application

Current interest in female crime and delinquency has led some theorists to reexamine social control theory. Proponents of the social control perspective contend that sex differentials in delinquency reflect variations in ties to the social bond. More precisely, females are less involved in delinquent behavior because they lack appropriate opportunities to engage in delinquency and because they have greater ties to the social bond. Females, for example, have a greater degree of attachment to parents because they are more closely supervised by their parents. This relatively higher degree of supervision results in less autonomy, thereby restricting the opportunity to engage in delinquency.

Girls are socialized to be more dependent on others and to develop closer and longer-lasting friendships than boys. Boys are encouraged to be more independent and achievement-oriented (Bardwick and Douvan, 1972). Thus, differences in **sex-role socialization** are said to promote varying degrees of attachment to significant others—which, in turn, influences involvement in delinquent activity.

Sex-role socialization practices are also thought to influence belief in the legitimacy of social rules. Differential practices instill greater acceptance of general moral standards in girls; boys are taught to be more individualistic and critical (Lynn, 1969). These practices have led at least one researcher to suggest that females are more likely to abide by legal norms than males (Turk, 1969). Thus, rather than sex itself, sex-role differences are thought to be instrumental in explaining adherence to the belief structure that, in turn, influences delinquency. Several studies have tested elements of the social bond in relation to female delinquency. We will examine one such study, that of Gary F. Jensen and Raymond Eve.

Jensen and Eve (1976) used the original data Travis Hirschi used in his book, *Causes of Delinquency*, to determine whether Hirschi's theory could account for sex differences in delinquency. The data were based on a survey of 4,000 California high school youth and included self-reported delinquency.

Jensen and Eve divided the sample into two groups, male and female. A distinct sex difference remained when the researchers examined the relationship between sex and delinquency, controlling for parental supervision, parental emotional support, attachment to the law, academic grade point average, and several other school-related variables. Simultaneous control of all these social control variables did not cause the sex-delinquency relationship to vanish completely; a significant relationship still persisted. Thus, although Hirschi's social control perspective received some empirical support from the data, Jensen and Eve were unable to account completely for the sex-delinquency relationship.

Although Jensen and Eve grounded their study very well within a plausible and appropriate theoretical framework, it does contain one serious limitation. Jensen and Eve relied upon the biological concept of **sex** instead of using the sociological concept of **gender**. The distinction here is not simply one of semantics. Sex is a biological concept based on chromosome differences; gender is a social definition based upon the human construction of what is masculine and what is feminine (Gould and Kern-Daniels, 1977). The distinction between sex and gender is important because it enhances theoretical precision and helps to avoid the error of tautological reasoning (F. Adler, 1975).

For example, Americans traditionally think of aggressiveness and violence as being typical male characteristics. If females were becoming more aggressive and violent in the commission of delinquency and crime (through assaultive behavior and carrying weapons, for example) and the researcher, without measuring masculinity, contended that the reason for this trend was that females were becoming more masculine, the error of tautological reasoning would have been made. In other words, the researcher, in the absence of measuring masculinity, uses the characteristics of the dependent variable to explain the dependent variable. The concept of gender is one way to avoid tautological reasoning in the area of female delinquency.

The Masculinity Hypothesis.   Sociologists such as Freda Adler have maintained that female rates of delinquency have increased because females have attained more "masculine" personality traits. This perspective is based on the view that masculine and feminine traits have been traditionally antithetical. Females were passive and dependent, and males were more aggressive and competitive. Delinquency was viewed as a typical male activity. But as females have become more independent, aggressive, and competitive—"more masculine"—according to this theory, there should be a corresponding increase in their commission of crime and delinquency.

This changing sex-role argument suffers from a serious defect that has been labeled the **ecological fallacy** (Cullen, Golden, and Cullen, 1979). This fallacy refers to the assignment of group characteristics to individual members. Although sociologists such as Adler have contended that increased female crime and delinquency are the result of

greater masculinization, it is important to note that this claim is made in the absence of any personality data. What is needed, then, are some studies that link individual sex-role changes to changing participation in delinquent behavior.

One such study was conducted by Peggy C. Giordano and Stephen A. Cernkovich. Giordano and Cernkovich (1979) attempted to examine the masculinity hypothesis by linking sex-role attitudes to self-reported delinquency. Using a sample of 740 high school girls and 187 girls in reformatories, the researchers found that most female delinquent acts were committed in groups with boys present. In other words, most of the self-reported female delinquency involved girls acting as accomplices to boys. At the same time, there were no strong correlations between nontraditional sex-role attitudes and female delinquency. Giordano and Cernkovich therefore questioned the attributed relationship between changing sex-role attitudes and delinquent involvement.

Although the Giordano and Cernkovich study departed from the practice of using biological sex as a substitute for the concept of gender, their sample consisted only of female adolescents. A better strategy would have been to include males in the sample in order to determine whether masculinity does correlate with delinquent activity. Fortunately, a study which does that has now been reported. Cullen, Golden, and Cullen (1979) surveyed 99 males and 83 females in order to test the masculinity hypothesis. After creating a masculinity personality scale, the researchers found a relationship between masculinity, independent of biological sex, and several types of delinquency. More important, Cullen et al. uncovered an interaction effect: That is, sex and gender worked together to explain delinquency involvement. Possession of male personality traits increased delinquency involvement for both males and females, but the effect was greater for males than females. This finding led the researchers to conclude that a theoretical model based solely on sex or gender differences was still incomplete.

Social Control Theory and the Masculinity Hypothesis: A Merger.   The studies that employed

Hirschi's social control perspective and the studies examining the masculinity hypothesis suggested that both explanations add something to our knowledge concerning the origins of female delinquency. However, the studies that used the social control perspective measured biological sex, and the studies of the masculinity hypothesis concentrated on gender traits. Several researchers have attempted to capitalize on the strengths of these two perspectives by integrating gender traits within the social control perspective. Shover, Norland, James, and Thornton (1979) surveyed 1,002 high school students to investigate whether the merger of social control theory and the masculinity hypothesis provided a better understanding of female delinquency. After separating the self-reported delinquency items into property and violent offenses, Shover and his associates found that male and female gender role expectations were not related to delinquency. Although the opportunity variable was not related significantly to delinquency, as one would expect on the basis of social control theory, attachment to conventional others and belief in the legitimacy of rules and laws were related significantly to both property and violent offenses. The data provided greater empirical support for social control theory than for the masculinity hypothesis.

Thornton and James (1979) reexamined the data analyzed by Shover and his colleagues to see whether further refinement would enhance the theoretical merger of social control theory and the masculinity hypothesis. In addition to self-reported delinquency, the researchers utilized a scale to measure the degree of masculine expectations that each respondent possessed. Scale items included such traditionally masculine items as fixing a car, paying for expenses on a date, and providing most of the family income after marriage. The results showed a moderate degree of association between masculine self-expectations and delinquency. When Thornton and James examined the relationship between sex and delinquency among those who identified themselves as high or low in masculinity, they found that males were still more likely to be delinquent than females, regardless of degree of masculinity.

Other statistical testings also indicated that masculine self-expectations were not related to delinquent involvement. Examination of such social control variables as attachment to school, attachment to parents, delinquent companions, parental control, belief, and commitment revealed very little change in the masculinity-delinquency relationship for both boys and girls. It would appear from this study that a merger between social control theory and the masculinity hypothesis is tenuous and requires further research before there can be a definitive verdict.

Another study has examined the question of whether increased rates of female delinquency can be attributed to the emergence of feminist political thought and action. Women who have favorable attitudes toward feminism are sometimes thought to be more likely to engage in criminal or delinquent behavior than women with more traditional attitudes. At the same time, it is quite possible that recent shifts have increased the availability of delinquent opportunities and the social support for such activities.

James and Thornton (1980) surveyed 287 high school girls in a small northwestern city. In order to do a more thorough examination, the researchers divided delinquency into three types: social, property, and violent. Social delinquency included the traditional status offenses of running away, alcohol consumption, and truancy. Property delinquency referred to burglary and larceny; violent delinquency included fighting, assault with a weapon, and armed robbery. The empirical results showed that attitudes toward feminism were independent of self-reported delinquency. The introduction of the social control variables (delinquent opportunities, parental social control, and social support for delinquency) modified the findings somewhat. Self-reported delinquency was influenced mostly by whether a girl's companions engaged in delinquency. Feminist attitudes, however, were related to both property and violent delinquency. Girls with positive attitudes toward feminism were less likely to engage in property and violent delinquency. Thus, contrary to popular belief, it would appear that positive attitudes toward feminism actually inhibited delinquency among girls.

The merger between Hirschi's social control

theory and the masculinity hypothesis has not greatly enhanced the understanding of female delinquency. At this point, it does appear that the social control perspective offers the most plausible explanation for female delinquency; but the social control variables themselves do not account completely for female delinquency.

Critique of Control Theory

Control theory suggests that juvenile delinquency is most likely to occur among those who have few internal or external controls on their behavior.[6] Adolescents who have not developed respect for themselves, for others, or for conventional society and have not accepted the social norms of conventional society are prime candidates. Control theory suggests that delinquent behavior can be prevented by increasing the effectiveness of those institutions that have the greatest influence on the socialization and control of youngsters. Rather than changing the individual, control theorists seek changes in the aspects of social life that promote or hinder the development of controls.

Although tests of control theory appear generally to confirm its tenets, the theory does have some logical and practical problems (see Wiatrowski, Griswold, and Roberts, 1984; Cernkovich, 1978; Segrave and Hastad, 1983). Many of the concepts employed by social control theorists are vague and difficult to "operationalize" (that is, to measure). Also, some of the variables employed in explaining the onset of delinquency appear to be part of the activity (delinquency) being explained. For instance, it is virtually impossible to measure internalized controls (inner containments or internalization of norms) independent of the behavior that is supposed to be controlled. As Weis (1977) has noted, "One has to infer inadequate inner containment (or poor self-concept, weak personal control, inadequate internalized control) from the observation of delinquent behavior" (p. 43). There is, then, the danger of circular reasoning in some forms of control theory.

Further, control theory is premised on a consensual view of society. In other words, control theory rests on the assumption that there is agreement on norms, values, and beliefs in society. Our discussion of conflict theories in Chapter 8 will show that some sociologists take issue with this view of reality and see much cultural diversity within American society. Additionally, as Edwin Schur (1969) suggested, there may actually be values that are "criminogenic"—criminal in and of themselves.

LABELING THEORIES

Remember Michael, at the beginning of this chapter? He faced problems in home, school, and community life. According to the theorists discussed thus far in this and previous chapters, Michael's troubles should be attributed to flaws in his biological or psychological makeup or in the social environment and his reaction to it. The labeling perspective, which attained popularity during the 1960s, took a radically different approach. From the labeling point of view, the important question is not what it is about Michael that led to his delinquency; instead, the question is why his acts are defined as delinquent at all.

Labeling theorists also ask what it is about the reactions of the community in general, the criminal justice system, and various significant individuals that seems to be leading Michael to a delinquent career. A foremost scholar of the labeling school, Howard Becker (1963), has written:

> Whether an act is deviant . . . depends on how other people react to it. You can commit clan incest and suffer from no more than gossip as long as no one makes a public accusation; but you will be driven to your death if the accusation is made. The point is that the response of other people has to be regarded as problematic. Just because one has committed an infraction of a rule does not mean that others will respond as though this had happened. (Conversely, just because one has not violated a rule does not mean that he may not be treated, in some circumstances, as though he had.) (pp. 11–12)

At the heart of the labeling perspective is the belief that behaviors are not intrinsically or inherently deviant. A behavior is "deviant" only when society so labels it. A child is "delinquent" only when members of a social group so define him or her. The basic tenets of the perspective are so eloquently stated by the novelist William Faulkner that Becker (1963) quoted Faulkner on the title page of his own book, *Outsiders:*

> Sometimes I aint so sho who's got ere a right to say when a man is crazy and when he aint. Sometimes I think it aint none of us pure crazy and aint none of us pure sane until the balance of us talks him that-a-way. It's like it aint so much what a fellow does, but it's the way the majority of folks is looking at him when he does it. (Faulkner, *As I Lay Dying*, 1930: 160)

Labeling theorists basically argue that so-called deviants, delinquents, and criminals are no different from the nondelinquent, noncriminal, or normal except that the former have been tagged with a deviant label. In all societies, labeling as deviant is a way of assigning moral inferiority. The deviant is tagged with an "essentializing label." It is as though the person had no other identity—to be labeled as deviant means to become a person whose entire personality can be reduced to one word, one label. It is a sociological shorthand that dehumanizes the person and separates him or her from the rest of the group. Rather than describing a person with a number of characteristics, such as "young, born in a large city, baptized a Catholic, attends high school," we forego that and get to the essentializing label: "a homosexual" or "a delinquent."

Although labeling theorists insist that delinquents are not unique in biological or psychological terms, they do of course suggest that there is a difference in the way society reacts to delinquents. Adherents also stress that children may come to regard themselves as delinquents in response to societal reaction.

Labeling concerned with the development of the self-concept was derived from a social psychological theory, **symbolic interactionism**. According to the founding father of symbolic interactionism, George Herbert Mead (1934), the child is born with a self-identity that resembles a clean slate, the *tabula rasa* we have alluded to. Through interaction with others, the slate is written on; the identity or self-concept emerges.

If a juvenile is confronted with consistent and recurrent treatment as a delinquent, eventually the conception of others will be incorporated: The child becomes a delinquent in his or her own eyes. Erikson (1962), one labeling adherent, has written that negative labeling results in a negative self-image. N. J. Davis (1975) has put it another way: "Labeling, then, is the social process that transforms one conception of the self (normal) into another (deviant)" (p. 173). Many critics have pointed out, however, that delinquents have successfully resisted the labeling or stigmatizing process and maintained a normal identity, and that other children think of themselves as delinquents without ever being officially labeled as delinquent. This criticism of the labeling perspective, as well as others, will be discussed later in this section. First we consider the work of three major proponents of labeling theory: Frank Tannenbaum, Edwin Lemert, and Howard Becker.

Frank Tannenbaum: The Dramatization of Evil

Perhaps the earliest formulation of labeling theory was set forth by the sociologist Frank Tannenbaum in his book *Crime and the Community,* published in 1938. Tannenbaum hypothesized that as early harmless acts of delinquency were interpreted unfavorably in the community, the child became viewed as evil or delinquent:

> In the conflict between the young delinquent and the community there develop two opposing definitions of the situation. In the beginning the definition of the situation by the young delinquent may be in the form of play, adventure, excitement, interest, mischief, fun. Breaking windows, annoying people, running around porches, climbing over roofs, stealing from pushcarts,

playing truant—all are items of play, adventure, excitement. To the community, however, these activities may and often do take the form of a nuisance, evil, delinquency, with the demand for control, admonition, chastisement, punishment, police court, truant school. (pp. 19–20)

According to Tannenbaum, the child's first encounter with the authorities was crucial in producing a change in the child's treatment by others in his or her own identity. After public recognition of misbehavior occurred, the juvenile was "tagged" or labeled as different from other children:

The process of making the criminal, therefore, is a process of tagging, defining, identifying, segregating, describing, emphasizing, making conscious and self-conscious; it becomes a way of stimulating, suggesting, emphasizing, and evoking the very traits that are complained of. (pp. 19–20)

Tannenbaum calls this process "the dramatization of evil."

Once tagging took place, wrote Tannenbaum, the juvenile was thrown into the company of other delinquents, and delinquent activities and associations became a "means of escape" from the negative reactions of the larger society. The harder that well-meaning parents, neighbors, teachers, and community workers tried to stamp out the "evil" behavior, the more the misbehavior was "hardened" and the more delinquent associations were sought to give the child security and satisfaction that could no longer be found in the "straight" world.

Considering Tannenbaum's assumptions about the causes of delinquency and criminal careers, his solution for the "problem" of delinquency is obvious. He thought that the less the evil is dramatized, the better. In other words, if the community avoids overreaction to initial misbehavior and resists the impulse to "tag" the juvenile, chances that the child will turn to delinquent acts and associates for satisfaction are diminished. The juvenile continues to think of himself or herself as "normal," and commitment to a delinquent or criminal life style is avoided (pp. 19–20).

Edwin Lemert: Primary and Secondary Deviation

Edwin Lemert, clarifying and expanding Tannenbaum's basic premise about the causes and nature of deviance, in 1951 published a book titled *Social Pathology*. In it he laid the groundwork for contemporary labeling thought with his concept of **primary** and **secondary deviance**. Lemert criticized earlier explanations of nonconforming behavior for "the preoccupation with the origins of [deviant] behavior" and "the fallacy of confusing *original* causes with *effective* causes" (p. 75). In other words, he argued that most theories of deviance, including those concerned with the causes of crime and delinquency, focus on the reasons why an individual comes to engage in the nonconforming behavior, or the "original causes." Using the alcoholic as an example, Lemert, however, observed that

a person may come to use excessive alcohol not only for a wide variety of subjective reasons but also because of diversified situational influences, such as the death of a loved one, business failure, or participation in some sort of organized group activity calling for heavy drinking of liquor. (p. 75)

Similarly, a child may engage in delinquent acts for any number of reasons—family troubles, failure in school, peer influences, deep-rooted psychological problems, desire for material possessions, and so on. Since the causes of initial, or primary, deviance are many and varied—"polygenetic," to use Lemert's term—it is somewhat futile to try to identify one major cause. Instead, wrote Lemert, sociologists and criminologists should concern themselves with how the societal reaction to initial misbehavior transforms a normal individual into a deviant or a normal child into a delinquent.

Although some anxiety and tension may be felt by a child engaging in an act that might be labeled delinquent, the child whose delinquency remains hidden from others is likely to suffer "no lasting impact." A juvenile who, for example, steals from a local store may be able to rationalize the behavior as necessary, called for, or excusable under the circumstances and to still consider himself or herself to be honest and a good kid. Juveniles may also continue to regard themselves as nondelinquents after notice is first given to the behavior of others. As Lemert (1972) summarized it:

> While it may be socially recognized and even defined as undesirable, primary deviation has only marginal implications for the status and psychic structure of the person concerned. Resultant problems are dealt with reciprocally in the context of established status relationships. This is done either through normalization, in which the deviance is perceived as normal variation—a problem of everyday life—or through management and nominal controls which do not seriously impede basic accommodations people make to get along with each other. (pp. 62–63)

There may come a time, however, when societal reaction to the child's behavior does have "a lasting impact" on the child's self-concept and on the concept others have of the child. When a person's "life and identity are organized around the facts of deviance," the child is a "secondary deviant" (p. 63). This form of deviance results from attempts to adjust to labeling as deviant and involves the adoption of the deviant role. Therefore, children who are continually arrested by the police, berated by family, school personnel, and neighbors, and treated by community members as bad may come to accept the negative label and view themselves as delinquents (Clinard and Meier, 1979; Lemert, 1972; Waugh, 1977).

Although the original delinquent behavior could be attributed to a number of factors in a child's life, the continuing delinquency, or secondary deviation, is a consequence of the way others react to him or her and the resultant changes in the child's self-image. Similarly, the drinker may initially drink for any one of a number of reasons, but drinking may continue because others have come to treat the drinker as a drunk. In both instances deviance, whether delinquency or chronic drinking, becomes part of a self-fulfilling prophecy. If everyone says Johnny is a mean kid, he may

eventually "come to believe that the label is true and begin acting according to the expectation of others" (Waugh, 1977: 136). Lemert (1951) traced the transition from primary to secondary deviation:

> (1) Primary deviation; (2) social penalties; (3) further primary deviation; (4) stronger penalties and rejections; (5) further deviation, perhaps with hostilities and resentment beginning to focus upon those doing the penalizing; (6) crisis reached in the tolerance quotient, expressed in formal action by the community stigmatizing of the deviant; (7) strengthening of the deviant conduct as a reaction to the stigmatizing and penalties; (8) ultimate acceptance of deviant social status and efforts at adjustment on the basis of the associated role. (pp. 77–79)

Good kids may avoid the child who has become a secondary deviant, and the labeled child may turn to other identified delinquents for acceptance and the enjoyment of similar activities. "The important point in this sequence is that labeling of a person as delinquent began the process in which the potentially false prophecy of delinquency was fullfilled" (Waugh, 1977: 136).

Lemert built on Tannenbaum's ideas about how the actions of well-intentioned relatives, criminal justice personnel, and community and school workers encourage, rather than inhibit, delinquency. These ideas form one cornerstone of the structure of labeling thought.

Howard Becker: The Social Production of Deviance

The work of Howard Becker on the definition and creation of deviance is another key part of the labeling perspective. In the 1960s the labeling perspective gained popularity among sociologists and other professionals concerned with the causes and cures of deviance. Becker and other experts agreed with Lemert that efforts to control deviance could produce deviant behavior and life styles. But Becker's book *Outsiders: Studies in the Sociology of Deviance*, published in 1963, took Lemert's analysis of the relationship of social reaction to the production of deviance a step further. Not

TABLE 7.1   Types of Deviant Behavior

	Obedient Behavior	Rule-Breaking Behavior
Perceived as deviant	Falsely accused	Pure deviant
Not perceived as deviant	Conforming	Secret deviant

Source: Becker (1963, p. 20).

only does the societal reaction to forbidden acts encourage further deviance, but according to Becker, "social groups create deviance by making the rules whose infraction constitutes deviance, and by applying those rules to particular people and labeling them as outsiders" (p. 9). Becker concluded: "The deviant is one to whom the label has been successfully applied; deviant behavior is behavior that people so label" (p. 9). Basically, Becker argued that no behavior is deviant in or by itself; it is only when people identify or classify the behavior as "abnormal," "illegal," or "delinquent" that a potentially neutral act becomes deviant.

The Definition of Deviance.   Pointing out that no act is intrinsically "wrong," Becker comments that whether or not an act is called "deviant" varies from time to time and depends "on who commits the act and who feels harmed by it" (p. 12). Truancy, for example, was not considered a delinquent act before school attendance was made compulsory for children. Similarly, many acts formerly permissible for children became forbidden when juvenile court acts were passed. Becker, giving an example of how the definition of deviance fluctuates depending on who commits the act and who is harmed by it, noted that although middle class children commonly engage in delinquent acts, they are far less likely to be detained by police or to be referred to the juvenile court than are lower class children. Becker used the example of a girl who is sexually active and unwed to stress the importance of the consequences of the behavior in the defining of the behavior as deviant. The girl who has intercourse but does not become pregnant rarely faces "severe punishment and social censure," but the girl who "gets caught" by an unwanted child is likely to encounter severe re-

action. Becker said that he made these "common-sense observations" to point out the difference between rule-breaking and deviant behavior. Behavior that violates any stated rule is rule-breaking, but behavior that is recognized and reacted to as rule-breaking is labeled "deviant" (pp. 12–14).

To clarify the distinction between rule-breaking and deviant behavior, Becker devised a chart reproduced here as Table 7.1. One of the four types of behavior, "not really deviant," is conforming behavior. If an adolescent obeys school and community rules and is recognized by others as obedient, he or she is a conformist. At the opposite extreme is the individual who breaks a rule and is perceived as breaking it. The child who pilfers from schoolmates' lockers and is thus considered a thief is the "pure deviant." Becker concludes, however, that it is possible for an individual to break rules without getting caught, and calls this person the "secret deviant."

In areas where homosexuality is a crime, many homosexuals are secretly deviant, as are many users of legally prohibited drugs. Several critics have pointed out that the "secret deviant" category does not make sense in light of Becker's own definition of deviance. If one only becomes deviant after public labeling, how can anyone be secretly deviant (Taylor, Walton, and Young, 1973)? Self-reports do indicate that most children are, to some degree, involved in delinquent activities and that most escape detection.

Becker calls the fourth category of behavior the "falsely accused." These individuals break no rules, but are perceived as having broken them. Apparently, children who were once caught in rule-breaking behavior and therefore labeled delinquent do face increased likelihood of being accused of delinquent acts they did not commit. According to Becker:

A boy who is innocently hanging around the fringes of a delinquent group may be arrested with them some night on suspicion. He will show up in the official statistics as a delinquent just as surely as those who have actually been involved in wrongdoing. (p. 21)

The Creation of Deviance.   After Becker explored the definition of deviance and its types in *Outsiders,* he looked at the reasons why certain rules came to be enforced at all. He suggested that specific rules, both informal and formal, "find their beginnings in those vague and generalized statements of preference social scientists often call values" (pp. 129–130). Values, however, are too general and vague to be used as "guides to action" or patterns for behavior. Rules must be deduced from values if conduct is to be regulated. In Becker's words: "Rules are the products of someone's initiative and we can think of the people who exhibit such enterprise as moral entrepreneurs" (p. 147).

Using the illustrative case of rules regulating the use of marijuana, Becker showed how **moral entrepreneurs** take general values and transform them into specific rules or, in the case of marijuana, specific legislation. Although there are many types of rule creators, Becker called the "crusading reformer" the prototype of those who want to create new rules "because there is some evil which profoundly disturbs [them]" (p. 147). Most often, these reformers are members of the upper classes. After rules are created, rule-enforcing organizations are developed to see that the rules are followed.

Becker's analysis seems particularly appropriate for an understanding of the creation of delinquency. Child-saving reformers, members of upper class and middle class women's groups, saw evil in the way children were treated at the hands of the criminal justice system and in the threats posed by poor, immigrant children wandering the streets. These moral entrepreneurs worked for a new set of rules to regulate the behavior of youth and achieved success when juvenile court legislation was passed. To enforce these new rules, organizations such as the juvenile court, juvenile institutions, and police sections were founded.

Summarizing his observations about the social production of deviance, Becker said:

> Before any act can be viewed as deviant, and before any class of people can be labeled and treated as outsiders for committing the act, someone must have made the rule which defines the act as deviant. . . . Deviance is the product of enterprise in the largest sense; without the enterprise to get rules made, the deviance which consists of breaking the rule could not exist. . . . Once a rule has come into existence, it must be applied to particular people before the abstract class of outsiders created by the rule can be peopled. . . . This job ordinarily falls to the lot of professional enforcers who, by enforcing already existing rules, create the particular deviants society views as outsiders. (pp. 162–163)

Becker concentrated on how rules are created and enforced; other sociologists have discussed the importance of rules and rule-breakers to the maintenance of a society. Labeling people as odd, peculiar, no good, hell-raisers, immoral, fat, or delinquent serves a positive function in society. When we see a deviant labeled as criminal, we are heartened by our own honesty. It indicates the boundaries of the societal control system. "They" are the bad guys; "we" are the good guys. Similarly, the label "fat" encourages the rest of us to believe we are in the "trim" category. The label "homosexual" reassures us that we are straight. The label "atheist" assures us of the rightness of our religious beliefs, "Communists" of the soundness of our democratic political system, "alcoholics" of the moderation with which we drink, and "hippies" of our commitment to the work ethic. As Erikson (1966) put it, deviance serves an important social function by showing "where the line is drawn between behavior that belongs in the special universe of the group and behavior that does not" (p. 11).

Labeling and the Juvenile Justice System

According to labeling adherents, processing by the juvenile justice system may exacerbate a child's so-called delinquent tendencies by the very reaction that is intended to inhibit further delinquency. In a study of San Francisco children who had been designated delinquent by the police and juvenile court, Victor Eisner (1978) noted several ways that labeling influenced the juveniles' behaviors. First of all,

> the difficulty was, and still is, that once a juvenile appears in juvenile court with an offense, his [or her] name and alleged offense became a matter of record in many states, even if the case is dismissed. A juvenile can acquire a label of delinquent whether or not he [or she] is actually guilty of an offense. This paradoxical situation does not mean that most of the juveniles seen in court were innocent, but it does mean that the court records and records of police contacts that constitute a "police record" and make a youth unemployable may include persons who have not been guilty of law violations. (p. 12)

Another way official agencies may increase rather than control the delinquency problem is through the application of the label of delinquent to children who have broken no adult laws, but who have instead transgressed only against standards of behavior that are not illegal for adults. As Eisner pointed out, "A boy who is picked up at 2 A.M. and cited to juvenile court for delinquent activities has not injured the community. The purpose of the citation is to prevent a serious law violation. Nevertheless, the boy has received a delinquency label" (pp. 12–13).

Eisner also pinpointed three law enforcement agencies that are involved in delinquency labeling: the police, the juvenile courts, and the adult courts (when jurisdiction over juvenile cases is transferred to adult courts). These agencies all keep files on the delinquent activities of juveniles. Although juvenile court records may be sealed and thus not available for public examination, the fact that a juvenile appeared before the court remains on the record. And as Eisner observed, sealed records may make the offense seem more serious than it actually was.

Although formal records are one way a child may be labeled, informal labeling can occur as

police, school officials, family members, and neighbors exchange information on the activities of a particular adolescent. Information on a child who has been labeled a troublemaker in school may be shared with the local juvenile officer. A father or mother who talks to neighbors about problems "controlling" a son or daughter may transmit the negative label. Similarly, police and court juvenile officers often contact school officials to gain "background information" when deciding how to handle a particular child's case. As information is transmitted through these various spheres of the juvenile's life, the negative characterization may become stronger and more resistant to change (Cicourel and Kitsuse, 1968).

When the teacher, police officer, next-door neighbor, and parents all begin to concur that the juvenile is "delinquent," the chances of a **self-fulfilling prophecy** are increased. The child who comes into contact with the juvenile justice system may accept the image of "deviant." In a study of parents, police, teachers, and children,

> Werthman gives the example of a young boy sent to a foster home because he came from a broken home and his mother (primary deviation) was declared an unfit mother. The boy missed school (truancy) to see his mother and broke the terms of his probation (secondary deviation) by seeing his mother without official approval. Thus, the label "delinquent" substantially increased the probability of future norm violating behavior. (Waugh, 1977: 139)

It is, of course, possible that the process of official labeling will cease before the label of "deviant" produces further delinquency. The label must first be reinforced "by other justice officials, school or agency personnel, parents, and peers" (Carter and Klein, 1976: 107) and accepted by the juvenile. Thus, "even if label application is high and label acceptance is high, impact of these processes on subsequent behavior (new offenses, new arrests) may depend on the process being repeated several times. That is, the entire process may be cumulative over several arrest episodes but unlikely to be very evident after only one" (p. 107).

Critique of Labeling Theory

In sum, labeling theorists are concerned with how deviance is defined by the creation of rules and the reaction of individuals and social organizations to rule-breakers, as well as with the reasons rules are instituted. (The rationales underlying the development and enforcement of certain rules will be more fully examined when we discuss conflict theories.) The labeling perspective also views the social reaction to deviance as productive of deviance, including crime and delinquency. McCaghy (1976) summarized these two themes: "The labeling perspective deals with two fundamental problems: the social production of deviance and the effect of labeling on behavior" (p. 80).

The statements of labeling theory presented by Tannenbaum, Lemert, Becker, and others have not escaped criticism. The tenets of labeling theory have been attacked, and the popularity of the perspective may have declined somewhat in recent years. Yet basic labeling principles are widely accepted and have provided the impetus for programs that seek to avoid official labeling by use of social services agencies and diversionary programs. But the shortcomings of the labeling approach still plague its adherents.

Although the effects of labeling on behavior are now well recognized, the perspective has been criticized for various problems in the logic and application of labeling principles. Criticism centers on the assumption, found in the work of Tannenbaum and Lemert, that labeling individuals as deviant inevitably results in a deviant identity and career assumptions. Also questioned are arguments concerning the inevitability of the progression from primary to secondary deviance. Other criticisms of the perspective relate to the possible deterrent effects of labeling and to the exclusion of the "initial (primary) deviance" or the "meaning the behavior originally had for the deviant" (McCaghy, 1976: 87; Ball, 1983).

Lemert's key argument has been a favorite subject for debate. According to Nanette Davis (1972), Lemert basically argued that "societal reaction in the form of labeling or official typing, and consequent stigmatization, leads to an altered identity in the actor necessitating a reconstitution

of the self" (p. 460). There is, however, no real evidence to support this proposition. Davis asserts that "this premise has not been adequately demonstrated empirically, inasmuch as the research focus is on those social persons and categories already known to have been labeled" (p. 460). It is likely that many individuals are labeled as delinquent or deviant in informal ways or even self-labeled without official reaction to original deviance (see Covington, 1984).

According to Foster, Dinitz, and Reckless (1972), one arrest or even a court appearance may not change the self-image for better or worse. Further, initial contacts with social control agents do not inevitably produce deviant careers. Hepburn (1975) observed: "For some, a deviant career commitment may be stabilized prior to the official labeling activity; for others, however, the labeling activity initiates either a reaffirmation of non-deviant career commitment or a transformation to a deviant career commitment" (p. 400). Hepburn also argued that career deviance may occur prior to, as well as following, official labeling. Summarizing these criticisms, Davis continued:

> Labeling theorists who claim that reactive processes of society provide the causal factor in deviance are thereby providing only a partial view of a highly complex problem. Public labeling may have little or no impact in many areas of life, while many unsanctioned "normals" may engage in illegal or aberrational behavior in regularized fashion. (p. 461)

Linked to criticisms about the inevitability of deviant careers and identities are criticisms of the deterministic stance of labeling theory. The picture drawn by labeling theorists is that once official reaction occurs, the individual is powerless to resist the deviant identity, association, or career. The individual's free choice and potential for the power to act are ignored.

There are critics of the labeling perspective who find that too little emphasis and time are given to the factors that bring about original rule infractions. Since official labeling is thought all-important in an explanation of deviant behavior, "whatever meaning the behavior originally had for the deviant is ignored as a contributor to subsequent behavior" (McCaghy, 1976: 87). McCaghy posed the question, "If a person first steals for thrills, do thrills fail to be a factor once societal reaction has taken its toll?" (p. 87). Similarly, Mankoff (1971) has argued that "the labeling model fails to seriously consider the possibility that deviant behavior may be persisted in even when the rule-breaker has every opportunity to return to the status of non-deviant, because of a positive attachment to rule-breaking" (p. 212). All these critics have urged that research be conducted to ascertain the original causes "of the creation, perpetration, and intensification of criminal and delinquent behavior" (Wellford, 1975: 343).

It has also been pointed out that, although labeling sometimes results in increased involvement in deviance, official reaction to an initial rule-breaking behavior may reduce subsequent delinquency. Studying the deterrent and reinforcing effects of contact with official agencies, Thorsell and Klemke (1976: 174) hypothesized that future deviance will be deterred:

1. If the labeled person is a primary rather than secondary deviant.

2. If the labeling is carried out in a confidential setting, with the understanding that future deviance will result in public exposure.

3. If the labeling has been carried out by an ingroup member or a significant other.

4. The more easily the label is removable when the deviant behavior has ceased.

5. The more the labeling results in efforts to reintegrate the deviant into the community.

6. If the label is favorable rather than derogatory.

Thus, the child whose parents quietly correct him or her or who is called in for confidential meetings with school counselors is probably less likely to experience the negative effects of derogatory labeling than the juvenile who is taken to the police station and who is "known about" in the community.

Acknowledging the multiple effects that stem from the social control of deviants, Taylor and his colleagues (1973) write that social control "may deter some," "propel others to action to change the nature of control," or "engender self-conceptions in those affected by social control in such a way that 'amplification' in fact does occur" (p. 161).

A final group criticism is offered by conflict theorists. Taylor, Walton, and Young, for example, have argued that societal reaction writers "fail to lay bare the structured inequalities in power and interest which underpin the processes whereby the laws are created and enforced" (1973: 168). They call it "unfortunate" that the labeling proponents have retreated from the issue of how power and powerful groups influence the making of law and the application of sanctions for supposed infractions. We discuss this area in more detail in the next chapter.

PHENOMENOLOGICAL THEORIES

Although the labeling perspective has been attacked by many critics, the influence of its general tenets continues to be heeded by sociologists, including Jack Douglas (1970, 1972, 1976), David Matza (1969), and Peter McHugh (1970), who have attempted to expand and refine the principles of labeling theory through phenomenological thought. As we have noted, the purpose of labeling theory is to focus on the societal reaction to norm violators. Phenomenologists, however, are interested in the individual's *own* reaction to his or her deviant behavior.[7] Activity, then, is studied from the viewpoint of the deviant, in this context the delinquent.

Phenomenology: Premises

Norman Weiner's (1970) study of the shoplifting episode of a young middle class female is an example of phenomenological research:

We walked outside, and I asked, "Why'd you take that?" [She said,] "Didn't you take anything?" I shrugged noncommittally. "No, really. Why'd you take it?" "I needed it." "But you could have paid for it . . . if you wanted it that badly." "This is easier." As we walked back to the car, she continued to talk. "Well, you know, I don't do it all the time. And I only get what I really need. Like that mascara. But not what I don't need, 'cause that's dumb. Nobody misses stuff in a store like that. I mean, everyone does it. It's easy to get things. Even like the dress." "What dress?" "Huh?" She seemed surprised I hadn't known. She opened the bag she had been holding, and there, along with the blouse she had paid for, was a dress. "But the bag was stapled." "I put it in the bag in the dressing room. With this." She opened her purse and showed me a stapler with a staple remover. She had opened the bag, put the dress in, and restapled it. "I thought you knew." I replied, "No, not really." We dropped the subject, and after brooding a moment on my innocence, she began to talk on as if nothing had happened. But she never told me about the glass ball she had taken. (pp. 215–216)

This example of phenomenological writing exemplifies the contrast between phenomenological and positivist approaches. Positivists are concerned with the factors that explain delinquency; phenomenologists "consider the deviant's subjective experience as the heart of deviant reality" (Thio, 1978: 63). A social control theorist, for instance, might concentrate on the young shoplifter's lack of attachment to conventional others or lack of belief in the law to explain her delinquency. From the phenomenological point of view, an examination of social bond variables such as attachment or belief tells us nothing about the delinquent activity as such. Instead, it points out the researcher's perception of what the activity really means. As Thio has written:

The real phenomenon, in phenomenologists' view, is the immediate experience and consciousness of the person under study. In order to become what the real phenomenon is, one has to rely on the person's subjective experience—to discover

how the person feels and what he or she thinks about his or her . . . deviant experience. (p. 64)

According to phenomenologists, *deviant reality* is essentially the subjective meaning the delinquent imputes to his or her own delinquent behavior. Reiterating this view, Douglas (1970) has argued that descriptions of the formal causes of a delinquent act do not tell us anything about what delinquency means to the participant or how delinquents organize their activities.

How do phenomenologists come to know the subjective experience of the delinquents they come into contact with? Might not the phenomenologist's view of the deviant's reality differ from the deviant's own interpretation of the experience? Also, is it possible that the delinquent's view of a given event is a distortion of what really happened? To reduce this possibility and to maintain objectivity, phenomenologists attempt to repress their own beliefs and ideas about a situation and "become totally receptive to the true meaning of the subject's experience" (Thio, 1978: 66–67). This is referred to as **phenomenological reduction, phenomenological bracketing**, or **theoretic stance**.

Phenomenological Research on Delinquency

David Matza, in his book *Becoming Deviant* (1969), utilized a phenomenological approach to analyze how individuals become marijuana users and why they intentionally run the risk of becoming delinquent or criminal. He suggested three stages in this process: affinity, affiliation, and signification.

In the first stage, *affinity*, the individual is attracted to a potentially deviant situation, in this case marijuana use. This attraction is mediated by circumstances in the youth's life, such as family background, social class, search for identity, or other factors. Contrary to positivist theories, these various circumstances do not automatically predispose a person to engage in delinquent behavior. According to Matza, the affinity remains latent until the individual makes a conscious choice to engage in deviant behavior. Then the individual may consciously seek an opportunity to try the drug. If the person succeeds in finding such an opportunity, he or she has chosen to *affiliate* with a deviant activity.

Although this individual may go on to regular use of marijuana, the user does not necessarily envision himself or herself as a deviant. A deviant identity occurs only if the person concurs with society's *signification* of smoking marijuana as an illegal activity. It is entirely possible that a youth may accept but later reject the label of delinquent drug user. Even if the smoker is caught, formally adjudicated, and confined to an institution, which would be the conclusion of the signification process, he or she can still reconsider and reject the imposed label. Thus, according to Matza and other phenomenologists, the process of becoming a deviant is by no means a predictable and static phenomenon.

Other studies of delinquency also rely on a phenomenological framework. Cicourel, in *The Social Organization of Juvenile Justice* (1968), sought to specify "observable and tacit properties making up the practical decision making both lay and law enforcement officials utilize when deciding some act or sequence is wrong" (p. 55). He pointed out that the day-to-day operations of control agencies (police, courts, and so forth) produce given rates of delinquency. These rates, he suggested, do not reflect actual amounts of crime, but rather are indices of the amount of deviance that is processed by the control agencies.

Several criminologists have phenomenologically examined the role of the offender caught up in the justice system (e.g., Giordano, 1976; Spencer, 1983). Ericson and Baranck's (1982) study of the accused in the Canadian crime control system offers a plausible explanation of the delinquent's view of the system. They write (p. 4):

The accused is best seen as a dependent rather than a defendant. The accused is acutely aware that he [or she] is subject to an ordering process which makes it wise for him [or her] to be passive, because there is little scope to act otherwise without being subject to further negative consequences. If he [or she] sits back and accepts the majesty, justice, and mercy of the law, he [or she] indicates a deference to the wider order of things that may reap for him [or her] the immediate reward of leniency. By remaining passive the accused makes a small testimony to that order and allows himself [or herself] to be used on behalf of the state's need to reproduce order. In return, he [or she] is reaccepted as part of that order.

At each stage of the system, juveniles learn that their best chances for survival involve "going along with the system." Replete with formal legal rules and a hierarchy of power, the system produces and forms its own version of reality. The juvenile offender, especially a neophyte to the system, is completely dependent on the authorities' perceptions of reality and soon realizes that his or her protestations will not result in a negotiated version of reality. This official definition of reality begins at the police stage and continues through the court and disposition stages. Much like Garfinkel's (1967) version of a degradation ceremony, the ritual in court serves as a culmination of the ordering and legitimization process.

Juveniles to a large extent have their role defined for them. That role becomes reified so that the child sees it as inevitable (Berger and Luckmann, 1967: 103). As a reified client, the juvenile is treated as an object who is acted upon rather than as an object who acts. "His [or her] own wishes and purposes are not considered except as symptoms" (Friedenberg, 1975: 19). Since there are gross differences in power between delinquents and control agents, it is appropriate to view transactions between the two as "characterized by manipulation and coercion, not negotiation" (Ericson and Baranck, 1982: 24).

Critique of Phenomenological Theory

The phenomenological perspective on delinquency and crime in the United States has a relatively small but faithful following. Phenomenologists have pointed to obvious inadequacies in positivistic theories of delinquency. For example, phenomenologists question the ability of positivists to be objective and to refrain from imposing their preconceptions of reality on the existing study. Phenomenologists claim that they, unlike positivists, can be successful in suspending all past beliefs and ideas concerning the area under study. But these assumptions have been criticized. A major critic is Thio (1978), who has posed the question: "Can phenomenologists . . . keep a totally open mind so as to experience, observe, and depict the essence of reality?" He has argued that they cannot.

Because they rely primarily on an observational method of studying subjects, phenomenologists have been criticized on two counts. First, it is argued that the observational method of data collection is severely limiting. Many covert types of delinquent activities simply cannot be assessed by becoming involved with delinquent individuals and groups. Second, it has been pointed out that the participant observation method does not lend itself to the study of more powerful subjects. Aside from Cicourel's study of social control agents, most of the research within a phenomenological framework has focused on powerless subjects such as drug addicts and homosexuals. The rich and powerful are ignored (Thio, 1974).

Finally, phenomenologists are attacked for viewing individuals as possessed of extraordinary powers of reason and logic. Delinquents and deviants generally are depicted "as highly sophisticated free-thinking and choice-making philosophers, very much like phenomenologists themselves." Thio has humorously observed: "These philosophical deviants are constantly engrossed in analyzing the intricate meanings of all that happens or threatens to happen to them. We may wonder how they, being bogged down with such heavy philosophizing, could ever find time for, or be interested at all in, deviant action" (1978, pp. 69–70).

SUMMARY

The theories in this chapter represent contemporary sociological efforts to explain crime and delinquency. These theories differ from classical sociological theories (and individualistic biological and psychological theories) by concentrating, for the most part, on significant others, social groups, and social institutions as causes of delinquency. Social control and labeling theory are representative of recent attempts to explain delinquency within a larger social context. Another contemporary theory, phenomenology, remains within an individualistic framework, somewhat more troubled by subjective data gathering.

Social control theorists, tracing their views back to Emile Durkheim, view delinquents as children who have not developed bonds to society. Unattached to society's norms, they are free to engage in a variety of deviant activities, including delinquency. According to control theorists, delinquency is prevented when there are adequate social controls. These controls may be personal or inward (inner controls or inner containment), or they may be external or outward (external controls or outer containment). Inner controls, including the internalization of societal norms, are deemed necessary for the proper functioning of outer controls. Outer controls are constraints on individuals, behaviors that encourage conformity to group or community norms. Sanctions may be applied to force individuals to conform to expected behaviors.

An adaptation of control theory, social bond theory identifies the causes of delinquency as rooted in the lack of attachment of the individual to significant others, such as parents or peers, and to the school. Similarly, the youth's commitment to and involvement in conventional action and belief in obeying the rules of the society are thought important in explaining delinquent behaviors.

Although tests of control theory appear generally to confirm its tenets, the perspective has not escaped criticism. Critics point to problems in measuring or operationalizing many of the concepts the theory is based on. Further, control theory is premised on an assumption of agreement on norms and values within the society.

The labeling perspective, which took a radically different approach from control theory, attained popularity during the 1960s. Labeling theorists ask why particular acts are defined as delinquent. They question from the outset the bases of the study of juvenile crime. In attempting to answer this question, labeling proponents point to the role of societal reaction in formulating definitions of deviance. They assert that a behavior is deviant only when society so labels it. A child is delinquent only when members of a social group so define him or her. Labeling theorists basically argue that deviants or delinquents are no different from nondeviants or nondelinquents except that the former have been tagged with a label. Many variations of this central theme have been discussed in the 1970s. Criticisms of labeling theory center on the assumption that the labeling of individuals as deviant inevitably results in a deviant identity and career. Similarly, critics argue that too little attention is given to groups that have the power to create definitions of deviance and to apply those labels to rule-violators.

In an effort to extend the explanatory power of labeling theory, phenomenologists direct attention to the individual's own perception of his or her deviant behavior. To explore the subjective meaning that individuals apply to their deviant behavior, activity is studied from the viewpoint of the deviant or delinquent. The techniques used by phenomenologists to ascertain the subjective experiences of delinquents have been attacked. Proponents of phenomenology attempt to repress their own beliefs and ideas about a situation and become totally receptive to the meaning the situation has for the subject. Their ability to remain objective has been questioned by positivist researchers.

PROGRESS CHECK

1. Social control theory is particularly indebted to the early work of French sociologist _____. (p. 144)

2. Albert Reiss found that delinquents placed on probation were more likely to fail under certain conditions. Which one of the follow-

ing is *not* correct, according to Reiss? (p. 145)
a. The delinquents came from an upper class home of considerable wealth.
b. The parents were divorced or one was dead.
c. There was an open breach or gross incompatibility with the natural parents.
d. Unfavorable moral ideas had been institutionalized.

3. List and differentiate by definition and illustration the five neutralizing techniques described by Gresham Sykes and David Matza. (pp. 146–148)

4. Note three components of inner control as explained by Walter Reckless. (p. 146)

5. Howard Becker, Frank Tannenbaum, and Edwin Lemert are most appropriately classified as: (pp. 153–161)
a. Social control theorists
b. Labeling theorists
c. Phenomenological theorists

6. According to _____, a person who is falsely accused but who engages in obedient behavior will be perceived as a deviant. (p. 157)

7. Using the eight "steps" in their proper sequence, trace the transition from primary to secondary deviance. (p. 156)

8. Relate the self-fulfilling prophecy to the assessments that control agents give to certain types of youth. (pp. 158–159)

9. Assess the strengths and weaknesses of phenomenological theories of crime and delinquency. (pp. 161–164)

10. Phenomenologists who study delinquency take whose view? (p. 161)

NOTES

1. Some theorists, such as Weis, classify social structural disorganization (Merton, 1938; Cloward and Ohlin, 1960; Cohen, 1955) and cultural disorganization (Shaw and McKay, 1942; Shaw, 1929; Sutherland and Cressey, 1978; Miller, 1958) as theories of delinquency encompassed by the social control perspective. Their perspectives rest on the basic idea that "deregulation" and "malintegration" are vital to an explanation of delinquent behavior, in that each emphasizes different aspects of ineffective social control. Rather than classifying these theories under social control theory proper, which is certainly feasible, we discuss the works of Hirschi (1969), Reiss (1951), Nye (1958), and Reckless (1961b, 1973) as separate, or pure, forms of "control theory." We believe this is the more preferred or common way of dealing with the subject; see Empey (1978) and Gibbons (1981). We add, however, that we rely heavily in this section on Joseph Weis' work on control theory. His review of the subject (1977) is excellent.

2. In Chapter 11 we discuss the influence of peers or companionship on the commission of delinquent acts. Much delinquency is of a group nature; for examples, see Hindelang (1976) and Erickson (1971). Daniel Glaser (1955), recognizing in his theory of differential identification the importance of the group, explains criminal and delinquent behavior as the extent to which people identify themselves with "real or imaginary persons from whose perspective his criminal behavior seems acceptable" (p. 440).

3. See also Schwartz and Stryker (1970).

4. The work on Travis Hirschi comes primarily from James (1977: 16–25) and Thornton (1977: 12–21).

5. Other theorists note the same thing. For examples, see Glueck and Glueck (1950), Jensen (1972), and Nye (1958).

6. Our discussion is limited to social control theorists. Psychologists have also contributed to control theory, albeit under a different label. Nettler has noted that "Eysenck (1964) and Trasler (1962), working independently of each other, have noted how training interacts with individually different conditions to affect conduct. With less emphasis upon constitutional differences, psychologists in Canada and the U.S., such as Bandura (1973) and Bandura and Walters (1959, 1963), have emphasized an aspect of training they call 'social learning' or 'modeling' " (1978: 309).

7. Several other phenomenologically oriented theorists could be cited here. For a sampling of those theorists, see Scott and Douglas (1972).

CHAPTER 8

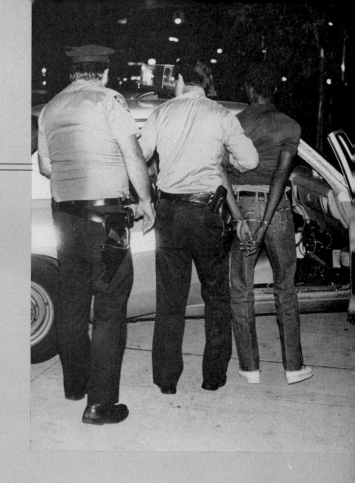

CONFLICT AND RADICAL THEORIES OF DELINQUENCY

CONSENSUAL POSITIVISTIC MODEL

CONFLICT AND RADICAL
CRITIQUE

CONFLICT CRIMINOLOGY VS.
RADICAL CRIMINOLOGY

HISTORICAL ROOTS OF THE
RADICAL AND CONFLICT
PERSPECTIVES

EARLY CONFLICT THEORIES (1930–
1960): PREMISES AND CRITIQUE

CONTEMPORARY RADICAL
CONFLICT THEORY (1960–1980):
PREMISES AND CRITIQUE

Eight promising young men—children of good, stable, white upper-middle-class families, active in school affairs, good pre-college students—were some of the most delinquent boys at Hanibal High School. While community residents and parents knew that these boys occasionally sowed a few wild oats, they were totally unaware that sowing wild oats completely occupied the daily routine of these young men. The Saints were constantly occupied with truancy, drinking, wild driving, petty theft and vandalism. Yet not one was officially arrested for any misdeed during the two years I observed them.

This record was particularly surprising in light of my observations during the same two years of another gang of Hanibal High School students, six lower-class white boys known as the Roughnecks. The Roughnecks were constantly in trouble with police and community even though their rate of delinquency was about equal with that of the Saints. (Chambliss, 1973: 24)

Why did the activities of the first group of boys go unnoticed, while the same types of activities by the second group were severely sanctioned by the community? Is there any difference in the community perceptions of the activities of these two youth groups and the way society generally reacts to the crimes of politicians or corporate heads and street criminals?

Radical and conflict theories of crime and delinquency draw our attention to the disparity in societal perceptions, definitions, and treatment of the behaviors of individuals representing different social classes or races.[1] They argue that our general approach to crime and criminal justice reflects the social relationships within a particular society or culture.

The conflict and radical perspectives of crime and delinquency suggest that the existence of different values, norms, and social experiences in society ultimately affects the definitions and causes of delinquency and crime. The radical explanation, which is a more specific expression of the general conflict perspective, stresses the fundamental power relationships between the ruling classes and the subjugated or exploited classes. Radical proponents are particularly critical of the unequal political and economic relationships that exist under capitalism. These theorists attribute the problem of delinquency to the alienation and powerlessness among youth—particularly among poor minority youth. They argue that crime and delinquency are the creation of the dominant classes and that the criminal justice system is a vehicle by which the dominant class controls the subordinate class.

The conflict and radical criminologists are noted for their roles as critics of mainstream criminology. They have raised issue with the basic assumptions of mainstream criminology. They have been particularly successful in uncovering some of the unconscious elements that underlie the development and operation of our social control institutions and norms.

CONSENSUAL POSITIVISTIC MODEL

Most of the theories discussed thus far, with the possible exception of the interactionist and labeling perspectives, are based on a "consensual" view of society. Assuming a consensual view of society, delinquent behavior is considered to be aberrant, irrational, or meaningless (Garofalo, 1978). Accordingly, the individual is psychologically maladjusted or physically abnormal, or the individual's immediate social and physical environment is inadequate, faulty, or disturbed. Any one of these situations or a combination may be used to account for delinquent behaviors.

Those who presume a consensual view of society take the social order within their own society for granted; they do not question the legitimacy of the institutions, laws, or social definitions that govern their society. Consensual or order theories share an image of a society based on a shared culture, including agreement on fundamental values and acceptance of the political organization (Dahrendorf, 1959; Horton, 1973). Although it is acknowledged that total stability within a society is never fully achieved (thus accounting for changing laws), it is believed that society is moving toward stability. The underlying assumption is that stability is the shared and desired goal of society.

Accompanying the consensual view of society is the idea that value-free science will uncover the objective, external properties of society. According to the positivistic **consensual model**, there is little disagreement over who or what a delinquent is. The delinquent in this model is defined as an individual who violates the state-prescribed law and thereby rejects the community or societal values and threatens the stability of the whole society (Empey, 1978). While the model admits that definitions of crime and delinquency can serve to reinforce the collective normative conscience and may even suggest when changes in the law are necessary, it emphasizes the dysfunctional effects of crime and delinquency.

Crime and delinquency are often discussed in terms of societal breakdown, lack of communication, improper socialization, lack of stability, and weakness in the boundary maintenance mechanisms. Hence most classical and contemporary delinquency theorists hold that deviance should be controlled in any manner deemed appropriate to protect society (Pfohl, 1979). William Chambliss (1984: 76) summarizes the consensual paradigm in the following propositions:[2]

1. The law represents the value consensus of the society.

2. The law represents those values and perspectives which are fundamental to social order.

3. The law represents those values and perspectives which it is in the public interest to protect.

4. The state as represented in the legal system is value-neutral.

5. In pluralistic societies the law represents the interests of the society at large by mediating between competing interest groups.

CONFLICT AND RADICAL CRITIQUE

Contrasted with the consensual theories of society and delinquency, conflict theories and radical theories propose other sets of assumptions that lead to different views of society and subsequently of crime and delinquency. Conflict and radical theorists hold that society is more typically conflictual in nature and full of dissension and contradiction.

Conflict and Radical View of Society and Delinquency

"Customs explain little" (Chambliss, 1984: 76). Some have argued that the apparent consensus, especially about crime, is manufactured (Quinney, 1970; Michalowski and Bohlander, 1976; Reiman, 1979: 162–168). Indeed, they suggest that our attitudes and beliefs about crime and social order are part of a "false consciousness." Most common, everyday images of crime and criminal justice are based on incomplete and selective information. Our common impressions, irrespective of how erroneous they are, influence how we define the problem of crime and what solutions we seek.[3]

Both the conflict and radical schools of thought maintain that crime and delinquency are socially rooted and are products of the conflict relationships among individuals that emerge when groups or classes with unequal power and differing interests come into contact. More specifically, conflict and radical theorists underscore the relevance of the concept of power in the understanding of criminal law and crime in society.

The following general statement by Marx and Engels, two nineteenth-century theorists who provided some of the major theoretical underpinnings of the conflict and especially the radical perspectives, has been applied to the field of criminology.

> The ideas of the ruling class are in every epoch the ruling ideas, i.e., the class which is the ruling "material" force of society is at the same time its ruling "intellectual" force. (Marx and Engels, 1970: 64)

Conflict and radical theorists argue that some societal members have control—specifically, economic and political control—over other members (Dahrendorf, 1959; Quinney, 1970). The amount of control a group possesses determines the probability with which the members of the group will be labeled criminal. Those with the least amount of control are most likely to find themselves among the criminal or delinquent population. This position does not intend to suggest that poverty (poor living conditions) and relative deprivation necessarily lead to crime. Rather, the position asserts that the ideas, values, and attitudes, including laws and sanctions, which are produced by the more powerful individuals usually dominate and become the norm for most groups. The powerful individuals in society are in a more opportune position to affect communication and education systems, and thus to determine the social consensus about crime according to their own interests.

First, it is in the interest of the more powerful factions in society to divert attention from their own behavior and to focus it on the behavior of the subordinate groups. Michael Foucault (1979), a French sociologist, illuminates this point in the following passage. Beginning with a discussion of crime among the underprivileged class, he goes on to say:

> But this criminality of need or of repression masks, by the attention paid to it and the disapprobation

surrounding it, another criminality that is sometimes its cause and always its extension. This is the delinquency from above, a scandalous example, the source of misery and the principle of revolt for the poor. "While misery strews your streets with corpses and fills your prisons with thieves and murderers, where are the swindlers of the fashionable world? . . ." But this delinquency of wealth is tolerated by the laws, and, when it does find its way into the courts, it can depend upon the indulgence of the judges and the discretion of the press. (pp. 287–288)

Second, since the economically or politically dominant population represents only a small fraction of the whole, making their dominant status numerically vulnerable, status maintenance is a constant problem. Over a long period of time, physical control or brute force alone cannot keep people (particularly the most disadvantaged individuals) in their subordinate and inferior position. In order to maintain a social hierarchy based on an unequal distribution of goods and services, psychological and sociological, as well as physical, control, must be established. If the disadvantaged can be made to accept the philosophy of "just deserts"; and if they can be convinced of the validity of such concepts as crime, insanity, and deviance, which are supposed to explain why some people are disadvantaged and somehow justify the deprivation of these individuals in society; and if they can be coopted into applying these concepts to themselves exclusively, the poor and powerless become part of the more subtle control mechanisms which protect the economically affluent and politically powerful.

By controlling the economic resources of a society, those in power manipulate social conditions so that the lower classes appear to be the major contributors to crime.[4] For example, in "The Saints and the Roughnecks," William Chambliss (1973) notes the relationship between a community authority structure (school officials, police, and the town's citizens) and two adolescent youth gangs—the upper middle class Saints and the lower class Roughnecks. Behaviorally, there were few differences between the Saints and the Roughnecks. Members of both groups were involved in delinquent acts such as truancy, reckless driving, excessive drinking, vandalism, and shoplifting. Wealth and the mobility that comes with wealth enabled the Saints to conduct their delinquent activities in places beyond the visibility of the townfolk. This, along with their upper middle class manners and a community bias in their favor, all helped keep gang members free from being labeled delinquent.

A pattern of class discrimination worked against the Roughnecks, whose acts were more apparent and whose manners and demeanor were considered defiant by community standards. While the activities of the Saints went largely unnoticed, the activities of the Roughnecks were stamped with a criminal label. This labeling affected the futures and the adult careers of the boys. Chambliss's study demonstrates how patterns of discrimination based on class affect individuals' life chances.

Schwendinger and Schwendinger (1976a) attempt to explain the emergence of different classes of youth. They claim the history of capitalistic economic and productive forces has affected the development of "the collective varieties of youth," each with their own respective community-predetermined brand of delinquencies that represent their class affiliations. This historical analysis suggests that the formation of lower, middle, and upper class youth groups has deep roots which are tied to the history of the capitalist division of labor and which continue to the present along historical class lines.

In a similar vein, Colvin and Pauly (1983) relate the formation of peer groups that lead to different paths of delinquency to the productive forces of society. Relying on the evidence provided by Kohn (1977), Colvin and Pauly conclude:

> Family compliance structures are class differentiated and . . . parent-child relations are profoundly shaped by parents' encounters with workplace compliance structures. (Colvin and Pauly, 1983: 514)

In other words, the experiences at work, which vary according to different occupational levels and associated work environments, affect or "shape the consciousness and behavior of parents who repeatedly produce and reproduce control relations with children" (Colvin and Pauly, 1983: 514). The theme of socialization is thus approached as a latent manifestation of the work relationships in society. The authors suggest that the work experiences of parents ultimately determine the way they interact with their children. Parents who are treated with hostility and disrespect, who are expected to conform and obey orders without question, and who are expected to assume subordinate, compliant positions in the labor hierarchy, in turn use similar expectations with their children.

Kohn (1977) reports that parents of lower socioeconomic status coming from work environments that are rigid and routinized are more punitive in their childrearing practices and stress conformity to external authority. Such parents tend to rely more on physical punishment and are more likely to punish their children for the consequences of their acts rather than the intent. These childrearing practices lead to the establishment of a control structure within the family comparable to the control structures encountered by parents at the workplace—both control structures and patterns of interaction represent more alienated bonds. Both lower class parents and children learn to respond to authority more out of fear of reprisals or calculation of consequences rather than out of respect or any internal commitment (see review of Kohn, 1977, in Colvin and Pauly, 1983: 535).

Parent-child interactions are different in families of higher economic status. Both parents and children are more "self-directed" and more likely to emphasize internal commitment and more intense bonding (Kohn, 1977; Colvin and Pauly, 1983: 536). The differential socialization experiences, especially the variable "coerciveness of family control structures, conditioned by parents' work experiences, contributes at least indirectly to the production of delinquency" (Colvin and Pauly, 1983: 537).

A parent's relative position in workplace control structures is the first factor that affects the direction or path of the socialization of the child. The child's first bonds, which are shaped by family control relations at home, in turn affect the child's position or placement in the control structures of the school. Different control structures at school imply different patterns of reward and punishment and affect the child's subsequent bond with the school. Adolescents who are less committed to the school and who experience reinforced alienated bonds are more available for recruitment by peer groups made up of alienated peers who "form peer group control structures" which are also built along class lines. Interaction with community and neighborhood further reinforces the alienated bonds and may create two types of delinquent involvement: (1) violent delinquent behavior, which stems from experiences of coercion and personal alienation; and (2) instrumental delinquent behavior, which stems from calculative bonds and the peer group's ability to provide alternative utilitarian incentives (Colvin and Pauly, 1983: 542–543).

Colvin and Pauly's approach to the role of socialization in delinquency is important, because it does not "view the delinquent outcomes of socialization sequences in undifferentiated terms" (p. 524). In essence they are questioning the uncritical rejection by some radical thinkers of the relevance of socialization theories on the grounds that socialization as a concept implies only a consensual model of society. Assuming that the processes of socialization differ depending on the class structures, the way is open to studying socialization from a radical perspective.

Radical criminologists claim that the criminal justice system is the tool the more powerful classes use to maintain control over what they perceive as the "dangerous classes" (Empey, 1978). For example, the point is frequently made that the laws are selectively enforced against the poor and especially blacks. In an experiment, fifteen college students with exemplary driving records put Black Panther bumper stickers on their cars. After 17 days, a total of 33 driving citations had been received by these students, who previously had none (Heussenstamm, 1971: 32). The stickers seemed to elicit a significantly stricter degree of law enforcement. Radical criminologists claim that blacks are treated more harshly than whites by the criminal justice system (Thornberry, 1973; Thomas and Fitch, 1975). At the time of arrest, blacks are more likely to receive official treatment—they are more likely to be detained and referred to court. During adjudication, blacks are more likely to be found involved in delinquency, and they are more likely to be sent to training school (Thornberry, 1973; Thomas and Fitch, 1975).

Radical criminologists have also noted a double standard at work in the treatment and processing of female delinquents. Young females are more likely than young males to be brought before the court for status violations (curfew, truancy, running away) (Chesney-Lind, 1978). Girls are also punished more harshly for relatively less serious offenses. The creation of the juvenile court, for instance, is seen by some radical criminologists as a device that maintains working class powerlessness, along with racism and sexism (Krisberg and Austin, 1978; Platt, 1974).

Krisberg and Austin (1978) in *The Children of Ishmael* suggest that adolescents themselves constitute a powerless, alienated, and subordinate class subject to a wide range of social control mechanisms that monitor their behavior and specify their limited range of rights. Greenberg (1981) holds that the exclusion of the young from the adult world (work and leisure activities) throws young people upon themselves for support and for validation of identity. Age segregation limits the development of solutions to the structurally induced frustrations and inferior status of youth. David Greenberg writes:

> If young people had a good understanding of the structural sources of their frustration and oppression, their response might well be different. Instead of individualistic and predatory adaptations, we might see collective, political and non-predatory challenges to their exclusion. (1981: 136)

Conflict and Radical View of Science and Reform

The role of age, race, gender, and social class in criminal justice and even the study of crime are indeed very complicated, requiring special attention to history and to the values and beliefs that underlie present social definitions and responses to crime. Advocates of the conflict and radical perspectives maintain that crime and the criminal justice system are not simple matters easily dissected by ahistorical, unidimensional, ex post facto methods of scientific investigation. Moreover, radical and conflict theorists have not been convinced that facts and values are separable. They raise questions with regard to the impartiality of science and the impartiality of scientific experts (including psychologists, social workers, and physicians who work for the criminal justice system) (Jenkins, 1982). Academic criminologists working on various crime control projects funded by private and government research grants are thought to perpetuate class inequalities and myths (Quinney, 1974).

Historically, criminologists have rarely been criticized for their acceptance and promotion, through theories, of the existing social class structure. Sociologist C. Wright Mills (1943) was an early exception. He argued in the 1940s that the smalltown, middle class background of most sociologists blinded them to the larger political, historical, and social aspects of major social problems, including delinquency and crime, within American society. Only recently, in the 1970s, have stronger attacks been directed against the sociology of crime and deviance. In a 1972 article, Liazos suggested that there has been a "fascination with the study of 'nuts, sluts, and perverts,' " to the exclusion of "unethical, illegal, and destructive actions of powerful individuals, groups, and institutions in our society" (p. 111). Discussions of violent crimes, for instance, center on only one type of violence, the dramatic and predatory; Liazos says that other types of violence, including racism, malnutrition, slum housing, and the like, are rarely discussed. According to radical criminologists, these other kinds of violence explain why we have crime and delinquency in our society. From the radical perspective, even the more recent theoretical explanations of delinquency and crime, such as the labeling approach, do not adequately address the political and economic basis of most lawbreaking (Wiles, 1977).

One of the primary contributions of the conflict and radical perspectives has been to debunk the facts and findings accompanying the widely held views of mainstream criminologists. Conflict and radical criminologists have criticized mainstream criminologists for upholding the dominant power structures of society and hence the perpetuation of crime and delinquency. The critique suggests that criminologists have been duped into rationalizing a system in which "the rich get richer and the poor get prison."[5]

CONFLICT CRIMINOLOGY VS. RADICAL CRIMINOLOGY

Conflict and radical criminologists study the content, context, and source of beliefs and values and actions associated with criminal law, criminal justice, and criminal theory as they are reflected in political, media, academic, or criminological treatments. The conflict and radical approaches are holistic; they rely heavily on historical and content analyses.

William Chambliss (1984) describes the conflict-oriented theories of crime in the following manner:

The starting point, then, for a conflict-oriented general theory of crime is *not* society but the political economy. The focus must be on whole political and economic systems rather than nation-states or societies. The analysis focuses on class relations (as opposed to social class as a category) as these are created and sustained by particular political economies. And, finally, the methodology of determinism as practiced by social science is replaced with the methodology of dialectical-historical materialism. (p. 78)

Conflict and radical criminologists do not compose homogeneous groups; they represent a wide variety of positions. Radical criminology, for example, has been associated with numerous other titles—the new criminology, Marxist criminology, materialist criminology, dialectical criminology, socialist criminology, critical criminology (Bohm, 1982a).[6] Conflict criminology, which has been confused with radical criminology (Bernard, 1981; Bohm, 1982b), has also been variously described—

as functional conflict theory (Simmel, 1955; Coser, 1956) and pluralist conflict theory (Sellin, 1938; Vold, 1958; Turk, 1969; McCaghy, 1976, 1980). While it is beyond the scope of this chapter to present all the shades of difference among the various writers, we will attempt to review the areas of commonality and the main points of departure.

Critique of the classical and positive criminologies has been one of the main preoccupations of both radical and conflict criminologists (Bohm, 1982a: 566). Both are conversant with Marxism. Conflict theorists, however, are less concerned with adhering closely to the orthodox writings of Marx and Engels. Conflict theorists assume a broad perspective; they do not attribute the causes of conflict or crime to any particular historical context or to the emergence of any specific economic or political system. Instead, they argue that conflict is inherent in all societies. Different theories emphasize different types of conflict relationships. Conflicts arising from age, gender, race, social class, ethnicity, and power are variously treated by different theorists.

Conflict theorists do not treat crime as primarily the by-product of capitalism. Nor do they consider the establishment of socialism as the only solution to the crime problem. "Societies have the criminals they merit," may be a maxim of the conflict perspective (Lacassagne, 1896/1977).

Radical criminologists are more specific in their approach; they locate the causes of crime within capitalism. Radical criminologists are more concerned with the applicability of the philosophy of Marx and Engels. They not only attempt to explain the existence of crime, but usually advocate political, social, and economic changes to eliminate crime. Although radical criminologists see some types of crime (common predatory crime) as a problem, they are not concerned with attempting to solve criminal behavior within the confines of the existing capitalist social system (Dod, Platt, Schwendinger, Shrank, and Takagi, 1976; Young, 1975). Rather, they give priority to "the transformation of capitalism and the establishment of a socialist society" (Garofalo, 1978: 21). The study of crime control therefore becomes secondary, only a means to the political-economic end.

Capitalism, particularly private property, is considered to be the root of most of our social problems, according to the radical perspective. The position, dating at least as far back as Sir Thomas More's *Utopia* (1516/1964), where private property and consequently poverty are the main causes of crime, asserts that the only solution is to change the economic and social structures of society (Schwendinger and Schwendinger, 1976). Presumably only a "good" society leads to "good" human beings! Contemporary radicals attack the existing system of crime and justice by demonstrating the extent to which obsession with private property is reflected in the laws and administration of justice. They point to the lopsided enforcement of laws the protection of private property has created.

Attacking traditional criminologists and their theories, radical proponents claim that radical reform of the existing criminal justice system is a contradiction in terms. Reform efforts aimed at the establishment of a more professional police force, more human correctional facilities, decarceration, and the like (Harring and McMullin, 1975; Scull, 1977; H. M. Solomon, 1976) are criticized by radical criminologists as attempts "by the ruling class to contain the contradictions of capitalism in a way that would preserve the stability of bourgeois rule" (Garofalo, 1978: 21).

HISTORICAL ROOTS OF THE RADICAL AND CONFLICT PERSPECTIVES

Conflict and radical theories have waxed and waned throughout history. The forerunners of the conflict and radical perspectives are many:

> There is no difficulty at all in finding people through history who wrote that poverty and inequality lead to crime, that social justice would diminish crime, or that the law and the justice system served the interests of a ruling class. (Jenkins, 1982: 368)

Plato, Sir Thomas More, Godwin, Holbach, Robert Owen, Karl Marx and Friedrich Engels, to name just a few, have all articulated this position

in some form.[7] The most commonly cited of these are Marx and Engels, who inspired many generations of writers. Some of the early writers dealing with a Marxist interpretation of crime include K. G. Kakowsky, August Bebel, Paul Lafargue, Bruno Battaglia, Joseph Van Kan, and perhaps the best known of the early Marxist criminologists, William Bonger (Greenberg, 1981: 11). We begin our history with the fundamental contributions of Marx and Engels.

Karl Marx and Friedrich Engels: Class Struggle and Crime

Karl Marx (1818–1883) and Friedrich Engels (1820–1895) concentrated most of their efforts on the political and economic changes and class struggles that accompanied the growth of nineteenth-century capitalism in Western societies. Neither Marx nor Engels dealt with the subject of crime and delinquency in any detail. They did, however, develop a model of human social interaction that was particularly sensitive to noting the effects of economic activities and interests on human consciousness and social institutions. They argued that capitalism (mature capitalism) accentuates economic relationships in society and permeates other relationships as well (family, religion, education, politics, law, leisure) (Marx and Engels, 1848; Marx, 1867–1894).[8] Marx's classical observations may be captured by the following quote:

> It is not the consciousness of men that determines their existence, but on the contrary, their social existence determines their consciousness. (1904: 11)

Marx found modern societies to be characterized by the incompatible economic interests of two groups, the **bourgeoisie** and the **proletariat**, who compete for material resources. In a capitalist society the bourgeois class owns and controls the means of production and seeks to maximize its profits by exploiting the working and propertyless or proletarian class. Through its wealth, the ruling bourgeoisie class has an inordinate amount of influence over a society's political institutions. Its members can create and enforce criminal law to protect its economic interests.

Marx predicted that as capitalism expanded, there would be a proliferation of criminal laws. These laws would invariably define as illegal behaviors that threaten the bourgeoisie. To enforce these laws, mainly against the working class, Marx believed that the ruling class had at its disposal the police, the courts, and the correctional systems. Marx further believed that only after the existing economic system was destroyed through a revolution emanating from the proletariat could a classless society, without exploitation, emerge.

According to Marx and Engels, crime is an inherent element of capitalism. In fact crime is "functional" in a capitalist society, but not in the way intended by functional or consensual theorists. Rather, it is indispensable to the capitalist hierarchical order. Without crime, capitalism would not survive. Contrary to the capitalist rhetoric, it is not in the interest of capitalists to eliminate crime. Indeed, as capitalism grows, so will crime.

Marx sarcastically addresses the "usefulness of crime" in this passage from *Theories of Surplus Value:*

A philosopher produces ideas, a poet verse, a parson sermons, a professor textbooks, etc. A criminal produces crime. But if the relationship between this latter branch of production and the whole productive activity of society is examined a little more closely one is forced to abandon a number of prejudices. The criminal produces not only crime but also the criminal law; he produces the professor who delivers lectures on this criminal law, and even the inevitable text-book in which the professor presents his lectures as a commodity for sale in the market. . . .

Further, the criminal produces the whole apparatus of the police and criminal justice, detectives, judges, executioners, juries, etc., and all these professions, which constitute so many categories of the social division of labor, develop diverse abilities of the human spirit, create new needs and new ways of satisfying them. Torture itself has provided occasions for the most ingen-

ious mechanical inventions, employing a host of honest workers in the production of these instruments.

The criminal produces an impression now moral, now tragic, and renders a "service" by arousing the moral and aesthetic sentiments of the public. He produces not only textbooks on criminal law, the criminal law itself and thus legislators, but also art, literature, novels and the tragic drama, as *Oedipus* and *Richard III*, as well as Mullner's *Schuld* and Schiller's *Rauber*, testify. . . . Crime takes off the labour market a portion of the excess population, diminishes competition among workers, and to a certain extent stops wages from falling below the minimum, while the war against crime absorbs another part of the same population. . . . The influence of the criminal upon the development of the productive forces can be shown in detail. Would the locksmith's trade have attained its present perfection if there had been no thieves? Would the manufacture of bank notes have arrived at its present exellence if there had been no counterfeiters? . . . Crime, by its ceaseless development of new means of attacking property, calls into existence new measures of defense. . . .

Leaving the sphere of private crime, would nations themselves exist, if there had not been national crimes? (Marx, 1964: 158–160)

By attacking theories of crime, all based on a consensual model of society, Marx attempted "to emphasize the criminal nature of capitalism" (Taylor et al., 1973: 212).

It was not Marx's intention to romanticize the criminal, for whom he had little sympathy. Marx did not see criminals as serving any positive function—or, more important, as aiding the cause of the proletariat. On the contrary, he called criminals the *lumpenproletariat* or the "dangerous class." The lumpenproletariat was described by Marx and Engels (1848) as a "parasite class living off productive labor by theft, extortion and beggary, or by providing 'services' such as prostitution and gambling" (Hirst, 1975: 216). In essence, "their class interests are diametrically opposed to those of the workers" (p. 216). Marx and Engels described the members of this class as dangerous in another way: They were open to bribes from the ruling class and could be recruited as police informers to infiltrate the workers (1848: 44).

Crime, according to Marx, is not necessarily a political act through which individuals consciously aim to redistribute wealth. Instead, it is an adaptation, made individually, by people who are "demoralized and brutalized by the day to day existence of employment (and unemployment) under industrial capitalism" (Taylor, Walton, and Young, 1973: 218). Criminals, then, are people who are trying to adjust to an inequitable capitalist system that exploits and dehumanizes them. Individual acts of crime are usually not forms of rebellion against the ruling order, but rather adaptations to it (Hirst, 1975; Quinney, 1977).[9] Marx devoted little attention to the individual offender. Crime was of interest to him "from the standpoint of political and ideological struggle" only (Hirst, 1975: 219).[10]

As many theorists have noted, Marx never created a full theory of criminality.[11] To the extent that he had an interest in crime, he appears to have looked at it simply as one aspect of human behavior. From his various writings it is possible to get some notion of how Marx viewed criminal activity. We should caution, however, that Marxist criminologists continually debate Marx's contribution to the study of crime and thus far have failed to achieve agreement.[12] Radical criminologists generally agree that Marx saw crime as a product of social conflict. He stressed that crime is inherent in the capitalist class structure and can be eliminated only by transforming capitalism and establishing a classless society.

Apart from the scant references to the criminogenic conditions of capitalism, little is said by either Marx or Engels about crime in the classless society. One may deduce from their general approach, however, that in a classless society many causes of crime will not exist, especially those causes that stem from capitalism itself. Both Marx and Engels did caution that communism is not to be equated with perfection or utopia, suggesting that communism overcomes social structural inequities and injustices but not nature's injustices—personal inabilities, shortcomings, failures, death, disease, and other natural limitations will not be overcome by communism. This leaves open the possibility that causes of crime not stemming from social structural roots may exist in a classless society. Marx and Engels, however, do not address the question of what types of crime will wither away in the development of communism and what will remain. They do not consider the causes of crime that stem from population growth, modernization, bureaucratization, and other processes which may be common to both Communist and capitalist nations (Plamenatz, 1966).

Critics of radical criminology claim that Marx's followers have stretched his original view of crime and romanticized the criminal by making the offender into some type of oppressed minority. Some of these critics assert "there is no 'Marxist theory of deviance,' either in existence, or which can be developed within orthodox Marxism" (Hirst, 1975: 204). Radical criminologists counter with the argument that their works are directed against the romanticization of criminality. They cite their attacks on labeling theory as an example (Liazos, 1974; Taylor, Walton, and Young, 1973; Thio, 1973). Regardless of arguments over what Marx really meant, most radical and nonradical theorists would agree that a radical approach to crime and delinquency accentuates the ways in which societal organization creates and perpetuates overt and covert violence that harms certain individuals and groups within the society. Radical theories may also erode individualistic explanations about the causes of crime and replace them with examinations of crime in relation to the broader sociohistorical relations within a society.

The radical solution to crime and delinquency through a restructuring of the capitalist state is a solution that has been questioned by many. Some critics have pointed to the patterns of crime in the Soviet Union, which closely parallel ours, as evidence against the radical Marxist position. This may not be valid, however, since those nations of the world that claim to be Communist or socialist do not provide adequate examples of Marx's notion of a classless society. Bohm (1982b: 45) writes:

> As history has well documented, there have been several "antitheses" of capitalism (e.g., social democracy, bourgeois socialism or state capitalism, Nazism or Fascism, bolshevism, Stalinism,

Maoism, etc.). Moreover, none of these "antitheses" of capitalism is Marx's conception of "socialism." Thus, as Becker and Horowitz (1972: 53) warn, "To demand allegiance to any social system as a mark of radical perspective is to ignore the 100-year history of inequality within what has passed for socialism."

David Greenberg (1981), addressing the parallel between Soviet and American delinquency patterns, adds:

> Since Soviet society is based on hierarchical domination and requires a docile, disciplined and stratified labor force, this parallel is not surprising. (p. 135)

Horton and Platt (1983) argue that the convergence noted in the comparisons of international crime patterns is linked to the history and interdependence of a world ecosystem of which all nations are a part (p. 18). They claim that a world system analytical perspective must be developed in order to understand both the commonalities and the anomalies in criminal activities and social responses to crime among different countries.

Many elements of Marxian theory have been widely debated. The main question Marx asks, however, is this: What is the source of social knowledge, including knowledge of crime? Whether or not we agree with his conclusions that knowledge is socially constructed and ultimately tied to societal superstructures, we cannot dismiss the importance of his original question. The Marxian perspective particularly takes issue with the assumption of neutrality associated with the state and even with technology and science, which he considered to represent the ideologies of the powerful class of society. Marx's favorite motto was *De omnibus dubitandum* (Everything must be doubted) (Fromm, 1970: 257).

William Bonger: Capitalism and Demoralization

William Bonger (1876–1940), a Dutch criminologist, was one of the first criminologists to develop a Marxist theory of crime. He analyzed the crime rates of European capitalist states during the early 1900s (Bonger, 1936). Although Bonger's thought diverged from orthodox Marxism in many respects, he did attribute criminal activity to the demoralization brought about by capitalism. Capitalist class structure, characterized by upper class use of economic and political force to exploit the working class, produces people who are greedy and selfish (egoistic). Since the bourgeoisie has the opportunity legitimately to satisfy its desires, crime is concentrated in the lower classes. The criminal justice system criminalizes the poor when it attempts to gain an advantage through the control of behavior that conflicts with the interests of those in power. Bonger argued that a socialist society would eliminate crime by promoting altruism within a society.

Bonger's theory has been criticized for being too individualistic to meet the requirements of pure Marxism (Taylor et al., 1973). Marx concentrated his efforts on the larger social implications of crime. He was not concerned with the individual offender, much less the offender's selfish desires. Additionally, critics point out that Bonger oversimplified the sources of criminal behavior. People commit deviant acts for reasons other than egoism (McCaghy, 1976). Juvenile gang offenders, for example, may fight other gangs to further the interests of their group, or for more prestige or turf.

Despite these criticisms, Bonger's theory of crime was an early forerunner of later conflict theories. His theory centered on the relationships between groups with differing social and economic interests and definitions of crime and delinquency, as did later conflict perspectives.

EARLY CONFLICT THEORIES (1930s–1960s): PREMISES AND CRITIQUE

Not until the 1930s, however, did conflict theory of a nonradical type surface in criminology. At that time, pluralist conflict theorists such as Thorsten Sellin rekindled an interest in the study of crime and delinquency, an interest that was later reiterated by George Vold in the late 1950s and Austin Turk in the 1960s. These theorists agreed that crime and delinquency are products of conflicts between groups of unequal power. But unlike Marx, these pluralists did not view society as split into two opposing camps, a ruling class and a powerless class. Rather, they saw a society divided into many groups that competed for power.

Thorsten Sellin: Pluralist Conflict Theory

In 1938 Thorsten Sellin published a short work entitled *Culture and Conflict in Crime*. Attempting to explain crime and delinquency patterns among the immigrant population of the United States, Sellin distinguished crime norms (embodied in criminal law) from conduct or group norms:

> The criminal law may be regarded as in part a body of rules, which prohibit specific forms of conduct and indicate punishments for violations. The character of these rules, the kind or type of conduct they prohibit, the nature of the sanction attached to their violation, etc., depend upon the character and interests of those groups in the population which influence legislation. In some states these groups may comprise the majority, in others a minority, but the social values which receive the protection of the criminal law are ultimately those which are treasured by dominant interest groups. (p. 21)

From this excerpt, we see that Sellin employed a rudimentary conflict approach to the study of crime. Those groups that are dominant in terms of nationality, ethnicity, or economics—and not necessarily mere numbers—are able to control and define the legal definitions of criminality. Problems arise when individual group members, abiding by their respective group or conduct norms, clash with the formal norms of other groups, particularly when a member of a less powerful group challenges a dominant or majority group. The more complex a culture becomes, the greater the likelihood "that the number of normative groups which affect a person will be large, and the greater is the chance

that the norms of these groups will fail to agree, no matter how much they may overlap as a result of a common acceptance of certain norms" (p. 29).

Thus, for every person, depending on the norms that establish values for his or her particular group, there is a normal and an abnormal way of reacting. Sellin proposed that "the study of conduct norms would afford a sounder basis for the development of scientific categories than a study of crimes as defined in the criminal law" (p. 30). Later social theorists, including advocates of the societal re-action perspective, obviously heeded this advice.

Sellin sought to explain immigrant criminality with the theory of culture conflict. As the foreign-born flooded the nation's cities, experts and the public believed that immigrant groups were largely responsible for rising crime and delinquency rates. In many of the earlier ecological studies noted in Chapter 6, conditions in transitional sections of cities, areas where a number of different ethnic groups and nationalities lived in close proximity, were depicted as major causes of crime and delinquency. Sellin thought that the physical closeness of many deviant groups and the invasion of one group into another provided an explanation of criminality in urban areas. He pointed out that when different ethnic groups remained homogeneous, experiencing little contact with "outsiders" but accepting the dominant culture, they maintained low delinquency and crime rates.

Since immigration to the United States has been severely limited over more recent decades, interest in Sellin's theory of immigrant deviance has declined. It has simply not been very useful for the explanation of contemporary crime and delinquency.[13] Sellin's work did, however, lead to a later version of conflict theory, that of group conflict.

George Vold: Group Conflict

In 1958 sociologist George Vold published *Theoretical Criminology*, the first criminology text in which certain types of crimes were attributed to social conflict.[14] Vold argued that the normal antagonisms and conflicts among human groups could be used as the setting or condition for explaining large amounts of deviant activity. Vold depicted society as a "congerie of groups held together in a shifting but dynamic equilibrium of opposing group interests and efforts," and described the endless series of moves and countermoves through which groups vie for power—for example, political and economic power. Various groups come into conflict when their interests and purposes overlap or encroach (1979: 283). Vold thought groups gain an advantage by political power and then influence the passage of legislation which will be beneficial to them and protect their interests. Through legislative majorities, they win "control over the police power and dominate the policies that decide who is likely to be involved in violation of the law" (p. 288).

Vold suggested that certain collective types of crimes, such as juvenile gang delinquency, or acts of political rebellion, such as sabotage, are adaptive means. Gang members and rebels band together for protection and strength because they are in some way "at odds with organized society and with the police forces maintained by society" (p. 289). According to Vold, delinquent gangs are "minority groups" because of their inability to achieve their objectives through regular channels or reliance upon the protection of the state. In this sense, the gang represents a united group in conflict with the "established world of adult values and power" which threatens the gang members (p. 290). Other kinds of criminal acts represent a more direct contact between groups seeking power within the political arena. These illegal acts include such diverse tactics as strike breaking and terrorism. The participants are likely to view their deeds as unpleasant but necessary to further the group's cause against the perceived enemy.

Vold's conflict theory, differing from Marxist or contemporary radical criminology, is used to explain certain types of crime and delinquency within the confines of an existing set of social relationships (Taylor et al., 1973). In Vold's theory, group conflict is normal, and therefore no radical change within the existing political social system is necessary. Vold's conflict theory is also limited "to those kinds of situations in which the individual criminal acts flow from the collusion of groups whose members are loyally upholding the in-group position" (p. 296). Individualistic impulses or irrational acts of criminality outside the context of a group cause cannot be explained by Vold's group conflict theory.

Austin Turk: Authorities and Subjects

Austin Turk is another representative of non-radical conflict theory. Turk rejects past attempts to explain crime in terms of specific behaviors. He has suggested instead that criminality is a status conferred on that behavior. In his work *Criminality and the Legal Order* (1969), Turk initially informs the reader that "no one is intrinsically criminal: criminality is a definition applied by individuals with the power to do so, according to illegal and extralegal as well as legal criteria" (p. 10). After making the now commonly accepted discrimination between rule-breaking behavior and acts defined as deviant, Turk presents a number of propositions. He asserts that criminality is a status, encompassing real or fancied attributes of people, rather than a specific behavior. He writes:

> The study of criminality becomes the study of relations between the statuses and roles of legal authorities—creators, interpreters, and enforcers of right-wrong standards for individuals in the political collectivity—and those of subjects—acceptors or resistors but not makers of such law, creating, interpreting and enforcing decisions. (p. 35)

Turk specifies "the conditions under which a subject in an authority-subject relationship will be defined as criminal" and enumerates the conditions under which individuals will accept and not accept authority (Taylor et al., 1973: 242). People, he suggests, learn and continually relearn that they are "occupants of superior and inferior statuses and performers of dominating and submitting roles" (Turk, 1969: 42). Only by learning (and accepting) these authority-subject relationships do people make social order possible.

If individuals learn their places in these authority-subject relationships, they will adhere to two sets of norms: *norms of domination* and *norms of deference.* These norms are historically well established within a society. Lawbreaking occurs "when rulers and ruled, decision-makers and decision acceptors, are not bound together in a perfectly stable authority relationship" (p. 48). In this situation, there is a failure in the patterns of domination.

In addition to domination and deference norms, Turk delineates *cultural norms* (publicized norms) and *social norms* (actual behaviors). Conflict and the assignment of a deviant label depend upon whether there is congruence or lack of congruence between these social norms and the cultural evaluation of the norms. For instance, when those in authority believe the use of marijuana is wrong and abstain from using it but younger members of a society believe the use of marijuana is acceptable and use it, the potential for conflict between the two groups is great. In this situation, there is a strong likelihood that those who use the drug will come to be defined as delinquent. On the other hand, if those in authority say that use of marijuana is wrong but use the drug themselves, the conflict between the two groups is more symbolic than actual. And the assignment of deviant labels is much less likely.

Turk also argues that certain social variables, such as age, sex, race, and ethnicity, determine the relative relationships of an individual with respect to the norms of domination. Similarly, the subject's degree of organization and degree of sophistication and the subject's ability to verbalize rationalizations for norm violations determine whether he or she comes into conflict with those in authority and subsequently becomes labeled as a norm resistor (Turk, 1969: 59).

Although Turk's brand of conflict theorizing alerts us to the individual and social factors that produce conflicts between authorities and subjects, the theory itself is so complex as to be virtually untestable. Whether the relationships between conflict and criminalization can be clarified through Turk's theory remains to be seen.[15]

CONTEMPORARY RADICAL CONFLICT THEORY (1960–1980): PREMISES AND CRITIQUE

As we have suggested, conflict theories of crime have waxed and waned in popularity throughout the history of criminology.[16] Beginning in the United States in the 1960s, a time of political unrest, there was renewed interest within the academic community in Marxist-oriented theories of deviance. The roots of radicalism were found in various political struggles—the civil rights movement, the Vietnam antiwar movement, the student movement, the women's movement, the children's rights movement, anti-imperialist movements, and in the writings of participants in these struggles (Platt, 1975).

Accompanying these movements was the rise of concern associated with growing social and economic problems. America's post-World War II optimism was giving way to disappointment and disillusionment as political corruption (Watergate) and U.S. military escalation in the world became more evident and as economic hardships in the midst of affluence became apparent. All this provided the context out of which radical criminology reemerged. Despite political-social constraints and anti-Marxist sentiment, radical criminology was able to flourish in many American universities between the late sixties and early seventies (Sinclair, 1983; Platt and Takagi, 1982).

The School of Criminology at Berkeley was considered by many to represent the highest quality of radical theoretical development and to be the center of radical scholarship (Platt and Takagi, 1982). Under the influence of the Schwendingers, Platt and Takagi produced the journal *Crime and Social Justice,* which emphasized the Marxian perspective.

However, growing conservatism in the late 1970s soon produced pressures to preclude the development of Marxist ideas which were perceived to undermine American traditions. The result was the closing of the School of Criminology in 1976. Most of those associated with *Crime and Social Justice* moved to different parts of the country. This dispersal of scholars might have severely hampered the communication and development of a coherent perspective had not ISLEC (the Institute for the Study of Labor and Economic Crisis), an independent research institute, been founded in 1977 to continue the support and the development of radical ideas. *Crime and Social Justice* continues to be published by the institute.

Platt and Takagi summarize the events of the late 1970s and early 1980s in the following passage:

> The representation and dispersion of the School of Criminology at Berkeley fundamentally disrupted the consolidation and development of radical criminology in the United States. . . . For a while, "radical" criminology became increasingly unguided and disorganized, reminiscent of Engels's description of the utopian socialists: "a mishmash permitting of the most manifold shades of opinion: a mishmash of the less striking critical statements, economic theories and pictures of future society." The terms "radical criminology" and "new criminology" were quickly coopted and diluted, for the most part emptied of their genuine radicalism, and used as a fashionable mantle to cloak everything from muckraking exposés to liberal reformism. Richard Quinney, who built his cases as the leading "radical" criminologist in the United States, added to the confusion by publishing huge amounts of materials which were generally crude, undigested and dogmatic. Not surprisingly, the opponents of "radical" criminology seized upon Quinney's shallow scholarship and opportunistically equated it with Marxism. (Platt and Takagi, 1982: 2; cited in Sinclair, 1983: 26)

Radical criminology, exemplified by the works of William Chambliss and Robert Seidman, Tony Platt, Herman and Julia Schwendinger, Barry Krisberg, and Richard Quinney, to name just a few, continues to receive mixed reviews in the United States.[17] Although many criminologists recognize the need to rectify inequities in the criminal justice and juvenile justice systems, as well as within political and economic institutions, they are unwilling to accept a theoretical orientation that advocates drastic reorganization of the existing society.[18] The emphasis on the reorganization of society as a solution to the crime problem has led to increased attention to cross-cultural comparisons. As a result, the radical school of criminology, perhaps more than any other school of thought, has been concerned with cross-cultural studies of crime and delinquency, and especially the theoretical contributions of criminologists from different countries.

In Europe, especially Britain, the 1970s also represented a period of growth and development of the radical perspective in criminology. In Britain, criminologists Ian Taylor, Paul Walton, and Jock Young developed a critical explanation of crime and delinquency based on Marxist principles. In *The New Criminology* (1973), which is frequently cited by American radical theorists, they outlined their theory as "one normatively committed to the abolition of inequalities of wealth and power, and in particular of inequalities in property and life circumstances [and breaking] entirely with [theories or methods of] correctionalism" (p. 281).

In Germany, the noted Frankfurt School of Sociology and such scholars as Habermas (1975) have mounted an attack on the role of science (positivism) in the formation of social policy, with warnings against the "false consciousness" that surrounds the scientific enterprise. In this context, false consciousness is associated with the results of scientific methods that serve to reduce complex human behavior and relationships to some numerical averages. There is a tendency to reify these averages (treat these statistics or estimates as if they are real). Problems occur when social policies are based on statistically created, mythical images that are derived from aggregate data rather than on the real people, whose individual needs become lost in the process of statistical abstraction.

Foucault (1979) from France has contributed a history of penology which demonstrates the association between the development of Western penology and capitalist modes of production. He concludes that reliance on institutional forms of state control go far back in history. State control has changed in form, not in substance—punishment is punishment irrespective of form. In the past, punishment was physically defined; now it is psychologically and medically defined.

More and more attention has been devoted to Soviet criminology. Soviet criminologists typically employ a Marxist critique in their analysis of Western crime or crime in capitalist nations. It is interesting to note, however, that they do not usually apply a Marxist explanation to their own crime problems (Voigt and Thornton, 1985). The Soviet approach to delinquency is primarily preventive, stressing youths' relationships with family, teachers, and peers. Their own explanations of delinquency closely resemble the social control theories popular among criminologists in many countries around the world, including American criminologists (Voigt and Thornton, 1985).

Moreover, despite differences in ideology between the USSR and USA, many observers (Connor, 1972; Juviler, 1976; Shelley, 1981a,b; Voigt and Thornton, 1985) have noted similarities in the patterns of crime and delinquency and the characteristics of the typical offender (young males from poorly educated, lower-income, single-headed families comprise the bulk of the statistics). This evidence is used by some to condemn the claim that socialism is the solution to crime. Yet what this evidence also suggests is that culturally specific paradigms of crime which assume that cultural systems are "fixed, pre-existing and independent" underestimate the influences of a world system of which most nations are a part (Horton and Platt, 1983). The overlap between the Soviet Union and the United States does not confirm or disconfirm any theories; it raises many more questions than it answers. A great deal more comparative work is necessary before we can understand the meaning of the commonalities and differences we document among countries.[19]

Our summary of the radical perspective is very brief, hardly touching upon the complexities and varieties of ideas that have been contributed by scholars all over the world. We have selected two well-known American theorists, Richard Quinney and Tony Platt. Quinney, one of the most prolific proponents of radical criminology, has been selected because his works offer a comprehensive statement of the radical approach to crime. Although his work focuses on adult crime, his theories may be applied to juveniles as well. Tony Platt has been selected because his work not only deals directly with a radical approach to delinquency, but also addresses some more recent criticisms of radical criminology.

Richard Quinney: Social Construction of Crime

Richard Quinney's numerous works on the subject of crime have in common one unifying element: "A Marxist analysis of crime begins with the recognition that crime is basically a material problem" (Quinney, 1977: 31). Quinney, like most radical criminologists, has argued that crime is affected by the social, the economic, and the political structures of the capitalist state.

According to this theory, competition for scarce resources between segments of a society inevitably leads to conflict. Powerful individuals have a clear advantage; they are able to formulate and manipulate public policy to protect their interests. Part of this manipulation process, as Quinney has written, is the ability to create an existing social reality of crime. His theory is an attempt to demonstrate the ways in which structures of power, authority, and interest make up a society's social reality of crime. Quinney has set forth six propositions:

1. *The official definition of crime.* Crime, as a legal definition of human conduct, is created by agents of the dominant class in a politically organized society. [In other words, people in power officially determine a definition of crime that is conferred upon other people. Such agents of the law as legislators, police prosecutors, and judges are responsible for formulating and administering criminal and juvenile law. Crime, then, is not inherent in behavior but is a

judgment made by some about the behaviors and characteristics of others.]

2. *Formulating definitions of crime.* Definitions of crime are composed of behaviors that conflict with the interests of the dominant class. [These definitions of crime—and delinquency—change as the interest of the dominant class changes. The more a group's behaviors conflict with the interests of the dominant class, the greater the likelihood that those groups will be sanctioned by the enforcing and administering of criminal law.]

3. *Applying definitions of crime.* Definitions of crime are applied by the class that has the power to shape the enforcement and administration of criminal law. [Rather than simply creating criminal laws, the dominant class must enforce and administer these laws to fully protect its interests.] The probability that definitions of crime will be applied varies according to how much the behaviors of the powerless conflict with the interests of those in power.

4. *Development of behavior patterns in relation to criminal definitions.* Behavior patterns are structures in relation to definitions of crime, and within this context people engage in actions that have relative probabilities of being defined as criminal. [The less powerful segments of society, who are not represented when the definitions of crime are created, are more likely to act in ways that will be defined as criminal. Once definitions of crime are established, these less powerful individuals may come to develop behavioral patterns and self-conceptions leading to future criminal behaviors.]

5. *Construction of criminal conceptions of crime.* Conceptions of crime are constructed and diffused in the segments of society by various means of communications. [Those in power construct and disseminate public conceptions of crime. The more the power-ful are concerned about crime, the greater the probability that criminal definitions will be created and that behavior patterns will develop in opposition to criminal definitions.]

6. *Constructing the social reality of crime.* The social reality of crime is constructed by the formulation and application of definitions of crime, the development of behavior patterns in relation to these definitions, and the construction of an ideology of crime. [This proposition summarizes the previous five.] (Quinney, 1970: 15–25; 1975: 37–41)

Inherent in Quinney's work is the assumption that there are two basic social classes: those with power and those without. Quinney has suggested that a politically organized society such as the United States may be viewed as having differential interest structures. By possessing authority within this interest structure, some groups are able to make their interests represented in public policy. Quinney argues that actual public policy is determined by a very small and very powerful group of economic interests. This segment is "that class which owns and controls the means of production and which is able, by virtue of [its] economic power . . . to use the state as its instrument for the domination of society" (1974: 53). For Quinney, the ruling class in the United States is not a monolithic entity, but rather a class composed of owners and controllers of the means of production, relatively small in number, and other interest groups that benefit from these policies. The primary interest of the ruling class is to preserve the existing order.

In *The Social Reality of Crime* (1970), and more specifically in *Critique of Legal Order* (1974), Quinney asserted that an official reality of crime exists to maintain order and stability in society; the official reality is basically a myth. Through the legal system, the capitalist order, including the welfare state associated with that order, can be preserved to protect the interests of the few. He suggested that even laws regulating morality (for example, status crimes of juveniles and victimless crimes) were intended to preserve the "moral and ideological basis of capitalism" (1974: 55–56). By reviewing the origins of such crimes as theft, vagrancy, antitrust violations, drunkenness, and drug use, Quinney tried to show how crimes pose a threat to the legitimacy of the ruling class even when the acts are perpetrated against members of the subservient class.[20]

Quinney has not specifically discussed delinquency, but his radical analysis is easily applied to an examination of the origins of juvenile delinquency.[21] Some sociologists see "the concept of juvenile delinquency as a bourgeois invention used to segment off for treatment those youth whose patterned acts [represent] threats to bourgeois hegemony" (Carter and Clelland, 1977: 4). As evidence for radical theory, it is pointed out that crime control focuses on working class rather than middle or upper class offenders. Quinney has said that agencies and programs such as LEAA (now phased out) and the President's Crime Commissions are devices used to maintain the economic interests of those in power (Quinney, 1970, 1974).

Crime (and delinquency) control, according to Quinney, encompasses the courts, the correctional establishment, and even criminologists, who eagerly compete for federal grants that further exploit certain classes of people. (Granting agencies decide what will be funded, and in the 1960s, for example, when many blacks were openly demonstrating, much research was conducted on riot control.) Quinney's views on crime control also include a consideration of the role of the victim.

> A victim cannot be taken for granted . . . in the larger social context we all engage in commonsense constructions of "the crime," "the criminal," and "the victim." In our minds we know who or what is the victim in any situation. At the same time, we exclude other contenders from our image of the victim. . . . Our conception of victims and victimization are optional, discretionary, and by no means innately given. . . . The conceptions we do hold, however, have consequences for . . . criminologists. And, moreover, such conceptions affect the ways in which we all live our lives. (Quinney, 1975b: 189)

Criminologists and victimologists often present limited constructions of crime and victimization (Quinney, 1975b: 192). They support particular perspectives while disregarding or minimizing competing positions. They selectively choose and emphasize certain variables while omitting others. Often, they arbitrarily cluster variables. They create typologies (imaginary criminals or imaginary victims) on the basis of a relatively narrow range of information.[22] Many research questions are simply unanswerable, given the very nature of the methods of data collection and the inherent difficulties associated with crime and victim data.

Victimological investigation suffers from difficulties in definition. For instance, the definition of victims in victim surveys does not include gang or delinquents' victimization of themselves.[23] Criminological thought generally precludes systematic consideration of any victims of oppression ("victims of the state of violence," "victims of the correctional system," "victims of the police force," "victims of war") (Quinney, 1975b: 196):

> The absence of empirical research is explicable on the ground that it may expose the unreality of the assumptions made about victims of crime. The confusion present in the various justifications proferred for legislative intervention becomes inevitable given the political goals that are based on these assumptions. (Miers, 1980: 14–15)

Delinquents are denied victim status because there is a rival alternative (offender status) that ultimately determines their treatment in society (Voigt and Thornton, 1982).

Tony Platt: From Child Saving to Child Stigmatization

In radical theory, delinquency, like adult criminality, is depicted as a bourgeois invention or an artifact of capitalism. When the rules that make certain behaviors "delinquent" are applied, certain youth are defined (labeled) as delinquent. Delinquent behaviors are those that are believed to be antithetical to capitalist interest. Most of the evidence supporting the critical view is historical, concentrating on the social and political conditions that led to the creation of the juvenile court. The work of Tony Platt (1969, 1974) is probably best known in this area.

Platt analyzed the child-saving movement through the late nineteenth century and argued that there are a number of prevailing myths about the origins of the juvenile justice system. Although the child-saving movement was depicted as successful in humanizing the criminal justice system's handling of juvenile offenders, the movement, according to Platt, did not attain its goals. More specifically, the child-saving movement was "coercive and conservatizing." The movement tried to do for the juvenile justice system what industrialists were trying to do for the economy—"achieve order, stability, and control while preserving the existing class system and distribution of wealth" (1974: 367).

Although the child-saving movement drew its most visible supporters from the middle class, Platt reported that it could not have achieved significant reforms without the financial and political support of the wealthy and powerful. The movement was only one of many massive changes taking place in the United States as the country shifted from laissez-faire to monopoly capitalism. The abolition of child labor, deemed by many as a major reform, was in reality "a means of driving out marginal manufacturers and tenement operators, hence increasing the consolidation and efficacy of business" (p. 369). In this same radical vein, the rise of compulsory education was also seen to be closely tied to the changing forms of industrial production (and social control). Education served to impose on the working class a "system which mirrored the ethos of the corporate workplace and was designed to provide an increasingly refined training and selection mechanism for the labor force" (p. 370).

As the United States emerged from the economic instability and industrial violence of the 1890s, efforts were made to stabilize the new capitalist order. Platt noted that one of these efforts involved the creation of an ideology equating chaos with crime and violence and proposing

a solution of social controls. Crime was viewed as coming primarily from so-called criminal classes, who recruited their rank and file from the lower classes. Delinquent youth were described as "little Arabs" or "vagabonds" who were "familiar with the vicious ways and places of the town" (p. 373). The prevailing theories of crime causation were grounded in evolutionary theory. Criminals were viewed as a "dangerous and atavistic class, standing outside the boundaries of morally regulated relationships" (p. 374). Some child savers advocated harsh methods of crime control—sterilization, criminal punishments, and permanent incarceration—but more moderate means generally prevailed.

Platt claimed that the concentration of the child-saving movement on youthful deviance drew attention to and thus created or invented new categories of youthful misconduct previously not deemed a problem. Threats posed by moral offenses, status, and victimless crimes, were included in these new categories of deviance. Status offenses were thought to threaten the existing value system, which induced stable participation in the workforce. Juvenile court legislation, passed in all but three states by 1917, was meant to prevent youthful offenders from engaging in the criminal careers that directly threatened the existing capitalist order. To accomplish this task, new programs of adjudication and control for "delinquent," "dependent," and "neglected" youth were formulated by the court. The **parens patriae** concept gave the court authority to intercede in the family life of children who appeared to be suffering from improper home conditions. Extending its concern far beyond the handling of juvenile offenders, the court amassed a tremendous amount of power which it increasingly used to control, in the legal sense, the children of working class and immigrant families.

Although many middle class people who were genuinely interested in the welfare of youth worked in and for the child-saving movement, the movement was seen by Platt as one "primarily concerned with regulating social behavior . . . and preparing [working class] youth as a disciplined and devoted work force" (p. 382). According to Platt, the contemporary juvenile justice system has continued the class exploitation. He has also depicted it as a device "to maintain racism, sexism, and working-class powerlessness" (p. 384). Middle class adolescents have recently been arrested in greater numbers than ever before, but most arrestees are still from the ranks of the urban poor, the lower classes, and minority groups.[24] Radicals charge that middle class youngsters avoid state institutionalization by the use of expensive attorneys, private psychiatrists, and referrals to military schools. They also assert that suburban youth in middle class white communities avoid referrals to the juvenile court through the informal handling of sympathetic local police.

Based on recommendations from the 1967 National Crime Commission, new strategies of control—some seemingly benevolent, others coercive and authoritarian—were directed toward "hard to reach" youth, often minority group members. The more benevolent strategies to control delinquent youth include youth service bureaus, community relations programs, and the use in juvenile courts of attorneys who specialize in juvenile law (Platt, 1974: 387). There is evidence, however, that these new programs are not as benevolent as they are depicted. Referral to youth service bureaus, for instance, can bring with it compulsory intervention in the lives of children and their families to a point where treatment is forced on unwilling juveniles without due process. In this process, the child's guilt or innocence is never determined (James and Thornton, 1978).

Even the right to counsel in juvenile proceedings, supported by the Gault ruling in 1967, has not had the expected impact. A study by Platt, Schechter, and Tiffany (1978) reported that public defenders in juvenile courts handled mainly poor and nonwhite youth and often labeled their clients as bad kids or good kids, proceeding accordingly. Youth who came from broken homes or homes where there was unemployment and youth who did not have the proper demeanor were likely to be labeled as unsalvageable. In reality, these juvenile attorneys "bring to their jobs commonsense notions about adolescence and troublesome behaviors . . . that are really no different from those of other adult officials (teachers, social workers, youth officers, etc.)" (Platt, 1974: 388).

Radicals also point to more coercive measures of dealing with what is referred to as the delinquency problem. According to Platt (1974): "The creation of police gang intelligence units, infiltration of youth groups by police spies, the presence of heavily armed riot and 'tactical' units, and the routine patrolling of urban schools by police guarantee the availability of coercive measures to support benevolent policies" (p. 389).

In summary, many radical criminologists see parallels between the early child-saving movement and contemporary efforts to perpetuate the juvenile justice system. They charge that acceptance of state definitions of delinquency continues to be unquestioned, accompanied by promotion of reforms within the framework of corporate capitalism, underestimation of the importance of historical and macroscopic analysis, and encouragement of defeatist attitudes about the possibility of radical change. According to radicals, a solution to juvenile delinquency is not to be found in existing institutions and token reforms. Only until these measures are replaced by institutions "which serve and are democratically controlled by the people," argue radicals, will juvenile crime be reduced in our society (Platt, 1974: 389).

Since the reconstruction of society does not appear close, Platt (1982: 41–44) has recommended some immediate measures to deal with serious street crime:

1. Bring equal justice to the bail system.

2. Abolish mandatory sentences.

3. Restore indeterminate sentences.

4. Combat racism in criminal justice professionals.

5. Prosecute corporate crime and racist violence.

6. Increase employment to lower the incarceration rate.

7. Restore funding for community alternatives to imprisonment.

Platt concludes:

> We need to do a great deal of difficult theoretical work, to escape from the intellectual straight-jacket of "criminology" and use the complex science of Marxism to get beyond muckraking radicalism. And given that Marxism is, after all, a guide to action, our policy proposals and theoretical enterprises must be informed by and tested in practice. (1982: 44)

The issue of immediate reforms presents a problem, particularly with respect to the long-term goal of reconstructing society. The immediate reforms may be viewed as leading to the false hope of reconciling the contradictions of capitalism. The short-range reforms are motivated more by general humanitarian concerns and less by ideological consistency.

Critique of Contemporary Radical Conflict Theory

Radical theory has mainly dealt with "criminal" adults; only rudiments of a radical delinquency theory exist. Examples of radical analyses of delinquency include the work of Platt (1974), especially his study of the early child-saving movement in the United States; the Schwendingers' (1976a) historical account of the varieties of adolesence and delinquency; Greenberg's (1977a) work on delinquency and the age structure. Other examples include the work of Carter and Clelland (1979), which represents an attempt to analyze juvenile corrections critically; Sinclair's (1983) radical Marxist historical overview of juvenile justice in the United States; and the work of Colvin and Pauly (1983) relating a structural Marxist framework to the process of socialization.

Two delinquency texts (Krisberg and Austin, 1978, and Schwendinger and Schwendinger, 1985) approach the study of juvenile crime from a "critical" perspective. There are, of course, other works that could be listed (Chambliss, 1973, and Krisberg and Austin, 1978). Certainly many studies, while not aimed specifically at a Marxist interpretation, offer evidence for radical writers.

Yet even these works, added to those included in our survey, do not constitute a comprehensive and integrated theory of delinquency.

The radical and conflict perspectives have been relatively successful in "explaining the distribution of crime rates among various groups in society" (Bernard, 1981: 367). However, explaining criminal behavior has not been among the central concerns of either the advocates of the radical or the conflict perspectives. The question of scientific research used in support of theories has been widely debated both by radical proponents and by critics of the radical perspective. Radicals have questioned the value-free premise of positivistic criminologists. On the other hand, radicals have themselves been charged with being biased. David Greenberg addresses this problem in the following statement:

> Where there is disagreement between Marxian and non-Marxian theory, then, the superiority of the Marxist analysis must be demonstrated.
> Such demonstration will not be easy because both Marxian and non-Marxian ideas are frequently hard to operationalize. Many of Marx's ideas are expressed in language that is metaphysical and ambiguous. Similar problems pervade non-Marxian criminology. Given this difficulty, we may end up evaluating theories on the basis of how congenial we find their untestable meta-sociological assumptions, but this circumstance is not one that should make us happy. (1981: 20)

More conservative criminologists have voiced numerous criticisms of radical theories and have pointed out alleged flaws of the radical approach.[25] Acknowledging the fact that some of the criticisms aimed against the radical perspective may be out of date and tend to be more author-specific, thus limiting their generalizability, we would like to offer some of the typical questions raised against the radical paradigm. Some critics have accused radicals of selective treatment of research citations, suggesting that they use research which supports their positions and reject evidence which goes against them on the ground that it is value laden.

It is alleged that radical writers rarely consider studies of self-reported delinquency which reveal that delinquent acts and crimes are committed by all classes of American (and non-American) youth. Radicals are faulted for ignoring the large volume of self-reported crimes committed by middle and upper class youth and for not looking at evidence which suggests that middle class juvenile offenders, especially female status offenders, are detained more often and treated more harshly in the juvenile court than lower class youth (Pawlak, 1977; L. E. Cohen, 1975).

Since radical criminologists see poverty and unemployment at the heart of the reasons for crime and delinquency, radical criminology faces a serious anomaly. Research shows that delinquency rates increase during times of prosperity, not during times of unemployment. As Empey (1978) has noted, "The loosened controls that are associated with increasing affluence and opportunity may be somewhat more important than poverty per se" (p. 389). Similarly, radical theorists claim that capitalism exploits the labor of poverty classes. Yet there has been a persistent decline in teenage employment and labor force participation over the years, especially among lower class youth (Greenberg, 1977a). Before radical theories can assume full legitimacy, empirical analyses that support general, sweeping statements about youth crime in capitalist society are needed.

Recent evidence on social class and criminality suggests that class-based theories of deviance should be reevaluated. Tittle, Villemez, and Smith (1978) have noted, for instance, that there has been a constant decline in the strength of the relationship between social class and crime-delinquency. This is especially true for self-report and official statistics studies done since 1970, in which essentially little relationship between social class and crime and delinquency has been found.[26]

In response to the question of the magnitude of the correlation between social class and crime, the Schwendingers (1982) argue that "it is not the concept of class, in principle, that is fundamentally at fault" (p. 71). They go on to claim that "the fault lies with the theories that dominate the field and the ways in which criminologists generally conceive of delinquent relationships" (p. 71). According to the Schwendingers, "the debate about social class and delinquency symbolizes a paradigmatic crisis in conventional theories about social class and delinquency" (p. 71). Juvenile crime and its causes are complex, and it is extremely unlikely that any one theoretical perspective, including the radical, can explain the problems by examining a select group of variables, no matter how encompassing they at first appear.

Some critics, such as Klockars (1979) and Akers (1979), fault the radical perspective for overstressing the conflict interests and dissensus associated with laws. They claim that laws cannot simply be viewed as representing the interests of the upper classes exclusively. In fairness, not all radical proponents hold this position without qualification. Chambliss (1969), for example, maintains that some laws reflect the interests of the general population (laws against the person, such as rape, murder, assault). Chambliss asserts that the effects of interest groups and power groups on the development of the laws represent one dimension of the explanation of the emergence of our legal codes.

Perhaps the solution offered by radicals to the crime problem has been questioned most. In his last proposition, *Critique of Legal Order*, Quinney (1974) claimed that the problem of crime cannot be solved within the confines of a capitalist society; a new society based on socialism would be the only way to eliminate crime. Although it is true that American criminology has been primarily "corrective" in its approach to criminals and delinquents (that is, trying to change them), Socialist and Communist societies are not crime-free utopias. As Klockars (1979) has indicated, Marxist criminologists have failed to address the issue of crimes, particularly crimes of violence, committed in Socialist and Communist societies.

Descriptions of Stalin's purges in the Soviet Union in the 1930s and Alexsandr Solzhenitsyn's descriptions of more recent USSR atrocities reveal that Soviet delinquency shares many similarities with delinquency in the United States and other Western countries (see Voigt and Thornton, 1985). Generally, "the age, types of offense, educational experience, and family background of the Soviet delinquent do not appear strikingly dissimilar from his [or her] counterparts elsewhere" (Connor, 1972: 92; see also Chapter 18). Cuba, though experiencing a reduction in many crimes since the 1959 revolution, has adopted a policy of arresting youths not working and not in school in order to force them to do productive labor. This concept of a solution to the delinquency problem is probably not what radical academic criminologists envision for crime-free society (Klockars, 1979: 499). Schichor makes the following observation:

> Overpolitization of juvenile delinquency and criminology by radical criminologists often leads to ideological criticism of others in attempting to arrive at causal explanations and concentrates on the analysis of capitalist societies without paying enough attention to the criminogenic attributes of socialist social systems. (1983: 96)

In response to such criticisms, Platt and Horton (1983) have begun to devise a framework based on a world system perspective to explain "crime and criminal justice under capitalism and socialism" (p. 3). However, the recommendation to consider cross-cultural studies should not just be directed to the radical criminologists. The area of cross-cultural comparisons is one that must be expanded (see Chapter 18). The potential for the cross-fertilization of ideas is great. Not until we begin to understand other cultural problems and adaptations will we be able to recognize the ethnocentricity contained in our own paradigms and solutions or begin to reconcile the differences we observe.

Although radical criminology makes no pretense of eliminating crime within a capitalist society, its failure to arrive at a consensus on what immediate policies to support, and its failure to explain the commission of violent and predatory crimes that are not politically or economically motivated, are shortcomings. Most personal crimes, such as murder, assault, and rape, are directed against members of the same social class (for example, lower class attacker against lower class victim). Some traditional criminologists claim that predatory street crimes have to be dealt with now; we cannot wait for the erosion of the capitalist state. Again, in fairness, some radical criminolo-

gists address this criticism and offer support for specific programs of reducing street crime (Dod et al., 1976; Platt, 1982). Many others, such as Quinney (1977), however, see such crimes as being "pursued out of the need to survive" and "a reproduction of the capitalist system." They are similarly depicted as "antagonistic to the capitalist order" (p. 54).

However, though crimes victimizing a ruling class may show political antagonism, it is difficult to accept the corresponding view that violent crimes committed by working class members against one another can be construed as antagonistic to the existing order. On the other hand, it may be argued here that the intraclass relationship between offender and victim (the primary offender and the primary victim share similar class, life style, and demographic characteristics, suggesting that each class, including the upper class, "rips off" and hurts itself) is evidence of the growing alienation being experienced by all in capitalist society.

The stress placed on the reconstruction of society as a solution to the crime problem has led to the allegation that "radical criminologists are less inclined to search for objective truth than to the quest for the overthrow of the capitalist system" (Bernard, 1981: 373). This, of course, brings us back to the question of the method of seeking and justifying political change.

Finally, there is disagreement about the nature of the ruling class, even among radically oriented theorists. Robert Lefcourt (1971), for example, concedes that pluralism in the United States, where varied groups compete and in which decision-making rests on give and take, has resulted in some positive changes. Through group pressure, interest groups have brought about civil rights legislation, regulations concerning pure food and drugs, strengthening of labor unions, and air and water pollution controls. True to a conflict perspective, however, Lefcourt contends that "the corporate elite, through its influence over law enforcement, insures that these new laws are not used to impair basic operations" (p. 34).

Whether radical and nonradical conflict perspectives will continue to receive attention, positive or negative, remains to be seen. One thing is certain: Charges of the gross control of the legal system by a select few corporate officials and government leaders "demand adjudication through evidence" (Gibbons and Garabedian, 1974: 57). Klockars (1979) has noted: "After class explains everything, after the whole legal order is criticized, after all predatory and personal crime is attributed to the conditions and reproduction of capitalism, there is nothing more to say—except more of the same thing" (p. 502).

SUMMARY

Conflict and radical criminologists, breaking with consensual explanations of society and deviance, argue that crime and delinquency are the products of the conflictual relationships and interests within society. Crime and delinquency are not attributed to individual or immediate environmental factors, but are believed to result from the conflict that emerges when groups or classes with differing power and interests come into contact. Conflict theorists, by definition, view dissension and conflict as ubiquitous; that is, they are everywhere. They argue that some societal members have control—specifically, economic and political control—over others.

Conflict theorists vary in their perceptions of the degree of dissension within a society. Pluralist conflict theorists, including Thorsten Sellin, George Vold, and Austin Turk, agree that crime and delinquency are due to conflict and that laws emerge from groups whose ethics and interests are not necessarily those of the majority. Each of these groups maneuvers to protect its own interests and has varying degrees of influence over the government and the criminal justice system. Pluralists, then, view American society as comprised of many groups who periodically encroach on one another's interests.

More radically oriented conflict criminologists, such as Richard Quinney, Herman and Julia Schwendinger, Tony Platt, William Chambliss, Ian Taylor, Paul Walton, and Jock Young, view American society as split into two opposing social classes: the ruling class, which is the bourgeoisie, and the working class, or proletariat. These radical criminologists ground their hypotheses about the nature of crime and delinquency in the philosophy of Karl Marx and Friedrich Engels. Both Marx and Engels postulated that the economic organization of society is the fundamental determinant of the structure and development of society. In every society there are two basic classes, one representing the powerful owners and controllers of production, and the other representing the exploited working class. Using this Marxist framework, radical criminologists argue that crime and delinquency are products of a class struggle in which the bourgeois rulers of a capitalist society (that is, a society in which the ownership of land, production and distribution of goods, and so forth are effected by private enterprise) define deviant behavior based on their own self-serving interests.

Radicals assert that by controlling the economic resources of a society, those in power manipulate social conditions so that the lower classes appear to be the major contributors to crime. While the early nonradical conflict theorists explored the normative conflicts between different groups within a complex society and recommended reforms, many radical criminologists have criticized reforms of the existing criminal justice system, arguing that they ultimately are used to maintain the status quo. For many radicals, the elimination of a class-based capitalist society is the only answer to the crime problem. Thus, radical criminologists, unlike traditional criminologists, propose a theory that not only attempts to explain the existence of crime, but also advocates drastic political, social, and economic changes to eliminate crime.

Traditional criminologists often agree with the tenets of radical theory about inequities within society, but question the feasibility and likelihood of such radical changes. They argue that delinquency and crime have to be handled in the here and now and that radical rhetoric can only raise questions for which more pragmatic solutions, based on the needs of current situations, must be found.

PROGRESS CHECK

1. Compare and contrast the consensual positivistic model of society and delinquency with the conflict and radical model. (pp. 168–172)

2. How are the conflict and radical perspectives distinguished? (pp. 173–174)

3. Evaluate the strengths and weaknesses of the conflict and radical theories of crime, being careful to differentiate between some of the various positions associated with each orientation. (pp. 173–174)

4. Why are radical theorists critical of science and reform? (pp. 172–173)

5. Outline and discuss the Marxian influence on conflict and radical theories of crime and delinquency. (pp. 174–177)

6. Who is credited with the following statement? "The ideas of the ruling class are in every epoch the ruling ideas, i.e., the class which is the ruling *material* force of society is at the same time its ruling *intellectual* force." What significance does that statement have for radical criminology? (p. 174)

7. Richard Quinney suggests that even those laws regulating morality—for example, victimless crimes and juvenile status offenses—are intended to preserve the "moral and ideological basis of _____." (p. 184)

8. According to the radical perspective, why do you suppose the *delinquent as victim* is not a popular subject even though evidence does suggest that the delinquent-victim interaction is actually very common and constitutes a very serious problem? (p. 184)

9. Outline and discuss Platt's description of the historical child-saving movement. To what extent is the movement still alive today? (pp. 184–187)

10. Discuss the overall contributions and weaknesses of the conflict and radical explanatory model of delinquency. (pp. 187–190)

NOTES

1. Criminologists vary in their use of the terms *conflict theory* and *radical criminology*. Takagi (1976) offers perhaps the most commonly accepted view. He concludes that a " 'conflict theorist' remains in the liberal tradition, albeit critical of a functionalist perspective" (p. 256). Conflict criminology is basically non-Marxist in its orientation, since many interest groups are seen to vie for power, and sweeping political changes are not advocated for eliminating crime. Marxist (also called radical) criminologists are proponents of the "new criminology" springing from a class structure based on Marxian philosophy. According to the radicals, crime cannot be dealt with within the confines of an existing capitalist society. Radical theorists believe that only the elimination of a class-based social system can solve the problems of crime. We will discuss the differences between the conflict and radical perspectives later in this chapter.

2. The consensual paradigm is also referred to as the Durkheimian or functionalist paradigm.

3. Not only radical criminologists have noted public inaccuracies in crime perception. Mark Warr (1982) states that "criminologists agree that public beliefs about crime are inaccurate, and some seem willing to abandon crime reduction as a policy goal in favor of strategies which affect public perceptions of crime" (p. 185).

4. See, for instance, Galliher and Walker (1978) for an analysis of the origins of drug laws. They marshall evidence which demonstrates that repressive and punitive drug laws are passed to help control a specific economic, ethnic, or racial minority. Also see Hagan (1980) for a review of several studies relating to the origins of drug and other laws aimed at specific groups in the population.

5. This phrase is taken from Jeffery Reiman's book, *The Rich Get Richer and the Poor Get Prison* (1979).

6. Robert Bohm (1982a) lists some of the more popular labels and their associated proponents: "the new criminology" (Taylor et al., 1974; Phillipson, 1973; Chambliss and Mankoff, 1976; Meier, 1976; Hackler, 1977; Bonomo and Wenger, 1978; Inciardi, 1979; Toby, 1979; Pelfrey, 1980); "Marxist" criminology (Young, 1976; Greenberg, 1976, 1981; Quinney, 1977; Beirne, 1979; Klockars, 1979; Akers, 1979); "materialist" criminology (Werkentin et

al., 1974; Taylor et al., 1975; Inciardi, 1979); "dialectical" criminology (Quinney, 1979); "radical" criminology (Wright, 1973; Gibbons and Garabedian, 1974; Young, 1975; Platt, 1975; Taylor et al., 1975; Turk, 1975; Gordon, 1976; Scull, 1977; Toby, 1979; Pelfrey, 1980); "socialist" criminology (Young, 1975); "critical" criminology (Wright, 1973; Sykes, 1974; Davis, 1975; Taylor et al., 1975; Schumann, 1976; Michalowski and Bohlander, 1976; Keller, 1976; Inciardi, 1979; Wollan, 1979; Pelfrey, 1980).

7. For an excellent history of the radical and socialist perspectives of crime and penology, see Jenkins (1982).
8. See Tucker (1978) for excerpts relevant to this discussion.
9. Joel Kovel in *The Age of Desire: Reflections of a Radical Psychoanalyst* (1981), using a Marxian psychoanalytic perspective, suggests that many common forms of behavioral adaptation required by capitalist society (e.g., striving for financial success) are the source of unhappiness and subsequently psychological malfunctioning. See Chapter 5 for comments on the radical view of psychoanalysis.
10. Redo (1979) suggests that greater attention should be devoted to the development of a Marxian theory of the criminal personality in capitalist society. Kovel (1981) has posited a general psychoanalytic theory of personality in capitalist society. Pearson (1975) warns that strict adherence to the Marxian macrostructural approach may result in a loss of concern for personal liberation. The fuller development of a Marxian psychoanalytic theory may fill the void (Pearson, 1975; Kovel, 1981).
11. See Hirst (1975), Summer (1977), and Taylor, Walton, and Young (1975).
12. The entire February 1979 issue of *Criminology* is devoted to the subject of radical criminology. In particular, see Klockars (1979); also see Hirst (1975) and Taylor and Walton (1975).
13. As we have suggested in other chapters, theories of criminality are tied to the historical period of their origination. Such theories, notes Thomas Kuhn (1973), are often "replaced" when they no longer can explain existing reality. For a discussion of the sociology of knowledge, see Mannheim (1936).
14. *Theoretical Criminology* was posthumously updated by Thomas Bernhard in 1979.
15. Also see Turk (1966, 1977, 1979).
16. Philip Jenkins (1982) offers an overview of radical and socialist reactions to rehabilitative or discretionary penology between 1890 and 1930, including the contributions of Clarence Darrow (1972), Edward Carpenter (1908, 1905), George Bernard Shaw (1946), Eugene Debs (1927), Robert Batchford (1913), and others.
17. See Chambliss (1969), Chambliss and Seidman (1971), Krisberg and Austin (1978), Platt (1974, 1975), Quinney (1970, 1974, 1977), and Schwendinger and Schwendinger (1970, 1974, 1976a, 1976b).
18. There is evidence which indicates that improvements have occurred as a result of the radical movement (Sinclair, 1983: 28).
19. See Chapter 18 on cross-cultural studies for an elaboration on this point.

20. Also see Chambliss (1964), Dickson (1968), and Hall (1952).
21. In a recent interview conducted by Clemens Bartollas, Quinney was asked about the theoretical needs of the field of delinquency. Quinney replied:
Our society emphasizes youth and the youth culture while at the same time increasingly excluding youth from gainful and meaningful employment. Youth are being relegated to the consumption sector—without the economic means for consumption. Education—including college—has traditionally provided a place for youth that are not essential to a capitalist society. But with the widening of the economic gap between classes, will education be an outlet and opportunity for the majority of adolescents and young adults? We are approaching a structural crisis (and personal crises) that will require a solution beyond what is possible in a capitalist society. Our challenge is to understand the changes that are taking place around us and the courage to be a part of the struggle that is necessary. (Bartollas, 1985: 230)
22. These terms were used by Schafer (1977).
23. Evidence exists suggesting that the problem of delinquents' victimization of themselves is significant (see Klein, 1969; Miller, 1975; Savitz, Lalli, and Rosen, 1977; Mawby, 1979; Duxbury, 1980; Singer, 1981; McDermott, 1983; Voigt and Thornton, 1982). The victim-offender intersection warrants much greater attention than it has received. Alcabes and Jones (1980) note that the victim is more or less transformed into a delinquent as a result of rationalizations based on concrete victimization and the relative inattention to victimization. They suggest that focusing on the needs of the victim instead of the transgressions of the offender "may break the cycle whereby the exploited become the exploiter" (p. 202).
The delinquent as victim is not a popular topic for media coverage or for social scientific investigation because, as Miller (1975) notes, the public's perceptions of delinquents' victimization of themselves does not appear to pose a direct threat. Since delinquents as victims are taken for granted, they do not inspire public interest. Hence official support (including government and private funding) is minimal.
24. Reports consistently show that blacks are overrepresented in arrest, conviction, and prison statistics. A similar trend is found when victimization statistics are used. While early self-report statistics generally fail to show a significant relationship between race and crime-delinquency, more recent self-report data which take into account both serious and nonserious crimes show a significant relationship between race and serious violent offenses. Peterson and Hagan (1984) conclude that the role of race in sentencing is more complicated than previously acknowledged. Research on class and crime also presents a problem not because of the direction of the correlation, but because the magnitude may be a paradigmatic problem (Schwendinger and Schwendinger, 1982).
25. See Clinard (1974b), Garofalo (1978), Gibbons and Garabedian (1974), Klockars (1979), Spitzer (1975), and Toby (1979).

26. As the methods of self-reporting have improved along with the measures of serious and nonserious crimes, results have been variable too. The contradictions in the research with regard to the relationship between delinquency and social class attest to the complexity of these phenomena. Similarly, the variable of race has been found to be a great deal more complicated (Peterson and Hagan, 1984).

PART 3

DELINQUENCY AND THE SOCIAL MILIEU

One day the monarch of a small kingdom assembled five blind wise men for consultation. The monarch took the five to a courtyard, where a huge elephant stood; and he commanded the men to describe the object that stood before them. The five wise men began to run their hands over the beast. "Sire," shouted the first sage, who was grasping the elephant's tail, "This is a very thick rope." The second blind sage felt the leg of the elephant, stood back, and proclaimed that the object was a thick, durable tree. The third blind man groped the soft, hairy belly of the elephant and declared, "This is a very fine woven rug." The fourth had been investigating the elephant's trunk. "Your majesty," he announced, "this specimen is clearly a water hose." The fifth, who had been searching the elephant's ears, proclaimed: "This object is a very large fan."

Sociologists who describe the importance of various aspects of the juvenile's social milieu or environment and how components of that environment relate to juvenile delinquency are similar to the five blind wise men. Some sociologists examine the family characteristics of delinquents and then argue that delinquency is the result of problems in family life. Others consider the school experiences of delinquents and contend that delinquency is produced by educational failures and dissatisfaction. Peer relationships are studied by some sociologists, who have concluded that these relationships hold the key to understanding delinquency. More recently, the effects of the mass media, primarily violent television programming, have been linked to the aggressive delinquencies

of youth. The use of alcohol and other drugs within the juvenile environment are delinquent acts themselves, and have similarly been associated with more violent criminal and delinquent activities.

In this section, we will discuss the discoveries of sociological researchers about each of these social components. Chapter 9 focuses on the family relationships of delinquents, relationships that appear very important in explaining the delinquency of some young people. As we will see, our conceptions of a "traditional" family may no longer hold true. Chapter 10 is concerned with the school experiences of delinquents and the ways schools may fail in the goal of teaching children to behave. Inadequacies in school curriculums are examined as a causal component of delinquency. Chapter 11 considers the importance of the peer group in explaining delinquency and shows how sociological interest in the subject changes periodically, reflecting the shifts in youth collectivities; there is a resurgence in interest in delinquent gangs, an area neglected for a number of years. Chapter 12 examines the role of the mass media and its possible influence on youth crime and delinquency. Historically, various mass media have been suspect as stimulating aggressive attitudes and behaviors in children. With the institutionalization of television and its preoccupation with violent programming, interest has focused almost exclusively on this medium in recent years.

In Chapter 13 we review the research that has been done on both "normal" and deviant adolescent drug use—the extent of abuse, reasons for abuse, and the relationship between drug abuse and other forms of delinquency. The drug-crime connection remains a clouded one, complicated by many factors.

In the final analysis, each chapter in this section offers a glimpse into important social structures in the juvenile's environment that have been related to delinquency. We must remember that none of these phenomena operate in isolation; they are intricately related in a dynamic social system.

CHAPTER 9

FAMILIES AND DELINQUENCY

Larry is a 16-year-old boy who lives with his father. Until Larry was 13, Larry's mother, an alcoholic, lived with Larry and his father. Larry's first contact with the police occurred when he was 6. Drinking half a can of beer, Larry's mother put the can into the refrigerator to finish later. Larry poured the beer out of the can when his mother was not looking, urinated in the can, and then replaced it on the refrigerator shelf. As Larry had planned, his mother drank part of the "beer." She then called the police and Larry's record of police contact began.

Several years later Larry's mother went off with one of her occasional men and changed the pattern of her affairs. This time she did not return home. The father remained with the children. Neighbors noticed that Larry and his brother and sister often had welts and bruises on their faces, arms, and legs, especially after the father's periodic alcoholic binges.

Over the years, Larry amassed a large number of police contacts, ranging from stealing his grandfather's new fishing rod to tearing down neighbors' fences with a dirt bike. When he was sent to a social service agency specializing in the reform of juvenile delinquents, he was on probation for breaking into an old woman's house. Larry's father complained to the workers at the youth agency that he could not control the boy and was "at the end of his rope."

L arry's case is typical of the family histories of many juvenile offenders. In this chapter we will examine the relationships between the family and delinquency. We will first discuss the importance of the family in the child's life and how the structure of families may relate to delinquent activities. We will then examine the effects of parental control practices, including supervision, discipline, and teaching, on the child's delinquency. Next we look at a number of family characteristics thought to be related to delinquency at one time or another. We will follow this discussion with an examination of changes taking place in the American family that call into question much of the research previously based on what a *typical* or *ideal* family should be like. We conclude the chapter with a discussion of family policy and its possible role in delinquency prevention and control.

THE INFLUENCE OF THE FAMILY

Social scientists generally agree that the family provides the most important social control in the child's early life. The way in which the family responds to the child's emotional, intellectual, physical, and social needs shapes the child's personality and transforms him or her from an amoral creature who does not know social norms to an acceptable social being who knows expected social roles. The process whereby a child learns the rules and beliefs of the society is called **socialization**. The family has the primary responsibility of socializing the child, especially during the early years of life. The family is the agency that most directly teaches the child what is right and wrong; what is expected by parents, other adults, and children; what behaviors are appropriate in various situations; and what ways of satisfying desires are socially acceptable. Later, of course, other influences, such as school and the child's peers, also become significant.

Families influence children not only through the imparting of standards of right and wrong, but also through *direct, internalized,* and *indirect controls.*

For example, if 5-year-old Eddie's mother tells him not to accept candy from strangers and Eddie obeys her, one of three control processes may have inhibited the forbidden behavior.

First, the mother might have been watching as Eddie started to accept the candy, in which case she undoubtedly would have rushed out to stop the potentially dangerous event. This intervention would be direct control. If the mother then scolded or spanked the boy, the punishment would also be direct control. But suppose Eddie's mother was blocks away when the candy was offered, and still Eddie refused. In this case Eddie's conscience may have led him to deny himself the candy. Perhaps he thought: "It is wrong to take candy from strangers. I'll be a bad boy if I do." Here, Eddie would have exercised internalized control. The parent's standard had become Eddie's standard.

Another process, indirect control, is also possible. Since Eddie loves his mother and wants her to be happy with his behavior, he would refuse the candy. If Eddie did not care about his mother or her expectations, he would have been free to follow his temptation and take the candy. Since he didn't, the mother exercised indirect control over Eddie's behavior. Thus, parents can exert influence on a child's behavior through direct, internalized, and indirect control (Nye, 1958).

Although sociologists tend to emphasize the control of the family, psychologists are likely to describe how parents affect the child's personality development. According to many psychologists, as we saw in Chapter 5, the "normal" child has the love of parents who consistently and fairly teach him or her to sublimate instinctual drives. If all goes well in this process, the child will exhibit a happy, healthy, law-abiding personality and develop traits that make it possible to get along with adults and other children.

Aside from shaping personality and applying controls, parents can have other, less direct, influences on the child's development. Sociologists can use the occupation and income of parents to determine the child's social class and link social class and position to many facets of everyday life. If the child's parents are lower class, chances are that the neighborhood the family lives in, the school the child attends, and the friends he or she makes are different from the neighborhood, schools, and friends of the child born to middle or upper class parents. Parents also affect their offspring by welcoming or rejecting the child's friends and by reinforcing or contradicting the teacher or the school.

If the influence of the parent is positive, the result is a child who conforms to societal norms and thus fulfills societal expectations. But parents are not uniformly and consistently conformist, as we saw in the case of Larry. The result is often a child who deviates from norms and becomes delinquent. Deviation in the form of delinquency is quite common among youth. In the next section we consider the effects of various aspects of family relationships on involvement in delinquency.

FAMILY STRUCTURE AND DELINQUENCY: INTACT VS. DISRUPTED HOMES

The family is important in many theoretical positions on delinquency. A wide variety of family characteristics has been linked to the misconduct of adolescents. Foremost among these characteristics are broken homes and conflict in the home.

Broken Homes and Official Delinquency

Sutherland and Cressey (1978) quote an African proverb that cautions, "If the old bird dies, the eggs are addled" (p. 215). According to studies on divorced families and delinquency conducted during the early part of this century, the negative effect of parental separation extends to children as well. Researchers made the assumption that intact homes, or families containing both natural parents, were somehow better at socializing and controlling children than broken households where one or both parents are absent due to death, divorce, separation, or desertion. On the basis of these assumptions, parents in the past were often advised, in the cliché, to "stay together for the sake of the children." Today millions of children

are now raised in single-parent families and from all indications, the great majority of these children suffer no ill effects.

Research on Broken Homes.   When juvenile courts were created at the beginning of this century, attention first focused on broken homes as causes of delinquency. Juvenile courts kept records of the children referred, and it soon became apparent that a large number came from homes where one or both parents were missing. Breckinridge and Abbott studied juveniles referred to the Cook County (Illinois) Juvenile Court in 1903 and 1904 and discovered that 44 percent lived in broken homes. In 1915, scrutinizing referrals to the same court, Healy reported that 36 percent of all referrals and 49 percent of referrals of repeat offenders came from structurally broken homes (that is, homes in which a parent was physically missing). From these figures, the conclusion was drawn that the absence of a parent was detrimental to the socialization of the child (Breckinridge and Abbott, 1970; Healy, 1915).

These studies were criticized because, even though they showed incomplete families to be common among delinquents, they did not prove that broken homes were more frequent among delinquents than among nondelinquents. Statistics on broken families are meaningless unless delinquents can be demonstrated to live less often with both parents than nondelinquents (Shaw and McKay, 1932; Sutherland and Cressey, 1978).

In one of the first United States studies employing nondelinquents as a control, or comparison group, Slawson (1926) found that 19 percent of the nondelinquents attending three public schools and 45 percent of the delinquents drawn from four New York correctional schools were from broken families. Burt (1929) examined the families of delinquents referred to the juvenile court in London, England, and the families of nondelinquent schoolchildren. Less than 26 percent of the schoolchildren and almost 58 percent of the delinquents lived in homes lacking one or more parents.

Shaw and McKay (1932) cast the first doubt on broken home accounts of delinquency when they questioned whether the control groups of nondelinquents could be validly compared to groups of delinquent adolescents in these earlier studies, since broken homes and delinquency are more common in certain ethnic and racial groups, social classes, and residential areas than in others. If delinquents more often come from those groups, classes, and areas associated with high rates of delinquency and incomplete families, broken homes may *appear* to influence delinquency, but may in fact have no direct effects.

To test their ideas about the relationship between broken homes and delinquency, Shaw and McKay compared the percentages of broken homes among schoolboys and adolescents referred to the Cook County Juvenile Court in 1927 and 1930. They statistically adjusted for differences in age, nationality, and residential area to make the two groups more directly comparable. Among the schoolchildren, the adjusted percentage of broken homes was 36, whereas 42 percent of the delinquents were from families that were in some way not intact. This difference was much smaller than the differences reported in other studies, causing Shaw and McKay to conclude that "the differences . . . are not sufficiently great to indicate that the broken home, as such, is a significant causitive factor in the cases of delinquent boys brought before the Cook County juvenile court" (p. 522).

In contrast to Shaw and McKay's findings, subsequent studies comparing delinquents and nondelinquents generally showed a consistent association between disrupted families and adolescent misbehavior. Peterson and Becker (1965) summarized studies conducted from 1929 to 1958. According to these studies, delinquents were one and one half to two times more likely to live separated from their parents than were adolescents who had never been officially processed for delinquency. Broken homes tended to be more common among officially delinquent girls and younger boys than among male adolescents.

In 1957 Toby reexamined Shaw and McKay's 1932 data, attempting to account for the discrepancy between their findings and the general trend of evidence. He noticed that Shaw and McKay's sample of delinquents and schoolboys consisted primarily of older male adolescents. When Toby evaluated more closely the delinquency of the younger males in Shaw and McKay's sample, he found a substantial relationship between delinquency and residence in a broken home. Shaw and McKay did not include females in their research, but Toby reported the findings of several projects that demonstrated broken homes to be more prevalent among female than among male delinquents (Monahan, 1957a, 1960; Toby, 1957).

From these facts, Toby developed an argument about why Shaw and McKay discovered little difference in broken homes among boys referred to the juvenile court and schoolboys. He pointed out that the juveniles studied by Shaw and McKay were the *least* likely to be influenced by broken homes. Such weak control is exercised over the male adolescent that there is little difference in supervision between an intact or a disorganized family. Girls and younger boys, on the other hand, are closely controlled by an intact family. A broken family may not—and may not be able to—provide the same degree of supervision that is possible in two-parent homes. Thus, differential supervision may account for the relationship between broken homes and delinquency among girls and preadolescent boys, though it does not affect the delinquency of older boys.

Criticisms of Official Data.   Generally, the findings of studies that compare the family backgrounds of delinquents and nondelinquents are consistent. Children referred to official agencies for involvement in delinquency are more likely to come from broken homes than children who have never come to the attention of authorities. Shaw and McKay's 1932 study is the major exception to this generalization, but the exclusion of girls and preadolescents from their sample may explain why their findings differ from those of other studies. Two developments have raised questions about whether broken homes are important causal factors in delinquency. First, studies of official agencies processing offenders have indicated that the relationship between broken homes and delinquency may result from the operating procedures of the agencies. Second, self-report data have suggested that broken homes have little or no effect on actual delinquent behavior. We have earlier discussed the highly discretionary world of juvenile justice. At every stage of the juvenile justice system, considerations other than the purely legal influence what will happen to a juvenile. The nature of the child's family is one of these extralegal factors important in the handling of juvenile cases.

Researchers have investigated the number of broken homes among juveniles at each successive stage in juvenile justice processing. Polk (1958) listed percentages of broken homes in relation to dispositions assigned by the Los Angeles Probation Department. About 43 percent of cases closed at intake, 50 percent of the juveniles placed on probation or under juvenile court supervision, and 58 percent of those institutionalized were from families where at least one parent was missing. Similarly, Nye (1958) noticed that 48 percent of the boys in a training school were from broken homes, while only 24 percent of the most delinquent boys attending a high school did not live with both parents. If broken homes were an important cause of delinquency, a similar percentage of broken homes would be expected among all delinquents, regardless of whether they had been caught and institutionalized (Sutherland and Cressey, 1978).

How would these selective factors in official processing act to distort the apparent relationship between broken homes and delinquency? If children from broken homes are more likely to be arrested, petitioned into court, and confined in institutions, studies would naturally find a greater proportion of broken homes than are present in the general population. But broken homes may not be an actual cause of delinquency; there may, in fact, not even be a significant causal relationship. Most studies that employ official data report that children from broken homes are overrepresented in juvenile courts and institutions (see Monahan, 1957a,b; Chilton and Marble, 1972; Rosen, 1970).

A recent study (Fenwick, 1982) that examined legal, social, psychological, and demographic variables as they influenced juvenile intake decision-making found that the "further [a juvenile] goes into the intake decision-making process, the more does family disaffiliation become the prominent independent variable" (p. 443). *Family disaffiliation*

in the study referred to prominent independent variables relating to family integration, including a broken home. Fenwick found, for example, that a juvenile's family disaffiliation was the *sole* determinant of the decision to deter a youth in a custodial setting (p. 447). Other factors, such as the youth's demeanor and the nature of the offense, were more important than family integration. Other research has similarly found that family variables are influential factors in the decision-making process at intake (Thomas and Sieverdes, 1975).

Additionally, broken homes are more prevalent in the lower social classes. Officially recognized delinquency is also more common in the lower classes. Since adolescents from lower social levels are more likely to be arrested and imprisoned and larger proportions of broken homes are found among the same adolescents, Nye has pointed out that a larger group of adolescents from broken homes "is listed on official records and placed in institutions" (Nye, 1958: 42).

The higher rate of broken homes among female rather than male delinquents has been attributed to the court referral process. Adolescents referred for certain kinds of offenses, such as "ungovernability," "incorrigibility," and running away, are highly likely to live in broken homes. Adolescent girls, more often than adolescent boys, are referred to court for these types of home-related offenses. When boys and girls referred for similar types of offenses are compared, the rate of female delinquents from broken homes more closely resembles the rate of male delinquents from broken homes (Kratcoski, 1974; Weeks, 1940).

To conclude, the evidence shows that the association between broken homes and officially reported delinquency is probably at least in part accounted for by court referral and processing. The police and courts apparently consider the circumstances of the child and family as well as the facts of the case in making dispositions.

Broken Homes and Self-Reported Delinquency

In much of the self-report research, surprisingly little investigation has taken place beyond the broken home and more global measures of self-reported delinquency (as opposed to *specific* delinquent offenses). Similarly, key variables such as sex, race, and social class have often been neglected in the specification of the relationship between the broken home and delinquency. Studies that have examined the broken home and delinquency through the self-report technique generally have not found that children from broken homes are significantly more delinquent than those from intact homes (Wilkinson, 1980: 22–23).

The first major research project investigating the association between broken homes and self-reported delinquent behavior, rather than official delinquency, was conducted by Nye in the 1950s. More than 3,000 youngsters attending public schools in three medium-sized towns in the state of Washington were questioned about a number of family relationships as well as their involvement in various types of delinquency. Nye concluded from this study: "The analysis of the data . . . indicates a relationship between broken homes and delinquent behaviors, although the relationship is a very small one compared to that found in the institutional population" (Nye, 1958: 45). Nye further suggested that broken homes were not the crucial link from the family to delinquency; other variables such as the happiness of the family and the parents' marital adjustment were potentially more important than a broken home.

Another study of broken homes and self-reported delinquency was conducted by Hirschi (1969) as part of a larger research project involving over 1,815 adolescent males in California. Hirschi found little difference in the self-reported delinquency of boys living with their natural fathers or those living without a father figure. "Only those living with step- or foster-fathers [were] more likely than children from 'intact' homes to be delinquent" (p. 24).

A 1978 study concentrated on types of delinquent behavior among middle class high school students. Hennessey, Richards, and Berk found almost no relationship between broken homes and each of the types of delinquent behavior in their study. In fact, juveniles from broken homes were, in several instances, a little *less* likely than juveniles from complete homes to commit delinquent offen-

ses. The conclusion reached from these data was that there was almost no relationship between broken homes and delinquency.

Self-reports that have examined more specific types of delinquent offenses (as opposed to global scales of delinquency) have shown mixed results. Dentler and Monroe (1961) found broken homes to be unrelated to theft. Austin (1978), however, found that father absence was associated with white girls' vandalism and assault. Hennessey et al. (1978) reported that broken homes were more related to marijuana use than to alcohol use, theft, or vandalism, although this association was very weak.

Self-reports that control for different types of juveniles based on their sex or race and ethnicity in relation to broken homes and delinquency reveal some variations. Females may, for example, be more affected by family instability than males (Nye, 1958; Gold, 1970; Austin, 1978). Some evidence to the contrary, however, can be found. Canter (1982b) reported that males may actually be more affected by certain family variables than females with respect to the commission of several types of delinquency (especially status offenses). Wilkinson (1980) discovered that minor differences existed between males and females from broken homes for the commission of ungovernable conduct (truancy and running away).

The child's race also has been singled out for differential impact on the relationship of the broken home and delinquency. Austin (1978) noted that the relationship between father absence and delinquency was stronger for white than for black girls. Wilkinson (1980), employing samples of Anglo and Chicano youth, found that father absence was more important for Anglo boys for truancy and running away and for Chicano boys for their reports of vandalism, marijuana use, and drinking. In contrast, for girls truancy and drinking alcohol were the only offenses where father absence was similarly associated for both ethnic groups. Assault and marijuana use were both closely associated with father absence for Anglo girls, but not Chicanos. However, vandalism, shoplifting, auto theft, and running away were more associated with father absence for the Mexican-American girls.

Studies that have controlled for the influence of social class on the relationship between broken homes and delinquency have been sparse. Using a classification of lower, middle, and upper class divisions from the Warner ISC scale, Rosen, Lalli, and Savitz (1975) examined the relationship for white and black youth. For both groups, there was some indication that the broken home had more impact on those from the lowest social classes. Interestingly, for the black group the broken home apparently had some effect on delinquency for those from the highest income levels.

Research on the broken home and delinquency also generally fails to specify the type of broken home that exists for a child (Johnstone, 1981). The most frequent definition employed refers to "the absence of at least one biological parent through death, desertion, divorce, or separation" (Rankin, 1983: 468). Even homes "reconstituted" by adoption or the inclusion of stepparents have been considered as broken because the child does not reside with his or her biological parents. Rosen (1970) has noted that the concept of "broken home" actually consists of two dimensions: (1) the *reason* for the breakup of the family (death, desertion, divorce, or separation) and (2) the *absence* of one or both parents (mother, father, or both).[1]

A recent study by Rankin (1983) examined the self-reported delinquency of samples of males and females with respect to these two dimensions. Singling out the offense of running away (only one of three offenses out of ten that significantly related to the "broken" family), he found no clear patterns of differences in running away for families that had broken up for specific reasons (death, divorce, or separation). The percentage of runaways from homes broken by death was *no* different from the percentage of runaways from homes broken by divorce or separation. He did, however, find that the probability of running away was significant depending on the specific *type* of broken home the juveniles resided in. Adolescents from intact homes (both biological parents) were least likely to run, followed by youth from homes in which *one* biological parent was absent, followed by reconstituted homes in which a stepparent replaced the missing biological parent and homes

in which both biological parents were missing (and not replaced by stepparents) (p. 476).

To conclude, although official data have indicated over the years a strong relationship between broken homes and delinquency, self-report studies have revealed that the association is weak if it exists at all. An examination of the juvenile justice system and its operating procedures provides some reason for the disparity in official and self-report findings. Although self-report studies have tended to deemphasize the importance of broken homes in causing delinquency, the influence of other family factors is not dismissed. A key finding that emerges from self-report studies was noted by Nye: "Less delinquent behavior was found in broken than in unhappy unbroken homes" (p. 51). The happiness of marriage was found to be much more closely related to delinquent behavior in children than whether the marriage was an original one, a remarriage, or a home where the child was living with one parent only.

Conflict in the Family and Delinquency

Although accentuated by the findings of self-report studies, the realization that family factors other than the structurally broken home might be important in explaining delinquency is not really a recent one. Many sociologists have cautioned that the concept of a broken home grossly over-simplifies the myriad family conditions possibly affecting a child's behavior. In the 1930s Shaw and McKay, for example, urged consideration not of breaks in the "normal" family structure, but of other aspects of family relationships.

The evidence mounting from a number of studies suggests that "psychologically broken homes"—that is, homes where there is a great deal of conflict and tension—are especially likely to produce delinquent behavior. Even in broken homes, the circumstances surrounding the break may be more important than the break itself. Browning (1960) summarizes the evidence: "[The] broken home, as generally defined, is ineffective and probably meaningless as an indicator of family disorganization and other characteristics of family life known to be associated with deviant behavior" (p. 43).

Quarreling in the home is reported to be more significantly related to delinquency than the absence of a parent (McCord, McCord, and Thurber, 1962). Of course, in many cases of divorce and separation there is a great deal of fighting before the break actually becomes formal. This kind of family conflict may account for the slight relationship between broken homes and delinquency observed in most self-report studies.

Grygier, Chesley, and Tuters (1969) surveyed juveniles confined to training schools in Ontario, Canada, and examined the effects of parental deprivation on these imprisoned juveniles. They reached the conclusion that separation from a parent did not really explain why a juvenile became delinquent. Separation combined with inadequate parenting before the break in the family or ineffective parenting on the part of the remaining parent was, however, quite common among the delinquents and appeared important in accounting for the delinquent behavior.

Grygier's research centered on officially identified delinquents. A study conducted in 1977 by Norland, Shover, Thornton, and James examined the relationship between conflict in the family and self-reported delinquency. About a thousand junior and senior high school students in a large southeastern city in the United States were asked to respond to the statement: "There is a lot of tension and conflict in my home"; they also answered questions about delinquent activities. Adolescents who said there was a high level of conflict at home were more delinquent than those who reported congenial family relationships. Where family conflict was relatively high, 64 percent of the males and 52 percent of the females were highly involved in delinquency. Conversely, 44 percent of the males and 24 percent of the females who experienced little family conflict admitted high frequencies of delinquency. It is interesting to note that family conflict was more common among delinquent girls in this study than among boys. Prior research supports the results of this study: Conflict is more prevalent among families of female delinquents (Norland, Shover, Thornton, and James, 1979).

Other self-reported studies compared the effects of a structural break in the home with the consequences of conflict in the home. An investigation by Biron and LeBlanc (1977) found that parental supervision of the child and communication between parent and child, two factors conceivably influenced by conflict in the home, were more closely linked to home-based delinquencies (for example, disobedience of parents, stealing from parents, staying out late) than was the absence of a parent. Dentler and Monroe (1961) disclosed that several aspects of parent-child relations were tied to juvenile thefts, but thefts were not more frequently found among children from broken homes. In Nye's study (1958), 38 percent of adolescents from broken homes and 48 percent of those from unhappy unbroken homes committed a large number of delinquent acts.

Two findings are consistent in both official and self-report data. First, conflict in the home is often related to self-reported delinquency. Second, a structural break in the home has less impact on delinquency than a psychological break. Apparently, unhappy intact families more often have delinquent members than happy broken families.

There are, however, many sources of conflict in the home and many indicators of unhappiness. In the first sentence of *Anna Karenina*, Tolstoy wrote that all happy families are alike, but each unhappy family suffers in its own way. It is certain that many factors may contribute to conflict in the home and to delinquent behavior. Three factors in particular—parents' marital adjustment, affection between parents and child, and psychological defects resulting from home deficiencies—have been related to conflict in the home and delinquency. We will examine each of these factors more closely.

Marital Adjustment.   To a large degree, tension in any particular family depends on the parents' marital adjustment—that is, how well the parents get along. If parents are constantly quarreling, they may not provide effective supervision or socialization of their children. A mother and father can be too concerned with each other's shortcomings and misdeeds to notice that their 11-year-old is down in the basement smoking marijuana in a pipe shoplifted from the local five-and-dime. Or another child, sick and tired of hearing that her mother is lazy and good-for-nothing or that her father is lazy and good-for-nothing, may be out vandalizing the local school.

Exploration of the relationship between marital adjustment and delinquency tends to confirm the notion that unhappy marriages are more apt than happy ones to produce delinquent children. Sheldon and Eleanor Glueck (1950) found that 65 percent of their nondelinquent sample, but only 37 percent of their delinquent group, lived in families where parents shared a good marital relationship. In another study contrasting delinquents and nondelinquents, Browning (1960) reported that the marital adjustment of parents of delinquents was less satisfactory than the marital adjustment of parents of nondelinquents.

Among the mothers and fathers of delinquents questioned by McCord, McCord, and Gudeman (1960), only a small percentage said they had affectionate relationships. Shulman's (1959) research revealed that parents of truants are often deeply disturbed with one another. These studies show poor marital adjustment increases the chances that children will be adjudicated delinquent.

Parental Affection.   Marital adjustment is one variable in family relationships that correlates with delinquency. Parental affection, by which we mean affection between parents and children, is another. When there is tension in the home, often the parent-child relationship as well as the husband-wife relationship suffers. Some researchers have found parental affection crucial. Others have found maternal affection as the more important link to delinquency. Regardless of the source of the affection, numerous studies have documented the importance of acceptance and affection between parents and their offspring in the prevention of juvenile delinquency (Glueck and Glueck, 1950; Andry, 1962; Stone, 1963). Generally, the more affection a parent shows for a child, the more affection and attachment will be returned by the child.

Psychological Defects.   Besides marital adjustment and parental affection, a third factor related to conflict in the home and delinquency is a child's psychological defects.

Psychoanalytic perspectives are generally characterized by the linking of emotional disturbances in the home with emotional defects and problems and, ultimately, delinquency in the child. This approach draws criticism because most delinquents show no signs of emotional disturbance. Since the research of most psychoanalysts is based on clinical practice, the delinquents observed tend to be the few who could be classified as psychologically "sick," rather than the many who are delinquent but reacting in a "normal" fashion to the social environment.

But whether or not delinquency is a symptom of a psychological disease, there are many points about families and delinquency on which sociologists and psychologists do agree. For example, delinquency is thought by both to result at least in part from homes that somehow do not effectively transmit values to children. From either perspective, socialization of the child is thought to be disrupted by family tension, making the child more susceptible to delinquent influences present in the social environment.

PARENTAL SOCIAL CONTROL AND DELINQUENCY

The broken home and conflict in the family are two aspects of family life that relate to delinquency. Another is parental social control over children. The practices of parents (or parental surrogates) in supervising, disciplining, and teaching children are particular elements of social control that are thought to influence delinquency.

Parental Supervision

Homes where there is a great deal of conflict may not keep the kinds of close tabs on children that are possible in homes where there is little conflict. Parental affection may also influence the amount and quality of parental supervision of young people. Hostile parents may be less likely to care about the child's whereabouts and activities. Further, adolescents who do not care about their parents may not consistently and honestly inform their parents about their activities and whereabouts.

Direct control of children by parents is thought by many sociologists and criminologists to check delinquent behavior. Reckless, Dinitz, and Murray (1956), for example, questioned the mothers of "good boys" (the samples were judged as low delinquency risks by teachers) and reported that the mothers knew the whereabouts of their sons at all times and kept close watch on the identities and reputations of their sons' friends. Similarly, Slocum and Stone (1963) found delinquent-type behaviors increased if the juvenile was permitted to go out every night and was not required to come directly home from school. Hirschi (1969) also reported a relationship between close supervision by mothers and self-reported delinquency among boys. He contended that the influence is direct: "The child is less likely to commit delinquent acts not because his parents actually restrict his activities, but because he shares his activities with them; not because his parents actually know where he is, but because he perceives them as aware of his location" (pp. 89–90).

If a parent restricts the kinds of friends the adolescent associates with and the child's activities outside the home, the chances of delinquent behavior in that child are lessened. It may be that the child simply has less time to be delinquent or to encounter delinquent influences. It is also possible that the effects may be indirect, as Hirschi (1969) suggested. Children who know their parents are aware of, or concerned about, their whereabouts may be more apt to consider the parents' reaction before committing a delinquent act.

Parental Discipline

Although supervision by parents relates to delinquency, the techniques parents employ to maintain and enforce supervision and control are equally, if not more, important. Conventional wisdom cautions "Spare the rod and spoil the child," but evidence about disciplinary practices and delinquency does not totally support this advice. In fact, it appears that the rod may be more often administered to delinquents than nondelinquents. Although the type of discipline does affect the misbehavior of adolescents, the manner of discipline—punitive, lax, or loving—is not as closely related to delinquency as the consistency with which discipline is applied.

Most studies explore at least four categories of discipline: (1) stern or physical, (2) lax, (3) erratic, and (4) strict but fair. The findings concerning stern or physical punishment are contradictory. Glueck and Glueck (1950) and Bandura and Walters (1958) argue that physical and harsh punishment foster aggression and delinquent behavior. It may be, of course, that parents more often resort to punishment with a delinquent child. Although Nye's self-report data show no relationship between physical punishment and delinquency, McCord and McCord (1958) suggest that consistent punitiveness inhibits delinquency for reasons we consider later. There is more consistency in the research findings about lax discipline. Extremely lax discipline is more common in the families of delinquents than in the families of nondelinquents. Both strict and lax punishment are more effective if they are consistently applied. Erratic discipline, shifting from strict to lax, relates more strongly to delinquency than any other form (McCord, McCord, and Zola, 1959).

The crucial link between discipline and delinquency is found in the development of internalized controls. According to Peterson and Becker (1965): "Capacities for internal control are complex but closely related to previously imposed external restraints. . . ." (p. 82). Fair discipline is thought to produce conforming behavior through the internalization of parental values, but consistent punitiveness may foster conformity because the child is afraid to deviate. In other words, the son or daughter who clearly understands the reasonable demands of loving parents tends to accept their standards and values, but the child who is ridiculed or physically punished will obey out of fear.

Abuse and Neglect

Extreme physical punishment and maltreatment, which may be legally classified as child abuse (or neglect) in some jurisdictions, have been linked to delinquent and criminal behavior later in life. According to some experts, the effects of childhood maltreatment haunt the individual well into adulthood. Fontana (1973) noted that such infamous public assassins as Arthur Bremer, Sirhan Sirhan, James Earl Ray, Lee Harvey Oswald, and John Wilkes Booth were all reared in abusive households. Steele (1976) reported that studies of individuals convicted of murder revealed "a demonstrable association between homicide and maltreatment in early childhood" (p. 22). Similar results have been obtained in other research with murderers (Gillen, 1946; Guttmacher, 1960; Palmer, 1962; Tanay, 1969). Groth (1979) reported that a third of the convicted rapists and child molesters he examined had been victims of sexual assaults when they were children.

One of the more popular links observers stress is that child abuse is a precursor of delinquency. Victims of child abuse internalize the use of violence as an appropriate remedy and subsequently engage in violent offenses. Researchers view the vicious cycle of violence begetting violence as a major social problem (Maden and Wrench, 1977; Mouzakitis, 1984).

However, despite a number of studies and testimonials which infer that various forms of maltreatment increase the probability of violence and like behavior among the victims of such abuse (Brown, 1984; Conger, 1980; Lynch, 1978; Reidy, 1977; Smith et al., 1980), much of the research is methodologically unsound. Any definitive statements alleging a maltreatment-delinquency link are wholly conjectural at this time.

One serious problem in specifying the relationship between maltreatment and delinquency involves the *type* of abuse the child receives. For example, Smith et al. (1980) hypothesize that physically abused and neglected youth are more prone toward violent offenses. However, other research indicates that neglect has less impact on the commission of violent offenses than overt physical abuse of a child (Reidy, 1977), but that neglect correlates highly with the commission of property offenses (Jenkins, 1968).

Another problem, at least with past research in this area, is the case history method, which has been used to examine a small number of children purportedly abused or neglected. This method is often based on self-reports that rely on the memory and veracity of the offender. In some cases, offenders may use stories of child abuse to justify their acts or gain sympathy for their situation. It is often impossible to verify past accounts of child abuse. Even if it were possible to overcome these obstacles, there is often no long-term follow-up of later deviant behavior (see the work of Hunner and Walker, 1981). More recent studies conducted by sociologists have attempted to link case histories of abused children with juvenile and criminal records later in their lives to gauge the impact of early life trauma (Alfaro, 1978; Lewis et al., 1976; Bolton, 1977; Wick, 1981; Mouzakitis, 1984; Harston and Hansen, 1984).

Value Transmission

The transmission of values from parent to child is a fundamental way in which discipline affects delinquency. One of the most important functions of childrearing is teaching children the appropriate norms, values, and expectations for behavior. During the socialization process, parents must teach children certain basic principles. Children learn that it is wrong to steal another child's tricycle or to push playmates out of trees to watch how they fall.

Both sociologists and criminologists have linked deficiencies in the family's teaching of law-abiding norms and values to delinquent behavior (see Sykes and Matza, 1957; McCords, 1958; Jaffe, 1969). In conflict-ridden homes, parents may be too busy with other problems to teach, control, and discipline their children. Sometimes parents do not agree on the standards children should be taught, with the result that children do not clearly understand what they are supposed to do. Additionally, a poor parent-child relationship can lead children to reject the parents and their values.

The nature of the values transmitted by parents to children as children grow up can be an important factor in children's acceptance or rejection of conventional, law-abiding values and in the shaping of delinquent and nondelinquent behaviors. Although the content of values is important, the manner in which values are taught appears to be more important in determining whether children follow them. Even if the parents are criminal, children tend to honor parents they accept and are accepted by with conformity to dominant societal values. On the other hand, parents who teach upstanding moral values but reject and inconsistently discipline the child risk the spurning of parental teaching and delinquency in the child.

FAMILY CHARACTERISTICS AND DELINQUENCY

Besides the broken home, family conflict, and parental social control, other family characteristics have been examined for a link to delinquency. These characteristics have included the mother who works outside the home, the size of the family, and the positioning of the child among the other children in the family.

Mothers, Employment, and Delinquency

The idea that delinquents frequently live in homes where the mother is employed outside the home has a long history. Since the number of mothers working and the rate of juvenile delinquency have both increased in recent years, the association between working mothers and delinquent children has been considered a direct cause and effect relationship by a number of writers in the popular press. According to such newspaper and magazine writers, the mother who works causes her child to be a delinquent (Friedan, 1963).

A major problem with this logic is that evidence does not support it. The Fluecks' (1950, 1962) data on 500 delinquents and 500 nondelinquents showed no relationship between full-time employ-

ment by mothers and delinquency in children. Twenty percent of the mothers of delinquents worked regularly, and 18 percent of the mothers of nondelinquents had full-time jobs. A greater percent of delinquents than nondelinquents were, however, from homes where the mother was only occasionally employed. As Maccoby (1958) has pointed out, homes where the mother was sporadically employed tended to be characterized by other factors that might influence delinquency, including emotionally disturbed fathers with poor work histories and parental incompatibility.

The key to the effect of the mother's employment on the child's delinquency in the Gluecks' study was not the fact of employment in itself, but the kind of supervision provided by the mother. If adequate supervision was arranged by a working mother, the chances were her children were less delinquent than the offspring of an unemployed mother who did not keep close watch on what her children were doing.

Studies of self-reported delinquency confirm the basic findings of the Gluecks' research. Nye (1958) discovered a slight relationship between working mothers and delinquent behavior, but felt the relationship should be attributed to some loss of direct control over children whose mothers worked outside the home. Similarly, Hirschi (1969) found that the children of employed mothers reported slightly more delinquency than the children of mothers who did not hold jobs. He suggests that the geographical proximity of mothers who stayed at home may have had a tendency to inhibit delinquency.

Still other studies report little or no relationship between a mother's employment, or lack of it, and delinquency. A mother's employment is one facet of the family structure that appears to have little influence on delinquency.

Family Size

Another aspect of family structure that researchers have investigated is family size. Many criminologists have argued that smaller families can more effectively control and fulfill the emotional needs of children. Nye (1958), for example, suggested that in a small family, "the parent-child relation is more intimate and affectionate. Closer parent-child affectional ties should, in turn, result in more effective indirect controls and, perhaps, more effective internalization as well" (p. 37).

The evidence from research on family size and delinquency supports the hypothesis that more delinquency is found in large families than in smaller ones. However, questions have been raised about the effects of large families on delinquency, because large families are more often found in the lower socioeconomic strata. The child from a large poor family may be delinquent not because the size of the family is large, but because poor children are more often adjudicated delinquent. Yet the self-report findings of Nye (1958), Hirschi (1969), and Slocum and Stone (1963) all indicate that children from large families are more likely to commit delinquent acts than children from small families.

Ordinal Position and Siblings

Most studies considering family size and delinquency have also explored the ordinal position of the child. These researchers ask: "Are firstborn, intermediate, or youngest children most likely to engage in delinquency?" The first studies of birth order and delinquency centered on the problems and inferiority of oldest children. Reasoning that first births are often the most difficult, that parents are less skilled with first children, and that trauma is associated with passing from the role of only child, researchers thought that first-borns were more delinquent than other siblings. Other researchers cast doubt on these studies because the studies sampled only small numbers of juveniles. Subsequent work indicates that intermediate siblings are most likely to be involved in delinquency (Nye, 1958; Hirschi, 1969).

Most research concerning sibling structure and delinquency has, however, been limited to studies of the birth order of siblings, with little or no emphasis on the sex of siblings with respect to delinquent behavior. Wilkinson et al. (1982) surveyed a sample of Arizona boys and girls and found a relationship between delinquent behavior

and sibling structure. Basically, this data indicated that birth order effects should not be considered without data on the sex of siblings. Youngsters sharing the same order of birth with brothers rather than sisters were not equally delinquent. They reported that, for example, "second born girls who have one older sister are not only much more delinquent than all other girls but also more delinquent than nearly all of the boys" (p. 228).

Research on sibling influence on delinquency is still in an exploratory stage. Wilkinson contends that other factors have to be examined to further qualify that relationship. For instance, the quality of the relationship between siblings may influence delinquent involvement, irrespective of sibling structure.

THE CHANGING AMERICAN FAMILY

Divorces and separation will increase until any profound differences between socially sanctioned marriages and illicit sex relationship disappears. . . . The main functions of the family will further decrease until it becomes a mere incidental cohabitation of male and female, while the home will become a mere overnight parking place mainly for sex relationships. (Sorokin, 1941: 776)

This statement, somewhat dismal in its predictions for the American family, was made some 45 years ago by Pitirim Sorokin, a prominent sociologist. Although Sorokin's assessment of the family as becoming a "mere incidental cohabitation" has obviously never materialized, the family has undergone certain changes which have affected all its members, parents and children alike.

To a large extent, criminologists have failed to study these changes in the American family and how they have related to juvenile delinquency and the juvenile justice system. Differing family structures such as single-parent families, joint-custody families, dual-career families, blended families, and the like have to a large extent been ignored in the delinquency literature. What has also been ignored is that the family—in whatever version we are addressing—is not an isolated unit necessarily set apart from the community. One criminologist who has studied the family in relation to juvenile delinquency argues that periods of acceptance and rejection of the status of the family reflect more the investigators' values regarding the sanctity of the family than objective evidence to the contrary or otherwise (Wilkinson, 1974).

Fewer and fewer social scientists argue that the family today is a major causal factor in explaining delinquency among American children. Yet popular views prevail that malfunctioning families produce problem or delinquent children. Juvenile justice practitioners make decisions affecting the lives of children based on their perceptions of what a *typical* or *ideal* family should be like. This family usually takes the form of a conjugal-nuclear family in which there is a traditional father who works and a traditional mother who devotes her full time to raising and caring for the children. This idealistic model is often used as a yardstick with which to compare deviations from the "norm." Whether this type of family ever existed, except on shows like *Father Knows Best,* is perhaps debatable.[2] However, in order to understand the differential assessment of the impact of the family on juvenile delinquency, we have to familiarize ourselves with some of the changes that have and are taking place in American families.

Single-Parent Families

Without a doubt, divorce is the key reason for today's single-parent family. No other family form has been increasing as rapidly. Between 1970 and 1979, the number of single-parent families increased by about 90 percent. Ninety percent of these families were female-headed. Of particular importance is that about 11.3 million children live in a single-parent family (Grossman, 1981). The chances are about 50–50 that a child will spend part of childhood in a single-parent family (Furstenberg and Nord, 1982).

Despite the prevalence of single-parent families today, they continue to be suspect because they deviate from the traditional intact nuclear family (Strong et al., 1983). As we noted at the beginning

of the chapter, the "broken home" has historically been linked to delinquency, even though much evidence suggests that other family factors more strongly relate to delinquency. Some problems, of course, do exist for single-parent families. Most of these families are female-headed and thus reflect the economic ramifications of sex discrimination in wages and job opportunities. Child support and alimony provide little help for these families, and as a result, economic uncertainty can put undue stress on them. Childcare for the working mother is another major difficulty faced by many.

There is evidence to suggest, however, that many single-parent families live in modified extended families consisting of their own children and another adult who is a relative, a boarder, or a cohabitant. Because of the necessity for dealing with financial and other logistical problems, single-parent mothers tend to develop extensive support systems to meet their children's needs, and these serve as positive socialization agents for the children (Strong et al., 1983).

An interesting variation of such a support system can be found in the black American family. Billingsley (1968) estimated that at least 25 percent of the black families in the United States are of an extended kinship type where relatives other than the child's natural parents (or parent) share in parental responsibility. Many of these families operate as single-parent units with a single, abandoned, separated, or divorced woman living together with the child and other relatives. These extended kinship networks have been neglected in the socialization of black children and may alter statements about the weakness of the black family (Johnstone, 1981: 86).

Children who live in a single-parent family generally have little contact with their nonresidential parent. Furstenberg and Nord (1982) report from their research that about 40 percent of the children they studied did not see their fathers in a five-year period. Whether the lack of a father role model is detrimental is still debatable. While the permanent absence of a parent does change the way the remaining parent relates to his or her children, this change is not necessarily negative. Research suggests that the single-parent mother generally becomes closer and more responsive to her children. Children may assume more egalitarian roles with the mother and more responsibility at an earlier age than children from intact families.

Joint Custody Families

A new type of family structure called **joint custody** or **divided custody** is now becoming popular. As opposed to the traditional "sole custody" status, where one parent has legal custody for the child's care, joint custody involves the child spending substantial periods of time with each parent on some type of alternating basis. The child basically "lives" with both parents, who each have legal responsibility for making decisions that affect the child, irrespective of which parent actually has possession. The child may spend two weeks with one parent and two weeks with the other parent, or live in some other time sharing arrangement.

Advocates of joint custody claim that it is psychologically more healthy for the child to be exposed to both parents rather than to just one. Furthermore, fewer demands may be placed on one parent in terms of finances, resources, and energy and time. Others argue that the decision to engage in joint custody should be approached with caution. The parents have separated or divorced because of serious differences, and it may be impossible for them to cooperate in terms of the planning that is needed to carry out a joint custody order. There is also the danger that one parent desires to have joint custody to "get back" at the other for alleged wrongdoing and pain caused by the marital breakup (Statsky, 1984: 280–281). Children in these "joint families" may find themselves caught between two families and experience both subtle and overt pressures to align themselves with one or the other.

Blended Families

Families that emerge from the remarriages of spouses are often called **blended** or **reconstituted**

families. Some 60 percent of these remarriages involve a parent with physical custody of one or more children. A number of potential problems that affect primarily children in these families can be noted. Anger and hostility on the part of the child for the breakup of the original family may be displaced to the new stepparent. The biological parent who lives outside the new family may interfere and feel threatened by the loss of his or her past position. The stepparent may be unsure of the role he or she is supposed to play with respect to the children. Should he, for example, be a father, a friend, or what to the children? Very few aspects of this blended family have been explored in relation to juvenile delinquency. Given that the majority of divorced individuals now remarry within about three years, the effects of blended families on children will no doubt attract more attention in the future.

Dual-Career Families

The impact of dual-career marriages on children is still only dimly understood. For discussion purposes, we refer to women in the dual-career family rather than men, since emphasis in the past few years has been on the entry of women into career roles. We also make the distinction here between women who work at jobs and women who work at careers.

Most women in the United States work. In 1980, some 50 percent of all married women held jobs in the United States. The vast majority of these jobs were low-paying positions and the supposition had been, right or wrong, that such women did not seek personal fulfillment from their jobs, but rather from their families. Career women, it is argued, possess different characteristics. They possess strong needs for achievement, recognition, and promotion. As a result of career demands, conflict between husbands and wives over the division of labor in household tasks and childcare may result.

The literature in the area has tended to concentrate on sex-role type arguments, suggesting that a woman's career is somehow at odds with her role as mother and wife. Such arguments appear senseless and biased. Many positive aspects of dual career marriages can be pointed out. Children in such families have more equitable role models to emulate. There is evidence to suggest that these marriages are actually less stressful than more traditional marriages, which may result in more "quality" time spent with children (Strong et al., 1983). As women more and more break down traditional sex-role barriers in the market-place, dual-career families will increase and add more variety to the ever-changing family structure.

Alternative Families

Throughout history there have been attempts at alternative family structures. While many of these structures are short-lived, reflecting cultural fads or experimental life styles, others have been more enduring. We actually know very little about the children raised in these alternative families.

Communes, popular during the 1960s, represented both economic and childrearing alternatives to traditional families. While youth-oriented communes of the 1960s often operated as a group marriage phenomenon, other communes abided by monogamous standards, sharing economic and childrearing functions rather than sexual partners. Communal life styles have, however, tended to be rather short-lived family alternatives.

Another alternative for which there is very little concrete data involves gay couples, lesbian women or homosexual men who "marry" or cohabit and raise children in homosocial households (Johnstone, 1981: 87). According to some research, there are striking similarities between homosexual and heterosexual couples. Each desires relationships that provide love, satisfaction, and security (Peplau, 1981). Some studies do indicate, however, that lesbian couples form more lasting relationships than do homosexual male couples and appear more committed to the relationship. Although such couples obviously cannot biologically produce children themselves, many gay people have had heterosexual relationships in their pasts and may have custody of children from such unions. Almost nothing is known about the rearing of children by homosexual couples.

As we have indicated, current changes taking place in the American family have been largely ignored by criminologists. Dichotomous categorizations of intact versus broken homes are not sensitive to the many variations now possible in parenting children. Whether some of these changes have any relationship to certain types of juvenile delinquency remains to be seen. However, given the importance that is placed on the family in our society, especially in light of the rapid changes taking place, some individuals have advocated that stricter control must be maintained over the family. Advocates of this view favor strict family policies that would guide and give direction to those attributes presumed desirable for the elimination of problem areas in the family.

FAMILY POLICY IN THE UNITED STATES

Despite an extensive history in Europe and other countries, "family policy" has not attracted organized interest in the United States. Family policy represents a more deliberate expression of a nation's acknowledgment of the importance of the family (Kamerman and Kahn, 1978: 1–2). Explicit family policy may be subcategorized into two areas: (1) "Specific programs and policies designed to achieve specified, explicit goals regarding the family, and (2) programs and policies which deliberately do things to and for the family but for which there are no agreed upon overall goals regarding the family" (p. 3). Implicit family policy, on the other hand, refers to "governmental actions and policies not specifically or primarily addressed to the family but which have indirect consequences" (pp. 1–2). Family policy efforts in the United States tend to be implicit as opposed to explicit.

Family policy was first employed in Europe through passage of legislation redistributing income favoring large families via family allowances or demogrants and income tax policies and passage of a population policy concerning long-term demographic projections.

Discussion of family policy for our purposes

obviously hinges on the belief that the family has as its primary function the task of nurturing, caring for, and socializing children. Major changes in families which disrupt that function eventually have a negative impact on all aspects of society.

The United States does not, like many other countries, have an explicit, comprehensive national policy. It does, however, have many social policies relating to family concerns—particularly those affecting children and young people. Some of these have been initiated by federal authorities as crises, needs, and problems have arisen. One could point to early federal programs in the 1930s, such as the Civilian Conservation Corps and the National Youth Administration for Depression-affected youth. The Army and Veterans Administration became central to youth in the 1940s and 1950s, as was the Office of Economic Opportunity in the 1960s. During the 1970s, the now defunct Law Enforcement Assistance Administration initiated and funded programs aimed at diverting potentially delinquent youth from the formal juvenile justice system. Since that time, various programs funded through the departments of Labor and Education have been directed toward youth employment and training, as well as a variety of health and mental health projects dealing with drug use and alcoholism.

Most of the more explicit family policies, however, have their roots in state programs and laws. In reality, the Tenth Amendment reserves to the states most of the powers that have become known as *family law*. Laws affecting marriage, divorce, annulment, abortion, parent-child relationships, adoption, foster care, child abuse and neglect, waywardness, emancipation of minors, child support, artificial insemination, and alimony, to name a few, have been within the realm of state family policies. Many of these laws relate specifically to the care and protection of young people and are constantly supplemented by the press, magazine articles, and sermons devoted to the specific problems of youth: high unemployment, drug use, crime, runaways, decline in basic skills, teenage pregnancies, sexual precocity, and so on.

To this we can add the role of the state in administering many federal-state programs in which funds are matched with respect to family-related matters: Supplementary Security Income (SCI); Aid to Families with Dependent Children (AFDC); unemployment insurance; housing; various educational programs; and many health programs (Kamerman and Kahn, 1978: 433).

Current family policies are predicated on the assumption that the traditional Caucasian family predominates. With few exceptions, these policies have neglected the needs of minorities. For example, when the number of white children began to decline, policies emphasized the older white cohort, which has been on the rise. The black and Hispanic young age cohort, however, has been expanding and is expected to grow in the future. Our family policies will be challenged by this emerging demographic trend (see Chapter 19).

Both past and current concern over juvenile delinquency in the United States has prompted a number of people to argue that more formalized control over basic socializing institutions such as the family through compulsory national family policies might alleviate the problem. Such individuals often point to the efforts of other nations as an example—the Soviet Union, for one. However, upon closer examination it is instructive to note that more formalized control over the family has resulted in relatively few changes either in the family or in those problems that affect youth from those families (Voigt and Thornton, 1985). A major drawback of most national family policies is that a concept of a "normal" functioning family unit is assumed. Given the rapidity of changes currently taking place and the many types of family structures which are emerging, caution must be used in formulating policies that are too narrow or biased.

SUMMARY

Research has shown that children who have been officially adjudicated delinquent are more likely to live in homes where one or both parents are absent than are children who have not been officially adjudicated delinquent. Apparently, this relationship results from the operating procedures of juvenile justice agents rather than from factors originating within the broken home. When self-reported delinquency studies are examined, little or no association is found between broken homes and adolescent lawbreaking.

Research has also shown that juveniles from unhappy unbroken homes are more likely to engage in delinquency than children from happy broken homes. Evidence from a number of studies suggests that homes with high levels of conflict and tension are especially likely to produce delinquent children. Similarly, when parents and children lack affection for each other, chances for effective supervision and socialization are diminished, and chances of delinquent behavior are increased. Parents who fairly and conscientiously supervise, discipline, and teach children decrease the likelihood of delinquent behavior in their offspring. Apparently, children of employed mothers are no more likely to be delinquent than the children of mothers who do not work outside the home. A more significant aspect of family life is family size. Children from large families have higher rates of delinquency than do children from small families. Intermediate children have been found to engage in more delinquency than either oldest or youngest children. However, studies employing birth order as causal factors in delinquency should probably not be considered without the inclusion of sex of siblings.

Most discussions of the relationship of the family to delinquency have employed a definition of the family that is very traditional. The intact, conjugal-nuclear family has become the ideal with which to compare other types of family structures. Changes in American society indicate that the concept of a family itself must be altered. Such things as single-parent families, joint-custody families, dual-career families, blended families, and alternative families have become more prevalent during the last decade. The effects of these types of families on juvenile delinquency, if any, have not been adequately explored.

Since the family is depicted as one of our most vital socializing institutions, there has been much discussion in the United States about developing more formal family policies as other countries have done. Although the United States does not have any comprehensive national family policies, each state has evolved a body of family law and policies that deal with matters pertaining to such things as marriage, divorce, childcare, abortion, adoption, foster care, and the like. Many of these policies are supplemented by federal legislation.

PROGRESS CHECK

1. The process whereby a child learns the rules and beliefs of the society is called _____ and is the primary responsibility of the _____ in the early years of life. (p. 198)

2. Define and illustrate three forms of parental control. (pp. 198–199)

3. Studies consistently show that children referred to official agencies for delinquency involvement are more likely to come from broken homes than children who have never come to the attention of authorities. (p. 200)
   a. True
   b. False

4. The first major research project investigating the association between broken homes and actual delinquent behavior rather than official delinquency was conducted by which of the following? (p. 202)
   a. Edwin Sutherland in the 1920s
   b. Clifford Shaw in the 1930s
   c. Thomas P. Monahan in the 1940s
   d. F. Ivan Nye in the 1950s

5. Evaluate the relevance of marital adjustment and family conflict to juvenile delinquency, utilizing research studies such as those of Biron and LeBlanc, Glueck and Glueck, McCord and McCord, Browning, and Shulman. (pp. 203–205)

6. According to the text, if a parent restricts a child's activities outside the home and the kinds of friends with whom the child can

associate, the chances of delinquent behavior in that child are increased. (pp. 205–206)

a. True

b. False

7. Compare and assess the relative strengths and weaknesses of parental discipline *and* value transmission as two key forms of delinquency prevention and control. (pp. 206–208)

8. According to the text, the effects of childhood maltreatment have never been associated with delinquency or later criminal activity. (p. 207)

a. True

b. False

9. Discuss the structure of the family as it is presently constituted, including references to the emerging trends of single-parent households, joint custody, blended, dual-career, and alternative families. How might these changes be related to delinquency? (pp. 209–212)

10. Distinguish between *explicit* and *implicit* family policy. Which type more aptly applies to the United States? (pp. 212–213)

NOTES

1. The concept of broken home also communicates a negative connotation. It carries with it an implicit negative value judgment. *Broken* suggests something requiring mending, not functioning, or out of order. Increasingly the term *broken* is avoided because it overstates the negative and understates any positive attributes of the family relationship.

2. The problem is that not only is the departure from the ideal type family not correlated with delinquency, it may not be correlated with "reality." The 1980 census indicates that only about 15 percent of American families resemble the "ideal type." An examination of research on the traditional family and delinquency indicates that most of this research was undertaken in the 1950s and 1960s. More current research will undoubtedly have to deal with new family structures.

PUBLIC SCHOOL 37

CHAPTER **10**

SCHOOLS AND DELINQUENCY

Ralph is a 15-year-old boy who was referred to a youth service bureau, an agency that provides counseling to children viewed by police, parents, or school personnel as problems. In an initial youth service bureau interview, Ralph's parents indicated that Ralph's problems with the school and the law developed recently, when Ralph entered junior high. At his new school Ralph had become a general behavior problem, throwing lunch trays, coming to class late, challenging teachers' authority, and fighting with other students. Ralph's difficulties were also apparent outside the school. Several neighbors accused Ralph of stealing tools and other items in their cars and yards. Ralph had also run away from home three times.

Interviews with school personnel, however, revealed that Ralph's school problems had begun long before his entry into junior high. According to school records, Ralph's misbehavior started in kindergarten. During third grade, the boy spent six weeks in the principal's office when the teacher was unable to control his disruptions. By seventh grade, Ralph hated teachers, wanted "to kill the principal," resented the school's restrictions, failed several subjects, managed to get suspended from school 100 out of 150 school days, and voiced the desire to drop out. "Who needs school anyway?" said Ralph. "I'm going to be a mechanic and they don't teach that in school."

On the day Ralph was to appear in juvenile court, Ralph's school problems took a new *turn. The principal told Ralph to put his cap in his locker and Ralph refused, knocking the principal down to underscore his refusal. Ralph was then suspended for the rest of the year.*

The juvenile court judge ordered Ralph to continue counseling at the youth service bureau. This counseling proved ineffective. Ralph's delinquent behaviors became more frequent and serious. After the year suspension, Ralph tried to go back to school, but his disobedience and fighting soon led to another expulsion. He made a few half-hearted attempts to find a job, but because of his age was always turned down. An older friend gave him some marijuana to sell, and now Ralph spends his time hanging out at his old school, selling marijuana to kids he used to go to school with and dreaming of becoming a big-time drug dealer.

Ralph's story illustrates the relationship between school experiences and involvement in delinquency in the life of one teenager. Many sociologists and criminologists believe that the school encourages conformity in some, but delinquency in others. Schafer and Polk, in a 1967 report of the President's Commission on Law Enforcement and the Administration of Justice, argued:

> Available evidence strongly suggests that delinquent commitments result in part from adverse or negative school experiences of some youth, and, further, that there are fundamental defects within the educational system, especially as it touches lower-class youth, that actively contribute to these negative experiences, thereby increasing rather than decreasing the chances that some youth will choose illegitimate alternatives. (p. 223)

It is not surprising to find the school at the forefront of accounts and explanations of delinquency because, after the family, the school assumes a major responsibility for much of a child's time and development, particularly from the age of 6 until, most commonly, 16 or 17. During the time children spend in school, they are expected to learn rules about social behavior as well as basic academic skills. Sociologist Talcott Parsons (1959) wrote that the rules taught by the schools included norms about **role responsibility**, "or the capacity to live up to other people's expectations of the interpersonal behavior appropriate to these roles" (p. 298). Basically, the child learns what behavior is considered acceptable and what behavior is not. Properly transmitted, these social norms are supposed to inhibit delinquency and deviance in the child and criminality in the adult.

In this chapter, we will first examine research evidence about the relationship between the school and delinquency; then we will evaluate delinquency theories that have incorporated this research evidence into general explanations of why school experiences relate to delinquency. We will also explore characteristics of individual schools that are thought by sociologists to influence the delinquency of the children who attend. Alternative schools and their programs are reviewed as one possible way of working with youth who have problems in more traditional settings. As a possible reaction to dissatisfaction with school, increased violence and vandalism have been reported in the nation's schools. We examine the types of crimes and the victims of crime in the schools and then look at possible means of preventing and controlling such crimes.

SCHOOLS AND DELINQUENCY: RESEARCH EVIDENCE

There is strong agreement among researchers that certain facets of the child's school career relate to involvement in delinquency.[1] These facets include school achievement, ability, ambition, misbehavior, truancy, and dropping out, each of which we will examine individually. Failure to achieve and conform in school has been particularly demonstrated to relate to delinquent behavior both inside and outside school. School conduct is regulated by many rules that tell students what they should and should not think and do while in school. In a study of school interaction, Schafer (1972) outlined some of the norms for behavior:

> All schools, for instance, are legally bound to require attendance until some specified age is reached, usually 16 or 17. And once in attendance, pupils are expected to perform at their highest possible levels in their schoolwork. This means that academic success goals are to be internalized and pursued by all youngsters, the height of those goals to be limited only by the innate capability of the student.
>
> In addition, and partly to insure maximum achievement, all students must achieve above a minimum academic level. . . .
>
> Associated with the expectation that [students] will learn is the further anticipation that [they] will do nothing to interfere with [their] learning. This is the common-sense concept of school discipline. (pp. 148–149)

A child who conforms to these rules for behavior is less likely to become delinquent than a child who breaks school rules. If Jack the class bully has failed three or more grades, brings home a report card liberally sprinkled with Fs, hates school, spits on the teacher, sees no relation between school and his vocational ambition of being a pimp, loves to skip school to hang out with the guys, and plans to drop out at the first available opportunity, his chances of being involved in delinquency are much greater than those of Joe the class president, who sports a straight A report card, perfect attendance, a high degree of school motivation, and has big plans for his occupational future. Some researchers go so far as to view the school as the most crucial factor in accounting for a child's involvement in delinquency (Elliott and Voss, 1974).

School Achievement

Academic achievement is an important factor in predicting whether or not a student will become delinquent. Research evidence indicates that the poorer a child's academic record (measured by grade point average, the prevalence of failing grades, and the number of years held back in school), the greater the likelihood of delinquency involvement. This is not to say that all students with bad grades engage in delinquency, but more failing than passing students are involved in delinquency.

In the last fifteen years the results of a number of studies have supported findings about the relationship between school achievement and delinquency (Empey and Lubeck, 1971a; Gold and Mann, 1972; Kelly and Balch, 1971; Polk and Halferty, 1972). For example, British researchers reported in 1973 that boys who do poorly in school have more police contacts (West and Farrington, 1973). In the United States investigators have also found that both official and self-reported delinquency is highly correlated with poor grades for both boys and girls (Gold and Mann, 1972).

School Ability

Besides academic achievement, another apparently important factor in explaining delinquency is school ability. School ability, or **intelligence**, has been variously defined as the inherited capacity to learn, the ability to perform a variety of mental operations, the intellectual result of socialization for middle class life, social adjustment, and the ability to behave in accordance with legal standards. Intelligence has also been called what intelligence tests measure. We will define intelligence as the ability to learn what the school teaches and what intelligence tests measure.

Throughout the years, designers of intelligence tests have tried to construct tests that measure *learning capacities* rather than *previous learning,* but there is doubt that any intelligence test can be totally free of cultural bias. Tests may measure the effectiveness of a child's socialization into middle class life or the amount of information already learned in school, rather than the actual ability of the tested child. Problems with the measurement of intelligence plague researchers who examine the relationship of school ability to delinquency.[2]

As we noted in Chapter 5, there is little

consensus about whether intelligence, however it is measured, relates to differential delinquency involvement. Although the meaning of the difference has been diversely interpreted, most research evidence does show that children with dull to normal intelligence, but few adolescents with superior intelligence, become delinquent (Caplan, 1965; Hirschi and Hindelang, 1977). This is particularly true of official delinquents and repeat offenders. If intelligence tests measure the ability to do well in school and if school achievement unquestionably relates to delinquency, it does seem feasible that intelligence would be expected to have some influence on delinquency and the societal reaction to delinquency. However, it is important to note here that the relationship of school achievement to delinquency is stronger than the relationship of intelligence to delinquency. In other words, delinquency relates more to the child's grades than to his or her score on intelligence tests.

Types of Intelligence.   Although most attention has focused on general intellectual competence and delinquency, there are indications that the relationship varies, depending on the aspect of intelligence under consideration.

For example, in 1963 Prentice and Kelly reviewed studies reporting the verbal and performance scores (psychomotor skills) of delinquents and nondelinquents and observed: "Almost without exception, these studies based largely on an adolescent population report significant elevation of Performance over Verbal IQs" (p. 333). Urging caution in interpreting this finding, Prentice and Kelly present evidence that nondelinquent populations also show the pattern of higher performance scores.

More recently, it has been proposed that **learning disabilities** are causes of delinquency. According to the National Advisory Committee on Handicapped Children: "Children with special learning disabilities exhibit a disorder in one or more of the basic psychological processes involved in understanding or using spoken or written languages." Learning disabilities are "not caused by low intelligence, emotional disturbance, physical handi-

caps, or incompetent teachers" (Murray, 1976: 11–12). In fact, no one is certain what causes learning disabilities; but some researchers think they relate to "minimal brain dysfunction." Learning disabilities are hypothesized to contribute to increasing chances of delinquency because learning-disabled children experience high rates of school failure. This hypothesis has not yet been adequately and systematically tested.

School Attitudes

Negative attitudes toward the school are another feature of the school career that has been repeatedly found to be more widespread among delinquents. Negative attitudes may include dislike for the school and teachers, apathy toward the school, feelings that teachers are not helpful, feelings that school is irrelevant, lack of confidence in ability to do well in class, and resentment of the school's authority.[3] The research evidence spanning some forty years clearly supports the view that delinquents dislike school more than nondelinquents (Wattenberg, 1947; Frease, 1973a).

School Ambitions

Although the relationship between school attitudes and delinquency is one of the oldest and most consistent in research into adolescent misconduct, the link between school ambitions and related vocational aspirations and delinquency is more controversial. Sociologist James Short, Jr., commented: "High educational and occupational aspirations . . . seem clearly not to pressure the boys toward deviance, despite limitations, perceived and objective, in opportunities for achievement of these aspirations" (1964: 115). Short, in a 1964 study of gangs, found that objective educational failure does not reduce the educational desires for either white or black gang or nongang members. In fact, high educational aspirations inhibit delinquency. Stinchcombe (1964), on the other hand, asserted that failure in school frustrates educational and occupational aspirations, and lowered ambitions for the educational and vocational future result in higher school rebellion and ultimately in increased delinquency.

Short and Stinchcombe agreed that lowered aspirations led to delinquency, but they disagreed about the influence of school failure or ambitions for future schooling and high-status occupations. The work of Kelly (1971) illustrates a third point of view:

> Once again, it may be that the immediate consequences of failure are more important than the long-run implications of low grades. Being grounded or kicked off the football team is a direct, immediate, salient consequence of failure. The inability to enroll in college or get a high-paying, prestigious job lies somewhere in the distant, and probably very hazy, future. (p. 501)

Polk (1972) reached similar conclusions and reported that in his sample of adolescents, rebellion appeared to occur as a "response to the immediate effects of failure rather than to its implication for future low status" (p. 114). Although educational failure appears to lower occupational and educational ambitions, the child's prospects for the future are not as strongly related to delinquency as are the realities of the present.

School Misbehavior

Another aspect of the school career that appears to serve as a precursor of delinquency among some adolescents is misbehavior. School life is regulated by sets of specific rules governing behavior. For instance, the student may be expected to be quiet and attend to his or her own work, to refrain from interfering with the learning activities of others, to raise a hand and be recognized before speaking, and to act in a deferential and respectful fashion toward teachers and other school personnel. Concern for obedience to these rules is reflected in the importance of the word "discipline" in the vocabularies of school personnel. Generally, the rewards offered to students by school—including grades, praise, and recognition—are reserved for students who conform to the conduct rules.

Several studies show more school misconduct among official delinquents than among nondelin-

quents. Havighurst and his associates (1962), for example, found that 66 percent of boys who are distinctively aggressive in school eventually become delinquent. Khlief (1964) matched juvenile court referrals and nondelinquent adolescents similar in age, sex, race, and first-grade teachers and reported that boys who became officially recognized as delinquent engaged in significantly more school misconduct in the first five years of school than did boys never referred to the juvenile court. On the other hand, Khlief more often characterized delinquent girls as "indifferent clients" than as active behavior problems.

Summarizing the connection between school misconduct and delinquency, Khlief concluded that delinquency relates not only to academic school performance, but also to social behaviors in school. Carrying this reasoning one step further, other researchers point out that the grades assigned by teachers are subjective interpretations of the student's work. These interpretations may be influenced by conduct, as well as academic performance. Future misconduct may then occur as a reaction against failure, especially failure considered by the student as unfairly assigned (Cicourel and Kitsuse, 1968; Rhodes and Reiss, 1969). Other studies demonstrate that school misconduct relates to social class, school ability, and involvement in teenage groups, as well as to school failure. Misbehavior in school also appears more widespread among young people who do not perceive school as relevant to their futures (Polk and Pink, 1972; Sexton, 1961; West and Farrington, 1973).

It may be that rebellious behavior in school and delinquency are both manifestations of the same pattern of disregard for rules, but the evidence strongly suggests that school misbehavior precedes delinquency. Schafer and Polk (1967), in fact, argued that the school's reaction to initial misconduct may itself cause future involvement in delinquency.

School Truancy

One of the most important school rules concerns attendance—a student is legally required to come to school until he or she attains an age set by statute. Much attention has been directed toward the relationship between chronic breaking of this particular rule and delinquency. Research findings demonstrate that the tendency to skip school is related to involvement in delinquency.

Walberg in 1972 surveyed Chicago high school students and observed that self-reported delinquency was more strongly associated with skipping school than with a number of other school characteristics. Reckless and Dinitz (1972) noticed that truancy often foreshadowed the development of delinquency among boys attending school in Columbus, Ohio, and hypothesized that "school attendance reflects motivation, goals, and perceptions of the legitimacy and the significance of the educational institution" (p. 108).

One school condition that is highly linked to truancy is academic failure. In a sample of adolescent boys in Oregon, Kelly and Balch (1971) reported that truancy is more common among unsuccessful than among successful students. Similarly, Essex-Cater (1961) discovered in a study of British schoolboys that "poor attendance sometimes originated from the despair which boys felt because of academic difficulties" (p. 145). When Roberts (1956) studied San Francisco truants, he concluded that school failure was both a cause and effect of truancy and suggested that "schools might well try to break the vicious cycle and attempt to find ways in which children might progress with their own social and age groups and at the same time be helped to achieve success in these groups" (p. 435).

In summary, truancy may relate to delinquency because truancy increases delinquent opportunities and contacts with delinquent companions. There may be a process of withdrawal from conventional social life. It does seem likely that if school experiences are frustrating and unrewarding, there may be a tendency to avoid the unpleasant situation. Perhaps truancy and delinquency are then linked because both in part result from academic failure.

School Dropout

Another characteristic of the school career that may represent a step toward delinquency is dropping out of school. School attendance is thought to inhibit delinquency for two primary reasons. First, going to school helps children learn specific information, skills, and values. Children who do not attend school may fail to learn rules that prohibit crime and delinquency. Second, as Schafer and Knudten (1970) have written: "Excessive absence may itself be a symptom of developing delinquency" (p. 234). In other words, the child who no longer goes to school is more likely to engage in delinquency than is the child who still attends.

Researchers report that the student who fails is simply more likely to leave school than the student who does well. When Kelly and Pink (1972), for example, studied school dropouts, they found that students who failed were more likely to drop out than students who passed. One researcher, Delbert Elliott (1966), presented evidence that experiences in school are related to tendency to drop out of school and to involvement in delinquency. According to Elliott, even able students engage in school avoidance and delinquency when they cannot or will not conform to the middle class values of the school and find themselves therefore locked out of the reward system. Elliott further argued that "as a result of unequal competition, lower-class youths develop feelings of insecurity, become frustrated and begin to search for some solution to their status problem" (p. 307). Elliott labeled the frustrated, insecure feelings that develop when children do not achieve **status deprivation**. He suggested that dropping out of school and engaging in delinquency are two ways to solve the problem of status deprivation.

One characteristic of school life that might contribute to dropout and delinquency is a discrepancy between what school personnel think the school should accomplish and what students think the school should accomplish. Studying juvenile court referrals in Britain, Power, Benn, and Morris (1972) compared the objectives of dropouts and their headmasters. The boys thought the school should:

1. Teach you things to help you get a good job.
2. Teach you how to manage money.
3. Teach you things of direct use on your job.

4. Teach you about jobs and careers so that you can select one.

5. Teach you to put things into writing.

The headmasters' objectives differed considerably. They wanted it assured that students were taught:

1. Character and personality

2. Proper speech

3. Independence

4. Confident behavior

5. Differences between right and wrong (128)[4]

Apparently these boys were not getting the education they thought most appropriate. Perceived irrelevance of education does seem to contribute to school leaving and misconduct. A U.S. Office of Education report cautioned that "school experience, irrelevant to life experience and to employment opportunities, contributes heavily to dropout rates. An unemployed dropout stands a good chance of becoming delinquent" (U.S. Department of Health, Education and Welfare, Office of Education, 1967: 278). However, a more recent study of the nation's schools, *A Nation at Risk*, conducted by members of the National Commission of Excellence in Education, reported that some 25 percent of the credits earned by high school students are in such things as work experience outside school and personal service and development courses on "Training in Adulthood and Marriage." The commission cautions that more academic courses must be offered (U.S. Department of Education, 1983: 19). This finding suggests that there must be an acceptable balance between academic courses and so-called job or life preparation courses.

SCHOOLS AND DELINQUENCY: SOCIOLOGICAL THEORIES

Thus far in the chapter, we have seen evidence that several aspects of the school career relate positively to delinquency. Regardless of the reason for leaving school, dropping out is related to delinquency. Other aspects of school life associated with delinquency include school failure, lack of school ability and ambition for schooling, negative attitudes toward school, school misbehavior, and truancy. Many theorists and researchers attempt to account for these relationships. They ask: "Why does the child's school career appear to relate to his or her involvement in delinquency?" Depending on their particular orientation, theorists answer this question differently. The relationship of school experiences to delinquency is especially considered by subcultural theorists, social control theorists, and labeling theorists.

Subcultural Theory

According to subcultural theorists, delinquency is the result of adherence to group norms. Educational frustration is thought to increase the likelihood that a child will be involved with a delinquent peer group.

Educational Frustration. In 1955, Albert Cohen published a book entitled *Delinquent Boys: The Culture of the Gang.* Cohen assigned the school central importance in his explanation of delinquency. According to Cohen, schools are middle class institutions, and all children who attend school are evaluated by "middle class" measuring rods. Boys from the lower class, however, are ill-equipped to compete in the middle class world, and failure in school almost inevitably results. Because they desire to attain the rewards the school offers but are prevented by their class backgrounds from achieving status there, lower class boys create a status system of their own. Delinquency is one valued behavior in this system.

Thus Cohen attributed delinquency directly to educational frustration encountered in schools. Using his reasoning, one would expect lower class boys to desire school success and bright occupational futures, but to engage in delinquency when school failure, rather than success, occurs. Delinquent lower class boys would further be expected to have unfavorable attitudes toward the school and high rates of truancy, dropping out of school, and school misbehavior as a reaction to school failure.

Schafer and Polk (1967) concurred with Cohen's theory about school-related causes of delinquency, noting that educational failure, combined with a desire for success, contributes to delinquency regardless of the social class of the child's family. According to Schafer and Polk, children from the lower classes are more affected by educational failure for two reasons. First, lower class children fail more often in school because their backgrounds do not adequately prepare them for the demands of school. Second, middle class children who fail in school are "held in" the legitimate system by pressures from parents, peers, and community.

Research evidence indicates that Cohen's ideas have some validity, at least as far as the relationship among social class, educational failure, and educational aspirations are concerned. Sexton (1961) has documented that two chief rewards of the school—good grades and the promise of occupational success—are largely reserved for the children of middle and upper class parents. College scholarships, extracurricular activities, and access to college preparatory programs are assigned not on the basis of ability, talent, and interest, but instead on the basis of the family's social class.

Other research indicates that even though lower class youngsters fail more often than middle and upper class ones, lower class children and their parents uniformly value educational success. In a study of low-income boys in Philadelphia, Lalli and Savitz (1972) discovered that 97 percent of the boys wanted to complete high school. Boys with delinquent histories were, however, less likely to aspire to a college education. By and large, these lower class boys did subscribe to middle class values, including getting a good job, having a nice home, owning nice clothes, and living in a good neighborhood.

There is, however, a growing body of evidence that disputes Cohen's ideas about the relationships among the school, social class, and delinquency. Although lower class children may desire school and occupational success but fail more often than middle or upper class children, studies have indicated that school failure, not social class, is the important factor in explaining delinquency. Self-reported delinquency studies contradict the assumption that lower class boys are more involved in delinquency than boys from other classes. Even Empey and Lubeck's research (1971a) on official delinquency among boys in Los Angeles and Utah failed to show that social class is related to delinquency. Instead, they reported that "performance in, and dropping out of, school, not social class . . . are related most strongly to official delinquency" (p. 48). The child who does well in school, regardless of social class origins, is less likely to be delinquent.

Reformulating Cohen's hypotheses, Stinchcombe (1964) proposed that a pupil's class origins are not as important as his or her future status prospects in explaining rebellious behavior. The student who fails "does not visualize achievement of long-run goals through current self-restraint" (p. 5). Among poor pupils, no payoff is seen from conformity to school rules and values. Stinchcombe further proposed that failure is more frustrating to the middle class children. School failure implies that the working class child will retain his or her present status in the future, but the middle class child will face the downward mobility of a working class occupation. Stinchcombe's data, gathered in a smalltown high school, supported his contentions. Failing middle class students were especially rebellious.

Other studies, however, have not duplicated Stinchcombe's findings. Both Polk and Kelly reported that downwardly mobile middle class boys are no more delinquent than their blue collar counterparts. Apparently, "immediate consequences of failure are more important than the long-run implications of low grades" (Kelly, 1971: 501). So in summary, grades seem more important in accounting for delinquency than class origin or future prospects.

Peer Influences.   Subculturists commonly argue that school failure, both academic and social, brings about identification with delinquent or peer groups, and that these associations result in increased delinquency. According to Karacki and Toby (1962), the values and activities of the peer group become more important to the failing student than school values and activities.

Polk and Richmond (1972) surveyed students with failing grades and remarked that failing students spent more time with peers, had more friends outside the school setting, and preferred activities involving friends to those involving school personnel. "Rejection by the school," according to Polk and Richmond, "leaves little room for any alternative but seeking out the society of peers" (p. 65). The result is "a subculture of alienated youth who work in concert both to provide effective neutralization and to generate trouble for the system" (p. 69). There is a high incidence of delinquency among students involved in this subculture of alienated youth.

Writing about the effects of the school and peer groups on adolescents, Parsons (1959) observed that, in most schools, there are two distinct subgroups of students: those identifying with teachers and those identifying with the peer group. This division of pupils parallels the division of those who later attend, or do not attend, college. Often, children who identify with other children rather than adults evolve and encounter standards of behavior that are disapproved by adults. From Parsons' viewpoint, the peer group is the "seed bed from which extremists go over into delinquency" (p. 305).

Although involvement with other students who "buy" the values of school may make the student more committed to conformity, entanglement with students who rebel against the school appears conducive to delinquency. Further, success in school is an important predictor of which group the student will find attractive. The commitment to adult values and positive attachment to the school that is characteristic of the "pupil" group is, according to social control theorists, the heart of the distinction between delinquents and non-delinquents.

Social Control Theory

In our discussion of social control theory (Chapter 7), we said that one of the most concise and complete presentations of the propositions of social control theory is found in Travis Hirschi's book, *Causes of Delinquency* (1969). Hirschi considered

commitment and attachment to the school critical in explaining involvement, or lack of involvement, in delinquency. Essentially, Hirschi argued that students who do poorly in school (more often than not because they lack the academic ability to do well) dislike school, and students who dislike school are more likely to be involved in delinquency. Hirschi, however, did not believe that dislike for school relates to delinquency because "delinquency is a means of relieving frustration generated by unpleasant school experience" (p. 122), but argued instead that a boy who dislikes school and does not care what teachers think of him probably rejects the values of the school and the school's right to tell him what to do. The student who has unfavorable school attitudes is unrestrained by the values and control of the school and is, at least to some extent, free to commit delinquent acts.

Hirschi's data supported his hypotheses and demonstrated that boys who dislike school reject the authority of the school. Hindelang's (1973) study of boys and girls living in rural areas also confirmed Hirschi's contentions about the relationship of attachment to the school and delinquency. And we have already viewed evidence strongly supporting the notion that unfavorable attitudes toward the school (what Hirschi called "lack of school attachments") are widespread among both official and admitted delinquents.

Hirschi and other control theorists have also emphasized the importance of lack of commitment to conventional goals and futures in accounting for delinquency. A student who is doing well in school is unlikely to jeopardize prospects for the future by involvement in delinquency. Conversely, the student who sees no relationship between school and occupational future or one who faces dismal job prospects does not have as much to lose through delinquent behavior.

Labeling Theory

Some labeling theorists argue that teachers, counselors, and principals make assumptions "about the abilities and conduct of young people" and categorize school children as "bright, culturally deprived, dull, troublesome, and so on" (Polk and Schafer, 1972: 4). These categories "are of fundamental importance in establishing the legitimate and illegitimate adolescent identities that can be identified in delinquent behavior" (p. 4).

The student who fails and misbehaves in school and who dislikes school and rebels against it faces the possibility of negative categorization, or labeling, by school personnel. Even children who have not broken specific school rules may be assigned a deviant label when they do not measure up to middle class standards of neatness, cleanliness, and verbal proficiency (Kelly and Pink, 1973). Tolerance limits for an individual child's behavior may depend "on such things as his own status characteristics, how he looks, who his friends are, and what his reputation is; on the situation; and on who is enforcing group standards" (Schafer and Polk, 1967: 227). Once the child has been categorized by school personnel, future deviant acts may be the result of adverse school-pupil interactions, rather than simply being individual acts of rebellion. The school may thus *encourage* delinquency and rebellion through negative labeling.

If a child is constantly treated as a "delinquent," a "troublemaker," or a "slow learner," the child's self-concept may be affected. The student often considers himself "bad" or "stupid" and behaves in accordance with the deviant identity. It is also possible that commitment and attachment to the school may lessen while association with other delinquents increases.

The deviant identities most commonly assigned by school personnel and sometimes adopted by students themselves relate to several kinds of so-called adolescent problems. When students are unable or unwilling to conform to norms of academic achievement, they may be labeled "underachievers" and "overachievers." On the basis of general misconduct in school, pupils may be called "delinquents," "hoods," or "troublemakers" (Cicourel and Kitsuse, 1968: 126). Once the student has been classified as an academic, emotional, or behavioral deviant, escape from the assigned label is very difficult.

One of the most important conclusions reached by labeling theorists is that the reactions of the school to failure or misconduct may increase, rather than deter, delinquency involvement. A cycle of failure, labeling, and rebellion has been described by Frease (1973a): "The rebellious behavior in turn leads to stigmas being attached to the rebels by the school officials, which then leads to more failure, which leads to an even more negative attitude of the school experience, which leads to even more rebellion, more stigmatization, more failure, and around again to rebellion" (p. 449). The school is not a hospitable place for the negatively labeled student. As a result of opportunities closed and identities altered by school labeling, misconduct may generalize from the school setting to the community.

In summary, all the theories we have reviewed concur that the school career in general is important in explaining delinquency. Although most advocates of particular theoretical perspectives tend to think that only their perspective can interpret the relationship of the school career to delinquency, each theory has a particular point of emphasis and is important in accounting for specific facets of the complex ways a child's school career can relate to delinquency. Generally, the child who fails in school is more likely to misbehave in school and dislike school than the child who is successful. Failure and subsequent negative labeling may decrease commitment to the goals and values of the school and increase delinquent associations. Lack of commitment and attachment to the school, delinquent associations, and the effects of negative labeling within the school may further increase the chances of delinquency.

SCHOOLS AND DELINQUENCY: SCHOOL CHARACTERISTICS

Thus far we have referred to "the school," considering all schools similar in goals, values, and practices. Most delinquency studies view the school as a "constant factor" and refer to the general institution of the school, not to specific schools. This tendency to regard all schools as similar in characteristics and interaction patterns has, however, been criticized; researchers have suggested that schools differ in many ways and that these differences are reflected in the delinquency rates of students attending particular schools. Power, Benn, and Morris (1972), for example, matched British schools on the basis of similarity of neighborhood and several external factors and still found differences in delinquency rates among schools.

A number of distinctive attributes of particular schools have been linked in one way or another to delinquency. We will consider three: tracking, teachers, and tolerance of misbehavior.

Tracking

Perhaps the presence or absence of "tracking" is most frequently mentioned as an important determinant of the delinquency rate in an individual school. *Tracking*, which is also called *streaming*, is the practice of assigning students to groups based on the school's assessment of the child's ability and potential for the future. Between schools, there are differences in the number of tracks, or streams. The major breakdown is generally between college-bound and non-college-bound students. Some schools elaborate further, assigning students to a number of tracks, in some cases to as many as six. According to Schafer, Olexa, and Polk (1972), "selection into . . . different tracks resulted from a combination of desires and aspirations, teacher advice, achievement test scores, grades, pressure from parents, and counselor assessment of academic promise" (p. 37). Classification has also been attributed to social class, racial background, school ability, and general deportment.

Several studies have related track position to probabilities of delinquency. Hargreaves (1967) studied an inner city British school and found that delinquency was more prevalent among the lower-stream boys. Similar findings have been reported by researchers in the United States (Kelly and Pink, 1973; Schafer, Olexa, and Polk, 1972).

Teachers

Research on differences between schools and the existence of delinquency has also focused on

characteristics of teaching staffs. Phillipson (1971), for example, reported that schools with high staff turnover and absenteeism rates have more than their share of delinquent children. According to Phillipson, high turnover and absenteeism generate confusion about authority figures, cynicism about teachers and the school, and low institutional pride among pupils. Further, schools may differ in predominating "types" of teachers. Some staffs may be dedicated and stable; others, apathetic and constantly changing. Phillipson hypothesized that teacher-type turnover influenced delinquency among pupils.

Tolerance

Characteristics of teaching staffs such as turnover and absenteeism, however, may not be most important in accounting for differences in delinquency patterns. Schools may also vary in tolerance limits for pupil behaviors and inclinations to label pupils negatively. On the premises of labeling theory, schools where teachers and other personnel are quick to stereotype and stigmatize students may encourage delinquency among pupils. Research relating differences between schools in terms of labeling and quality of instruction to school delinquency rates is, however, sketchy and inconclusive. More subtle factors, including the quality of teaching, characteristic teacher-pupil interactions, the relevance of curricula, and the appropriateness of teaching methods, may also more effectively explain differences between the delinquency rates of schools in similar neighborhoods.

SCHOOLS AND ALTERNATIVE EDUCATION IN THE PREVENTION OF DELINQUENCY

As a reaction to problems that some children experience in more traditional school settings (poor self-esteem, poor grades), some educators and criminologists have argued that certain alternative educational programs may be a promising means of preventing and treating delinquent behavior (Gold, 1978; *Prevention of Delinquency Through Alternative Education*, 1980). Basically this philosophy suggests that "delinquent behavior is a manifestation of [psychological defenses] against threats to self-esteem and [that] a substantial part of those threats originates in school experience" (Gold 1978: 290). Students who have little stake in achievement and in conformity to the rules of conventional schools may become alienated and more likely to engage in delinquent activities. Also, they are more likely to join the ranks of the unemployed and remain there. Schools, it is argued, must provide problem youth with the opportunity to receive "alternative educational experiences geared to developing constructive interests relative to their environment," while at the same time imparting basic information that they will need to survive in a complex, urbanized society (*Prevention of Delinquency*, 1980: 3).

Alternative educational programs need not, as some have suggested (Papagiannis, Bickel, and Fuller, 1983; Henslin, Henslin, and Keiser, 1976; Nasaw, 1979), be designed to maintain a stable working class by socializing certain children to lesser life styles or to lower grades of information. Rather, such programs can embrace subject matter and teaching methods that are not generally offered to students in a traditional school setting. Alternative programs attempt to facilitate student success, while at the same time evoking positive growth and development in academic, vocational, and social skills. They may be instituted more often in so-called high risk communities characterized by high rates of crime and delinquency, high rates of unemployment, substandard housing, and so on.

Although the concept of alternative education is relatively new, many of the techniques are not. The alternative school employs such techniques and practices as individualized instruction; the establishment of warm, caring relationships; smaller class or school size; competence in teachers and administrators; and the use of reward systems. Given that the nation's school systems are under scrutiny and review at the present time, the role of alternative education should be examined for possible delinquency prevention and control.

SCHOOLS AND VIOLENCE, THEFT, AND VANDALISM

The traditional conception of the school has generally been that it is a haven for children where learning and continued socialization can occur. While accounts of students talking back to teachers and other school personnel were inevitable, the idea of teachers being assaulted or otherwise victimized was incomprehensible. Similarly, an occasional fight might occur on the playground or in the halls, but premeditated assaults on students by other students just didn't happen. Petty thefts and minor vandalisms might occur, but large-scale stealing and major acts of vandalism were infrequent.

Although for the most part both public and private schools continue to be orderly institutions where learning takes place, evidence does indicate that we cannot take it for granted that all schools fit this model (Toby, 1983; *Crime and Disruption in Schools*, 1979; *Criminal Victimization in Urban Schools*, 1979). According to two national studies of school crime, there is enough evidence to indicate that both students and teachers are victims of crime to the extent that it has become a serious problem meriting immediate attention. In addition, acts of vandalism directed against schools themselves have become extremely expensive (U.S. Department of Health, Education, and Welfare, 1978; *Criminal Victimization in Urban Schools*, 1979).

Types of Crime

Most research on school crime indicates that violence and property destruction in the nation's schools increased from the early 1960s through the early 1970s and then began to level off. Researchers have suggested that this time period reflected particularly volatile times for the country in general (the Vietnam war, racial unrest, and the growing youth movement) and that school crimes, especially acts of vandalism, were simply symbolic reflections of the hostilities and frustration young people felt. Another reason for increased disruption in the schools during this time has been blamed on the "baby boom" generation.

The sheer size of this generation has increased the probability that a certain amount of disruption would occur in the schools after the relative calm of the 1950s (*Violent Schools/Safe Schools*, 1981: 149).

Predictions that school disruption would decline substantially have not, however, been forthcoming. The problem remains serious, though not epidemic, and particularly manifests itself in large urban and suburban schools.

Offenses against Students, Teachers, and Schools. Based on victimization surveys from both students and teachers collected by the National Institute of Education in 1976, most school crime is of a nonviolent nature. Both teachers and students run much greater risks of losing their property through theft rather than assault or robbery.[5]

According to principals' reports of estimates of offenses against school property, some 24,000 of the nation's 84,000 public elementary and secondary schools report various property offenses, including trespassing, breaking and entering, theft of school property, and deliberate property destruction (vandalism). The average cost of an act of vandalism is $81. Breaking and entering costs in a given month averaged about $183. Interestingly enough, "the rate of burglary for schools is about five times as high as that for commercial establishments such as stores, which have the highest burglary rate reported in the National Crime Survey."

Estimates of the annual cost of school crime run from $50 to $600 million. Based on the National Center for Education Statistics (NCES) figures, the average cost per year is around $200 million for the replacement and repair of school property and equipment (*Violent Schools/Safe Schools*, 1981: 150–151).

Attempted Solutions

A broad range of strategies has been tried by the schools to deal with school crime. Since schools vary tremendously in their locale, student makeup, and community values, a successful program at one school may not necessarily be replicated at another school (*School Crime*, 1979). As a result, several different approaches have been developed to prevent or control school crime throughout the nation. They range from increased security in the schools to more community-oriented efforts where parents and other concerned citizens are used as resource people to deal with problems before things get out of hand. The latter approach is predicated on the view that school crime is seldom an isolated phenomenon; it originates in the community and therefore must be solved through community efforts.

CRISIS IN AMERICAN EDUCATION: A COMMENT

As succinctly stated in the National Commission on Excellence in Education Report, "A Nation at Risk," there is a "widespread public perception that something is seriously remiss in our educational system" (U.S. Department of Education, 1983: 1). The commission confirmed that mediocrity in American education has become the norm. Indeed, evidence is cited which suggests that regardless of race or class, many of America's children are educationally handicapped:

Some 23 million American adults are functionally illiterate by the simplest tests of everyday reading, writing, and comprehension.

About 13 percent of all 17-year-olds in the United States can be considered functionally illiterate. Functional illiteracy among minority youth may run as high as 40 percent.

Average achievement of high school students on most standardized tests is now lower than 26 years ago when Sputnik was launched.

Many 17-year-olds do not possess "higher order" intellectual skills we should expect of them. Nearly 40 percent cannot draw inferences from written materials; only one-fifth can write a persuasive essay; and only one-third can solve a mathematics problem requiring several steps. (U.S. Department of Education, 1983: 3–5)

Since the school is seen as one of the basic socializing institutions in our society, one which to a large extent prepares individuals for the eventual life styles they will live, weaknesses in the school dramatically affect the total society. Young people perceive that a basic promise is not being kept. Many are emerging from high school not ready for work or for college. This predicament, notes the commission, "becomes more acute as the knowledge base continues [to expand], the number of traditional jobs shrinks, and new jobs demand greater sophistication and preparation" (p. 12).

The commission makes a number of recommendations, many of which urge the schools to adapt more rigorous and measurable standards and parents and students to work to their maximum capacity in attaining the knowledge and skills that will enable youth to live productive lives. We suspect that the imposition of more rigorous standards in and of itself is not the answer to the problem. More traditional educational techniques, at least with the present generation of children, appear not to be working. This being the case, an eye toward incorporating some of the alternative programs we reviewed earlier may be a step in the right direction.

The relationship between events in the nation's schools and juvenile delinquency is a complex one, one not lending itself to simple solutions. Although no one can predict the future, history suggests that when education achieves some degree of relevance and prepares individuals for satisfying life styles, at least at a rudimentary level, other accompanying social problems diminish. This may indeed be the case with juvenile delinquency.

SUMMARY

Schools play a key role in socializing children and are charged not only with the responsibility of teaching academic skills, but also with that of instilling acceptable social behavior.

Delinquency has been related to many aspects of the school career. Research studies indicate that the failing child is more likely to engage in delinquency than the successful child. There is, however, dispute about the causes of school failure.

Some researchers attribute school failure to lack of ability to do well in school and maintain that below-normal intelligence, as well as school failure, causes delinquency involvement. Most investigators agree that the child who fails in school and the child who dislikes school face greater likelihood of delinquent behavior. Further, the child who expresses a lack of educational ambition and does not relate current schooling to future success is more probably delinquent than the child who strives for educational and occupational attainments. Finally, children who misbehave in school, engage in truancy, and drop out before graduation are more likely to commit delinquent acts.

The school is assigned importance in several general theories about the causes of delinquency. The most important interpretations of delinquency and school experiences include those concerned with subcultures of delinquency, social controls, and labeling.

Albert Cohen's subcultural theory emphasizes failure of lower class boys in the middle class institution of the school and the reaction of these boys to that failure. According to Cohen and others, delinquency is an attempt to gain status that cannot be achieved in the school. Although there is evidence that lower class boys do fail more frequently, many investigators have shown that school failure influences involvement in delinquency of students of *all* social classes. School failure is the crucial factor, not social class.

Subcultural theories focus on the effects of school failure on the child's peer associations. Many subcultural theorists hold that school failure, both academic and social, brings identification with delinquent peer groups, and that these associations result in increased delinquency. Failing students may be drawn into delinquent groups, and successful students may be further locked into conventional life through relationships with other students who subscribe to adult values and goals.

Social control theorists such as Travis Hirschi suggest that commitment and attachment to the school influence delinquency. The child who dislikes school may reject the authority of the school, as well as the rules and values taught in school, thus "freeing" himself or herself to engage in delinquency. Moreover, the child who is doing well in school is unlikely to jeopardize his or her prospects for the future by involvement in delinquency.

Finally, it is argued that the tendency of school personnel to label failing students negatively increases delinquency within that school. If a child is constantly treated as a delinquent or troublemaker, conventional opportunities may be closed and the child may adopt a negative self-concept. Social typing by school personnel may in fact launch students on delinquent careers.

Although most delinquency researchers consider all schools similar in goals, values, and practices, some stress the differences in individual schools that apparently result in variations in delinquency rates among schools, even those having similar types of students and neighborhoods. The practice of tracking is thought to increase delinquency among students assigned to lower tracks. Teacher turnover and absenteeism, as well as the tendency of school personnel to label students negatively, are also viewed as important effects on rates of delinquency within individual schools.

Since some children experience problems in traditional settings, it has been argued that alternative educational programs may be a promising means of preventing and treating delinquent behavior. These programs do not "track" problem youth into vocational fields, but rather offer a variety of innovative techniques which allow these children to excel at their own pace and experience many of the same rewards children in more traditional programs may experience. However, problems in the entire educational system reveal that many children are not experiencing the rewards past generations of Americans took for granted.

Some schools have been plagued with both violence and vandalism. While most school crime is of a nonviolent nature, evidence from victimization surveys indicates that both teachers and students are victimized in proportions great enough to merit immediate attention. In addition, acts of student vandalism against the nation's schools run into the millions of dollars in any given year. A variety of approaches have been devised to deal with these problems; they range from increased security and surveillance to educational programs aimed at helping students understand why they behave as they do and other ways to solve their problems. The latter approach appears the more promising in preventing and controlling school crime over the long haul.

Our discussion of the relationship of the schools and delinquency cannot remain an isolated one. The nation's school system has fallen into a state of disrepair so great that an entire generation of individuals lacks both academic and work skills for adequate life styles. This course of events suggests that changes are going to have to take place in the schools so that all children will be given an opportunity to lead productive lives.

PROGRESS CHECK

1. What is meant by the concept of *role responsibility*? (p. 217)

2. Academic achievement is an important factor in whether or not a student becomes delinquent. (p. 218)
   a. True
   b. False

3. How does the text define *intelligence*? (pp. 218–219)

4. During the past forty years, researchers have established a consistent relationship between school attitudes and official delinquency. (p. 219)
   a. True
   b. False

5. Discuss the relative contributions to the understanding of juvenile delinquency of: (pp. 220–221)
   a. School misbehavior
   b. School truancy
   c. School dropout

6. Several studies bearing on Albert Cohen's view of schools and social class are cited. Summarize the empirical evidence provided on this issue. (pp. 222–223)

7. Britain, Power, Benn, and Morris found that dropouts had different ideas about what schools should offer when compared with their headmasters. Discuss these differences. (pp. 221–222)

8. Utilizing the research of such authors as Karacki and Toby, Thrasher, Polk and Richmond, and Gold (and others you consider relevant), discuss the relationship of peer influence to schools and delinquency. (pp. 223–224)

9. List and discuss the factors associated with violence and vandalism in schools. In your discussion, please consider the significance of the national study entitled *Violent Schools– Safe Schools*. (pp. 227–228)

10. Why is American education in a state of crisis? What are the recommendations of the National Commission on Excellence in Education? (pp. 228–229)

NOTES

1. For example, see Empey and Lubeck (1971a), Ferguson (1952), Glueck and Glueck (1950), Hirschi (1969), Kelly and Balch (1971), Polk and Halferty (1972), and West and Farrington (1973).
2. See Caplan (1965), Hirschi and Hindelang (1977), Vold (1979), and Woodward (1955).
3. See Gold (1973), Hindelang (1973), Hirschi (1969), and Reckless and Dinitz (1972).
4. From "Neighborhood, School and Juveniles Before the Courts," M. J. Power, R. T. Benn, and J. N. Morris, in *British Journal of Criminology*, 12, No. 2 (April 1972), p. 128. Copyright © 1972 The British Journal of Criminology and contributors. Reprinted by permission.
5. In response to the Education Amendment Act of 1974 (Public Law 93-380), Congress mandated that the secretary of the Department of Health, Education and Welfare conduct a study to access the incidence and seriousness of school crime. Based on this mandate, the National Institute of Education (NIE) designed a three-phase study. In the first phase, principals in a representative national survey of over 4,000 public elementary and secondary schools were asked to report in detail on the incidence of illegal or disruptive activities between February 1976 and January 1977. In the second phase, a nationally representative sample of 642 public and junior and senior high schools was surveyed, including the responses of students and teachers about their experiences as victims of violence and thefts in the reporting month. The third phase of the study selected 10 schools for more intensive scrutiny. These schools had initially reported serious problems with crime and violence.

CHAPTER 11

PEERS AND DELINQUENCY

PEERS AND DELINQUENCY: THE CLASSICAL PERIOD

PEERS AND DELINQUENCY: THE THEORETICAL PERIOD

PEERS AND DELINQUENCY: THE COMPANIONSHIP PERIOD

PEERS AND DELINQUENCY: CONTEMPORARY GANG RESEARCH

It was a sunny, hot spring day in a small rural town in North Carolina. Jeryl, a senior at Washington High, drove his old red Jeep to school and waited in the parking lot. He had an idea. As Eddie and the other guys arrived one by one, Jeryl explained his plan. "Let's cut school today, buy some beer, and drive over to the other side of the river." Not needing much persuasion, everyone piled into the old Jeep. After driving the forty or so miles through the countryside, the boys came upon a deserted farmhouse, obviously vacant for a number of years. The boys got out of the Jeep and surveyed the weather-beaten wood structure. They shoved open the door and walked around the creaking old house. Leaning against the bannister of the staircase, Jeryl, well on his way to being drunk, noted, "It wouldn't take much to tear this place down." Eddie, seizing upon Jeryl's statement, added with excitement, "Hey, that's not a bad idea." "What do you mean?" Jeryl and the others asked in unison, looking at Eddie. "Why don't we see if we really can tear this place down?" Inspired by the thought and the beer, the group began the task. Methodically, the boys knocked out windows, kicked in doors, and as a coup de grace, pushed down the chimney with the Jeep. After a couple of hours work, the farmhouse was demolished.

Later in the week, a front page article appeared in the local paper, headlined "Civil War Home Destroyed." The article told of a 125-year-old house, slated for reconstruction, that had been wantonly vandalized beyond repair. Irreplaceable hand-blown glass windows, handcrafted doors, and a colonial brick chimney, imported from England, were destroyed. Monetary value could not be placed on the damage. In the small rural community, word eventually got out, and the youths were caught and punished for their delinquent act.

In Chicago, six teenage boys, who called themselves members of the Black P. Stone Nation, broke into a dozen of their neighbors' houses and raped a 12-year-old girl in one of the homes. This was all in a week's work for Tommy, Bob, and three or four other teenage

232

boys who prided themselves on being tough. Although the group did not actually have a leader, Tommy, age 14, usually chose the targets for the group's "attention." The youths attacked their victims swiftly in the street or in the victims' homes and then vanished into the surroundings. The youths were primarily after money and salable goods. But other "diversions," such as an occasional rape or assault, were not beyond their capabilities. Tommy particularly liked to pick elderly victims as targets because they were slow and didn't fight back. Neither Tommy nor his "associates" were ever caught by the police.

Although the types of delinquent acts committed by these two groups of youths are different, the incidents have one thing in common—the acts were committed, as sociologists would say, by "collectivities of youth." Delinquency research, spanning a period of sixty years, has consistently shown that much delinquency is of a collective nature, which means it is committed by juveniles in the company of their peers. Research done in the 1930s and 1940s indicated that from 70 to 85 percent of male delinquencies were committed by at least two boys working together. Recent evidence suggests that delinquency is still a group phenomenon, in which the small clique appears to predominate. Delinquents appear to prefer the social and moral support of other delinquents when they engage in deviant activities.

Sociological concern with peers and delinquency can be divided into four general periods. The first period, often termed the classical period of delinquency, was dominated by the **Chicago School** of sociologists. This group, working out of the University of Chicago from the 1920s through the 1940s, studied several social problems by "research into the distribution of areas of work and residence, places of public interaction and private retreat, the extent of illness and health, and the urban concentrations of conformity and deviance" (Taylor, Walton, and Young, 1973: 110). These sociologists hypothesized that residents of transitional inner city slum areas culturally transmit attitudes and behaviors—especially about crime and delinquency—from one generation to the next. An immense body of data on peer delinquency, especially gang behavior, was collected by such sociologists as Frederick Thrasher (1966), Clifford Shaw and Henry McKay (1942),

Frank Tannenbaum (1938), and William Whyte (1943). Through descriptive case histories, personal documentation, and several prevention-oriented programs, their research into lower class delinquency in the central city produced a body of data that set the tone for later theorizing in the field.

A second period of interest in peers and delinquency, what we will call in this chapter the theoretical period, extended from 1950 to 1960. During this time sociological research focused on the study of gang delinquency, and theoretical rationales for explaining delinquent and criminal behavior were sought. Very little empirical research (that is, research where data are collected) was conducted during this era. Instead, sociologists such as Albert Cohen, Richard Cloward, Lloyd Ohlin, Herbert Bloch, Arthur Niederhoffer, Walter Miller, and Lewis Yablonsky made theoretical generalizations about what causes gangs to emerge in society and offered ideas about how these groups were structured.

A third period of sociological concern with peers and delinquency began in the 1960s. At that time sociological emphasis generally shifted away from studies of the delinquent gang, which had predominated during the two earlier periods, and was aimed instead toward the more general topic of the relationship of companions or peer influence and delinquent behavior. The interests of this generation of sociologists were primarily directed toward disproving past conceptions of lower class subcultural delinquency. In contrast to the theoreticians of the second period of peer studies, researchers in the third period emphasized empirical research. These sociologists, armed with new data collection techniques such as self-report delinquency inventories, found that delinquency was prevalent among all social classes, and not just among lower class youth.

A fourth and relatively new period of research on peers and delinquency began in the early 1970s with renewed interest in and concern about juvenile gangs. The research of this period, extending into the 1980s, is generally atheoretical, reflecting more the particular interests of specific researchers and the interests of social control agents, rather than contributing to major theory testing or policy development. Miller's national study of youth gangs, conducted between 1972 and 1974, serves as a starting point for this period.

In this chapter we will examine the interests, observations, and conclusions of each of these four periods of sociological research on peers and delinquency.

PEERS AND DELINQUENCY: THE CLASSICAL PERIOD

The classical period of research on delinquency was defined by an interest in delinquency-producing conditions inherent in certain residential areas and in descriptions of gangs and gang members. Juveniles were seen to be members of well-organized gangs in which most of their delinquent pursuits were carried out. Three sociological researchers in particular can be singled out as major contributors during this period: Frederick Thrasher, Clifford Shaw, and Henry McKay.

Frederick Thrasher: Gangs in Chicago

One representative of the early Chicago School, Frederick Thrasher, is credited with one of the most comprehensive and colorful investigations into gangs and gang activities ever done. His research, although suffering from serious flaws according to contemporary research standards, is rich in its descriptive detailing of 1,313 gangs in Chicago during the 1920s. An account of gang conflicts in Chicago's North Side "jungles" is an example of Thrasher's work. Here we see how early notions of competition for turf became synonymous with gang conflict:

Edmond Werner, fifteen, self-styled leader of the roving Northwest Side gang which carries the cognomen of the "Belmonts" . . . prefaced his story of the gang fighting between the Belmonts and the Elstons, which Saturday resulted in the death of Julius Flosi, eleven, with this bitter statement today.

He told me of the innumerable battles of fists and bricks which have been staged for the possession of the lonesome bit of railroad trackage at California and Elston avenues, in the last two years, and describes how, when the two gangs realized the impotency of bare knuckles and ragged stones, each turned to firearms.

In the show-down scrap Saturday between Werner's Belmonts and the Elstons, Flosi was killed by a bullet from a 22-caliber rifle. He was an Elston.

"Dey picked on us for two years, but even den we wouldn't a shot if "Stinky"—the big guy and the leader of the Elstons—hadn't jumped out of his dugout in a coal pile Saturday and waved a long bayonet wid a red flag on one end of it and an American flag upside down on de udder and dared us to come over de tracks." (Thrasher, 1966: 121)

Thrasher believed gangs were formed naturally during adolescence from spontaneous play groups. Group members were transformed into a gang by conflict with other groups of children or with common enemies such as the police. Through this conflict, the gang became integrated and developed a "tradition, unreflective internal structure, esprit de corps, solidarity, morale, group awareness, and attachment to a local territory" (p. 46). The gang was characterized by several types of behavior: face-to-face interactions, milling, movement through space as a unit, conflict, and planning. Thrasher's definition and characteristics of gangs laid the foundations for theorizing through the 1960s.

Clifford Shaw and Henry McKay: Cultural Transmission

Clifford Shaw and Henry McKay (1929, 1930, 1931, 1936, 1942) were also interested in the group context of delinquent behavior. They gathered data on official delinquents in Chicago for the period from 1900 to 1940 by analyzing police records, court hearings, and institutional commitments. After plotting more than 60,000 cases on city maps, they found that delinquency rates were "highest in the low rent areas near the center of the city and decreased with distance from the center of the city" (Sutherland and Cressey, 1978: 187). Delinquency rates were also high around the railroads and stockyards and in the industrial and steel districts. Much of this delinquency was committed by boys in gangs. The delinquency of girls, though not nearly as widespread as the delinquency of the boys, was also more frequent in these central city districts.

Shaw and McKay (1942) drafted two basic generalizations about delinquent gangs, basing their research on the personal accounts of gang members. First, children learn their delinquent behavior from other individuals, both peers and adults. These delinquent behaviors are often condoned by the community. Second, these delinquent traditions are culturally transmitted from one generation of gang members to the next and can account for the high delinquency rates in these areas.

Shaw's concern with the people in these areas led him to develop the Chicago Area Project, in which he sought: (1) to develop "youth welfare organizations among residents of delinquency areas"; (2) to utilize families, peers, and neighbors to work directly with predelinquents and delinquents; and (3) to gain the maximum effectiveness of such agencies as the schools, the police, and the courts by stressing cooperation with community residents (Kobrin, 1959: 20–29). The social services project was later criticized as nothing more than a Band-aid when radical surgery was required (Empey, 1978: 257). In other words, only the lesser symptoms of community problems were addressed. The project helped people adjust to unacceptable conditions rather than attacking the actual causes of the unacceptable conditions—inequities in the socioeconomic and political sectors of the society.

Summarizing this early period of gang research, we note two areas of contribution: First, Thrasher, Shaw, and McKay gave us a wealth of detail on the characteristics of gangs. Second, these sociologists emphasized that the existence of gangs can be explained by social conditions in the community, rather than by biological or psychological factors.

PEERS AND DELINQUENCY: THE THEORETICAL PERIOD

In the second period in the study of gangs, gang delinquency was viewed primarily as a lower class phenomenon. The Chicago School studies attempted to establish that most crime and delinquency was committed by individuals from lower socioeconomic backgrounds. Most of this interpretation was based on official data, police and court statistics. Only later, primarily in the 1960s, when other sources of data, especially self-report delinquency studies, were made available, did it become apparent that the middle and upper classes also committed large amounts of crime and delinquency.

The studies of Cohen, Cloward and Ohlin, Miller, Bloch and Niederhoffer, and Yablonsky, limited to conclusions drawn from more traditional data sources, are typical of the second period of study.

Albert Cohen: The Culture of the Gang

Cohen, like other sociologists of the time, viewed delinquent behavior as primarily a lower class problem. As you recall from Chapter 6, he conceptualized the gang as a subculture with its own value system, which differed from the value system of middle class society. This value system was created as a means of reaction and adjustment to the middle class standards by which working class boys were judged. Working class boys developed a delinquent subculture as a means of recouping self-esteem destroyed by institutions dominated by the middle classes.

Richard Cloward and Lloyd Ohlin: Delinquency and Opportunity

Cloward and Ohlin (1960) attempted to specify how delinquent gangs arise and persist. Like Cohen, they presumed that gang behavior is typically found among adolescent males in lower class areas of large urban centers (p. 1). Unlike Cohen, however, these sociologists defined much delinquent behavior as rational and utilitarian. Relying on the work of another sociologist, Robert Merton, Cloward and Ohlin asserted that when legitimate opportunities to achieve or advance are denied to lower class youth, the result is a state of "anomie," or strain. Although lower class youths may desire middle class rewards in the form of good jobs, material possessions, and so on, they lack the opportunities to achieve these goals. One adaptation to this situation is the creation of delinquent gangs (see Chapter 6).

Walter Miller: Gangs and Focal Concerns

Miller (1958) viewed gang behavior not in terms of access to certain opportunities, but as a result of learned patterns of conduct acquired from lower class socialization. He theorized that delinquent gangs do not result from community disorganization; instead, gangs are a direct consequence of a lower class way of life, which is characterized by a set of focal concerns (or values) differing dramatically from middle class values.

As indicated earlier, young lower class males learn a set of values or focal concerns prevalent in the adult community. These values are often unacceptable by middle class standards, and include trouble, smartness, toughness, fate, excitement, and autonomy. Through expression of these focal concerns, young males are basically adhering to the existing adult set of norms. Status is achieved not by hard work or deferred gratification, but in gang membership.

Lewis Yablonsky: Near-Group Theory of Gangs

Unlike most of the work of the theoretical period, Yablonsky's original "near-group" theory of gangs was based on an actual study of gangs. Yablonsky collected data on New York City gangs from 1953 to 1958. Based on his work, first published as an article in 1959 and as a book, *The Violent Gang*, in 1962, Yablonsky asserted that gangs are not, in reality, groups as portrayed in the media or by earlier social scientists like Thrasher, Shaw, and McKay. Much of what is known about gangs was, according to Yablonsky, essentially mythical, based only on press and public overreaction to isolated incidents.

Yablonsky described the gang as a "near-group." He defined gangs as generally "diffuse and malleable" structures having mixed values and goals, with a membership that is impermanent and limited cohesively (Yablonsky, 1959: 116). In other words, collectivities of delinquents do not possess characteristics ordinarily found in full-fledged "groups" or "mobs," as those terms are defined by sociologists. In terms of organization, gangs fall midway on a continuum between mobs and cohesive groups. Table 11.1 presents Yablonsky's theory of the gang as a near-group. One property of the near-group is impermanent and shifting membership. Another is membership roles that are not clearly defined. Further, the members of near-groups exhibit a minimum of consensus, and leadership is vague.

Studying thirty gangs, Yablonsky found three levels of membership. In the first level are "psychologically disturbed youth who desperately need a gang to solve their personal problems" (Cartwright, Tomson, Schwartz, 1975: 17). Gang leadership comes from these disturbed boys, who constantly plan activities for the other youth. These boys tend to exaggerate membership size. A second level contains youth who claim affiliation with the gang, but in actuality associate with the gang only when they encounter emotional disturbances, such as conflicts with their parents. A final level consists of boys who do not claim membership with the gang, but who occasionally join in various gang episodes.

Also included in Table 11.1 is a column for what Yablonsky described as a distorted view of gangs. Here, he noted that the public, social workers, and authorities often portray gangs as stable groups when in fact gangs are nothing more than loose collectivities without a definite name. Only when apprehended by officials do these collectivities assume a grouplike organization. Yablonsky reported one case where a social worker told two boys, who were both perceived gang

TABLE 11.1   Yablonsky's Theory of the Gang as a Near-Group

| Property | Continuum of Organization as a Group | | | |
	Mob	Near-Group	Gang (Distorted view of)	Group
Life of group	Temporary	Impermanent	—*	Relatively permanent
Membership size	Undetermined	Shifting	Measurable number of members	Relatively stable
Expectations of members	None	Limited	Defined	Defined
Leadership	None	Disturbed	Clear, direct	Clear, direct
Members' role definitions	None	Diffuse	Specified	Clear
Cohesion	None	Limited	—	High

* Note that Yablonsky's work did not mention matters related to the categories shown by dashes.
Source: Cartwright, Tomson, & Schwartz (1975, p. 17). Devised from information in Yablonsky (1959).

leaders, that he would have a bus ready to take them on a trip. Although the gang had virtually no membership or organization, thirty-two "members" were ready for the trip when the bus arrived. Thus, a near-group became a more structured group in reaction to the social worker's intrusion.

Yablonsky's theory was criticized by other sociologists, and he revised his formulation in his 1962 work, *The Violent Gang.* In this later work, Yablonsky limited the near-group phenomenon to gangs organized primarily for emotional gratification and violent activities. Other types of gangs, the social and delinquent gangs, were not characterized as near-groups. According to Yablonsky, "nonviolent" delinquent gangs are driven to illegal acts such as burglary, petty thievery, and car theft by a profit motive. These gangs have tight primary group structures and relatively permanent memberships. Social gangs are different from both violent and nonviolent gangs; they revolve around conventional activities, and their members seldom participate in illegal behaviors (Haskell and Yablonsky, 1978).

Herbert Bloch and Arthur Niederhoffer: Gangs and Adult Strivings

Bloch and Niederhoffer's work on gangs differs from the work of Cohen, Cloward and Ohlin, Miller, and Yablonsky because they did not conceive of gang behavior as a primarily lower class

phenomenon. Instead, they viewed gang behavior as a universal and normal adolescent striving toward adult status. In their book *The Gang,* published in 1958, Bloch and Niederhoffer wrote that the formation of gangs is widespread in societies, such as the United States, that fail to make preparation, formal and otherwise, for the induction of adolescents to adult status. Gangs, delinquent as well as conventional, serve a basic function for their members by providing a substitute for the formalized puberty rites found in some societies.

As Cartwright and associates (1975) have noted: When compared to the middle classes, "the [delinquent] gang may be the lower-class adolescent's only means to accomplish the transitional growth expected at adolescence" (p. 26). However, middle class youth are also involved in gangs. Middle class youth are "not as apt to have the formal, almost military, structure characteristics of certain lower class 'war gangs' . . . yet they do have similar well-defined patterns of leadership and control" (Bloch and Niederhoffer, 1958: 9).

Although Bloch and Niederhoffer's theory offers an explanation for the development of gangs, other explanations may be just as plausible. Adolescent groups or gangs could be attributed to such factors as common interests, frequent association in school, or parent-youth conflict. Bloch and Niederhoffer's theory is vague about the "origin of delinquent activities and the relationship of the adolescent peer group to the distribution of gang delinquency in the social class structure" (Cartwright et al., 1975: 25).

We can summarize the work done in the second period of the study of gangs by stating that the sociologists of this period generally considered the gang to be an important facet of delinquency. This assumption, however, was sharply challenged by third-period researchers.

PEERS AND DELINQUENCY: THE COMPANIONSHIP PERIOD

When we consider the work thus far reviewed, one conclusion is inescapable: The term *gang* has been employed with considerable variation and imprecision. Apparently gang researchers have found little need for formal explanation of the concept of the gang because the term is assumed to be one everyone knows. This imprecise terminology led to a change in emphasis among criminologists working in the 1960s. Research into the collective nature of delinquency shifted from the study of gangs, or delinquent subcultures, and instead concentrated on the companionship factor in the etiology and continuation of delinquency. In other words, juveniles were thought to commit their delinquent acts in the company of other youth, though not necessarily in an organized gang.

Most of the companionship studies do not include theoretical explanations for research findings. Often the work of this third period is totally atheoretical, but sometimes attempts are made at **middle-range**, or limited, theoretical explanations of the data at hand. Most of these works are basically empirical—that is, they are primarily involved in collecting data through scientific investigation, and they are designed to answer a specific research question about delinquent behavior.

Networks and Subcultural Transmission

Paul Lerman conducted a study, published in 1967, that dealt with 700 boys, aged 10 through 19, in New York City. Lerman argued that past delinquency research had displayed a disproportionate interest in gangs and that this attention to gangs had hindered understanding of peer-based delinquency. Lerman suggested that where membership boundaries are vague between youth but interaction regularities can be identified, the concept of *network* rather than gang best describes the phenomenon. Examining the nature of these networks, Lerman postulated that units within the network are in the form of pairs or triads.

Through the use of self-report techniques, Lerman determined that, until age 14 or 15, either the pair or the triad appeared to be the dominant interaction pattern. A smaller percentage of young adolescents belonged to regular groups, and a small minority classified themselves as loners. Lerman observed a shift at age 14 or 15 toward membership in a regular group. He also noted that at ages 16 through 19, more boys could be classified as loners. The pair and triad types, however, remained dominant at all stages of adolescence.

Relating this finding to delinquent activities, Lerman concluded that in his sample, "a majority of youth at all ages engage in illegal behaviors alone, rather than with others" (p. 70). However, he suggested that boys who agreed on appropriate terminology or slang and deviant values, such as admiration of toughness and the ability to keep one's mouth shut to the cops, tended to participate in delinquent activities in pairs or triads. Thrasher (1966) had indicated as early as 1927 the importance of pair and triad relationships in the lives of delinquent youth.

Although it involved a relatively small sample, Lerman's study suggested that partners in delinquency may be chosen on the basis of friendship or "palship," rather than on the basis of gang membership. Other work has supported these conclusions (Jensen, 1972; Hindelang, Hirschi, and Weis, 1981; Thornton and Voigt, 1984; Shannon, 1982). The studies cited in the next section explored further the role of companionship in the commission of delinquent acts.

Self-Report Data and Group Violations

We noted earlier that much of the past research on gang delinquency had been based on official data. These findings have generally supported the notion that "delinquency is typically a group phenomenon" (Erickson, 1973a: 128). Recent research using self-report techniques has produced conflicting results about the role of companions in the commission of different types of delinquency. Some of these studies support the assumption that delinquency is more common when teenagers are in groups. Other studies indicate that it varies, depending on the specific offense.

Shapland (1978) used self-report delinquency interviews to investigate the pattern of delinquency among boys in British secondary schools. She interviewed the boys at ages 11 and 12 and again two years later, at ages 13 and 14. As indicated in Table 11.2, the delinquency items ranged from status offenses like truancy to petty theft.

In Table 11.2, we see that the percentage of offenses perpetrated in groups ranges from zero (taking money from home) to 91.4 (shooting fireworks in the street). Offenses with high rates of group participation included vandalism (91.3), breaking windows (90.67), and trespassing (85.19). More serious offenses such as breaking into a store, assaulting strangers, and escaping from the police also were very likely to occur as group activities.

Also using self-reports, Erickson and Jensen (1977) surveyed high school students in four separate Arizona communities that ranged from rural to urban. With the exception of assaults and fights, some similarity existed between their findings and those of the Shapland study. Serious offenses, such as burglary, vandalism, and auto theft, were usually reported to be committed within a group context. Erickson and Jensen noted that assaults and fights received low group violation scores. Less serious offenses such as drunkenness, drinking, and marijuana use happened in the company of others in 84 to 98 percent of the cases.

Erickson and Jensen also reported that girls as well as boys and rural as well as urban youth are more likely to engage in delinquent acts when accompanied by companions than when alone. Females in both rural and urban settings tend to have higher rates of group violations than males. For ten offenses—burglary, shoplifting, vandalism, smoking, truancy, auto theft, defiance, drinking, drunkenness, and marijuana use—the female group

TABLE 11.2 Self-Reported Delinquency in Boys Aged 11 to 14

Number	Brief Description	Percentage Group Involvement
17	Stealing from clothes	43.75%
18	Stealing from slot machines	71.21
19	Smoking	64.52
20	Going to "X" film	89.39
21	Trespassing	85.19
22	Stealing bicycle	54.55
23	Stealing school property	31.25
24	Struggling to escape from police	81.82
25	Receiving stolen property	31.82
26	Littering	90.32
27	Stealing from small shops	63.04
28	Stealing from big stores	75.44
29	Drinking alcohol in pubs	16.67
30	Going into pubs	16.67
31	Using weapon in fight	73.68
32	Breaking windows	90.67
33	Attacking an enemy	85.08
34	Stealing from cars	80.00
35	Vandalism of public property	91.30
36	Taking money from home	0.00
37	Assaulting strangers	84.48
38	Fireworks in street	91.40
39	Paying wrong fare	49.52
40	Not paying fare	56.31
41	Playing truant	57.41
43	Riding cycle without lights	31.29
44	Driving vehicle on roads	47.62
45	Joyriding	62.50
46	Breaking into store, etc.	75.00
47	Carrying weapon	56.79

Source: Shapland (1978, p. 263).

violation rates exceeded those of the males living in both rural and urban settings. Michael Hindelang (1976), in a comparable study, found that rural and urban males had similar group involvements in delinquency, but that females exhibited a different pattern. Urban females more often than rural females were accompanied by companions when committing delinquent activities. Also, urban females participated in delinquency with friends with greater frequency than urban males. The reverse was true for rural males and females. Rural males more often than urban males committed delinquent acts in the company of others. From this evidence, it appears that although girls commit fewer delinquent acts than boys, girls are just as likely as boys, and even perhaps more likely, to be delinquent in the company of companions.

The idea that adolescents who are delinquent in groups face increased risks of arrest has been discussed extensively in recent delinquency literature. Erickson (1977) suggested that violation of the law in groups increases the likelihood of official detection and reaction, including apprehension, arrest, and court appearance. This hypothesis has been dubbed the *group hazard hypothesis.*

Since most delinquency based on official statistics shows high rates of group violations, Erickson suggested that perhaps "violating the law with others increased the probability of being apprehended" (1973a: 128). If the group hazard hypothesis is correct, then we would expect official records to reflect high rates of group delinquency. To test this hypothesis, Erickson compared the group violation rates of an institutionalized sample of male delinquents with those of a sample of male high school students, assuming that group violation would be found more frequently in the histories of the incarcerated adolescents. His findings, however, generally failed to support the group hazard hypothesis. There was little or no difference between the institutionalized and noninstitutionalized groups in overall group violation rates (the total number of self-reported violations for fourteen delinquent offenses that were group violations). A more recent study by Feyerherm (1980) likewise found limited support for the hypothesis.

Hindelang (1976), however, found evidence to support the group hazard hypothesis. By questioning a sample of 140 sheriff's deputies, Hindelang discovered that a large number of the deputies believed juveniles generally commit offenses in groups. Hindelang collected data which indicated that juveniles who engaged in delinquent behavior in groups are more likely to have contact with the police than offenders who carry out illegal behaviors alone. He found this trend to hold even when the seriousness and frequency of the offenses were similar.

Morash (1984) examined a sample of youth drawn from school, police, and court records in Boston. She found that a greater proportion of youth without a peer group had no contact with police than those with a peer group. Moreover, those individuals fitting the common image of a delinquent and potentially dangerous person— being a male in a predominantly male, delinquent peer group—increased their chances for arrest. Based on self-reports, Morash found that compared with juveniles who did not have encounters with the police, those who did also tended to have higher incidences of self-reported delinquency. Those juveniles who were questioned and arrested by the police were generally white (males) and belonged to groups that were more "ganglike" (engaged in group fighting, drug involvement, and so on). Although the reported relationships are complex and, in some cases, contradictory, it does appear that most juveniles have "a little help from their friends" when engaging in delinquency.[1]

Partly in response to the narrowness and imprecision of past gang research, a number of contemporary sociologists have directed their attention to the study of the group nature of delinquency. Although by no means consistent, their findings have raised questions about the amount and type of undetected and actual delinquency committed by youth of all classes.

PEERS AND DELINQUENCY: CONTEMPORARY GANG RESEARCH

Although sociologists over the past sixty years have gradually shifted from the study of gangs to the relationship of peer or companions' influence and delinquency, recent accounts of youth gang violence have rekindled interest in the study of gangs. A 1983 *New York Times* article entitled "Youth Gangs Rob Fans After Show" attracted national attention to the problem:

> Bands of roving youths attacked and harassed fans leaving the Diana Ross concert in Central Park and others strolling nearby on Friday night. . . . A total of 171 people filed complaints, most of

them reporting beatings and robberies, the police said. . . . In one incident after the concert a dozen youths invaded the patio of the Tavern on the Green, a restaurant on the western edge of Central Park, tipping over tables and assaulting patrons. (Daley, 1983: 1)

The varying attention criminologists have given to youth gangs over the years, according to some researchers, cannot be explained entirely by the actual seriousness and extent of gang delinquency. Bookin, Weiner, and Horowitz (1983) argue that prevailing ideological concerns and social conditions may influence the way the public, crime experts, and social control agents perceive and treat certain types of crimes.

For example, during the 1950s, when gang delinquency became almost synonymous with delinquency, the political ideology of the country was generally conservative, or "law and order" oriented. Delinquent gangs were seen as attacking the very heart of conventional values and norms. During the mid-1970s and early 1980s, the prevailing political currents were generally conservative under Ronald Reagan, and much attention was devoted to such things as crime control and fear of victimization. The *Attorney General's Task Force on Violent Crime* included in its report the recommendation that "the use of federal investigative and prosecutorial resources now directed against traditional organized crime activities [now be directed] to the serious criminal activities of youthful street gangs now operating in metropolitan areas of the country" (1981: 84).

The intensity of the recommendation suggests the possible direction research on gang activity will take in the present decade. Since the political Right perceives "crime to be the result of the failures of social institutions, inadequate deterrence, and insufficient incapacitation," we might speculate that funds will not be given for the study of the dynamics of gangs, but rather to those individuals interested in preventing youth from joining gangs and in controlling gang violence (Bookin, Weiner, and Horowitz, 1983: 598).

The task of obtaining, verifying, and presenting accurate data on delinquent youth gangs in the United States is a difficult one. Many studies are small in scale, and their capacity to be generalized to other youth and areas of the country is questionable. Comprehensive national studies have been virtually nonexistent. Most of these studies have relied on control agents' estimates of the number and types of delinquent gangs in certain cities.

Walter Miller: Youth Gangs

In the mid-1970s, criminologist Walter Miller (1975) conducted the first nationwide study of youth gangs and youth gang violence. Miller's work represented the "first attempt to compile a national-level picture of youth gang and youth group problems, based on direct site visits to gang locales" (p. 4).

Miller concentrated primarily on a dozen large metropolitan areas in the United States. Half of these were classified as having gang problems and were subjected to in-depth study. Miller reported that gang violence was at high levels in New York, Chicago, Los Angeles, Detroit, Philadelphia, and San Francisco. By analyzing available data, he estimated that the extent of youth gangs in these cities ranged from a low of 760 gangs and 28,500 members to a high of 2,700 gangs and 81,500 members. Statistics from various criminal justice and social service agencies within these cities showed 525 gang-related murders in the period from 1972 through 1974, a number representing roughly 25 percent of all juvenile homicides in these cities.

By interviewing personnel from the agencies, Miller sought to obtain a working definition of the term *gang*. The criteria most frequently associated with a gang were "violent or criminal behavior as a major activity of gang members; group organized, with functional role division and chain of command authority; identifiable leadership; continuing and recurrent interaction or association among group members; identification with and/or claims of control over, some identifiable community territory or territories" (Miller, 1975: 9). Miller noted that respondents were able to distinguish between "law-violating youth groups" and more formalized gangs. The term *gang* was reserved for those groups who fit the criteria previously mentioned.

Youth Gang Violence In California

Although Miller's research indicated large numbers of both loosely formed law-violating groups and delinquent gangs in major United States cities (as well as in smaller cities of over 10,000), much of the in-depth analysis of gang behavior has been conducted in the state of California. Miller reported that at least one city in California, Los Angeles, had a high estimate of about 1,000 gangs operating in the city between 1973 and 1975.

As a reaction to the assumed escalation of youth gangs in California beginning in the late 1960s, the California State attorney general's office organized a Youth Gang Task Force in 1981 which assessed statewide problems resulting from youth gang activity (*Report on Youth Gang Violence in California*). While the intent of the task force was the development of ways to identify, prevent, and control violent gangs, a great deal of data were collected about the structure and types of gangs in operation throughout the state. Using a technique similar to Miller's, the task force conducted a survey of local law enforcement agencies throughout the state to determine the extent of the youth gang problem.

A *youth gang*, according to the task force, is a loose-knit organization of youth between the ages of 14 and 24, with the leader being the strongest or boldest member. The gang has a name, claims a specific territory, and usually is involved in criminal activity involving violent assaults against other gangs, as well as crimes against the general public (1981: 4). Based on reports from local law enforcement agencies, it was estimated that there were approximately 765 gangs with a membership of about 52,400 operating in the state. Although the responding agencies reported that most youth gang activity occurred in the metropolitan areas of the state; rural communities were also experiencing problems.

The task force found that gang members are usually males, aged 18 through 24, who joined the gang by committing a crime or by undergoing an initiation procedure. Their motivation for joining the gang may be identity or recognition, protection, fellowship and brotherhood, or intimidation. There is some evidence that the prison gang influence on youth gangs is increasing; however, very few studies have substantiated the allegation that prison gang members have actively recruited juveniles into their organizations.

The structure of youth gangs can range from loose-knit groups of juveniles who know one another and commit crimes together to formal organizations with specific leaders, and formal rules and regulations that specify expected behavior and disciplinary actions when that behavior is violated.

Gang leaders usually acquire their positions by virtue of their past reputations as being the "baddest" guys around or by possessing some leadership abilities. The leadership usually comes from the ranks of the "hard core" members, often the most violent and destructive. Involvement of members in a gang varies, but in general several levels of membership can be discussed. The "hard core" include those youth who need and thrive on the activity of the gang. These members instigate and participate in violent activities and other gang endeavors. The "associates" are those individuals who associate with the group for status and recognition. They may wear club jackets, attend social functions, and have tattoos. "Peripheral" members move in and out of the gang on the basis of interest and activities (*Report on Youth Gang Violence in California*, 1981: 1–15).

The youth gangs of California are organized along ethnic lines and are comprised of Asian, black, Hispanic, and Caucasian groups. Although they organize themselves according to ethnicity, the gangs do not necessarily represent the ethnic communities of which they are a part.

Female Gangs

Although there appears to be a consensus of opinion that most gang members are male, female gangs and gang members have recently become popular topics. This interest in the female gang parallels a rise in attention given to women's rights and women's social status. There is no evidence, however, that the feminist movement has contributed to any increase in female gang delinquency.

For traditional sociologists, the idea of a "female gang" is almost a contradiction in terms. As Albert Cohen argued in his book, *Delinquent Boys: The Culture of the Gang* (1955): "Again the group or the gang, the vehicle of the delinquent subculture and one of its statistically most manageable earmarks, is a boy's gang. . . . If, however, female delinquents also have their subculture, it is a different one from that which we have described. The latter [gang] belongs to the male role" (pp. 46–48).

Cohen and most sociologists attributed female delinquency not to group conduct and standards, but instead to the personal problems of the individual girl. It seemed inconceivable to early sociologists, given the evidence reported in most gang studies, that girls could band together for the purpose of delinquent activities. Yet more recent studies suggest that although females may not commonly form organized gangs, their delinquency is just as likely to be group-based as is the delinquency of boys. Giordano (1978), for example, studied a sample of institutionalized delinquent girls and emphasized the importance of group support and companionship. She further noted a strong relationship between the group affiliations of the girls and their self-reported delinquency.

Miller's study of gangs in the 1970s reported findings that concur with the results of earlier research. Many male gangs studied had female auxiliaries that bore a feminized version of the male gang name. For example, the boys' gang Crips had a female auxiliary called the Cripettes, and the boys' gang Disciples a female auxiliary known as the Lady Disciples. There were only a few reports of gangs comprised totally of females acting without the sponsorship of a male gang. Miller (1975) reported that female "gang" members were rarely involved in assaults, and that even though they had "bad reputations," they were not really that bad when compared to their male counterparts (33–34). Other research, however, has found evidence that female gang members may in some cases be as violent as their male counterparts. Brown (1978) studied a black female gang

in Philadelphia and found that this gang was quite violent and aggressive. We might note that research on female gang delinquency is quite contradictory.

Bowker and Klein (1980) also studied a group of black gang girls in Los Angeles and found that females present at the site of delinquent activity had a suppressing effect on the scene. They also reported that the females never planned a gang activity; this was done by the males, who usually excluded them. The girls would, however, participate in violent crimes and other incidents like drug use.

Quicker (1983) studied Chicano gang girls in East Los Angeles and described four salient aspects of these Hispanic girl gangs. First, he found that female gangs do not occur without a connection to a boys' gang. More specifically, the girls do not acquire independence from the boys' gang and derive their name from the boys' gang. A recent study of Hispanic gangs in San Diego (1982) similarly found that female gangs in that city participated in an auxiliary or support role for male gangs (*Juvenile Violence and Gang Related Crime*, 1982). Second, girls are not coerced into the gang. They must prove their loyalty and undergo a severe initiation procedure. Third, the girls have rather diverse leadership and generally operate in a democratic manner. Fourth, there is strong loyalty to the gang to the point of rivaling the girl's family. Most friends come from within the gang.

In the same study, Quicker explains the structural pressures placed on the girls with respect to joining a gang. He argues that both social and economic pressures have weakened the ability of school and family to socialize and control the girls. The gang, in a sense, fills this void and offers "warmth, friends, loyalty and socialization." It is a rational adaptation to an irrational situation (see Quicker, 1983).

We must emphasize that the study of female gangs is still in its infancy. This is possibly due to the less menacing activities of the female gangs, less press coverage, or because there are relatively few of these gangs when compared with male gangs. The activities of female gangs, however, represent a very small proportion of the amount of female delinquent behavior committed with companions. Although there are far fewer female than male gangs, the relationship of female gangs to the total female group-based delinquency is similar to the relationship between male gangs and male group-based delinquency. Among males as well as females, gang delinquency is a dramatic, attention-getting form of delinquency. But most group delinquency is not gang delinquency.

Gang Reduction Programs

As criminologist John Quicker (1982a) notes, there are some major ideological differences between contemporary gang reduction programs and those of the past. Current programs, he suggests, are basically atheoretical in orientation. They are conservative and pragmatically oriented, with the prime goal being containment of gang violence. Past programs, like those in the 1960s, attempted to incorporate the theoretical perspectives in vogue at the time. Thus the works of Cloward and Ohlin (1960), for example, were used as a framework from which to understand as well as control gang influence. Malcolm Klein (1981) probably expressed the greatest differences between past and present approaches to gangs when he indicated that contemporary programs are "deterrence oriented," whereas earlier programs were "transformation oriented."

> Deterrence—the basic elements . . . are the provision of heightened street visibility/surveillance of project staff, area rather than specific gang focus, violence rather than general delinquency as a focus, and intergang mediation efforts . . . the essence of the matter is the reactivation of visible, community controls and the rapid increase to violence and crisis events.
>
> Transformation—the basic element [is] the assignment of "detached workers" to established, traditional gangs to transform their structure and value systems into more acceptable forms . . . often other components [stress] community connections—schools, jobs, recreation. (Klein, 1981: 4–5)

Although many things are responsible for the changed orientation toward generally more punitive control of gangs, one key reason is that the "transformation" programs of earlier decades simply did not work, or were accused of actually contributing to an increase in gang membership (Quicker, 1982a: 4; Poston, 1971). These beliefs, coupled with reports of increases in gang violence, have led policymakers and criminal justice practitioners to develop a variety of techniques for dealing with the gang problem. These techniques have generally focused on law enforcement solutions, such as special gang units assigned to patrol high gang areas of a city. However, other approaches, such as the use of detached youth workers, have had some success. *Detached youth workers* are individuals who inhabit the area where known gangs are operating and attempt to become intimate with gang members in the hope of diverting the gang's efforts into legitimate channels.

Based on some sixty years of efforts to deal with the problem of juvenile gangs, one thing seems inescapably clear: Piecemeal programs based on punitive law enforcement techniques or dissolution of gangs via community refocusing have been less than successful. Most experts on gangs argue that much broader solutions have to be employed before the conditions that breed gang formation, and hence gang dissolution, can come about. Thus, whenever social conditions lead to economic deprivation, status deprivation, racism, and the like, gangs will form (Quicker, 1982b). Gangs represent an adaptation to the modern urban environment.

SUMMARY

Sociological study of peers and delinquency can be divided into four periods. During the first period, the Chicago School described the characteristics of gangs and related gang activity to residence in slum and transitional areas of cities. Sociologists during the second period concentrated on the causes of gang delinquency. Generally, gang delinquency was viewed as the result of lower class boys' blocked access to middle class avenues of success. The sociologists of the second period drew parallels between lower class life and gang delinquency. There were, however, several dissenters during this period. Yablonsky viewed gangs as "near-groups" rather than tightly structured groups, and Bloch and Niederhoffer postulated that gangs were universal means of coping with the transition from adolescence to adulthood. Emphasis during the third period of peer research shifted to an interest in the group nature of delinquency. Empirical studies indicated that gang delinquency in the traditional sense of the term was relatively rare, but delinquency carried out by networks and small groups was common. Although there was some evidence that group delinquency was more often detected by authorities than solitary delinquency, most group delinquency remained undetected and unreported. Lower class adolescents stood a greater chance of apprehension for delinquency whether their acts occurred alone or in groups. A renewed interest in gangs comprises the fourth period of peer research. Much of the research in this period is directed toward the social control of violent youth gangs.

Interest in this latter period of peer research was stimulated by the work of Walter Miller. Miller conducted a nationwide study of youth gangs and reported that gang members create serious problems in many urban areas throughout the United States. Drawing their membership primarily from young, poor males who are members of ethnic and racial minorities, these gangs have become increasingly violent in recent years. Research conducted by other individuals and groups substantiates many of Miller's claims. In particular, studies of gangs in the state of California indicate a resurgence, with violent incidents being everyday occurrences in certain ethnic and racial communities and neighborhoods. There is some evidence that recruiting takes place in both juvenile and adult correctional facilities and serves to perpetuate the existence of stable membership in many gangs. Most gang activity appears to still be a male phenomenon, although females do commonly engage in delinquent activities in the company of their peers.

Increased attention to gang violence and victimization has led to the creation of gang reduction and gang control programs. Gang reduction programs commonly revolve around law enforcement efforts to prevent gang violence or to apprehend gang offenders. Gang control programming, while encompassing some of the same goals as reduction, places greater emphasis on social work functions, with workers seeking to rechannel gang activities into more normal activities.

As many criminologists have come to realize, piecemeal efforts to deal with gangs and their activities have not been very successful over the last several decades. Until some of the structural conditions such as inequality and economic deprivation are corrected, and in general a satisfying and rewarding life style can be offered to all youth, gangs will continue to exist.

PROGRESS CHECK

1. Identify the four general periods of sociological concern with "peers and delinquency." (pp. 233–234)

2. Present and discuss the early contributions of Frederick Thrasher to our understanding of the gang. (p. 234)

3. What is meant by the term *cultural transmission*? Who were its principal proponents? What was the Chicago Area Project? (pp. 234–235)

4. During the theoretical period of gang study, gang delinquency was viewed primarily as a phenomenon of what social class? (p. 235)

5. Outline and compare Albert Cohen's view of delinquent gangs with that of Richard Cloward and Lloyd Ohlin. (pp. 235–236)

6. Lewis Yablonsky described the gang as a "_____," characterized by generally incoherent structures, with mixed values and goals, and having a membership of limited cohesive quality. (p. 236)

7. Describe and assess the research on peers and delinquency undertaken during the companionship period, commenting on: (pp. 238–240)
   a. Paul Lerman's "networks"
   b. Self-report data

8. According to the *Report on Youth Gang Violence in California*, "what" is a gang and "who" is most likely to be a gang leader? (p. 242)

9. Summarize in the form of at least three generalizations what could be considered solid conclusions about female gangs. (pp. 242–244)

10. Describe the conflicting goals of past and contemporary gang reduction programs. (p. 244)

NOTES

1. One well-known criminologist, Franklin Zimring (1981), argues that while the empirical evidence for the hypothesis that adolescents commit their crimes as they live their lives, in groups, is overwhelming, much of this research has been ignored, especially when policies are made regarding delinquency control.

CHAPTER 12

MASS MEDIA AND DELINQUENCY

THEORIES OF MASS
COMMUNICATION

THE MASS MEDIA AND
DELINQUENCY: HISTORICAL
CONCERNS

THE MASS MEDIA AND
DELINQUENCY: SOME
CONTEMPORARY CONCERNS

In California in 1974, 9-year-old Olivia Niemi was sexually assaulted with a bottle by four other children. The assault occurred three days after the NBC prime time broadcast of "Born Innocent," in which girls in a reform school "raped" another young girl with the handle of a plumber's plunger.

In 1977, during an attempted burglary in Miami, 15-year-old Ronald Zamora killed his 82-year-old neighbor in a manner that was said to resemble a slaying in an episode of "Kojak," Zamora's favorite program. The boy's lawyer pleaded him innocent by virtue of "television intoxication," but a jury found him guilty of murder.

In 1981, the number of "Deer Hunter deaths" compiled by the National Coalition on Television Violence grew to more than 22 young people shot and 19 dead playing Russian roulette after that movie was shown on television.

In April 1981, a 14-year-old boy in Sandwich, Mass., was shot by a friend as they played with a gun while watching a slow motion replay of Reagan's assassination attempt on television (Terror, 1982: 1).

Scouts from a troop taught and sponsored by IBM in Milwaukee used their home computers to penetrate a dozen computers in the U.S. and Canada. Included were Security Pacific National Bank in Los Angeles and the nuclear weapons laboratory in Los Alamos, New Mexico. The event occurred after the showing of War Games, a movie where a bright teenager uses his home computer to gain access to the key U.S. military computer. (Time Magazine, 1983: 14)

We might ask what all these events have in common. Each of the crimes committed, ranging from violent crimes against the person to sophisticated computer crime, are linked to a mass media event—in these cases, television or the movies. In earlier times, similar accounts of delinquent and criminal acts committed by juveniles were attributed to the influence of comic books, pulp magazines, radio dramas, and the movies. As technological advances were made in the field of mass communications, attention generally shifted from the print media (newspapers, comics, and magazines) to the sound (radio) and then to the visual media (movies and television).

The commonly held assumption has been that there is some causal connection between media representations of violence and crime and the actual perpetration or the condoning of these acts in the real world, especially by impressionable children. Studies of the relationship of the mass media to criminality now almost exclusively focus on the role of television. Within less than twenty-five years, television has, according to many researchers, become the "cultural arm" of American society, rivaling the influence of other socializing institutions such as the family and the school (Gerbner and Gross, 1976).

Ever since television became a public phenomenon, its critics have decried the disproportionate amount of programming devoted to crime and violence. Even such seemingly benign programs as children's cartoons reveal large amounts of violence and mayhem. Given these events, television became an early target for its possible influence on delinquency. The first congressional hearing on television took place in 1952. Since that time, several national commissions have examined the television industry and found evidence of increased violence in programming and linkage of this violence to actual behavior, some of which is of a delinquent variety.

Given the ubiquitous nature of television compared to previous mass communication devices, modes of thinking and research rooted in the expressions of other media simply do not apply to television. Unlike the print media, television does not require literacy. Even infants may have direct access to the full range of programming. Unlike the movies, television is "free" and virtually continuous and uncontrollable in who may watch its contents. And unlike radio, television does not just describe, it shows—now in living color (Gerbner and Gross, 1976).

The evidence for and against the influence of the media remains controversial and inconclusive. The causal effects of earlier media influences on delinquency were never clearly understood. Now a large body of scientific research, much of it done in the last decade, has sought to clarify the nature of the relationship between television and violence.

Although much of the research has dealt more with the general topic of violence and aggression than with types of juvenile delinquency, most of the studies have concentrated on juveniles' deviant behaviors as influenced by the media. Despite elaborate research designs, social scientists find it extremely difficult to factor out the influences of the televised media from other cultural phenomena that affect children's attitudes and behaviors. Numerous nagging questions remain partially answered:

1. Is there a direct or indirect relationship between viewing violence in the media and engaging in those activities?

2. Does the viewing of violence weaken the internal or external controls on aggressive behavior?

3. Does the viewing of violence desensitize an individual to reactions against violence?

4. Does viewing the violence result in a cathartic effect, whereby people experience a vicarious release of aggressive tendencies?

5. Do the media provide fake information about the extent and nature of crime and delinquency in the real world?

In this chapter we examine the research which has tried to answer these and other questions pertaining to the influence of the mass media on delinquent behavior. We first discuss the nature of mass communications in general and then explore historical accounts of how early media were thought to relate to juvenile delinquency. The remainder of the chapter focuses on television as a contemporary medium which has been singled out as a potential and possibly powerful factor in delinquency. Television has been charged not just with influencing behavior, but with creating a world view that may be far removed from the real world.

THEORIES OF MASS COMMUNICATION

Before the advent of modern mass media—devices for disseminating information to large masses of people—most humans lived their entire lives in local communities and were largely dependent on information from personal, face-to-face interactions with their neighbors. In the frontier days of our country, it often took several months for people to learn of significant national and world developments. After the War of 1812, for instance, when the treaty had been signed, it took three more weeks for word of Andrew Jackson's victory to reach Washington (Zanden, 1970: 30).

As America changed from a rural agrarian society to a complex industrialized society, mass communications became central to the functioning of the nation. Prior to 1830, books and newspapers were produced only for the educated elite. It was not until later that technological developments in printing and in the manufacture of paper made it possible for these materials to be distributed to larger audiences, who were by then better educated. By the end of the nineteenth century, several magazines had achieved a circulation of several hundred thousand subscribers.

Major technological advances in electronics and cinematography eventually led to split-second broadcasting of vast amounts of information to millions of people. Television, radio, and the movies began to appear in the twentieth century. Movies came first; by the late 1920s, radio was common in most American homes. Public use of television was delayed by a number of years because of World War II, but by the late 1950s nearly 50 percent of Americans had television sets.

It would be difficult now to imagine life without newspapers, magazines, radio, television, and other forms of mass communication. Mass communications link major institutions in the society together into a dynamic social system. Mass communications provide a major means for advertising and marketing goods and services. They provide both entertainment and educational services to the country. Major businesses such as the print and broadcast industries have developed from the mass communications explosion, providing jobs and investment opportunities for millions of Americans (Defleur and Ball-Rokeach, 1975).

Given the positive benefits that mass communications have for society, it may seem inconceivable that the phenomenon has been targeted by some critics as a social problem in need of drastic reform (Hubbard, Defleur, Defleur, 1975). Two charges are usually leveled at the media: (1) that the various media themselves create problems by stimulating aggressive behaviors and attitudes, or (2) that regardless of the media's influence, some of the material is in and of itself objectionable (violent acts and pornography). The purpose of this chapter is to explore these charges as they relate to delinquency. Before doing this, however, we need to understand the processes by which the media are thought to influence people. Why do people select certain media content to read, observe, or hear; and once the selection is made, how does it shape a person's opinions, attitudes, or behaviors?

Patterns of Selective Exposure

One person may never miss an episode of "Cagney and Lacey," a popular television cop show, while another watches only Masterpiece Theater presentations on the public educational channel. Someone else may read the *Wall Street Journal* exclusively and listen only to classical music on the radio. Obviously, the media will have different effects on each of these types of individuals. Evidence suggests that media selectivity is shaped by at least three major kinds of factors: individual differences, social categories, and social relationships.

Individual Differences.   Each individual has a distinct personality, an organization of emotional, motivational, and learning characteristics that functions in a certain way and interacts with the environment. The components of personality are products of both heredity and environmental influences, some of which may begin before birth. The unique nature of personality development ensures that no two people are exactly alike. Some individuals, for example, may have a greater ability to reason and solve problems; others may not. These differences, coupled with a unique set of learning experiences, may help explain why people select specific forms of mass media and interpret the contents as rewarding or not rewarding. A child who is extremely bright, constantly seeking new knowledge, may find cartoons boring and unchallenging. A youngster who is having difficulties in school, who has not developed an inquisitive mind, may enjoy the fantasy world of cartoons, where he or she may escape from reality for a few hours on Saturday morning.

Social Categories.   By virtue of being a member of society, each of us belongs to distinct social categories, where we share a consciousness of kind with others who possess similar characteristics. Some of these characteristics are conspicuous and visible, such as skin color, age, and sex. Others, such as religion, occupation, and education, are not. Social categories that possess distinctive ways of thinking, feeling, and acting that in a number of respects set members apart from the larger society may be said to form subcultures. By being a member of a specific subculture, such as an upper class professional or a lower class unskilled laborer, we possess very distinct preferences and tastes for select types of media. Some research suggests, for instance, that lower class adolescents express a preference for more violence-oriented types of television programs when compared to their middle and upper class counterparts (Thornton and Voigt, 1984).

Social Relationships.   Since each of us interacts with other individuals through social relation-

ships—with family members, peers, co-workers, and neighbors—these ties may strongly influence our exposure to mass communications. Children who are raised in families in which reading is stressed or where television programs are rigidly controlled will probably be affected quite differently by the media than children raised in more promiscuous families. Group ties may not only affect the selection of media and its content, but may actually shape the nature of the interpretation of that content. Family members or other influential people may tell you about a program that they viewed on a particular night which you may have missed. Rather than forming an opinion of the program from experiencing the event yourself, you form an opinion based on *their* interpretation of the event. This pattern is called the *two-step flow* of communication and appears to be a common phenomenon (Defleur, 1983: 576–580; Weimann, 1982).

Each of these sources of selectivity—individual differences, social categories, and social relationships—is important in determining the types of media content people choose.

THE MASS MEDIA AND DELINQUENCY: HISTORICAL CONCERNS

Historically, the mass media have come under attack for their presumed negative influence on juveniles. Criticism of such media as comic books, radio, and the movies as contributors to delinquency has waned since the arrival of television, which now receives the full brunt of the charges. However, in order to better understand the arguments against television and its influence on human behavior, we briefly review some of the early research which focused on comics, the movies, and radio, and their presumed effects on juvenile delinquency.

Comic Books

Criticism of comic books as being causal or at least contributory factors to delinquent behavior has declined since the 1950s, when television hit the American scene. Comic books in the 1980s are essentially a thing of the past, with only expensive versions of the old Dell "ten centers" still available. There is little concern about their influence on children's attitudes or behaviors.

However, at the peak of their popularity, from the 1930s through the 1950s, comic book sales were purported to be over 60 million copies per month, with a publishing list of some 600 titles (Larsen, 1968: 21). During this time, when public concern was exceptionally strong over violence in comic books (and movies), numerous studies were conducted to see what effect the reading of comics had on the youth of the day. Much like the current arguments over television, no agreement was ever reached on the actual effects of comics on children's behavior, deviant or otherwise.

The research of Frederick Werthman (1948, 1953, 1954) perhaps attracted the most attention during this era of concern over comics. Based on his clinical experience, Werthman, a psychiatrist, was unrelenting in his belief in the negative influence of comics on children. He wrote:

> [The comics] often suggest criminal or sexually abnormal ideas, create a mental preparedness or readiness for temptation; suggest the forms a delinquent impulse may take; may act as the precipitating factor of delinquency or emotional disorder; may supply rationalization for a contemplated act which is often more important than the impulse itself; set off chains of undesirable and harmful thinking in children; and create for young readers a mental atmosphere of deceit, trickery, and cruelty. (Sutherland and Cressey, 1960: 214)

Werthman's findings, however, tended to be more sensational than scientific, and his case study approach made generalizations to a larger population of children extremely difficult (Werthman, 1948, 1953, 1955).

More rigorous examination of the comic book phenomenon can be found in the literature. Hoult (1949) conducted a survey in which known delinquents and nondelinquents were asked such things as the types and quantities of comics they read.

He found that a sample of delinquents reported reading a total of 2,853 harmful and questionable comics, while the nondelinquents reported reading only 1,786 similar types of comics. Hoult classified the various comics into the categories of (1) crime and gangsterism, (2) general blood and thunder, (3) supernatural action, (4) jungle adventure, (5) cowboys and Indians, (6) young romance, and (7) animated cartoons. Delinquents, according to Hoult, read "many more of the crime, the blood and thunder and the supernatural action books" than did the nondelinquents (p. 282). Hoult emphasized that his findings do not show any causal relationship between juvenile delinquency and the reading of certain comic books, but only that apparent differences do exist between his two samples.

Despite some research finding no differences between delinquents and nondelinquents (Cavanagh, 1949; Pfuhl, 1956), other research did support the finding that children who preferred criminal- or violence-oriented comics expressed behavioral or attitudinal differences (presumably antisocial) when compared to children who preferred less violent comics (Wolfe and Fishe, 1948; Lovibond, 1967; Hirschi, 1969).

As we have indicated, the early research examining the influence of comics on delinquency experienced difficulty in establishing causality between comics and delinquent behavior. While evidence was found of a relationship between the reading of certain comics and, say, a history of delinquency, the finding could be spurious, or false, when other factors were examined (such as social class, age, peer group). Pfuhl (1956) reported, for example, that when intimate peer group relationships of children were held constant, the effects of comic books were marginal in explaining delinquent behavior patterns.

Radio

Early arguments about the detrimental effects of radio on children's attitudes and behaviors were generally based on editorial commentaries rather than any empirical data. Radio critics commonly attacked the violent content of various radio dramas. Much like television, early broadcasts were thought to contain a disproportionate amount of violence in their programs (Preston, 1941). In addition, some critics argued that young children learned delinquency and criminal methods from listening to the broadcasts (Rowland, 1944).

A study conducted by the Chicago Recreation Commission (Shanas, 1942) reported that children from known delinquent areas in the city, such as the lower North side, reported listening to crime programs proportionately more than children from nondelinquent areas such as Hyde Park. It was suggested, however, that "the same economic and cultural factors which produce delinquency also produce a greater number of juveniles who enjoy crime drama" (Rowland, 1944: 214). Other research (Preston, 1941) concentrated on young radio "addicts" and concluded that "nervousness and emotional instability" were a result of the steady diet of crime and violence. Little, if any, of this research found any concrete evidence of a link betwen listening to certain radio programs and actual delinquent behavior.

Movies

Since motion pictures predated television by some fifty years in their ability to present visual dramatizations, the motion picture industry very early attracted the attention of individuals concerned with problems affecting children. Basically, the same concerns were voiced about the effects of violence, crime, and sex on the screen that were voiced about comics and radio; in order of chronological concern, movies actually came under attack before comics and radio.

Based on research that has analyzed the content of movies over long spans of time, there can be no denying that much of the content has indeed been violent in nature. Clark and Blankenberg (1972) sampled several hundred movies released between 1930 and 1969 and concluded that 35 percent could be coded as violent. Despite fluctuations from year to year, the trend in violence has been upward since the 1930s, leading some people to speculate that this was an effort on the part of the movie industry to compete with television, which also had a history of accentuating violence in its programming.

One of the first empirical studies that examined the effects of movies on juvenile delinquency was conducted by Blumer and Hauser (1933). They examined both the indirect and direct effects of motion pictures on the behavior of delinquent and nondelinquent males and females. The researchers suggested that "by arousing desires for easy money, by inducing a spirit of bravado, toughness, and adventurousness, by fostering the day dreaming of criminal roles, by displaying techniques of crime, and by contributing to truancy, motion pictures may lead or dispose [children] to crime" (p. 70). Their conclusions, based on interviews with known delinquents, were offered as support for the indirect influence of movies on certain types of delinquency. Movies could, for instance, play a role in both male and female delinquency by arousing sexual passions or by evoking longings for expensive consumer items viewers could not afford.

More direct influences on delinquency were thought to occur when movies depicted accounts of crimes which "furthered and fortified the development of criminal conduct" (p. 35). Thus, such things as the skill and cleverness with which a crime was carried out, the enjoyment of money and the adventure of carrying out a crime, might, according to the researchers, incite certain individuals to criminal or delinquent behavior (p. 35). They reported that 49 percent of the male delinquents questioned indicated that the movies gave them a desire to carry a gun; 28 percent that the movies taught them methods of stealing; and 21 percent that they learned ways to fool the police.

Blumer and Hauser emphasized, however, that while motion pictures may create attitudes favorable to crime and delinquency, they may likewise engender attitudes unfavorable to them. Delinquent influence from motion pictures is, they suggested, dependent on how strong other institutions such as the family, school, and church are in transmitting socially acceptable attitudes and values. In a sense, various patterns of selective exposure were posited by Blumer and Hauser.

Other early research reported negative findings about the presumed effects of movies on children's attitudes and behaviors (see Pfuhl, 1970). As we will see in our discussion of television and delinquency, many of the earlier concerns about the influence of movies are still hotly debated.

THE MASS MEDIA AND DELINQUENCY: SOME CONTEMPORARY CONCERNS

The belief that certain mass media either directly or indirectly affect juveniles' deviant attitudes and/or behaviors continues to intrigue researchers. Most of the research today concentrates on the role of television and its influence on all aspects of American culture, including family life, education, politics, advertising, and especially crime and delinquency. The ubiquity of television cannot be denied. "More Americans have television than have refrigerators or indoor plumbing" (*Television and Behavior*, v. 1, 1982: 1). Probably less than 2 percent of all households do not possess at least one television set; over half have two or more (Sterling and Haight, 1978).

Furthermore, the amount of exposure per individual to television viewing is enormous. One national study reports an average viewing time of about 29 hours per week (Comstock et. al., 1978). This figure is probably much higher for selected groups such as children. Some research reports that the majority of children watch television regularly even before the age of 4 (Adler et al., 1980: 15).

Average viewing time is more than four hours a day in some instances, but may be greater for certain categories of children (those of lower socioeconomic status). It is not inconceivable that children's viewing time may equal or surpass the amount of time they spend in school each day. These findings take on added significance when we realize that much of the broadcasting involves shows that are heavily laden with crime and other types of violence. We will examine the intricacies of the television-crime relationship shortly. Much of this research has been preoccupied with aggression and violence, whether of a delinquent or criminal variety or not.

Content of News Presentations

A topic that does not deal specifically with media and crime causation per se but that is intimately related to our study of the media involves the reporting of crime news (specifically newspapers and television news). While this is certainly not just a contemporary concern (Holmes, 1929–30; Highfield, 1926–1927; Lombroso, 1911), there has been recent interest in how crime coverage in the newspapers and television can affect a person's estimate of the frequency of crime as well as the interpretations of crime. In a sense, as criminologist Richard Quinney puts it, a "social reality" of crime may be created by the media that does not reflect how crime actually occurs in the "real world" (1970).

The amount of crime depicted in the media has little relationship to the amount of crime actually occurring. Thus, media coverage of certain types of crimes and the individuals associated with those crimes in both an offender and victim capacity can influence our perceptions dramatically. Overreporting of violent, sensational juvenile delinquency, for instance, may signal to the public a belief that all juvenile crime is on the rise, when in fact this is not the case. Similarly, stereotyping of "typical" juvenile offenders may be gleaned from media accounts which are false.

Amount of Crime News.   The general public fails to realize just how selective the media are in reporting news. Rivers (1973) studied a large metropolitan newspaper and found that the city desk normally handled about 150,000 words (about 900 potential news stories), of which only about 12 percent were actually printed. In essence, the editors of the paper served as *gatekeepers* of the news by selecting and filtering out those stories that would reach the public (Lewin, 1947). Given that the one goal of the newspaper industry is to sell papers, those stories which have the broadest appeal or are the easiest to obtain often get into print (or are broadcast on the air).[1]

Interestingly enough, the same media may provide varying and often divergent portrayals of crime. A striking example of this was illustrated by Bachmuth, Miller, and Rosen (1960). In their content analysis of two newspapers in New York City over a three-month period, they found that the *New York Daily News* presented nearly twice as many items about juvenile delinquency as the *New York Times*. Even more dramatic was the finding that each newspaper reported the same delinquent acts in a different manner. The *Daily News* headlines tended to be more emotional and sensationalistic: "Cops Nab Two in Cat-Mouse Roof Top Chase," "Hunt Two Boy Bullies Who Killed Lad." The *New York Times*, on the other hand, reported the incidents in a more matter-of-fact manner: "Museum Theft Laid to Delinquents," "Third Slain in Youth Violence" (1960: 47–51).

An additional consideration in examining the criteria used in reporting news involves problems in the gathering of news (Cumberbatch and Howitt, 1974; Cumberbatch and Howitt, 1975). Since news can be very expensive to obtain, journalists are often dependent on official processors of crime (the police, the courts) for a ready supply of cheap news. In a content analysis of juvenile crimes reported in the *Arizona Republic* (a major Phoenix newspaper), Sager (1983) found that the police were quoted three times more often than other sources (including the victims of crimes). Other research indicates that some two-thirds of newspaper items on crime are based on court reports that tend to exaggerate the clearance rates for crime in the press. Similarly, crime that is threatening to the official source may go "undetected" (Cumberbatch and Beadsworth, 1976: 82).

Studies which have attempted to measure the amount of space (in newspapers) devoted to crime news vary in their estimates. Some researchers examine only reports of specific criminal events, while others include editorials and features (Garofalo, 1981: 321). Despite these variations and the considerable time spans these studies cover, there is a high degree of stability in the amount (percentage of total space) of crime news in newspapers. Most important, perhaps, is the finding that overall there is a relatively low proportion of total news space devoted to crime. Most of the figures indicate that it is normally in the range of 5 to 10 percent of news space (Harris, 1932; Davis, 1952; Swanson, 1955; Hauge, 1965; Deutschmann, 1959; Otto, 1963; Roshier, 1971; Croll, 1974), although some studies report higher percentages ranging as much as 20 to 30 percent (Roshier, 1973; Graber, 1980).

Given that the media devote a certain amount of space or attention to crime news, the next question to ask is how closely this coverage corresponds to actual crime rates. Obviously this is a difficult, if not impossible, question to answer, since the measurement of crime itself is an inexact science (see Chapter 3). Some evidence does exist, however, to suggest that media reporting of crime (primarily newspapers) is grossly unrelated to changes in "actual" crime trends. In a comparison of juvenile crimes reported in the *Arizona Republic* for 1962 with official crime figures, Sager, for example, found that violent offenders accounted for 57 percent of all juvenile offenders in the newspaper, whereas they accounted for only 4 percent of total juvenile arrests according to official statistics (1963: 17).

Images of Crime, Criminals, and Victims in the News.   Just as the media may affect the public's perception of the amount of crime, so too may they affect the public's image of the types of crime and their accompanying offenders and victims.

Almost without exception, violent personal crimes—especially murders—are disproportionately represented in news media depictions of crime in the United States (Croll, 1974; Antunes and Hurley, 1977; Graber, 1980; Sherizen, 1978) and in other countries (Van Dijk, 1979; Dussuyer, 1979). Graber's (1980) analysis of *Chicago Tribune* stories for 1976 is a good case in point. *Tribune* reporting of murder accounted for 26 percent of crimes reported; robbery, assault, and rape accounted for another 20 percent. On the other hand, common property crimes of burglary and larceny or theft accounted for about 5 percent of crimes mentioned, while vandalism, sex offenses, and child abuse accounted for less than 3 percent (p. 41). Examining exclusively juveniles, Sager's analysis of the *Republic* revealed that some 15 percent of juvenile offenders reported in the paper for 1982 were involved in murder, whereas official statistics indicated that only 0.04 percent of total juvenile arrests for the same year were for murder (1963: 18).

Usually only the most sketchy details about crime offenders are given in media accounts. Despite some exceptions (such as Dussuyer, 1979), younger individuals appear less often than one might expect in the media. Graber (1980) reported that the *Tribune* identified about 30 percent of criminals as under age 25, another 30 percent as 25 to 35, and the rest as over 35. Racial characteristics of offenders, when reported, were very close to the distribution found in national arrest statistics (Graber, 1980). Similarly, the sex distribution of offenders also corresponded closely to official statistics, with females composing no more than 10 percent (Roshier, 1971). The evidence on social class is ambiguous. Generally newspaper accounts suggest an overreporting of higher-status offenders (Graber, 1980; Hauge, 1965; Roshier, 1971), although there are some exceptions (Cumberbatch and Beadsworth, 1976).

Generalizations about victims of crime from news sources are incomplete because few studies have analyzed victimization characteristics. Graber (1980) indicated that with respect to age, the *Chicago Tribune* reported that 39 percent of the victims were over age 35. A British study of the *Manchester Evening News* conducted by Cumberbatch and Beadsworth (1976) showed that about 22 percent of the reported victims were over age 60. Both these studies found that there were more male (60 percent) than female victims (40 percent). Graber also reported that about two-thirds of the *Tribune* victims were white and that about 20 percent were reported as being unemployed or in unskilled jobs.

A chief concern of many criminologists deals with the link between media depictions of crime and public beliefs about crime. Some researchers have argued that there is a direct causal connection between media images and public beliefs about crime and delinquency (Quinney, 1970; Gerbner, 1972a). The argument is proffered that the public allegedly accepts the media's version of crime (crime reported in the news), since most people have minimal contact with delinquents and criminals during their lives. As with most of the mass media research, contradictory evidence can be found. Generally speaking, however, most studies that address the problem of the relationship between media images and public attitudes about crime find relatively little evidence to support the view that the mass media dramatically influence our perceptions about crime and the criminal justice system.

Content of Television Entertainment

Although there are some similarities between accounts of crime, criminals, and victims and the operation of the criminal justice system as reported in the news media and as represented in television crime dramas, the contents of news and entertainment presentations are quite different. The news media simply summarize and offer information on crime events, commenting on the "relevant" facts. Television drama unfolds a story for the viewer to experience firsthand (Garofalo, 1981: 325). Very little research suggests that news coverage of crime "contributes" to criminal activities as television dramas do. In the drama, some information is given about the events preceding the crime, about the interaction between offender and victim, and about the consequences of the crime.

Garofalo notes that, "as in any form of storytelling, the links between motives, means, and ends are more central than in the array of items comprising newspapers or news broadcasts" (1981: 325). Because of the differences between news and entertainment presentations of delinquent and criminal events, stories, and items, and due to the paucity of research on television news broadcasts in general, we treat television dramas separately. We first examine crime in primetime television entertainment.

Crime in Primetime Television.   Since the late 1950s, crime has become a staple component of primetime television entertainment. By 1975, nearly 40 percent of the three major networks' primetime holdings contained shows dealing with crime and law enforcement. Despite fluctuations in this figure, shows dealing with crime remain the "bread and butter" of the television industry (Dominick, 1978: 115).

Numerous studies, hearings, and commissions have documented the ubiquity of crime in television shows over the years. Since 1967, George Gerbner and his associates have conducted some of the most thorough studies about the portrayal of crime in television drama. In 1967, for example, criminals numbered 10 percent of all television characters; they made up 20 percent of the killers and 24 percent of those killed. Some 82 percent of all criminals were violent; law enforcement agents were a close second, with 70 percent (Gerbner and Gross, 1974). When crime was featured, it was almost always violent. A more recent study in 1973 conducted by Dominick analyzed a week's worth of primetime programming and similarly found that murder, assault, and armed robbery were the most frequently portrayed events in programs. Focusing on crime dramas exclusively, Barrile (1980) reported that 60 percent of crime victims were murdered, while another 23 percent were subjected to attempted murder.

Differing from official statistics, television research suggests that by and large, the young, blacks, and people of low socioeconomic status are underrepresented as offenders in television programs (Barrile, 1980; Dominick, 1973). Middle and upper class white males in their mid-adult years comprise the bulk of criminal offenders and victims (Pandiani, 1978). Some researchers have suggested that those types of characters are over-represented to create an audience for the advertisers of television products (Graber, 1980).

Just as offenders and victims differ from official statistics about crime, so do other aspects of crime in television entertainment. In the television world, for example, the legal process usually ends when the offender is captured. Very rarely do viewers see such things as arraignments, bondings, hearings, requests for bail reduction, plea bargaining, jury selection, and the like. Overwhelmingly, the law enforcement role is overrepresented in television crime dramas. Police officers comprise some 17 percent of major characters' occupations (Head, 1954; Gerbner et al., 1978). Much like Dudley Dooright of the Royal Mounted Police, the police usually (and quite unrealistically) "get their man" (or woman). In doing so, they use unnecessary violence, violate constitutional rights, and summarily depict the police as freewheeling agents answerable to no one (Barrile, 1980; Culver and Knight, 1979; Dominick, 1973, 1978; Gerbner, 1972a).

The interactions between criminals and "law enforcers" in television dramas provide more than just action-packed entertainment for audiences. According to some critics, television is an "agency of the established social order and as such serves primarily to extend and maintain rather than alter, threaten, or weaken conventional conceptions, beliefs, and behaviors" (Gerbner, 1976: 175). Thus, law enforcement officials always triumph, and the legitimacy of the system is reaffirmed. Gerbner argues that in contrast to the usual concerns of media researchers about the stimulation of real-life aggression by television violence, we should examine more critically the role of television with respect to the power it has in socializing people to the dictates of the power structure.

Violence in Television Entertainment. Public interest about the issue of violence on television programs is certainly not a new concern. Based on reports of excessive violence and sexual provocativeness in programming, the first congressional hearing on television programming took place in 1952 (*Television and Behavior*, v. 1, 1982: 36). Television as a cause of delinquent behavior became a central focus of inquiry. During the next twelve years, the Senate Committee on the Judiciary held other hearings, and Congress as a whole suggested that excessive violence on television may be a contributor to juvenile delinquency or at the very minimum may be damaging to young viewers. The period between 1952 and 1967 witnessed numerous analyses of television programs which found that violence was rampant. One study conducted in 1954 reported an average of 11 threats or acts of violence per hour (Remmers, 1954). Later research confirmed that television violence was increasing most rapidly on programs that large numbers of children preferred (Greenberg, 1969).

Two separate government commissions examined the problem of television violence in the late 1960s. The National Commission on the Causes and Prevention of Violence issued a report in 1969 summarizing existing information about the prevalence of violence on television and its potential negative effects. Based primarily on laboratory studies, the commission concluded that viewing violent programs increases the likelihood of a viewer behaving violently (Baker and Ball, 1969). A similar conclusion was reached by the Surgeon

General's Scientific Advisory Committee on Television and Social Behavior in 1972.

The committee commissioned George Gerbner to analyze violence in television entertainment (Baker and Ball, 1969). Gerbner and his associates began analyzing weeks of primetime and weekend morning dramatic programs representing three seasons, 1967, 1968, and 1969 (1972a). Using a definition of violence as "the overt expression of physical force, with or without a weapon, against self or other, compelling action against one's will on pain of being hurt or killed, actually killing or hurting," they introduced their famous *violence index,* which summarized the quantity of violence in a given body of programming (Comstock, 1982: 111). In addition, they collected data on tabulations of murder rates and other acts of violence by program categories, classifications of violence by setting and characteristics of perpetrators, and the ratio of violence perpetrated by violence suffered by characters of a particular age, sex, or ethnicity. From this information, they generated a *victimization ratio* which reflected "the degree to which characters of a given sort are portrayed as powerful or powerless" (Comstock, 1982: 103).

This work for the Surgeon General's committee demonstrated that involvement in violence is common for programming on all three major networks (1976). The committee concluded that "the convergence of evidence from laboratory and field studies [suggests] that viewing violent television programs contributes to aggressive behavior" (*Television and Social Behavior,* 1972). A more recent review of research examining violence in television programs during the past ten years substantiated this finding (*Television and Behavior,* 1982, vols. 1 and 2).

Gerbner and his associates continue to monitor the major networks, and much of their earlier findings reported in the 1972 *Television and Social Behavior* series still stand, even a decade later (Gerbner et al., 1977a,b,c; Gerbner et al., 1979a; Gerbner et al., 1980a, b, c). The frequency of violent acts did not change except for a slight decline in fatalities and injuries; cartoons and weekend daytime programming, which include all children's programs, were more violent than primetime general audience programming. Some differences in quantity of violence between the networks were discernible. About 40 percent of leading characters' victims were injured or killed as a result of their earlier violence. Victimization remained frequent and more common than the committing of violence. When violence was committed, it was usually carried out by an American middle or upper class unmarried male, in the prime of life. All in all, the potential for violence was much greater in television drama than in real life.

Assessments of the amount of violence in television programming are controversial, to say the least. The television industry is especially sensitive to measures that rank one network's programming as higher in violence than others'. Gerbner's violence index is criticized, for instance, by the major networks for ignoring the "dramatic context" in which the violence occurs. They argue that some violence, say in the defense of life, is "justified." This type of violence is somehow different from violence used in a less legitimate or illegal manner. As a result, CBS began monitoring its own television programming, using methods it claims are more accurate than Gerbner's (CBS, 1977, 1980). The other networks have also conducted their own content analyses of programming.

Television, Aggression, and Violence

In the quest to discover the effects of media violence on subsequent behavior and attitudes, the research to date, spanning roughly twenty-five years, is immense. Given the amount of attention that has been aimed at the mass media in their presumed role of eliciting or inciting antisocial behaviors and attitudes, it is surprising that criminologists conspicuously fail to take the media into account in their theories of crime and delinquency causation. As a result, much of the research has not been conducted by criminologists and examines antisocial behavior that may not in many cases be considered delinquent or criminal in terms of strict legal criteria, using instead broad categories of aggressive or violent behavior.

While it is beyond the scope of this chapter to review this body of research, several works offer excellent summaries (Andison, 1977; Comstock et al., 1978; Eysenck and Nias, 1978; Liebert et al., 1973; Murray, 1980). Andison, for example, surveys 153 studies relating to violence and viewer aggression from 1956 through 1976. He reports that despite the use of differing research methodologies, "it seems quite clear that there is at least a weak positive relationship between watching violence on television and the subsequent aggression displayed by viewers of that violence" (p. 323). Although some contradictory findings exist (Milavsky et al., 1982a,b), more recent reviews generally offer similar (and stronger) findings. Huesmann (1982) notes, for instance, that "the evidence [from recent studies] seems overwhelming that television violence viewing and aggression are positively correlated in children" (p. 128).

A word of caution should be given in interpreting research which examines the relationship between viewing violence on television and aggression. The obvious question regards the causal ordering of the variables. Does viewing violence produce aggression or, as some researchers suggest, do children who are aggressive simply prefer violent material (Garofalo, 1981)? Much of the research which addresses this issue has relied on cross-sectional designs, measuring a sample of people at one point in time, rather than longitudinal designs, where data are collected over an extended period. The cross-sectional studies generally find a positive association—moderate to strong relationships—between children's viewing behaviors and aggression. However, such findings do not infer causality—that amount of violence viewed somehow *contributes* to real violent predispositions. This can be ascertained only through full-fledged longitudinal designs where knowledge about subjects' prior exposure to television violence can be linked to later delinquent behaviors. Because of the cost of longitudinal designs, relatively few of the studies on mass media, at least until recently, utilized this more time-consuming and expensive methodology.

Generally, four types of effects of media violence have been studied over the years: (1) learning of new behaviors (modeling or imitation); (2) disinhibition (the weakening of internal or external controls on aggressive, violent, or delinquent behaviors); (3) desensitization (the weakening of emotional reactions to violence); and (4) catharsis (where a viewer's drive to perform aggressive behaviors is reduced by watching actors behave aggressively).

Modeling, Imitation, and Social Learning. Advocates of this view suggest that through observational learning, children learn to behave aggressively by watching violent role models on television, much in the same way that they learn acceptable behaviors from parents, peers, and other significant and generalized others. Much of this research has involved laboratory-type experiments where children are exposed to aggressive or violent behaviors through screen depictions (such as a violent cartoon character, another child engaging in aggressive behaviors, and the like).

One of the first experiments conducted in this area was done by Bandura and his associates at Stanford University (1963a,b). Children who were exposed to a film of an aggressive model who was rewarded, a small boy who took toys away from and beat up another little boy, were found to imitate the aggressive behaviors themselves. Since Bandura's original experiments, a number of other experiments and field studies have attempted to test his theories. There have been many variations of the theme (regarding punishing the aggressive role model, rewarding and punishing the subjects, degree of identification of the subject with the aggressive role model, persistence of learning over time, and so on).

Milgram and Shotland (1973), for instance, engaged in field experiments to see if individuals (including teenagers) would imitate stealing behavior from a charity display they observed on television. Control groups were used in which subjects observed neutral shows; various experimental groups were used in which subjects saw the television thief punished or not punished. Although the experimenters did report that subjects stole from the charity box after viewing television, the type of program viewed apparently had no effect on theft rates.

This type of experimental research has given us insight into how the media can influence aggression by its contents. While there is still much to be learned about the cognitive aspects of an imitation-aggression link, there is ample evidence to indicate that under certain conditions, children do learn, retain, and imitate aggressive and violent behaviors they observe in the media. The intensity of the modeling influence of television programs is obviously affected by the viewer's own social situation, including class, cultural definitions of appropriate behavior, and individual differences.

One weakness of laboratory studies, however, involves responding to charges about the generalizability of sterile laboratory settings to the "real world." Numerous researchers have engaged in observational and field studies seeking to further specify the positive relationship found between violence viewing and subsequent aggression in laboratory studies. This research has employed both cross-sectional and longitudinal designs and often includes self-reported delinquency inventories as a means of assessing television viewing of violence (see Chapter 3 for a description of the technique). Few of these studies utilize comprehensive self-report delinquency inventories in relation to viewing televised violence. In fact, a review of the literature suggests that rather selective self-report inventories are employed, often neglecting certain types of offenses that may or may not be construed as violent in nature. Many of these inventories are heavily laden with behaviors that are relatively minor in nature and do not reflect serious delinquent behavior. This makes it difficult to make inferences about a full range of deviant behaviors thought to be related to the media.

However, despite these weaknesses and despite rather broad interpretations of delinquency, the bulk of the research to date generally reports moderate to strong relationships between viewing television violence and certain types of children's aggressiveness. Some research on social learning further suggests that the content of the media and the violent role models presented in the media may influence certain children in ways we do not yet fully understand. For instance, lower class adolescents, upon seeing middle and upper class characters heavily involved in career crime on television, may gradually neutralize their commitments to conventional society (assuming that they

exist in the first place). Evidence suggests that lower class youth generally spend more time watching television than middle and upper class kids and generally prefer programs that are more violence-oriented (Dominick and Greenberg, 1972). It is not inconceivable, then, that television provides a major vehicle for learning dominant social norms—in this case, norms favorable to law violation (Green and Bynum, 1982).

Disinhibition.   The research examining the disinhibition hypothesis postulates that exposure to media violence can influence proneness to engage in aggressive or violent behaviors. We assume that most children are inhibited from being aggressive by proper socialization. However, if they watch a lot of television, so the argument goes, they may lose their inhibitions against violence—they become *disinhibited* (Dominick and Greenberg, 1972). More important, the attitude change may manifest itself by a greater expectancy of becoming involved in real violence. The mere acceptance of aggression on television may make it likely that children will themselves be more aggressive. Both laboratory and field research has been used to test the disinhibition hypothesis (Hoyt, 1970; Berkowitz, 1962). There is considerable support for the disinhibition of aggression after viewing even a single act of violence (Eysenck and Nias, 1978: 59).

One of the more comprehensive field studies supporting the disinhibition hypothesis, funded by the Columbia Broadcasting System (Belson, 1978), collected data on 1,565 teenage boys (aged 12 through 17) in London. By employing matched subgroups, Belson sought to determine the amount of exposure to 98 violent television shows broadcast between 1959 and 1971 and youth's involvement in self-reported violent behaviors. Belson concluded that exposure to certain types of television violence (violence for a good cause, fictional violence) and not others (sport and cartoon violence) increased the degree to which boys engaged in serious violent behavior (during the last six months). He indicated that his research is strongly suggestive of a disinhibition process whereby inhibitions against being violent ordinarily built up through socialization are progressively broken down by the continual presentation of violence on television.

Desensitization.   Another area of research involves the hypothesis that extensive exposure to violence through the media serves to make people less sensitive (it desensitizes them) to the violence they encounter in the real world. Several laboratory studies have shown that after viewing violent presentations or dramatizations, sensitivity to subsequent violence is indeed dulled (Thomas et al., 1977). This dulling may occur at a physiological level (Cline et al., 1973) or at an attitudinal level (Drabman and Thomas, 1974; Thomas and Drabman, 1975).

In an experimental study conducted by Cline et al. (1973), boys who regularly watched programs with a high violence content displayed less physiological arousal when exposed to new scenes of violence than did a control group of boys. Rabinovitch et al. (1972) let children watch either a violent or a neutral television program. Each child was later shown violent or neutral scenes; the violent group was less likely than the neutral group to notice the violent pictures. Some studies have gone on to suggest that violence arousal via television actually heightens a person's propensity to behave aggressively (Green and O'Neil, 1969; Zillman, 1971). At the very minimum, there is a danger that viewers come to tolerate aggression in their daily lives as perfectly normal behavior (Drabman and Thomas, 1974).

Catharsis.   Contrary to the other theories we have reviewed, the catharsis argument predicts that aggressive behavior will be reduced after exposure to television violence.

Catharsis proponents often argue that all of us need periodic doses of visual violence to keep us from repressing our own aggressive tendencies. The popularity of violent sports, violent movies, and violent television is given as evidence of the need for "outlets" for aggression. Thus, after watching a particularly violent film, some people report feeling more relaxed. While this could be

catharsis, it might just as well be attributed to the distracting effects of the film, diversion from troubles, and so on (Eysenck and Nias, 1978: 62).

Generally, most of the research to date posits results directly opposite to the catharsis hypothesis and is more supportive of the view that television has a facilitative role in producing rather than retarding aggressive behavior in children and other individuals.

Specifying Factors.   As we have indicated, the results of research which has examined the effects of the media on aggression taken as a whole indicate that the media do indeed have an effect on children's deviant attitudes and behaviors. The weight of the evidence strongly suggests that observational learning and attitude changes induced by television violence contribute to the positive relationship between media violence and actual violence. However, the nature and degree of that relationship have been found to differ substantially among certain categories of people (age, social class, family background). Very little of the research considers a wide range of factors that may specify the original finding, and much of it examines only the direct influence of select media variables, violence of programs or heavy television viewing, on deviant behavior (violence) or attitudes (willingness to use force), paying little attention to the indirect influences of the media.

Several possibilities, only peripherally explored in the research, exist. We suggest that an examination of social control variables (see social control theory in Chapter 7) in relation to key media variables may be a fruitful approach to the television-delinquency connection. Since television is, according to many, a new socializing agent for children, it seems logical to examine certain media variables in light of several core social control variables to see what effects, if any, they exert on delinquent behavior.

Only a few studies examine a full host of social control variables in relation to media and delinquency (or violence and aggressiveness). Some researchers, however, have begun preliminary work in this area. McLeod, Atkin, and Chaffee (1972b) included several social control variables in their self-report study of aggressive behavior and violence viewing. They reported that low school performers watch more violent television, have stronger reactions to the content, and behave more aggressively. Parental efforts to influence the child's television behavior by controlling types of programs and by interpreting violence had little effect on reported aggressive behavior. Children well integrated with their peers, interestingly, tended to display higher levels of violence viewing and aggressive behavior (see also Chaffee and McLeod, 1972; McLeod, Atkin, and Chaffee, 1972a; McLeod, Chaffee, and Eswara, 1966).

Thornton and Voigt (1984) examine both media variables (preference for violence-oriented television programs and average viewing hours) and core social control variables (attachment to parents, attachment to school, parental social control, involvement in conventional activities, and belief in the legal system) in relation to several types of self-reported delinquency (ranging from minor delinquency such as petty theft to serious delinquency such as assaults, breaking and entering). Their results suggest that simultaneous controls for all the variables—looking at how each variable affects every other variable in the model—revealed more evidence for the *indirect* influence of the media variables on delinquent variables rather than *direct* influence.

For instance, adolescents who were strongly attached to their parents, committed to school, involved in many extracurricular activities, and who held traditional beliefs about law and the legal system tended to report a preference for less violence-oriented television shows and watched less television than youth who scored low on the social control variables. These youth also reported engaging in less delinquency in general and in particular less serious delinquent activities. Youth who were not strongly attached to their parents, who were less committed to school, not involved in conventional activities and the like, reported engaging in greater quantities of delinquency—especially of a serious nature. Although Thornton and Voigt could not infer causality from their cross-sectional design, the research did strongly

suggest that any study of television and its presumed influence on children's behavior and attitudes must take into consideration the interaction of key social control variables with media influence.

Researchers will undoubtedly continue to try to understand how television affects children's behaviors and attitudes. Not all the research has been negative; some has pointed out the positive or educational features of the medium. Enough negative evidence, however, has been collected over the past twenty or so years to cause alarm over the influence of television on the American public. If nothing else, the ubiquitous nature of the phenomenon should force us to further scrutinize the effects of television on individuals.

We must realize, however, that children do not grow up in a vacuum and that they are constantly being exposed to numerous other factors which can affect them just as strongly as television. We have just entered the computer revolution and cannot even comprehend the magnitude of the impact this technological development will have on children. In all probability, there will be negative consequences attached to this seemingly benign creation. Similarly, the videogame craze has already been linked to truancy and inattention in school.

SUMMARY

Scientists have been interested in the possible negative effects of mass communications on behavior for a long time. A great deal of this research effort was devoted to discovering how certain mass media affected the deviant behaviors and attitudes of juveniles. Early attention was focused on the role of movies, comics, and radio in causing delinquency. These media were thought to contribute to the delinquencies of adolescents. While no conclusive results were ever obtained regarding the direction or degree of impact of these media on delinquency, pressure was put on each industry to institute various codes of self-regulation.

With television's debut in the 1950s, attention generally shifted to the television industry. Literally hundreds of studies have examined television's influence on a wide spectrum of attitudes and behaviors of the viewing population, with many of them focusing on the effects of the medium on aggression and other forms of deviant behavior, many of which could be classified as "delinquent." More recently, researchers have extended their research to the broader topic of how television creates a "social reality" of crime, criminals, victims, and the criminal justice system which may differ dramatically from the real world.

While this social reality may be created by other media, such as newspaper reporting of sensational or bizarre crimes, because of television's ability to create a plot and develop a story line, its programs can project powerful messages about the established social order, what types of people violate that order, and what happens to them when they do.

The research which has examined the assumed relationship between television and aggression has by and large found moderate to strong support for the finding that television does indeed contribute to aggressive and violent attitudes and behaviors in children and adolescents who are exposed to disproportionate amounts of screen violence. However, there remains controversy over the processes involved in the effects of the media on those attitudes and behaviors.

One area of research suggests that through modeling or imitation of violent role models depicted on television, children learn to behave aggressively much in the same manner that they learn normal behaviors from parents and other role models. Another perspective postulates that exposure to media violence disinhibits children's inclinations to behave in a socially acceptable manner, making them prone to violent behavior. Still other research posits that extensive exposure to media violence may desensitize children to violence in general and possibly make them susceptible to solving their own problems in a violent manner when all else fails. Support for all these hypotheses has been found in the research. Relatively little support has been offered for the catharsis argument, which postulates that aggressive behavior will be reduced after a person is exposed to concentrated violence on the screen.

Although we have some insights into how the media affect individuals, in many ways we are still very ignorant of the cognitive processes that intervene between exposure to the media and real life activity. Media research will no doubt remain a popular endeavor.

PROGRESS CHECK

1. List and discuss the three major factors that shape individual selections of television programs. (pp. 249–250)

2. Discuss how certain media, such as comics, radio, newspapers, television, and movies, are thought to affect crime and delinquency. (pp. 250–252)

3. What are the effects of the print media on the public's perceptions of crime (e.g., amount and type)? (pp. 253–254)

4. Review and discuss the research connected with television crime shows during primetime. Has the research shown a relationship between these shows and *real* crime and delinquency? (pp. 255–256)

5. How do media researchers measure violence in television programs? Why have these measures come under attack? (pp. 256–257)

6. What is the issue regarding the causal ordering of viewing violence and engaging in violence? (p. 258)

7. List and discuss the four ways media are thought to affect individuals' attitudes and/ or behaviors. (pp. 258–260)

8. According to the catharsis theory of media influence, aggressive behavior is increased if a person is exposed to violence on television. (p. 260)
   a. True
   b. False

9. Does the viewing of violence desensitize an individual to violence? (p. 260)

10. Is there a direct or indirect relationship between viewing violence in the media and engaging in those activities? Discuss and cite appropriate research. (pp. 260–261)

NOTES

1. An example of the more sensational crimes that usually make the front page include bomb threats (Mazur, 1982) and terrorism (Bassiouni, 1981).

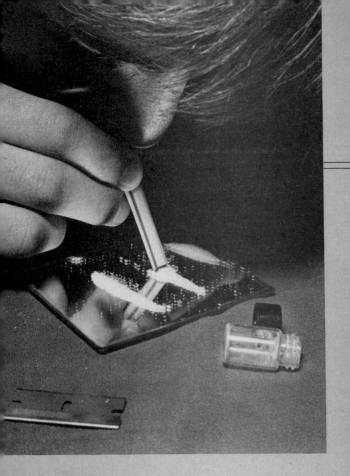

CHAPTER 13

DRUGS AND DELINQUENCY

DRUG TERMINOLOGY

VARIABLES INFLUENCING DRUG EFFECTS

COMMON DRUGS: EFFECTS AND USE

RECENT TRENDS IN DRUG USE AMONG ADOLESCENTS

DRUG ABUSE AND DELINQUENCY

REASONS FOR DRUG ABUSE

CHARACTERISTICS OF DRUG ABUSERS

SOCIETAL REACTION TO SUBSTANCE ABUSE

A young man injects some cocaine and proceeds to rob a gas station at gunpoint. A 15-year-old juvenile smokes two marijuana cigarettes and rapes his 6-year-old niece. A man and woman drink wine and sniff glue together at the beach; he "blacks out" and awakens to find his hands around the neck of his strangled companion. A witness to a fatal stabbing is admittedly intoxicated with phencyclidine (PCP) but claims to remember clearly all the events. A young man "nods out" after injecting heroin and awakens to find his grandmother has hidden his stash; he proceeds to brutally beat and strangle her. Two brothers smoke PCP and argue over who will kill their father; one gives a gun to the other who proceeds to shoot the father in cold blood. A middle-aged woman takes some cocaine which has been adulterated with PCP and tries to rob a bank armed only with a broom which she manipulates as if it were a gun. The plaintiff in a civil suit claims he was under the influence of nitrous oxide when diagnosed as "psychotic" and institutionalized against his will. (Velmen and Haddox, 1983: 52)

The idea that drug use is associated with criminality is widely held. Some people are convinced, especially after hearing about cases like those above, that drugs are a cause of criminal behavior. But these cases primarily sensationalize the relationship between drugs and criminality. They are usually based on erroneous information and thus generally contribute to confusion rather than understanding of the problem. The alleged relationship between drug use and crime has been of interest to researchers, law enforcement officials, and the public for a long time. But the research dealing with this relationship, extensive as it is, tends to expose the complexities of the problem rather than provide definitive evidence.

Early studies concentrated primarily on the extent of criminal records among officially known addicts or evidence of substance abuse among samples of prisoners (or mental patients). Other research has attempted more succinctly to define what the parameters of legitimate and illegitimate use (abuse) are and to account for the great variety of pharmacological effects of different drugs on individuals. While an extensive body of research has examined the link between drugs and crime, until recently little has been done on the relationship between drug use and delinquent (and criminal) behavior among adolescents.[1]

The relationship between delinquency and drug use is complicated by the fact that an adolescent's use of drugs, including alcohol and in some instances cigarettes, which are outlawed for minors and not for adults, is by itself a delinquent act. When an adolescent uses any drug without a doctor's prescription, he or she has committed a delinquent act. The sale and purchase of drugs by teenagers are also delinquent (and criminal) acts.

While relatively little is written about the connection between drug use and adolescent delinquent behavior, a great deal of attention, including popular media coverage, has been devoted to the more general topic of drug use among the young. The information that has accumulated over the years covers a wide range, so it is not uncommon for people to be confused over what is myth and what is reality. Consider the following statements: Which conclusions are supported by more recent research, and which are not?

1. The high cost of illicit drugs leads the drug user into income-producing crime.

2. Drugs have the effect of lowering normal inhibitions, which increases the likelihood of violent, aggressive behavior.

3. Drug abuse is directly linked to certain types of delinquency.

4. Most drug sellers do not use drugs themselves.

5. Involvement in delinquent activities increases chances of being exposed to drug use and thus the likelihood of drug abuse.

6. Heroin is the most dangerous drug.

7. Most marijuana users graduate to the hard core drugs.

8. Among the 3 age groups studied (12–17 years; 18–25 years; 26 +), the 12–17 age range has the largest number of users.

9. Males far outnumber females in all categories of drug use.

10. The most recent trends suggest that drug use among the young is on the rise.

11. Significantly more youth and at a younger age are using such drugs as LSD, PCP, and heroin.

12. Marijuana use leads to aggressive and violent behavior.

13. Cigarettes are not classified as drugs.

None of these statements is simply true or false. However, without careful consideration or further explanation, they are all false. Each of these topics, as well as others, will be discussed in this chapter. We will review the types of drugs most commonly used by young people, concentrating on the effects of the drug and the extent of the use. We will also focus on the relationship of substance use to more general delinquency patterns, and outline the reactions of the criminal justice system to young substance users. Reasons for drug use and the characteristics of young drug users will also be explored. Finally, we will discuss various forms of treatment aimed at "curing" substance abuse.

DRUG TERMINOLOGY

Much of the terminology used to describe the effects of drug use is scientific, complicated, and confusing. Drug experts rarely agree on the definitions of such key terms as **addiction, tolerance, dependency,** and **drug abuse.** Indeed, even the term **drug** is difficult to define. There is no definition general enough to encompass the great variety of substances to which the term refers and which at the same time serves to distinguish substances that are to be excluded. Many definitions have been proposed. Goode (1984) provides a list which includes the main dimensions qualifying chemicals to be given the added label of *drug:*

1. *Medical utility:* Substances currently accepted and used in conjunction with healing the body or the mind by physicians (examples: penicillin, aspirin, Thorazine)

2. *Psychoactivity:* Substances that have a direct and significant impact on the processes of the mind, that influence emotion, thinking, perception, feeling (LSD, alcohol, amphetamines)

3. *Recreational use:* Substances used for their subjective effects, to get "high" (alcohol, marijuana, cocaine)

4. *Illegality:* Substances whose possession, use, or sale are against the law for the general public (heroin, LSD, cocaine)

5. *Public definition:* Substances most people think of when they are asked to provide examples of what a drug is (heroin, cocaine, barbiturates) (Goode, 1984: 17)

Some substances qualify under several definitions. Other drugs may be exclusively categorized under one definition. It is evident from this list that the term *drug* is not entirely an objective or pharmacological category. Its use depends on some objective as well as subjective judgments made by many different types of professionals (physicians, psychiatrists, police, judges, sociologists, criminologists), as well as the general public. Many political and social issues may be implied in any particular use of the term, making general statements about "drugs" tenuous. The use of terms and their implied meaning or ideological context must be carefully scrutinized. In reviewing and comparing research, especially delinquency and drug studies, one must begin with the researcher's operational definitions of the concepts under study.

Another term that is difficult to define is addiction. Addiction is defined "as the periodic or chronic abuse of a drug characterized by physical dependence, psychological dependence, and tolerance" (Weissman, 1978: 47). According to drug experts, **"physical dependence** is an altered physiological state, caused by repeated consumption of a drug in which the drug is needed to maintain 'normalcy'; abstinence from the drug will result in a **withdrawal syndrome"** (Weissman, 1978: 47). The nature of the withdrawal syndrome depends on the nature and amount of the particular drug upon which the user is dependent. Typically, the dependent user experiences symptoms such as irritability, diarrhea, or stomach cramps when the drug is withdrawn.

Psychological dependence on a particular drug, also called **habituation,** also characterizes the drug addict. This form of dependence differs from physical dependence because there is no withdrawal syndrome when the drug is withheld. The psychologically dependent user does, however, experience a craving for the drug, "a psychological state characterized by preoccupation with drug procurement and compulsive drug use necessary to the maintenance of an acceptable level of well-being" (Weissman, 1978: 47). Some drugs, such as marijuana, do not produce physical dependence, but may produce psychological dependence. The user of a drug who has formed a psychological dependence cannot be called an addict because physical dependence is an essential element in the definition of addiction.

Addicts also develop **tolerance** to the drugs they use. "Tolerance means that the drug must be taken in progressively larger doses in order to achieve the desired result" (Pittman, 1974: 210). Some drugs that do not produce physical or psychological dependence do produce tolerance.

The term **drug abuse** has a broader meaning than do the terms addiction, dependence, or tolerance. According to psychologist James Coleman, "Drug abuse is used to indicate excessive use of a drug, regardless of whether an individual has reached the point of true dependence on it" (Coleman, Butcher, and Carson, 1980: 313). A drug addict is a drug abuser, but not all drug abusers are drug addicts. Any person who uses drugs illegally or for other than medically accepted reasons is a drug abuser. The most commonly abused drugs are alcohol, marijuana, stimulants, sedatives, hallucinogens, and narcotics (Pittman, 1974).

For some experts, the exclusively medical definition of drug abuse is insufficient (Goode, 1984). Drug abuse is also a social label with a negative connotation. Use of the term frequently suggests that a substance is harmful and that the harm may be measured. Thus, the medical meaning may be misleading because "it claims clinical objectivity, and it discredits the phenomenon it categorizes," while at the same time blinding people to the effects of other substances which it does not categorize (Goode, 1984: 23). For example, Goode (1984) notes:

> Alcoholism certainly destroys more human life; cigarettes may kill nearly as many people each year as the total number of heroin addicts in existence. There are more people addicted to barbiturates and tranquilizers than heroin. . . . (p. 226)

Yet because alcohol and cigarettes and prescription drugs are legal, we sometimes underestimate their danger and overestimate the danger of other drugs because they are illegal. Some experts insist that in order to control for bias, the term *drug abuse* should be employed when medical, psychiatric, or social damage can be objectively established.

VARIABLES INFLUENCING DRUG EFFECTS

Before we review some of the pharmacological effects of drugs, let us consider some of the other factors that come into play (Goode, 1984: 27–33). Effects are determined first by the nature or *identity* of the substances; what exactly is being ingested is not as simple a question as it first appears. Especially in the case of illegal drugs or street drugs, one may not know what substance is actually procured. *Purity* is an issue closely tied to identity. Frequently drugs are mixed with other substances. Purity refers to "the percent of the batch which is actually composed of the drug in question" (Goode, 1984: 31). Drug combination or drug mixing is also an important consideration. Sometimes people take drugs in combination with other drugs; different combinations may create different effects.

The amount of the drug taken is also a vital factor in determining the type(s) of effects experienced. The questions to be considered in this context include these: What are the normal dosage levels? What effects are associated with different levels of intake? What is the *potency* of the drug? The less the dose required to produce a given effect, the more potent the drug. Street drugs are sometimes unpredictable in their effects because their relative purity and potency are unknown.

The *method of intake* similarly results in very different types of effects. Custom often dictates the methods popularly associated with certain drugs: Marijuana is usually smoked, and cocaine is typically snorted. Sometimes the dangers of drugs are connected more with the method of intake rather than the drug itself. (Many people still envision a dirty hypodermic needle when heroin is mentioned.) Moreover, different intake methods, even of the same drug, may lead to variable effects. The methods include smoking, snorting, mixing with food, mainlining (intravenous injection), skin popping (intramuscular injection), and taking a tablet. The "normal" dosage levels vary according to the different methods. Generally, the direct application of a drug to the bloodstream, as in intravenous injection, brings the most rapid and efficient (smallest dose for greatest effect) results.

Individual tolerance levels also produce variable results. Body weight and other physical characteristics affect different reactions. Steady use over time of certain drugs resulting in drug buildup in the body can affect the rate and nature of the drug experience. Frequent users may require a greater quantity or dose of a particular drug in order to get results comparable to those of a first-time user.

Finally, the individual's emotional and mental state may influence the type of effects certain drugs produce. The terms *set* and *setting* are used to refer to the individual and social variables that influence the drug experience. Set includes mood fluctuations, personality factors, level of intelligence, personal expectations, and the like. Setting refers more to the physical surroundings and the social context in which the drugs are taken. Is the setting a small party with friends or a large party with strangers? Is the person alone, hiding and fearful of being caught? Is the person at a school dance with small groups of friends who are being observed by judging peers and adults? Setting, of course, may affect one's own set. The special circumstances and associated meaning may determine the nature and assessment of the drug experience.

COMMON DRUGS: EFFECTS AND USE

The drug user's diet of altering chemicals is potentially quite varied. Drugs consumed to fall asleep may be followed by drugs to wake up in the morning. There are drugs that numb the senses, reduce pain, and bring on lethargy, and others that take the initiate on a journey into inner space. Some drugs are widely used, both in moderation and to excess. These drugs, their effect,

and the incidence of their use form the topic of this section. The effects, legal controls, and patterns of use of some of the major drugs of abuse are summarized in Table 13.1.

RECENT TRENDS IN DRUG USE AMONG ADOLESCENTS

Given the variety of drugs available on the streets, how extensive or pervasive is drug use? The following materials attempt to answer that question by presenting information obtained from a variety of sources, particularly official statistics and national survey data. Although the data contain some limitations, they tend to sensitize us to the magnitude of drug and alcohol use among American youth.

Official Statistics

Table 13.2 presents the national distribution of juvenile arrests for drug and alcohol offenses for 1975 and 1984 by sex. The table shows a large decline in drug abuse arrests for both sexes. While drunk driving arrests have increased for males, they have soared over the decade for females. Liquor law violations have proportionately increased more for females than for males. Interestingly, arrests for drunkenness decreased for juveniles over the 1975–1984 period.

The national statistics would seem to indicate that juvenile arrests for drug violations have declined. Even the number of deaths attributed to drug use among teenagers shows a marked decrease over the past few years (Hindelang et al., *Sourcebook*, 1981: 325).

Unfortunately, official crime statistics are vulnerable to several criticisms. First, these figures show only those crimes that have come to the attention of the local authorities. Second, arrests represent the product of police work. If police are deployed in order to concentrate on other crimes, it is understandable that victimless offense arrests would decline. Third, it is possible that police make fewer arrests in these areas because the police

TABLE 13.1 Drugs of Abuse

Drugs	Often Prescribed Brand Names	Medical Uses	Dependence Potential – Physical	Dependence Potential – Psychological	Tolerance	Duration of Effects (hours)	Usual Methods of Administration	Possible Effects	Effects of Overdose	Withdrawal Syndrome
Narcotics										
Opium	Dover's Powder, Paregoric	Analgesic, antidiarrheal	High	High	Yes	3 to 6	Oral, smoked	Euphoria, drowsiness, respiratory depression, constricted pupils, nausea	Slow and shallow breathing, clammy skin, convulsions, coma, possible death	Watery eyes, runny nose, yawning, loss of appetite, irritability, tremors, panic, chills and sweating, cramps, nausea
Morphine	Morphine	Analgesic	High	High	Yes	3 to 6	Injected, smoked			
Codeine	Codeine	Analgesic, antitussive	Moderate	Moderate	Yes	3 to 6	Oral, injected			
Heroin	None	None	High	High	Yes	3 to 6	Injected, sniffed			
Meperidine (Pethidine)	Demerol, Pethadol	Analgesic	High	High	Yes	3 to 6	Oral, injected			
Methadone	Dolophine, Methadone, Methadose	Analgesic, heroin substitute	High	High	Yes	12 to 24	Oral, injected			
Other narcotics	Dilaudid, Leritine, Numorphan, Percodan	Analgesic, antidiarrheal, antitussive	High	High	Yes	3 to 6	Oral, injected			
Depressants										
Alcohol	None	None	High	High	Yes	Variable	Oral	Slurred speech, disorientation, drunken behavior without odor of alcohol	Shallow respiration, cold and clammy skin, dilated pupils, weak and rapid pulse, coma, possible death	Anxiety, insomnia, tremors, delirium, convulsions, possible death
Chloral hydrate	Noctec, Somnos	Hypnotic	Moderate	Moderate	Probable	5 to 8	Oral			
Barbiturates	Amytal, Butisol, Nembutal, Phenobarbital, Seconal, Tuinal	Anesthetic, anticonvulsant, sedation, sleep	High	High	Yes	1 to 16	Oral, injected			
Glutethimide	Doriden	Sedation, sleep	High	High	Yes	4 to 8	Oral			
Methaqualone	Optimil, Parest, Quaalude, Somnafac, Sopor	Sedation, sleep	High	High	Yes	4 to 8	Oral			
Tranquilizers	Equanil, Librium, Miltown, Serax, Tranxene, Valium	Anti-anxiety, muscle relaxant, sedation	Moderate	Moderate	Yes	4 to 8	Oral			
Other depressants	Clonopin, Dalmane, Dormate, Noludar, Placydil, Valmid	Anti-anxiety, sedation, sleep	Possible	Possible	Yes	4 to 8	Oral			

TABLE 13.1 Drugs of Abuse (Continued)

Drugs	Often Prescribed Brand Names	Medical Uses	Dependence Potential		Tolerance	Duration of Effects (hours)	Usual Methods of Administration	Possible Effects	Effects of Overdose	Withdrawal Syndrome
			Physical	Psychological						
Stimulants										
Cocaine†	Cocaine	Local anesthetic	Possible	High	Yes	2	Injected, sniffed	Increased alertness, excitation, euphoria, dilated pupils, increased pulse rate and blood pressure, insomnia, loss of appetite	Agitation, increase in body temperature, hallucinations, convulsions, possible death	Apathy, long periods of sleep, irritability, depression, disorientation
Amphetamines	Benzedrine, Biphetamine, Desoxyn, Dexedrine	Hyperkinesis, narcolepsy, weight control	Possible	High	Yes	2 to 4	Oral, injected			
Phenmetrazine	Preludin	Weight control	Possible	High	Yes	2 to 4	Oral			
Methylphenidate	Ritalin	Hyperkinesis	Possible	High	Yes	2 to 4	Oral			
Other stimulants	Bacarate, Cylert, Didrex, Ionamin, Plegine, Presate, Sanorex, Voranil	Weight control	Possible	Possible	Yes	2 to 4	Oral			
Hallucinogens										
LSD	None	None	None	Degree unknown	Yes	Variable	Oral	Illusions and hallucinations (with exception of MDA), poor perception of time and distance	Longer, more intense "trip" episodes, psychosis, possible death	Withdrawal syndrome not reported
Mescaline	None	None	None	Degree unknown	Yes	Variable	Oral, injected			
Psilocybin-Psilocyn	None	None	None	Degree unknown	Yes	Variable	Oral			
MDA	None	None	None	Degree unknown	Yes	Variable	Oral, injected, sniffed			
PCP‡	Sernylan	Veterinary anesthetic	None	Degree unknown	Yes	Variable	Oral, injected, smoked			
Other hallucinogens	None	None	None	Degree unknown	Yes	Variable	Oral, injected, sniffed			
Cannabis										
Marihuana	None	None	Degree unknown	Moderate	Yes	2 to 4	Oral, smoked	Euphoria, relaxed inhibitions, increased appetite, disoriented behavior	Fatigue, paranoia, possible psychosis	Insomnia, hyperactivity, and decreased appetite reported in a limited number of individuals
Hashish										
Hashish oil										

† Designated a narcotic under the Controlled Substances Act.
‡ Designated a depressant under the Controlled Substances Act.
Source: U.S. Department of Justice, Drug Enforcement Administration, *Drugs of Abuse* (Washington, D.C.: U.S. Government Printing Office, n.d.).

TABLE 13.2   **Juvenile Arrest Trends for Drug and Alcohol Offenses, United States, 1975–1984**

	Males under 18			Females under 18		
	1975	1984	% Change	1975	1984	% Change
Drug abuse	75,090	42,357	– 44	14,841	7,854	– 47
Driving under the influence	11,642	12,204	+ 5	1,000	1,990	+ 99
Liquor laws	63,344	57,592	– 11	16,680	20,443	+ 23
Drunkenness	26,811	14,197	– 47	4,041	2,784	– 31
Total	176,887	126,350	– 29	36,562	33,071	– 10

Source: Adapted from FBI (1985, p. 167).

themselves have a more liberal attitude toward substance abuse or because officers feel the juvenile justice system would not respond appropriately to those arrested. In any event, official statistics are not necessarily an accurate barometer of drug-related illegal activity. One way to double-check observations based on official data would be to examine self-reported drug and alcohol usage.

Self-Report Statistics

The limitations associated with official crime data have prompted criminologists to utilize alternative sources to check interpretations reached with official statistics. As you know from earlier discussions, self-reports, although subject to their own biases, constitute an important source of information.

Annual High School Surveys

Starting in 1975, Johnston and his colleagues began collecting a variety of self-report data from a cross-sectional random sample of high school seniors in the United States. Although the sample does not include individuals who have dropped out of school, the data do allow a comparative analysis of substance abuse over a time (Johnston et al., 1984: 32). The results of the annual survey for nine years appear in Table 13.3.

The figures in Table 13.3 indicate relative stability in high school seniors' use of these substances over the years. Not surprisingly, alcohol consumption leads the list. Unfortunately, these figures do not differentiate between such practices as drinking a glass of wine at the family Thanksgiving meal and drinking alcohol at a weekend party when adult supervision is absent. The table also shows that student use of marijuana rose from its reported low of 40 percent in 1975; it continued rising until 1979, when it peaked at 50 percent, and then began to decline in the 1980s. Similarly, there was a rise in the use of cocaine and other stimulants, and more recently a slight decline can be noted. PCP, a relative newcomer to the drug scene, is used less often, probably because of its relative lack of availability. In summary, the more recent trends seem to suggest an overall decline for most drugs.

National Survey on Drug Abuse

Every year researchers (see Fishburne et al., 1981; Miller et al., 1982) conduct a national random sample of adults (26 years of age and older), young adults (18 to 25 years old), and youth (ages 12 through 17) to determine the prevalence of drug use in the United States. The use of comparative age groups allows more sense to be made of observed changes. As Table 13.4 shows, marijuana consumption has recently decreased for the 12–17 age group and for the 18–25 age group, but increased for the 26+ group. However, the largest user group is the 18–25 age category. Use of cocaine, hallucinogens, inhalants, and stimulants is relatively constant and is significantly lower for juveniles than for young adults. The young adult group (ages 18–25) reported the largest usage. According to Table 13.4, heroin is

TABLE 13.3   Trends in Annual Prevalence of Sixteen Types of Drugs

	Percent Who Used in Last Twelve Months									1982–1983 Change
	Class of 1975	Class of 1976	Class of 1977	Class of 1978	Class of 1979	Class of 1980	Class of 1981	Class of 1982	Class of 1983	
Approx. N =	(9,400)	(15,400)	(17,100)	(17,800)	(15,500)	(15,900)	(17,500)	(17,700)	(16,300)	
Marijuana/hashish	40.0	44.5	47.6	50.2	50.8	48.8	46.1	44.3	42.3	-2.0
Inhalants*	NA	3.0	3.7	4.1	5.4	4.6	4.1	4.5	4.3	-0.2
Inhalants Adjusted†	NA	NA	NA	NA	9.2	7.8	6.0	6.6	6.7	+0.1
Amyl & Butyl Nitrites‡	NA	NA	NA	NA	6.5	5.7	3.7	3.6	3.6	0.0
Hallucinogens	11.2	9.4	8.8	9.6	9.9	9.3	9.0	8.1	7.3	-0.8
Hallucinogens Adjusted**	NA	NA	NA	NA	12.8	10.6	10.1	9.3	9.3	0.0
LSD	7.2	6.4	5.5	6.3	6.6	6.5	6.5	6.1	5.4	-0.7
PCP‡	NA	NA	NA	NA	7.0	4.4	3.2	2.2	2.6	+0.4
Cocaine	5.6	6.0	7.2	9.0	12.0	12.3	12.4	11.5	11.4	-0.1
Heroin	1.0	0.8	0.8	0.8	0.5	0.5	0.5	0.6	0.6	0.0
Other opiates§	5.7	5.7	6.4	6.0	6.2	6.3	5.9	5.3	5.1	-0.2
Stimulants§	16.2	15.8	16.3	17.1	18.3	20.8	26.0	26.1	24.6	-1.5
Stimulants Adjusted§,§§	NA	NA	NA	NA	NA	NA	NA	20.3	17.9	-2.4ss
Sedatives§	11.7	10.7	10.8	9.9	9.9	10.3	10.5	9.1	7.9	-1.2s
Barbiturates§	10.7	9.6	9.3	8.1	7.5	6.8	6.6	5.5	5.2	-0.3
Methaqualone§	5.1	4.7	5.2	4.9	5.9	7.2	7.6	6.8	5.4	-1.4ss
Tranquilizers§	10.6	10.3	10.8	9.9	9.6	8.7	8.0	7.0	6.9	-0.1
Alcohol	84.8	85.7	87.0	87.7	88.1	87.9	87.0	86.8	87.3	+0.5
Cigarettes	NA	NA	NA	NA	NA	NA	NA	NA	NA	NA

Note: Level of significance of difference between the two most recent classes: s = .05, ss = .01. NA indicates data not available.
* Data based on four questionnaire forms. N is four-fifths of N indicated.
† Adjusted for underreporting of amyl and butyl nitrites.
‡ Data based on a single questionnaire form. N is one-fifth of N indicated.
** Adjusted for underreporting of PCP.
§ Only drug use which was not under a doctor's orders is included here.
§§ Adjusted for overreporting of the nonprescription stimulants. Data based on three questionnaire forms. N is three-fifths of N indicated.
Source: Johnston et al., 1984: 32.

TABLE 13.4 Reported Drug Use among Age Groups by Type of Drug, United States, 1972–1982

	1972		1974		1976		1977		1979		1982	
		N		N		N		N		N		N
Marijuana												
Age 26+	7%	(1,613)	10%	(2,221)	13%	(1,708)	15%	(1,822)	20%	(3,015)	23%	(2,760)
Age 18–25	48	(772)	53	(849)	53	(882)	60	(1,500)	68	(2,044)	64	(1,283)
Age 12–17	14	(880)	23	(952)	22	(996)	28	(1,272)	31	(2,165)	26	(1,581)
Inhalants												
Age 26+	—		1		2		2		4		—	
Age 18–25	—		9		9		11		17		—	
Age 12–17	6		9		8		9		10		—	
Hallucinogens												
Age 26+	—		1		2		3		5		6	
Age 18–25	—		17		17		20		25		21	
Age 12–17	5		6		5		5		7		5	
Cocaine												
Age 26+	2		1		2		3		4		9	
Age 18–25	9		13		13		19		28		28	
Age 12–17	2		4		3		4		5		7	
Heroin												
Age 26+	—		1		1		1		1		1	
Age 18–25	5		5		4		4		4		1	
Age 12–17	1		1		1		1		1		*	
Stimulants												
Age 26+	3		3		6		5		6		6	
Age 18–25	12		17		17		21		18		18	
Age 12–17	4		5		4		5		3		8	
Alcohol												
Age 26+	—		73		75		78		92		88	
Age 18–25	—		82		84		84		95		94	
Age 12–17	—		54		54		53		70		65	

— = Not available.
* = Less than 0.5%.
N = Sample size.
Source: Adapted from Brown, Flanagan, and McLeod, 1983: 362–363.

rarely used by any age group, and alcohol is the leader of all substances by far. Interestingly, all three age groups showed a leap in alcohol consumption between 1977 and 1979, although even these trends seem to be tapering off.

The National Youth Survey is another example of a major self-report study based on a nationally drawn sample of youth aged 11 to 17 in the United States (Gold and Reimer, 1975; Elliot and Huizinga, 1983). While there was some respondent attrition over the years, the samples remained largely intact during the study periods. Gold and Reimer's (1975) analysis of drug use responses showed a large and dramatic rise for both males and females surveyed between 1967 and 1972. Continuing this line of inquiry by analyzing the 1976–1980 National Youth Survey data, Elliott and Huizinga (1983) also noted a rising trend. Generally these results conform to the other data sources for corresponding years which we have discussed above. Reports for the 1980s which are now available are showing a decline. It will be interesting to see if the National Youth Survey covering the late 1980s confirms these results.

DRUG ABUSE AND DELINQUENCY

Sociologists and criminologists have been particularly interested in the consequences of drug *abuse* vs. drug *use* in the younger segments of the population. Although drug abuse is a problem in all age groups, drug use, with the exception of illicit drugs, is primarily a problem for the young.

Use of any drug whose possession or sale is prohibited by law or possession or sale of drugs that may be legally prescribed in violation of regulatory statutes governing their sale and distribution is a crime. A young person who possesses or sells a drug illegally has committed a delinquent act and may be arrested and adjudicated a delinquent by the juvenile court. Any person who buys or possesses alcohol before attaining the minimum age set by the laws of the particular state has committed a status offense. Alcohol purchase or consumption is a status offense because it is not illegal for adults to buy or drink alcohol, but it is illegal for juveniles to engage in these behaviors. Illegal use of other drugs by young people is not, however, a status offense because an adult who illegally uses these other drugs is committing a criminal act.

Most young people are never apprehended for drug violations. Several self-report studies indicate that 80 to 90 percent of high school students have illegally used one or more drugs (Beschner and Friedman, 1979). The majority of young people, therefore, are candidates for adjudication as delinquents because they have broken drug laws.

The relationship of drug delinquency to other forms of delinquency has also been explored in numerous studies. Some criminologists have argued that drug use can lead to other forms of delinquency. Drug abuse and especially addiction have been hypothesized as being related to criminal behavior. One assumption has been that the drug addict must steal to support his or her habit. It has also been argued that addicts commit crimes to experience the thrill of stealing. Somewhat like the measles or chicken pox, addiction is thought to spread when student addicts draw criminals

(drug sellers) to the school. Sellers are usually recruited from among the students and are themselves users. Of course, the students who use drugs become delinquent when they obtain the drugs.

The 1967 President's Commission Task Force Report on Narcotics and Drug Abuse asserted that "a state of addiction cannot be maintained without running afoul of the criminal law. On the contrary, the involvement of the addict with the police is almost inevitable" (p. 10). According to the 1967 report, most crimes by addicts are "fundraising" activities. Some have reasoned that males may resort to property crimes and females to prostitution to obtain money for drugs. Another argument linking the effects of drugs to crime is formulated on a pharmacological basis—that violent aggressiveness is caused by certain drugs through the relaxation of normal inhibitions.

The opposite position, that delinquency or criminal behavior leads to drug use, has also been considered by some researchers. This view suggests that delinquent activities and associates provide circumstances and exert pressures to try drugs. What this theory suggests is that in the cases where a drug-delinquency connection exists, the delinquency usually precedes any drug use.

Finally, there are researchers who claim that no causal relationships can be posited between drugs and delinquency. Both drugs and delinquency encompass a vast array of behaviors as well as sociocultural meanings. A search for more general associative concepts such as deviance or certain cultural patterns is usually the focus of this type of orientation.

Let us now look at some of the research that has been done to test the various hypotheses or theories. These hypotheses, among others, have been the subject of several national self-report surveys (Huizinga and Elliott, 1981; Brennan, Elliott, and Knowles, 1981). The general findings of the inventories imply that most adolescents have either "no involvement in delinquent behavior or have no involvement in drug use," suggesting that in the majority of cases drug use is not associated with delinquency (Huizinga and Elliott, 1981: vii). However, among those cases where both behaviors are manifest, there appears to be an "association between drug use patterns ordered by the frequency and number of drugs used and various types of problem behaviors, delinquency, and measures of bonding to conventional groups' norms and activities" (Brennan, Elliott, and Knowles, 1981: iv).

Similarly, Huizinga and Elliot (1981) conclude:

> Among youth who both use drugs and are engaged in delinquent behavior, the levels of delinquency are lowest among alcohol users, higher among alcohol and marijuana users, and highest among users of alcohol, marijuana, and other drugs. (p. vii)

These researchers also found that for those who are involved in both delinquency (especially minor offenses) and drug use, the delinquency usually preceded drug use (p. vii).

These longitudinal studies suggest, however, that any global generalizations regarding the drug use-delinquency relationship remain problematic. Different temporal orderings pertaining to each type of behavior (drug use and delinquency) severely complicate the causal relationships. Consistent with previous research, the National Youth Survey on drug use and delinquency concludes:

> Strong evidence for any of the three explanatory hypotheses (drug use leads to delinquency, delinquency leads to drug use, or both are dependent on pre-existing deviant orientations) is not contained in the analyses provided. . . . Global generalizations about the drug use/delinquency relationships within the youth population are likely to be inaccurate. (Huizinga and Elliot, 1981: viii)

A variety of other types of studies, including those which are drug-specific (marijuana and delinquency; barbiturates and delinquency) have been conducted over the years. A general review of some of this literature follows. Some apparent inconsistencies may be noted in the findings, reflecting the difficulty we experience in trying to generalize from the results of different data sources. Conclusions vary according to the goals of the research, the type of sample drawn, the time periods studied, and the way terms are defined. Let us now review the findings on the relationship between specific drugs and delinquency.

Marijuana use, as has been noted, is associated with the category of behavior we call criminal because the marijuana user has automatically committed a delinquent or criminal act. People sometimes smoke marijuana before committing planned illegal acts to relax and reduce fear; but in general marijuana use is "believed to reduce the inclination of the individual toward physical tasks, particularly those requiring sustained effort." Further, "marijuana is believed to act as a deterrent to those criminal acts which require continuing physical effort and concentration" (National Commission on Marijuana and Drug Abuse, 1973: 158).

Barbiturate users are also unlikely to be involved in criminal activities, particularly when doses are low. High doses may, on the other hand, "cause irritability and unpredictably violent behavior in some individuals" (National Commission on Marijuana and Drug Abuse, 1973: 159). The other side of the "ups" and "downs" cycle is the amphetamine. Amphetamine users are more likely than nonusers to be involved in violent crime, but whether amphetamine use actually *causes* criminal behavior is unknown. Support for the position that amphetamine use contributes to violent tendencies is found in Japanese experience in the 1950s, when amphetamines were widely used and the normally low rate of violent crime among the Japanese skyrocketed.

The connection between consumption of alcohol and involvement in criminal activities is much more certain. At least half of homicides and other assaultive offenses are committed by individuals who are under the influence of alcohol. Most often, violence occurs when family and friends are drinking together. This pattern holds true for youth as well as adults. Among schoolchildren, drinking also relates to poor grades and work records and excessive fighting (National Commission on Marijuana and Drug Abuse, 1973).

Relationships between drug use and delinquency were recently explored in a study of drug use called "Drugs and American Youth." Data on youth backgrounds and characteristics were collected in 1968, 1969, 1970, and 1974. Included in the study was the collection of information on self-reported drug use and other delinquency. Both property and violent theft-vandalism offenses were discovered to be higher among serious drug users. In 1974 there was little difference in aggression among marijuana abstainers and marijuana users. Marijuana smokers were more likely than abstainers to engage in property crimes, but marijuana users committed property crimes far less often than users of other illicit drugs (Johnston et al., 1978). Johnston, O'Malley, and Eveland (1976) also found no evidence of an association between marijuana use and increased delinquency. On the contrary, the delinquency patterns of marijuana users paralleled those of abstainers when followed over time.

Another study, the National Youth Polydrug Study (1976–1977), collected data on a sample of 2,750 adolescents in drug abuse treatment programs and also found that adolescents who have used drugs were more likely to report involvement in private property offenses than adolescents who have not used these substances. A greater number of arrests for property offenses occurred among youth who engaged in serious drug use (heroin, cocaine, hallucinogens) than among youth who used only marijuana (Leukefeld and Clayton, 1979).

The overall conclusion reached in the Drugs and American Youth Study was that

> nonaddictive use of illicit drugs does not seem to play much of a role in leading users to become . . . more delinquent. . . . The reverse kind of causation seems considerably more plausible, that is, that delinquency leads to drug use. For example, . . . it is quite possible that delinquents who, because of their delinquency, became part of a deviant peer group are more likely to become drug users because drug use is likely to be an approved behavior in such a peer group. (Johnston et al., 1978: 155–156)

Although impressive, the Drugs and American Youth study has limited generalizability because it

involved an analysis of confirmed drug abusers. Given the pervasiveness of marijuana consumption by American youth, it would be expedient to focus on the marijuana-delinquency connection. Thornton (1981) did just that. Utilizing self-report data from a sample of high school students, Thornton found that smoking marijuana within the past year correlated positively with status offenses, property crime involvement (burglary and larceny), as well as with aggressive delinquency (battery, weapons offenses, and robbery). However, further specification altered the findings somewhat. When other common correlates of delinquent activity were examined (age, sex, education), marijuana use retained its primacy only for property offenses.

While results like these are commonly thought to lend credence to the "crime to support a drug habit" position, other studies (Jacquith, 1981) suggest that one's social relationships influence use patterns. Consequently, the question remains as to whether marijuana use is a cause or an effect of various processes involved in causing delinquency.

As hinted earlier, three possible explanations exist for the substance abuse and delinquent behavior relationship. First, there is the causal order implying that drug use causes delinquency. Second, an equally feasible explanation is that delinquency involvement produces drug use. The final model is that delinquency and drug abuse are similar activities produced by similar processes. Although this line of questioning has garnered criminological interest (Weissman and DuPont, 1982; Inciardi, 1981), the issue is still not resolved. Huizinga and Elliott (1981), who analyzed responses from the 1977–1979 National Youth Surveys, found that most of the juveniles had no involvement in either delinquency or substance abuse. For those youth who indicated involvement in both delinquency and substance abuse, delinquency generally preceded alcohol and marijuana involvement.

A more intensive analysis of the 1979 National Youth Survey data, however, suggested that chronic delinquents were responsible for a disproportionate amount of illegal activity (Johnston et al., 1984). These youth registered heavy drug involvement.

Thus, it would appear that the drug-delinquency connection is a relevant issue mainly for a handful of delinquent offenders. Moreover, this small number of individuals is responsible for an overwhelming number of offenses. It would seem, then, that the drug-delinquency causal connection is of paramount importance when dealing with chronic delinquents, but not for delinquent youth in general.

Researchers do acknowledge a pressing need for more incisive research in the area of drugs and delinquent behavior. Clayton and Tuchfeld (1982), for example, propose a fourfold agenda for future research. First, there is a need for research focusing on careers in drugs and crime. Little is known about development stages of "drug using criminals and criminal drug users" (p. 161). Second, we need a better understanding of the economics underlying drug user life styles. As Clayton and Tuchfeld (1982: 161) point out, "Little is known about how much money addicts and criminals have, the sources from which money is obtained, and how decisions are made about the expenditure of money." A third area of concentration concerns drug use and delinquency. While many studies concentrate on the addict, not enough attention has been paid to the relationship of drugs to delinquency progression, both in terms of volume and seriousness of offenses. Finally, there is a need to examine multiple drug use and crime. Heavy users generally do not confine their appetite to one type of drug. Researchers need to determine the types of drug mixes that are used and the kinds of impact these mixes have, particularly with respect to aggressive and predatory crimes.

REASONS FOR DRUG ABUSE

The reasons adolescents abuse drugs are no easier to understand than the reasons for other problems of adolescence. In a national drug abuse survey, 13- to 17-year-olds commented about why they used drugs: "What else is there to do?" "It makes you feel you're in another world." "It doesn't hurt you and it feels good, so why not?" "People

are funnier and get along better stoned." "I like it; I'm funny and can really talk." "Nothing bothers me when I'm stoned." "When I'm stoned, I can't think about the things that bring me down; I'm somewhere else, where there's no bring-downs, like my family." "It's easier to make friends getting stoned" (Beschner and Friedman, 1979: 8). Statements such as these show some of the reasons adolescents give for using drugs. Some youth obviously use drugs, especially alcohol and marijuana, for pleasurable effects. These drugs are often used in a group setting among friends and peers. Youth may also use drugs, such as barbiturates and amphetamines, to cope with family problems or to escape from the tensions and anxieties of adolescence. Psychedelic drugs are sometimes taken in an effort to expand awareness.

Adolescent drug use patterns are constantly changing. These changes are affected not only by the availability of various substances at a given time, but also by the patterns and habits of drug use that become popular among various groups of young people.

Normal Drug Use

Although there is controversy about the reasons adolescents use drugs, one fact is inescapable: Nationally, the United States is a drug-oriented society. It is therefore quite logical to find that the young people of this country use drugs. The journalists Allen Geller and Maxwell Boas succinctly argued this point in 1969:

Today's teenagers entered a world in which mood-changing substances were in existence; sleeping pills, stimulants, tranquilizers, depressants and many other varieties of mind-altering chemical compounds had long been absorbed into the nation's pharmacopoeia, and [popping] pills, swallowing capsules, and downing tablets were a national habit. Our youngsters' indulgence in drugs can hardly be blamed on some sinister outside influence; they witnessed firsthand the tranquilizer-amphetamine-barbiturate boom of the fifties as their parents took eagerly to psychic delights. They grew up regarding chemicals as tools to be used to manipulate the inner mind. Some youngsters were even recipients of these drugs; until the dangers were clearly delineated, it was not uncommon for parents to dose their children with half a barbiturate tablet so that they would be sure to go to sleep. (p. xvi)

This description of adolescents raised in the 1950s applies also to children raised in the 1970s and 1980s. The United States has been and is a nation of pill takers. Modern medicine has made the use of drugs highly legitimate, "as something to be taken casually and not only during moments of acute and certified distress" (Simon and Gagnon, 1968: 60). Children who use drugs, "far from being in revolt against an older generation, may in fact be acknowledging how influential a model that generation was" (p. 60).

The drug industry in particular has been a motivating force in spreading the idea that drugs can solve all sorts of problems. First, companies have pushed the use of drugs through professional advertisements to physicians. The companies have urged doctors to treat every conceivable physical and psychological problem through drug prescriptions. Many of these drugs are beneficial and save lives. The widespread prescribing of other drugs, especially the psychoactive drugs that are used to help individuals cope with life problems ranging from depression to anxiety, has been questioned. Many drugs are absolutely useless; see Wolfe and Coley's *Pills That Don't Work* (1981). According to psychologist Henry Lennard and his colleagues, the drug industry has not limited its market to adults:

[A] journal has an advertisement that advises a physician on how he can help deal with such everyday anxieties of childhood as school and dental visits. This advertisement, in the *American Journal of Diseases of Children*, portrays a tearful little girl, and in large type appear the words: "School, the dark, separation, dental visits, 'monsters.' " On the subsequent page the physician is told in bold print that "The everyday anxieties of childhood sometimes get out of

hand." In small print below he reads that "A child can usually deal with his anxieties. But sometimes the anxieties overpower the child. Then, he needs your help. Your help may include Vistaril (hydroxyzine pamoate)" [a drug that relieves anxiety and tension]. (Lennard, Epstein, Berstein, and Ransom, 1970: 438)

The drug industry also contributes to the drug abuse problem by advertising directly to the public hundreds of drugs that can be bought without prescription. The advertisement of common drugs such as aspirin, cold capsules, cough medicines, and the like promotes the idea that problems can be solved by taking drugs. The drug companies have fostered the view that for every ailment there is a remedy waiting at the local drugstore or supermarket (Seidenberg, 1976).

Thus, young people in the United States are raised in a social setting where drug taking is considered natural and normal. Given the prevalent advertisement and use of drugs, it is not surprising to find that youth turn to drugs for what they consider recreation. Drugs are used to alleviate boredom, provide excitement, and ease fears about social interaction—just as they are used to relieve headaches, coughs, and colds.

Youth Drug Subculture

Drug use among young people has often been attributed to the youth subculture. A **subculture** is a distinctive pattern of norms, beliefs, attitudes, and values that characterizes a certain group. Although not all adolescents adhere to the beliefs and values of the youth subculture, including attitudes about drug use, sociological researchers have found that many young people do have similar values, especially about the use of drugs. According to sociologists, a "subculture owes its existence to the fact that it provides a solution to certain problems of adjustment shared among a community of individuals" (O'Donnell, 1966: 73). Sociologists view drug use by members of the youth subculture as part of a solution for the various problems of maturing.

Marijuana in particular became a favored drug of the youth subculture in the 1960s, a decade strongly affected by revolt. In 1980 marijuana use and other drug consumption remained an integral part of the youth subculture. Some of the same functions fulfilled by drug use in the 1960s are still fulfilled by the drug use in the 1980s. One function of drug taking has been called the *ritual of rebellion* (Dobkin de Rios and Smith, 1977: 271). The ritual of rebellion is behavior that contradicts society's usual or socially acceptable behavior forms. Drug taking is one of these rebellious behaviors. Note Dobkin de Rios and Smith:

> Whether intended or not, such [drug-taking] rituals may serve the ultimate stability of a society by providing an outlet for chronically frustrated impulses. In stratified societies through the world, underground use of . . . stimulants and psychedelics may be a way in which such rebellion is manifested. Youthful chugalugging of alcohol in large quantities in a group setting may be yet another example. The emergence of drug-culture language may in part be motivated by the illegality of the particular drug practice. It reaffirms the rebelliousness of the subgroup, and provides a value on things and acts which are in keeping with the values of the practitioners of the ritual, particularly when the values are different from those held by the dominant society. (p. 271)

When examined from this perspective adolescent drug taking serves as a tension release form of expression through rebellion.

Similarly, drug use rituals among the young fulfill the functions of offering support and understanding from peers. The motivation for drug use in many cases is the desire for social acceptance, intimacy, or status (Fadely and Hosler, 1979). It is often through peer groups that adolescents are introduced to drugs and within peer groups that they are likely to participate in drug-taking activities.

Deviant Drug Subculture

The youth subculture we have previously discussed is composed primarily of middle class adolescents who use drugs as one aspect of their life style. Although some of these adolescents may acquire serious drug problems and all of them are breaking the law by their use of illegal drugs, these members of the youth subculture stand in contrast to members of deviant subcultures for whom drug consumption becomes a way of life. In these deviant subcultures, often found in urban ghettos, serious criminal acts may be committed to maintain habits, especially heroin habits.

Sociologists have at one time or another attributed almost every social ill to urban ghetto residents, who are often minority group members. To some degree, sociologists have exaggerated the ills of ghetto life. There is, however, some evidence that youth living in ghetto areas experience social conditions that contribute to serious drug problems and other criminal activities. In a study of heroin users in a large metropolitan area, sociologist Leroy Gould and his associates obtained the following statement from a street-wise youth:

> My father never lived with my mother, but he used to come by to visit me and my mother. I especially remember one time—I guess I was eleven or twelve—when he took me aside and told me, "It looks like you're growing up and maybe you need some spending money." So he took out his wallet and gave me all the money in it—two dollars. My older brother was dealing shit [selling heroin] and stepping fast—and he used to give me twenty dollars just to shine his shoes. It didn't take many smarts to figure out where the action was. (Gould, Walker, Crane, and Liz, 1974: 23–24)

From an early age, this adolescent associated heroin with a fast, good life. In the ghetto, use of drugs, including heroin, may be socially acceptable behavior. Further, there may be pressures on ghetto adolescents, especially males, to live up to certain ideals: "toughness, strength, daring, and the willingness to challenge the bleak fate of being poor" (Feldman, 1968: 132–133). The achievement of these ideals brings prestige and good reputations. Adolescents who do not attempt to achieve these ideals may find themselves ranked very low in the ghetto status hierarchy (C. Brown, 1965; Feldman, 1968; Smith and Gay, 1972).

As a drug user becomes physically addicted to a drug, he or she usually becomes more involved with the deviant drug subculture. His or her closest associations are with other users who share a preoccupation with drugs. Most activity and conversation center on the drug habit. The more mundane aspects of life, such as eating or sleeping, become secondary to obtaining a drug supply. The addict's involvement in the drug subculture makes it extremely difficult to "kick" the drug habit. Those who stop using a drug, either voluntarily or involuntarily, stand a poor chance of remaining drug-free if they return to their old environment. But since this is usually the only world the individual has known, he or she may have no other place to go after the habit is "kicked" (Lindesmith, 1968).

CHARACTERISTICS OF DRUG ABUSERS

Social scientists have attempted to discover the social and psychological characteristics of young drug abusers. It is, however, difficult to accurately collect data about adolescents who engage in drug consumption because drug abuse is an illegal and primarily secret activity. Despite this obstacle, researchers have provided information on the characteristics of young people who abuse drugs. These characteristics include the age, sex, race, and social class of young drug abusers (Beschner and Friedman, 1979; J. Green, 1979).

Age

Drug abuse increases with the age of the adolescent. Relatively few 12- to 13-year-olds are regular users of drugs. Regular use is much more common among 14- to 18-year-olds. In a national drug study conducted in 1976, Abelson and Fishburne reported that drug use peaks in the early twenties. There is also evidence that as adolescents get older, there

is a greater probability that they will engage in simultaneous use or several different drugs.

Sociologists have offered explanations for the increase in drug abuse as young people get older. Drugs may become more available to older adolescents, and decreasing parental supervision may afford more opportunities to use drugs. Parent-child conflict is a common experience as adolescents get older, and use of drugs may be one way young people attempt to deal with these problems. Similarly, peer pressure to use drugs may become greater as the child gets older.

Sex

Until the 1970s, most research indicated that males were more likely than females to abuse drugs. In the 1970s researchers began to find increased drug abuse among females and less difference in rates for male and female drug abuse. Males, however, were still more likely to become involved in extended and serious types of drug abuse, such as alcoholism and heroin addiction (J. Green, 1979; Rosenberg, Kasl, and Berberian, 1974; Smart, Fejer, and White, 1970).

Race

Very few studies that focused on the race of young drug abusers considered the possible influence of social class or peer groups on the relationship between race and drug abuse. As a result, the findings of most studies are unreliable (J. Green, 1979).

Until the past two decades, researchers tended to find more drug abuse among white than among black youth. In the past two decades, researchers have found similarities in the patterns of drug use of black and white youth. O'Donnell, Voss, Clayton, Slaton, and Room (1976) reported that 51 percent of the black males they studied and 49 percent of the white males had used marijuana. This finding was corroborated by Abelson and Fishburne (1976) in their national drug survey. They reported no overall differences in past or present use of marijuana between white and black juveniles.

Differences have been reported in several studies of alcohol use among white and black adolescents. The data collected in these studies suggest that a greater number of young whites engaged in alcohol consumption (Blacker, Demone, and Freeman, 1965; Globetti, 1967; Short, Tennyson, and Howard, 1963).

Social Class

Studies of adolescent drug abuse among different social classes have reported contradictory findings. Part of this controversy may be the result of different measures of social class employed in different studies.

Some researchers have concluded that people from the lower social classes, especially males, are more likely to drink heavily than are people from the middle or upper classes. Other researchers have discovered that young drug users are most typically upper or middle class. Higgins et al. (1977) found few differences in the frequency of drinking alcohol among male and female black teenagers from the upper, middle, and lower classes. Like black males and females, white males from all three social classes tended to drink similar amounts of alcohol. But upper class white females differed, tending to drink more frequently than either middle or lower class white females.

A. Y. Cohen and Santo (1979), analyzing data from the National Polydrug Study, concluded that when social class was measured by parental educational attainment, which is one indicator, middle class teenagers used a wider variety of drugs than lower class teenagers. The researchers speculated that the greater affluence of middle class young people allowed them access to a wider variety of drugs. With one exception, no differences were found in frequency of drug abuse among young people from different social classes. Youth from lower class families, however, indicated more frequent use of inhalants. Some researchers have argued that youth from poverty environments prefer drugs that dull the senses, such as opiates, barbiturates, and inhalants; upper and middle class youth prefer drugs that intensify experiences, such

as marijuana, stimulants, and hallucinogens. This hypothesis, however, was not confirmed by the data analyzed by Cohen and Santo.

SOCIETAL REACTION TO SUBSTANCE ABUSE

Social scientists, law enforcement personnel, and the general public agree that something should be done to prevent and to correct substance abuse among the young. Some experts hold the position that substance abuse is a purely medical problem which requires treatment. Others argue that the criminal justice system should impose harsh penalties to punish and deter abuse and institute policies that would prevent drugs from being available to those who abuse them.

Control of Drug Abuse

The 1967 President's Commission Task Force Report on Narcotics and Drug Abuse asserted: "Since early in the century we have built our drug control policies around the twin judgements that drug abuse was an evil to be suppressed and that this could most effectively be done by the application of criminal enforcement and penal sanctions" (p. 11). Control efforts include agencies that attempt to reduce the amounts of drugs available for illicit use. The agencies, the Food and Drug Administration and the Drug Enforcement Administration, oversee the administration of the Controlled Substances Act (CSA), a federal law that took effect in 1971.

The CSA divides drugs into five categories based on the drugs' potential for and actual abuse, extent of medical knowledge about effects, the significance and scope of abuse, and dependency potential. To regulate the flow of drugs to illegal markets, the Controlled Substances Act imposes controls on the manufacture, sale, and use of drugs through registration of drug handlers; recordkeeping requirements; quotas on amounts manufactured; restrictions on dispensing, distribution, and imports and exports; conditions for storage; reports of transactions to the government; and criminal penalties for trafficking (U.S. Department of Justice, Drug Enforcement Administration, 1976).

The CSA affects youth drug abuse by controlling the supply of drugs available to young users. The penalties portion of the act applies only to adults. Young people arrested for drug offenses are subject to juvenile court. According to two drug researchers, one group of juvenile justice personnel holds the position that drug-abusing youth "are 'rotten kids' and represent that proportion of every birth cohort that one might expect to make 'trouble' for the system, those who have already jumped on a treadmill of failure" (Leukefeld and Clayton, 1979: 225–226). They advocate punishing juvenile abusers in institutions or "treating these youths as if they were adults under the law. They say that the most appropriate response to illegal and deviant behavior is swift and certain punishment" (p. 226).

The "penalty" approach is criticized by those who point out that the use of drugs is not a "rational, albeit illegal business venture in which risks of prosecution become part of the business calculation. More often than not, drug abuse is the result of mental instability, group pressure, or unwise adolescent curiosity" (Haislip, 1970: 13–14). If these are the major reasons for drug abuse, it is not surprising to find that penalties do not deter. Other sociologists point out that addicts and users bear the brunt of the penalties, but international and interstate traffickers go unapprehended or unpunished (Haislip, 1970; President's Commission, 1967c). The most important criticism, however, is that attempts to control drug abuse through law enforcement have failed. Pointing out the limits of law enforcement, Schroeder (1975) has written:

> The tragic error is to believe that law enforcement alone can do the job. The "get tough" mentality . . . appears to be counterproductive. It doesn't work, and if it did, it would have drastic results. A decline in the heroin supply, it has been amply demonstrated, leads to a marked increase in the taking of other drugs. (pp. 173–174)

A further indictment of the penalties and enforcement approach to handling drug users is found in the experience of New York, where a harsh state law was passed in 1973. Based on the new law, penalties for narcotics and many other drug-related offenses were severe and mandatory. Several years after the law was enacted, an evaluation of its effects was conducted. It was reported that heroin use did not decline from 1973 to 1976 and that the pattern of use in New York City, which has a large heroin-using population, resembled the pattern in other major cities out of state. There was an immediate deterrent effect when the law went into operation, but a reduction in the use of heroin was not sustained. By 1974, in fact, use had actually climbed.

The law also appeared to fail to "deter prior felony offenders from committing additional crimes" (Joint Committee on New York Drug Law Evaluation, 1978: 9). According to the researchers, the new law did not increase the fear of apprehension because there was only a low risk of arrest and conviction after indictments declined. Prison terms, on the other hand, became more likely and were generally lengthened. After the new law, the New York City courts experienced backlogs in drug cases and long court delays. Consequently, "the risk of imprisonment was lower after the 1973 revision than it had been before the law was enacted" (Joint Committee, 1978: 22). Thus, controlling drugs appears to be a very difficult task indeed.

Treatment of Drug Abuse

The limited success of the punishment approach to drug abuse is frequently brought up by those who hold the opinion that the drug user is "sick" in a medical sense and in need of a "cure." Often, the young person who is apprehended for drug use is thought to need counseling and social services rather than punishment. The adolescent user is a particularly likely candidate for "treatment," since the juvenile justice system is supposedly based on a treatment, not a punishment, philosophy. The youthful drug offender may be diverted from the juvenile justice system to treatment programs and services. Diversionary programs will be discussed fully in Chapter 17; here our interest is in basic methods of "cure" thought appropriate for drug users.

Three researchers conducted an extensive study of drug treatment programs for adolescents in the United States. They found that "only a small percentage of youths get into federally supported treatment programs compared with the percentage of adults in these programs" (Smith, Levy, and Striar, 1979: 538). Of the 224,959 people in federally funded drug treatment programs in 1975, only 12.3 percent were people under the age of 18. Most of these youths were treated in outpatient rather than residential settings. Very few young people received methadone maintenance treatment, a form of treatment in which heroin addicts are given methadone to ease their withdrawal from heroin. Because methadone maintenance programs substitute dependence on methadone for dependence on heroin, the federal government has been reluctant to recommend youth for methadone programs. Much more commonly, young drug abusers are referred by police and court personnel to counseling services. Four types of counseling programs predominate: individual, group, family, and peer counseling.

Many types of individual counseling approaches have attempted to "cure" the young drug abuser. According to the drug treatment survey done by Smith, Levy, and Striar, "These approaches include the traditional psychoanalytically oriented 'intensive' or 'deep' interpretive psychotherapy, as well as the nondirective and reflective; the informational, instructional and problem-solving; the behavior modifying; the active-supportive; the reality oriented; the environmental manipulative; authoritative-persuasive; confrontative," and so on (Smith, Levy, and Striar, 1979: 541). Generally, in all these therapies the counselor tries to establish a relationship of trust with the young person. It is often difficult to establish trust and rapport between the counselor and young person because the young person does not consider drug use, especially marijuana use, to be a "problem." The only reason the young person submits to counseling in many cases is the pressure of parents, police, or court workers. The effectiveness of the various forms of individual counseling has not been tested.

Another type of counseling offered to young drug users is group counseling. Group counselors believe that "many young drug clients are more likely to be influenced by group pressure and peer influence than through a one-to-one relationship with an adult" (p. 542). The thought is that the drug abuser not only "receives support and guidance from others with similar problems," but can "help others as well, thereby improving his or her self-image" (p. 543). There are many different varieties of group counseling, including informational, problem-solving, guided group interaction, confrontational, encounter, role-playing, and so on. Group counseling programs, like individual counseling programs, have rarely been evaluated.

Family counseling has also been used to treat young drug abusers. The idea is to work with the entire family, because most youth "live emotionally, socially, and economically as part of their families" (p. 545). Often, however, the family members of young drug abusers are unwilling to participate in this type of counseling, preferring instead to turn the youth over to treament agencies. This form of counseling, however, may be most appropriate when family members can be persuaded to participate and when family conflict appears to be contributing to the drug abuse.

Peer counseling is another way young drug abusers have been treated. Peer counselors are generally ex-addicts and nonprofessionals of the same ethnic, racial, cultural, and social backgrounds as the drug-abusing youth. Supporters of these programs believe that these untrained counselors may be able to help those who distrust professionals.

Other treatment programs have used vocational training, work programs, educational services, residential homes, medical clinics, and school programs in attempts to cure drug abuse. The effectiveness of these programs has not been tested, but many programs have experienced problems in treating young people who have been referred by juvenile courts. "Adolescents directed by the criminal justice system into treatment may demonstrate a lack of motivation or interest in participating in a serious and authentic way in the therapeutic process" (Smith, Levy, and Striar, 1979:565).

Many drug experts think that efforts to cure

drug abuse and addiction are futile and that prevention of drug abuse is the only solution to the problem. Drug abuse education is often recognized as central to prevention efforts. The 1967 Task Force Report on Narcotics and Drug Abuse recommended making clear, accurate information on drugs available to all. Although the report suggested that education efforts should begin in school, the members of the task force believed that the entire community should participate if information is to be effectively disseminated.

SUMMARY

Drug abuse is one type of delinquency that has captured the attention and concern of the general public, law enforcement personnel, and delinquency experts. Although drug abuse is considered to be a problem among adults and youth alike, it is thought particularly harmful for youth because they are still developing physically and psychologically and are thus more susceptible to the potentially damaging effects of substance abuse. Many types of drugs are available to the teenage user, but some are more favored than others. Currently, alcohol and marijuana are the most popular drugs among adolescents.

When use is not sanctioned by a doctor's prescription, young people are prohibited from consuming any drugs. Drug use can be, then, a type of delinquent act. Further, it has been a common belief that drug use leads to other forms of delinquency, but research on drug use among juveniles suggests that nonaddictive use does not necessarily lead to delinquency. Adolescent drug users, particularly hard core users, do have higher delinquency rates than nonusers. Addiction to a particular drug is thought by criminologists to result in delinquent acts because the addict may engage in illegal behaviors to support the drug habit.

Young people abuse drugs for many reasons, including the influences of a drug-oriented culture and peer pressure. Older adolescents are more likely to abuse drugs and to abuse a greater variety of drugs. Until the past two decades, males were more likely than females to abuse drugs. Now females have begun to abuse more drugs on a regular basis. Statistics for the 1980s suggest that male and female youth exhibit increasingly similar patterns of drug abuse. White young people tend to abuse more drugs with a greater frequency than black young people. There is evidence that youth from the lower social classes may drink more heavily than youth from the middle or upper classes, but youth from the middle or upper classes may abuse other drugs with greater frequency.

The criminal justice system has attempted to control drug abuse by imposing penalties for use and by restricting the available supply. The Controlled Substances Act mandates nine different drug control mechanisms and applies these control techniques differentially, depending on the nature of the particular drug. But some drug experts argue that law enforcement schemes to combat drug abuse have failed.

The limited success of the punishment approach to drug abuse control and alcohol abuse control has given rise to treatment programs. Commonly, the juvenile who is arrested for substance abuse is thought to need counseling and social services rather than punishment. The adolescent user is a particularly likely candidate for treatment, since the juvenile justice system is based on a treatment rather than a penal philosophy. The young substance abuser is often diverted from the juvenile justice system to treatment programs and services, especially counseling programs.

PROGRESS CHECK

1. Define each of the following terms: addiction, tolerance, dependency, drug abuse. (pp. 266–267)

2. What three variables influence how a particular drug might affect an individual? (pp. 267–268)

3. Liquor law violations have apparently increased more for _____ than _____ through the mid-1980s. (p. 271)
   a. Males
   b. Females

4. Discuss the findings of the annual high school surveys and the National Survey on Drug Use. (pp. 271–272)

5. Based on the discussion in the text, respond to the following statement: Marijuana use has been shown conclusively to relate to the commission of violent crimes. (pp. 275–276)

6. What is meant by the term "normal" drug usage? (pp. 277–278)

7. How have certain types of drug use been linked to the "ritual of rebellion"? (pp. 278–279)

8. What is a deviant drug subculture? (pp. 279–280)

9. On the basis of the data provided in the chapter, construct a profile of the young drug *abuser*, incorporating the dimensions of age, sex, race, and social class. (pp. 280–281)

10. How is drug abuse treated? (pp. 282–283)

NOTES

1. A review of this extensive body of literature on the topic of crime and drugs was recently conducted by Gandossy, Williams, Cohen, and Harwood (1980). Although somewhat dated, Elliott and Ageton (1976) provide a review of the literature on the adolescent drug and crime connection. Kandel (1978) reviews work done on youthful drug use and its association with deviant behavior. Blane and Hewitt (1977) particularly review studies which consider the relationship between alcohol use and delinquency.

PART 4

DELINQUENCY AND THE JUSTICE SYSTEM

The juvenile justice system in the United States today is characterized by tension and change. Both academics and juvenile justice practitioners are seeking to define the proper role of the juvenile justice system in dealing with delinquent and dependent juveniles. As juveniles acquire more of the legal rights of adults, the rethinking and reevaluation of the operation of all components of the juvenile justice system will continue.

In this section, we will examine four components of the juvenile justice system: (1) the police, (2) juvenile law, (3) the juvenile court, and (4) juvenile corrections.

Chapter 14 presents the dual role of the police in reacting to referrals from the community of juveniles who commit delinquent acts and seeking out delinquent behavior as it takes place in the community. As the gatekeepers of the juvenile justice system, the police have a great deal of discretionary power in deciding how a particular incident will be handled. Juvenile offenders may be dealt with informally or referred to the juvenile court for processing.

Major Supreme Court decisions about the constitutional rights of juveniles are discussed in Chapter 15. The impact of these decisions on the workings of the juvenile court are examined. The factors influencing court handling of juvenile cases and the weaknesses of the current juvenile justice system are also considered.

The current state of juvenile correctional institutions in the United States is presented in Chapter 16. A history of juvenile correctional institutions and types of contemporary facilities are discussed in light of the changing goals of juvenile institutions. The types of youth imprisioned in these facilities, the types of treatment they receive, and the effect of the inmate subculture on institutional effectiveness are also examined.

Chapter 17 traces efforts in the United States to find alternatives to juvenile institutions. The chapter describes diversionary programs and community-based correctional programs and the extent of referrals to these programs. The effectiveness of diversionary and community corrections programs is also evaluated.

CHAPTER 14

THE POLICE AND JUVENILES

POLICE–JUVENILE CONTACTS

SPECIALIZED POLICE FOR JUVENILES

JUVENILES AND POLICE DISCRETION

While on patrol, police officers Myers and Rawls received a dispatch directing them to proceed to 509 South Elm Street, where there had been a complaint concerning a "neighborhood disturbance." As the officers approached the residence, a well-kept two-story brick house, an elderly man ran to the car. "There ought to be a law," he said. "Those damn kids have been going strong since five o'clock this evening. No one on the block can sleep with that stereo blasting away. Lord knows what else they are doing over there." After assuring the man that they would take care of the matter and sending him home, the officers approached the house in question and knocked on the door. A young man of about sixteen or seventeen opened the door and was obviously shocked by the appearance of the police, despite his apparent state of intoxication. "What . . . what's the matter, officer? Is there anything wrong?" The police replied that there had been a complaint about the loud noise and asked the boy's name and address. "My name is Toby Smith, sir, and I live here." When the officers found out that Smith's parents were out of town overnight, Myers and Rawls asked for permission to enter the house. Once inside, they saw boys and girls about Smith's age in the living room of the house. An assortment of beer cans was scattered about. The pungent odor of marijuana hung heavy in the room. After questioning several of the youths, Myers and Rawls determined that an "end of the school year" party had been in progress and that nothing appeared suspicious—aside from the signs of beer drinking and marijuana use. Each youth, although apprehensive and, in varying degrees under the influence of beer or marijuana, responded respectfully and courteously to the officers.

During the same patrol shift, officers Myers and Rawls cruised the east section of town, a transitional area of ethnically mixed neighborhoods. Unlike the middle class area of their earlier call, this section of town was known by the police to be a "high crime" district. Before the evening shift, a grocery store in the area was robbed. All officers were on notice for possible suspects, two black male teenagers. As they approached the corner of Canal and Carrollton streets, Myers and Rawls saw a gathering of black teenage males, passing around *a bottle of some sort. Pulling alongside the curb, Rawls asked one of the youths what they were doing. The reply from an older boy was "What's it to you, man? We ain't hurting nobody." The other boys responded with similar comments, all expressed in an obviously hostile tone. Myers informed the youth that open liquor drinking was against the law, but if the group dispersed, he would let them off with a warning. All of the group started moving except the older boy who spoke first. "I got a constitutional right to stand where I want to," he replied. "You jerk cops are always picking on us down here. Why don't you go hassle somebody else for a change?"*

How would the police handle both cases? Obviously, specific laws or ordinances were violated both by Toby Smith and his friends and by the group of youths openly drinking in public. Legally speaking, laws were broken in both instances, and the suspects should be handled accordingly. Yet is the issue that clear-cut? Would such factors as respect shown toward the police, the seriousness of the offense, the age, race, and social class of the suspect, and the area of town in which the incident occurred sway the officers' judgment? Might these factors, as well as numerous others, influence the officers to let one suspect off with a stiff warning and formally process the other, even though the offenses are similar?

Although the extent of police authority depends on the particular powers given a local police department by law and on judicial interpretation of that law, police officers have a great amount of discretion in choosing how to deal with such situations. Perceptions about "types" of juveniles and juvenile misbehaviors do influence decisions about appropriate legal or extralegal dispositions. If we are to accept the evidence of past studies of police-juvenile encounters, chances are that the lenient disposition of informal reprimand would be given to Toby Smith, the middle class white youth, rather than to the outspoken black youth from a "known" criminal section of town.

In this chapter we will investigate police-juvenile encounters. We will consider the procedural aspects of screening and referral of juveniles by the police and the dispositional alternatives available to the police in handling juvenile matters. Then we will turn to factors that are thought to affect police discretion in disposing of juvenile incidents.

POLICE–JUVENILE CONTACTS

The first contact with a juvenile suspected of engaging in illicit behavior is usually made by the officer on the juvenile officer's beat. Although some departments have active juvenile patrol officers attached to a police juvenile division on the street, most juvenile contact is made by regular patrol officers. If a police officer decides formally to process a youth suspected of a delinquent or criminal act, the officer must follow certain procedures. In most states, statutes determine the police and juvenile court procedures in the processing of juvenile offenders. Several United States Supreme Court decisions require that the police ensure the protection of minors' rights at certain stages during the investigating process if a case is to continue to a formal adjudicatory level. A large number of juvenile cases, however, never reach an advanced stage. There are a number of decision points in the police handling of juveniles, and these range from outright release of the juvenile to referral to the juvenile court.

Number of Police–Juvenile Contacts

Statistics on the total number of police-juvenile contacts are difficult to obtain. The problems encountered here are perhaps as great as those described in Chapter 3 when we tried to determine the total amount and types of crimes committed by juveniles. The self-report studies discussed in Chapter 3 suggest that youth engaging in delinquent behaviors actually stand only a slight chance of getting caught. But the risk of police contact increases with the seriousness of the offense. If the behavior is reported by a complainant or observed by the police, the risk is, of course, also increased. According to Black and Reiss (1970), 72 percent of the police-juvenile encounters they witnessed in Boston, Chicago, and Washington, D.C., were citizen-initiated. Police on patrol initiated the remaining 28 percent. A replication of the study in another city by Lundman, Sykes, and Clark (1978) reported similar findings.

Although statistics from a variety of studies give us some indication of percentages of youth who come into contact with the police, in reality we do not know how many youth have encounters with the police in a given year. Not all police-civilian contacts become recorded as incident reports. Arrest or custody statistics in the *Uniform Crime Reports* represent only those youth who are actually taken to the police station or referred to the juvenile court or some other agency. As reported in the 1985 *UCR*, roughly 1,160,233 youths came into contact with law enforcement agencies *reporting* in the year 1984. Most of these contacts, almost 1 million, were in cities. Suburban areas and rural areas reported fewer police-juvenile encounters. In terms of overall statistics, over 50 percent of the official police-juvenile encounters resulted in referral to the juvenile court in 1984. Approximately 4 percent of juveniles coming into contact with the police were referred to adult courts, a figure that has been increasing substantially over the last decade. Just about one-third of the police-juvenile encounters were handled with the juvenile being released. An important point to remember here is that many departments keep records only of *formal* juvenile-police encounters and do not record informal dispositions, such as reprimands or warnings given in the field. Informal dispositions are *not* reflected in official statistics such as the *UCR*. Influenced by factors such as the youth's age, race, social class, prior record, demeanor, and so on, the decision to formally detain or informally to reprimand is to some extent a function of the officer's discretion.

Taking Youth into Custody

Thus far, we have avoided the use of the word *arrest* in our discussion of juvenile-police encoun-

ters. The phrase **taken into custody**, rather than arrest, is used in most jurisdictions to protect the child from having a criminal record. Theoretically, the youth who in later life fills out job applications and other forms that ask whether the applicant has been arrested can legally reply in the negative (Eldefonso, 1967). For all practical purposes, though, custody is tantamount to an arrest in the field. It is the officer's intent to detain the juvenile; the juvenile reasonably feels that he or she is not free to leave; and the officer takes physical control of the child.

What are the conditions under which a youth may be taken into custody? Most states usually specify two circumstances under which a child may be detained: The child may be taken into custody with a court order or without a court order. Taking a child into custody with a court order is deemed necessary in several specific instances. Florida statutes (Chapter 39.03) stipulate:

(1) A child may be taken into custody:
    (a) Pursuant to an order of the circuit court issued pursuant to the provisions of this chapter, based upon sworn testimony, either before or after a petition is filed.
    (b) For a delinquent act or violation of law, pursuant to Florida law pertaining to arrest.
    (c) By an authorized agent of the department when he has reasonable grounds to believe a child in a community control program has violated in a material way a condition or term of the program imposed by the court or otherwise required by law.

Florida law also distinguishes two types of youth who may be taken into custody by court order: those alleged to have committed a delinquent act or to have violated the court's jurisdiction, and those deemed in need of care or supervision. Cases of abused or neglected children fall into this latter category. When considering whether to issue a court order to take a child into custody, the terms "verified complaint" and "reasonable grounds" become important. A **verified complaint** is one with accurate information about the nature of the youth's alleged offense or alleged need for supervision and care. It further specifies that, as can best be determined by the available facts, the child is a danger to the community or is in personal danger.

A youth may be taken into custody without a court order by a law enforcement officer or a probation officer of the court if the officer has **reasonable grounds** to believe that:

1. The child has committed a delinquent act, pursuant to the laws of arrest;

2. The child is suffering from illness or injury or is in immediate danger from his surroundings and that his removal is necessary;

3. The child has run away from his parents, guardian, or custodian;

4. A child on probation has violated in a material way a general or specific condition of probation imposed by the court;

5. The custodian of a child under protective supervision has violated in a material way a general or specific condition of the placement imposed by the court;

6. The child is absent without authorization from school. (Florida Statutes, Chapter 39.03)

According to this statute, then, the police officer who observes a youth in the act of committing a crime has reasonable grounds to take a child into custody without a court order. Legal intervention is also allowed in cases of neglect, truancy, and runaway.

Because a child taken into custody is, for all intents and purposes, under arrest, law enforcement personnel must grant the youth certain privileges normally granted an adult: "The laws of arrest apply to juveniles as well as adults" (Kobetz, 1971: 105). What this means is that certain protections in the form of procedural rights and safeguards have to be applied to the "arrested" youth. This also means, however, that the police have the authority to secure and search the juvenile taken into custody as they have with the arrested adult.[1] There are, however, some differences between juvenile processing and adult criminal processing. Most states have some statute in their juvenile codes specifying that upon taking a child

into custody, there must be an "immediate and maximum effort to notify the juvenile's parents or guardians" (Hahn, 1978: 250).

Upon taking the child into custody, the police must "immediately notify the youth of his or her constitutional rights and refrain from any action that would abridge or deny these rights" (Hahn, 1978: 250). Again, juveniles theoretically have many of the rights afforded adults. We must caution, however, that there has been much controversy over extending adult rights to juveniles. It remains unclear, for example, whether juveniles who have not been taken into custody may be searched. Although clarification of juvenile arrest procedure is needed in certain areas, the United States Supreme Court has set down guidelines for many aspects of juvenile procedure. According to several Supreme Court decisions, when a juvenile is taken into custody for a felony offense—or *any* offense that may result in a delinquency adjudication and possible commitment to a correctional institution—the juvenile suspect is entitled to certain rights.

The **Miranda ruling** (1966), stemming from the 1964 *Escobedo* v. *Illinois* decision, in which it was held that arrested suspects must be informed of their right to counsel, required that suspects be advised of their rights before interrogation. If suspects were not told about these rights, their testimony would not be admissible in court. The Miranda ruling spelled out several specific rights that must be told to the suspect. The police officer must inform the suspect of his or her right to remain silent and his or her right to consult with an attorney. Further, the Miranda decision requires the court to supply counsel if the suspect cannot afford to hire a private attorney. The suspect must also be told that, should he or she waive these rights, whatever he or she says may be used against him or her.

The Miranda warning contains two distinct provisions: the right to remain silent and the right to counsel. *Miranda* applies whenever the officer wishes to conduct an interrogation of the suspect. Several federal Supreme Court cases control these circumstances. One exception to the Miranda warning concerns a "spontaneous expulsion"— when the suspect blurts out an incriminating statement either before the officer realizes that the individual is the suspect or before the officer can reasonably administer the warning. For example, an officer responds to a disturbance. Two persons are fighting. Upon arrival, the officer observes the victim lying face down in a pool of blood. Before the officer can say anything, the assailant stammers, "I didn't mean to kill him." Because the officer did not knowingly invite what amounts to a confession, that confession was issued voluntarily and would be admissible in court.

One of the primary functions of *Miranda* is to ensure that confessions are not coerced and are made voluntarily. Once a person invokes the right to confer with counsel, the police may not initiate any further questioning (*Edwards* v. *Arizona*, 1981). However, if the subject begins talking of his or her own accord, the police may continue the interrogation.

Contrary to popular belief, the Miranda warning does not have to be read verbatim to the individual (*California* v. *Prysock*, 1981). This ruling emerged from a case involving a juvenile accused of homicide. The interrogating officer began to explain the rights to the juvenile when the juvenile inquired as to whether his parents could be present during the interrogation session. The officer discussed this aspect with the juvenile and then returned to the interrupted point and completed the Miranda warning. The federal Supreme Court overturned an earlier court ruling and declared that the Miranda warning did not have to be read word for word by the officer. Instead, all the court required was that the substance of the warning be conveyed in an adequate fashion.

Law enforcement officers received a stern reminder to preserve the voluntariness of any confession in what has become known as the "Christian burial speech" (*Brewer* v. *Williams*, 1977). The defendant, a murder suspect, had refused to make any incriminating statements while in custody. One of the officers, knowing that the defendant was a religious person, mused how shameful and degrading it would be that the victim, whose body was undiscovered, would not receive a decent, respectable Christian funeral. After hearing that statement, the defendant disclosed the location of the corpse. The U.S. Supreme Court eventually

ruled that the "Christian burial speech" amounted to psychological coercion and therefore the confession was not voluntarily produced and was suppressed.

Following the 1967 Gault decision, which extended the right to counsel and the right against self-incrimination to minors, serious questions were raised about the ability of certain youth, especially the very young and immature, to understand the consequences of a waiver of rights (see Chapter 15 for a discussion of research that deals with juvenile comprehension of constitutional rights). Although there is still some debate over this issue, the requirement that the police contact the child's parents immediately after arrest serves in most instances to overcome the objection that children are not knowledgeable enough to waive their rights. Some states require that parents and juveniles sign a waiver or nonwaiver of the youth's rights.[2] If the child is later referred to the probation department or to the juvenile court, the intake probation officer may administer the Miranda warnings a second time to ensure that the child's constitutional rights have been protected to the fullest extent possible.

Police Investigations

Obviously, all juveniles taken into custody by the police do not end up in juvenile court. Whether an alleged offender becomes further enmeshed in the juvenile justice system is, to a large extent, the decision of the police officer. In reality, if all juvenile cases were referred to the court, it is doubtful that the available personnel in most jurisdictions could handle the caseload.

When the officer decides to do more than merely stop and warn the youthful suspect, certain information must be obtained about the youth and his or her alleged offense. This information is collected by the juvenile division of the police department and is used to determine the best course of action in the case. The child may be returned to the family, referred to a social service agency, or, if the facts warrant, transferred to the juvenile court. If the juvenile's case is petitioned into juvenile court, juvenile probation personnel assume responsibility for further investigation.

The procedures of police investigation vary from locale to locale. For the most part, police investigations include the gathering of data about the child and the offense and the interviewing of both child and parents.

The interview part of the investigation actually serves two purposes. Relevant information for the written report about the child is collected, and the details of the alleged violation are clarified. Since the police often hope to obtain admissions of guilt from youth accused of offenses, especially serious offenses, officers must inform children of their rights, as established in the Miranda and Gault rulings.[3] To ensure intelligent waiver or exercise of rights, the child's parents are advised to attend the interview (Kobetz, 1971).

During the interview, the youth is encouraged to admit guilt, a practice that reflects the treatment orientation of the juvenile justice system. Operating under the concept of *parens patriae*, juvenile courts have traditionally argued that "strict adherence to procedural regularity might prevent their obtaining total disclosure of a child's character and the offense in question. Full disclosure was seen as necessary to design an effective treatment plan" ("Juvenile Confessions," 1976: 198). A youth who persistently denies guilt despite incriminating evidence is thought to be beyond rehabilitation. Thus, the youth's recognition of the consequences of the delinquent behavior in fact partially determines the consequences. Those who refuse to confess and those who refuse to name accomplices are often referred to the court rather than being informally reprimanded.

The initial interview is usually performed by juvenile officers and is not a formal hearing in any sense of the term. Even though juvenile hearings are informal, the youth is entitled to have an attorney present if he or she or parents so desire. Police rarely welcome the presence of attorneys at interviews, because police fear that attorneys will instruct the juveniles to remain silent, thus hampering the investigation from the police viewpoint (Kobetz, 1971). Although the police have no legal authority to force the juvenile or the parents to attend an informal hearing or to accept a restriction on the youth's rights, the police do have a certain amount of leverage. They can inform the juvenile and the parents that the alternative to the hearing, and the possibility of station adjustment (that is, handling the incident informally at the police station), is immediate referral to the juvenile court. Often, both parents and youth would rather take their chances with the police than with the court.

Detention

Youths who are taken into custody pending police investigation of their cases may be released to their parents or held in appropriate detention facilities. A case deemed serious enough to merit **detention** is automatically within the jurisdiction of the juvenile court. Placing a youth in detention is one way the police can handle and dispose of juvenile cases. The detained juvenile now becomes the court's responsibility.

A distinction is usually made between predispositional detention and dispositional detention. **Predispositional detention** occurs when a minor is held in custody before a decision is made in his or her case. **Dispositional detention**, on the other hand, involves the result of court sentencing. The youth has been sentenced by the court to detention for a specific or indeterminate period of time in a juvenile correctional institution or in a foster home.

The practice of predispositional detention has undergone attack in recent years. Coffey (1974), a juvenile justice administrator, pointed out that the National Council on Crime and Delinquency recommends predispositional detention of a youth in only a few cases. Specific evidence must show that the youth is "likely to flee" from the jurisdiction, that he or she is likely to commit another offense, or that he or she is in danger of harming himself or herself (p. 104). Generally, the police have a strong voice in the initial decision to detain. Certain practical considerations also influence the decision to place a child in detention. Small police departments, for example, may seldom detain juveniles because of lack of facilities. Edward Pawlak (1977), a delinquency researcher, found higher rates of police referrals to courts with juvenile detention facilities than to courts lacking detention facilities.

Several studies have shown that girls are more likely than boys to be detained after arrests. Kratcoski (1974), for example, found that 31 percent of the females, but only 24 percent of the males, in his sample of juvenile court referrals in a midwestern city were held in detention. Chesney-Lind (1977), examining national data on juvenile arrests and detention in 1971, reported that girls comprised 22.3 percent of arrests, but 33 percent of detentions. In 1971, 75 percent of girls held in detention were charged with status offenses. Only 20 to 30 percent of boys charged with status offenses were held in detention. A study of the juvenile justice system in two cities, Dever and Memphis, found that girls accused of criminal offenses were less likely to be detained than were boys charged with status offenses (Cohn and Kluegel, 1979a).

Chesney-Lind (1978) also assembled evidence that girls were held longer in detention facilities. According to the findings of a Philadelphia study, female status offenders were detained for longer time periods than either male or female criminal offenders. A study conducted in New York also reported that (1) status offenders were more likely to be detained for longer than thirty days than were criminal offenders, and (2) girls were more likely to be charged with status offenses. Thus, girls charged with offenses that would not even be criminal if committed by an adult faced increased chances of detention and longer periods of detention. Teilmann and Landry (1981: 64) also reported that female delinquents in one Arizona jurisdiction spent almost three days more in detention than their male counterparts. After considering this evidence, Chesney-Lind (1977) concluded: "Girls who have not violated the law are punished more severely after arrest than either boys or girls charged with crimes. Like good parents, the family court officials feel the need to 'protect' their 'daughters'—usually from sexual experimentation" (p. 125).

Referrals by the Police

The police officer, having made a thorough investigation of a delinquency case, is in a position to choose an appropriate **disposition** for the youth. The police usually have initial contact with youth in trouble with the law or in need of some sort of supervision. This initial contact gives the police at least some power in determining the disposition of cases. Police action is also dictated somewhat by factors extraneous to the offense and the offender, including the availability of community services and departmental policy. Within these constraints, there are several dispositional alternatives available to most police. Five dispositions are most often employed by juvenile officers. We will discuss each separately.

Outright Release. Minor incidences involving only simple violations or status offenses often result in warnings and immediate release. Police generally deem warnings and advice to be appropriate sanctions for noncriminal offenses. The juvenile is informally interviewed and usually not taken to the station.

Release Accompanied by an Official Report. This type of police disposition differs from the outright release because the officer files an official report. It outlines the circumstances of the encounter and is forwarded to the juvenile division, unless a juvenile officer made the initial contact with the juvenile. When a juvenile officer makes an official report, it is forwarded directly to the juvenile division. According to official statistics, such as the UCR, release is the second most common form of police disposition.

Release to Parents or Guardians. Unless the offense committed is very serious, most authorities feel that the best place for juveniles is in their own homes. Police officers tend to release youngsters to parents under the following circumstances:

1. The offense is minor in nature, and there is no apparent need for treatment.

2. The child shows no habitual delinquency pattern.

3. The family is stable.

4. The relationship between the child and the parents is good. The parents seem aware of the child's problems and are able to cope with them.

5. Adequate help is available from public or voluntary agencies in the community. (Eldefonso, 1967: 101)

A variation of this type of disposition is release to parents on the condition that the youth receive help for his or her problem from a nonauthoritarian treatment source (for example, a drug education agency) or an agency such as a youth service bureau, which treats a juvenile's particular problem within a community setting.

Referral to Social Service Agencies.   Juveniles who are determined to be "in need of supervision" or in actual danger because of their home environments can be referred to specific social service agencies. Police automatically refer cases of child abuse and neglect to local agencies. Additionally, police officers refer children for treatment in family service agencies, child guidance clinics, mental health clinics, public service agencies serving families and children, visiting teaching services, church groups, and other similar organizations.

Referral to the Juvenile Court.   Usually, referral to the juvenile court is reserved for those who persistently get into trouble, often by committing very serious offenses. The Conference of Chiefs of Police has agreed on the following justification for juvenile court referral:

1. The particular offense committed by the child is of a serious nature.

2. The child is known or has in the past been known to the juvenile court.

3. The child has a record of repeated delinquency extending over a period of time.

4. The child or the child's parents have shown themselves unable or unwilling to cooperate with agencies of a nonauthoritative (social agency) character.

5. Casework with the child by a nonauthoritative agency failed in the past.

6. Treatment services needed by the child can be obtained only through the court and its probation department.

7. The child denies the offense and the officer believes judicial determination is called for, and there is sufficient evidence to warrant referral, or the officer believes that the child and his [or her] family are in need of aid.

8. There is apparent need for treatment. (Cavan and Ferdinand, 1975: 317)

By way of summary, Figure 14.1 depicts the various decision points that police encounter when handling a juvenile case. From the material presented in this section, we see that the actual number of juvenile-police encounters is difficult, if not impossible, to obtain. Although the police are guided somewhat by recent Supreme Court decisions and by state juvenile codes, a number of alternatives are available to the police in handling a particular incident. Depending on the officer's evaluation of a juvenile and his or her alleged delinquent act, the police officer has a tremendous amount of power in deciding whether the child becomes enmeshed in the juvenile justice system or whether the incident ends with the initial police encounter. For this reason, the police are often called the *gatekeepers* of the criminal justice system.

SPECIALIZED POLICE FOR JUVENILES

Within the last thirty years, police organizations have begun to place particular emphasis on work with juveniles. This has led to the development of specialized juvenile services within police departments. Although many departments in smaller towns and communities have specialized youth police attached to investigative branches, many larger city departments have developed separate

FIGURE 14.1   Decision Points in Police Handling of Juveniles

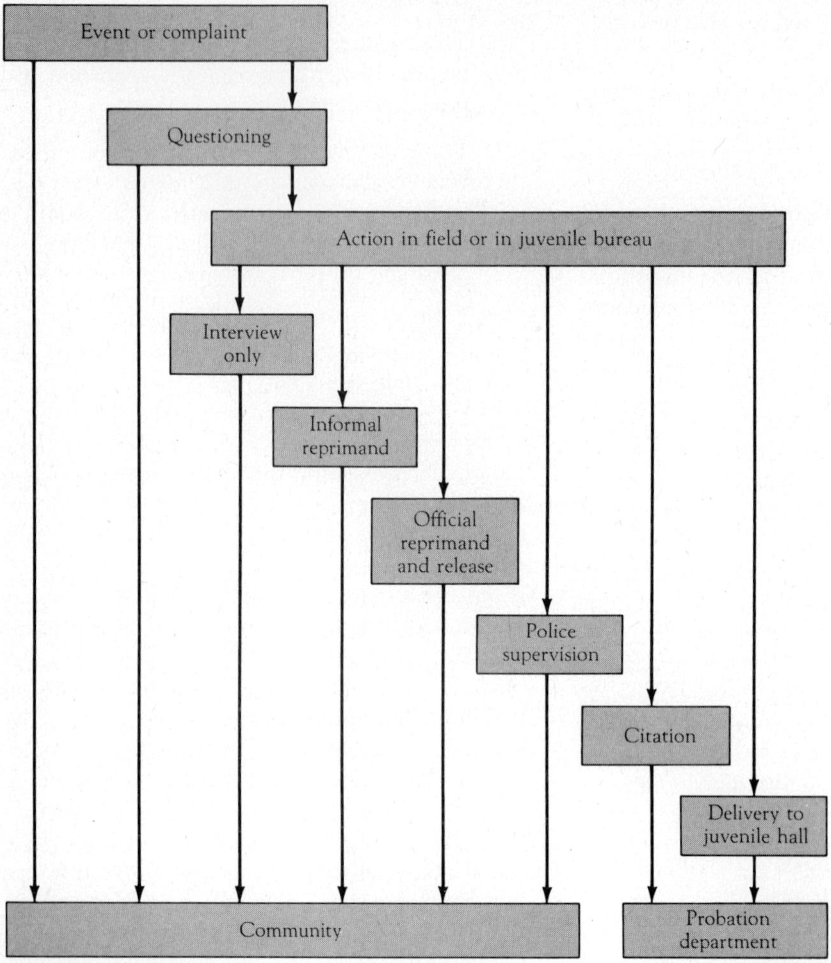

Source: Carey, Goldfarb, Rowe, and Lohman (1967, p. 62).

departments, or *juvenile control units,* to handle all matters relating to minors. These units are commonly called crime prevention bureaus, juvenile bureaus, youth aid divisions, or juvenile divisions. Underlying the decision to specialize is the general assumption that a juvenile specialist, because of superior knowledge and more intimate acquaintance with youth problems, can do a better job of handling juvenile cases than can the regular patrol officer (Eldefonso, 1972; Shepard, 1972).

Specialization has, however, created certain problems for the police administrator. In the past, the absence of clear policies for dealing with juvenile offenders set juvenile bureaus apart from the rest of their departments, causing isolation of bureau personnel and policies. Specialization also produced the tendency for nonjuvenile officers to neglect their share of the reponsibilities for dealing with youth. When a department has a juvenile bureau, regular officers often consider that youth are no longer within their sphere of influence (Kobetz, 1971). Another problem is found in attitudes toward juvenile officers. There is some indication that officers associated with juvenile bureaus are viewed by fellow officers as holding an inferior position in law enforcement. Since juvenile police do not deal with "real criminals," juvenile officers are not held in high esteem by other law enforcement officers.

Each police organization has more or less defined its own specific functions or duties. Controversy continues about the proper roles and responsibilities of juvenile bureaus and centers on the question of whether juvenile bureaus should assume strictly law enforcement roles, strictly crime prevention roles, or a combination of both.[4]

JUVENILES AND POLICE DISCRETION

Throughout the process of selecting and implementing a disposition, the police officer is allowed discretion. There has been debate about the extent and possible control of this discretionary power. Joseph Goldstein (1960), for example, argued in an influential paper that police use of discretionary power should be limited. He pointed out that "because police [officers] often make decisions that are essentially 'invisible' and subject to no review, especially when they decide not to make [an] arrest . . . they should be brought under the control of some subsidiary rules, compliance with which would be insured by the scrutiny of an official agency" (Bittner, 1970: 3).

Although other experts agree with Goldstein that police discretion should be controlled, most have questioned his proposal to limit discretion by adding new bureaucracy. As Egon Bittner (1970) has written: "While the proposal that discretion should be reviewable is meritorious, the hope that its scope can be curtailed by the formulation of additional norms is misguided. Contrary to the belief of many jurists, new rules do not restrict discretion but merely shift its locus" (p.31).

Attempting to explain how the police employ discretion, sociologists have directed attention toward the role of the police subculture. Peter Manning (1972) has described an occupational culture as representing all the "norms, values, attitudes, and material paraphernalia that are shared by and are typical of the practitioners of a named set of work tasks" (p. 234). The police, for example, are thought to learn a set of strategies from other officers that often take precedence over recommended formal practice.

Since police handling of juveniles, unlike police handling of adults, is not regulated by a comprehensive code, it is perhaps understandable that informal practices, subject to the officer's discretion and learned from other officers, have developed over the years. Although discretion is to some extent necessary and understandable, the problem comes when legislative changes to protect the rights of youth are short-circuited by the police sticking to customary procedures. It is at this point that police discretion is often attacked as excessive.

Similarly, law enforcement officers are taken to task for the ways in which they "police" certain types of youth and certain areas of a city. Studies reveal that the police come to perceive and define certain groups and categories of individuals as "potential troublemakers" or as "dangerous classes." Lower class individuals and neighborhoods are especially categorized as likely to be involved in crime. The police have been criticized for their tendency to overpatrol lower class neighborhoods and to single out the residents of lower class areas for particular scrutiny, especially when crimes have been committed somewhere in the area.

Although there is some validity to these charges, it is possible that the police simply reflect the attitudes and stereotypes of members of the larger society (Piliavin and Briar, 1964; Suttles, 1968; Werthman and Piliavin, 1967). Thus, the application of discretion becomes a source of trouble when the officer allows it to erode into discrimination.

In an effort to understand how the police make dispositional decisions regarding suspected delinquents, we will look at several variables that are thought to affect police discretion. The first group of variables focuses on the police. The second group concerns types of juvenile offenses and characteristics of juvenile offenders.

Police Factors Affecting Discretion

All police departments engage in *proactive* law enforcement activities when they actively seek to prevent crimes in the community. Police departments also engage in *reactive* law enforcement when they simply respond to crimes that take place in a community. Although both functions take place in all police departments, the organizational structure of a particular department determines to what extent these duties are fulfilled. To this end, police departments are often described as having distinctive "styles" of policing. These styles are thought to influence directly the types of dispositions juvenile law violators receive. In addition, individual officers develop their own personal "style." One major factor, the types of calls the police receive about a juvenile incident, has been shown to affect the disposition decisions the police make regarding a given incident.

Styles of Community Policing.   Although it is impossible to predict how a particular officer will respond to any given event, studies suggest that rather distinctive styles of community policing do develop (J. Q. Wilson, 1973).[5] The style of a community police agency is the result of a combination of expectations. Community groups, legal codes, and the organizational structure of the police agency all reflect expectations about police performance. Sometimes these expectations clash, and the police officer may experience *role conflict*. That is, the officer occupies one status for which there are two or more opposing sets of expectations. For example, the law may require that a certain offender be released, while public opinion demands retribution against that offender.

Given that a certain amount of role conflict develops from the differential expectations of police performance, the individual officer, and the police department as well, must make some form of adjustment. For the police officer, adjustment to role conflict often takes the form of discretion

in disposing of juvenile cases. Two juveniles accused of the same offense may receive vastly different treatment.

The police department can attempt adjustment to conflicts of expectations by setting and revamping agency policy (Kuykendell, 1974). Studies indicate that top police administrators establish both formal and informal guidelines about the extent to which certain laws and ordinances should be enforced. For example, James Q. Wilson (1970), a retired police administrator, studied police in two cities and found that the chief of police in "Eastern City" formulated a policy where officers were told to process formally only those youth who committed particularly violent crimes, such as brutally assaulting the elderly or engaging in wanton violence. This was not the policy in "Western City," where juveniles were far less likely to be released with just a reprimand.

Wilson characterized encounters between the police and citizens as either order maintenance or law enforcement situations. **Order maintenance situations** reflected an implicit concern with "keeping the peace." In these situations, the concern of the officer was to restore order and not necessarily to make arrests, even if the law has been broken. Prescribed procedures for officers were often lacking for such situations, and power was wide. Rowdy teenagers in public places or noisy parties disturbing neighbors fell into the category of order maintenance situations. In **law enforcement situations**, emphasis was not just on maintaining order, but on enforcing the law, and the officer was afforded less discretionary power. Police had established procedures to follow, and arrests were likely (Bittner, 1967; J. Q. Wilson, 1973).

Using these two police-citizen encounters, Wilson developed a threefold typology of police organization or community styles of policing: watchman, legalistic, and service. Although no police department is totally organized around one of these styles, all departments have characteristics of each. However, it is possible to classify police departments generally as following a watchman, legalistic, or service style of policing.

Order maintenance is the primary function of a police department operating according to a

watchman style. Police administrators attempt to influence the discretion of patrol officers through directives, either formal or informal, informing the officers to ignore many garden-variety violations such as traffic and juvenile offenses. More serious offenses, especially victimless crimes such as vice and gambling, may also be somewhat underenforced. From a watchman perspective, juveniles are expected to misbehave as part of "growing up." Unless juveniles commit particularly serious crimes or become labeled as chronic offenders, incidents are handled informally.

In sharp contrast to the watchman style of policing, the **legalistic style** emphasizes interpretations of situations in law enforcement terms. Although officers cannot measure all disturbances against some specific legal standard, they are expected by police administrators to handle situations with legal processing whenever possible. Thus, a "legalistic department will issue traffic tickets at a high rate, detain and arrest a high proportion of juvenile offenders, act vigorously against illicit enterprises, and make a large number of misdemeanor arrests even when . . . the public order has not been breached" (Pepinsky, 1976: 33).

In departments with a **service style**, "the police take seriously all requests for either law enforcement or order maintenance but are less likely to respond by making an arrest or otherwise imposing formal sanctions" (J. Q. Wilson, 1973: 200). Instead, alternatives to formal processing, including referral to social service agencies, traffic education programs, and drug education programs, are preferred. Wilson defined this style of policing as suited to homogeneous, middle class communities where the citizens agree on the need for protection of the public order but pressure on the police for a legalistic type of enforcement is lacking.

The dispositions of cases in a police department are influenced by departmental organization and departmental policy establishing a style of policing. Smith (1984) categorized twenty-four local police agencies according to degree of bureaucratization and degree of professionalization. When he examined the outcomes of police-civilian encounters, Smith discovered that victim, suspect, and situational characteristics achieved differential emphasis according to the type of police department. Confirmation of the notion that oganizational style affects the work product also comes from Reppetto's (1975) analysis of two different police departments. Thus, departmental organization appears to be a salient variable that molds the working environment and imparts a style of law enforcement on its members when they interact with the public.

Individual Styles of Policing.   Wilson's concentration on organizational styles of law enforcement prompted other researchers to investigate the existence of individual police styles. Broderick (1977), for example, argues that officers can be differentiated on the basis of their regard for due process and their perception of the need for social order. Broderick's typology produces four types.

The first type is the *idealist*, who has a high respect for individual rights and a corresponding acute recognition that law and order are necessary. Generally, this type of officer is quite dedicated, but often feels powerless to protect society. The second type is the *enforcer*. The enforcer shares the idealist's concern for preserving law and order, but is not hindered by legal technicalities. The enforcer's goal is to clean up the beat in his own way, since the courts have lost sight of the proper goal of protecting law-abiding citizens. The third type is the *optimist*. The optimist religiously remains steadfast to the notion of due process. At the same time, though, the optimist scores low on social order. This type of officer wants to help people and downplays the crime fighter image. The final type, the *realist*, is the recluse. Recognizing how the courts have taken and elevated the individual's constitutional rights over the protection of society and society's interest in eradicating crime, this individual retreats and develops a defeatist attitude.

A second typology has been developed by Muir (1977) and differs somewhat from Broderick's. Muir delineates two different considerations: the ability to empathize and the ability to use force in certain settings. The *professional* (similar to Broderick's idealist) understands other people's lot in life. The professional wants to help whenever possible, but recognizes that he or she can only accomplish so much. The *enforcer*, on the other hand, has a cynical outlook and is not loath to use violence if necessary. This type of supercop has one goal only: to catch criminals. Anything else lies outside the purview of this individual's job. The *reciprocator* (similar to Broderick's optimist) is people-oriented. This officer is reluctant to use force, but wants to help other people with their problems. The final type, the *avoider*, is uncomfortable with the potential to use force and does not understand even the smallest human problem. This type tends to avoid civilian contact whenever possible.

Unfortunately, there is not much research in this area. The research that does exist, however, questions the empirical value of these typologies. Researchers have not been able to isolate these different types of individual officers on the basis of attitudinal and value judgment tests (Hochstedler, 1981a; Hochstedler, 1981b; Talarico and Swanson, 1980). One huge limitation, though, has been the failure to determine whether actual street behavior differentiates between these police types.

Types of Police Calls.　　When an officer confronts a juvenile suspect because a particular citizen has complained about that juvenile's behavior, the complainant affects the type of disposition eventually given to the youth's case. Black and Reiss (1970), for example, stated that citizen complainants exert an important influence on the police officer's disposition. Searching for justice, complainants often make demands on an officer that the officer cannot ignore. Further, the complainant may witness the police officer's behavior and then use this information to contest an officer's version of a juvenile encounter or to file an official complaint against the officer. Since a large number of police calls dealing with juveniles are based on citizen complaints, the importance of the citizen complaint cannot be minimized.

The central role of the public complaint is illustrated when considering differences in types of dispositions assigned to the cases of black and white juveniles. Black and Reiss attributed differences in the dispositions of cases of black and white suspects to the greater number of complainants on the scene in police encounters with black juveniles. These complainants often requested severe dispositions. When no citizen complainant was present, the race difference in arrest rates of juveniles narrowed to the point of being negligible—14 percent of black juveniles were arrested, and 10 percent of white juveniles. The presence of complainants when police confronted white juveniles apparently did not influence the dispositional decisions of officers as much as the presence of complainants in police encounters with black juveniles. Overall, more black juveniles were involved in encounters with complainants than were white juveniles, and most of the citizens initiating police encounters with black juveniles were also black. Similarly, most complainants in white cases were white.

The research of Lundman, Sykes, and Clark (1978) supports the conclusions of the Black and Reiss study. In the police-juvenile encounters observed by Lundman, Sykes, and Clark, more black suspects than white were confronted by complainants. Also, more black than white complainants lobbied for formal police action. Regardless of the race of the suspect and complainant, there was a greater frequency of arrest when a suspect and a complainant were both present than when only the suspect was present. According to the researchers, citizens not only initiate police dispatches and remain at the scene of an offense until the police arrive, they also exert pressures on police decisions that can directly affect official delinquency rates.

We see, then, that the structure of a police department as well as the types of officers and types of calls the police receive about juvenile incidents can affect an individual officer's disposition of a juvenile case. Departments organized around a watchman or service style of policing are probably less likely formally to process juveniles than departments organized around a legalistic style. Similarly, different officers, depending upon their style of policing, are likely to render different dispositions in juvenile encounters. In any police department, however, the types of complaints officers receive about particular youths will to a large extent determine the dispositional outcome suspects receive.

Offender and Offense Characteristics Affecting Discretion

Several variables relating to characteristics of juveniles and the offenses they commit are thought to affect the decisions police officers make regarding how best to handle a given delinquent incident. These variables are (1) seriousness of the offense, (2) prior record, (3) demeanor of offender, (4) social class, (5) race, (6) age, and (7) sex. Although there is no definitive evidence that all officers make decisions based on these factors, separate studies do indicate that each of these variables influences officers' decisions about the disposition of juvenile cases.

Seriousness of Offense.   There is a great deal of evidence suggesting that youth who commit serious acts or crimes stand the greatest chance of being taken into custody or being arrested (Ferdinand and Luchterhand, 1970; McEachern and Bauzer, 1967; Terry, 1967a, b). Ariessohn (1972) asked police juvenile officers, probation officers, and juvenile court judges to rank a number of factors according to their importance as dispositional criteria. Police ranked the seriousness of the present offense as the most important factor.

Utilizing police records in four cities, Goldman (1963) found that in three of the four cities the police were more likely to refer serious cases to the juvenile court than they were to refer less serious cases. Some offenses were almost always reported to the court: robbery, larceny, motor vehicle theft, assault, burglary, and sex offenses. Two out of three youths carrying concealed weapons were referred to the court. When police thought that an offense, particularly a serious one, was premeditated or carefully planned, they were also likely to refer to the juvenile court. Such offenses were considered more criminal than those committed on the spur of the moment. Similarly,

the probability that the police would deal harshly with the youth increased when the offense committed was sophisticated or when weapons or tools were used.

Black and Reiss (1976) reported that among black and white juvenile offenders, the arrest rate was twice as high for felonies as it was for serious misdemeanors. Further, the arrest rate for more serious misdemeanors was double the rate for less serious offenses such as juvenile rowdiness. All in all, Black and Reiss found that "the dispositional pattern for juvenile suspects clearly follows the hierarchy of offenses found in the criminal law, the law for adults" (p. 68). In their replication of this study, Lundman, Sykes, and Clark (1978) reported similar findings: The probability of arrest increased with the legal seriousness of alleged juvenile offenses. Each of the alleged felony encounters that were observed by the researchers ended in attempted or actual arrest, but less than 5 percent of the rowdiness encounters and none of the noncriminal encounters resulted in an arrest.

A classic study by Piliavin and Briar (1964) also found that as the magnitude of the offense committed by the youth increased, the chances of being labeled a confirmed delinquent and subsequently being formally processed also increased. However, these researchers discovered that the demeanor of the youth in some instances was of more importance to the police than the offense itself.

To summarize, research results document the relationship between the seriousness of an offense and the likelihood of a harsh police disposition. The serious offense may result in arrest because police are likely to investigate serious offenses. Often, serious offenses involving someone who may summon the police and identify the offender tend to be very visible.

Prior Record.   Several studies have found a positive relationship between a juvenile's prior record and the severity of the police disposition when he or she has committed a crime (McEachern and Bauzer, 1967; Piliavin and Briar, 1964; Terry, 1967b; Williams and Gold, 1972). Apparently, those who have a prior record of delinquency often have a history of committing serious crimes. Thus, the two factors combine to influence the likelihood of formal processing. The police in Ariessohn's (1972) study ranked prior record as the third most important dispositional criterion out of nine possible criteria. A prior record is also a criterion that influences the police to refer a youth to the juvenile court.

Police officers tend to label serious repeat juvenile offenders as unsalvageable and therefore not amenable to less authoritarian types of treatment. Accordingly, the police often recommend referral of these offenders to the juvenile court or transfer to an adult court for the commission of a felony. Aaron Cicourel (1968), a sociologist, suggested that the police group cases into several categories with an ascending order of seriousness. The types are: (1) dependency cases; (2) family and juvenile problems, including incorrigibility and runaways; (3) "minor" misdemeanors or "normal" juvenile delinquency, including drinking, sexual activity, curfew violations, and fighting; (4) normal misdemeanors, including petty theft, malicious mischief, joyriding, and battery; and (5) serious offenses and general felonies (p. 118).

Cicourel argued that the police spend less time with the youth as the offenses become more serious because youth who commit serious offenses are perceived by the police to be "hard core" offenders who are routinely involved in systematic criminality. These offenders are usually referred directly to the juvenile court. There is also evidence that these youth are routinely held in detention. A study by E. J. Pawlak (1977) revealed that youth who have a number of prior juvenile court contacts have increased probabilities of detention, regardless of sex, race, or offense. Such youths are seen as threats to the community.

Demeanor.   The effects of a youth's attitude or demeanor on an officer's eventual disposition of the youth's case are difficult to measure. Since the assessment of demeanor depends on the police officer's perception of the juvenile, a rather intangible entity, descriptions of how these perceptions affect dispositional decisions are often imprecise.

Cicourel did, however, explain why officers need all the information they can gather in a given encounter. The police have to categorize a given encounter and the individuals involved in it into socially and legally relevant categories before they can make decisions about how to handle the case. Although initial investigatory procedures and prior assumptions provide the officer with a preliminary categorization, such things as the suspect's body motions, facial expressions, voice intonation, and the like can alter or push the interpretation of events into categories calling for more or less "serious" action. Thus, a juvenile who is the suspect of some particular crime and who "appears" guilty in his or her speech or expression may not be given the benefit of the doubt, although a youth who has what Cicourel terms a more "normal appearance" may receive lenient treatment.

Many delinquency studies have indicated that a juvenile's demeanor influences his or her treatment by the police (Hohenstein, 1969; Lundman, 1976; Westley, 1970). On the basis of a nine-month period of observation, Piliavin and Briar (1964) concluded that the key factor in determining how a boy is approached by the police is his resemblance to a delinquent stereotype. This stereotype is constructed from elements of demeanor and appearance and is based on cues that the police receive from the youth.

> The cues used by police to assess demeanor were fairly simple. Juveniles who were contrite about their infractions, respectful to officers, and fearful of the sanctions that might be employed against them tended to be viewed by patrolmen as basically law abiding or at least *salvageable*. For these youths it was usually assumed that an informal or formal reprimand would suffice to guarantee their future conformity. In contrast, youthful offenders who were fractious, obdurate, or who appeared nonchalant in their encounters with patrolmen were likely to be viewed as "would-be-tough-guys" or "punks" who fully deserved the most severe sanction possible—arrest. (pp. 210–211)

Lundman, Sykes, and Clark (1978) discovered that when there was no direct evidence about the offense in encounters, the demeanor of the youth became the most important determinant of whether formal action was taken. Both black and white juveniles who were antagonistic to the police were more likely to be arrested. But among white suspects, the very deferential were actually arrested more than the very antagonistic. The small number of very deferential black suspects made impossible any meaningful comparison to the very antagonistic black suspects. The authors concluded that the higher rate of extremely deferential juveniles was perhaps the result of police suspicion of their overly contrite manner. Similar findings were reported in the Black and Reiss study. Juveniles who behaved antagonistically toward the police stood a greater chance of being arrested than youth who were civil or polite to the police. In their study, however, this pattern held for black youths rather than white.

Some researchers have suggested that juveniles—and adults—who are hostile to police and those who fail to show the proper respect for officers are arrested because these attitudes arouse the "moral indignation" of the officer (Reiss, 1972: 137). Wayne LaFave (1965), for instance, suggested that arrests are often used to (1) maintain respect for the officer, (2) maintain an image of full enforcement of the law, or (3) deter or punish persons known to be violators (p. 437). Regardless of whether there is sufficient probable cause to arrest the juvenile, the officer wants justice done in order to punish the disrespect shown to his or her authority.

Even though the police may have a great deal of experience with individuals of divergent values and life styles, most police still retain definite ideas about how people *should* behave, especially toward an officer of the law (Hudson, 1970). As Goldman (1963) noted, "The police officer is concerned with the proper recognition of his [or her] authority. An assault on [the police officer's] self-esteem will lead quickly to punitive action. Almost all officers agreed that 'defiance on the part of a boy will lead to juvenile court quicker than anything else' " (p. 106).

In many instances, a direct affront to the officer's legal authority can result in consequences more serious than merely hurting the officer's pride.

Relatively minor encounters can escalate into dangerous situations if the police lose control. If the officer, by permitting his or her authority to be challenged, loses the initiative in the situation, the result can be bodily injury to suspect or officer. Thus, challenges to police authority in the form of backtalk, aspersions on the officer's character, and insults are often dealt with by swift arrest, especially if there are other people on the scene who could become involved in the encounter.

Officers on assigned beats or patrols who must interact with citizens day in and day out cannot afford to lose face too often. There may be, however, unintended consequences when arrest is based on an affront to police authority rather than the facts of the specific offense. Werthman and Piliavin (1967) studied gang members and the police and observed that when boys find "themselves arrested for insolence rather than for any specific offense, they are doubly outraged. Under these circumstances, the legitimacy of the interrogating patrol officer is all but destroyed" (p. 96).

Social Class.   The results of studies that attempt to relate the social class of the offender to the severity of police dispositions are mixed. Evidence generally indicates that the lower the individual's social class, the greater the probability that the individual will have contact with the police. Observing the police in high-crime areas, Black and Reiss discovered that "police encounters with citizens are more likely to involve police-suspect interaction when blue-collar citizens are involved than when the participants are white collar" (Garret, 1972: 34). Further, "when the police initiate contact with white-collar citizens on the street, the citizens are less likely to be seen by the police as suspects than are blue-collar citizens" (p. 34).

What is it about lower class citizens, including youth, that increases their probability of having contact with the police? An extensive body of empirical research suggests that people living in the poor sections of cities are more closely scrutinized by the police than people residing in affluent sections. Apparently police believe, perhaps with some warrant, that urban slum areas hold the greatest potential for the commission of crimes and thus need the heaviest coverage by police patrols (Bittner, 1970; Bouma, 1969; Werthman and Piliavin, 1967). Since large numbers of ethnic and racial minorities live in the lower class slums, these groups are often labeled as the "types" of people most likely to perpetrate crimes.

When police attitudes are examined, studies tend to indicate that the police "hold a consistent view that most delinquency occurs among lower class boys, and that the view is closely matched by patterns in official police-juvenile contact records" (Garret and Short, 1978: 102). Garret (1972), for example, found that most of the police she investigated in three cities tended to view lower class boys as much more likely to engage in delinquent behavior than boys from higher social class backgrounds. When Garret asked the police in "Western City" to predict the likelihood that boys from several social classes would repeat a delinquent offense, she found that the police thought the lower status boys would repeat and the higher status boys would not.

In reality, the accuracy of officers' predictions about recidivism—that is, youths engaging in future delinquency—was low. Social class was not itself a powerful predictor of recidivism. Garret argued that other factors often coincide with lower class and thus increase the chances of police contact and possible formal dispositions among lower class youth. Unkempt appearance, long hair, loitering on streetcorners, appearing visibly rattled when near a police officer, hitchhiking, walking in groups, and taunting the police were included in the cues that aroused an officer's suspicion and associated the youth with membership in the lower classes.

When assessing the relationship of social class to police dispositions, sociologists have found conflicting research results. Terry (1967b) reported that social class was unrelated to the severity of police dispositions. Similarly, Polk, Frease, and Richmond (1974) found no relationship between social class and referrals to the juvenile court. Although differences in the rates of referral were not great, Shannon (1963) did discover a tendency for police in Madison, Wisconsin, to refer more lower class juveniles for official processing (for

example, to the probation department) than middle and upper class youth. Further, Williams and Gold (1972) related that lower social class girls received harsher dispositions than higher class girls, but no relationship was reported between social class and the outcome of boys' cases.

Although the research shows no clear-cut, direct link between social class and the harshness of police dispositions, it is possible that social class relates to other factors which then link directly to police dispositions. Garret (1972) pointed out that, although lower social class may not itself influence police dispositions, the characteristics and attitudes of poorer youth may increase their chances of being singled out by the police for investigation. At least to some degree, police perceptions of lower class youth can account for the presence of these youths in official statistics.

Race.   A number of studies report that black juveniles receive harsher police dispositions than those received by white juveniles for the same offenses. Ferdinand and Luchterhand (1970) discovered that black teenagers are labeled as delinquent by the police and referred to the juvenile court disproportionately more than their white counterparts. This was especially true in the case of serious offenses and offenders. Although black youth were treated more harshly than white youth, black offenders were less antisocial and less aggressive than white offenders in the inner city neighborhoods. The one exception to this finding was "authority rejection," an attitude found more often among blacks.

According to the researchers, the trait of authority rejection was very likely to influence police dispositions. Piliavin and Briar (1964) arrived at a similar conclusion, citing the uncooperative demeanor of the black youth as the prime factor that resulted in the comparatively harsh dispositions of young black offenders. Both the Black and Reiss study (1970) and the Lundman, Sykes, and Clark study (1978) revealed that the arrest rate for black juveniles was higher than that for white juveniles. The researchers noted, however, that there was no evidence that the police utilized the race of the youth in deciding whether to arrest.

According to the researchers, the higher arrest rate for black juveniles could be attributed to the prevalence of black complainants who lobbied for formal police action.

Goldman (1963) found that black youth who were arrested were referred to the juvenile court twice as often as white juvenile arrestees. He also observed that a black child arrested for a minor offense had a greater chance of being referred to the court than did a white child. Hepburn (1978), though not dealing exclusively with juveniles, found that "nonwhites [were] more likely than whites to be arrested under circumstances that [could] not constitute sufficient grounds for prosecution" (p. 66). In other words, the race of the offender was an important factor in the decision to arrest when there was insufficient evidence in the case.

Hepburn attributed this finding not to race itself, but to the powerlessness of the nonwhite: "Powerless persons are more likely than powerful persons to be arrested on less sufficient evidence" (p. 69). However, other researchers examining the case flow process from the police to the juvenile court level did find a correction factor. Dannefer and Schutt (1982) reported that although race achieved a prominent status in police dispositions, the effect of the juvenile's race declined when examining juvenile court dispositions. This type of finding lends credibility to the street justice adage, "You may beat the rap, but you won't beat the ride."

Other studies, however, have not found race to be a significant factor in police dispositions (E. Green, 1970; Weiner and Willie, 1971). Two studies by Terry (1967a,b) and one by McEachern and Bauzer (1967) concluded that other variables, including the seriousness of the offense and the age and previous offenses of the suspect, had greater influence on officers' dispositional decisions than race. E. J. Pawlak (1977) also found some evidence that blacks are not always treated more harshly than whites.

Age.   Research studies have generally indicated that older juveniles receive harsher police dispositions. Goldman's investigations in four cities revealed an underrepresentation in court of juveniles below the age of 12 and an overrepresentation of 16- and 17-year-old offenders. Generally, the frequency of referral to the juvenile court increased with the age of the offender. The cases of younger juveniles were more often disposed of by police release.

Williams and Gold (1972) similarly report that police officially process older offenders more often than younger ones. They suggest that this is due, in part, to "the greater frequency of their delinquent behavior in a given period of time and their longer life-span . . . [resulting] in more of them being caught more than once" (p. 223). Thus repeaters, usually the older youth, are more often put on record. The researchers also state that the older youth are caught at more serious offenses than the younger ones. The suggestion here is that older youth, when caught by the police, are perceived as "knowing better" or are "not frightened by a warning," and thus stand a greater chance of referral to court. Conversely, younger offenders who commit serious delinquent acts are either not caught as often as older serious offenders or are given a warning and a second chance. According to Goldman, because the police are loath to refer younger children to court, police use referral as the last resort.

Sex.   Traditionally, criminologists have argued that police were less likely to take female offenders into custody because the police were presumed to have a "chivalrous" attitude toward women (see Visher, 1983). Otto Pollak commented in his classic book on female criminality in 1950 that "men hate to accuse women and thus indirectly send them to their punishment, police officers dislike to arrest them, district attorneys to prosecute them, judges and juries to find them guilty" (Pollak, 1950: 151). However, as Chesney-Lind (1976) pointed out, Pollak and other criminologists rarely based their observations about male chivalry on scientific research.

Currently there is conflicting evidence relating to police dispositions of female juveniles. Although the patterns of behaviors condoned for males and females are possibly changing, female adolescents have had a much narrower range of acceptable behaviors from which to choose. Noted Chesney-Lind (1973: 54): "Even minor deviance [by girls] may be seen as a substantial challenge to the authority of the family, the viability of the double standard, and to the maintenance of the present system of sexual inequality." Basing her contentions on a study of juvenile court referrals in Honolulu, Chesney-Lind concluded that most adolescent females were referred to the court for committing relatively minor offenses. Running away and sex offenses alone accounted for 60 percent of all the female delinquency referrals in 1964; only 27 percent of the males were referred for such status offenses.

This finding has been supported by other research. McEachern and Bauzer (1967), for example, reported that police tended to file petitions to the juvenile court when females were accused of status offenses and males were accused of adult offenses. The President's Commission on Law Enforcement and the Administration of Justice, in *The Challenge of Crime in a Free Society* (1967a), found that "more than half of the girls referred to juvenile court in 1965 were referred for conduct that would not be criminal if committed by adults; only one-fifth of the boys were referred for such conduct" (p. 56). These findings suggest that females who commit minor offenses are more harshly dealt with than males who commit the same acts.

Trojanowicz (1978) explained this by saying that "in many ways, the juvenile justice system not only reflects, but actively reinforces the values and assumptions of society at large in regard to the behavior of females, so that standards for protection and care may be considered different for girls than boys" (p. 138). In fact, until recently many states maintained provisions in their juvenile codes establishing a longer period of juvenile court jurisdiction for girls than for boys. As of 1974, only three states (Oklahoma, Texas, and Illinois) still had such statutes, but these statutes were declared unconstitutional by the state courts (Levin and Sarri, 1974).

When encounters between female juveniles and the police are examined, evidence can be found suggesting that females often receive preferential treatment. Monahan (1957a) noted that Philadelphia police released a greater proportion of girls apprehended for law violations than boys. According to Chesney-Lind, this research, when added to self-report studies showing that girls admit to engaging in the same offenses as boys, "suggest[s] that police indeed have the paternalistic mindset which says that girls should be treated chivalrously and released unless they need 'protection' " (1974: 45).

It should be noted, however, that police discretion in dealing with females can be influenced by factors other than paternalism. Since the police often base their dispositional decisions on the perceived dangerousness of a suspect, they may feel that females are a better risk than males and are less likely to get into future trouble. Further, official statistics report that males are three times more likely to become involved in the juvenile justice system and seven times more likely to become involved in the adult system. Thus, there is "some reason to believe that females are less likely to continue into adult criminal careers than males." (Trojanowicz, 1978: 139).

SUMMARY

To a large degree, the police play the important role of gatekeepers in the juvenile justice system. The police are usually the first agents of social control to come into contact with youth who have violated the law. Police dispositions and recommendations determine the fates of thousands of juveniles each year in the United States. Although police dispositions are guided by the legal precedents that are set forth in state juvenile codes and several recent Supreme Court decisions, the procedures for handling youthful offenders are by no means as clear and definitive as those provided for adult offenders. Only since the early 1960s have some of the constitutional rights afforded adults been extended to juveniles.

Although there has been some recent clarification of juvenile rights and procedures, police still have a large amount of discretionary power when they confront juveniles suspected of violating the law. The police may decide to release suspects with or without a formal reprimand. Should the offense be more serious, the officers may elect to release offenders into the custody of their parents or refer them directly to a social service agency. Referral to the juvenile court is reserved for youths who persistently get into trouble or who have perpetrated particularly serious crimes. Court referral may be accompanied by the recommendation to release the juvenile to the parents until a court date is set or the recommendation to detain the child when there is evidence that the child may flee or has a criminal history.

In the past thirty years police organizations have begun to place particular emphasis on work with juveniles. As a result, many departments have evolved special juvenile divisions where officers trained in juvenile affairs routinely handle all matters regarding youthful offenders. These special units or bureaus developed from the recognition that juveniles, by virtue of their youth, require a special type of handling. Included in juvenile bureau functions have been programs aimed at preventing delinquency through diverting early offenders from the juvenile justice system. At present, the success of many of these programs is debatable.

Police dispositions may be influenced by the predominant style of policing adopted by a particular department. Although harsh dispositions are often given by legalistically oriented departments, departments operating with watchman and service styles often give informal reprimands or warnings. Other factors affecting police dispositions include the individual officer's style of policing, the nature of the offense, the characteristics of the youth, and his or her environment.

Youths who commit more serious offenses and those who have a history of involvement with the law face a greater probability of juvenile court referral than that faced by first-time offenders who are accused of a status offense. Further, the juvenile who exhibits the stereotypical demeanor of the delinquent and comes from a lower social class family runs a greater risk of receiving a harsh disposition from the police. Evidence suggests that police are influenced by the apparent disorganization of lower class slum neighborhoods. Simi-

larly, black and older youth, regardless of other factors, experience heightened probabilities of formal processing by the police.

Even though females are less represented in police-juvenile encounters than are males, a disproportionate number of females are referred to the juvenile court for relatively minor or status offenses. Finally, youth committing crimes in which a complainant is involved stand a greater chance of being taken into custody than those involved in situations where a citizen complainant is not present. Black youth confronted by black complainants are particularly likely to be taken into custody. Although there have been calls to limit police discretion, the nature and goals of the juvenile justice system inherently involve discretion on the part of police officers.

PROGRESS CHECK

1. In most jurisdictions, juveniles are _____ rather than arrested. (p. 290)

2. Based on the _____ Supreme Court decision, juveniles (like adults) must be informed of their right to be silent, their right to consult with an attorney, and told that whatever they say can be used against them. (p. 291)

3. Distinguish between *predispositional* and *dispositional* detention. (pp. 293–294)

4. Are girls more likely than boys to be detained after they are taken into custody? Cite appropriate research. (p. 294)

5. Cite the dispositional alternatives available to a police officer once he or she comes into contact with a juvenile who has come to attention for the possible violation of a law. (pp. 294–295)

6. What do we mean by *police discretion?* Why is this particularly important in our discussions of juvenile delinquency? (pp. 297–299)

7. What do we mean by *styles of community policing?* According to criminologist James Q. Wilson, there are three such styles. What are they? Briefly explain each in relation to delinquency. (pp. 299–300)

8. Distinguish between an *idealist* police officer and an *enforcer* police officer. (pp. 299–300)

9. Briefly explain several factors that might affect the type of disposition a police officer gives a juvenile offender. (pp. 301–305)

10. Assess the role of specialized juvenile police in dealing with juvenile offenders. (pp. 295–296)

NOTES

1. We should note the controversy over the searching of juveniles by police. Hahn says: "In view of a trend toward applying to juveniles the Fourth Amendment guarantee against unreasonable search and seizures, the provision in the Uniform Juvenile Court Act, Sec. 27(b), that 'Evidence illeglly seized or obtained shall not be received over the objection to establish the allegations made against him (the child), . . .' caution should be observed in making a search for evidence when taking a juvenile into custody. Even when the child is taken into custody for his own welfare, there may be a question as to using fruits of a search as evidence to substantiate allegations that he has committed an unlawful act" (Hahn, 1978: 316). However, one exception to the need for a search warrant, commonly referred to as a search incidental to a lawful arrest, is usually triggered by an arrest situation. The rationale behind this exception is to protect the officer from any weapons the person in custody may have secreted. Generally, this exception is predicated upon three conditions: (1) a bona fide arrest, (2) custodial situation, and (3) the search is contemporaneous to the arrest. The safety feature becomes more important when police fatality statistics are borne in mind. Of the 1,566 law enforcement officers killed in the line of duty from 1972 through 1982 in this country, approximately 8 percent ($n = 119$) of the attackers were under the age of 18 (FBI, 1982).

2. Part of the Gault decision (387 U.S. 1, 70, 1967) requires that the juvenile know about his or her Fifth Amendment privilege before confessing. While *Gault* did not directly hold that the Miranda warnings must be given, courts have so held—possibly to ensure that the juvenile is aware of his or her rights. Further, language in *Gault* points to the need for "certainty and order" in receiving a confession. It further cites *Miranda* as a procedure necessary and capable of ensuring constitutional rights ("Juvenile Confessions," 1976: 200).

3. "*Gault* held that a confession must meet two criteria to be admissible into evidence. First, the confession must be voluntary. Second, it must not be made in ignorance of one's Fifth Amendment rights. The same considerations which created the "voluntariness" test in adult courts support *Gault's* requirement that juvenile confessions be voluntary" ("Juvenile Confessions," 1976: 199).

4. Some states limit the power of the police and the court to fingerprint and photograph juvenile offenders by restricting such activities to juveniles who have received a court order to be fingerprinted and photographed or to juveniles who have been accused of a felony.

5. For a general discussion of aspects affecting police behavior, see Sherman (1980).

CHAPTER 15

JUVENILE LAW AND THE JUVENILE COURT

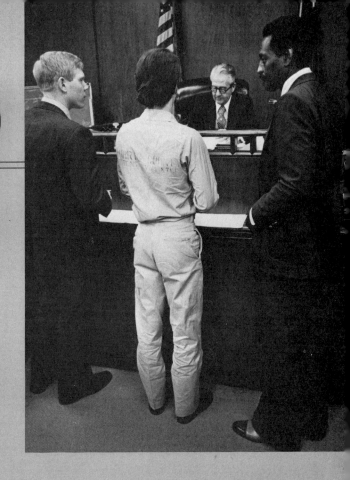

DEVELOPMENT OF THE JUVENILE COURT

LANDMARK SUPREME COURT DECISIONS

THE IMPACT OF LANDMARK DECISIONS

THE JUVENILE COURT PROCESS

JUVENILE COURT PERSONNEL

KEY ISSUES FOR THE JUVENILE COURT

"Attention, all units. Burglary of an auto just occurred at 618 Chapel Drive, Wheeler Apartments, Fort Lauderdale. The complainant, Mr. John Pittman, advised that three white male juveniles entered several parked automobiles. The subjects fled on two bicycles when he approached them. Subjects last seen traveling north on Woodward. Subject One wearing blue jeans, white T-shirt, and baseball hat. Subject Two had on cut-offs and no shirt. No description for Subject Three."

As the patrol car approached a shopping center four blocks north of the apartments, Officers Dill and Williams scanned the center parking lot. "Hey, Dill, there's a couple of bicycles and three kids in front of the laundromat." "Sure enough," responded Dill. "One's without a shirt and the other has on a baseball cap and a white shirt."

Officer Dill pulled the patrol car into the parking lot and the three boys began to pedal away. "Hey, fellas, come over here for a minute," ordered Officer Williams. The three boys approached the police car. "What are your names?" asked Williams. The biggest boy answered, "I'm Billy Richards, this is my little brother Tommy, and he's my cousin Joe." The smallest boy was starting to quiver and was obviously scared. "What are you doing here?" inquired Officer Dill. Again, the biggest juvenile answered, "Just riding around." Dill

309

turned to the little fellow, "You been over at the apartments down the street?" Little Tommy became more nervous and blurted out, "Yeah, but I didn't go in any of the cars." At this point, the two bigger boys chimed in with conflicting stories. "Okay, fellas, everybody in the car. Let's take a ride over to the apartments. Williams, read them their rights."

"All right, fellas, listen carefully. You have the right to remain silent. Anything you say can and will be used against you in a court of law. You have a right to an attorney. If you cannot afford an attorney, one will be provided to you at no cost. Do you understand these rights as I have explained them to you?"

When Officers Dill and Williams arrived at the apartments, Mr. Pittman was standing next to his car. "Those are the boys I saw," he told the officers. The only damage he could find was that the tape deck had been removed from the car but had been dropped on the pavement outside the car. The tape deck was badly dented and would not fit back into the holder.

"Well, Mr. Pittman, we'll take these kids down to the juvenile bureau and file a report on the incident," explained Officer Dill.

"What about my tape deck? It cost me over $200 and now it's worth nothing. It's not even insured."

"We'll turn the case over to the juvenile authorities, Mr. Pittman, and they'll take it from there. Right now, we can't do anything about your tape deck. We'll make out a stolen property report and the investigators will contact you later and take it from there. Sorry, but there's nothing else we can do. Good night, Mr. Pittman."

The three boys looked at each other. The littlest one, Tommy, shivered and wondered what now. What would the police do next? What would Daddy say? When would he be able to go home? Would they lock him up?

What did happen to Billy, Joe and Tommy? Because the three boys were under 18 years of age (the age of juvenile jurisdiction in many states), they were brought into the juvenile justice system for processing. In this chapter, we will trace the cases of Billy, Joe, and Tommy through the system. First we will examine briefly the history and development of the juvenile court and review some of the more important United States Supreme Court decisions governing the constitutional rights of juveniles. We will also review some studies of the impact these decisions have had on juvenile court functions. We will next explain how the juvenile justice system works, how it aims to protect those brought into it, and how, in this way, it differs from the adult criminal justice system. Finally, we will discuss the influence of key juvenile court personnel—the judge, the lawyer, and the probation officer—and conclude with a consideration of the major issues facing the juvenile court today.

DEVELOPMENT OF THE JUVENILE COURT

Prior to the establishment of the juvenile court, children were placed under the jurisdiction of the adult criminal court. They were tried and sentenced as adults and in some cases were even executed. Growing dissatisfaction with juvenile recidivism led some reformers to open New York City's House of Refuge in 1825. It served as a correctional rehabilitation facility that isolated juvenile from adult prisoners. Rehabilitation consisted mostly of manual labor. Children were contracted out to farmers and factory owners, in theory to learn the value of a virtuous life. However, many overseers physically abused and mistreated their wards. As a result, reformers grew skeptical of this punitive approach to juvenile crime. They sought instead a new approach, one that would focus on true rehabilitation of youthful wrongdoers. The reformers' efforts finally led, in Illinois in 1899, to the establishment of the first statewide juvenile court in the United States.

The concept of a separate juvenile court gained momentum. By 1925 virtually every state had a juvenile court (President's Commission, 1967c). This new juvenile court had a completely different orientation from the adult criminal court. It operated under the *parens patriae* doctrine. Instead of focusing on the question of guilt or innocence, the juvenile court focused on whether the child was in need of treatment. Since the goal of the juvenile court was to rehabilitate children instead of punish them, the normal constitutional safeguards afforded adults were relaxed. Gradually over the years, though, critics drew attention to the fact that juveniles could lose their freedom not for what they did, but for who they were (Kittrie, 1971). In fact, it had begun to appear that the juvenile court was dealing with its clients in a capricious manner. However, it took several U.S. Supreme Court decisions during the mid-1960s to curb some of these practices (see Gottfredson, Chandler, and Cohen, 1983).

LANDMARK SUPREME COURT DECISIONS

The period extending from the early 1960s to the early 1970s was marked by several major United States Supreme Court decisions concerning the constitutional rights of citizens who become involved in the American justice system. The highest court in the land made a concerted effort to ensure that the constitutional rights of Americans were not being usurped by overzealous guardians of the legal system. The Court ruled, among other things, that the Constitution protected adult citizens from unreasonable **search and seizure** (*Mapp* v. *Ohio*, 1961), afforded accused persons the right to an attorney (*Escobedo* v. *Illinois*, 1964; *Gideon* v. *Wainwright*, 1963), prohibited **cruel and unusual punishment** (*Robinson* v. *California*, 1962), allowed citizens the privilege against self-incrimination (*Wong Sun* v. *U.S.*, 1963), set down guidelines concerning pretrial identification (*Gil-*

bert v. *California*, 1967; *U.S.* v. *Wade*, 1967), specified stop-and-frisk practices (*Terry* v. *Ohio*, 1968), and established proper warnings to be given prior to a custodial investigation (*Miranda* v. *Arizona*, 1966).

The expansion of constitutional rights and safeguards was not limited to the adult criminal justice system. A series of U.S. Supreme Court rulings extended many similar constitutional rights to juveniles during this same period (see Zimring, 1982). Four decisions that have had a pervasive impact on juvenile processing were those in the Kent, Gault, Winship, and McKeiver cases. A recent Supreme Court decision, *Schall* v. *Martin* (1984), has been assailed by child advocates, however, as a blow to the constitutional rights of children.

Kent v. United States

One of the first juvenile court procedures to come under scrutiny by the United States Supreme Court was waiver. As we indicated in Chapter 1, **waiver** is the process whereby the juvenile court judge can transfer a case to the adult criminal justice system so that the juvenile can stand trial as an adult. The power to waive a juvenile's case is limited by the age of the child and the seriousness of the current offense. In Florida, for example, a juvenile can be waived to stand trial as an adult if he or she is at least 16 years old and has a prior record of two felonies (Florida Statutes, Ch. 39.02).

The major case concerning waiver of a juvenile to the adult court involved Morris Kent, a 16-year-old male (*Kent* v. *U.S.*, 1966). Kent broke into an apartment in Washington, D.C., raped the female occupant, and stole her wallet. The police took Kent into custody three days later, on September 5, 1961. Kent's mother retained a lawyer almost immediately. The attorney had Kent examined by two psychologists and a psychiatrist, who certified that Kent was in need of psychiatric care and was a suitable candidate for rehabilitation. Armed with these reports, the attorney filed for a hearing on the question of waiver. The question of waiver was of tremendous importance. If the waiver failed, Kent would remain under the protection of the juvenile court until he reached majority age, 21 at that time. If the waiver was successful, Kent would be tried as an adult and would face a maximum sentence of the death penalty.

A short time later, the juvenile court waived jurisdiction and remanded Kent to the jurisdiction of the United States District Court for the District of Columbia. The juvenile court never held a hearing on the question of waiver; nor did the judge confer with Kent, his parents, or his attorney. The jury found Kent guilty of breaking and entering, but found him insane at the time he perpetrated the rape. The judge placed Kent in the custody of a mental institution with the stipulation that Kent face a thirty- to ninety-year sentence after regaining his sanity.

Kent's attorney appealed the case to the United States Supreme Court. The Court ruled in 1966 that the juvenile court had not conducted a complete investigation prior to the waiver decision. In addition, the Court specified four guidelines for future waiver hearings: (1) A waiver would require a full hearing before the juvenile court. (2) Counsel could be present at the waiver hearing. (3) Counsel should have access to all reports and records that the juvenile court considers when making the transfer decision. (4) The presiding judge must issue a statement outlining the reasons for permitting the waiver to adult court.

It is important to note that the Supreme Court did not question the validity of the waiver law. Instead, the Court questioned the procedure and the lack of constitutional safeguards at that point. Thus, *Kent* marked the first time in American history that the United States Supreme Court vested juveniles with the right to due process. However, it was not until *Gault* that the Court extended constitutional rights to other portions of the juvenile justice system.

In re Gault

This case began when a Mrs. Cook contacted the Gila County Sheriff's Office in Arizona to complain that she had been receiving obscene phone calls. After an initial investigation, the sheriff's office took Gerald Gault, a 15-year-old male juvenile, and a companion into custody at approximately 10:00 A.M. on June 8, 1964. Both of Gault's parents worked during the day and they were not notified of the action, so they had no knowledge of their son's whereabouts when they returned home. His mother sent one of her other children around the neighborhood to find Gault and to bring him home to eat. One of the neighbors informed the Gaults that the sheriff's office had taken Gerald Gault away that morning. Gault's mother went to the detention center and spoke with Probation Officer Flagg. Flagg informed her of the circumstances surrounding her son's detention and told her that a hearing would be held the next day in juvenile court.

On Tuesday, June 9, Flagg filed a delinquency petition with the court. During the hearing on the petition, Gault told Judge McGhee that he had dialed the telephone but that his friend Ronald did all the talking. Officer Flagg informed the judge that Gault had earlier admitted speaking into the phone in a suggestive manner. After listening to the parties, Judge McGhee declined to issue a ruling. Instead, he ordered Gault to remain in detention at the juvenile hall. Three days later, the youth was released and driven home without any explanation, but relaying a note from Officer Flagg to Gault's mother. That note, written on a plain piece of paper with no official seals or letterhead, informed Gault's mother of the time and day for the next hearing.

The judge scheduled another hearing in the case and listened to more testimony on June 15. At that time Gault's mother requested that the complainant, Cook, be ordered to appear before the court. Judge McGhee replied that it was not necessary. After concluding testimony, Judge McGhee reviewed a report prepared by the probation officer and remanded Gault to the custody of a reform school until he reached majority age. Majority age was 21 at the time. In effect, then, Gerald Gault received a six-year sentence for making a lewd phone call. Had he been an adult, the maximum sentence the judge could have levied would have been a $50 fine or a 60-day jail term.

Although Arizona law at that time did not

provide the right to appeal a juvenile court decision, Gault's parents appealed the case to the Superior Court and later to the Arizona Supreme Court. Both courts failed to reverse Judge McGhee's earlier ruling. Finally, the Gaults petitioned the United States Supreme Court, which granted a hearing and issued its ruling on May 15, 1967, nearly three years after Gault had first been picked up and taken into custody (*In re Gault*, 1967).

The appeal contended that Gerald Gault's constitutional right to due process had been violated by the juvenile court. The appeal to the Supreme Court outlined six areas of infringement: the right to an adequate notice of charges, the right to counsel, the right to confront and cross-examine witnesses, the right against self-incrimination, the right to a transcript of the proceedings, and the right to appellate review.

Right to Adequate Notice of Charges. The Court noted that the Arizona authorities failed to safeguard Gault's right to an adequate notice of charges. For example, his parents were not notified that the sheriff's office had taken their son into custody. Furthermore, Officer Flagg never informed the senior Gaults of the charges in writing. Thus, Gerald and his parents had no knowledge of the specific charges, and as a result could not prepare an adequate defense.

Right to Counsel. Neither Gerald Gault nor his parents were advised that they had a right to legal representation during the juvenile court proceedings. The Arizona Supreme Court contended that the juvenile did not need such protection, since the juvenile court was acting in the best interests of the child. The United States Supreme Court disagreed. The federal justices maintained that there was no difference between an adult proceeding and a juvenile proceeding where the accused has a chance of losing his or her freedom. Consequently, the U.S. Supreme Court ruled that juveniles do have the right to counsel, but only in those cases where they face the possibility of commitment. Although some observers interpreted this portion of the ruling as a victory, some

critics were concerned with the narrow circumstances under which the Court allowed legal representation (Kittrie, 1971).

Right to Confrontation and Cross-Examination. Cook, the complainant, never appeared at the hearings to offer her testimony. She did, however, talk with Officer Flagg, who relayed her comments to the judge. When Gault's mother requested the presence of Cook at the proceedings, Judge McGhee ruled that Cook's presence was not necessary. The net result was that Gault never had the opportunity to cross-examine Cook under oath. The U.S. Supreme Court ruled that Gault should have had the right to cross-examine witnesses.

Right against Self-Incrimination. The U.S. Supreme Court carefully reviewed the admissibility of Gault's confession. The justices noted that Officer Flagg obtained a confession without Gault's parents being present, without an attorney being present, and without advising Gault that he had the right to remain silent. The Court also noted that Gault's confession formed the only basis for a legal judgment in the case. Thus, the Court disagreed with the earlier courts and ruled that Gault's right against self-incrimination should have been protected. Although this ruling is important, the Court restricted its consideration to those juvenile cases that carry a potential loss of freedom. The Court ruled against compulsory testimony. However, it failed to go so far as to recommend the presence of counsel during interrogation in order to ensure a voluntary confession should any confession be forthcoming.

Right to a Transcript of the Proceedings. The United States Supreme Court failed to issue a definitive ruling on this question. However, the Court did caution that in those instances where a transcript is not kept, the burden of proof falls on the juvenile court in subsequent hearings. Courts that keep records would not have to reconstruct the proceedings or have the presiding judge subject to cross-examination at later hearings; both procedures are conceivable in juvenile courts that do not keep transcripts.

Right to Appellate Review. The Arizona system did not provide for the right to appeal a juvenile court order. The U.S. Supreme Court elected not to review this point. The Court reasoned that since it had struck down the earlier rulings in this case and had invalidated certain other procedural practices, the issue of **appellate review** was moot. However, Arizona did modify its statutes after the Gault ruling to include an appeal process for juveniles.

In re Winship

Samuel Winship, a 12-year-old boy from New York, stole more than $100 from a woman's pocketbook, which had been stored in a locker. The juvenile court judge found Winship delinquent and committed him to a training school for an intitial period of eighteen months, subject to yearly extensions until he reached 18 years of age. In other words, Winship received a six-year sentence for the crime of larceny. In reaching this verdict, the judge rejected the argument that due process required "proof beyond a reasonable doubt." Instead, the judge relied upon a section of the New York juvenile statute which used the criterion "a preponderance of evidence." Subsequent appeals to the Appellate Division of the New York Supreme Court and to the New York Supreme Court were futile. The United States Supreme Court heard the case and overturned the earlier rulings in 1970 (*In re Winship*, 1970).

The opinion stated that the standard "proof beyond a reasonable doubt" was a constitutional mandate and as much a requirement in the administration of justice as the constitutional safeguards affirmed in *Gault*. According to Justice John Harlan, the portrayal of the juvenile court as a civil, not criminal, procedure produced the divergence in standards. The "preponderance of evidence" rule is a suitable yardstick in **civil cases** because the outcome is expressed in monetary damages. In **criminal cases**, however, the more stringent determination, "proof beyond a reasonable doubt,"

should be applied in order to prevent the erroneous conviction of an innocent party. The Supreme Court chose the "proof beyond a reasonable doubt" criterion because "it is far worse to convict an innocent man than to let a guilty man go free." Since the Winship case involved the potential loss of freedom, the more appropriate rule was the stronger "proof beyond a reasonable doubt" criterion. The importance of the Winship case lies in the Supreme Court's determination that the rehabilitative powers of the juvenile justice system could not be imposed upon a juvenile unless the juvenile was found guilty of a criminal offense.

McKeiver v. Pennsylvania

Joseph McKeiver, a 16-year-old male, was taken into custody in May 1968 and charged with robbery, larceny, and receiving stolen goods. His attorney requested a trial by jury, but the request was denied. In an unrelated case, another juvenile, Edward Terry, was charged with assault and battery upon a police officer and with **conspiracy**. His lawyer also asked for a trial by jury, and the request was also denied. Both attorneys appealed their cases, and the Supreme Court of Pennsylvania consolidated the cases. The issue to be examined was whether juveniles possessed a constitutional right to a jury trial in the juvenile court system. The Pennsylvania Supreme Court turned down the appeal, and the case was then accepted by the United States Supreme Court.

The United States Supreme Court issued its ruling in 1971 (*McKeiver v. Pennsylvania*). The Court decided against McKeiver and ruled that trial by jury was not a constitutional right at the juvenile adjudication stage. The Supreme Court chose this route for several reasons. First, the Court had never issued a flat ruling asserting that juveniles possess the full range of constitutional rights afforded adults. Each case we have reviewed—*Kent, Gault,* and *Winship*—had dealt with only a narrow range of constitutional rights. Second, the justices expressed the fear that granting the right to jury trial would transform the juvenile court system into an adversary process and spell the end of the *parens patriae* doctrine. Third, the

President's Commission on Juvenile Delinquency and Youth Crime (1976c) never recommended the use of jury trial in the juvenile justice system, since it would undermine the very premise of the system itself. Fourth, a trial by jury was not a necessary ingredient for a fair and equitable criminal process. Fifth, there was nothing that precluded a juvenile court judge from impaneling an advisory jury if conditions warranted such a practice. Sixth, the Court noted that at least twenty-eight states denied the juvenile a right to a jury trial and that there was no evidence this denial impeded the pursuit of justice.

Finally, the underlying issue was whether the juvenile proceeding could be equated with a criminal proceeding. Such an equation, the justices noted, would tend to deny the informality and paternal attention of the juvenile justice system. Thus, the Supreme Court denied McKeiver's appeal on the basis that a trial by jury was not a fundamental constitutional right of juveniles.[1]

Schall v. Martin

The most recent Supreme Court decision affecting the rights of juveniles was handed down on June 5, 1984. The Court reversed two lower federal courts and reinstated a New York law, similar to laws in all fifty states, under which juveniles charged with delinquency may be held before trial to prevent them from committing additional crimes.[2] In a 6 to 3 ruling, the Court gave its first decision on the approach to pretrial confinement, often referred to as "preventive detention." Differing from traditional bail statutes, which allow judges to set bail in the amount necessary to ensure that a defendant will appear at trial, preventive detention takes into account the *danger* that the defendant will commit future crimes while awaiting trial. Thus, 14-year-old Gregory Martin, who robbed and assaulted another youth, and who subsequently filed a class action suit on behalf of all children in preventive detention in New York state, was confined in a detention facility not to ensure his appearance at trial, but because he was regarded by the juvenile court judge as a serious risk to commit new crimes while waiting for his case to come up.

Justice William Rehnquist, writing for the majority, was careful to confine the opinion to juveniles; the Court has never ruled on the legality of preventive detention laws for adults. Rehnquist wrote that "Society has a legitimate interest in protecting a juvenile from the consequences of his/her criminal activity—both from potential physical injury which may be suffered when a victim fights back or when a policeman attempts to make an arrest and from the downward spiral of criminal activity into which peer pressure may lead the child" (Rehnquist, 1984: B5). Rehnquist added that a juvenile's right to freedom from outside control is reduced by the fact that "juveniles, unlike adults, are always in some form of custody." He further emphasized that juvenile rights were protected during detention by a number of safeguards, including the right to a free lawyer, a full record of the proceedings, and the requirement that within three days the state establish "probable cause" that the juvenile committed the offense charged (Margolick, 1984: B5).

Needless to say, the opinion of the court elicited both positive and negative reactions. Alfred Regnery, director of juvenile programs for the Justice Department, stated: "It [the decision] recognizes that juvenile crime is serious business that needs to be dealt with seriously" (Serrill, 1984: 76). Martin Guggenheim of the New York University Law School, the attorney who appealed the case, called the ruling a "devastating blow" for young people and indicated that "kids are being harmed under the guise of doing them good" (Margolick, 1984: B5).

THE IMPACT OF LANDMARK DECISIONS

Five major Supreme Court decisions have focused on the constitutional rights of juveniles. As a result of the Kent decision, juveniles received the right to due process during waiver. As a result of the Gault decision, juveniles were given the right to notice of charges, the right to counsel, the right to confront and cross-examine witnesses, and the privilege against self-incrimination. As a result of the Winship decision, juveniles could not be found delinquent unless there was "proof beyond a reasonable doubt." As a result of the McKeiver ruling, juveniles were said not to possess the right to a trial by jury. Finally, as a result of the Schall ruling, juveniles can be held in detention before trial to prevent them from committing additional crimes.

Many legal revisionists or strict constitutionalists hailed the Kent, Gault, and Winship decisions as decisive victories that ushered in a new era of safeguarding juvenile constitutional rights. Other observers were more reserved. Juveniles still lacked the right to bail, protection against **double jeopardy,** the right to jury trial, and protection from **grand jury** indictment. They were still subject to status offenses and also to vague standards for arrest, search, and detention.

But legal revisionists had won the battle for the extension of certain constitutional rights to juveniles. On paper, juveniles now possessed some constitutional rights. But what about in practice? Were the juvenile courts making these constitutional rights available? Was the law as it appeared on the books being transformed successfully into living law? We can find a partial answer to these questions by looking at studies of several juvenile courts that attempt to assess the degree of impact the Supreme Court decisions have had on the day-to-day business of the juvenile justice system.

The Impact of *Gault*

As we mentioned earlier, the Gault decision provided juveniles with many of the safeguards adults possess. The more prominent rights extended to juveniles included the right to counsel, the right to confront one's accusers, and the right to remain silent. In order to determine the impact of the Gault decision, researchers have monitored the presence of defense counsel, whether juveniles were being advised of their rights, and whether juveniles understood these rights. As we will see, some courts have adopted routines which, on the surface, appear to conform to the Gault requirements. In practice, however, the attempt to comply with the Supreme Court's ruling rings hollow and leaves much to be desired.

Reasons: The Presence of Counsel.   Charles F. Reasons, a criminologist, conducted an analysis of 3,225 juvenile court cases in Columbus, Ohio (1970). He divided the cases into two groups: those handled in the year prior to *In re Gault* (June 1966 to May 1967), and those handled in the year after the decision (June 1967 to May 1968). Reasons found that the overall retention of lawyers increased from 13 percent in the pre-*Gault* period to 29 percent after *Gault.* The percentage of cases involving a defense attorney similarly increased. There was a substantial decrease in the number of serious charges against juveniles, but at the same time a large increase in minor charges. For example, although auto theft charges dropped from 311 to 107 cases, operating a car without the owner's consent rose from 13 cases during the pre-*Gault* period to 106 cases after *Gault.*

Reasons explained this change by noting that the Supreme Court ruling carried a more stringent requirement for the determination of guilt after *Gault:* "An increase in the presence of counsel and a reduction in the number of cases reaching adjudication and disposition [indicated] a shift toward legal fact finding" (p. 171). Further, "a reduction in the number of juveniles placed on probation and an increase in the use of fines [indicated] less emphasis on treatment" (p. 171). Reasons noted that although treatment is not incompatible with a more legalistic orientation, "treatment must be based on an accurate determination of guilt" (p. 171). Reasons concluded that the Gault decision had the desired impact on the Columbus Juvenile Court.

Reasons' study, however, left many questions unanswered. The Gault decision extended to juveniles the right to adequate notice of charges, notification of the right to counsel, and the right to confrontation and cross-examination, as well as the protection against self-incrimination. Reasons' study did not provide a very accurate basis for determining whether the Columbus court actually complied with the Gault guidelines. For example, there was no information concerning how many juveniles received a notice of charges, how many juveniles were informed of their right to examine witnesses, or how many were advised about the protection against self-incrimination.

Instead, Reasons inferred that the court changed its process by counting the number of cases with legal representation. A more suitable approach would have been to determine whether juveniles were being advised of their rights and if so, in what manner. Fortunately, such a study is available.

Lefstein and Associates: Judicial Circumvention. Lefstein, Stapleton, and Teitelbaum (1969) studied the juvenile courts in three anonymous cities during the latter part of 1967 to determine the impact of *In re Gault*. The sample was limited to cases involving a delinquency petition in which commitment was a possibility and the juvenile lacked legal counsel. Thus, the sample met the basic conditions under which the juvenile court should apply the Gault ruling.

The Supreme Court decision in *Gault* instructed that both the juvenile and the parents be informed of the right to counsel and that an attorney would be provided if the family could not afford one. Two of the courts in this study mailed a notice to the juvenile's parents informing them of the right to counsel. However, neither notice informed the parents that a court-appointed attorney was available if they could not afford their own. In adult cases, the judge is obligated to advise the individual of the right to counsel. Observers at the three courts found that the judge made no mention of the right to counsel in 85 percent of the cases in Gotham City, 32 percent of the cases in Metro City, and 6 percent of the cases in Zenith City (Lefstein, Stapleton, and Teitelbaum, 1969). These figures indicated that two of the three courts failed to apply the Gault standards systematically as far as the advisement of the right to counsel was concerned.

The figures cited in the study do not necessarily indicate full compliance with the Gault standards. A judge could still discourage the election of the right to an attorney simply by phrasing the inquiry in a leading manner. Consider the following excerpt from a report of an actual case:

"At this time, I'd like to inform you that you have a right to have an attorney. If you cannot afford an attorney, I'll appoint an attorney for you. Or, on the other hand, if you'd like, we can have the case heard today." The woman said something and the judge said, "I can't hear you." Then the woman said that she would like to have it heard today. The judge said, "Let the record show that Mrs. G _____, the mother of A _____, waives the right to an attorney." (Lefstein, Stapleton, and Teitelbaum, 1969: 512)

The Supreme Court ruled during *In re Gault* that juveniles could not be required to incriminate themselves. If a juvenile does not invoke the privilege of self-incrimination, the judge must inform the child that this right is available. Judges in the Gotham court failed to advise a single juvenile of the privilege against self-incrimination. Such advice was given in only 29 percent of the Metro court cases and in 33 percent of the Zenith cases. Again, the way in which the judge informed the child of this constitutional protection can color the spirit of the law. The following case report is an example:

Initially, the judge made comments to the effect that all boys were involved in the arson, although some may have taken part in different ways. After these statements, the judge stated, "Now none of you have to answer anything. You don't have to say anything. I'll start with A _____." The judge asks A _____ if he was involved, saying, "A _____?" And A _____ says, "Yes." (Lefstein, Stapleton, and Teitelbaum, 1969: 522)

In re Gault also extended the right to confront and to cross-examine witnesses. Thus, for example, if the owner of a stolen car fails to appear in court, the judge can dismiss the case. The survey revealed that the judges failed to dismiss several cases in which essential witnesses failed to appear. Again, this practice was contrary to the guidelines laid down by the Supreme Court.[3]

The conclusion reached by Lefstein and his associates was that none of the juvenile courts studied was operating in full compliance with the standards promulgated by the Gault decision. More recent evidence also suggests that juvenile courts have not fully afforded to juveniles the rights upheld in *Kent* and *Gault*. Sprowls (1980) reported in his study of juvenile courts in seventeen Pennsylvania counties that "there was not one reference to counsel in any of the case files reviewed" (p. 66). Moreover, after interviewing members of the juvenile court staff, Sprowls concluded that the juvenile court staff became particularly defensive and uncooperative when queried about the role of counsel in the juvenile courts studied.

Sprowls (1980), Stapleton and Teitelbaum (1973), and Canon and Kolson (1971) have suggested that a juvenile's decision to be represented by counsel may, in some cases, be "the kiss of death. . . . Representation by counsel, particularly aggressive, adversarial representation [may produce] dispositional outcomes inconsistent with the client's interests" (Sprowls, 1980: 17–18). This is especially possible in situations where the court "disapproves" of such representation. Taking an opposite view, some critics of the juvenile justice system have argued that full compliance with Supreme Court guidelines concerning proper legal counsel for juvenile defendants has made the juvenile court too much like an adult court. The result is that the original philosophy of the juvenile court, including the notion of the court as "nonadversarial, nonlegal, and nonpunitive," has been lost (Sagatun and Edwards, 1979: 18). Some critics argue further that youthful law offenders who are willing to admit their guilt may be persuaded not to do so by the presence of a defense attorney (Bogen, 1980).

Grisso: Cognitive Barriers to Justice.   Even when the juvenile court operates in full procedural compliance with the Gault requirements, the outcome may be substantially less than what the Supreme Court had envisioned. While examining compliance in the St. Louis juvenile court, Grisso (1981) was amazed to find that virtually all the juveniles interrogated by the police had waived their Miranda rights. Intrigued by this observation, Grisso wondered whether juveniles were even "capable of providing a meaningful waiver of their rights to avoid self-incrimination and to obtain legal counsel" (p. 38). After collecting comprehension data from a sample of juveniles, Grisso found that almost everyone younger than 14 and half the juveniles in the 15 to 16 age bracket had less than adequate understanding of what their

Miranda rights entailed. Consequently, if a substantial number of juveniles simply do not possess the competence to understand the typical Miranda advisement, then these juveniles could not make a valid waiver of rights (see Ferguson and Douglas, 1970).

In light of juveniles' inability to comprehend just what it is that they are waiving, it would appear incumbent upon the court to alter its routine practices. But just what should be done? Grisso explores several possible solutions and their ramifications. One proposal might be to rephrase the Miranda warning to make it more comprehensible. As attractive as a rewriting might appear, it would not be practical. Even though juveniles understood they had the right to remain silent, they did not realize it was an absolute right. The way one juvenile explained it was: "If I'm in court, I have to tell the truth, the whole truth, and nothing but the truth. So when the judge asks you what you done, you got to tell him even if you don't want to" (p. 124). Thus, increasing the comprehensibility of the warning would not automatically ensure that subsequent waivers would be valid.

A second solution might be to include a mandatory law education course in the school curriculum. However, having such a requirement would not guarantee mastery of legal rights. A third possibility would be to assess the child's understanding prior to waiver. Law enforcement officers would object strenuously, since this practice would erect another barrier to police investigations, particularly in those situations requiring immediate action. Furthermore, some juveniles might deliberately flunk preinterrogation comprehension tests in the hope of achieving greater leniency. A fourth proposal would be to require parents or guardians to be present at the time of waiver. Unfortunately, many parents are not legal experts and are not versed in juvenile law. In addition, Grisso's analysis of parent-child communication showed that a large number of parents would not allow their children to heed their Miranda rights. Instead, these parents would virtually force the child into confessing even though it would be self-incriminating.

Given all these objections, what possible solutions would work? Grisso (1981: 202–205) suggests two. The first proposal calls for state legislatures to pass a law requiring either a blanket exclusion of all juvenile confessions or that an attorney be present during questioning, particularly if the child is under 14 years old. These recommendations would be consistent with the results of Grisso's study and mirror the *mens rea* assumption employed by the juvenile justice system. Undoubtedly, Grisso's endorsement would meet with strong opposition. For example, the costs associated with mandatory provision of an attorney would be enormous. In addition, there is the problem of role conflict that needs some type of resolution. Does the attorney represent the child as client, or is the attorney an advisor to the court? The role conflict inherent in this proposal will receive greater attention later in this chapter.

The suggestion of providing a blanket exclusion for all juvenile confessions would come under fire also. The law enforcement community would view it as a serious hindrance to police investigation. A quick look at the criminal statistics in Chapter 3 shows that arrest and clearance rates would decrease dramatically. At the same time, juvenile judges would object to the erosion of their discretion and the impediment to the court's attempt to fulfill its *parens patriae* mission.

Grisso's other recommendatioin is more compatible and traditional. It is suggested that the juvenile judge spend considerably more time probing the juvenile's competence and the conditions under which a waiver was obtained. Such an approach could be implemented immediately, would not hamper law enforcement investigations, would avoid many of the earlier objections, and would permit a more individualized assessment. Of course, one could raise a more penetrating objection. If juvenile court judges have been able to circumvent the *Gault* protections mandated by the United States Supreme Court, why would one expect the issue of competence to fare any better?

The Impact of *Kent*

One of the more pressing issues confronting the juvenile court is the critical accusation that it coddles future criminals. While juveniles are af-

forded the luxury of a system that basks in its *parens patriae* philosophy, academicians and practitioners both bemoan the fact that rehabilitation has not worked. In other words, the promisers of rehabilitation have failed to deliver tangible results. Consequently, public officials have attempted to patch the problem by introducing harsh, "get tough" policies. Examples of such proposals include efforts to lower the maximum age of juvenile court jurisdiction and the passage of new statutes governing waiver mechanisms. The purpose of both proposals is to expel serious delinquents who have eluded all rehabilitative efforts and to propel them into the adult system.

The case of *Kent v. United States* recognized the dramatically divergent goals of the juvenile and adult court systems. Since waiver had such important implications for his client, Kent's attorney wished to keep the case within the juvenile justice system. Because the juvenile court had violated the sense of fair play, the federal Supreme Court agreed with Kent's attorney. In addition to specifying the proper procedural safeguards applicable to waiver, the Court appended a variety of criteria that should guide the waiver decision. One direct consequence was that state legislatures considered the enactment or revision of waiver provisions and adhered to the suggested guidelines. Once a child is waived to the criminal court, all the constitutional rights an adult possesses attach to the child. Some of these available rights include trial by jury, bail, and stricter rules of evidence.

Legislative Reaction.   There are two types of waiver, judicial and legislative. The *Kent* case, for example, involved judicial waiver. *Judicial waiver* occurs when a juvenile court judge decides that a juvenile is either dangerous or not amenable to rehabilitation and transfers the case to the adult system. *Legislative waiver* compels the juvenile court to remand certain youths who commit specific offenses to the adult court. These individuals then must face charges as if they were adults.

In an effort to curb judicial discretion in transferring juvenile offenders to the adult court, many states have sought to handle the problem by emphasizing strictly objective criteria in the waiver process that either automatically exclude certain juveniles from juvenile court jurisdiction or create a presumption in favor of exclusion. At least one study suggests that "despite its defects and potential for abuse," the traditional discretionary process [judicial waiver] appears to be more successful . . . in identifying the more serious juvenile offenders [than legislative waiver] (Osbun and Rode, 1984: 199). However, other research cautions that a strict judicial decision regarding juvenile transfer to the adult court is inconsistent and discriminatory (Feld, 1983; Bortner, 1986).

As mentioned earlier, many states conformed to the Kent criteria when considering change in waiver laws. Florida's waiver provision, fortunately, is quite representative of the various state waiver statutes. Florida statutes instruct the state attorney that a motion for waiver can be submitted within one week of filing a delinquency petition and prior to the hearing stage only if the child meets three conditions. The conditions include a chronological age of at least 14 when the act was committed, a previous delinquency adjudication for a violent crime (murder, sexual battery, robbery, aggravated battery, or aggravated assault), and that the present charge is murder, sexual battery, robbery, aggravated battery, or aggravated assault. After receiving the state attorney's motion, a waiver hearing is scheduled.

The criteria warranting consideration focus on the offender, the offense, and the prospects of rehabilitation. Offender characteristics include the youth's prior involvement with the juvenile justice system and whether the child possesses an adequate *mens rea.* Offense characteristics focus on offense seriousness, particularly if the crime was a violent offense, whether the crime was perpetrated in a heinous fashion, prospects for successful conviction in the adult court, and whether other accomplices have been transferred or tried in the adult court. Finally, the judge must consider whether the juvenile constitutes a menace to society and what the chances are that the juvenile court can find an appropriate strategy which will rehabilitate the child.[4]

Should the juvenile court judge transfer the youth to the adult court, Florida statutes [Chapter 39.12(6) (a)] stipulate that the transfer must not

be construed as to indicate the accused is guilty. In addition, the state attorney may not inform the jury that the accused was waived by the juvenile court. In the event the waived youth is found guilty of the charges, Florida statutes allow the juvenile to be treated like an adult offender in the event of recidivism.

Waiver Studies. Despite the awesome consequences associated with the outcome of waiver, criminologists have neglected this research area. Consequently, only very basic questions have been examined in the available literature. Some of these basic considerations include who gets waived, why, and what happens in terms of sentencing dispositions.

After the enactment of Florida's waiver provisions, the Florida Department of Health and Rehabilitative Services (1980) monitored a sample of waiver cases. The result showed that only "40% of the cases involving a request that the case be transferred actually resulted in the case being transferred" (pp 18–19). Although filing a motion for waiver does not automatically produce a transfer, 3.4 percent of the juvenile court cases eventually were transferred to the adult court. Over half the cases involved legislative or judicial waiver, while the state attorney accounted for 27 percent of the cases and grand jury indictments produced 17.4 percent of the cases (p. 23). The remaining transfers included self-request (0.6 percent) and previously waived youth (4 percent). Interestingly, only 71 percent of the waivers involved felony charges. The misdemeanor cases involved petty larceny, shoplifting, trespass, loitering and prowling, and possession of marijuana less than 5 grams.

As noted earlier, waiver invites the attachment of constitutional rights normally reserved for adults. Half the children were unable to make bond even though they had the right to bond, and all were represented by counsel in the form of private (3 percent), court appointed (16 percent), or public defender attorneys (81 percent). Despite the statutory admonition that waiver should not be equated with guilt, the state was able to post a 96 percent conviction rate (p. 27). Approximately two-thirds of the cases resulted in a jail or prison term, with the average period of confinement being slightly over two years.

A more comprehensive study in terms of coverage was a 1978 census of all juvenile courts in the United States. Hamparian and her associates (1982) reported tremendous difficulty in compiling standardized information given varying state statutes, different jurisdictional practices, and the varying minimum and maximum jurisdictional ages in the states. In any event, 7,881 juveniles were subjected to waiver in calendar year 1978 (p. 105). Most of these defendants were male (92 percent) and white (61 percent). While the majority of offenses were serious, 43 percent of the cases in Oregon, for example, were for drug violations, liquor violations, and other public order offenses (p. 107). In addition, 16 percent of the waivers in Missouri were based on status offenses, traffic offenses, offenses against the family, and other minor transgressions (p. 107). Thus, one might question the basis for transferring these "serious" offenders to the adult court (see Bortner, 1986).

In terms of court outcome, virtually all (91 percent) of the waived youth were convicted (p. 112). Of those found guilty, 54 percent were placed on probation (p. 112). Thus, over half the offenders considered too serious to be handled by the juvenile court received a minor disposition. Of those juveniles subjected to major sentencing dispositions, none incurred the death penalty.[5] While a quarter received a sentence of less than one year, it is estimated that at least half of the waived defendants spent less than eighteen months in confinement (p. 114). Of course it is difficult to draw any conclusions in the absense of comparable adult data. However, it does appear that the mere fact of waiver does increase the certainty of punishment (See Rudman et al., 1986).

One study of Philadelphia homicide cases included both juveniles certified as adults and adult offenders. Eigen (1981) found that certification was more likely to occur in cases involving a white victim–black offender and in cases where there were multiple offenders. Waived juveniles were just as likely to be found guilty of felony murder or manslaughter as were adults. Sentencing differentials were virtually nonexistent. In fact, "all juveniles tried in criminal court for felony killings

were convicted and sentenced to prison with a median minimum sentence of three-to-five years. The fact that no juvenile received probation further underscores the impact of waiver for juveniles arrested in felony murder" (p. 1084). In terms of non-felony murders, waived juveniles were somewhat more likely to be found guilty and sentenced to somewhat longer terms than were comparable adults. Thus, it would appear that waiver increased the certainty of punishment.

The Deterrent Effect of Waiver.   While conducting a field study of delinquent activity, Glassner and his research team (1983) noticed a sizable decrease in illegal activity once adolescents observed their sixteenth birthday. When the researchers investigated this pattern, most juveniles explained their lack of involvement in criminal activity in terms of court jurisdiction. At the time of the study, the juvenile court in that state relinquished original jurisdiction to the adult court when the juvenile reached age 16. Consequently, these youths, if caught by the police, would face charges as adults. As one youth explained:

> When you're a teenager you're rowdy. Nowadays you aren't rowdy. You know, you just want to settle down, because you can go to jail now. [When] you are a boy, you can be put in a detention home. But you can go to jail now. Jail ain't no place to go. (p. 219)

Other information elicited by the researchers led them to conclude that most juveniles viewed adolescence as the time to experiment in illegal activity. However, criminal involvement after attaining legal adulthood was perceived as carrying a heavy penalty. Although one commentator (Feld, 1983: 206) criticizes the trying of juveniles in adult criminal court as creating "instant virgins" in the sense that the judge does not have access to waived juveniles' prior histories and must treat them as first offenders, the possibility of an appearance in adult court deterred these adolescents from continued criminal activity. As Glassner and colleagues wrote:

It is ironic that juvenile courts appear to serve some of their intended purposes, despite the many problems that have been noted about them. They are juxtaposed to adult courts, at least in the mythology of adolescents: by appearing benign compared to adult courts they may prevent some criminality, and possibly thwart criminal careers. (p. 221)

THE JUVENILE COURT PROCESS

The juvenile justice system is distinctly different from the adult criminal justice system. The aim of the juvenile court is to protect and safeguard children from embarking upon a criminal career, rather than to prosecute children. This ideological difference is reflected in a special legal vocabulary for the juvenile court. Instead of being arrested, a child is "taken into custody." Instead of being sent to jail, a juvenile is "placed in secure detention." A child is not indicted on criminal charges; instead, the child "has a petition of delinquency filed on his or her behalf." An adult goes to trial, where the verdict is guilty or not guilty. The juvenile has a hearing where the outcome is "adjudication as delinquent" or "adjudication as nondelinquent." If adjudicated delinquent, the child is not sentenced to a penitentiary; rather, the child is "institutionalized" or "committed to a reformatory."

The juvenile justice system, as outlined in Figure 15.1, consists of a series of four stages referred to simply as **custody, intake, adjudication,** and **disposition**. Not all children are funneled through the entire system. Depending on the circumstances of the case and what decisions are made, a juvenile can be processed through the entire system or make an early exit prior to the dispositional stage.

Custody: Entering the System

Most children enter the juvenile justice system through contact with the police. Let us return to the case of Billy, Joe, and Tommy. Officers Dill

and Williams were on routine patrol when they received a burglary of an auto complaint from the dispatcher. While en route to the crime scene, the officers observed three boys in the neighborhood who matched the descriptions of the suspects. Upon investigation, the officers had reason to believe that these three were the suspects involved in the complaint. The officers, after talking with the boys, took them into custody.

What was the legal basis for the actions taken by Officers Dill and Williams? After sighting the boys, the officers had grounds for reasonable suspicion. *Reasonable suspicion* means that the officers encountered circumstances "which reasonably indicate that such person(s) has committed, is committing, or is about to commit a violation . . . of any law" (Dade County Public Safety Department, 1977: 26). The observation of three juveniles on two bicycles in the vicinity of the crime location matching the description radioed by the dispatcher gave the officers grounds for reasonable suspicion. Under the **stop-and-frisk** law, an officer with reasonable suspicion may temporarily detain a subject in order to find out who the person is and what that person is doing at the present location (Florida Statutes, Chapter 901.151, 1979). Thus, when Officer Williams ordered the juveniles to approach the patrol car, he was invoking the "stop-and-frisk" powers.

During the course of conversation, little Tommy proclaimed his innocence before the officers told the juveniles what they were investigating. Tommy's statement immediately gave the officers probable cause. **Probable cause** means that there is "a reasonable ground of suspicion, supported by circumstances sufficiently strong in themselves to warrant a cautious [person] in believing the accused [person] to be guilty" (Dade County Public Safety Department, 1977: 26). As soon as Tommy denied his participation in the crime, the officers had probable cause to believe that these three boys were the ones who had committed the crime. Because larceny over $100 is a third-degree felony, the officers were justified in taking the three juveniles into custody, even though the offense had not taken place in their presence (Florida Statutes, Chapter 812.021 (5)g, 1979).

After taking the three juveniles into custody,

FIGURE 15.1   **The Juvenile Justice System**

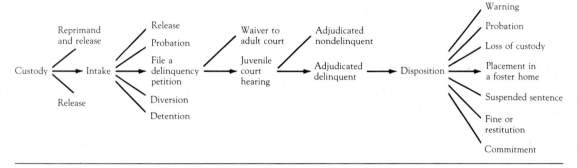

Source: Adapted from the Florida Bureau of Criminal Justice Association.

Officer Williams advised them of their constitutional rights by reading the Miranda warning. The use of the Miranda warning arose from a 1966 United States Supreme Court ruling which stipulated that suspects must be advised of their right against self-incrimination and their right to counsel prior to custodial interrogation (*Miranda* v. *Arizona*, 1966). The *In re Gault* decision extended several constitutional protections to juveniles who faced a potential loss of freedom. Although the Gault ruling did not explicitly connect the Miranda warning to police interrogations, the police routinely inform all suspects of their constitutional rights after custody in order to ensure that any subsequent confession is voluntary.

After taking the three juveniles into custody, Officers Dill and Williams conducted a **field investigation**. In Florida and some other states, if a suspect is apprehended within two hours of a crime and in the vicinity of the crime location, he or she may be transported back to the scene of the occurrence in order to determine whether the eyewitness can make a positive identification (Dade County Public Safety Department, 1977). The suspect does not have the right to an attorney during this confrontation procedure. Thus, when the officers returned Billy, Joe, and Tommy to the apartments, the victim identified the juveniles as the perpetrators. At the same time, Officers Dill and Williams gathered the information necessary for their report.

Having concluded the field investigation, Officers Dill and Williams faced a decision. What should they do with the three juveniles? As explained in Chapter 14, a police officer has six available options at this point. The officer can (1) simply conduct an interview, (2) informally reprimand the child, (3) give an official reprimand and release the child, (4) place the child under police supervision, (5) give the child a **citation**, or (6) transport the child to the juvenile bureau.

Officers Dill and Williams made the decision to transport the three juveniles to the juvenile detention facility because the alleged offense was a felony. Once inside the detention facility, the police officers prepared a crimes-against-property incident report and a probable cause statement. The incident report contained the name and address of the victim and a description of the incident, including when it took place and where it happened. In addition, the officers indicated what action they took to conclude the case. The second report, the probable cause statement, outlined the activities undertaken by the officers and the reasons for taking the three juveniles into custody.

In Florida, if the juvenile is accused of a felony, as in this case, he or she will be fingerprinted and photographed. The fingerprint cards and the photographs must be kept at the juvenile facility and stored in a nonpublic record. Should the judge later find the juvenile not to be delinquent, the judge can order the fingerprints and photographs destroyed. If the judge finds the juvenile to be delinquent, copies of the fingerprints and photographs will be released to the state department of law enforcement, the county sheriff's department, and other local police departments (Florida Statutes, Chapter 39.03 (6) (a), 39.03 (6) (b), 1979). Once the fingerprints, photographs, and reports are completed, the officers turn the juvenile over to the authority of the juvenile court.

To summarize, custody represents the culmination of a field investigation by law enforcement officers. After establishing that a crime took place and what the surrounding circumstances were, the police may temporarily detain likely suspects for a short field interrogation. If the police officer established probable cause during the interrogation, the officer can take the suspect into custody and advise the suspect of his or her constitutional rights. The officer then has the duty to transport the juvenile in custody to the juvenile detention center for further processing.

Intake: Analyzing the Situation

The first processing point the child encounters within the juvenile justice system is the intake procedure. The purpose of intake is to determine whether the child falls within the juvenile court's jurisdiction and if so, what course of action ought to be pursued. The intake probation officer first determines whether the juvenile court has proper jurisdiction. The officer checks the juvenile's age to make sure he or she is a minor and whether the alleged offense took place within the geographical boundaries of the court. If both conditions are met, then the juvenile court in that locale can process the case.

The second task the intake officer faces is deciding what to do with the juvenile. About half the children referred to the juvenile court system are not funneled through the system. Instead, they are diverted away from a formal hearing. The other half remain within the system and receive formal handling.

What happened to Billy, Joe, and Tommy? After the officers finished their paperwork and left, the intake officer began to interview the boys. The officer filled out an information form on each,

asking for their parents' names, addresses, and phone numbers, their full names, and the addresses where each child was living. After gathering the necessary information, the officer called the boys' parents to advise them of their children's whereabouts.

Depending upon the time of day and the staffing situation, the intake officer may place the child in detention overnight or ask the parents or guardian to come down to juvenile hall for an interview. At such an interview, the intake officer advises both parents and child of the constitutional rights under *Miranda*. The Miranda case, in conjunction with the Gault decision, stipulated that a person in custody has the right to an attorney, has the privilege against self-incrimination, and has the right to remain silent, following the warning that anything the person in custody says can and will be used against him or her in a court of law.[6] Usually at this point the intake officer will ask the parents and the child to sign a form which states that they have been advised of their constitutional rights. Should the parents or child refuse to sign this form, the intake officer will simply mark the form "Refused to Sign."

If the interview continues, the intake officer reviews the police report and obtains the child's version of the incident. In addition, the officer probes to see how well the child is doing in school and whether the child is experiencing any other emotional, family, or adjustment problems. The officer also reviews his or her decision options at this point. These options include (1) filing a **delinquency petition**, (2) giving a lecture and then releasing the juvenile, (3) referral or diversion to a noncourt institution, or (4) informal probation. Since half the juveniles are processed formally and the other half are processed informally, we will review some studies concerning what factors influence the intake officer's decision to file formal charges.

Researchers investigating the decisions made by intake officers generally focus on two sets of variables. The first set are commonly referred to as *legal variables*. They include such things as the type of offense; whether it is a felony, misdemeanor, or status offense; the seriousness of the offense; and whether the child has a prior record.

The second set of indicators, *social variables*, include such factors as race, age, sex, family stability, socioeconomic status, and school status. The strategy researchers typically use is to determine which set of variables is more influential with respect to the outcome of the intake interview. If some social variables, such as race or social class, appear to be more important predictors of the decision to process juveniles through the court stage than do the legal variables, such as prior record or seriousness of current offense, researchers generally conclude that some form of discrimination exists. If the legal variables appear to be more influential than the social variables, researchers generally conclude that discriminatory practices are generally absent.

Thornberry (1973) utilized data from the Philadelphia juvenile justice system to see whether blacks and lower class children received differential treatment at various stages of the juvenile justice system. His analysis of 3,475 delinquent cases revealed that the police referred 41 percent of the black youths and 21 percent of the white youths to the juvenile court intake office. Intake officers filed delinquency petitions against 58 percent of the black youths, compared to 53 percent of the white youths. When Thornberry considered the seriousness of the offense, he found that some differences persisted. Intake officers did not refer more blacks than whites for a court hearing when the offense was serious. However, blacks were somewhat more likely to draw a court hearing when the offensed was minor. When Thornberry considered the number of previous offenses, he found no real difference. Court referrals generally increased as the number of prior offenses increased. Thus, the data did not indicate that blacks systematically received more severe dispositions at the intake level in comparison to whites.

Meade's (1974) analysis of the intake decision for first offenders in the Atlanta juvenile court produced similar results. Race and class were not significantly related to the intake decision of whether a child should go before a judge for a formal hearing. In other words, being black or coming from a lower social class did not increase the odds of receiving a formal court hearing for first-time juvenile offenders. In addition, being a

school dropout, coming from a broken home, being male, being older (ages 15 to 16), or committing a nonstatus offense had no impact on the intake officer's decision. Meade concluded that intake counselors in the Atlanta juvenile court approached each case on an individual basis to determine which course of action would be more advantageous to the child.

An analysis of another juvenile court intake office indicated that both legal and social variables exerted an influence on the outcome. Thomas and Sieverdes (1975) reported that seriousness of offense became an important consideration when the child was a male, had a prior record, was black, was older, or had committed the offense with a companion. Similarly, whether or not the child was a recidivist, a repeat offender, was an important consideration when the child was black, came from a lower social class, committed a felony offense, had an accomplice, or was over the age of 16. These findings led Thomas and Sieverdes to conclude that intake officers considered both legal and social factors when deciding whether to handle a case formally or informally.

In another study of juvenile court intake decisions, the researcher divided juveniles into those children being referred for a status offense and those children being referred for a nonstatus offense (T. J. Carter, 1979). He found that two legal variables, number of prior court appearances and prior record, and two social variables, age and social class, were important determinants of formal processing for nonstatus offenders. For status offenders, age, sex, and previous police contact predicted formal processing. Thus, it appeared that a mixture of legal and social variables influenced the intake decision.

An appropriate question at this point is why these reports contain divergent findings. One research team suggested two possible answers (Cohen and Kluegel, 1979b). First, earlier studies contained a variety of methodological deficiencies and were not very sophisticated. Second, not every court takes the same philosophical stance toward juveniles. Some courts are legalistically oriented and adhere to a "due process" model; that is, they give the child all his or her legal rights and treat each equally. Other courts are treatment oriented;

they try to give offenders individualized treatment, depending on the circumstances of the case. Consequently, it would be consistent for some juvenile courts, especially those emphasizing a treatment orientation, to weight social variables more heavily than legal variables in intake decisions.

To investigate these two possibilities, Cohen and Kluegel undertook a detailed analysis of intake decisions during 1972 at two different locations, Denver and Memphis. The Denver juvenile court emphasized the "due process" model and stressed a legalistic orientation. In contrast, the Memphis court was more traditional and approached each case from a therapeutic model.

An analysis of 2,654 cases from the Denver court and 5,963 cases from the Memphis court identified some jurisdictional differences at the intake point. The treatment-oriented Memphis court was, overall, more likely to handle juveniles informally than the legalistic Denver court. At the same time, the treatment-oriented Memphis court was more apt to formally process alcohol offenders, drug offenders, and property offenders than was the Denver court. Although some social variables were important, the researchers found evidence of neither race nor class biases at the intake decision. There was, however, a sex bias in the handling of juveniles in both courts. Females were more likely to receive formal handling when referred for alcohol, drug, and other decorum offenses. Thus, despite the difference in orientation, this social variable was an important consideration in both courts.

One could conclude from these studies that race and class discriminatory practices are not rampant at the intake level. It also appears that the philosophical orientation of the local court has an important bearing on screening decisions. What is missing, though, is a thorough understanding of the process by which juvenile intake counselors screen cases.

Researchers conducting secondary analyses of juvenile court intake decisions generally make three basic assumptions (Needleman, 1981). First, these analysts assume that court referral is the most serious available alternative to the intake counselor. Second, researchers think that intake personnel look for certain personal characteristics and that the presence or absence of these characteristics dictates an appropriate line of action. Third, it is commonly thought that official court records, including field case notes, accurately reflect case handling. Acceptance of these three assumptions guides researchers during the course of their research. Unfortunately, these assumptions may be false and, as a result, damaging to the research product.

Needleman (1981) spent two years working with and observing juvenile court intake officers in order to determine just how these court officials do their jobs. Her experiences directly contradicted the three assumptions just discussed. Contrary to popular belief, court referral is not always the most severe outcome at intake. In fact, some counselors fear that court referral might culminate in more lenient and ineffective treatment for the youth. Instead of scheduling a case on an already crowded docket for an appearance three months later, some probation officers prefer to deal immediately with a juvenile's problem. Thus, a period of supervised probation allows the counselor to keep close tabs on a child who would normally go home and return three months later at the appointed hour to see the judge.

Another erroneous assumption is that the juvenile offender is the focus of attention at intake. Researchers typically analyze the social characteristics of the arrested youth, but neglect factors pertinent to the offender's social situation. For example, probation officers in Needleman's study decided how to handle a quarter of the juveniles without even having seen the child. The counselors already had collected background information as to whether there were family problems or trouble in school. According to Needleman: "If a cursory check of the child's family and social circumstances reveals adequate supervision and support, the PO will usually decide not to spend much time on the case. The PO may interview the child only briefly, or not at all, in making this determination, because it is the child's social situation that is being judged. Again, the offender and the offense itself may be almost irrelevant" (pp. 254–255). Thus, lack of a statistical relationship between seriousness of current offense and intake decision in some studies becomes more understandable.

The final assumption made by researchers is that official records accurately reflect case histories. According to Needleman (1981), some of the variables recorded in the intake files actually take place after the probation officer has decided upon an appropriate dispositional alternative. For example, intake counselors may contact the victim and convince him or her through a series of arguments to drop or to press charges. While the intake counselor played a dominant role in this type of decision, only the victim's wishes about prosecution would be recorded in the file. Thus, researchers not familiar with the activities of probation officers might falsely interpret the records as "real" data.

The observations recorded by Needleman (1981) pose serious questions as to the reliability and validity of earlier empirical studies of intake results. Although these observations may detract from earlier studies, some other questions do remain. As we mentioned previously, half the juveniles are funneled into the system at intake, and the other half avoid a formal court hearing. Where do these children go? What happens to them? The intake officer can dispose of a case in five different informal ways.

First, the intake officer can dismiss the charges for a variety of reasons. The legal evidence may be lacking, the offense may be petty, the victim may have received restitution, or the intake officer may believe that further processing would be of no benefit. Second, the intake officer may give the juvenile a short warning lecture and then release the child. Third, the child may be placed on informal probation with a consent decree. A *consent decree* places the individual on temporary probation, usually for a six-month period. If the juvenile abides by the terms of the probation, the delinquency petition is dismissed. But if the juvenile violates probation or commits another offense during this time, he or she can be returned to the juvenile court for a formal hearing on the initial petition. In a sense, a consent decree involves serving one's sentence prior to, and under

threat of, adjudication. Fourth, the intake officer may refer the child to another agency, such as a mental health clinic, for attention. The fifth alternative is diversion. The intake officer usually uses the diversion option when he or she perceives the violation to be minor or the child to be predelinquent. A *predelinquent* child is one who has not yet committed a delinquent act but exhibits signs of becoming involved in delinquency in the future. The intake officer may use the diversion strategy to prevent future delinquency and to cure current ills. (We will discuss diversion as an alternative in Chapter 17.)

What happened at intake to Billy, Joe, and Tommy? The juvenile court intake officer decided to file delinquency petitions against the boys. Billy had a record for truancy, and Joe had been in trouble once before for breaking windows at a housing construction site. Tommy, the youngest of the three children, had no record but seemed to the officer to be very impressionable. In addition, the alleged offense was a felony, a serious charge. The victim, Mr. Pittman, lost an object worth a considerable amount of money and was adamant about recouping his loss. After reviewing all the particulars of the case, the juvenile officer decided that the most appropriate route would be to file a delinquency petition and hold a formal hearing. Billy, Joe, and Tommy would have to see the judge.

Adjudication: Going to Court

A hearing for Billy, Joe, and Tommy was set for two weeks later. At the appointed time, the three boys and their parents would come to the juvenile facility for an adjudicatory hearing. The purpose of the **adjudicatory hearing** is to determine whether a child is delinquent. The judge has three options: The case can be dismissed, adjudication can be withheld and the child placed on probation or referred to another agency, or the judge can find the child to be delinquent. When a judge finds the child to be delinquent, a **disposition hearing** is scheduled for the near future.

The juvenile adjudicatory hearing bears some

resemblance to the adult process. When the judge enters the hearing room, he or she is wearing the traditional black robe of the office. The bailiff orders everyone to stand and announces that the juvenile court is now in session.

The hearing usually begins with the juvenile probation officer recounting the details of the alleged incident and the decisions in the case to date. After the probation officer completes the informational report, the judge conducts a waiver inquiry. The U.S. Supreme Court decision *In re Gault* guarantees juveniles the right to adequate notice of charges, the right to counsel, the right to confront and cross-examine witnesses, and the privilege against self-incrimination. The *waiver inquiry* is held to ensure that child and parents understand these rights and to determine whether child and parents wish to exercise or waive all or any of these constitutional rights.

Once the judge completes this inquiry, testimony begins. The judge hears the testimony of both victim and witnesses and then discusses these materials with the juvenile. The judge will obtain the child's version of the incident and usually stresses the gravity of the situation to the child. After reviewing the case, the judge makes a finding in the case and decides whether to adjudicate the child as delinquent.

The first thing the judge did with Billy, Tommy, and Joe was to determine whether they understood what the charges were. All the boys nodded yes. Turning to the parents, the judge made the same inquiry and received the same answer. While conducting the waiver inquiry, the judge reminded the three boys and their parents that the court would provide free legal counsel. All indicated they did not wish the services of an attorney. After hearing testimony from Mr. Pittman and Officers Dill and Williams, the judge questioned the boys. The boys were quiet and passive. After reviewing the papers in front of him, the judge announced his finding, saying that it was quite clear that a crime had occurred and that the three boys had been involved in the incident. However, it seemed that all three boys agreed that little Tommy had nothing to do with the decision to loot the cars; nor had he entered any of the cars. Tommy was a passive observer, simply accompa-

nying his older brother Billy. Essentially, Tommy had done nothing wrong except for being in the wrong place at the wrong time. The judge decided in view of these surrounding circumstances to dismiss the petition against Tommy and to return him to the custody of his parents.

The involvement of Billy and Joe was somewhat different. These two boys had talked about searching cars and seeing what they could take. Although only one of them, Billy, actually entered Mr. Pittman's parked car without permission, Joe served as the lookout. Thus, both boys were equally involved in the crime. The judge noted that both boys had been involved in minor incidents before. As a result, the judge decided that both were delinquent and should return to the same court in ten days for a disposition hearing.

Disposition: Determining the Outcome

Most juvenile courts separate the adjudicatory hearing from the disposition hearing. This allows the probation officer some time to complete a *Presentence Investigation Report*, commonly known as a *PSI.* The PSI contains information concerning the child's home life, the stability of the family, health and medical information, school history, problems the child is experiencing, and a general history of the child's life. The PSI also contains a disposition recommendation to the judge. The alternatives available to the court cover a wide range and include (1) a simple warning from the judge, (2) probation, (3) removing the child from the custody of the parents and placing the child in a foster home, (4) a suspended sentence, (5) a fine or restitution order, or (6) commitment to a juvenile correctional facility. This stage is a critical point in the juvenile court process. Several studies have attempted to determine what variables influence the outcome.

Previously, we discussed two sets of variables that influence the intake decision, legal variables and social variables. Researchers studying intake decisions are interested in determining which of the two sets of variables is more important in explaining the outcome of the intake process. Researchers who study juvenile court dispositional outcomes employ a similar strategy. They too are interested in seeing whether legal or social variables are the most important predictors of sentencing. If social variables, such as race or class position, appear to be more important explainers of the dispositional decision, then researchers generally assume there has been some form of bias or discrimination. If legal variables appear to be more influential, researchers generally assume there has been no bias or discrimination.

An analysis of dispositions rendered in the Philadelphia juvenile court system showed the presence of some racial bias. Thornberry (1973) found that black juveniles were more likely to be sentenced to a reformatory than whites. When Thornberry controlled separately for seriousness of offense and for prior record, racial differences still persisted. When the social class background of the child was examined, it appeared that lower class juveniles were more likely to be institutionalized than upper class children. As a result, Thornberry rejected the hypothesis that legal variables are important explainers of institutionalization. Instead, he contended that the data indicated the presence of a racial and social class bias in the Philadelphia juvenile court system.

Arnold (1971) conducted a similar analysis of juvenile records in an unnamed southern city. The results showed that blacks were more likely to receive harsher sentences than whites, while social class had no significant influence. Even when black and white youths had similar family backgrounds and committed similar types of offenses, blacks received harsher sentences. Although juveniles with a prior record were more likely to receive a harsher sentence, blacks were still institutionalized more often than whites. As a result, Arnold concluded that blacks received the severest juvenile court dispositions.

Several studies have found that girls may serve longer sentences than boys. Armstrong (1977) reported that in 1964 the average time served by a female offender was 10.7 months, compared to 8.2 months for males. Similar sex differences were also reported in an analysis of New York State Family Court records during the 1965 to 1974 period (Conway and Brogdan, 1977). These sentence differentials existed in spite of the fact that most of the females were serving time for noncriminal status offenses.

Another study of a southern juvenile court separated cases according to status and nonstatus offenses. T. J. Carter (1979) found that the most important variables for understanding judicial dispositions of status offenders were having a previous court referral and coming from a lower social class. The most important variables for the nonstatus offenders were social class, previous court referrals, and multiple petitions. The most consistent finding in this study was the impact of social class on disposition decisions. This finding was of considerable interest because Carter, instead of using an objective indicator of social class like income, used the probation officer's perception of the family's social status after visiting the juvenile's home.

As previously noted, Cohen and Kluegel (1978) conducted an analysis of intake decisions in the legalistic Denver court and in the treatment-oriented Memphis court. These two researchers conducted another study in which they compared disposition outcomes in the two courts. Using a sophisticated statistical technique, Cohen and Kluegel could find no evidence of race or class bias. That is to say, blacks and lower class youths did not receive harsher sentences in comparison to whites and middle to upper class juveniles. The researchers did find that the Memphis court issued more severe sentences than the Denver court for similar types of offenses. Sentencing practices did distinguish the "due process" court from the "treatment" court. However, both courts employed similar criteria and placed a similarly strong emphasis on the existence of prior records and the type of current offense. Thornberry and Christenson (1984) also found strong support for the significant influence of prior offenses on the court dispositions of juvenile offenders.

At least one research team would argue that pitting social variables against legal variables in a search for discriminatory sentencing patterns is an inappropriate model for analyzing juvenile court dispositions. The juvenile court, in its quest for individualized treatment, must focus on some extralegal variables in order to fulfill its mandate. Horowitz and Wasserman (1980) analyzed Newark juvenile court dispositions and found two important background variables: family problems and school problems. Although these variables are neither legal nor social, they figured prominently in judicial decisions. "In every category of offense, juveniles with family and/or school problems are more likely than those without problems to be put on probation and sent to institutions and less likely to receive the most lenient dispositions" (p. 420). In terms of arrest history, all offenders, "but especially the most chronic offenders, receive more severe dispositions when they have family and/or school problems" (p. 420). Thus, it appears that the court strays from a model emphasizing legal variables and includes extralegal variables in order to become better informed about the child's situation. As a result, Horowitz and Wasserman (1980: 422) chide researchers to take into account the juvenile court's mission in order to reach a fuller understanding of juvenile court dispositions.

When weighing the evidence, we can safely conclude that race and class biases appear to be operating in some, but not all, juvenile court jurisdictions. A similar finding was reached in the discussion dealing with the impact of Supreme Court decisions on everyday juvenile court operation. Some juvenile courts have implemented the Gault standards to the letter, but others have been found to use practices that indirectly circumvent the guidelines laid down by the Supreme Court. These observations lead us to a very valid point: The juvenile courts scattered throughout this country are not part of a monolithic structure. Instead, each local jurisdiction is independent and proceeds in its own manner. So it should not come as a surprise that researchers studying different courts in varying locations come up with a variety of results.

Returning to the case of Billy and Joe, we see that the juveniles and their parents appeared at the juvenile court on the scheduled day and at the appointed time. After the bailiff announced that the court was in session, the judge began the **docket**, the schedule of cases for the day. When the judge came to the case of Billy and Joe, the probation officer recounted the circumstances surrounding the incident and reviewed the decisions to date before giving a summary of the PSI. After

reviewing the records, the judge sternly lectured Billy and Joe, emphasizing the amount of damage sustained by Mr. Pittman. The judge also reminded the two boys and their parents that the court had the power to institutionalize them and that it would do so if either boy became involved in another serious delinquent act.

In view of the good homes from which the boys came and in light of the fact that neither boy had engaged in serious delinquent acts in the past, the judge announced that he was going to place Billy and Joe on probation for eight months, or until the boys made restitution to the victim. Since both boys were involved equally in the incident and the total damage came to $200, each boy was required to make restitution in the amount of $100. Failure to make restitution during the probation period would result in another hearing for contempt of court, and the boys would be subject to commitment to a juvenile institution. Having pronounced the sentence, the judge asked if there were any questions. Hearing none, the judge concluded the case and adjourned the hearing.

JUVENILE COURT PERSONNEL

We have so far treated the official participants in the juvenile justice system in an abstract way. For example, reference has been made to the fact that some juvenile courts are more legalistically oriented than others and that court officers have a great deal of discretionary power in handling cases. It would be appropriate at this juncture to ask who the key people in the juvenile justice system are and what influences the part they play in the system.

The Judge

Although the United States Supreme Court imposed some procedural obligations on the juvenile court and questioned its basic treatment philosophy, the juvenile court judge still retains a great deal of discretion. The degree to which the organization and structure of a particular court resemble the legalistic or the treatment model largely depends on the orientation of the presiding judge (Stapleton, Aday, and Ito, 1982).

Schumacker and Anderson (1979), for example, surveyed juvenile court judges in Illinois and found that judges' backgrounds influenced their attitudes about delinquency. Judges who had assumed the bench prior to the Gault decision expressed more punitive attitudes toward delinquents, while judges who began hearing cases after 1967 were more interested in the rehabilitative aspects of the court. Another survey of Minnesota juvenile court judges uncovered a similar philosophical split. Kittel (1983) reported that about two-thirds of the judges embraced rehabilitation as their major goal. The remainder were more inclined to favor a due process and a punitive model of justice.

Based on these surveys and other studies, it seems safe to conclude that although some juvenile court judges still adhere to a more punitive crime control model, many judges follow social work philosophies of treating and protecting juveniles. The role model for these judges is that of the doctor-counselor, not the lawyer. Supporting the social work philosophy inherent in the modern juvenile court, the National Council of Juvenile Court Judges reacted unfavorably to the recent Supreme Court decisions about procedural requirements. According to the council, adversary proceedings—that is, hearings where lawyers plead defendants' cases—will destroy the informality and paternal quality of the court (Platt, 1969; Walther and McCune, 1965).

Other judges, however, are very careful about legal traditions of rules of evidence and burden of proof. Studying a court with dual "legal and social agency models of the institution," Emerson (1969) concluded that this court's adherence to certain legal procedures and standards was based on the "personal conviction of the judge" (p. 26). The point is that the role of the juvenile court judge as defined by law allows the judge a great deal of latitude in reaching decisions. This discretionary freedom has been criticized by legal reformers who believe it may unfairly affect the life of the child

and by social workers who are concerned that judges are trained in law and lack the scientific knowledge of social work required to treat juveniles (Fisher, 1960; Numberg, 1958).

Just who are the men and women in control of juvenile court discretion? In 1974 K. C. Smith attempted to answer that question in "A Profile of Juvenile Court Judges in the United States." Comparing the results of 1963 and 1973 surveys of juvenile court judges, Smith portrayed the average juvenile court judge of 1974 "as over 50 years of age, married with children, male, Protestant, a law school graduate, having a long career of public service, and spending less than one-fourth of his judicial time on juvenile matters" (p. 38). Although most of the judges had a legal education, only 8.2 percent majored in the behavioral sciences as undergraduate students, a fact which lends some support to the charge that even though juvenile court judges may subscribe to a treatment approach, they are not trained to treat juveniles.

Perhaps most interesting is the finding that "86.4% of the judges with juvenile jurisdiction in the 1973 survey devoted half-time or less to juvenile matters and 66.7% spend one-fourth of their time or less" (p. 33). When asked about the pressing problems of the juvenile court, the judges ranked "the need for alternatives to institutionalization" as their greatest concern. Ironically, the demand for "alternatives to institutionalization" was the banner cry of reformers in the movement to establish the House of Refuge in 1825 and in the movement to establish the first juvenile court in 1899. It would appear that achieving real alternatives to institutionalization is a difficult task indeed (see Rubin, 1985).

Appointed or elected, the juvenile court judge is particularly susceptible to political and public pressure. A judge who tries to follow treatment principles may be criticized for being soft on crime, and a judge who adheres to legalistic procedures may be thought to let too many kids off on technicalities. Further, the role of the juvenile court judge is plagued by low prestige and pay. Thus, the juvenile court has been hampered in its attempt to seat judges who are knowledgeable in both law and human behavior.

The Lawyer

In the last section, we discussed the extensive discretion allowed juvenile court judges. Critics of this discretionary power advocate the presence of lawyers in juvenile court to provide procedural justice for the child in the juvenile court. Evidently in agreement with this criticism, the U.S. Supreme Court rendered several decisions in the late 1960s which required that juveniles be informed about the right to counsel and provided with counsel if children and parents could not afford to retain private counsel (Alers, 1973; President's Commission, 1967c).

From the standpoint of the role of the lawyer, these decisions have wrought great changes in the juvenile court. Prior to the Court rulings, a Philadelphia study found that lawyers were present in 1 to 5 percent of all juvenile cases; representation in the 1970s in some areas was as high as 40 percent. According to a California study, use of representation has increased from 3 to 15 percent, and in some areas the percentages have been much higher. The proportion of juvenile offenders represented by counsel has traditionally been low. Juvenile court judges have discouraged the presence of lawyers in their courts because lawyers have been thought to undermine the basic treatment goal and the overriding tone of friendliness and concern in the juvenile court. "The child needs a judge, not a lawyer," insisted one judge. Thus, in the past, juvenile court personnel did not deny lawyers to juveniles, but they discouraged their use. As a result, lawyers have not been very familiar with juvenile court procedures, and uneasiness about the proper role of lawyers has been found among both lawyers and court personnel (Cayton, 1972; Coxe, 1967; Siler, 1965).

Since the presence of lawyers has become more common in juvenile court, problems stemming from role ambiguity have emerged. A study of California lawyers participating in juvenile courts indicates that attorneys in these courts tend to assume one of three roles: the traditional lawyer, the counselor or rehabilitative person, or a combination of the two (Phelps, 1976). Some observers contend that the traditional lawyer role can be dysfunctional to the court's goal of rehabilitation.

The role of a defense counsel is to work for an acquittal even though the client might in fact be guilty.

According to Bogen (1980), this stance might not be in the best interest of the child or society: "In cases where defense counsel was successful in gaining dismissal of the petition despite the fact that the minor would have been willing to tell the truth in court, the outcome was essentially the same as if there were a law permitting minors to commit crime with impunity" (p. 20). Setting a guilty juvenile free due to technicalities does nothing more than instill a warped sense of values in the child. The alternative approach, the counselor or rehabilitative style, also suffers from serious drawbacks.

Many attorneys receive very little formal training in juvenile law while in law school. In fact, some public defender offices routinely assign new and inexperienced lawyers to a stint in the juvenile court so they can get some courtroom seasoning (McAnany, 1978: 39). The question of competence, coupled with the inherent dilemma of whether these representatives should take the posture of guardian, advocate, or friend of the court, has led some commentators to issue a plea for better law school preparation and more role specificity (McAnany, 1978; Streib, 1980). The issue of legal counsel, raised in such a simplistic and clear-cut fashion in the 1967 Gault decision, is punctuated by a host of attendant questions that are just now surfacing and being debated in legal circles.

In some instances, the presence of lawyers has influenced the disposition of cases. Writing about lawyers in juvenile court, Coxe (1967) cited a Philadelphia incident in which eight juveniles were adjudicated delinquent in one 15-minute hearing; the event occurred before the Gault decision. In this hearing the minors were not informed of the charges, said nothing in court, and heard no evidence that they had indeed committed the act. When the same cases were heard again with counsel present, six cases were dismissed, and the hearings lasted three to four hours for each child. After the increase of counsel in Philadelphia courts, fewer juveniles have been detained before their hearings, and fewer have been committed to institutions. But a backlog of 7,000 cases awaiting disposition was created.

Even though the Philadelphia study showed that lawyers can aid children appearing in court, there are limits to the benefits of counsel in juvenile court. Some judges resent the intrusion of a defense attorney who takes a watchdog approach to judicial actions. Consider the following conversation one researcher held with a juvenile court judge:

> As the judge in one county explained to me, however, and as he would undoubtedly explain to counsel, the court had the right to commit the juveniles in question to a state youth-development center for an indefinite period. The judge asserted that if his decision were in error, it erred in the direction of excessive leniency. Were an objection to his practice of sentencing juveniles to weekend detention filed, he suggested that he would regrettably be forced to commit those juveniles to institutions. He made no acknowledgment of the possibility that the alternative to weekend detention might be probation. Given this type of intimidation and the court's authority to carry out its threat, it would appear to be ethically impossible for a lawyer to object to his client's sentence to weekend detention. (Sprowls, 1980: 83–84)

When unbridled judicial discretion proceeds in this manner, legal representation in juvenile court is tantamount to a "kiss of death"—or at best cannot have a noticeable impact on the outcome (Canon and Kolson, 1971; Hayeslip, 1979; Walter and Ostrander, 1982). In contrast, research done in California shows that lawyers "do their clients some good" by reducing the number of wardships and increasing the number of dismissals and suspended sentences. But the study confirmed that "dismissals were not proportionately numerous, and moreover they clustered among cases alleging neglect by parents or unfit homes" (Lemert, 1967: 103).

Lawyers in juvenile court may be unwilling to help a child accused of delinquency " 'beat a case' and may therefore do less defending and more accommodating . . . to the system of personal relationships, the philosophy, and the organiza-

tional needs of the juvenile court" (S. J. Fox, 1970: 1236). A recent study by Marshall et al. (1983) similarly found that the juvenile court tended to operate much like the adult court system with the role occupants, especially attorneys representing juvenile offenders, bowing to social and organizational pressures leading to cooperation and accommodation to "get the job done."

The Probation Officer

The probation officer is at the very heart of the juvenile justice system. The probation officer is the decision-maker who determines whether a juvenile should receive formal or informal handling. This agent of the court prepares presentence reports and makes dispositional recommendations to the judge. In addition, the probation officer is responsible for administering probation and aftercare. In short, the role of the probation officer is to keep the juvenile court functioning smoothly.

Like judges and attorneys, probation officers are not immune to external pressure. One of the more perplexing bureaucratic demands that probation officers encounter is paperwork. Probation officers commonly claim that the paperwork and documentation that accompany a case pose a hindrance to counseling. Time spent shuffling paper, they claim, could be better spent in counseling sessions. However, one study concluded that the amount of time spent on bureaucratic details was unrelated to the amount of time spent counseling juveniles (Gillham and Bersani, 1976). In other words, counselors perceive themselves to be caught in a dilemma between the intrusion of paperwork and the goal of rehabilitating youth, although in fact this is not the case.

Professional orientation also affects job performance. Anderson and Spanier (1980) surveyed juvenile probation officers in Pennsylvania and found a distinction between counselors with a treatment orientation and those with a legal orientation. Probation officers with a higher educational level were more likely to stress a rehabilitation orientation and recommended fewer legal dispositions. These probation officers were also more likely to define juveniles as in need of treatment rather than as delinquent. Thus, a probation officer's educational background appeared to be an important determinant of the type of handling a juvenile receives within the juvenile court.

KEY ISSUES FOR THE JUVENILE COURT

In the 1960s and 1970s, the juvenile court became the focus of much debate. Just about every facet of court procedure and rationale was examined and, most often, criticized by correctional workers and academic and legal observers. Criticism of the court centered on four major issues. One was the broad jurisdiction of the court, specifically the question of noncriminal offenses. Another was the failure of the court to prevent rising delinquency rates. A third was the reliance of the court on so-called treatment programs as a solution for delinquency in light of how little was really known about the causes and prevention of delinquency. The fourth was the court's continued willingness to institutionalize children, particularly the practice of detaining children with adult offenders. We will now examine each of these four areas of criticism.

The Broad Jurisdiction of the Court

The intention of early child-saving reformers was to provide needed help to children, regardless of the nature of each child's difficulty. After all, a child could be in trouble for a number of reasons, including truancy, crime, ungovernability, neglect, and so on. To early reformers there was little difference in the categories of delinquency, neglect, and dependency. All three were thought to represent steps on the stairway to crime: The court was intended legally to intervene in the lives of these types of children (President's Commission, 1967c).

In the late 1960s critics began to attack the broad jurisdiction of the juvenile court and the rationale on which this jurisdiction was based.

The court's influence over children who committed acts that would not be illegal if committed by adults was particularly challenged. The commission appointed by President Lyndon B. Johnson (1967c) charged:

> In view of the stigma and disabilities that accompany being labeled a delinquent and the growing doubt about the need for intervention in many cases . . . the youth who has once been through the process and comes out a delinquent is more likely to act delinquent again. (p. 23)

Further, it was suggested that the juvenile court's jurisdiction over noncriminal offenses may have the unintended consequence of producing criminal conduct among juveniles who were originally involved only in noncriminal offenses (Handler, 1965).

Similarly, removal of court jurisdiction over cases of dependency has been advocated because the cases of children whose parents cannot take care of them appear to belong in social work agencies, not in courts "whose latent structure is criminal." There is evidence that the stigma of juvenile court processing extends to those children adjudicated dependent or neglected as well as those termed delinquent. At one time, the lack of social work services provided a rationale for the court's broad reach. Today, social welfare agencies abound, and

> [The] net conclusion is that incorrigibility, truancy, and running away should not in themselves be causes for assuming juvenile court jurisdiction over children. There is much reason to believe that the bulk of such problems can be handled successfully by referrals, demonstrated by an inquiry in the District of Columbia where it was found that non-court agencies took responsibility for 98 percent of the total identifiable or reported runaways, 95 percent of truancies, 76 percent of sex offenses, and 46 percent of youth termed ungovernable. (Lemert, 1967: 99)

The solution suggested by reformers, then, has been to eliminate juvenile court jurisdiction over noncriminal offenses. However, juvenile court judges who fear a diminution of jurisdiction and an erosion of court philosophy have opposed such a change (Handler, 1975; Lemert, 1967; S. Rubin, 1976). This fear has continued throughout the 1980s.

Rising Delinquency Rates

When a juvenile court was first opened on July 1, 1899, the event was supposed to mark the dawn of a new day. Treatment philosophies had defeated punishment and retributive ideals, and the hope for diminishing delinquency finally seemed realizable. But just as the treatment purpose of the court has been questioned, so has its efficiency in reducing delinquency rates. The criticism is not a recent issue. In 1949, William Healy reported that "occasionally the value of the juvenile court is challenged because there is no evidence that delinquency has decreased since the establishment of the court" (p. 18). Discontent with the court's role in the reduction of delinquency rates has, however, gained momentum in the past few years. With newspaper headlines and television portraits of violent teenage crime abounding, public attention has increasingly been drawn to the subject of rising delinquency rates. It is not surprising that the court, an agency supposed to handle delinquency, is the subject of criticism.

Official rates of delinquency· have indeed increased over the years, regardless of the source of the official data. Both arrest rates and petitions filed in juvenile court show more delinquency in the adolescent population now than in the past. Does this official rise reflect real or apparent events and trends? Throughout this book, we have stressed the limitations of official data in accurately identifying the true occurrence of delinquent behaviors. It is unclear whether actual delinquency is growing or diminishing. Therefore, it seems premature to accuse the juvenile court of a shortcoming that has not been verified.

But even if delinquency rates are increasing, is it logical to blame the juvenile court? Has the juvenile court become a community scapegoat? Answered Pena (1978):

The main reason for this negativism is that the public has been led to expect too much of the juvenile courts. Even those who administer the courts, for the most part, believe that if they are provided with the necessary ancillary personnel, they, the courts, will be the panacea for the social ills of children. The harsh fact that history has taught us is that even in those juvenile courts where the full panoply of social workers, intake and probation officers, and other trained personnel are totally utilized, the overall result must be judged something less than desired. This is so because the phenomenon of juvenile delinquency is a response to deep social, cultural, and political currents quite beyond the influence and control of the juvenile court or, indeed, the juvenile justice system. (p. 634)

Similarly, Fisher (1960) has charged that "many belabor the court for failure to overcome the blight of delinquency, a patently absurd charge" (p. 80). A statement from one delinquent perhaps best summarizes the limitations of the court's effect on delinquency:

You can't do anything for me, doctor, and the court can't. Would you be the yellow kid on our street when the gang yells, "Come on, let's get some dough"? I'll betcha in a couple of months I'll be in court again. (Healy, 1949: 18)

Although it may be unrealistic to blame the court totally for increases in official delinquency rates, there is some logic in the argument of labeling theorists that the stigma of juvenile court processing may lead to repeat offenses. Yet court processing is but one of many influences on conforming and deviant behaviors and acceptance or rejection of a delinquent label. Thus, we would question the extent of the court's influence on rising rates of delinquency.

Scientific Knowledge about the Causes and Cures of Delinquency

Could the court prevent delinquency even if its influence over the child were total? Critics have said no. From its beginning, the juvenile court was supposed to apply scientific knowledge to treating the delinquents who appeared before it. Underlying the treatment philosophy of the court was the assumption that scientific knowledge was sufficiently advanced to reveal why children were delinquent and how they could be made to conform. This assumption has been increasingly questioned. Critics of juvenile courts' past records of what has been called scientific accomplishment would appear to agree with Oscar Wilde, who said: "They show a want of knowledge that must be the result of years of study" (1925: 223). We have reviewed many theories about the causes and cures of delinquency and pointed out their weaknesses. It should be obvious that no one theory explains delinquent behavior and that practical applications of the theories have not been successful in preventing delinquency.

Lacking any real answers, the juvenile court could not be expected to prevent delinquency even if it did exert control over more aspects of the child's life. Some critics have taken their arguments one step further. They have charged that the court, through ignorance, employs practices that have been scientifically identified as encouraging delinquency:

> Official action may actually help to fix and perpetuate delinquency in the child through a process in which the individual begins to think of himself [or herself] as delinquent and organize his [or her] behavior accordingly. That process itself is further reinforced by the effect of the labeling upon the child's family, neighbors, teachers, and peers, whose reactions communicate to the child in subtle ways a kind of expectation of delinquent conduct. (President's Commission, 1967c: 8)

At least one observer (Feld, 1981, 1983) contends that the juvenile court is placed in an impossible situation. As mentioned earlier, two criteria considered by the judge during waiver are amenability to treatment and dangerousness. As Feld noted:

> Assessing a youth's amenability to treatment raises some of the most fundamental and difficult issues

of juvenile jurisprudence. First, are there any forms of treatment that will systematically bring about improved social adjustment in juvenile offenders; and second, if there are, is there a basis, via diagnosis and classification systems, for clinically distinguishing those youths who are amenable to treatment from those who are not? Legislation instructing a court to determine a youth's amenability to treatment is based on the assumption that there are such treatment programs, that there are classification systems that differentiate the treatment potential of various youths, and that there are validated and reliable diagnostic tools that will enable the clinician or juvenile court judge to determine the proper disposition for a particular youth. These are all problematic assumptions. (1983: 198)

As for the characteristic of dangerousness, Feld (1983) observed:

> The lack of reliable psychological or clinical indicators to predict dangerousness almost invariably results in overprediction through the erroneous classification as dangerous of many young offenders who do not commit further offenses. (p. 199)

Since we know so little about the causes of delinquency, juvenile courts have been called experimental laboratories. What we do know suggests that these laboratories may aggravate the problems they are seeking to cure.

Detention and Institutionalization

Some of the worst effects of juvenile courts are, according to critics, seen in the continued use of detention with adults and institutionalization. Thus, a fourth focus of criticism of the juvenile court has centered on those court processing practices that relate to the child in custody.

Ironically, in spite of the intent of the early child-saving reformers to remove children from adult jails, there is evidence that juveniles are still detained in jails with adults. Some children are detained in jails and juvenile detention centers because they are abused and neglected and have no other place to go. Other children in detention are those who have committed noncriminal status offenses. In fact, they are more likely to be placed in detention than those accused of criminal offenses. The detention of status offenders has been criticized because criminologists fear that noncriminal offenders will learn techniques and attitudes that will lead to criminal involvement (Sarri, 1974; Schultz, 1974).

Institutionalization of juvenile offenders in reformatories and prisons, a disposition imposed by court power, has been shown to be a dismal failure in deterring or reducing delinquency, and the juvenile court has been attacked for its continuing commitment of juveniles to institutions. Often, however, the detention of juveniles both in adult jails and in juvenile and adult prisons is the result of a lack of alternatives. If diversionary programs are undeveloped and separate juvenile detention facilities missing, it is difficult for the court to change its detention and institutionalization practices.

The juvenile court, then, is in a state of flux. Social work and legal functions vie for predominance. Facing a difficult task, the juvenile court judge, lawyer, and probation officer attempt to balance these competing positions. Change is occurring not only with a turn to more legalistic orientations, but also in a redefinition of the court's jurisdiction, goals, expectations, and practices. As the court comes to more closely resemble a court of law and as court jurisdiction narrows, the social work orientation of the court will probably decrease. It is doubtful, however, that the individualistic treatment philosophies upon which the court was founded will entirely disappear.

SUMMARY

During the 1960s and early 1970s, the United States Supreme Court vested juveniles with a variety of constitutional protections earlier extended only to adults. These rulings met with mixed reactions. The more traditional proponents of the *parens patriae* doctrine decried them as

spelling the end of an institution whose duty it was to protect children. Legal revisionists, however, criticized the Supreme Court for not going far enough. The clash between these two philosophical schools was reflected in the way in which various juvenile courts began to modify their procedures. Although some courts stuck to the letter of the law in ensuring newly gained constitutional rights, other courts found indirect ways to circumvent the intention of the law.

The juvenile court process is relatively standardized despite the orientation toward the legal rights of juveniles of any one particular court. Most children enter the juvenile justice system through contact with the police. Once inside the system, children are sent to the intake officer, who must decide how to process them, informally or formally. The decision whether the juvenile is to be handled informally or formally depends upon a variety of social and legal variables. Juveniles who are retained in the system at intake face an adjudicatory hearing where the judge determines whether or not the child is delinquent. If found delinquent, the juvenile faces a disposition, or sentencing, hearing. Again, research indicates that some social variables, especially race and social class, influence the disposition decision; but legal variables, such as prior record and seriousness of the offense, are more commonly considered.

Whether a juvenile court emphasizes the legalistic or the treatment model depends on the presiding judge's orientation. Judges retain considerable discretion in the courtroom. Some feel that their function is to treat the child, and view lawyers as an intrusion into their domain. However, there is some evidence that attorney representation does discourage rash judicial action. Perhaps the most important agent in the system, however, is the probation officer, since he or she determines the flow of a case. Whether a probation officer has a treatment or legalistic orientation does influence whether a child is processed formally or informally.

The contemporary juvenile court has become the focus of much debate. There have been four major criticisms. First, given the labeling perspective, some observers have contended that the juvenile court should stop processing status offenders in order to avoid adverse stigmatization. Second, there has been some question about the efficacy of the juvenile court, especially in view of apparently rising juvenile delinquency rates. Third, the lack of a cumulative body of scientific literature has stymied the search for a way to end the problem of juvenile delinquency. Fourth, there has been some concern that the institutionalization of juveniles has not had the desired rehabilitative effect. In summary, then, the juvenile court system is in a state of self-evaluation and change.

PROGRESS CHECK

1. Outline the principal features and findings of *Kent* v. *United States*. (pp. 311–312)

2. List and describe the six rulings of the U.S. Supreme Court in the 1967 case of Gerald Gault. (pp. 312–314)

3. In which of the following cases did the U.S. Supreme Court rule that juveniles should be entitled to the safeguard of "proof beyond a reasonable doubt"? (p. 314)
   a. *Kent* v. *United States*
   b. *In re Winship*
   c. *In re Gault*
   d. *McKeiver* v. *Pennsylvania*

4. The Supreme Court, in the McKeiver case, ruled that trial by jury is a fundamental constitutional right of juveniles. (p. 314)
   a. True
   b. False

5. Cite the latest Supreme Court ruling regarding *preventive detention* for juvenile offenders. How does this decision compare with other Supreme Court cases since *Gault*? (p. 315)

6. Summarize the findings of Charles F. Reasons' study of the juvenile court in Columbus, Ohio. (pp. 316–317)

7. What are the principal conclusions reached by Lefstein, Stapleton, and Teitelbaum in their study of the juvenile courts in three cities? (pp. 317–318)

8. Outline the principal features of the intake officer's role in the processing of juvenile offenders referred to the juvenile court. (pp. 322–327)

9. Discuss the six dispositional options available to the juvenile court judge. (p. 329)

10. Four key issues for today's juvenile court are discussed in the latter section of this chapter. Rank these issues in terms of your assessment of their relative importance. What is your rationale for your ranking? (pp. 334–338)

NOTES

1. For a general discussion of the *McKeiver* v. *Pennsylvania* ruling, see P. S. Smith (1978).
2. New York law provides that: (1) at the initial appearance, the court in its discretion may release the respondent or direct his detention; (2) the court shall not direct detention unless it finds and states the facts and reasons for so finding that unless the respondent is detained; (a) there is a substantial probability that he will not appear in court on the return date; or (b) there is a serious risk that he may before the return date commit an act which if committed by an adult would constitute a crime (New York Family Court Act, 320.5).
3. Michael Vitiello (1976), an attorney, explored the legal impact that the earlier Kent decision had upon the juvenile courts during the ten years following the ruling. He concluded that courts as well as legislatures have sought to avoid compliance with the holdings of the Kent decision in a number of ways. These include (1) failure to specify substantive criteria for waiver out of a junvenile court, (2) failure to delineate the meaning of the terms "amenable to treatment" and "best interest," and (3) almost total reliance on such factors as the seriousness of the crime or the juveniles' past contact with the juvenile court system.
4. Although state legislatures have been willing to enact excluded offense provisions (i.e., specific crimes that automatically exclude the juvenile from juvenile court jurisdiction), many of the statutes that have attempted to more objectively define those juveniles rely only on age

and present offense and not on prior record. Thus many juveniles who are arrested initially for serious, violent offenses will not face repeated charges of the same kind. In addition, there is the possibility that when present offense is emphasized many first time offenders who may not recidivate and for whom no treatment has been attempted will be drawn into the criminal justice system beyond the point of return (Zimring, 1981).

5. While no juveniles have been executed as of 1983, of the 1,058 inmates on the nation's death rows, 17 were under the age of 18 when they committed their crimes and had been transferred to the jurisdiction of the adult courts. *Eddings* v. *Oklahoma* [102 S. Ct. 869 (1982)] urged the Court to adopt a blanket prohibition against the imposition of death sentences on juvenile offenders since it was cruel and unusual punishment in violation of the Eighth and Fourteenth amendments. While the Court granted *certiorari* in *Eddings* solely to consider the constitutionality of imposing the death penalty on juvenile defendants, the Court failed to address the unresolved and increasingly contested issue in its opinion (Greenwald, 1983: 1525).

6. T. Rubin (1980) noted: "The 1967 *In re Gault* decision by the United States Supreme Court expressly noted that its procedural requirements for the adjudicatory stage had no necessary applicability to the preadjudication treatment of juveniles. However, the *Gault* mandate of the right to defense counsel at the time led to greater prosecution representation of the community interest at adjudicatory hearings. This set in motion another development which is now eroding probation officers' informal, discretionary practices at the intake stage. State legislatures, responding to public concerns regarding juvenile crime, are rapidly placing prosecutors in decisional roles at juvenile intake, using various models in accommodating and accomplishing this. This development portrays yet another example of the replacement of historic juvenile court informality and *parens patriae* practice by a legal process model." (p. 299)

CHAPTER 16

JUVENILE CORRECTIONS: THE INSTITUTIONAL SETTING

At sunrise, the children are warned, by the ringing of a bell, to rise from their beds. Each child makes his own bed, and steps forth, on a signal, into the Hall. They then proceed, in perfect order, to the Wash Room. Thence they are marched to parade in the yard, and undergo an examination as to their dress and cleanliness; after which, they attend morning prayer. The morning school then commences, where they are occupied in summer, until 7 o'clock. A short intermission is allowed, when the bell rings for breakfast; after which, they proceed to their respective workshops, where they labor until 12 o'clock, when they are called from work, and one hour [is] allowed them for washing and eating their dinner. At one, they again commence work, and continue at it until five in the afternoon, when the labor of the day terminates. Half an hour is allowed for washing and eating their supper, and at half-past five, they are conducted to the school room where they continue at their studies until 8 o'clock. Evening Prayer is performed by the Superintendent; after which, the children are conducted to their dormitories, which they enter, and are locked up for the night, when perfect silence reigns throughout the establishment. The foregoing is the history of a single day, and will answer for every day in the year, except Sundays, with slight variations during stormy weather, and the short days in winter. (Society for the Reformation of Juvenile Delinquents, 1835: 6–7)

At Mixer . . . the day's schedule for all boys except those confined to cottages or security cells was awakening; supervised dorm cleanup, lineup, counting and marching back to the dorm; more supervised dorm cleanup, lineup and marching off to classrooms or job locations; and so on. At neither Mixer nor Dick (at least for the bigger boys) were the inmates supposed to talk during meals, and at Mixer the mealtime task of one staff member was to see that they did not take more than the allotted number of bread slices. Neither institution permitted inmates to move in unsupervised groups, except while on some special assignment or when granted special privileges like those of the "trustee" in the adult institution. (Street, Vinter, and Perrow, 1966: 154)

These two descriptions depict the daily routine of youth incarcerated in a juvenile institution. The first describes a typical day in the life of a youth confined in a New York House of Refuge, an early juvenile institution, in the 1830s. The second depicts life in a contemporary juvenile correctional facility.

Although there have certainly been changes in juvenile correctional facilities over the decades, the basic philosophy that underlies the institutionalization of youths has not changed appreciably. Juveniles labeled a threat to themselves or to the community have been confined in special institutions. The intent of confinement has been rehabilitation, a process aimed at transforming errant youth into useful and productive citizens.

The regimentation of the daily routine—the marching in step, the ringing of bells, and the inflicting of swift and severe punishment for any transgression—illustrate the goals of the 1830s juvenile institution. These facilities focused on bringing about changes in behavior through regimentation of daily activities. Early proponents of special institutions for juvenile offenders emphasized that such places could put order and predictability back into the lives of youthful offenders and that "any resident could not help but be programmed into moral and right ways of living" (Bartollas, Miller, and Dinitz, 1976: 5).

Despite years of evidence indicating that these procedures do not aid in the rehabilitation of youthful offenders, many contemporary institutions, including the one represented in our second example, continue to operate as **total institutions,** in which the aim is to control every aspect of the inmate's life. The inmate is treated with regimentation, isolation, and brutality—much as in the 1830s.

The effectiveness of such juvenile correctional institutions has been questioned in recent years. Contemporary critics have argued that such facilities are unduly harsh and that incarceration should be limited to juvenile offenders who commit serious offenses. A push to find alternative, community-based methods for the treatment of less serious offenders has resulted.

In this chapter we will study juvenile correctional facilities. We will review the history of juvenile institutions, examine the types of correctional institutions currently in use, and explore the goals of these establishments, particularly the contradictions in the goals of custody. We will also describe the characteristics of inmates, consider the effectiveness of available treatment (therapy) programs, and investigate the inmate sub-culture. Finally, we will explore the rights of juveniles in confinement.

HISTORY OF JUVENILE CORRECTIONAL INSTITUTIONS

Two special institutions were created in the United States as humane establishments to reha-bilitate youthful offenders, houses of refuge and reformatories. These institutions, which have been with us for nearly two hundred years, have been plagued with many problems. Though attempts have been made over the years to improve juvenile facilities, they have not been fundamentally suc-cessful. Many of the same problems continue to exist in contemporary facilities.

Houses of Refuge

Historical accounts of life in colonial America indicate that early Americans had little need for specialized institutions serving juveniles. Not even adults were in need of prisons, as criminals in the colonies were either expelled from the community or subjected to penalties of corporal punishment, fines, mutilations, and death. Imprisonment was rarely used. Some jails were maintained to detain offenders before trial, to serve as holding places for debtors, and to ensure that individuals con-victed of particularly serious crimes remained avail-able for the carrying out of their sentences (Scull, 1977). Before the 1790s, no effort was made to segregate the less serious offender held in jails from the more hardened criminal (Amos and Manella, 1965).

In the eighteenth century, youthful offenders were for the most part dealt with informally by the family, the church, and a strong network of community relations that served to check the behavior of the community's inhabitants. The informal networks, when they functioned properly, were thought to spare towns the turmoil of crime

and to ensure a high degree of social order and stability. For this reason, "Families were to raise their children to respect law and authority, the church was to oversee not only family discipline but adult behavior, and the members of the community were to supervise one another, to detect and correct the first signs of deviancy" (Rothman, 1971: 16).

According to eighteenth-century law and prac-tice, public authority to handle juveniles was subordinate to the authority of the family. In Massachusetts, for example, youthful offenders appearing before a magistrate were referred back to the family for the actual execution of the punishment, a court-observed whipping.

Since early colonial towns were small and their populations initially homogeneous, informal meth-ods for dealing with deviants worked extremely well. By the late eighteenth century, however, the colonial towns were growing, and methods of social control based on personal contact and similarity of standards became ineffective (Mennel, 1973). With the coming of independence and the establishment of the new nation, the situation worsened. The large influx of immigrants, partic-ularly to the eastern cities, further enlarged the population, creating a need for a more structured and more formal means for handling crimes. Crim-inals from all along the eastern seaboard used the slums of these cities as havens from the law (Cavan and Ferdinand, 1975). In the poorer areas of the cities, where the new immigrants lived, juvenile gangs roamed at will. Large numbers of neglected and abandoned children were also found in these areas.

The first organized efforts to treat youthful offenders and to lower the juvenile crime rate centered around the founding and development of houses of refuge in New York, Boston, and Phil-adelphia in the 1820s. Impetus for the founding of these early institutions came from private phi-lanthropists who sought to save juveniles from urban chaos and mold them into useful citizens. The New York Society for the Reformation of Juvenile Delinquents, led by some members of the Society of Friends, in 1825 opened the first public institution for boys and girls in the United States, the New York House of Refuge. This institution, as well as those opened in Boston (1826) and Philadelphia (1828), accepted destitute and orphaned youth and children convicted of crimes in local and state courts.

Life in these institutions was spartan. If the parents of incarcerated youth were alive, they were seen as too poor or too degenerate to provide their children with the necessities of life (Simonsen and Gordon, 1979). The institutions therefore stood **in loco parentis** (in place of the parents) to children and had the right to place them in a family or to bind them to apprenticeship whenever staff believed placement outside the institution was preferable to treatment within the institution (Dean and Reppucci, 1974).

Although the early houses of refuge offered shelter and sanctuary, their main purpose was to "train and rehabilitate [their] charges" (Rothman, 1971: 210). Techniques of reformation focused on a strict regimen of religious instruction, education, and hard work. The following description of typical work tasks in early institutions shows the emphasis on labor as a means of correcting the child:

> The refuges established and supervised large workshops where the boys, whose labor was contracted to local entrepreneurs, made brass nails, cane chairs, and cheap shoes; delinquent girls were occupied with domestic chores in a separate part of the building. The children labored approximately eight hours a day and spent most of the remainder of their waking hours learning how to read, write and cipher. After delinquents had been trained "for usefulness," the institutions often apprenticed them to local artisans and farmers. Girls were bound out as housemaids and older, more intractable boys were indentured to ship captains in the whaling or merchant service. Those who rebelled against the authority of their foster family were either returned to the refuge or sent to jail. (Bremner, 1971, Vol. 1: 672)

Although hard work was lauded as building character in children, the belief in the salutary influence of hard work on the offender had certain practical benefits for the institution. Ninety per-

cent of children released from institutions were apprenticed, and under this system, children's earnings from apprenticeship were paid to the releasing institution (Mennel, 1973).

Every detail of the early house of refuge was designed to inculcate order and regimentation into the lives of inmates. Upon entering the institution, recruits were stripped and washed, and their hair cut to a standard length. They were dressed in coarse, drab uniforms. The facility itself was as monotonous as the daily schedule. The buildings were usually four stories high. Each story had two long halls containing rows of cells, one after another. Cells were commonly 5 feet wide, 7 feet high, and windowless. With the emphasis on order and discipline, refuge administrators vigorously defended strict punitive measures for any infraction of rules. Apparently, few inmates were spared the whip, the ball and chain, or solitary confinement.

In the philosophy and educational practice of the times, behavior, especially criminal behavior, was held to be entirely a matter of self-control. Thus, institutions were designed to foster such self-control in youths through adherence to strict and detailed routines that governed every minute of inmates' lives. Inmates spent the bulk of their day at work, had only a few hours of school, and even less time for exercise or recreation (Rothman, 1971).

Several factors encouraged the decline of the house of refuge and the subsequent rise of a new type of institution, the reform or training school. The records of a two-year period in the history of the New York Refuge indicate that about 40 percent of the children either ran away from their apprenticeships or were constantly returned to the refuge by their foster families.

Aside from the questionable effectiveness of treatment programs, the institutions were badly overcrowded. It was difficult to control the large numbers of youth committed to institutions with inadequate staff and funds. Violence, purportedly brought on by increases in the numbers of hard core delinquents committed to the institutions, was reported to be widespread (Mennel, 1973). By the 1850s, there had been enough erosion in confidence that the houses of refuge could alter delinquents' behavior that another new approach to handling delinquents, reformatories, came into existence.

Reformatories

Reformatories, also called training schools, developed in the mid-nineteenth century. The development of the reformatory paralleled new theories about the causes of delinquency. Both poverty and delinquency were seen as the result of degraded environmental circumstances. Early refuge houses were based on the belief that poverty and delinquency were matters of free choice and inmate wickedness. Reformatories, on the other hand, were influenced by the increasing numbers of scientific theories about the causes of crime and delinquency. Attempts were made to translate scientific findings into school programs. These early scientific programs included strict military discipline, tough physical conditioning, religious training, and the forced learning of a trade. As the medical model of delinquency gained favor and the "new science of the mind," psychology, won converts, numerous treatment strategies aimed at altering behavior were instituted.[1] The medical model and the science of psychology continue to guide new modes of treatment being developed and tested today.

The new reformatories were, for the most part, indistinguishable from the early houses of refuge. The reformatories stressed a longer period of schooling, usually half a day. But the regimented workshop routines continued, and the contracting of inmates' labor assumed a more exploitative character. Manufacturers were allowed to control inmates during working hours, and reports of cruelty and violence against juveniles flourished.

Despite abuses, states continued to build reformatories. In 1847 Massachusetts established the first state-oriented training school, the Lyman School for Boys at Westborough. In 1856 the State Industrial School for Girls at Lancaster, Massachusetts, was opened. New York built a state agricultural and industrial school in 1849, and

Maine opened a training center in 1853. By 1870, Connecticut, Indiana, Maryland, Nevada, New Hampshire, New Jersey, Ohio, and Vermont had separate institutions for delinquents. By 1890, nearly every state outside the South had some type of reform school for delinquent juveniles or destitute youth (National Conference of Superintendents of Training and Reformatories, 1962; Simonsen and Gordon, 1979). No provisions were made for the separate handling of juvenile offenders in the South until after the Civil War.

Some reformatories presented innovations in design and treatment. Following the European lead, Massachusetts and Ohio founded reform schools based on the cottage, or family, plan. Both the Massachusetts State Industrial School for Girls (1856) and the Ohio Reform or Farm School (1857) operated on a system that divided children into small families of forty or fewer children. Each family had its own cottage and autonomous schedule (Mennel, 1973). In these cottage institutions, there was at least some effort to segregate youth by factors such as age and type of offense, which the congregate, or single-building, schools did not provide. Cottage parents were employed to create a homelike atmosphere that would reduce the effects of institutionalization. Emphasis on education and vocational pursuits was primary, but inmates were still required to work, usually at agricultural tasks. With some variations, this cottage school remains the most popular type of juvenile institution.

In many ways the early reformatories continue to serve as models for contemporary correctional facilities. Some of the early reform schools are actually still in existence. Contemporary therapeutic techniques are considerably more advanced than the methods used in early reform schools; they range from individualized psychotherapy to group and milieu therapy. Other recent innovations in juvenile corrections include halfway houses, group homes, and reception-diagnostic centers. Yet even after a century of effort to treat juvenile delinquency, there is little evidence that treatment programs are successful in preventing repeat offenses (Hood, 1967; Robison and Smith, 1971).

TYPES OF CORRECTIONAL INSTITUTIONS

There are several types of correctional institutions in the United States today: (1) detention centers, (2) shelters, (3) reception-diagnostic centers, (4) reformatories, and (5) work camps. No one description of institutional organization applies to all juvenile facilities. Facilities differ dramatically in size, age, groups served, services provided, nature of personnel, extent of financial resources, and attitudes of the surrounding community. The basic functions of these institutions, however, are similar.

Of all the areas in juvenile justice, the field of juvenile corrections most lacks a regularized and comprehensive means of accumulating accurate and current information about institutional populations and programs. "It is difficult to think of any other sector where so little information is routinely and systematically enumerated, reported on, and analyzed for use in planning and administration" (Vinter, Downs and Hall, 1976: 1). Until recently, the only current data on the number of youth incarcerated in correctional facilities or the actual number of facilities were in the *Statistics on Public Institutions for Delinquent Children* series, published by the U.S. Department of Health, Education, and Welfare. The Office of Juvenile Justice and Delinquency Prevention now publishes *Children in Custody*, a series that covers statistics on youth incarcerated in nonfederal juvenile detention and correctional facilities in the United States.

Funded through the now defunct Law Enforcement Assistance Administration and other sources, the National Assessment of Juvenile Corrections (NAJC) worked out of the University of Michigan to conduct a 1974 survey of state-supported juvenile correctional facilities and programs (Vinter and Sarri, 1976). Findings from NAJC provide valuable information about the types of youth involved in correctional programs that include community-based residential and day treatment agencies, institutions, and aftercare services. The paucity of information on juvenile correctional programs, especially since the *President's Commission Task Force Report: Corrections* (1967b), has not only severely hampered the assessment of correctional programs, but also limited the spread of knowledge about developments and trends from state to state.

Detention Centers

Detention centers are **short-term facilities** that provide temporary care in a physically restricting environment for juveniles in custody pending court adjudication and for juveniles who have been adjudicated delinquent and are awaiting transfer to a long-term facility. Most detention centers are secure to the extent that they have locked doors, high fences or walls, and other devices to prevent escape. Detention facilities do not attempt to correct or treat offenders, but simply serve as holding areas until the child can be further processed. The U.S. Supreme Court's latest decision, *Schall* v. *Martin*, upholding the right of judges to lock up juveniles who present a "serious risk" of committing another offense before trial, may increase the number of juveniles held in detention.[2]

Shelters

Juvenile shelters differ from detention centers because shelters do not employ physical restraint. Boarding houses or similar child welfare institutions fall into this category. Another distinction between shelter care and detention is that both the juvenile court and child welfare agencies may refer a child to a shelter. Only the court may refer a child to official detention centers. The differences indicate that shelters are designed to care temporarily for neglected or abused, rather than delinquent, children.

According to the OJJDP publication *Children in Custody*, there were 459 *short-term* correctional facilities, including detention centers, shelters, and reception-diagnostic centers in 1982 (see Table 16.1), holding 15,203 juveniles. The number of private short-term facilities was much smaller: 164 holding 1,667 juveniles, as shown in Table 16.2.

TABLE 16.1 Number of U.S. Public Juvenile Detention and Correctional Facilities and Juveniles Held, by Type of Facility, 1971, 1973, 1974, 1975, 1977, 1979, 1982

Type of Facility	Number of Facilities						
	1971	1973	1974	1975	1977	1979	1982
All Facilities	722	794	829	874	992	1,015	1,023
Short-Term Facilities	338	355	371	387	448	464	459
Detention centers	305	319	331	347	NA*	NA	NA
Shelters	17	19	21	23	NA	NA	NA
Reception or diagnostic centers	16	17	19	17	NA	NA	NA
Long-Term Facilities	384	439	458	487	544	551	564
Training schools	191	187	185	189	NA	NA	NA
Ranches, forestry camps, and farms	115	103	107	103	NA	NA	NA
Halfway houses and group homes	78	149	166	195	NA	NA	NA

	Number of Juveniles						
	1971	1973	1974	1975	1977	1979	1982
All Facilities	54,729	45,694	44,922	46,980	44,096	43,234	48,701
Short-Term Facilities	14,280	12,706	12,566	12,725	11,929	12,185	15,203
Detention centers	11,767	10,782	11,010	11,089	NA	NA	NA
Shelters	360	190	180	200	NA	NA	NA
Reception or diagnostic centers	2,153	1,734	1,376	1,436	NA	NA	NA
Long-Term Facilities	40,449	32,988	32,356	34,255	32,167	31,049	33,498
Training schools	34,005	26,427	25,397	26,748	NA	NA	NA
Ranches, forestry camps, and farms	5,471	4,959	5,232	5,385	NA	NA	NA
Halfway houses and group homes	973	1,602	1,727	2,122	NA	NA	NA

* NA means not available.
Source: Adapted from U.S. Department of Justice, National Criminal Justice Information and Statistics Service (1977, p. 17; 1979b, p. 2); U.S. Department of Justice, Office of Juvenile Justice and Delinquency Prevention, National Criminal Justice Information and Statistics Service (1983, p. 5).

Reception–Diagnostic Centers

According to the 1975 *Children in Custody* (CIC) census (Table 16.1), there were only 17 reception-diagnostic centers in the United States. This small number reflects the newness of the reception-diagnostic center concept. More and more, juvenile correctional staffs are emphasizing the diagnosis and classification of juveniles prior to the determination of an appropriate treatment program and assignment to a correctional facility.

Reception-diagnostic centers are based on the idea that classification of offenders is necessary before treatment plans can be determined. They make it possible to release a substantial number of juveniles on probation; theoretically, this should happen before the negative effects of institutionalization develop.

Each child entering the center is evaluated by an intake team that includes mental health specialists—psychologists, psychiatrists, psychiatric social worker–teachers, and a staff member from the child's living unit at the center. The intake team, after being provided with all relevant available data on the child's case, including court records, probation reports, school records, and any other pertinent information, takes a few weeks to diagnose the child and see that appropriate placement is accomplished.

The small number of special reception-diagnostic centers presently in existence means that most states must diagnose and classify offenders within correctional facilities. After diagnosis and classification at specialized diagnostic centers or in separate sections of correctional institutions, the juvenile most frequently is placed in a reform-

TABLE 16.2 Number of U.S. Private Juvenile Detention and Correctional Facilities and Juveniles Held, by Type of Facility, 1974, 1975, 1977, 1979, 1982

Type of Facility	Number of Facilities					Number of Juveniles				
	1974	1975	1977	1979	1982	1974	1975	1977	1979	1982
All Facilities	1,337	1,277	1,600	1,561	1,877	31,749	27,290	29,070	28,688	31,390
Short-Term Facilities	76	66	126	75	164	797	830	843	733	1,667
Long-Term Facilities	1,261	1,211	1,474	1,486	1,713	30,952	26,450	28,227	29,955	29,723
Training Schools	61	65	NA*	NA	NA	4,078	3,660	NA	NA	NA
Ranches, forestry camps, and farms	395	295	NA	NA	NA	16,955	13,094	NA	NA	NA
Halfway houses and group homes	805	851	NA	NA	NA	9,919	9,706	NA	NA	NA

* NA means not available.

Source: Adapted from U.S. Department of Justice, National Criminal Justice Information and Statistics Service (1977, p. 19; 1979a, p. 3); U.S. Department of Justice, Office of Juvenile Justice and Delinquency Prevention, National Criminal Justice Information and Statistics Service (1984, p. 6).

atory, more often referred to today as a training school.

Public and Private Training Schools

The training school is a **long-term** custodial residential facility. State training schools were originally intended to be small reformatories, providing a place where youthful offenders could be prepared for a productive future. Larger reformatories, like that in Elmira, New York, were generally intended to house and treat offenders who fell between the juvenile and adult categories. Although many modern training schools provide educational and vocational opportunities for youth in pleasant surroundings, many others remain little more than miniature prisons.

The physical features of training schools vary tremendously throughout the country. Older schools are often large, unattractive, prisonlike structures that house all inmates together. More modern institutions have a completely different organization. In recently built facilities, housing usually includes: (1) a reception unit combined with an infirmary, (2) a security unit close to the reception and infirmary units, (3) dormitory units or cottages for housing, (4) dining hall or kitchen areas, (5) academic and vocational schoolrooms, (6) a library, (7) an auditorium-gymnasium, and (8) other facilities, such as a craft shop, barber shop, and commissary.

Licensed by state agencies, private training schools have been particularly innovative in the development of treatment strategies. By employing a selective intake policy that bars the admission of emotionally disturbed or extremely aggressive juveniles, private institutions can devote more time to programs rather than to control. Also, private schools are freer from political pressures and can be more flexible in hiring qualified staff and trying new treatments.

Although the number of public training schools increased slightly in 1975 (see Table 16.1), the general trend since the early 1970s has been a decrease in training school institutions. The 1984 *Children in Custody* census, though not itemizing correctional facilities by type, revealed an increase

of only 20 new long-term facilities in the United States since 1977 (see Table 16.1). However, we do not know whether this increase was in training schools or less secure facilities, such as halfway houses and group homes. There was a larger increase in the number of private long-term facilities between 1977 and 1982, as shown in Table 16.2.

An examination of Table 16.1 indicates that public training schools housed 26,748 juvenile offenders in mid-year 1975.[3] Except for a 5 percent increase in public training school populations in 1975, there have been decreases in the number of youths incarcerated since 1971. Figures for the CIC census since 1975 do not break down long-term facilities into specific categories (with training schools as a separate type of facility), as they did previously. However, admissions of juvenile offenders to long-term facilities (the great proportion being training schools) have continued to decrease since 1975, with an increase taking place between 1979 and 1982. This trend shows that despite the substantial increases in the number of youths in public, community-oriented programs over the last few years, the use of secure facilities continues as the most prevalent means of handling delinquents. Between 1975 and 1979 there was a decrease in the total number of juveniles confined in long-term private facilities followed by a slight increase through 1982.[4]

Although the general trend appears to be a decline in the number of juveniles in state correctional institutions, it is more difficult to trace what has happened to youth who are diverted from institutions. The extent and nature of alternative dispositions are particularly hard to document because of the very inadequate statistics on the subjects. Obviously, many youth are reaping the benefits of the decarceration movement through placement in community treatment programs. In late 1970 the push to decarcerate continued to gain momentum despite some public pressures to the contrary. At the same time, other youth were being transferred from public to private facilities.

In general, however, we see a trend in juvenile corrections where delinquent offenders, those adjudicated delinquent by the juvenile court, are committed in greater numbers to public and private

TABLE 16.3   **Top Ten States in Rate of Admissions to Training Schools, 1971, 1974, 1979**

1971		1974		1979	
State	Rate per 100,000	State	Rate per 100,000	State	Rate per 100,000
(1) District of Columbia	2,313	Alaska	1,865	Alaska	2,349
(2) Alaska	1,980	District of Columbia	1,077	District of Columbia	2,043
(3) New Hampshire	736	New Hampshire	854	New Hampshire	777
(4) Delaware	666	Maryland	822	Maryland	682
(5) Vermont	645	Vermont	648	Delaware	605
(6) Nevada	510	Rhode Island	618	Oregon	532
(7) Rhode Island	499	New Mexico	488	Wyoming	518
(8) Wisconsin	434	North Carolina	450	Rhode Island	480
(9) North Carolina	402	California	399	Arizona	472
(10) Florida	346	Minnesota	390	Maine	449

Source: *Children in Custody* series, U.S. Bureau of the Census; B. Krisberg, P. Litsky, and I. Schwartz (1984: 160).

training schools, whereas status offenders, those whose conduct would not be a crime if performed by adults, are not incarcerated. For instance, of the 33,498 juveniles incarcerated in long-term correctional facilities in 1982 (according to CIC statistics), 31,388 were held for committing a delinquent offense (of a property or violent nature).

Utilizing CIC rates of admission for training schools, Krisberg and his colleagues found large variations in state admission rates to training schools. Table 16.3 shows the top ten states in rates of admission for the years 1971, 1974, and 1979. These states have for the past decade been consistently high in their admission rates. In attempting to explain such large variations between states, Krisberg (1984) hypothesized that states having the highest juvenile crime rates would logically have the highest confinement rates. He found virtually no relationship here between juvenile arrests and admission rates to training schools. In a further attempt to account for state variations in admissions to training schools, Krisberg examined teenage unemployment rates and the bed capacity in training schools, reasoning that states with large facilities may have a tendency to keep these institutions at peak capacity. He found that the three variables combined—serious youth crime, teenage unemployment, and bed capacity—explained only about 33 percent of the variation in state admission differences. In other words, roughly two-thirds of the variation among state training admissions was *not* explained by the three variables scrutinized.

Krisberg surmised that given his findings, it might be wise to characterize the state of juvenile correctional practices as "justice by geography." There are some 3,000 separate juvenile court jurisdictions across the nation, each making decisions about juveniles in a highly pluralistic and decentralized way. He argues that we must develop more uniformity and internal consistency within the system if we are to stop idiosyncratic differences in the practice of juvenile justice from state to state.

Work Camps

Since the 1940s, various kinds of small, work-oriented camps have been used to treat less seriously delinquent youth. According to the 1975 CIC census of correctional facilities (Tables 16.1 and 16.2), several thousand youth, mainly boys, were admitted to work camps, including forestry camps, ranches, and farms.

Most camps are situated in state forests or parks, where boys are assigned to work on the construction and improvement of park facilities or fight forest fires. Work projects are often supervised by state conservation service personnel (Galvin and Karacki, 1969).

Youth Held in Adult Jails and Prisons

Unknown to the average citizen, in any given year large numbers of juveniles are held for short to long periods of time in adult jails and prisons. While there has been no systematic attempt to compile information about youth held in adult prisons or jails, a number of different sources indicate that this is a common practice throughout the United States. The 1970 *Jail Census* reported that as of March 1970, some 7,800 youth were being detained in the 4,037 facilities surveyed (National Jail Census, 1971). Although some 66 percent of these juveniles were being detained temporarily, about 34 percent had actually been sentenced to these facilities.

The 1973 Census of Prisoners in State Correctional Facilities (1976) is the only available source of information citing national statistics regarding youth under 18 held in adult prisons. According to this early report, of the nation's total prison population of 178,835, youth under 18 numbered 1,970, or 1.1 percent of the national total. A study conducted by the Children's Defense Fund (*Children in Adult Jails*, 1976), which surveyed 449 jails in 126 counties and 9 cities in Florida, Georgia, Indiana, Maryland, Ohio, South Carolina, Texas, and Virginia, found 350 children incarcerated in these facilities. Perhaps more dramatic than the numbers of jailed children was the finding that only about 12 percent of the juveniles in these facilities had been charged with a serious offense.

In order to obtain more accurate and up-to-date data about the number of youth held in adult facilities and characteristics about such youth and their offenses, The National Center on Institutions and Alternatives (1980) conducted a comprehensive survey of youth in adult prisons in the fifty states and the District of Columbia. In addition, it randomly sampled 525 jails for the number of juveniles held and then used forecasting methods to make projections about average incarceration rates throughout the United States. The center found that in comparison to the 1973 Census of Prisoners in State Correctional Facilities, the proportion of younger inmates has decreased slightly. Of the 273,389 inmates in adult prisons as of the survey date (1979), 2,697 were aged 17 or younger;

inmates under 18 therefore accounted for only 0.98 percent of the total prison population. It was found that of this total number of juvenile inmates, only 1,052, or 39 percent, were sentenced to prison for crimes against people, including murder, manslaughter, rape, robbery, aggravated assault, kidnapping, and other sex offenses. Crimes involving property accounted for 1,112, or 41.2 percent, of the total number of offenses, followed by 3.5 percent for the commission of public order offenses (narcotics offenses, prostitution, and other minor crimes). Offenses for the remaining juvenile inmates could not be obtained.

Based on the center's jail survey, it was estimated that about 4,061 juveniles under 18 would be sentenced to adult jails in the United States as of the 1979 survey date. Most of these, about 58 percent, would be incarcerated for crimes involving property, not crimes against the person (about 17 percent).

Reasons for the incarceration of juveniles in adult jails and prisons vary. One study indicated that some 93 percent of all juvenile court jurisdictions reported that they used adult jail facilities to detain juvenile offenders temporarily because there were no other places to house them (President's Commission on Law Enforcement and the Administration of Justice, 1967b). Another possible reason that large numbers of youth are sentenced to adult prisons is because they were either tried under adult jurisdictions based on the crimes they committed or were transferred from juvenile to adult courts via new waiver laws (see Chapters 1 and 15). This situation, however, begs the question of why so few violent juvenile offenders are sentenced to adult prisons and why there are so many property and minor offenders incarcerated.

GOALS OF CORRECTIONAL INSTITUTIONS

Juvenile correctional institutions have multiple and somewhat contradictory goals. The major formal goals of institutionalization include keeping the delinquent in custody and away from the community and treating or rehabilitating the delinquent.

Custodial functions have in the past been accompanied by punishments. Treatment or rehabilitative goals, on the other hand, focus on curing the delinquent or deterring the delinquent from future delinquent acts. A number of means to these ends are practiced.

Institutions with the dual goals of custody and treatment may have difficulty reconciling these two somewhat incompatible aims. The maximization of one leads to inadequate fulfillment of the other (Zald, 1960). Thus, overemphasis on security and custody may create an organizational environment antithetical to treatment.

More and more, the organizational character and institutional climate of correctional facilities have been shown to affect dramatically the internal dynamics of the institutions. The relationship of staff members to other staff, to administrators, and to inmates is defined by the goals of the institution. Similarly, inmates' perceptions of the institution influence their susceptibility to treatment, their relationships with staff and one another, and eventually their adjustment to community life.

Institutional Climates: Custody, Reeducation, and Treatment

Several schemes have been devised to categorize juvenile correctional institutions. These attempt to assess inmate and staff activities in relation to the primary goal or goals of the institution.

One of the more comprehensive works in the area is that of Street, Vinter, and Perrow (1966), who studied the organizational climates of six different juvenile and correctional institutions from 1958 to 1960. They classified institutions as oriented toward (1) custody, (2) reeducation, or (3) treatment of inmates.

Custody.   In an institution stressing custody, inmates were to be changed through *conditioning*. Obedience and conformity were emphasized. In such an environment, the staff maintained undifferentiated views of the inmates, emphasized immediate accommodation to external controls, and relied on high levels of staff domination with many negative sanctions.

Reeducation.   In an institution stressing reeducation and development, inmates were to be changed through *training*. Changes in attitudes and values, acquisition of skills, the development of personal resources, and new social behaviors were sought. Compared to the custodial institution, in which obedience and conformity were important, the reeducation institution provided more gratifications for inmates and maintained closer staff-inmate relations.

Treatment.   In an institution stressing treatment, inmates were to be changed through *psychological therapy*. Since the treatment institution focused on the psychological reconstitution of the individual, it attempted to change the inmates' personalities more than the other types of institutions did. To this end, the treatment institution emphasized gratifications and varied activities for inmates, with punishments relatively few and seldom severe. There were two types of treatment institutions. In the individual treatment type, considerable stress was placed on self-insight and two-person psychotherapeutic practices. In the milieu treatment type, attention was paid to both individual and social controls, since the aim was not only to help the inmates resolve personal problems, but also to prepare them for community living (p. 21). Street, Vinter, and Perrow hypothesized the existence of a fourth pattern of institutional aims, the *mixed goal type*, which centered on both custody and treatment. This type, however, did not clearly fit any of the institutions surveyed.

Street and his colleagues found that different institutional goals had consequences for staff perceptions about inmates, staff-inmate authority relations, and the patterns of social relationships and leadership that emerged among inmates. In the custody institution, where obedience and conformity were important, the staff maintained a strict measure of social distance from inmates and kept them under constant surveillance. As a result, the inmates had relatively negative perspectives about the institution and the staff, especially when compared to the attitudes of inmates in treatment institutions (see Poole and Regoli, 1983). Relationships among inmates and inmate solidarity were generally less developed in the custodial institutions. In contrast, the atmosphere between staff and inmates in the treatment institutions was generally permissive and cordial.

The staff developed close relationships with the inmates and attempted to alter inmate behavior through incentives and rewards rather than strict discipline. Inmates' relations with each other were more friendship-oriented and less predatory than in the custodial institutions. Staff-inmate relations in the reeducation institutions stressed obedience and social distance, but were tempered by personal and moral considerations. For this reason, inmate response to these institutions was similar to inmate response to the treatment-oriented institutions.

Social climate indices such as that of Street, Vinter, and Perrow may be valuable because they provide the administration and staff of correctional institutions with feedback about program effectiveness. However, these scales do not supply information about the long-term effects of programs on youth released from institutions. (Other researchers have also assessed the effects of social climates in correctional institutions; see, for example, Jesness, 1975; Wink and Moos, 1972.)

The Effectiveness of Rehabilitation

"If you don't know where you are going, how do you know when you get there?" This is an appropriate question for institutions that supposedly function for the purpose of rehabilitating the juvenile offender (Edwards, 1971).

The assumption that delinquents break the law because they are somehow sick has been prevalent since the beginning of the reformatory era. Further, it has been believed that the so-called sickness can be cured if properly treated (Jarvis, 1978). The influence of the medical model has been particularly strong in correctional practices of the past forty years (Allen and Simonsen, 1978). As William Wayson (1974) remarked:

The social sciences, guided by an empirical philosophy, led corrections to the individual in the search for the causes of crime, because he was "sick," "antisocial" or "deprived." One only had to describe the etiology of the disease and prescribe appropriate "cures." . . . The objective of corrections, particularly incarceration, was to rehabilitate. (pp. 26–27)

Social workers, psychologists, and psychiatrists have devised literally dozens of treatment modes aimed at curing juvenile delinquents. With the recently renewed interest in biological theories of delinquency, medical doctors have joined the battle against the putative disease of delinquency. Given current uncertainty about the causes of delinquency, however, attempts to eliminate it through curing delinquents seem somewhat unrealistic. Although we have clues about the causes of youthful lawbreaking, we cannot explain why juvenile delinquency occurs; nor can we predict who will engage in it. For these reasons, the medical model has been increasingly criticized (see Gendreau and Ross, 1983–84). It is claimed that institutions do not rehabilitate, that most inmates are not sick, and that treatment is a myth. Some criminologists argue that "nothing works" (see, for example, Martinson, 1977: 518). Others argue that we should not summarily dismiss all treatment programs, but rather address the issue of which programs work and why they succeed (Gendreau and Ross, 1983–84: 32; Ross and Gendreau, 1980).

Criteria for Determining Program Effectiveness

In order to determine whether correctional institutions are effective in rehabilitating youthful offenders, we must first establish criteria to measure effectiveness. The rehabilitative success of correctional facilities has been judged in terms of several factors. One of the more popular of these is measuring the recidivism rates of released inmates. Based on the findings of recidivism studies, conclusions about the ability of correctional institutions to reduce recidivism have been very pessimistic. In a controversial article that reviewed more than 200 studies on rehabilitation attempts,

Robert Martinson (1977) came to the following conclusion:

> I am bound to say that these data, involving over two hundred studies and hundreds of thousands of individuals as they do, are the best available and give us very little reason to hope that we have in fact found a sure way of reducing recidivism through rehabilitation. This is not to say we have found no instances of success or partial success; it is only to say that these instances have been isolated, producing no clear-cut pattern to indicate the efficacy of any particular method of treatment. And neither is this to say that factors *outside* the realm of rehabilitation may not be working to reduce recidivism—factors such as the tendency for recidivism to be lower in offenders over the age of 30; it is only to say that such factors seem to have little connection with any of the treatment methods now at our disposal. (p. 518)

Other researchers have arrived at similar conclusions about the effectiveness of rehabilitation. After reviewing a number of correctional programs, Robison and Smith (1971) concluded that there was no evidence to support any claims of rehabilitative efficacy. Baily, in a 1966 study, surveyed 100 projects and reported disappointing results.

Specific data on the recidivism rates of released juvenile inmates are piecemeal at best. Although statistics vary from institution to institution and can be differentially interpreted, "most experts agree that about half of the persons released from juvenile training facilities can be expected to be reincarcerated" (President's Commission, 1967b: 142). Some researchers consider this 50 percent figure to be inflated, but spot checks of specific studies do suggest that recidivism rates are indeed high for most correctional facilities.[5] In a study of three female juvenile institutions, Giallombardo (1974) found that rates of previous institutionalization ranged from a low of 13.6 percent to a high of 50.9 percent. Following up 443 consecutive training school releases, Miller (cited in Bartollas, Miller, and Dinitz, 1976) found that the recidivism rate increased with number of years after discharge; four years after release, the rate was approximately 54 percent.

Two separate studies, one by Hood (1967) and the other by Jesness (1970), concluded that differential treatment efforts made little difference in subsequent criminal behavior. The Jesness study reported that recidivism rates for treated juveniles were identical to the rates for untreated inmates. More positive findings with recidivism rates ranging from 30 to 60 percent can, however, be found in the juvenile correctional literature (see Alexander and Parsons, 1973; Chandler, 1973; Lee and Haynes, 1980; Phillips et al., 1973; Ross and McKay, 1976; Walter and Mills, 1979).

Part of the problem in using recidivism rates to gauge the effectiveness of institutional treatment programs is that the influence of other variables can negate any improvement in the institution. Youth are often returned to unstable family environments, delinquent friends, and bitterly hostile generalized others, such as teachers, neighbors, and the police. Thus, any positive effects of training school programs may be nullified when the child is returned to the environment in which he or she got into trouble in the first place. Very few evaluation studies, at least until recently, have considered the impact of family and community situations on training school effectiveness. There is some evidence now that juvenile offenders released from institutions need advocates to help them deal with their parents, teachers, and others in the community so that any positive changes that might have occurred in confinement will continue to be reinforced (see Bartollas, 1985: 167). Finally, we might add that many previously incarcerated youths commit delinquent acts for which they are never apprehended. These behaviors, obviously, do not show up in recidivism rates. Thus, youth who are actually involved in delinquent behaviors may be counted as successes (Lerman, 1968; Wilson, 1978c).

A second criterion used to assess institutional effectiveness is the measurement of alleged personality changes in institutionalized youth (Zald, 1960). Hostile juveniles whose relationships with staff and other inmates become more controlled are deemed improved as a result of the treatment program. Slaikeu (1973) reviewed twenty-three studies on group treatment, a technique used to bring about personality change in both juvenile and adult offenders. He noted that "it is impossible to conclude that group treatment in correctional institutions is an effective rehabilitation mode" (p. 87). There are two basic problems with this type of measure. First, assessments of presumed personality changes are based on subjective appraisals by clinicians. At the present time, personality assessments are far from accurate. Further, many youths realize that in order to obtain release from correctional institutions, they must show signs of what is deemed improvement. Second, changes in the personalities of youths in institutional settings cannot be construed as predictive of how the juvenile will behave once he or she is released. A follow-up study on each child would be necessary to determine whether any personality change was temporary, contrived, or permanent.

A third evaluative criterion closely related to personality change assessments involves behavioral assessments in which delinquent offenders show improvements in any number of areas, including problem-solving, quality of interpersonal relationships with peers and staff, anticriminal verbalizations, social skills, and ability to deal with authority figures. Most of the programs designed to alter inappropriate behaviors follow a behavior modification format and generally have a better success record that other types of treatment modalities. From an evaluation standpoint, positive behavioral changes are difficult to assess once a juvenile has left a correctional facility unless there are effective follow-ups on his or her behavior.

A fourth criterion utilized to evaluate institutional effectiveness involves evaluation of the degree to which the correctional facilities meet standards that are supposed to ensure success. For instance, custodial facilities deemphasizing treatment may measure program effectiveness in terms of the number of runaways each month; fewer runaways mean that the institution is meeting its goals. Although the parent agency may be pleased and citizens in the surrounding community placated, it is debatable whether decreased numbers of runaways indicate effective rehabilitation.

A fifth approach used to test the effectiveness of institutionalization employs rating schedules administered to juvenile inmates and staff. Both youths and staff are asked to assess the impact of institutional treatment on those about to be released. Eynon, Allen, and Reckless (1971) used this technique at the Training Institution, Central Ohio (TICO), in Columbus, Ohio. Six different areas of hypothesized institutional impact were measured. These areas ranged from total rejection of the institution to self-labeling of oneself as an inmate. In general, the perceptions of the departing youths varied from somewhat unfavorable to slightly favorable. Staff ratings of boys were much more favorable than the ratings given by the youth. Beset with problems of subjectivity and removed from the child's community environment, this technique of assessing institutional impact has not met with much success.

All in all, research evidence points to one inescapable conclusion: Treatment programs predicated on the notion of sickness and cure are ineffective. Regardless of the measure, recidivism rates, personality assessments, compliance to goals of staff, or inmate attitudes, the results of studies of institutional effectiveness indicate that rehabilitation is an elusive phenomenon. Although some youth do not engage in repeat crimes, many others do so in spite of any treatment they might have received in an institutional setting.

CHARACTERISTICS OF YOUTH IN INSTITUTIONS

It is difficult to obtain accurate information on the types of juveniles confined in correctional facilities. The *Children in Custody* (CIC) series provides some information on the characteristics of institutionalized juveniles. In order to obtain a detailed view of the characteristics of youth held in correctional facilities, we will also consider data analyzed by Rosemary Sarri and Robert Vinter (1976) from the 1973–1974 National Assessment of Juvenile Corrections (NAJC) survey.

Sarri and Vinter report the race, age, sex, social class, and prior correctional experiences of a sample of youth involved in three types of correctional programs: (1) *closed institutions*, where youth are in secure custody all the time; (2) *community residential facilities*, where youth can interact with the surrounding community; and (3) *day treatment*, where youth live at home but are required to participate in supervised programs.

Sex

According to Sarri and Vinter (1976), males account for almost 75 percent of all youth in juvenile correctional programs. This sex-based disparity in correctional commitments corresponds to CIC's 1984 figures, which report that males represent well over three-fourths of all juvenile confinements in public and private facilities. The differences between male and female commitment rates are heightened when offense patterns are examined.

Age

The mean, or average, age of youth held in correctional facilities in the NAJC survey was 15.8 years; ages ranged from 8 to 24 years. In the CIC survey, the mean age was also approximately 15 years (for public and private facilities). Youth confined in institutional settings were slightly younger than those committed to community programs. According to Sarri and Vinter (1976), these findings refute the popular notion that institutions are places of last resort for older offenders.

Race

More than half of the juveniles in the NAJC sample (55 percent) belonged to minority groups, with blacks constituting the largest single category (32.2 percent of the total sample). Day treatment programs, involving 66 percent nonwhite juveniles, show the greatest racial differences. The high involvement of nonwhite youth is probably due to the location of these programs, many of which are within the central districts of major metropolitan areas. Similar to the findings of other studies, the data collected by the NAJC survey suggest an increase in nonwhite participation in correctional programs during the past decade.[6] Since the minority percentage of the total national population is around 15 percent, the NAJC data

clearly indicate that juvenile correctional programs disproportionately represent minority populations. The 1984 *Children in Custody* series reported that 39 percent of all juveniles confined to public long-term facilities were black; 24 percent of blacks were in long-term private facilities. From available evidence it is impossible to determine whether or not this discrepancy results from greater delinquent activity among minority juveniles. It is possible that biased enforcement of the laws by the police and selective reporting of crimes by the public result in overrepresentation of minority group members in correctional institutional programs.

Social Class

NAJC data indicate that in both secure institutional settings and day treatment programs, juveniles from the lower social classes, as measured by parents' employment record, predominate. A slightly smaller proportion of lower class youth are involved in community residential programs. These findings support previous reports suggesting that the police often single out members of the lower class for closer scrutiny because lower class neighborhoods, and often the demeanor of lower class individuals, arouse public suspicion.

Prior Correctional Experience

Prior correctional experience, according to Sarri and Vinter (1976), is commonly reported by youth held in correctional institutions, especially those held in secure institutional settings. Juveniles now confined in correctional institutions report frequent past contact with the juvenile justice system. Such experience ranges from arrests to prior institutionalization.

Commitment Offense

An examination of patterns of offenses resulting in commitment to the three types of correctional programs reveals several findings. The number of status offenders in each type of program is high. Females are particularly likely to face institutionalization for status offenses. Fifty percent of confined females are committed for involvement in status offenses. Further, females who have committed status and minor offenses are more likely to be sent to correctional and detention centers than are male offenders with the same types of adjudications. Drug and alcohol commitments are also higher among females in closed institutions and community facilities than among males in these facilities.

Regardless of the offense, females in the NAJC sample stand a greater chance of being institutionalized than males. Since the NAJC study was conducted, many states have enacted legislation prohibiting the incarceration of status offenders. CIC figures for 1982 indicate that 1,629 youths were confined in long-term public and private facilities for the commission of status offenses.

Although males are more frequently committed than females for serious crimes against the person, only 15 percent of total male commitments to programs in the NAJC study result from involvement in these serious crimes. Property crimes, which include such offenses as larceny, theft, and shoplifting, account for the largest percentage of male commitments to institutions.

The more serious offender is found not only in custodial institutions, but also in the other types of programs. One of the more provocative findings of the NAJC-based programs reports no greater difficulty in controlling youth involved in serious delinquency than did staff in traditional institutions.

Overall, the NAJC describes a gradual decline in juvenile inmate populations held in public institutions over the past decade. Concurrent with these declines in institutional residents have been increases in the populations of community-oriented programs. There appear to be two primary reasons for this shift: (1) the decarceration movement, which has gained momentum since the early 1970s, and (2) the awareness of monetary savings when offenders are placed in community programs instead of institutions. Despite increases in community programs, training schools in most states continue to handle the largest numbers of juvenile offenders. Only time will tell the full effect of

the decarceration movement on the treatment of juvenile delinquents and the future of correctional programs.

TREATMENT STRATEGIES IN INSTITUTIONS

There are numerous strategies aimed at treating juvenile offenders. These strategies range from social to psychological and attempt to discover methods to alter the behavior of juvenile offenders. Both individual and group variations of these approaches have mixed degrees of success and failure. In this section, we briefly summarize treatment modes currently employed in correctional facilities. These techniques are also employed in nonsecure and community types of correctional programs.

Insight Therapy

Insight-oriented therapy is directed toward helping young offenders understand why they behave as they do in light of past actions or behaviors. Individual psychotherapy and transactional analysis are two insight techniques.

Individual Psychotherapy.   Psychotherapy is one technique employed by psychiatrists, clinical psychologists, and psychiatric social workers to treat the emotional problems of juvenile inmates. Psychotherapists, using the framework of psychoanalysis, encourage individuals to explore the past and to draw links between the past and the present. When this process is successful, it is thought that emotional problems, often acted out in delinquent behavior, will end. According to Gibbons, the following premises underlie psychoanalytic treatment:

1. Most causes of personal maladjustment are rooted in early life experiences, particularly those involving parent-child interaction;

2. these causes are only dimly understood, at best, by the patient;

3. a skilled analyst or therapist can discover the causes of maladjustment through the therapeutic relationship;

4. the patient will experience "catharsis" or emotional relief when he is led to understand the source of his difficulties by the therapist. (Gibbons, 1965: 144)

The therapist tries not only to represent authoritative figures in the youth's past, but also to assume an accepting and sympathetic stance toward the offender. By showing the youth that all adults are not domineering or hostile, the therapist hopes to influence the child in a positive manner and to point out faulty perceptions acquired in early life. The final stage of analysis occurs when the child uses this newly acquired insight to alter present behavior.

There are three main problems with this approach. First, most institutions lack qualified personnel to administer the therapy. Second, commitment times may not be long enough. And third, once the juvenile is released from the facility, there may be no therapists available to continue the treatment.

Transactional Analysis.   Transactional analysis (TA) is a method aimed at interpreting and evaluating interpersonal relationships. Eric Berne (1961), originator of TA, suggested that transactions between people can be seen as "pastimes or games" (p. 23). According to Wolberg (1967), a psychologist, transactional analysis is based on the assumption that a person's "ego states"—that is, how the person acts at certain times—relate to his or her game playing.

1. Human relationships consist of competitive acts of social maneuvers which serve a defensive function and yield important gratifications. Such maneuvers are called "pastimes" or "games."

2. Manifested in all persons are three different "ego states": first, the *child*, a regressive relic of the individual's past; second, the *parent*, whom the person has incorporated through identification with his or her parents; third, the *adult*, who is the mature, reasonable self.

3. Each of these three aspects of the person perceives reality differently: the child prelogically, the parent judgmentally, and the adult comprehensively on the basis of past experience.

4. The three states are constantly operating in response to the needs of the person and the kinds of pastimes and games he or she is indulging in at the time. (Wolberg, 1967: 257–258)

Using TA principles, some correctional staffs attempt to teach juvenile offenders to interact with others in a mature fashion. When delinquents are treated through TA, the strategy is to define the offender's game in terms of the three categories of adult, parent, and child. Therapy sessions attempt to reinforce or strengthen the adult component of the youth's ego state. The assumption is that an overemphasis on the child component results in delinquent behavior.

Despite the popularity of TA and some limited success in reducing discipline problems and juvenile parole violations, there are problems in implementation (Jesness, 1965). TA does not work well with emotionally disturbed youth, the grossly immature, or the educationally handicapped. These groups are, of course, often represented in the populations of juvenile institutions.

Behavioral Therapy

Behavioral therapies concentrate on the offender's current or present problems, for the most part ignoring past behaviors. Reality therapy and behavior modification are two of the more popular behavioral techniques currently in use.

Reality Therapy.   Reality therapists try to fulfill certain basic and previously unfulfilled needs of the young delinquent. According to William Glasser (1965), the originator of this therapy, delinquency can be arrested through the development of meaningful relationships between the offender and a therapist who cares about the youth and who requires the youth to be responsible. By stressing reality, responsibility, and differences between right and wrong, reality therapists propose to find solutions for the unfulfilled needs of the youth. Reality therapy differs from traditional psychotherapy in that it largely ignores the past and is not concerned with unconscious motives. Treatment involves movement through three levels of relationships between client and therapist. First, honest personal relationships between the counselor and client are established. Second, therapists indicate that negative behavior is understood but not condoned. Third, the therapists teach offenders better ways to fulfill needs within the existing social setting (Glasser, 1965). Since institutional commitment is for a limited time, efforts are made to move through the three steps and to produce behavior change as quickly as possible.

There is little information on the effectiveness of reality therapy when it is applied to delinquents. Some success was reported by Glasser with a sample of delinquent girls at the Ventura School, a juvenile correctional facility near Ventura, California. He reported in his 1965 work that out of a total of 370 girls undergoing reality therapy, only 43 were recidivists. A more recent application of reality therapy at the Glades Correctional Institution in Florida reported fewer behavioral problems in the facility; no mention was made of the carryover effect of the treatment upon the juveniles' release (Williams, 1976).

Behavior Modification. Another technique focusing on present behavior and future actions is behavior modification. *Behavior modification* is the systematic application of principles of conditioning and learning to the remediation of certain undesirable behaviors. The behavioral model presumes that all behavior is learned, maintained, controlled, or extinguished by rewarding or punishing consequences. A number of behavioral techniques

are employed to reinforce positive, or desirable, behaviors and to extinguish negative, or undesirable, behaviors. These techniques include modeling, aversive stimulation, systematic desensitization, reinforcement schedules, counterconditioning, and the use of token economies, behavioral contracts, and point systems.

Behavior modification differs from most treatment strategies by concentrating only on overt behaviors—that is, readily observable behaviors—ignoring such concepts as repressed desires and unfulfilled needs. By gradually withholding reinforcers as privileges and rewards, behavioral therapists seek gradually to alter negative behaviors. Within the juvenile institution, behavior modification programs have enjoyed either very good success or dramatic failure. Those programs that have been unsuccessful generally had the following features: (1) They were imposed on the offenders who were never involved in the development of the program; (2) the target behaviors (those behaviors to be altered) were antisocial rather than prosocial, thus giving antisocial behaviors inordinate attention and in some cases reinforcing such behaviors; (3) they failed to neutralize or use in a positive manner the offender's peer group (Ross and McKay, 1978; Gendreau and Ross, 1983–84). Behavior modification programs that have succeeded either avoided or minimized these negative phenomena.

Behavior modification seems to work well in the controlled environment of the training school if certain conditions are met, but seems to have little permanent effect on offenders once they are outside the school. Also, since consistency is a crucial element in behavioral therapy, all staff must systematically provide the necessary reinforcers if the treatment is to be effective.

Group Therapy

Several types of group therapy techniques are currently employed in correctional facilities across the country. The most important of these are group psychotherapy, guided group interaction, positive peer culture, psychodrama, and milieu therapy.

Group Psychotherapy.   Group psychotherapy is a treatment strategy based on the assumption that delinquents exhibit unfavorable attitudes, self-images, and behaviors because of their associational networks. Further, since peers are important, group psychotherapists argue that attempts to change youth without taking their peers into account are unrealistic. Group psychotherapists, who are most commonly psychiatrists and clinical psychologists, also argue that treatment which involves the offender's close associates is likely to have more impact than some other form of treatment (Gibbons, 1965). Group therapy encourages members of the group to put pressure on each other for attitudinal and behavorial changes in order to attain a more equal balance of power between therapist and client. Juvenile offenders are, in a sense, therapists and clients.

Not all youth, however, are suitable for group psychotherapy. For best results, group membership should be voluntary, and care should be taken to diminish the control of manipulative offenders over other participants. Although group therapists assume that the groups in which one is involved influence behaviors, it should be remembered that inmates do not voluntarily associate with one another. Institutionalized inmates are members of contrived groups that may not be as important to the youth as voluntary associations. Inmate groups, however, can influence juveniles greatly, especially those at the bottom of the peer power hierarchy.

Research findings about the effectiveness of group psychotherapy are mixed. Slaikeu (1973) reviewed group treatment studies from 1945 to 1970 and observed some positive results with group techniques.[7] However, he concluded that it is impossible to know whether group techniques achieve their rehabilitation purpose.

Guided Group Interaction.   Like group psychotherapy, guided group interaction (GGI) is a therapy based on the notion that juvenile inmates can be helped to solve problems through group processes. GGI programs involve offenders in frequent and intensive group discussions of their own and each others' problems and experiences.

Supported by the idea that the peer group can exert a great deal of pressure on its members, GGI allows inmates to gradually assume power and decision-making functions in the group (Center for Studies of Crime and Delinquency, n.d.).

Residents participating in cottage sessions are often given considerable say in determining when group members should be released, granted home visits, or granted off-campus leaves. Similarly, inmates are sometimes allowed to suggest how other members should be punished or sanctioned for infractions of cottage rules. GGI is used in at least eleven states, including New Jersey, South Dakota, Minnesota, West Virginia, Illinois, Georgia, Florida, New Hampshire, Maryland, Michigan, and Kentucky. While the technique is used in correctional institutions, it is more prevalent in nonresidential programs (Bartollas, 1985: 133–134).

Positive Peer Culture.   Positive peer culture (PPC), like guided group interaction, is a therapy utilizing peer influences to effect behavioral changes. The therapy utilizes groups of nine youths under the guidance of an adult leader. PPC is aimed at changing a negative youth subculture and using the power of the peer group in a positive manner (Vorrath and Brendtro, 1974). The goal of the group, which meets in ninety-minute sessions five times a week, is to redirect peer pressures and to diminish the we-they battle between inmates and staff. PPC does not attempt to uncover deep-seated psychological problems, but instead tries to help clients acquire better modes of handling immediate needs and enable them eventually to function in a nondelinquent community.

Youth entering the group initially tell their "life histories." Thereafter, at the beginning of each session, group members decide which youth is going to be discussed and why. The person selected is referred to as "having the meeting." After discussing the way he or she has handled particular problems throughout the day, the group points out behavioral and attitudinal areas in need of improvement and any additional problems not discussed. Participants are urged to refer to improvements in the behaviors or attitudes of peers as "intelligent" or "great"; negative behaviors are referred to as "childish" or "immature" (Dean and Reppucci, 1974).

Mitchell and Cochrum (1980) examined the effectiveness of PPC in an adolescent treatment facility and generally found that the technique could be associated with fewer incidents and a smoother running facility. PPC has been successful in reducing the recidivism rates of such facilities as the Red Wing Training School in Minnesota (McKinney, Miller, Beier, and Bohannon, 1978). But the technique is not free from criticism. There are problems in obtaining qualified PPC leaders, upon whom the treatment hinges, and in detecting real versus contrived improvements in group members.

Psychodrama. Psychodrama is a technique through which clients act out past, present, and future situations with the goal of analyzing relationships with other individuals. Jacob Moreno originally conceived the technique in 1925 as a means of bringing the patient's social situation into the psychiatrist's office. Although not used extensively in juvenile correctional facilities, the strategy has had limited success with serious delinquents (Haskell and Yablonsky, 1978). In a group setting analogous to a stage, youth are allowed to play themselves in various relationships, particularly those in which they have experienced difficulties. Group members form the audience and, after the performance, discuss the actors' experiences and problems (Haskell, 1967). Group members are encouraged to refer to their own experiences.

Most correctional facilities lack therapists trained in this rather novel treatment mode. Thus the use of this technique in juvenile correctional programs has been hampered. The Rahway Treatment Unit in New Jersey has utilized psychodrama in its ROARE program (Reeducation of Attitudes and Repressed Emotions) with sex offenders (*Treating Sex Offenders*, 1974). The effectiveness of the therapy remains to be seen.

Milieu Therapy. Milieu therapy refers to several rehabilitative strategies designed to make every aspect of the juvenile inmate's environment a part of his or her treatment. These strategies include reducing the distinctions between custodial staff and treatment staff, creating a supportive, nonauthoritarian and nonregimented atmosphere, and enlisting peer influence in the formation of constructive values (Martinson, 1977). Milieu therapy is eclectic in its implementation and seeks to produce an institutional environment that will facilitate positive and meaningful general changes in the juvenile offender.

Polsky (1962), for example, sought to implement a more therapeutic community in Hollymeade, a custodial institution, and recommended that a professional clinician reside in the cottage with staff and inmates in order to develop a more comprehensive treatment program. Other techniques include educational and vocational training as well as social group work as a part of milieu therapy. Many other specific treatments are used to supplement the milieu therapy.

Reports of the results of the effectiveness of milieu therapy are conflicting. Some researchers, such as Goldberg and Adams (1964), report positive findings in reducing behavioral problems. Others, like Jesness (1965), have found less positive results. Jesness reported that the technique had no significant effect on recidivism among a sample of twenty boys at the Fricot Ranch School for Boys, a California Youth Authority facility. Eighty percent of the youth undergoing milieu therapy experienced trouble—that is, recidivism—within three years after treatment. Approximately 80 percent of a sample of youth not exposed to the therapy also experienced trouble.

Social Skills Therapy

Although it may not be technically correct to classify skill development programs in juvenile correctional facilities as a specific type of "therapy," these types of programs have enjoyed a certain measure of success compared to other more theoretically based treatment schemes. As Clemens Bartollas (1985) notes: "These programs are concerned with developing communication, daily living and survival, educational advancement and study, and career skills" (p. 148). In short, such programs provide juvenile offenders with very specific and concrete skills that they will need to make it throughout the rest of their lives. Dennis Romig outlines a model for a typical skill development program:

1. Get the youths' attention
2. Obtain input using staff who have empathy
3. Objectively diagnose
4. Set a behavorial goal
5. Teach youths new behavior using effective teaching methods:
    a. Individualized diagnosis
    b. Specific learning goal
    c. Individualized program based upon personally relevant material
    d. Teach basic academic skills
    e. Multisensory techniques
    f. Sequential presentation, breaking complex skills into simple steps
    g. Initially rewarding youths' attention and persistence
    h. Differential reinforcement of learning performance
6. Teach skills in the following areas:
    a. Communication skills
    b. Daily living and survival skills
    c. Educational advancement and study skills that result in a diploma or certificate that supports career goals
    d. Career skills, such as career decision-making and career advancement
7. Practice skills in problem-solving
8. Differentially reinforce
9. Family training in communication, problem-solving, and disciplining skills
10. Follow-up skill training and reinforcement (Romig, 1978: 109)

Critics of social skills development training point out that "both practitioners and administrators must recognize the limitations of the technique; it cannot cure the 'causes of [youth] crime' " (Henderson and Hollin, 1983: 337). It can, how-ever, be quite beneficial for some young offenders who have never developed even rudimentary interpersonal skills.

An Assessment of Therapy Programs

Evaluation of the effectiveness of these therapies suggests no definitive success in altering either the attitudes or behaviors of juvenile offenders. Selected cases of improvement, however, have been reported in the literature. The limited success of therapeutic programs does raise questions about the medical model approach to delinquency and about the extent of our knowledge concerning its causes and cures.

"The theoretical premises, or constructs, of most correctional intervention have been largely unexamined" (Bartollas, 1985: 168). Such theoretical premises are often derived from conventional wisdom, with very little thought given to what a particular program can realistically expect to accomplish with a group of juvenile offenders. Greenberg (1977c) describes many of the theoretical assumptions underlying current treatment interventions as "bordering on the preposterous." Thus, adhering to simplistic notions about "curing" delinquent offenders without regard to "circumstances precipitating the crime, the offender's characteristics and predilections, the social conditions affecting the offender, and the environment in which treatment is to take place" inevitably result in failure (Bartollas, 1985: 169).

THE INMATE SUBCULTURE

Beginning with Donald Clemmer's initial account (1940) of how inmates come to adopt the culture of the prison community, numerous works have contained hypothesized explanations of the emergence of the inmate social system. Regardless of whether the inmate subculture arises because of the **pains of imprisonment** or is imported from the outside, evidence suggests that the inmate community can seriously affect rehabilitative efforts in the institution (Clemmer, 1940; Irwin and Cressey, 1962; Schrag, 1961; Sykes, 1958; Thomas,

Hyman, and Winfree, 1983; Larson, 1983). Giallombardo (1974), a sociologist, has suggested that the consequences of the inmate social system include: "(1) a sharp cleavage between the staff and the inmates that oppose staff values and emphasizes loyalty to fellow inmates, (2) an inmate world that, although not a 'war of all against all,' is nevertheless notable for violence, struggles for power, and involvement in illicit activities; (3) the emergence of social roles defined in the argot [special vocabulary] of the prison community" (p. 1).

Only a few studies have investigated the effects of inmate social systems on juvenile institutions. However, these studies suggest that very real and powerful inmate codes affect both inmates and staff in juvenile institutions. Similarly, both inmates and staff use institutional social roles to categorize residents of the institution (see Ross, 1981).

Inmate Social Codes

In a study of an Ohio Youth Commission institution, Bartollas, Miller, and Dinitz (1976) observed very strong inmate codes of behavior that were understood by most residents. A close examination of the interactions of boys and staff suggested that practically every behavior had a corresponding rule defining the appropriate actions. What emerged was a normative code—one all newcomers came to know as they tried to figure out how to adapt to institutional life. This code was made up of a series of general tenets for day-to-day living and was passed from one youth to another. Following are the contents of the inmate informal code at a state institution for boys in Columbus, Ohio, as described by Bartollas, Miller, and Dinitz:[8]

1. *Exploit whomever you can*: The conduct norms suggest that the powerless may be victimized in any conceivable way. Exploitation of others is justified because inmates feel they have been victimized all their lives.

2. *Don't kiss ass*: This tenet warns inmates not to be dependent on staff and to treat youth leaders, social workers, and schoolteachers with distrust and suspicion.

3. *Don't rat on your peers*: To betray a peer is to break a very serious norm. Ratting on peers can result in serious consequences. Inmate leaders or "heavies" can, however, break these norms without fear of repercussion.

4. *Don't give up your ass*: Since a boy who is sexually exploited often runs the risk of becoming the cottage scapegoat, youths usually fight rather than submit to the pressure.

5. *Be cool*: This involves not "whining" when things are not going well or not running away from a fight.

6. *Don't get involved in another inmate's affairs*: This maxim promotes granting as much social distance as self-contained cottage living permits.

7. *Don't steal "squares"*: Stealing cigarettes is a serious offense and youth caught doing it are often seriously assaulted.

8. *Don't buy the mind-fucking*: Here youth guard against repeated treatment attempts made by staff to modify boys' behaviors and values.

Although there is evidence that the inmate code, to a degree, unites inmates against staff, inmates are by no means a cohesive unit. A great deal of victimization occurs, with the targets generally the newcomers and the weak. In any case, the overall effect of inmate codes is to undermine attempts at treatment and rehabilitation (Wellford, 1967).

Inmate Social Types

Informal inmate codes are one aspect of the inmate subculture affecting institutional life. Inmate social roles or types are also typical of juvenile institutions, and these roles often identify who is to be the exploiter. At the top of the social order are the more highly esteemed roles, and at the bottom are the more unacceptable. Bartollas, Miller, and Dinitz (1976) noted the following social roles, presented in order of diminishing prestige:

1. *Heavy*: A cottage leader who can maintain power by aggression, physical prowess, or by intelligence and cooperation. In addition, staff give privileges to heavies for cooperation in controlling the other inmates.

2. *Lieutenants*: These youths are the heavies' assistants. They may have similar traits to the heavies and are the next highest in inmate prestige.

3. *Slick*: Inmates who are highly esteemed by others for their ability to manipulate staff. Until close to release, slicks maintain their social distance from staff and other inmates.

4. *Booty Bandit*: Youths who sexually exploit others. These youth are generally black and are both older and more mature than the average inmate.

5. *Peddler*: Generally, one inmate from a cottage who trades goods from one cottage to another. He often extorts goods from weaker peers and deals in cigarettes.

6. *Messup*: Besides making mistakes, violating institutional rules, and creating conflicts with peers, this youth has a remarkable penchant for doing and saying the wrong thing. Both staff and other inmates discriminate against him and dislike the messup.

7. *Thief*: In spite of his lowly status, the thief, who steals from other inmates, is found in every cottage. These youth are frequently violently assaulted by other residents.

8. *Queen*: These are overt homosexuals.

9. *Scapegoat*: The lowest-ranking social role. A youth who becomes isolated from the group because of his amenability to exploitation, especially sexual exploitation. (pp. 105–128)

Most of these roles are recognized by both staff and inmates, and the names become a part of the institution's argot. Polsky's (1962) study of Hollymeade, a residential treatment juvenile institution for delinquent boys, revealed similar social roles.

Before 1965, very little correctional research dealt with female institutions. A few early and scattered studies noted the existence of a female inmate subculture in both juvenile and adult female institutions (Ford, 1929; Otis, 1913; Selling, 1931). These subcultures were reported to often take the form of pseudofamily role relationships in which young women assumed roles with one another as brothers, sisters, mothers, fathers, and so on. In 1965 David A. Ward and Gene G. Kassebaum published a book on a California women's prison and found no evidence of pseudofamilies, although much overt homosexuality was observed. A year later, Rose Giallombardo (1966) released her work on a West Virginia federal women's institution. Giallombardo found convincing evidence of a distinct female inmate subculture in which women assumed pseudofamily roles.

Later she conducted research in three correctional institutions for juvenile girls and reported a unique set of social roles for female inmates (Giallombardo, 1974). Relationships among inmates were less exploitative and were defined primarily in kinship terms. In one eastern institution, inmate social relations were structured by courtship, marriage, and kinship ties and provided functional substitutes for normal relationships with family and friends of both sexes. Two close girls, for example, might "go for sisters" and for all practical purposes treat one another as sisters. In addition, inmates were also broken into "types" similar to those found in male institutions— heavies, lieutenants, and so forth.

One of Giallombardo's (1974) concerns noted earlier was whether the organizational structure of the institution affected the type of inmate adaptation. Propper (1978: 269) had found that female homosexuality rates ranged from 6 to 30 percent over the seven institutions. In a subsequent study, Propper (1982) compared institutional characteristics to determine their impact on female homosexual practices and found several interesting points. First, female inmates in coed institutions were just as likely to participate in pseudofamilies and homosexuality as were inmates in all-female institutions. However, membership in a pseudofamily did not necessarily lead to an active homosexual role. Rather, it appears that pseudofamily membership and homosexual encounters represent two diverse adaptations to imprisonment.

Second, male inmates within coed institutions were often incorporated into the structure of pseudofamilies as brothers and fathers. Third, homosexual marriages in which females assumed the male role were extremely rare. Only 4 percent of the female inmates reported that they had assumed a traditional male sex role, either partially or exclusively. Finally, most pseudofamily roles took the relational form of mother-daughter and sister-sister ties.

Such patterns of inmate roles are important aspects of institutional life. Although formal goals of the facility may center on treatment, informal inmate roles, as in the case of informal inmate codes, may undermine treatment attempts.

THE RIGHTS OF JUVENILES IN CONFINEMENT

Concern over the effects of the inmate subculture on inmates has grown concurrently with attention to the rights of incarcerated juveniles. Interest in inmates' rights reflects the influence of the broader **children's rights movement** (Thornton, 1978). Recent court decisions, especially the Gault ruling (1967), reflect this renewed concern with the rights of juveniles. Thousands of youth are confined in public and private correctional institutions in the United States. Their rights have been recently reevaluated. Through new interpretations of the Constitution and through state and federal court rulings, legal protections for institutionalized youth are more extensive now than in the past. There are four major rights—the right to treatment, the right not to be treated, the right to be free from cruel and unusual punishment, and the right to release from an institution.[9]

Right to Treatment

Commitment of a juvenile without treatment is a violation of the Eighth and Fourteenth Amendments. In *White* v. *Reid* (1954), the court held that juveniles could not be held in facilities that did not provide for their rehabilitation. Although not dealing specifically with juveniles, *Rouse* v. *Cameron* (1966) ruled that "involuntarily committed mental patients have a constitutional right to treatment, since the purpose of hospitalization is not to punish but to help the patient" (Silbert and Sussman, 1974: 611). Several federal rulings dealing specifically with juveniles in training schools require that treatment include, at the minimum, the following: adequate food, shelter, and clothing; academic, vocational, and physical education; medical care; social services; psychiatric services; supervision by trained child-care staff; recreation; and opportunities for visits and telephone calls (see *Robin R.* v. *Wyman*, 1971).

Right Not to Be Treated

Although the two rights appear contradictory, the right to treatment is linked to the right *not* to be treated. Institutional programs that degrade, dehumanize, punish, or humiliate inmates cannot be condoned, even if they fall within the realm of treatment.[10] According to the Institute of Judicial Administration of the American Bar Association (IJA-ABA) standards, children may voluntarily refuse services except in three cases: "services juveniles are legally obliged to accept (such as school attendance), services required to prevent clear harm to physical health, and helpful services mandated by the court as a condition to a nonresidential disposition" (Swanger, 1977: 22).

Right to Be Free from Cruel and Unusual Punishment

Although certain Bill of Rights freedoms are not extended to juveniles (for example, the right to trial by jury), the Eighth Amendment barring cruel and unusual punishment unquestionably does apply to children.

Federal courts have ruled that extended periods of solitary confinement, as well as the use of Thorazine and other medications for the purpose of control, constitute cruel and unusual punishment. Similarly, most states prohibit the use of corporal punishment in any form. Also, the confinement without treatment of noncriminal offenders may violate the Eighth Amendment.[11]

Right to Release from an Institution

Keeping a child incarcerated when he or she is no longer in need of treatment is an unnecessary deprivation of liberty.[12] Since its conception, the juvenile justice system has been based on the idea that correctional institutions should treat rather than punish juveniles (Silbert and Sussman, 1974).

An Assessment of Juvenile Rights

Even though rulings in favor of children's rights have been made, judicial recognition of the rights of incarcerated juveniles does not guarantee that legal protection will be afforded youths. In most correctional facilities there is no channel of communication through which juvenile inmates can voice their complaints. Such a protective outlet is necessary. Currently, institutional bureaucracies often stifle complaints before they can reach the proper authorities.

SUMMARY

Past and present juvenile facilities have aimed at treating juvenile offenders in order to transform them into useful, productive citizens. The ostensible goal of institutionalization is rehabilitation. However, social scientists have increasingly questioned the rehabilitative effectiveness of juvenile facilities.

Before the late eighteenth century, young offenders were primarily handled informally by family, church, and community. By the end of the eighteenth century, informal methods of social control were rapidly becoming ineffective. In the 1820s, a new institution, the house of refuge, came into being in the progressive centers of New York, Boston, and Philadelphia. These early houses of refuge offered shelter and sanctuary, but their main purpose was to train and rehabilitate juvenile offenders through a strict regimen of religious instruction, education, and hard work. The harshness of life in these institutions led to their decline and to the rise of reformatories, also known as reform or training schools. Reformatories were supposed to provide treatment based on new, scientific theories of delinquency. However, in practice these facilities shared many of the same problems as the earlier refuge institutions, the science being less advanced than its advocates' hopes.

As the 1980s began, juvenile correctional facilities included these basic types: (1) detention centers, (2) shelters, (3) reception-diagnostic centers, (4) public and private training schools, and (5) work camps. Detention centers are short-term, physically restricting facilities that provide temporary care for juveniles, pending court adjudication. Shelters, on the other hand, do not employ physical restraints and are designed primarily to care for neglected or abused children. Reception-diagnostic centers attempt to explore and classify juvenile problems and to prescribe appropriate treatments. Training schools, also called reform schools and reformatories, are the most common type of facility. They are long-term residential centers that may be treatment- or custody-oriented. Work camps are also used for long-term residential care of less seriously delinquent youth. Despite much controversy, large numbers of juveniles are held in adult jails and prisons throughout the United States.

The typical offender committed to a residential program is male, about 15 or 16 years old, a member of a minority group, and from a lower social class; he often has a prior record and previous correctional experience. Females committed to residential programs are likely to be status offenders. More males are placed in residential programs for larceny, theft, and shoplifting violations than for involvement in any other kinds of offenses.

Juvenile correctional institutions have multiple

and often contradictory goals. These may include treatment as well as custodial goals. Although many types of treatments, oriented toward both individuals and groups, exist in juvenile correctional institutions, questions have been raised about the effectiveness of these treatments. It is charged that institutions do not rehabilitate, that most inmates are not sick, and that treatment itself is a myth.

Within all types of institutions, an inmate subculture develops. Regardless of whether the inmate subculture arises because of the "pains of imprisonment" or is imported into the prison world from the outside, evidence suggests that inmate codes and social roles may have adverse effects on treatment efforts made by institutional staff.

As part of the broader children's rights movement, attention to the rights of incarcerated juveniles grew in the 1960s and 1970s. Court decisions have supported the rights of institutionalized children to challenge various aspects of the treatment they receive or do not receive in correctional facilities.

PROGRESS CHECK

1. What are the implications of a *total institutions* approach to juvenile incarceration? (p. 341)

2. Historical accounts of life in colonial America indicate that early settlers had little need for specialized institutions to serve either juveniles or adults. (p. 342)
   a. True
   b. False

3. The Society of Friends opened the first public institutions for boys and girls in the United States in _____ and _____; its name was _____ . (pp. 342–343)

4. Trace the development of the reformatory (training school) movement in this country, giving particular attention to developments in Ohio and Massachusetts. (p. 344)

5. Distinguish among the three major types of short-term juvenile facilities in terms of the roles they play in contemporary youth corrections. (pp. 345–346)

6. Which of the Street, Vinter, and Perrow institutional classifications is characterized by an emphasis on respect for authority, the technique of conditioning, and an undifferentiated view of inmates? (pp. 351–352)
   a. Custody (obedience—conformity)
   b. Reeducation
   c. Treatment
   d. Mixed goal

7. Summarize the characteristics of institutionalized youth in terms of the following features: (pp. 355–356)
   a. Age
   b. Race
   c. Commitment offense

8. Which of the following treatment approaches was developed by Eric Berne to focus on behavior as pastimes or games, linked to ego states? (p. 357)
   a. Reality therapy
   b. Behavior modification
   c. Transactional analysis
   d. Psychodrama

9. Explain how inmate social codes may be antithetical to treatment in juvenile correctional institutions. (p. 362)

10. The chapter lists four rights of juveniles in confinement. Describe these in the order of importance you believe each should have, providing a rationale for your sequence. (pp. 364–365)

NOTES

1. During the latter 1800s, psychiatrists and psychologists in the United States and Europe became interested in the psychological characteristics of delinquent youth. As noted

by Cavan and Ferdinand (1975), "In 1909 the Juvenile Psychiatric Clinic was founded in Chicago with Dr. William Healy as its director, and by World War II similar clinics for the study of delinquents were opened in Massachusetts, Ohio, and Michigan. In Europe, August Aichhorn was developing a psychoanalytic theory of delinquency, and, in 1918, he opened an institution for delinquents near Vienna" (p. 399).

2. The Supreme Court in its decision upheld a New York law allowing judges to engage in "preventive detention." Similar laws exist in most states and the District of Columbia. Under these laws, judges may also lock up juveniles who are deemed poor risks for appearance at trial.

3. Annual periods for counts are generally for the calendar year, although some data in the CIC series may be based on the fiscal year. One-day counts are as of June 30 for 1974 and 1975 and December 31 for 1977 and 1979. The most recent one-day count, i.e., CIC counts for 1982, was changed from December 31 to the following February 1 to obtain a more representative enumeration of residents after the fluctuations of the holiday period. This change makes comparisons between years in terms of short-term and total custody populations problematic. Also, in the original CIC publications, "average daily number of residents" may include both juvenile and adult residents. Only *juvenile* residents are included in Tables 16.1 and 16.2 (see U.S. Department of Justice, December, 1984).

4. In 1978 *Corrections Magazine* conducted a survey of the number of juveniles held in state secure and semi-secure facilities. Although there are some differences in the findings of this survey and those of CIC surveys, the *Corrections Magazine* survey shows a decline in the number of juvenile offenders incarcerated in state correctional institutions (at least through 1978). This survey estimated the 1978 inmate population at about 26,000. All but 7

states showed decreases of 30 percent or more in their institutional populations, and 11 states had declines of 50 percent or more (R. Wilson, 1978a.)

5. See Clarke (1975), Kassebaum, Ward, and Welner (1971), Lipton, Martinson, and Wilks (1975), and Seckel (1965).

6. See, for instance, U.S. Department of Justice, Law Enforcement Assistance Administration (1975).

7. See, for instance, Persons (1966). His study reports that youth treated with group psychotherapy, as compared to individual psychotherapy, did considerably better on parole than untreated inmates.

8. This excerpt is from *Juvenile Victimization: The Institutional Paradox* by Clemens Bartollas, Stuart Miller, and Simon Dinitz. Copyright 1976, pp. 60–70 and 105–128, reprinted by permission of the publisher, Sage Publications (Beverly Hills/London) and the author.

9. Our review is drawn in part from Silbert and Sussman (1974). For a more detailed coverage of the rights of juveniles, see S. M. Davis (1980).

10. For more on this subject, see Kittrie (1971) and *Lollis* v. *N.Y. State Department of Social Services* (1970).

11. See *Lollis* v. *N.Y. State Department of Social Services* (1970), Rogers (1977), and *U.S. ex rel. Stewart* v. *Coughlin* (1971).

12. A child placed in an institution by a court has the right to challenge his or her initial confinement. In the case of *Morales* v. *Turman* (1971), two juvenile correctional facilities in Texas were ordered closed by the court because they failed to provide proper rehabilitative treatment. As noted by Silbert and Sussman (1974), "confinement may be challenged by direct appeal, by a writ of habeas corpus [that is, bringing an accused party immediately before a court or judge], or by a civil rights action in a federal court under section 1983 of title 42 of the United States Code" (p. 606).

CHAPTER 17

JUVENILE CORRECTIONS: THE COMMUNITY SETTING

DIVERSIONARY PROGRAMS

COMMUNITY-BASED
CORRECTIONAL PROGRAMS

A typical day at Achievement Place begins when the manager awakens the boys at about 6:30 in the morning. The boys then wash their faces, brush their teeth, and clean their bathroom and bedrooms. The manager, who is elected by his peers : . . , supervises these morning chores by assigning specific cleaning tasks to his peers, by monitoring the completion of these tasks, and by providing point consequences for their performance. While some of the boys are cleaning their rooms and bathrooms, other boys are helping prepare breakfast.

When a youth enters Achievement Place he is introduced to the point system that is used to help motivate the youths to learn new, appropriate behavior. Each youth uses a point card to record his behavior and the number of points he earns and loses. When a youth first enters the program his points are exchanged for privileges each day. . . . Because there are nearly unlimited opportunities to earn points, most of the youths earn all of the privileges most of the time.

After breakfast the boys check their appearance . . . before leaving Achievement Place to attend the local public schools. Since Achievement Place is a community-based facility, the boys continue to attend the same schools they had problems with before entering Achievement Place and the teaching-parents [the adults in charge of the day-to-day operation of the facility] work closely with the teachers and school administrators to remediate each youth's problems in school.

When the boys return to Achievement Place, they have their after-school snacks before starting their homework or other point-earning activities. In the late afternoon one or two boys usually volunteer to help prepare dinner. During the meal or just after the meal, the teaching-parents and the youths hold a family conference. . . . During a family conference the teaching-parents and the youths discuss the events that occurred during the day, evaluate the manager's performance, establish or modify rules, and decide on consequences for any *rule violations that were reported to the teaching-parents. These self-government behaviors are specifically taught to the youths, and they are encouraged to participate in discussions about any aspect of the program.*

After the family conference the boys usually listen to records or watch TV before "figuring up" their point cards for the day and going to bed about 10:30. (Fixsen, Phillips, and Wolf, 1973: 107–108)

Achievement Place is one example of a community-based juvenile correctional facility, a place where juveniles are to be rehabilitated without encountering the negative aspects of the traditional total juvenile institution. Such community-based alternatives developed as a result of widespread criticism of traditional correctional institutions in the 1960s. Those in favor of the removal of juvenile offenders from institutions argued that incarceration failed to rehabilitate juvenile offenders and thus should be reserved only for the hard-core, seriously delinquent offender. The movement to put juvenile offenders in community-based programs rather than traditional institutions came to be known as **decarceration** or **deinstitutionalization**. Decarceration has become one of the major innovations in treatment, with juvenile offenders being referred to community-based correctional programs increasingly since the 1960s.

Diversion, another alternative to the traditional handling of juvenile offenders, has also developed since the 1960s. Inspired by labeling theory, criminologists and juvenile justice workers argued that many juvenile offenders should not be handled by the juvenile justice system, but rather diverted from it. They contended that most youths who were found to be engaged in less serious delinquent offenses should just be sent home by police or court workers without any further official intervention or—at most—referred to social service programs where they could be treated. Since their introduction in the late 1960s, such diversionary programs have become increasingly available to juvenile court and police personnel. Their purpose is to solve emotional, family, school, or vocational problems of the delinquent and thus prevent future involvement in delinquency.

As with community-based correctional programs, diversion programs have developed because of the recognition by criminologists that the institutionalization of juvenile offenders failed to rehabilitate them and the belief that programs in the community could be more effective in rehabilitating offenders. However, these alternative programs have not been without their critics.

In this chapter we discuss the types of diversionary and community correctional programs, the extent of referrals to these programs, the reasons for the programs, and the criticisms that have been leveled against them. We will examine the experience of Massachusetts, the first state to attempt totally to deinstitutionalize juvenile corrections. Our discussion will begin with diversionary programs, which attempt to stop delinquency before it becomes severe.

DIVERSIONARY PROGRAMS

One of the most important and widespread trends in juvenile justice in the last twenty years has been the diversion of juvenile offenders from the juvenile justice system. President Lyndon Johnson's Commission on Law Enforcement and the Administration of Justice (1967a) recognized the diversion of juvenile offenders away from avenues of official processing as an essential part of juvenile justice reform. The commission stated that "in place of the formal system, dispositional alternatives to adjudication must be developed for dealing with juveniles, including agencies to provide and coordinate services and to achieve necessary control without unnecessary stigma" (p. 81).

First offenders, status offenders, and minor offenders are most often judged appropriate for diversion away from official processing. The hope is that early or spur-of-the-moment delinquency will either correct itself or be alleviated through counseling and vocational, recreational, educational, and medical services. Although referral to the juvenile court may produce the labeling of **delinquent** or **PINS (persons in need of supervision)**, diversion is thought to leave the child's public reputation and self-concept unblemished (Gough, 1977; National Advisory Commission on Criminal Justice Standards and Goals, 1976a).

Diversion away from formal processing may occur at several points. First, police officers may release a child after warnings about the possible consequences of engaging in illegal or annoying behaviors. Second, the child may be taken to the police station and his or her parents called. The juvenile may then be warned and released into the custody of the parents. These dispositions are examples of true diversion. Third, referral to social service agencies or community programs may occur after initial investigations by court intake workers or before official petitions are filed.

Thus, diversion can occur with or without referral to other agencies, although referral to social service agencies is not really true diversion. True diversion results in no further involvement with official agencies, whereas referral ensures future involvement with at least one community agency. Diversion accompanied by referral to another agency is a relatively new form of handling juvenile offenders, but diversion unaccompanied by referral has been a frequent practice throughout this century.

Types of Diversionary Programs

Many different types of diversionary programs have been devised. These include agencies offering family and individual counseling, programs specializing in crisis intervention, and agencies attempting to assess the offender's needs and provide answers for those needs. In San Francisco, for example, a diversion plan was begun for juvenile auto thieves. "Under the plan, the youth and his parents signed a contract enrolling the offender for six months in a community counseling program sponsored by [such] agencies as the YMCA" ("Children and the Law," 1975: 72). In other communities police have initiated informational programs in the schools and summer camps for predelinquent youth, juveniles who have begun to exhibit troublesome behavior in the home, school, or community, but have not yet had contact with official agencies.

Other programs have been instigated by juvenile courts and probation departments. The 601 Project of the Probation Department in Sacramento, California, was designed to provide short-term family counseling for status offenders, truants, runaways, and incorrigible youth (Bartollas and Miller, 1978; Feeney, 1977). The Vera project, located in New York City in the Bronx, accepted referrals of delinquent youth between the ages of 12 and 15 from court workers and judges. A youth diverted to the project was given an advocate, "generally a person less than thirty years old who lives in the youth's neighborhood . . . [and] counsels him and directs him to outside aids such as temporary home, school, or part-time work" (Nejelski, 1976: 401). The project also employed a "forum," a panel of community volunteer judges who addressed "the problems arising from minor offenses committed by neighborhood juveniles" and helped "resolve problems between parents and children" (p. 401).

More innovative diversionary programs involve attempts to shock delinquents into law-abiding behavior through visits to prisons and confrontations with prisoners serving life sentences. The lifers aim at "scaring" the juvenile "straight." One of these "scared straight" programs, conducted at Rahway Prison in New Jersey, was highly praised. However, there is evidence the shock experience does not reduce delinquency (Buckner and Chesney-Lind, 1983; Lewis, 1983; Finckenauer, 1979).

One diversionary agency that the President's Commission on Law Enforcement and the Administration of Justice considered most promising was the **youth service bureau**. According to Bartollas and Miller (1978), "the first youth service bureaus were established in Chicago and in Pontiac, Michigan, in 1958. Several agencies came in 1967 when the President's Commission . . . recommended [their] establishment" (pp. 180–181). Youth service bureaus were charged with "a broad range of services and certain mandatory functions" (President's Commission, 1967a: 83). In the words of the commission report (1967a), youth service bureaus were to act as "central coordinators of all community services for young people . . . [and] also provide services lacking in the community or neighborhood" (p. 83). Youth service bureaus, receiving referrals from police, courts, schools, and other sources, were supposed to function primarily through "individually tailored work with trouble-making youths" (p. 83).

The commission (1967a) recommended that at least half the cases handled by the juvenile court be referred to youth service bureaus. State, federal, and local agencies accepted this reasoning, and the number of YSBs burgeoned from 6 in 1967 to 150 in 1971 (Howlett, 1973). Several hundred such bureaus were estimated to be in operation by the mid-1970s. The federal agency involved in the funding and promotion of YSBs was the Law Enforcement Assistance Administration, no longer in existence. According to a 1975 LEAA report on YSBs, most were located in communities with a population of under 10,000; in such communities, they served fewer than 500 youths a year. About 14 percent of the youth bureaus served more than 1,000 youths a year. Most referrals came from the juvenile justice system; but schools, parents, and the young people themselves also were sources of referrals. There has been a decline in youth service bureaus in the late 1970s and early 1980s paralleling declines in federal funding.

Extent of Diversionary Programs

One goal of criminologists and juvenile justice personnel who recommend diversion from the juvenile justice system is to reduce the number of offenders involved with official agencies. There is no doubt that diversion has traditionally been used to achieve this aim. According to one researcher, "out of every 500 possible juvenile arrests, there are 200 police contacts, resulting in 100 arrests; of these, only 40 youths reach the intake stage, only 20 appear before a judge, and only 2 or 3 are sent to a correctional institution" (Nejelski, 1976:

394). Thus, more than half the juveniles who are candidates for court processing because they have committed a delinquent act are apprehended. Of those who experience police contact, only half are taken into custody, and of those taken into custody, only one-fifth have a court hearing. At each stage of juvenile justice processing, then, a large proportion of cases is diverted from the official system.

One research team graphically documented the diversionary processing using statistics collected in Pennsylvania in 1971. The team established that 90 percent of all Pennsylvania juveniles, or 1.4 million young people, had committed one or more delinquent acts, but only 92,000 young people were arrested by Pennsylvania police. According to the researchers, "most of [the delinquent acts were] never detected by anyone. . . . Many of their delinquent acts [were] noticed by parents, neighbors, shopkeepers, school teachers, child welfare workers, social workers, and others who decide[d] *not* to invoke the process of law. . . . *The process of diversion begins in the community, not in the patrol car*" (Katkin, Hyman, and Kramer, 1976: 134). Of the 92,000 juveniles arrested, 52 percent (47,000) were released, meaning that "police divert known juvenile offenders as frequently as they detain them" (p. 135). Of the 45,000 young people referred to the juvenile court, only 15,000 were adjudicated delinquent or neglected, and only 3,750 were institutionalized. The researchers concluded that "at all stages, more youngsters are diverted out of the system than are sent on for further processing" (p. 36).

There is little information on the numbers of juvenile offenders throughout the United States who are referred to diversionary programs. According to the well-known delinquency researcher LaMar Empey (1978), the movement of the past two decades to establish diversionary programs "has not resulted in leaving kids alone, as labeling theorists have recommended. Rather, hundreds, if not thousands, of new programs have been set up to give juveniles even more, rather than less, 'service' " (p. 539). Empey cited a California study of police diversion programs indicating that there are 150 to 200 of these programs in California alone. The California study, conducted by Klein and Teilmann, reported that most of the referrals to the diversionary programs would have been released, not petitioned into juvenile court, if there had been no diversionary program. Klein and Teilmann (1976) argued that " 'true' diversion—turning offenders away from the system who would otherwise be inserted into it—has been displaced by the provision of referral and treatment for offenders who otherwise would have been simply released" (p. 11).

Reasons for Diversionary Programs

Those in favor of diversionary programs have relied on three closely connected assumptions as evidence for their propositions. First, they are dissatisfied with the juvenile court and feel that referral to diversionary programs is a significant improvement over juvenile court adjudication. Second, they feel that diversionary programs are more successful in handling and reducing the number of offenders involved with criminal justice agencies at any one point in time. Third, they feel that diversionary programs prevent future involvement in delinquency. We will consider each of these assumptions more closely.

Dissatisfaction with the Juvenile Court.   The beginnings of the diversionary concept can be traced to mounting dissatisfaction with the juvenile court in the treatment and prevention of delinquency. Just as the juvenile court was designed to resolve the inequities of trying and incarcerating juveniles as adults, diversionary programs were designed to solve the evils of juvenile court adjudication. The criticism of juvenile courts focuses on several aspects of court operation, including the effects of incarceration and the effects of labeling on offenders.

Incarceration, one of the dispositional alternatives used by the court in controlling delinquency, has been sharply criticized by correctional specialists. As a result, an aversion to the use of prisons and correctional institutions has developed among correctional specialists (Duffee and Fitch, 1976). The trend toward community treatment

has never been stronger than at the present time; and at the juvenile justice level, the rise in diversionary programs has paralleled this trend. Diversionary programs avoid incarceration at early stages of juvenile justice contact and attempt to prevent eventual incarceration for repeat or serious offenses by working with the youth in a community setting. Since the diversionary programs are not connected with incarceration, these programs are thought to provide a more humane alternative to juvenile court adjudication.

Juvenile courts have also been criticized for the negative effects of the labeling process. Delinquency prevention and diversionary efforts, on the other hand, have received much of their theoretical backing from the precepts of labeling theory. Broadly, it has been argued that being officially labeled as deviant, more specifically delinquent, results in increased likelihood of recurring deviance. Following this reasoning, contact with the juvenile court and the concomitant formal labeling increase, rather than reduce, subsequent delinquency. Diversion away from court processing has been thought to avoid the "potentially stigmatizing consequences of formal processing" as well as the inequities of incarceration (Lundman, 1976: 430; see also Bullington, Sprowls, Katkin, and Phillips, 1978; Nejelski, 1976). Thus, diversionary programs have been reported to offer an alternative to the delinquency-producing actions of juvenile courts and institutions.

Management of Delinquency.   The assumption that diversionary programs are more successful than the juvenile court in handling delinquency is based on the view that these programs can help manage delinquency and delinquents in a particular community. Sociologist Kai Erikson (1966) discussed the management and amount of deviance existing in any community, writing that "it is simple logistic fact that the number of deviances which come to a community's attention are limited by the kinds of equipment it uses to detect and handle them, and to that extent the rate of deviation found in a community is at least in part a function of the size and complexity of its social control apparatus" (p. 24). In other words, the volume of deviance will match the community's ability to process deviance officially. Diversionary programs are viewed as means of aiding the courts and community in "managing" delinquency by reducing the numbers of children involved with agents of the justice system.

A study conducted by Esbensen (1984) reveals evidence of the reduction in juveniles officially processed by the juvenile justice system. Esbensen analyzed data from the National Evaluation of Diversion Programs (Dunford et al., 1981) for the years 1974 to 1979. Data allowed historical comparisons of the flow of youth through three different juvenile justice systems. In two of these systems, diversion programs succeeded in substantially reducing the number of youths penetrating (being processed through the system) and being maintained by the system. A third diversionary program decreased penetration rates in the system, but those youth who were processed were likely eventually to be formally processed. Esbensen attributes the latter to a change in personnel (an aggressive juvenile prosecutor) and organizational policy regarding the handling of juvenile offenders.

Another study of a diversionary project in a midwestern city by Bynum and Greene (1984) reported dramatic reduction in the use of adjudicative alternatives for first offenders, particularly status offenders and shoplifters. Only 24 percent of all first offenders were formally adjudicated during the first year of the project, compared to 43 percent before the project was implemented.

There is little doubt that true diversion, or outright release of the child by the police or court workers, does reduce the number of juveniles involved in the juvenile justice system. Therefore, true diversion is recognized as a widespread, useful practice. Since self-report studies demonstrate that 90 percent of youth have been involved in some form of delinquency and most of these juveniles are never picked up by police, true diversion is probably the most frequent means of handling delinquent acts. True diversion also occurs quite often after police-youth contact. About 50 percent of juveniles are released after the initial involvement with the police. In sum, correctional specialists view diversion as the only way to handle large numbers of juvenile arrests and to prevent

the courts from being clogged (Bullington et al., 1978; Nejelski, 1976).

Prevention of Future Delinquency. Another argument given in support of diversionary programs centers on the prevention of future delinquency among young people, particularly the poor, who have been apprehended for delinquent offenses. As some criminologists have argued:

> The recent increase in expanded systems of diversionary justice seems to be motivated by three beliefs: (1) diverted youngsters are less likely than institutionalized juveniles to persist in delinquent careers; (2) the benefits of current diversionary practices are disproportionately bestowed upon white or affluent youths, and (3) social services from community agencies are purchased by many of the offenders not diverted from the juvenile justice system. (Bullington et al., 1978: 64)

The rationale for public diversionary programs is, then, class-based. Publicly funded programs are supposed to offer services to poor youth. Thus, public agencies are designed to control the delinquency of the poorer classes. Studies of types of juveniles involved in delinquency prevention programs show a primarily lower class clientele. The hope is that diversion will retard delinquency among these youth. Supporters of diversionary programs point to official statistics which show that lower class youth are more involved in delinquency than are middle and upper class juveniles (Lerman, 1978). This differential involvement is in part attributed to the social and psychological services the parents of middle and upper class youth can afford to buy for their sons and daughters.

Criticisms of Diversionary Programs

Critics of diversionary programs have questioned the advisability of increasing referrals to there programs for several reasons.[1] They argue that these programs do not avoid the problems of the juvenile court. On the contrary, they may magnify court problems. Critics also assert that diversionary programs do not reduce the number of juveniles involved with official agencies. If the labeling perspective has any validity, these programs may actually increase delinquency rates. Only true diversion, which arbitrarily removes an apprehended child from any agency contact and thus from any recorded delinquency, can reduce the number of officially involved youngsters and avoid the adverse effects of negative labeling. Further, there is no evidence that these programs prevent delinquency in the target population of poor youth.

Advantages of Court Processing.   Although supporters of diversionary programs have confidently praised the ameliorative effects of diversionary programs (Binder and Geis, 1984), other criminologists and juvenile justice officials have questioned whether diversionary programs are substantially more effective and less stigmatizing than the juvenile court. First, there is evidence that incarceration, a disposition available after court processing, may be more effective in controlling delinquency. Some studies report a relationship, similar to those cited by behavioral theorists, between the *certainty* of punishment and reduced rates of offenses, suggesting that punishment should be swift and closely linked to the deviant behavior if it is to negate future recurrences of the crime. Thus, if certain punishment acts as a deterrent to delinquency, diversionary programs may actually increase delinquency, since no punishment is involved (Allen and Simonsen, 1978; Lundman, 1976).

Second, although diversion to community treatment is defined as an alternative superior to incarceration, treatment in the community raises an interesting question. As one criminologist (Greenberg, 1975) put it: "One might ask why, if the community is so therapeutic, the offender got into trouble in the first place" (pp. 4–5). Clearly, questions remain about whether, in terms of controlling the number of illegal acts or rehabilitating offenders, community treatment is a more effective disposition than incarceration.

Third, although diversionary programs are based on the assumption that diversion avoids the in-

herent labeling of formal processing, there is no reason to believe that the effects of labeling are limited to juveniles appearing before the juvenile court. Lundman (1976) pointed to evidence that diversion does not reduce labeling effects and that labeling does not explain delinquent careers. If participation in programs identifies youths as being involved with an agency, children referred to the diversionary programs may become publicly known as predelinquent or delinquent. Any detrimental effect from labeling would likely apply to juveniles referred to what have been called "delinquency agencies," regardless of the nature of the particular agency. "There is no reason to believe that the labels imposed by Youth Service Bureaus and other instruments of diversion will be nonstigmatizing" (Bullington et al., 1978: 66).

Fourth, the juvenile court appears to have an advantage over diversionary programs in one major regard. A common practice in diversion programs is the transferring of children from "police to treatment, without benefit of judicial processing" (Nejelski, 1976: 405). In police-juvenile contacts, the juvenile is often assumed guilty and then arrested, released, or referred to another agency. Police use their own discretion in assigning dispositions. Often, these decisions are based on extralegal factors (Nejelski, 1976; Piliavin and Briar, 1964).

Although some degree of due process of law has been required in juvenile court proceedings since the 1967 Gault decision and other U.S. Supreme Court rulings, police referral to diversionary programs occurs before proceedings and without legal protection. Referral to diversionary programs may intervene in the lives of children and their families without due process and force treatment on unwilling juveniles. Most important, the child's guilt or innocence is never determined (Bullington et al., 1978; Nejelski, 1976).

In fairness to the drafters of the 1967 President's Commission report, it should be mentioned that this drawback of diversionary programs was recognized as the report was written. To avoid the appearance of coercion, many diversionary programs were designed to treat only volunteers. In reality, "voluntary" participation is often the result of a choice by the juvenile of the least evil alternative. A juvenile who is allowed to volunteer for a diversionary program in order to avoid court processing is not really volunteering. The informal dispositions of police often involve "subtle forms of coercion that generally influence a child to agree with any suggested discretionary technique" (Marion, 1976: 464).

The problem of due process in discretionary handling of juvenile cases implies that juvenile court processing, since recent due process reforms, is superior in certain aspects to diversionary treatment programs. Nejelski (1976) has pointed out that the juvenile court at least provides "a measure of accountability and formality to decision making," noting as well that "in the juvenile system, machinery does not exist for the review of administrative decisions about stationhouse release or dismissal at probation intake" (p. 405). Howlett (1973), describing the due process problem in wider terms, argued that community intervention in the lives of children "should relate directly to the child's rights as well as to his needs" (p. 486).

Thus, although the juvenile court and diversionary programs may produce problems similar to those associated with labeling, diversionary programs are criticized for additional reasons. These programs rely on a referral system that clearly violates children's rights to due process. They also bring criticism from advocates of certain punishment, who believe that diversion removes punishment and thus removes deterrents to crime. Individuals questioning the effectiveness of community treatment also criticize diversionary programs.

Widening the Nets.   The crux of the rationale for diversionary programs is the removal of young people from the justice system—yet diversionary programs may produce the opposite result. These programs may also encourage the involvement of a larger number of juveniles with official agencies (Austin and Krisberg, 1981; Blomberg, 1980). Rather than removing young people from the justice system, diversionary programs may actually widen the net. "In fact, no one is diverted. The subjects of diversion would never have been adjudicated under the previous system—their cases would have been dismissed" (Nejelski, 1976: 397).

The result is a decrease in the number of juveniles directly released to their families.

Most basically, diversionary programs may become just another way of sanctioning children for their involvement in behaviors that offend the community's morality, but not its law. As one critic has argued:

> Diversion does not respond to the denial of basic rights of individuals—the right to associate with those of their choice and to engage voluntarily in acts that harm no one but themselves. The misbehaving child likewise has a fundamental right to be a child, and if he [or she] has committed no act that would be considered criminal if he [or she] were an adult, why seek recourse through the courts and why create another agency to divert [such a child] from the courts? (Howlett, 1973: 489)

Besides questioning whether or not diversionary programs reduce the number of officially involved offenders, critics also draw attention to the measures of delinquency employed when correctional specialists assert they are managing delinquency. Diversionary programs commonly aim at the reduction of recidivism, as measured by police and court contact. Most programs equate the reduction of official delinquency with reduction in actual delinquency. But only self-report studies can evaluate actual reduction in delinquency, and self-report studies of the effectiveness of diversionary programs are noticeably lacking. Rather, diversionary practitioners simply evaluate official delinquency.

That being so, this oversight on the part of diversionary program evaluators illuminates one of Kai Erikson's (1966) basic points: "When the community tries to assess the size of its deviant population, then it is usually measuring the capacity of its own social control apparatus and not the inclinations toward deviance found among its members" (p. 25). It appears that the community is interested in isolating and treating certain individuals, rather than reducing delinquency among the adolescent population in general.

Since diversionary programs entangle more individuals in public agencies without attacking actual delinquency, the assumption that diversionary programs are useful tools in reducing delinquency and the number of individuals involved with official agencies is open to question. One major effect of diversionary programs is the extension of the parameters of the social control apparatus referred to by Erikson, a result rather different from a reduction in the volume of delinquency.

Failure to Prevent Delinquency.   One goal of diversionary programs is to prevent future involvement among young people, especially poor young people. It is difficult to assess how well diversionary programs achieve this goal, because diversionary efforts are not frequently evaluated.[2] Even when conducted, most evaluations suffer from serious "political, theoretical, and methodological" problems (Wright and Dixon, 1977: 35). Such evaluations are criticized for "(1) the utilization of pre-experimental research designs, (2) subjective assessment techniques and (3) the absence of measurement" (Lundman, McFarlane, and Scarpitti, 1976: 304; Frazier, 1983). These problems render most evaluation efforts unreliable.

Success in reducing recidivism is not often reported when studies employ minimally adequate evaluation techniques. Lundman (1976) examined the results of labeling research and presented evidence that diversionary treatment programs fail to reduce recidivism. He concluded that "in addition to not reducing recidivism, diversion units also possibly magnify existing problems" (p. 437). Similarly, a survey of twenty-five articles on delinquency treatment programs found that even though many subjective studies report positive results, objective evaluations indicate "little or no success in preventing delinquency" (Lundman, McFarlane, and Scarpitti, 1976: 305). Wright and Dixon (1977) analyzed ninety-six studies and concluded: "Even when adequate evaluation is performed, few studies show significant results" (pp. 54–55). Other research has revealed the same negative findings (Beng and Shichor, 1979).

Given the state of current knowledge, it is not surprising to find that diversionary programs are unsuccessful in changing behavior, including delinquent behavior. There is no scientific basis for the belief that attitudes or behaviors can be changed. Further, "we do not now understand what causes delinquency. Existing theories of delinquency are, at best, imprecise and, at worst, contradictory" (Lundman, McFarlane, and Scarpitti, 1976: 307–308).

Diversionary programs are clearly not the panacea for the ill-defined problem of delinquency. These programs share dilemmas with older dispositional alternatives available to police and juvenile court workers. It has become evident that diversionary programs, like institutional commitment and other means of treating juvenile offenders, can be ineffective and unfair. There has been some suggestion on the part of criminologists that the theory behind diversionary programs is indeed valid, but that such theory can rarely be put into practice (Osgood and Weichselbaum, 1984). Also, there is such variability among diversion programs with respect to service delivery that it is difficult to make generalizations about the success or failure of programs (Whitaker and Severy, 1984).

COMMUNITY-BASED CORRECTIONAL PROGRAMS

Community-based correctional programs are another type of alternative disposition for juvenile offenders, a type of disposition that has been increasingly employed by police and juvenile court workers since the 1960s. The term **community corrections** is vaguely and inconsistently used, but in general community corrections are "any activity in the community directly addressed to the offender and aimed at helping him to become a law-abiding citizen" (Boesen and Grupp, 1976: 9). The President's Commission on Law Enforcement and the Administration of Justice (1967a) recommended that "[c]orrectional authorities should develop more extensive community programs providing special . . . treatment as an alternative to institutionalization for both juvenile and adult offenders" (p. 171).

According to the National Advisory Commission on Criminal Justice Standards and Goals (1974), "[I]t . . . seems clear that many persons can serve their sentences in the community without undue danger to the public" (p. 113). It is argued by the commission and other supporters of decarceration that many juveniles are inappropriately sent to institutions in the first place, with many of that group detained for excessive time periods (Lerman, 1975). Reflecting these concerns, the trend has been toward shorter periods of institutionalization and decreased assignment of juveniles to reformatories. Although the use of institutionalization as a dispositional alternative is declining, commitment to traditional types of juvenile correctional facilities is still widespread.

Another trend, the deinstitutionalization of status offenders, is also based on the growing belief that institutions are botched experiments (see Kobrin and Klein, 1983). When committed to reform schools, status offenders have been particularly singled out for harsh treatment, including longer periods of institutionalization. Increasingly, judges have been barred from sending noncriminal juveniles to training schools. Whether or not alternatives to institutionalization in large residential centers are more effective and fair than the traditionally ineffective training schools remains an open issue. Perhaps commitment of status offenders to *any* kind of program is just another way to sanction behavior that would not be prohibited for adults (Alper, 1973; Lerman, 1975).

Some correctional specialists who follow the community treatment model have advocated, and in certain areas accomplished, decentralization of large institutions. Hahn (1978), for example, argued: "we must decentralize the large mass-custody type institution. We must bring it from its remote and unrelated location to as close to the offenders' community as possible. Its programs must contain as many ingredients closely resembling normal life situations as can possibly be arranged" (p. 359). There is some indication that Hahn's suggestions have been implemented. According to data collected by Vinter, Downs, and Hall (1976), the number of state-related, community-based residential programs, as well as the population of offenders assigned to such programs, has increased, though large numbers of juvenile offenders are held in the traditional large, remote training school facilities.

The Massachusetts Experience

The reforms of deinstitutionalization, decarceration, decentralization, and community programs have not gone far enough for some sociologists and criminologists. There are suggestions, indeed demands, that institutions, having outlived their usefulness, should be put to rest. Chief among spokespersons for closing correctional institutions has been Jerome Miller, the man who orchestrated the 1972 shutdown of Massachusetts training schools and later directed changes in the Illinois and Pennsylvania juvenile correctional systems. Before ordering the closing of the Massachusetts facilities, Miller attempted "to create a humanized and therapeutic climate within the existing institutions" (Coates, Miller, and Ohlin, 1978: xvi). His efforts were hindered by the bureaucracy of the correctional system and by finances, and Miller soon decided that more radical changes were necessary. He resolved to remove juveniles from training schools and to place them in alternate facilities.

The Closing of Juvenile Institutions. Miller's ideas about closing institutions were not actually new. During the 1950s and 1960s, several short-term residential projects, including Highfields, Essexfield, and Pinehills, were reported as initially successful in the rehabilitation of offenders. The changes in Massachusetts were, however, unusually rapid and drastic. Miller closed one traditional institution in 1971; in January 1972, with the state legislature in recess, he shut down two more. The previously incarcerated offenders, transported in a caravan of cars, were spirited from the confinement of the two institutions to Amherst to live for a month with the students of the University of Massachusetts School of Education. The stay in the Amherst area allowed time for the placement of youngsters who could not be immediately released. Miller then closed two detention centers, and with that, the juvenile institution era in Massachusetts juvenile justice ended (Coates, Miller, and Ohlin, 1978; Scull, 1977).

The end of one epoch in Massachusetts' juvenile justice system signified the beginning of another.

We have described how juveniles were removed from training schools and transported to alternate placements. The idea seemed clear enough, but there was at least one basic problem with the implementation of the decision: what to do with offenders who could not be immediately paroled. According to Coates, Miller, and Ohlin: "Detention and reception centers were used, and Oakdale, which had been closed for young boys in 1971, was made into a reception center to provide more options. Only a few group homes were available. . . . No mechanism had been set up for processing youths into new facilities" (p. 26).

The situation was "chaotic at best. Adequate placements in sufficient numbers did not exist" (p. 26). Another criminologist, Andrew Scull, commented:

> Only *after* taking this action did the department begin the task of creating community-based alternatives. Almost proudly, the current Assistant Commissioner concedes that this was standard operating procedure. As he puts it, "destroying a system *before* creating alternatives to it was a characteristic mode of action for the department." (1977: 53)

Coates, Miller, and Ohlin's account of the transitional period documents the problems encountered when the need for alternatives to institutions suddenly burgeoned: "Youths had been dispersed widely across the state without a uniform day-to-day tracking system that permitted administrative staff to know where many youths were" (1978: 28). Part of the confusion was created by the vast increase in the use of purchased services to place and treat juveniles. The researchers observed: "The extensive use of purchase-of-services arrangements placed a great burden on a state bureaucracy not equipped to establish rates of payment and quickly process the payments to private vendors" (p. 28). Also lacking were methods of monitoring juveniles placed in private facilities. By mid-1973, however, placements were no longer so unpredictable, and bureaucratic procedures became more routine.

However, personnel changes in 1973 and 1974 wreaked more havoc on a system that had just recently reestablished equilibrium. Miller accepted a job in Illinois, an act leading to an exodus. His assistant, John Leavy, was appointed as Miller's replacement, but for more than a year Leavy's appointment was not confirmed. Leavy was dedicated to the community corrections philosophy, and he attempted to carry on Miller's reform; but heavy criticism about his organization, or lack of organization, of the department led to his resignation in 1975. In 1976 John Calhoun, an outsider to the Massachusetts system, took over. *Corrections Magazine* quoted Calhoun as saying at the time of his inauguration that "there were about 40 bills in the legislature calling for the abolition of DYS [Massachusetts Department of Youth Services]" (R. Wilson, 1978b: 13).

Discontent with DYS centered on the lack of secure facilities. The number of runaways from community programs was high, and the "get toughers" were demanding more control of offenders and protection of law-abiding citizens. Judges began to transfer more youths to adult courts to ensure that they were not committed to the DYS. Calhoun established a twenty-one-member task force to answer those persons and groups fearing a crime wave attributable to the so-called molly-coddling of delinquents.

The task force studied the cases of offenders who were considered prime candidates for institutionalization and reached the following conclusion: "The vast majority of DYS youth can be effectively and appropriately placed in the broad and diverse range of non-secure community-based settings and alternatives without detriment to public protection" (R. Wilson, 1978b: 13). The task force recommended that only 11.2 percent of the cases studied be remanded to secure placements. In the late 1970s the clamor for the demise of the Massachusetts DYS subsided; more juveniles were by then institutionalized than were institutionalized when Calhoun took over as commissioner. The chief difference was that far fewer were committed to secure facilities in the late 1970s than was the case ten years earlier.

The Aftermath of the Closings. By 1978, most Massachusetts juveniles were sent to community-based programs. However, many of these programs were "as isolated as the old training schools" (R. Wilson, 1978b: 14). Calhoun, realizing that just because a program was nonsecure did not mean that it was linked to the wider community, encouraged what he called "meaningful ties" between young offenders and the community. He persuaded "program staff members to involve young offenders with the local youth groups, schools, recreation programs and in community activities in their neighborhoods" (R. Wilson, 1978b: 14). Recidivism studies conducted within the Massachusetts system in the late 1970s have shown that programs isolating offenders from the community, such as therapeutic group homes, have been less successful than programs prodding the offender to adjust within the community, as must be done in home care and foster care systems.

Even when treatment facilities are nonsecure and integrated into the community, there may be problems in implementing programs. Citizens in many communities find it a threatening idea to have offenders actually living next door or down the block. Impassioned battles have been fought by communities that want to protect themselves against the scourge of having offenders in the particular communities. The resistance of respectable middle and upper class neighborhoods to the presence of community correctional facilities has, according to Scull (1977), produced a "concentration of community programs" in lower class neighborhoods where community organization and power are lacking.

Types of Community-Based Programs

There are a number of different kinds of community-based programs. Among these are probation, community service/restitution, nonresidential treatment, group homes, and foster homes.

Probation.   Probation was one of the forerunners of the development of a totally distinct juvenile justice system. In the early days of the juvenile justice system, as now, probation provided an especially appropriate alternative for nondangerous

offenders who could safely remain at home while under court supervision. A probation officer, acting as a representative of the court, is assigned a child's case and is involved with the child and the family from intake of the case to adjudication and disposition. Typically, the probation officer meets at regular intervals with the child and the parents. Traitel (1974), writing about the functions of the probation officer, concluded that he or she "serves two primary and often difficult . . . roles: legal officer of the court and counselor (helper) to the youngster and family" (p. 22). These are ambiguous and sometimes conflicting roles. The problems produced by role ambiguity include mixed goals. They are compounded by the unusually heavy caseloads of probation officers and the maze of paperwork associated with the job.

Most offenders and probation officers meet in traditional probation agencies where visits are cursory and infrequent. Several new programs, called *intensive* or *individualized probation*, however, have attempted to lower caseloads and increase supervising time. Intensive probation programs generally reduce the number of cases per probation officer and increase the frequency and intensity of visits to chronic, home-based offenders.

The use of *volunteers in probation* is another innovation. According to Traitel, these volunteers "are a force of probation [personnel] that supplements the paid professional staff, enabling more intensive intervention with increasing numbers of youngsters" (p. 23). *Group probation* is a third innovation. Here, groups of probationers attend scheduled group meetings led by the probation officer.

Innovations have also been used in providing incentives to persuade communities to place young people in county-run probation programs rather than state-run institutions. The California Probation Subsidy Program monetarily rewarded communities that increased the use of probation and decreased referrals to institutions. "According to the California legislation of 1965, funds could be authorized for distribution to a county, from general state revenues, on the condition that a county reduce its actual first commitments to state correctional facilities below its expected rate of commitments" (Lerman, 1975: 13). To qualify for funds, communities also had to set up probationary units that offered intensive supervision.

After studying the effects of the California program, Lerman concluded that fewer offenders were committed to spend more time in institutions at a state level and more offenders were sent to local detection facilities for shorter institutional stays. But the overall effect of the California program appeared to be an increase, rather than a decrease, in a juvenile's chances of being locked up. Thus, a probation subsidy plan may not achieve its intended purpose of reducing institutionalization of juveniles. There is evidence, however, that juveniles who were placed on probation instead of in institutions presented no great danger to public safety.

Community Service/Restitution. The idea that the offender should pay the community back through services rendered or pay the specific victim of his or her crime for damages (restitution) is a popular practice in community corrections. Since offender restitution often involves the payment of a specific sum of money to a crime victim, this practice is used less frequently with juvenile offenders, the presumption being that the juvenile lacks financial resources to make payments. However, the use of community service restitution—the payment of damages via unpaid work in the community—is frequently used with juvenile offenders. The underlying philosophy of community service restitution is popular with the public because it appears to offer a realistic punishment which helps the juvenile see in a direct way the extent of the cost he or she has incurred by the commission of the deviant act. To juvenile justice practitioners, community service, at least theoretically, offers a viable alternative to more traditional and less meaningful correctional options. Some critics of community service restitution argue that despite the humanitarian rhetoric about the practice, in reality juvenile court judges often use the alternative as a further sanction to probation.

Although juvenile community service programs were hard hit with the demise of LEAA (between 1978 and 1981, the LEAA gave some $30 million to set up programs in 85 counties and states),

variations of the program can still be found in most states (Krajick, 1982). Bartollas (1985) describes the operation of a community restitution program for youthful offenders in Hennepin County (Minnesota): First-time property offenders are assigned to Saturday work squads for a period of forty hours. Supervised by staff from the probation department, groups of youth engage in a variety of pursuits: janitorial work, cleaning bus stops, planting trees, working in city parks, and the like.

The effectiveness of community restitution programs in terms of preventing future youth crime remains open. Despite the appeal of such programs, relatively little evaluation has been undertaken. We should note, however, that since the mid-1960s, the Office of Juvenile Justice and Delinquency Prevention has been offering training seminars around the country through its RESTTA program (Restitution, Education, Specialized Training and Technical Assistance). These seminars provide local agencies expert advice on the use of restitution as an alternative to harsher sanctions. The effectiveness of these programs should be forthcoming in the immediate future (see Regnery, 1986).

Nonresidential Treatment. Nonresidential treatment programs are based on the premise that some juveniles need more control than is given by probationary supervision, but less than is found in residential programs. In these programs the juvenile participates in counseling, vocational, and academic sessions during the day and returns to community or family at night. Nonresidential programs allow substantial amounts of time to work with offenders, but avoid the costs of institutionalization and the isolation from the community of residential programs. In 1961 California led the way in the founding of day treatment plans, beginning a nonresidential community treatment program.

Empey reported that the experimental study conducted by the California Youth Authority showed a decrease in recidivism among boys who remained in the community. These findings are not definitive, however, because it appears that staff reacted more favorably to home-based boys than they did to the institutionalized boys and boys released from institutions but still under the supervision of correctional authorities. According to Empey (1973), correctional agents supervising nonresidential boys may have been less likely to revoke parole than the parole officers of institutionalized boys.

Another well-known project that utilized the day treatment approach was the Provo experiment, which was conducted in Utah over a ten-year period. It had two basic aims: the execution of a community-based delinquency treatment program, and research about the relative effectiveness of the program. The boys sent to Pinehills, the program center, by a juvenile court judge were "repeat rather than first-time offenders, ages 14 to 18 years. In fact, many were candidates for a reformatory" (Empey and Erickson, 1972: 7). Rather than living at Pinehills, the boys returned home in the evening after school or work and an afternoon group meeting. Originally, it was intended to contrast boys sent to Pinehills by a juvenile court judge with boys put on probation or institutionalized by the same judge. However, the judge sent so few youths to the reformatory that it became necessary to substitute a comparison with the entire population of the reform school for the planned comparison with juveniles placed in reformatories by one judge.

While at Pinehills during the day, the boys received intensive treatment based on the theory that delinquency is a group phenomenon. According to the designers of the program, LaMar Empey and Maynard Erickson (1972), the Provo program used the delinquent peer group to treat juvenile offenders.

> A treatment system will be most effective if the delinquent peer group is used as a means of perpetuating the norms and imposing the sanctions of the system. The peer group should be seen by delinquents as the primary source of help and support. The traditional psychotherapeutic emphasis on transference relationships is not considered the most vital factor in effecting change.

Empey and Erickson also cited three goals of these peer interaction programs:

(1) to make conventional and delinquent alternatives clear; (2) to lead delinquents to question the ultimate utility of delinquent alternatives; and (3) to help conventional alternatives assume some positive value for them. (p. 5)

Boys were strictly disciplined for rule infractions, such as failure to report on time to the program center each day. If a boy broke certain rules, the consequence was immediate transfer to the state reformatory.

How well did this particular community-based program do in preventing recidivism? To determine the effectiveness of community treatment, Empey and Erickson (1972) selected 71 boys slated for probation but sent to Pinehills, 79 boys assigned to probation, 44 boys slated for the reformatory but sent to Pinehills, and 132 boys actually confined in the reformatory. Four years later, a follow-up study was conducted on each group. Apparently, Pinehills treatment did not reduce the recidivism rates of boys thought suitable for probation. However, Pinehills boys who would have been institutionalized did somewhat better than boys actually institutionalized. Empey and Erickson stated that:

> The data indicate clearly that incarceration was not successful for a significant minority of the boys who received that kind of treatment. The extent and seriousness of their delinquent acts strongly suggest the need for other alternatives. Not only had their lives been disrupted, perhaps spoiled for as long as they live, by repeated crimes and confinements, but they were an obvious danger to society. (p. 197)

Even though the community-based home-care treatment at Pinehills did not reduce recidivism more than the other community-based program, probation, it was more successful apparently than incarceration. Significantly, the Provo project team reported that "at least while delinquents were a part of the experimental organization their delinquent acts were curtailed" (p. 257). Pinehills provided community protection during the intervention phase that was almost as completely effective as incarceration, indicating that some community programs may have results superior to those of institutionalization.

Group Homes.   There are, however, some juveniles who are regarded as needing more supervision and control than can be provided in nonresidential treatment. Other youth may have difficulties that stem from the home situation itself. Thus, a home-based placement might aggravate delinquent and troublesome behavior. In these cases, the child might be sent to a group home, a small, publicly funded residential treatment center.

Group homes are employed to give structure to and control over the child's life while allowing access to community resources and attempting to reduce or prevent delinquency involvement (see Murray and Cox, 1979). They are generally run by a married couple or other houseparents, some with professional training, and are often located in a residential area. Some four to twelve young people may be cared for at one time. The care is generally short-term.

Group care is also found in halfway houses. These are larger facilities, housing perhaps twenty to fifty young people, often operated by the juvenile court to give supervision similar to that of an institution, while maintaining offenders' ties to the community. Juvenile offenders may be sent to halfway houses after a period of time in a correctional institution to allow them to readjust to life in the community while close supervision over their activities continues.

The treatment methods employed in group homes are diverse and oriented toward a specific type of troublesome youth. Group counseling and interaction techniques, especially Guided Group Interaction (GGI), are popular treatment plans. Groups are composed of residents who are "expected to support, confront, and be honest with one another to the end that they may be helped with their own problems" (Bartollas and Miller, 1978: 159). Emphasis is also placed on educational programs in most group homes and on vocational and employment assistance in some.

One of the first small group facilities was the Highfields project, established in New Jersey in 1950. The small residential facility of twenty boys, ages 16 and 17, was directed by Lloyd McCorkle and opened on the old Anne Morrow–Charles Lindbergh estate in rural New Jersey. A small staff supervised the youth. Strict routines were at a minimum, and no guards were employed. Residents, most of whom were on juvenile probation, worked at a nearby mental hospital during the day and attended GGI sessions in the evening. At first glance, the effectiveness of the Highfields program appeared promising. When Highfields "graduates" were compared to a group of boys who had been incarcerated in the New Jersey State Reformatory at Annadale, the Highfields program seemed more successful. Of the training school inmates, 33 percent were apprehended for delinquency during the first year after release. Of the Highfields youth, only 18 percent were apprehended in the first year after release.

Some criminologists, however, questioned the comparability of the Highfields and training school groups. Highfields youth were slightly younger, somewhat less delinquent, and from higher social classes than were the reformatory boys. However, even though the recidivism rates of youth committed to state reformatories and to the Highfields program may have been similar, the Highfields curriculum accomplished the same results in a shorter period of time, at less expense to the state, and at much less personal cost to the youth. As a result, other residential centers of the Highfields type have been created in New Jersey.

The Silverlake experiment in Los Angeles was another ambitious group home program. Up to twenty youths at a time were assigned to a large house in a middle class neighborhood. Residents lived in the house during the week and attended school and then returned to their families on weekends. Daily group sessions allowed youth to share in decision-making about residential conditions (Bartollas and Miller, 1978).

Sociologists LaMar Empey and Steven Lubeck (1971b) compared the recidivism rates of youth involved in the Silverlake group home with those of randomly selected nonprogram youth who were assigned to a "small custodial, educationally-oriented private institution" (Empey, 1973: 45). The

Silverlake group home appeared to offer no advantage over the other program. According to the findings of a first-year follow-up study, both types of programs had low recidivism rates. What the official figures did not show, however, said Empey (1973), was that "these residential but noncustodial programs had high runaway and failure rates. Approximately half the boys who started each program did not finish" (p. 45). Apparently, the tendency of boys to run away related to the residential nature of the treatment. In contrast to nonsecure residential homes, nonresidential programs have very low runaway rates. These comparisons influenced Empey's conclusion that non-residential programs may be superior to residential programs in certain respects.

High runaway rates may contribute to public opposition to group home programs. Citizens resist establishment of group homes in their own neighborhoods mainly because children housed in such programs are viewed as threats to the safety of persons and property. The degree of opposition from the community can influence the group home's chances of success or failure. According to Coates and Miller (1973), three basic strategies seem to alleviate community opposition: "(1) maintaining a low profile; (2) focusing communication at a significant few [community members]; and (3) focusing communication both at a significant few [community members] and at the local residents" (p. 76).

Foster Homes.   Although community opposition may be a major problem in the establishment of group homes, there is often less community resistance to another type of community-based residential care, *foster homes*. The use of foster homes to house chronic offenders who cannot remain with their own families has been growing in recent years. Foster homes have traditionally served as placements for dependent and neglected youth. The juvenile court has, during the past two decades, turned to foster homes as dispositional alternatives for delinquents. One criminologist who conducted extensive research on foster homes pointed out that "the last ten years have seen a

bold effort by some juvenile courts at recruitment and use of existing families in the community as foster families for adolescent delinquent youngsters" (Traitel, 1974: 30). Usually, juvenile offenders who are not considered dangerous and are thought capable of living with a family but whose "home circumstances preclude (at least for the foreseeable future) remaining with their own natural family" (p. 29) make appropriate candidates for foster care. Probationary supervision, counseling, and educational and vocational services are available to juveniles living in a foster home. Foster parents generally receive some sort of training prior to receiving custody of a juvenile offender.

Extent of Community-Based Programs

In Chapter 16 we discussed the two basic sources of information on the numbers of children involved in correctional programs in the United States. The first source is the *Children in Custody* series, published since 1971. The second source is the National Assessment of Juvenile Corrections (NAJC), conducted in 1974 by a research team at the University of Michigan with LEAA funds.

From 1971 to 1975, the *Children in Custody* series contained statistics on the number of community-based residential facilities—that is, the number of halfway houses and group homes. In 1971 there were only 78 of these facilities in the United States. They housed only 973 juvenile offenders. In the period between 1971 and 1975, commitments to public halfway houses and group homes increased 118 percent and the number of facilities increased 150 percent. The marked increase in community-based placements paralleled the decrease in commitments to training schools during these years. The *Children in Custody* census included privately operated group homes and halfway houses in 1974 to 1975 (from 805 to 851) and a very slight drop in the number of juveniles held in the facilities (from 9,919 to 9,706). Because private group homes were not included in the 1971, 1972, and 1973 censuses, it is impossible to determine whether the number of commitments to these facilities increased throughout the 1970s. A comparison of the number of juveniles held in public and private community-based programs in 1975, however, revealed that more than four times as many young people lived in private as in public group facilities.

The most recent *Children in Custody* census (U.S. Department of Justice, 1983, 1984) did not present data on the children held in halfway houses and group homes. Instead, a new classification was adopted. Correctional facilities were classified as *institutional*—detention centers, diagnostic centers, training schools, and a significant proportion of ranches, or *open*—shelters, group homes, and some ranches. According to the 1982 count, there were 402 public open facilities and 621 public institutional facilities. There were 1,690 private open facilities and 187 private institutional facilities. The new classification system made it impossible to compare these figures to earlier figures. It was, however, apparent that private residential facilities were far more likely to be community-based than were public facilities.

In the 1974 NAJC survey, Vinter and others provided data on involvement in community-based correctional programs and institutional facilities, stressing the differences in the number of commitments to the two types of programs. According to the Vinter survey's findings: "Only four states assigned at least as many youth to [community-based programs as to] institutional settings, thirty-six had less than 25% in community programs, and six did not provide such services" (Vinter, Downs, and Hall, 1976: 50). There were only 5,663 juveniles held in state-related community-based residential programs in 1974; 28,001 juvenile offenders were confined in institutions, ranches, and camps in 1974.

Reasons for Community-Based Programs

Several assumptions form the basis of the search for substitute methods of handling juvenile offenders and the placement of juveniles in community-based programs. First, institutions have been criticized for brutality, inhumane treatment, and for serving as the home of the dangers of the inmate subculture. The opinion of criminologists and sociologists often is that anything is better than confinement in an institution. Second, institutional treatment has been demonstrated to be ineffective in reducing recidivism. Third, the assumption that treatment in the community automatically brings beneficial results is held by many criminologists. Balch (1976) concluded:

> Criminologists argue that offenders should be kept close to their families and friends. They should be able to secure a job and develop some stake in conformity. It has become apparent to many that imprisonment only cuts a man [or woman] off from his [or her] community and makes his [or her] eventual reinstatement more difficult than ever. (p. 56)

Accepting these ideas, supporters of community corrections implicitly expect noninstitutional programs, such as probation, community service, nonresidential treatment, group homes, and foster homes, to produce reductions in rates of recidivism.

Fourth, criminologists have argued that the cost of community-based services is lower than the cost of institutional care. Vinter and his colleagues amply documented the potential cost benefits of small residential programs over traditional institutions. The mean cost of community-based programs was $5,501 per offender-year in 1974, whereas institutions averaged a cost of $11,657 per offender-year. However, some states spent substantially more on community programs. Coates, Miller, and Ohlin (1978), for example, reported an average daily cost of $29 for each confined offender and a daily cost of $30 for each juvenile involved in a community-based program in the mid-1970s. But the costs varied widely, depending on the nature of the program.

In general, "programs that are most community-based, such as foster care and nonresidential facilities, were the most economical to operate" (pp. 177–178). Although some community treatment plans may be more expensive than others, and some states may spend more on community programs, the basic feeling of criminologists was that community-based facilities were cheaper than institutional commitments. With institutional costs running around $21,926 per offender as of 1982, there is some merit to this argument. One criminologist has suggested that the emergence of the community corrections movement can be traced to the cost savings of community treatment:

> Once the drive for control of soaring costs is seen as the primary factor underlying the move towards decarceration, both these and a number of other aspects of this change which formerly appeared either fortuitous or inexplicable become readily comprehensible. For one thing, this perspective allows us to see the spread of the policy of deinstitutionalization to the criminal justice sector, and the rise of efforts to decarcerate criminals and delinquents, as part of a single, unitary phenomenon. . . . But by the late 1960s, as the pressure to alleviate the upward spiral in relief costs mounts; as the magnitude of the capital expenditure otherwise required for new prisons and reformatories becomes apparent; and as the size of the savings community approaches can produce on current outlays is documented; so there begins a rapid expansion of programs designed to divert the criminal and the delinquent away from the institution. (Scull, 1977: 140)

In other words, the rising costs of maintaining and constructing institutions have made community programs especially appealing to policy-makers. There is evidence, however, that these cost savings are more hypothetical than actual. Although some community plans cost less per offender than institutionalization, states adopting decarceration policies tend to continue to spend about the same amount on the juvenile correctional system. Asking why deinstitutionalized states fail to manifest greater savings, Vinter, Downs, and Hall concluded: "Deinstitutionalization as implemented in the states generally does not result in significant economies for a combination of reasons. Few deinstitutionalized states have decreased usage of institutions commensurate with [the] development of community programs . . ." (1976: p. 56). "[m]any states appear to be supplementing rather than supplanting institutional corrections for juveniles" (p. 59). Similarly, Lerman (1975) found that although the California Community Treatment Project was designed to

save money, "the program did not follow the design and proved to be much more costly" (p. 5). Apparently, reduced numbers of offenders were institutionalized for longer periods of time. Thus, the costs of community corrections may be higher than anticipated.

Criticisms of Community-Based Programs

Throughout our discussion of various types of community programs—probation, community service, nonresidential treatment, group homes, and foster homes—we have made observations about the relative success of these programs and about the impact of community plans on correctional systems and residential areas. Before summarizing the results of research on community programs, we must caution that a selection process is often involved in the assigning of dispositions. Certain types or categories of offenders are sent to certain forms of programs. Thus, the groups are often not strictly comparable because something about those selected for community treatment and those selected for other commitments could be affecting recidivism rates. In such cases, differences in the two groups would not be attributable to the treatment facilities.

Putting these reservations aside, we can conclude that although community programs in some cases have lower recidivism rates than institutions, the residential community programs also have high runaway and failure rates. The Provo experiment demonstrated, however, that nonresidential community facilities may provide nearly as much protection to the community as secure institutions. Since community treatment may produce fewer repeat offenders and may afford almost as much protection to the community during the intervention period, there is much to be said for noninstitutional programs.

Yet, as Lerman (1975) cautioned, the institution does not necessarily disappear simply because community-based treatment increases. Community correctional programs, as well as diversionary ones, may widen the nets. Juveniles are still committed to institutions. Although some of the juveniles assigned to community facilities have been candidates for institutions, a substantial portion of community corrections clientele would have been released without commitment in earlier days. Further, the cost benefits of community programming may be canceled by the costs involved in operating institutions for reduced numbers of offenders who stay longer than the inmates of earlier days.

Some criminologists have sought to evaluate the success of the Massachusetts experiment in juvenile corrections, the first large-scale transition to a community-based correctional system, in the reduction of delinquency and recidivism rates. In 1978 Coates, Miller, and Ohlin reported about the Massachusetts system that

> when looking at indicators of recidivism over time, representing the training-school system of the late [1960s] and the community-based system of the middle [1970s], we saw that the absolute rate had increased slightly. Numerous explanations are possible for this increase, reflecting changes in the DYS [Department of Youth Services] population over time, broader societal trends in youth crime, changing attitudes toward females, and changes in police and court resources. Nonetheless, it is clear that the reforms in DYS did not bring about a decrease in the recidivism rate, and it is equally clear that the reforms did not generate an explosive youth crime rate. (p. 172)

Even though Coates and his colleagues argued that other factors might account in part for the recidivism rates, they also acknowledged that Massachusetts probably did not go far enough toward establishing a community-based correctional system. Perhaps group homes that are removed from the juvenile's own community and family do not establish the offender's ties with the community any more than institutionalization does. Or it may be that we simply do not know enough about reducing recidivism to actually accomplish it.

Clearly, community corrections are not solutions to the problem of delinquency. The movement may have widened the nets of juvenile justice, just as diversionary efforts certainly did.

Considering the treatment orientation of most of these community programs, it would be surprising to find that the rights of offenders not to be treated are protected. Because community programs exist, juveniles in some locations may face greater chances of waiver of their cases to the criminal court or commitment to a private institution. Moreover, evidence does not support the theory that community corrections are substantially more effective in rehabilitating offenders in the long run.

However, even though all the claims of community corrections proponents cannot be substantiated, community care provides two unquestionable benefits. First, if used strictly, community systems can reduce the cost of corrections. Second, community-based programs are in many respects more humane than institutionalization and do not appear to endanger the public significantly more than do traditional programs. Thus, although there have been some public objections to the noninstitutional treatment of offenders, community corrections seem here to stay.[3]

SUMMARY

Criticism of the juvenile justice system by criminologists and juvenile justice personnel has proliferated in the past two decades. There have been two major responses to these criticisms, the development of diversionary programs to remove noncriminal and early offenders from the juvenile justice system, and the development of community-based correctional programs to place offenders in various types of treatment programs in their communities, rather than in traditional institutions.

Diversionary programs include police recreational and counseling programs, juvenile court counseling and advocacy programs, and youth service bureaus. There is evidence, however, that these attempts to divert youngsters from the juvenile justice system have resulted in a reduction in the number of young offenders who are truly diverted—that is, released by police and court personnel—and have not reduced the number of young people petitioned into juvenile court. It is also argued that diversion programs share, and possibly extend, the problems of court processing. Although supporters of diversionary programs contend that these programs are successful in reducing delinquency, research has not demonstrated that the programs do in fact reduce delinquency.

Types of community-based programs include probation, community service, nonresidential day treatment, and foster and group homes. The closing of institutions, decentralization of correctional systems, deinstitutionalization of status offenders, and establishment of community-based programs have all been advocated and, in some areas, accomplished reforms. Although the use of alternatives to institutions is urged by those who point to the failure of institutions, these noninstitutional programs are underdeveloped in most states. Many youths are still confined in large facilities. It is doubtful that community correctional programs are effective in rehabilitating offenders, but it appears that these programs can be less expensive than institutional programs (though that has not always been the case in practice) and that community programs do not threaten public safety.

PROGRESS CHECK

1. Diversion from formal juvenile justice system processing may occur at several points. Locate four such points. (p. 370)

2. Name and briefly describe three different types of diversionary programs. (pp. 370–371)

3. Utilizing the statistics provided by Nejelski and by Katkin, Hyman, and Kramer, describe the "flow and dropout" rates from arrest to correctional institution. (pp. 371–372)

4. The authors of this book hold that referral of juveniles to social service agencies instead of to the court is not really true diversion. (p. 375)
   a. True
   b. False

5. Employing a pro-con format, provide three arguments for and three against diversionary programs. (pp. 372–373)

6. List three reasons why most evaluations of diversionary programs are unreliable. (pp. 373–376)

7. Although the use of community residential programs has been increasing, most institutionalized juvenile offenders are still placed in traditional, large, remote training school facilities. (p. 377)
   a. True
   b. False

8. After reading about the Massachusetts experience with the closing of traditional juvenile correctional institutions, what conclusions would you reach? (pp. 377–379)

9. Compare, in approach and results, the California Probation Subsidy Program with the Provo experiment. (pp. 379–380)

10. Note the several assumptions which form the basis of handling juvenile offenders in community-based programs. (pp. 384–385)

NOTES

1. Binder and Geis (1984) have recently argued that most of the major criticisms of diversionary programs come from sociologists, as opposed to psychologists and others. They suggest that sociologists have been overly critical of such programs for three reasons. First, sociologists have generally been suspicious of the use of psychological treatments to effect behavioral changes. More radical sociologists eschew any piecemeal programs which fail to take larger social structural conditions into account and which place major emphasis on the individual. Second, sociologists have been deeply distrustful of the police. And third, sociologists have had strong sentimental identification with the underdog, "who tends to be seen as a

romantic force engaged in a liberating struggle with retrogressive establishment institutions" (p. 327).

2. Several researchers (Stanford, 1984; Blomberg, 1982; Chen and Rossi, 1980) advocate a multigoal evaluation strategy for diversion programs. Basically this approach is based on two assumptions: (1) Every program has some effects and (2) *a priori* knowledge and social science theory can adequately anticipate these effects and evaluation can therefore be designed to access these effects (Stanford, 1984: 60).

3. One area particularly neglected in discussions of community corrections involves a lack of knowledge about the most important ingredient for the success or failure of programs—the community. Differences in community structures have been shown to play a vital role in the effectiveness of delinquency prevention and control programs (Spergel, 1976). For example, programs which ignore the makeup of the community—its solidarity, its ethnicity, its kinship ties, its support structure—are destined for failure. In an effort to take these important factors into account, Warren (1978) isolated "six types of neighborhoods based on identity, internal organization and external linkages and suggest[ed] different change agent roles and activities for each" (Sundean, 1983: 16). He found, for instance, that in a western county, with a large minority population, the creation of a community deinstitutionalization program sponsored by the probation department nearly failed because probation department officials neglected to establish contacts with local agencies that controlled the community-based service centers. These agencies were staffed primarily with minority persons who saw the official probation agents as not being sensitive to the needs of the community service center clients (Sundean, 1983: 16).

Sundean (1983) offers a model format for analyzing significant community characteristics which are vital for the success or failure of various community correctional programs. Basically, his scheme examines several characteristics relevant to juvenile justice with respect to (1) socio-demographic variables, (2) crime patterns, (3) communal values and attitudes toward delinquency, (4) support of youth-serving agencies, and (5) relevant organizational environment.

PART 5

DELINQUENCY: INTERNATIONAL DIMENSIONS AND THE FUTURE

With the beginning of the 1980s, the juvenile justice system marked eighty years of defining and handling delinquency in the United States. During this period, delinquency has been attributed to various causes, and many solutions to the delinquency problem have been proposed, attempted, and in some cases, abandoned. Many sociologists and criminologists contend that little more is known about the causes of and solutions to delinquency now than was known in 1900. Few experts, however, are willing to give up the struggle to discover the reasons for delinquency and the key to preventing and controlling it.

Recently, American criminologists have become interested in youth crime and delinquency in other cultures. Reports from other nations, especially those experiencing rapid modernization and industrialization, indicate that various types of youth crime have been on the increase since the end of World War II. Despite numerous cultural differences between countries, there appears to be a high degree of similarity in causal explanations for youth problems, especially delinquency. Many of these explanations focus on changes taking place in basic socializing institutions such as the family and the school, and on the lack of opportunities for certain types of youth within a society. Chapter 18 discusses the comparative methods utilized in cross-cultural delin-

quency research. World crime and delinquency trends are reviewed, and delinquency and the juvenile justice systems in select countries are examined in detail.

In Chapter 19 ways that delinquency will be affected by the position of children through the 1980s and 1990s in American society are considered, and the future of delinquency prevention and control is reviewed. Special attention is given to the four approaches to delinquency control that are likely to influence the future of the juvenile justice system.

The first approach views delinquents as afflicted with a disease that requires the curative techniques of psychiatry, psychology, and social work. Widely criticized, this perspective on delinquency causes and cures has lost support in recent years, but is still in evidence among correctional and clinical personnel. A second approach, the "get tough," "lock 'em up" movement, has garnered support from a rather large public and from some government officials. The current philosophy of national crime agencies espouses a "get tough" view, especially with violent juvenile offenders. The third approach blames the juvenile justice system itself for juvenile crime. To achieve the goals of delinquency control, supporters of this perspective argue for a "hands off" approach in which juvenile justice processing is kept to a minimum. Proponents of the fourth approach see debilitating social situations as responsible for delinquency and recommend broad social changes as the only solution.

Since social change is constantly taking place within American society, at a seemingly faster pace stimulated by technological advances, concomitant changes will be occurring in major socializing institutions. Both the institutions of the family and the school, long linked to juvenile delinquency, have already felt the impact of social change. We must realize that change is not necessarily negative, but that along with such change must occur alterations in our traditional ways of thinking. For example, the traditional nuclear family, still a viable institution, is no longer necessarily the model that we have to use when we discuss a stable environment for children. Single-parent families, blended families, and joint-custody families are increasing in number to the extent that we must no longer define these structures as "novel" or "crisis-oriented." The American public school system, on the other hand, does appear to merit the label "crisis-oriented." Our educational system, at least in many areas of the country, does not appear to be meeting the academic, social, or psychological needs of today's children. We have come to a point in history where a rethinking and revamping of the existing educational system is a necessity. The solutions to this problem will not be easy nor simple; they will, however, dramatically affect the future of American youth.

Two other key socializing structures are also noted in our final chapter on the future of delinquency. The church in American society, we suspect, has not utilized its full resources and expertise in helping youth meet the demands of contemporary society. We suggest that this vitally important institution take a more worldly stance in dealing with some very practical social problems, delinquency being one of them. Finally, the socializing role of the mass media, we argue, must constantly be monitored for its content and possible negative impact on children.

CHAPTER 18

CROSS-CULTURAL DELINQUENCY

COMPARATIVE RESEARCH
METHODS

WORLD CRIME AND DELINQUENCY
TRENDS

CRIME AND DELINQUENCY IN
DEVELOPED AND DEVELOPING
COUNTRIES

DELINQUENCY IN SELECTED
FOREIGN COUNTRIES

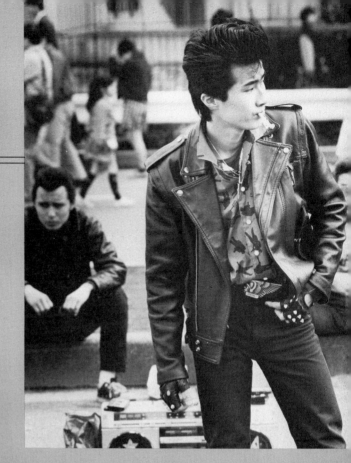

The study of comparative criminology, of which comparative delinquency is a part, has not been a major concern of criminologists (Archer and Gartner, 1984). American criminologists have, at least until recently, been myopic in their exclusive study of crime in their own country. Given that social scientists since the time of Auguste Comte (1853) have recognized the utility of comparative analysis, it is indeed surprising to find such a dearth of cross-cultural research on youth crime (Friday, 1971).[1] An obvious reason for this includes the insularity of attitudes or ethnocentrism on the part of social scientists convinced that their culture is the only one worth studying and analyzing (Johnson, 1983). To some extent, this has been the case with all countries, not just the United States (Klein, 1984). By examining research on delinquency in only one society and at one point in time, however, we cannot hope to understand all aspects of the phenomenon, which itself serves as a barometer of a changing social order.

Comparative criminology may be defined as the cross-cultural study of all aspects of crime and criminal justice in two or more societies. A researcher conducting cross-cultural research may analyze crime in a particular country by focusing on any one of several analytical units including the individual offender, the specific offense, national crime trends, and the criminal justice system and/or personal, scholarly contributions, and popular attitudes.

A review of the history of world criminology indicates that before World War II, European criminologists dominated the theoretical study of crime using primarily an individualistic approach concentrating on biological, psychological, and legalistic factors. Such a focus required relatively little contact with the larger world and limited the study of crime to one society, usually at one point in time. However, with the emergence of American criminological thought as part of a larger sociological tradition, crime research shifted from a focus on the individual criminal to the broader social conditions thought to be associated with certain forms of criminality. Since we have come to realize that crime, including delinquency, is at least in part a reaction to social, political, and economic conditions that impinge on a society as part of a broader macro system of changes which have accumulated since World War II, the idea that crime (and its study) is an international phenomenon has finally been accepted (Alper and Boren, 1972; Mannheim, 1965; Shelley, 1981a: xx–xxxiv). Acceptance and legitimation of this orientation have served to stimulate an interest in comparative criminology. Juvenile delinquency has been of particular interest, probably because of the glut of children born immediately after World War II.

For the most part, comparative criminology today operates on the premise that crime is inherent in the social structure of a society and that changes in crime patterns can be attributed to changes in this structure. Variations in types of criminality and in types of crime control systems are therefore studied as reflections of different social, political, and economic conditions.

A comparative approach to causation explanations may expose any theoretical shortcomings, may suggest plausible rival hypotheses, or at the very least, may lead to more comprehensive lists of relevant variables. Yet the comparative approach leads to some interesting dilemmas for criminologists. For instance, crime in Communist societies should theoretically become nonexistent as they progressively move toward the elimination of social and economic inequities. However, from all indicators, some Communist societies such as Russia and Cuba are experiencing delinquency patterns very similar to those of class-structured capitalist nations (young males residing in urban cities coming from working class broken homes represent the bulk of the statistics). Both the USSR and the USA have been experiencing general increases in criminal activity. The USSR

and the USA are among the nations of the world that have the largest number of prison populations. Some criminologists accounting for the relatively higher rates of crime in modern industrial nations have convincingly argued that crime is associated with industrialization, modernization, and population growth.

Why is it, then, that middle-sized cities in the Soviet Union have larger crime rates than their largest cities? How does one explain the fact that Japan, which has undergone unparalleled industrialization, modernization, and population growth, has experienced a decrease or stable rates in crime from 1976 to 1980? In order to explain what at first glance appear to be contradictions, an understanding of the respective cultures under study is necessary, as well as access to data about crime trends from both historical and contemporary times. These problems accentuate some of the difficulties and complexities criminologists face in conducting comparative criminology.

In this chapter we examine the parameters of juvenile delinquency in several foreign countries, documenting along the way some of the problems involved in conducting cross-cultural or comparative criminological research.

COMPARATIVE RESEARCH METHODS

At the present time, there is no comprehensive research methodology available to the criminologist interested in studying crime and delinquency in various cultures. Given that professional criminologists may include social scientists, legal scholars, historians, or criminal justice practitioners, it should come as no surprise that comparative "criminologists" employ a variety of research methodologies based on their particular orientations.

Comparative methodology can generally be classified into five categories: (1) comparative analysis of official statistics and archival data; (2) comparative content analysis of theoretical and popular literature; (3) comparative research utilizing immigrant accounts; (4) comparative intensive case studies; and (5) comparative studies employing various standardized research techniques (interviews, self-reports). The use of one technique over another depends on the goals of the research and on the logistical problems associated with different methodologies, including sample selection, validity and reliability testing, financial limitations, and the level of national or international organizational support. The first three strategies do not necessitate visits to the countries under study, although visits are certainly desirable. Some knowledge of the culture, history, and language of the country under study is a prerequisite for all the strategies listed.

Statistical and Archival Data

The first type of comparative methodological technique uses existing *statistical* and *archival data,* such as various official crime statistics, to make inferences or generalizations about crime trends in a particular country or between countries. Numerous problems arise in this type of research. In the case of youth crime, differing legal definitions of juvenile delinquency exist from country to country (and in some cases from region to region in one country).

For instance, in some countries, such as France, criminal responsibility depends not only on the age of the offender, but on the type of offense committed. A youth between the ages of 15 and 18 can be held fully accountable if the judge feels the circumstances of the case warrant a full penal sanction. If the youth is between 13 and 14 and the offense is serious, a penal sanction may be considered; however, the Penal Code holds that the sentence in such cases must be shortened (Terrill, 1984: 165). In Sweden, criminal responsibility is set at 15. Youths under the age of 15 are not subject to penal sanction or prosecution. Generally youthful misbehavior is the concern of the social welfare agency of a particular district and is not usually handled by police or courts (Terrill, 1984: 234). In India, there is a lack of parity between age distinctions from state to state. The Indian Penal Code includes an important

distinction between nonoffending and offending juveniles. Offending delinquents are those youth who break the law (the most common offenses being pilfering, stealing, petty thieving, robbery, and housebreaking), and nonoffending children include the socially handicapped (destitute and homeless children) and uncontrollable children (behaviorally maladjusted youths who cannot be controlled by parents and guardians) (Nagle, 1979). The increased rate of delinquency in India is mainly in the nonoffending category. Generally the largest groups of referrals are among the "nonoffenders" (Hartjen and Priyadarsine, 1984). This may account for the emphasis on the social defense orientation rather than the penal orientation in India (Gokhale and Sohoni, 1976; Kulkarni, 1981).

Since delinquency is defined and approached by every society in terms of its own cultural values, often reflected in various delinquency and criminal codes, there may be little consensus on what constitutes a juvenile crime. It is difficult to go beyond the definition that it is basically conduct that violates criminal laws or codes as defined by adults or otherwise includes acts detrimental to children. There may even be dissensus among societies over something as seemingly clear as the concept of "child." In Israel, for example, a "child" refers to a person under the age of 14 years, a "young person" refers to a person above 14 and under 16 years; and a "juvenile adult" refers only to a female person who is above 16 and under 18 (Mueller, Gage, and Kupperstein, 1969).

Such legal variations make comparisons between countries, and sometimes within countries, extremely difficult (see Wolfgang, 1967). The possibility of adopting a universal definition of delinquency was discussed during the Second United Nations Congress for the Prevention of Crime and Treatment of Offenders (New Forms, 1960), but little progress was made in this direction. Generally, the congress agreed to limit delinquency (for analytical purposes) to those actions that are violations of the criminal law, thereby eliminating those cases which represent need or neglect, and so on (Mueller, Gage, and Kupperstein, 1969: 11).

Even when common definitional ground can be found, some countries do not systematically maintain regular—or any—crime statistics. Further, as with any official statistics, the true volume of juvenile delinquency can never be determined, and the statistics may reflect more the operational procedures of the collecting agency than crime rates. Some statistics, even if available, are not made available to outside researchers. The Soviet Union is a good case in point. High juvenile crime rates might be embarrassing to a given political order (Voigt and Thornton, 1985).

One of the first studies that attempted to compare delinquency trends in several countries was conducted by the United Nations. In its "worldwide" survey of juvenile delinquency, undertaken by the Secretariat of the United Nations, five regional reports were prepared dealing with delinquency in North America, Europe, Central America, Asia, the Far East, and the Middle East (*Comparative Survey of Juvenile Delinquency*, 1950; 1952; 1953; 1958; 1965). Recently the *World Survey of Crime Trends and Patterns* for the years 1970–1975 has been compiled (United Nations, 1977). Moreover, an updated *World Survey* has been scheduled.

Although some of the available results may be outdated, various official crime statistics (e.g., court data, police data, and data from associations for the protection of children) were utilized to describe the extent of the problem and to offer suggestions for improvement of existing juvenile justice systems and treatment techniques. A more moderate international study of juvenile delinquency conducted under the auspices of the United Nations Social Defense Research Institute and the World Health Organization (1976) likewise employed official records to investigate the extent of juvenile crime in several foreign countries (*Juvenile Justice*, 1976). The International Criminal Police Organization (Interpol) collects and disseminates information on crime and delinquency, particularly on issues pertaining to police functions. Interpol data include information and statistics for 127 countries. In this chapter, much of the comparative data on juvenile delinquency and juvenile justice will come from recent studies that utilize official statistics in some capacity.

Professional and Popular Literature

Another approach to the comparative method involves the examination of both professional and popular literature from a particular culture under study. Researchers must become familiar with major journals, monographs, government publications, and textbooks, if available, which address crime and delinquency issues. The assessment of original contributions by the comparative researcher reveals dominant theoretical paradigms in vogue at a particular time and may lead to the discovery of the circle of elites (scholars) who dominate the field in the country under study. If such material cannot be acquired by visiting the country under study, it must be obtained through alternative means, such as various university specialty libraries and networks of colleagues and national or international organizations interested in the exchange of materials and information.

Some of the international organizations (International Society for Criminology, United Nations, the Council of Europe, World Health Association, International Society of Social Defense, International Criminal Police Organization) allow opportunities for information exchange between scholars.[2] Since the great majority of written works dealing with crime and delinquency in various countries are not in English, the researcher must be conversant in the language of the culture he or she is studying or have the material translated. Knowledge of all aspects of the foreign culture is essential, since crime obviously does not occur in a vacuum.

Content analysis of more popular literature such as newspapers, magazines, and other sources also provides insight into the nature of the crime problem, the popular causative theories, and the trend patterns of a nation's crime problem. Even propaganda accounts may reveal invaluable data for the comparative researcher. Sometimes what is *not* said is just as important as what *is* said. Propaganda changes constantly and may reflect certain patterns of concerns within a country. For example, in the Soviet Union the underlying message of propaganda is closely tied to certain social policies. The emphasis placed on prevention and the proper upbringing of youth is stressed in both popular and scholarly writings.

Immigrant Accounts

A third comparative technique employs accounts of immigrants who have recently immigrated to another country. Such individuals are in the enviable position of being able to compare two cultures with respect to any number of variables relating to crime or delinquency. Obvious problems regarding the generalizability and representativeness of immigrant accounts to the population that has remained in their country of origin exist. This is especially the case when individuals leave their homeland for religious or political reasons. However, at the very least immigrant accounts make comparative researchers sensitive to certain social and political issues of a foreign country that cannot be obtained in any other way.

Voigt and Thornton (1985) interviewed a nonprobability sample of 130 families who had recently immigrated from the USSR to the United States about their perceptions and knowledge of delinquency problems in the Soviet Union. The researchers were particularly interested in the respondents' views about the "common persons" explanations of delinquency and the extent to which the Russian people were aware of propaganda—the Party line—and its possible connection to *juvenile hooliganism* (used loosely to refer to juvenile delinquency). Surprisingly, while most of the respondents considered the adult criminal justice system to be a political control tool (the government's use of criminal sanctions to control "crimes against the central plan," "crimes against community property," and "crimes against community distribution of goods"), the juvenile justice system was viewed as a community agency dealing with a "real" (nonpolitical) and serious growing problem in the Soviet Union—juvenile crime. Juvenile hooliganism was thought to be a problem over which both government and citizens were concerned.

In other words, they did not perceive delinquency to be "politically constructed" or used by the Party hierarchy to manipulate and persecute certain groups or categories of people. This information proved vital to the research effort and led to a careful separate treatment of crime and delinquency problems in Soviet society. Indeed, social reactions to crime and delinquency are distinct and are reflected in the different methods of official response and treatment. The Soviet juvenile system, as we will see, is almost entirely in the hands of the community and staffed mainly by volunteers.

The respondents' replies to questions pertaining to what explanations of delinquency dominate in the Soviet Union were also insightful. Their responses led to a search for causes other than just the Marxian variety (those related to capitalistic influences) (Voigt and Thornton, 1985).

Voigt and Thornton concluded that their Russian respondents addressed factors for delinquency not unlike those isolated by the American public (breakdown of family relationships, lack of discipline, problems in education, lack of direction, and boredom were listed among the causes of delinquency). The Russian immigrants' emphasis on lack of family control over children as a cause of delinquency was also found to be congruent with the current crime theories employed by many contemporary Russian criminologists uncovered through a content analysis of Russian delinquency literature. Thus, while the immigrant accounts did not provide a basis on which to make generalizations about Soviet society, these accounts proved instrumental in developing relevant questions for the study of delinquency using other sources.

Case Studies

The case study method uses an intensive situation to gain insights about why juveniles engage in certain illegal activities and how they possibly perceive their delinquent deeds. Jackson Toby, an American criminologist, used the intensive case history method in a study of affluence and adolescent crime with delinquent offenders in Japan, Switzerland, and Israel (1981). By comparing the accounts of juvenile offenders from each of these cultures, he found support for the theory that as a country becomes industrialized, the sociocultural gulf between adolescents and adults widens, with one result being that social controls over adolescents break down. In addition, economic deprivation increases with the rise of affluence in such a way that the "have nots" experience relative deprivation when compared to the more fortunate and engage in delinquent behaviors to "even the score."

One obvious problem with the case history method is that the researcher must know the language and culture of the host country to gain access to a sample of adolescents—in the case of Toby, delinquent offenders. Even if these problems are overcome, it may be difficult to offer support for a particular theoretical explanation of crime based on a small number of case histories. In other words, it may be hard to generalize to a larger population of delinquents based on a few case studies. Nevertheless, the method provides crucial insights into certain details or dimensions of a problem area and offers a level of comprehensiveness which is difficult to obtain using other strategies. The case history method is particularly useful in specifying the cultural meaning behind some statistics or policies.

Other Standardized Research Methods

Comparative studies employing a variety of standardized research methods (survey techniques, self-reports) comprise the final major category of comparative crime methodology. Such studies may test specific causal theories of delinquency from either a micro or macro theoretical level or simply describe or systematize information about some aspect of delinquency or juvenile justice, such as the juvenile court structure. The international study conducted by the UNSDI (1976) supplemented official crime data with a multicountry survey which collected descriptive data on a variety of topics dealing with juvenile delinquency and juvenile justice in each country. Respondents were asked about their perceptions of delinquency.

Junger-Tass (1977) examined "hidden delinquency" in Belgium by employing self-report delinquency measures with a sample of Belgian and other European adolescents. He basically found that a large percentage of his sample reported engaging in delinquencies for which they were not caught (primarily property offenses) and committed their offenses in small group settings. His findings correspond quite closely to the bulk of self-report delinquency studies conducted by American criminologists. Other criminologists have employed the self-report technique to sample the amount of "hidden" delinquency in various countries (Hartjen and Priyadarsini, 1984; Shlapland, 1978; Burkhuisen et al., 1966; Junger-Tass, 1976; Junger-Tass et al., 1983).

Since studies of this type are very expensive and since institutional affiliation or legitimacy is often necessary to gain access to certain types of samples, the success of original comparative surveys frequently depends upon organizational or governmental support or sponsorship. Such organizations as IREX (International Research Exchange) have supported and sponsored numerous projects around the world. One of the requisites of program support is that scholars from the United States establish relationships (correspondence) with scholars in the countries to be studied prior to any exchange.

Despite some of the difficulties and drawbacks associated with cross-national studies, there is evidence that interest is increasing. The growing interest is indicated by the greater numbers of books, professional, and popular journal articles devoted to cross-cultural studies of delinquency and crime published each year. The American Society of Criminology recently established a new Division on International Criminology, and the Academy of Criminal Justice has sponsored the development of university curriculum projects on international criminal justice systems.

The value of the development of cross-cultural understanding of crime and delinquency is great. The experiences of others may inform our own policy decisions and planning. Speculation about the roots of delinquency, of course, is given added depth if tested against the backdrop of other cultural contexts. Confidence in theories is possible only when the results of similarly oriented research from other societies correspond.

In our analysis of juvenile delinquency in select countries, we draw heavily from cross-cultural materials that employ each of the comparative techniques we have discussed.

WORLD CRIME AND DELINQUENCY TRENDS

Although we will examine various delinquency statistics from several different countries later in the chapter, it would be informative to have some general ideas about world crime trends. Do societies as they change, expand, and develop, for instance, assume new crime patterns? Do they experience increases or decreases in certain types of crimes?

In order to obtain such data, the United Nations embarked on an ambitious information-gathering exercise which was called the World Crime Survey. Based on surveys given to sixty-seven member nations, the United Nations obtained data on the total number of offenders, males and females, juveniles and adults, for the years 1970 through 1975.[3] In addition, information about select types of offenses and certain new forms of criminality was reported. Ten offenses were provided for crime classification: intentional homicide, assault, sex crime, robbery, kidnapping, theft, fraud, drug abuse, illegal traffic in drugs, and alcohol abuse. These offenses were collapsed into three broad categories: property crimes, crimes against the person, and drug-related crimes. In most instances, data came from official police statistics supplied by the participating countries. Since the World Crime Survey was not geared to the study of juvenile delinquency exclusively, much of the material presented fails to delineate specific, detailed data about worldwide delinquency trends. For example, we do not know for which specific offenses juveniles were arrested (in comparison with adults).

Despite the limitations of the study, we can gain some insights into world crime trends that simply were not available in the past. One inescapable conclusion emerged from the final report: "Crime is increasingly becoming a major world problem: its extent, variety and impact, both nationally and internationally, cannot be underestimated" (United Nations, 1977: 4).

Based on the information obtained from the participating countries, it was concluded that the overall crime rate for the years 1970–1975 was approximately 900 offenders per 100,000 popula-

FIGURE 18.1 World Rate of Criminal Offenders (per 100,000 population), 1970–1975

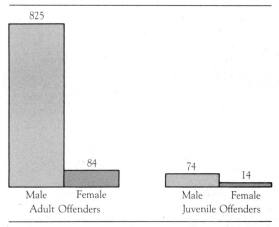

FIGURE 18.2 The World Crime Picture: Proportions of Total Crime According to Broad Crime Categories

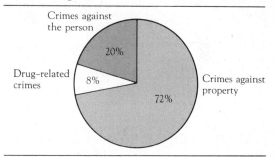

tion. From Figure 18.1, we can see that the overwhelming proportion of the adult offenders were males, with a rate 10 times that of females. For juvenile offenders, the male rate was 5 times greater than for females. Figure 18.1 also demonstrates that the offender rate was higher for adults than for juveniles, although these rates were computed using the total population as a base, rather than specific age groups of the population. If the specific crimes are grouped into the three categories of crimes against the person, crimes against property, and crimes involving drugs, crimes against property make up the greatest proportion of all crimes committed (see Figure 18.2).

CRIME AND DELINQUENCY IN DEVELOPED AND DEVELOPING COUNTRIES

The variations among countries included in the World Crime Survey allowed researchers to make comparisons between those countries experiencing rapid economic development (developing countries) and those countries which have reached a degree of economic stability (developed countries). As less developed countries seek to bring about transformations, often in one or two generations, that have taken industrialized countries centuries to accomplish, numerous social repercussions are often a consequence, crime being among them.

Marshall Clinard (1973) noted many of the problems facing nations in this period of rapid social change. For instance, industrialization usually affects both the direction and the nature of urbanization. Physical, organizational, and financial facilities necessary to support a growing industrial sector become concentrated in cities. Population shifts to the cities, stimulated by an influx of people seeking employment, may create huge urban ghettos in which numerous social problems exist, including overcrowding, disease, lack of housing, unemployment, and crime. Migration of predominantly rural, agricultural people to urban areas often leads to disruption of family and community ties and controls. Even as far back as 1955, the United Nations world delinquency survey reported that in such developing countries as Africa, Asia, and Central America, "juvenile delinquency [was becoming] a problem of concern in those countries when industrialization [had] increased and when urban centers [had] been established" (Clinard and Abbot, 1973: 11).

An examination of the overall rate of criminal offenders for developing countries according to the World Crime Survey was approximately 800 per 100,000. The rate of increase was about 2.5 percent each year. Figure 18.3 shows the largest proportion of adult offenders were males; likewise, the largest proportion of juvenile offenders were males. Grouping the crimes into property, person, and drug-related offenses, crimes against the person

FIGURE 18.3 **Crime Rates (per 100,000) population) for Developing Countries by Offender Characteristics, 1970–1975**

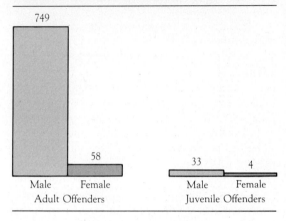

FIGURE 18.4 **Crime Picture for Developing Countries: Proportions of Total Crime According to Broad Crime Categories, 1970–1975**

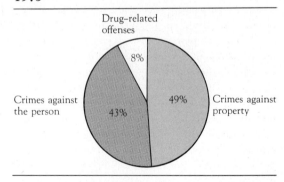

and crimes against property accounted almost equally for 90 percent of all reported crimes in developing countries (Figure 18.4).

When we look at the same data for developed countries, the overall rate of criminal offenders for the five-year period was approximately 1,000 per 100,000, with a rate of increase of 1 percent annually. From Figure 18.5, we see that most adult and juvenile offenders were males. Crimes against property account for 82 percent of total offenses, with crimes against the person and drug offenses

FIGURE 18.5 Crime Rates (per 100,000 population) for Developed Countries by Offender Characteristics, 1970–1975

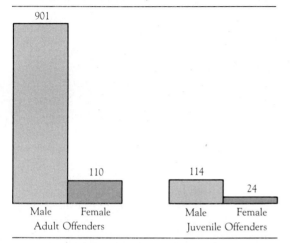

FIGURE 18.6 Crime Picture for Developed Countries: Proportions of Total Crime According to Broad Crime Categories

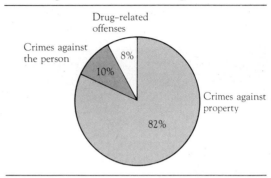

comprising the remainder almost equally (Figure 18.6).

The United Nations report emphasizes that the results of the first survey are tentative and provisional. However, some general statements regarding certain categories of crime in relation to certain macro-level variables can be made. For example, a high rate of homicide tends to occur in countries having a low gross domestic product per capita and a high proportion of the work force in agriculture. In contrast, countries with a high rate of property crime often accompanied a high gross domestic product per capita and a low proportion of the work force in agriculture. Drug offenses presented a similar pattern. Regarding juvenile delinquency, some countries that have high rates of illiteracy also have low rates of juvenile crime. Low juvenile offender rates are also displayed by countries with a high proportion of the work force in agriculture.

These findings have broad ramifications for explaining differential crime rates in countries. Rapidly changing social and economic conditions were identified by the United Nations respondents in developing countries as the main factors related to the increases in crime—especially delinquency. Developed countries singled out no particular

elements, suggesting that the factors were multifaceted. Those factors seen as being most related to lower crime trends were the presence of a close kinship system and the controlling effects of religion (see Evans and Scott, 1984). The developed countries saw the presence of community organizations and other local groups as having a beneficial effect on crime prevention (United Nations, 1977: 17–19).

DELINQUENCY IN SELECTED FOREIGN COUNTRIES

Delinquency in Japan

Japan is an island nation in the western part of the North Pacific, off the coast of East Asia. It occupies four main islands, Hokkaido, Honshu, Shikoku, and Kyushu, and numerous smaller ones. Japan covers an area of 143,706 square miles (approximately the size of Montana) and has a population of approximately 119,670,000.

Less than a century ago, Japan was a feudal state existing in self-imposed isolation. By the beginning of the twentieth century, it had become a world power. Since its defeat in World War II, Japan has become the third greatest industrial power in the world.

An emperor has reigned over Japan since its early feudal days. The emperor ruled the country with the aid of *shoguns*, or military dictators. When the country emerged from seclusion in the nineteenth century, the shogunate was abolished and the emperor resumed his position as the head of government. Western parliamentary forms were gradually introduced. The structure of the Japanese government is defined in its new constitution, drafted in 1946 by the occupation authorities, which vested sovereign power in the hands of the people and delineated a list of political rights guaranteed to them (Ogden, 1976). The government today is a constitutional monarchy in which the emperor reigns but does not rule, performing only ceremonial functions. The criminal justice code has undergone a long history of evolution. However, in its present form the code reflects the influences of both the Romano-Germanic tradition and the Anglo-American tradition.

Classification and Extent of Delinquency.   Unlike other countries that have experienced rapid growth and industrialization, the total volume of crime has generally been decreasing in Japan. The number of overall penal code offenses known to the police actually decreased from 1,561,000 in 1948 to 1,288,000 in 1979. Among industrialized nations, Japan has the lowest crime rates and is considered to have one of the best criminal justice systems in the world (Ames, 1981: 1). For instance, the average Japanese clearance rate for all penal offenses is between 68 and 71 percent, which is significantly higher than the average American clearance rate of 19 percent. Moreover, 99 percent of the cases brought before the court are prosecuted (Fenwick, 1984–85: 26). Prison recidivism rates are also substantially lower than those in the USA (Webb, 1984).

However, the crimes committed by juveniles under 20 years of age have not shown a steady decrease, but actually have increased during certain time periods (Suzuki, 1981: 78). Minoru Yokoyama (1981), however, does stipulate that part of the rise in statistics for juvenile offenses is related to an increase in the concentration by police on juvenile misbehavior, which affects the arrest rates.

But this does not mean that the amount of delinquency has changed. Nevertheless, what is significant is that even in Japan, where adult crime rates have been relatively stable or have declined, there is growing concern over youthful misbehavior.

Japanese juvenile law applies to three categories of youth: (1) "juvenile offenders," persons 14 years or over but under 20 who have committed criminal offenses; (2) "law-breaking children," children below the age of 14 who have committed acts which would be considered criminal if committed by those 14 or older; and (3) "predelinquent juveniles," persons under 20 who are prone to commit criminal acts in light of their character and involvement in certain questionable activities (frequenting unsavory places, associating with criminals, disobeying parents) (Shikita and Tsuchiya, 1976: 56–57).[4]

In the years following World War II, when Japan was disrupted both socially and economically, juvenile crime was high (Table 18.1). After attainment of economic recovery and stabilization, there was a significant decrease in juvenile crime. However, beginning in 1964, when large numbers of Japanese youth emigrated from the rural sections of the country to urban areas seeking jobs in chemical and heavy manufacturing companies, juvenile crime increased. This increase has been attributed to the rapid urbanization, coupled with enormous changes in the economic, social, and family structures in Japanese society (see Adler, 1984). As the economy stabilized, juvenile crime again decreased until about 1973 when it started to rise again, this time because of economic depression and increases in commodity prices stimulated by the worldwide "oil crisis." While economic conditions have to some degree stabilized, delinquency still remains higher in Japan compared with the past (Suzuki, 1981: 80–81).

A closer examination of Japanese delinquency reveals several important trends. First, attention to delinquency has shifted to include juveniles from the more affluent classes. For example, the proportion of students among juveniles arrested for penal code violations increased from 48 percent in 1966 to 75 percent in 1979. Similarly, the rate of juveniles coming from poor families fell from

TABLE 18.1   Nontraffic Penal Code Offenses for Juveniles and
Adults, 1951–1979

Year	Juveniles		Adults		Proportion of Juveniles
	Number	Rate*	Number	Rate*	
1951	126,505	12.1	380,142	8.2	25.0
1954	85,496	8.2	340,436	6.8	20.1
1960	121,408	11.2	279,911	5.0	30.3
1964	151,083	12.0	260,635	4.3	36.7
1969	107,992	9.5	267,140	3.9	28.8
1975	117,037	12.3	244,631	3.2	33.4
1976	115,875	12.3	241,204	3.1	32.5
1977	119,411	12.4	241,555	3.1	33.1
1978	137,021	14.1	242,544	3.1	36.1
1979	143,572	14.6	222,635	2.8	39.2

* Rate per 1,000 population.
Source: Suzuki, 1981: 79.

26 to 14 percent during the same time period. There was also an increase in the proportion of females arrested during this time (Suzuki, 1981: 81–83).

Second, there has been an increase in the number and rates (per 1,000 population) of younger aged juveniles arrested for delinquency. Between 1970 and 1979, juveniles aged 14 to 17 who were identified as delinquents increased some 40 percent; there was a substantial decrease in the number of juveniles aged 18 to 19, as well as "young adults" aged 20 to 24, arrested for delinquency.

Third, the increase in juvenile crime is largely due to an increase in the amount of property crime committed by juveniles. An examination of Table 18.2 reveals that there has actually been a decrease in the number of serious crimes committed by juveniles since 1955. An exception to this finding (not in Table 18.2) has been a reported rise in violent episodes in Japanese schools. In 1979, for example, 1,208 cases of assault in middle and high schools (some against teachers) were reported. There are also reports of violent attacks by children on their parents, something incomprehensible in traditional Japanese culture.

Another cause of alarm involves the delinquent activities of so-called juvenile hot rodders or collectives of young Japanese who congregate around their cars and motorcycles. Their number was estimated to be about 25,000 in 1979. In addition to violating traffic laws, they are accused of engaging in gang fights (leading to reported cases of murder), as well as attacking innocent bystanders.

A fifth area of concern deals with drug abuse by Japanese juveniles. Unlike America, the use and availability of hard drugs like heroin has never been a serious problem for the Japanese. However, the use of toluene and other organic solvents by adolescents to get high or reach states of euphoria is reported to be on the increase. There were more than 40,000 instances of such abuse noted by the police in 1979 (Suzuki, 1981: 82–84).

The Juvenile Justice System. Japanese children are handled by two different systems: a child welfare system and a juvenile justice system. The welfare system, operating under the Child Welfare Law of 1967, basically deals with matters involving children below age 18 who are in need of care and protection. The system is administered by 47 prefectures and other local entities under the supervision of the Ministry of Health and Welfare (Shikita and Tsuchiya, 1976: 55–57).

The juvenile justice system deals with the three previously noted categories of juveniles who get into trouble with the law. Family courts, handling both civil and criminal cases, investigate all cases involving juvenile delinquents. The present ju-

TABLE 18.2 **Japanese Juveniles Identified for Penal Code Offenses by Types of Crime for 1955 and 1979**

	1955	1979		
Types of Crime	Number	Number	Percent Change from 1955	Proportion of All Offenders
Total	96,956	192,065	198%	22.9
Murder	342	92	27	5.0
Robbery	1,969	566	29	31.3
Bodily injury	10,090	6,816	68	20.3
Assault	3,700	5,752	155	28.4
Intimidation	474	150	32	10.8
Extortion	3,903	3,496	90	42.6
Theft	58,458	110,540	189	47.3
Fraud	3,651	458	13	3.6
Embezzlement	2,218	7,910	357	50.3
Rape	2,078	916	44	33.2
Indecency	420	562	134	14.6
Arson	163	163	90	17.3
Negligent homicide and bodily injury by traffic accidents		48,493		10.2
Other	9,471	6,151	65	17.3

Source: Suzuki, 1981: 83.

venile justice system was created in 1948 and was greatly influenced by the American juvenile court movement, having its basis in the *parens patriae* concept. The system focuses on the rehabilitation of juvenile offenders. Proceedings in the family courts are informal, and there are no real efforts to abide by legal requirements for enforcing the procedural rights of the accused juvenile.

Figure 18.7 outlines the processing of certain categories of juvenile offenders in Japan. When the police have knowledge of a juvenile offender, they can refer less serious cases directly to the juvenile court; more serious offenses go first to the public prosecutor, who conducts further investigation and if the evidence warrants, sends the child to the family court.[5]

Once the child is referred to the family court, court personnel conduct a detailed investigation, including social, medical, and psychological assessments. If the court decides that the evidence is sufficient to continue proceedings, a closed hearing is held in which the judge can decide to

(1) dismiss the case; (2) refer the child to a child guidance center (bringing him or her under the Child Welfare Law); (3) refer the case back to the public prosecutor; or (4) place the child under protective measures (see Comparative Survey: Asia and Far East, 1953; Yanagimoto, 1973).

The decision to refer the child to the public prosecutor is predicated on the opinion that the act committed by the child is serious enough to be handled by normal criminal procedures.[6] The case is then tried in a district or summary court (adult criminal court) in which legal protections applicable to adults are triggered. Juveniles sentenced to imprisonment (with or without labor) are usually given an indeterminate sentence within the limits detailed by the law. Terrill (1984) reports that a very low proportion of Japanese juveniles receive a sentence of imprisonment and an even smaller number actually serve. The main reason for the low rate of imprisonment among juveniles is that youths under 16 by law cannot be imprisoned (p. 289).

FIGURE 18.7   **Japanese Juvenile Justice System**

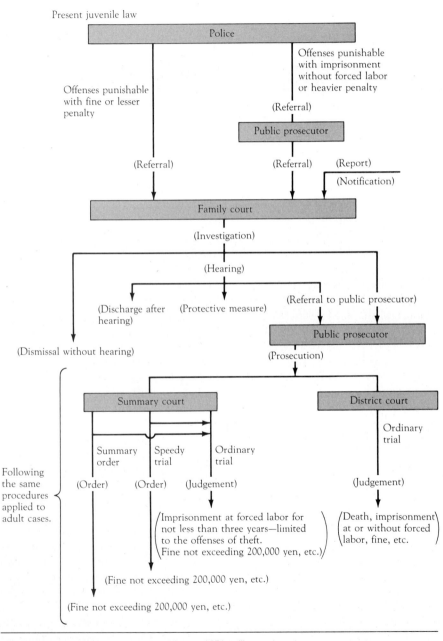

OUTLINE OF PROCEDURES

Source: *Juvenile Justice: An International Survey*, 1976; xviii.

The last decision, placing the child under protection, offers several options to the judge. The juvenile may be placed under probationary supervision by the Probation-Parole Supervision Office until he or she is 20 years old. Stricter protection results in the juvenile being placed in a Child Education and Training Home or a Home for Dependent Children. The most extreme ruling would be incarceration in a Juvenile Training School to age 20 where correctional education (school courses, vocational training, guidance, and so on) is given (Shikita and Tsuchiya, 1976: 57–81).[7] Less than 1 percent of all juveniles handled by the family court are referred to training schools (Suzuki, 1979).

Causal Theories and Policies.   The study of crime in Japan is not as fully developed a discipline as in the United States. No Japanese university has a separate department of criminology; courses that examine crime are peripheral in nature and emanate from specific disciplines, such as psychiatry, psychology, sociology, and the law (Tokoro, 1983: 409–410). This situation, in part, may be a reason why the Japanese do not have fully developed etiological theories for the study of juvenile delinquency.

Nevertheless, several sociocultural conditions have been linked to the recent rise in Japanese delinquency: parental discipline, urbanization, school achievement, migration into the cities, changing sex roles, to name a few (Tokoro, 1983: 419; *Juvenile Delinquency*, 1981). One study attempted, for example, to explain the rise in middle class delinquency by hypothesizing that a low level of parental concern which was characteristic of the lower class now exists in the middle classes (Hoshino, 1966).

Other studies likewise have pointed to family factors for an explanation of delinquency (see Hayashi, 1963). Discipline of children by parents is thought to be eroded when individualism is emphasized as a major value in contemporary society (Suzuki, 1981: 84). Parents who indulge their children are charged with conditioning them to have low tolerance for self-control. A study of delinquent and nondelinquent Japanese juveniles found that the delinquent sample seemed to have grown up expecting more freedom with regard to drinking, smoking, and staying out late than the nondelinquent sample, the implication being that parental controls were lacking in the delinquent families. Studies of the *ryunyu shonen*, migrant juveniles living in the cities without their parents, found that there is a greater propensity for these juveniles to commit crimes than for those living with their parents (Clifford, 1976: 114). However, those *ryunyu shonen* who maintained family ties over long distances by sending money to their parents tended not to get into trouble when compared to similar youth who broke their family ties.

Similar to the American case, some Japanese research has found that delinquent companions or delinquent peer influence is a strong determining factor in criminal involvement. An early study in 1968 revealed that out of 10,750 juveniles arrested for delinquency, almost half had broken the law with another person (Ministry of Justice, 1970; Clinard and Abbott, 1973: 195). Youth gangs, especially automobile gangs (*bosozoku*—reckless driving gangs) are reported to be quite prevalent in Japan. A 1975 *Japan Times* article estimated that there were 800 of these gangs, with over 2,500 members. Besides being a nuisance on the highway, these gangs are increasingly, from all reports, committing robberies, rapes, and other serious crimes. A police survey in 1975 interviewed 741 members of youth auto gangs and found that close to 75 percent joined these gangs to find companionship with peers (Ames, 1981: 85).

Unlike America, overemphasis on academic achievement in school due to stiff competition for entrance to advanced education forces Japanese youth to study hard after school hours (*Police White Paper*, 1976). Some researchers have speculated that as a means of venting the pressure or as a way of expressing failure, more Japanese youth engage in deviant behaviors.

Indeed, after a close inspection of delinquency in Japan and in the USA, the latter by far has a more serious problem. Comparative analysis of the Japanese delinquency trends and juvenile justice system is especially challenging because it raises questions with regard to the hypothesized relationship between such independent variables as industrialization, modernization, and population growth and the dependent variable, delinquency. Charles Fenwick summarizes this point well in the following:

> Japan is modernized, affluent, congested and highly urbanized with a standard of living that is similar, to a degree, to some Western societies. Moreover, comparisons are not minimized by differences in the number of social structural characteristics, i.e., levels of complex technology, rates of literacy or dominant modes of capitalistic production. In fact, after reviewing the Japanese experience, one should really start to question a number of specific independent variables that have been hypothesized in the explanation of increasing rates of interaction, modernization, industrialization, violent past national history and high levels of television violence. All of these factors have been present in Japan and their levels have been somewhat equivalent or even higher than ones in the United States. (Fenwick, 1984–85: 27)

While the Japanese example does not entirely negate the influencing or consequential effects of industrialization and modernization on delinquency, it does expose the explanatory complexities and the need to consider the mitigating or intervening conditions.

Delinquency in England and Wales

England and Wales are two countries that occupy the southern part of the island of Great Britain. Together with Scotland and Northern Ireland, they constitute the United Kingdom of Great Britain. While England and Wales have been politically integrated since the 1500s, each country maintains its own name and identity. In purely geographic terms, England and Wales may be referred to as south Britain. The total area of England and Wales is 58,350 square miles, of which Wales accounts for about 8,000 square miles.

The British Constitution is the product of more than a thousand years of evolution. The Constitution is unwritten in that its major rules cannot be found within a single document, but are derived instead from such things as statutes, judicial decisions, parliamentary law, and custom. The key doctrine of the Constitution is the sovereignty of the conjoint body of the Crown, the House of Lords and House of Commons, which together constitute Parliament. Parliament possesses unlimited legal authority over all matters, persons, and territories within its jurisdiction.

A high degree of local autonomy can be found throughout Great Britain. Local authorities are responsible for police, fire service, civil defense, education, public health services, housing, and so on. At a higher level, Wales and Scotland have considerable administrative autonomy, and Northern Ireland has a large measure of regional autonomy.[8]

The United Kingdom is a highly industrialized country and a major trading country. In the mid-1970s it ranked as the world's seventh largest producer of goods and services. The social structure of the United Kingdom may be described generally as homogeneous. Although there are differences in inherited wealth, social position, and education among the classes, they have become steadily less evident in the twentieth century.

Classification and Extent of Delinquency. Under English law there are no specific juvenile offenses, only those offenses defined in the ordinary criminal law. Thus, the terms "delinquent" and "delinquency" are not actually legal terms. Law violators are, however, subject to prosecution from the age of 10, but those under 14 are protected by a common law presumption (subject to rebuttal) that they do not know right from wrong. A juvenile who is under age 17 and who has not committed a grave offense such as homicide, rape, or arson is remitted to a juvenile court (Cavanagh, 1981: 47).

British criminologists face the same problems of measuring the extent of juvenile crime as do American criminologists. Basically, three tech-

TABLE 18.3 **Offenders Found Guilty of, or Cautioned for, Indictable Offenses and Number per 100,000 Population by Sex and Age Group, England and Wales, 1978**

Sex and Age	Number of Offenders			Number per 100,000 Population		
	Found Guilty or Cautioned	Found Guilty	Cautioned	Found Guilty or Cautioned	Found Guilty	Cautioned
Males						
Aged 10 and under 14	56,479	20,347	36,132	3,442	1,240	2,202
Aged 14 and under 17	97,127	65,020	32,107	7,858	5,258	2,597
Aged 17 and under 21	101,344	97,949	3,395	6,685	6,461	224
Aged 21 and over	180,600	174,710	5,890	1,122	1,054	37
All ages	435,550	358,026	77,524	2,125	1,747	378
Females						
Aged 10 and under 14	15,364	2,396	12,968	987	153	833
Aged 14 and under 17	19,044	8,309	10,735	1,617	705	912
Aged 17 and under 21	13,447	12,749	698	925	877	48
Aged 21 and over	47,499	42,582	4,917	267	239	25
All ages	95,354	66,036	29,318	434	301	133
Total	530,904	424,062	106,842	1,250	999	252

Source: Statistics of the Criminal Justice System: England and Wales, 1979: 23.

niques are employed: official statistics (from the Home Office), self-reports (Belson, 1978; Gibson, 1971; Shapland and Campbell, 1977; West and Farrington, 1973), and victimization surveys (Mayhew and Hough, 1983; Smith, 1982; Sparks, Genn, and Dodd, 1977).[9] For the purposes of examining long-term trends in youth crime, official crime statistics collected by the Home Office (comparable to American *Uniform Crime Reports*) offer the most comprehensive figures. As with all statistics collected by official agents, problems of bias and unreported crimes must be taken into consideration.

An examination of Table 18.3 reveals the number of males and females found guilty or cautioned in 1978 for indictable offenses. The number of male offenders (in all age groups) was about five times the number of female offenders.[10] Cautioning was used most often for juveniles (especially females) under 17; 64 percent of the male offenders under age 14 and 84 percent of the female offenders in the same age category were given cautions.[11] More males than females at all

ages were found guilty of the commission of indictable offenses.

For the ten year period 1968 to 1978 (Figure 18.8), there was an average yearly increase of 4 percent in the number of male offenders per 100,000 population at all ages. Throughout the period, the highest rate of offending was by males aged 14 and under. From Figure 18.9 we can see there was an average annual increase of 8 percent in the number of female offenders. Females aged 14 and under generated high rates of offending (based on a different scale than the males). There was a general rise for females in all age groups for the decade, with little indication of leveling off. For all age groups, both males and females, the rate of offending generally increased up to about 1974, except for males over 21.

Table 18.4 shows the proportion of offenders by sex found guilty of or cautioned for specific categories of indictable offenses of theft and handling of stolen goods—the proportion being higher for females than males. Of all female offenders, over half committed shoplifting offenses. For males,

FIGURE 18.8   **Males Found Guilty of, or Cautioned for, Indictable Offenses per 100,000 Population, England and Wales**

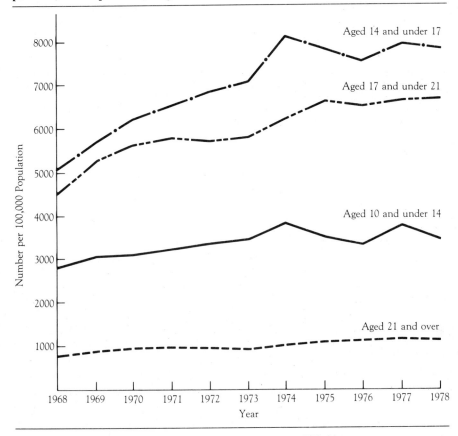

Source: Statistics of the Criminal Justice System: England and Wales, 1979: 26.

burglary was the next most frequent offense, ac-counting for about 25 percent of offenders aged under 17 and slightly less for those above 17. Low proportions of males (and females) under age 17 were involved in crimes of violence against the person.

The Juvenile Justice System.   Barring an official caution, a juvenile in England and Wales under age 17 who commits a violation is referred to the juvenile court. Such courts were established in 1908 and were initially special sessions of magis-trates' courts to hear cases of children under 16

years.[12] The juvenile court remains basically the same but perhaps more specialized now than in the past. It is the lowest level of courts with the most localized jurisdiction in the English judicial system still, like all magistrate courts, maintaining both criminal and civil jurisdiction (care proceed-ings).

Children between 10 and 17 are subject to the criminal jurisdiction of the juvenile court. When possible, as stipulated in the 1969 Children and Young Persons Act, civil jurisdiction of the ju-venile court invoked by a care proceeding is a preferred method of handling juvenile offenders (Parsloe, 1978: 147). The courts are staffed by

FIGURE 18.9 **Females Found Guilty of, or Cautioned for, Indictable Offenses per 100,000 Population, England and Wales**

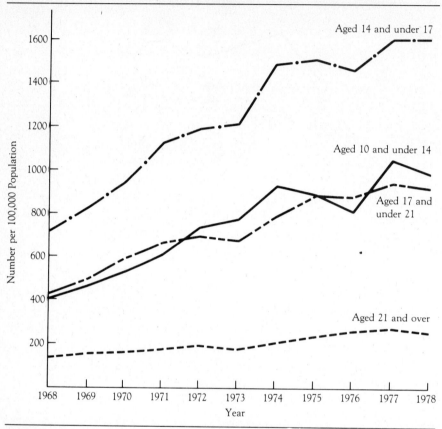

Source: Statistics of the Criminal Justice System: England and Wales, 1979: 27.

magistrates—individuals, often women, who are not professional or career judges possessing special legal qualifications, but rather individuals from all walks of life. Two or three of these magistrates, appointed by the Lord Chancellor on the advice of a local nonpolitical advisory committee, sit together on a juvenile court panel (Cavanagh, 1981: 52–53).

According to the 1908 Children's Act, juvenile cases must be physically separated from adult hearings. Although procedural modifications designed to aid children in understanding the proceedings have been instituted (such as using ordinary language), the fundamental legal basis of the British juvenile court is the same as that of

the adult court. Juveniles enjoy the same procedural protections as adults, including: (1) specific definition of charges; (2) proof beyond a reasonable doubt; (3) legal aid; (4) prohibition of hearsay and involuntary admissions as evidence; (5) the prevention of bias; (6) sentencing in proportion to the offenses; and (7) rights of appeal (Cavanagh, 1981; Parsloe, 1978).

While the underlying philosophy of the British juvenile justice system is generally to prevent juveniles from being referred to the juvenile court, statutory restrictions dictate whether the juvenile is subject to a criminal charge or a care proceeding. According to the Children and Young Persons Act of 1969 (section 5), a juvenile is brought to

TABLE 18.4 Proportion of Offenders Found Guilty of, or Cautioned for, Indictable Offenses by Offense Group, England and Wales, 1978

	Males				Females			
Offense Group	Aged 10 and under 14	Aged 14 and under 17	Aged 17 and under 21	Aged 21 and over	Aged 10 and under 14	Aged 14 and under 17	Aged 17 and under 21	Aged 21 and over
Violence against the person	2	5	11	12	2	6	6	4
Sexual offenses	1	2	2	3	—	—	—	—
Burglary	23	25	18	11	6	6	5	2
Robbery	—	1	1	1	—	—	—	—
Theft and handling stolen goods	62	56	50	52	89	82	74	82
Fraud and forgery	1	1	3	7	1	2	9	7
Criminal damage	11	10	14	11	3	4	5	4
Other indictable offenses	—	—	1	2	—	—	1	1
All indictable offenses (= 100%)	56,479	97,127	101,344	180,567	15,364	19,044	13,447	47,499

Source: Statistics of the Criminal Justice System: England and Wales. 1979: 28.

a juvenile court for a criminal charge only when a "qualified" person (a police officer) brings a formal charge. Before the formal accusation is made, the police officer making it must inform the local authority that this action is being considered, listen to recommendations, and be sure that the complaint cannot be handled by a formal caution or by some other means. When a decision is made, the police officer issues a summons or arrests and officially charges the juvenile.

Care referrals to the juvenile court can be instituted by a local authority, a constable, or some other authorized person. After a thorough investigation of the case in which opportunities for working with the child in the community are explored, thereby avoiding a court order, a formal care order may be issued.

Once the juvenile court has found a juvenile to have committed an offense or to be in need of care, a variety of dispositional options are available, including discharging the case, fining the juvenile or parent, issuing a service order, issuing a detention center order (if the youth is 14 or over), or issuing a youth custody order (if the youth is 15 or over) (see Figure 18.10).[13]

Much like the United States, the British have wrestled with the role of the juvenile court—whether it should be punitive or rehabilitative. The Children and Young Persons Act of 1969 was supposed to represent a compromise between these two positions, ensuring that the juvenile's welfare is not at stake, but that procedural protections are also guaranteed (Tutt and Giller, 1983).

However, the actual implementation of the provisions of the act has not occurred. The 1969 act, which called for a shift from a punishment orientation to the expansion of care services offered by social workers, has not been financially supported and has led to an ideological battle between the magistrates, who generally represent a more conservative and punitive orientation, and social workers, who lean toward a more liberal model of community control. Observers claim that these conflicting views among the decision-makers and implementers of policy in the juvenile justice system have resulted in a serious crisis (Terrill, 1984).

A similar conflict may be noted among scholars and practitioners in the United States. The more conservative factions are in support of a more punitive orientation, particularly with regard to serious and repeat offenders. The more liberally oriented are more focused on issues of diversion and prevention, especially of status offenders. Chapter 19 deals further with this issue in the American context.

Causal Theories and Policies. The British have a very well developed study of criminology which has encompassed both theoretical and practical criminal justice concerns about delinquency. Juvenile delinquency is often associated with the growth of towns and cities, and England has a rich history of urban development spanning several centuries. The social problems associated with urbanization—unemployment, poverty, disease—served as a catalyst for various criminal activities. Large numbers of criminal and destitute children stimulated early reformers to want to control these wayward youth and at the same time help them. Early on, then, the British, like the Americans, associated lower class poverty with criminality. As a result of this thinking, the juvenile justice system in Britain inherited ideas and institutions predicated on certain types of individuals, pauper children, constituting the juvenile crime problem. Obviously, with the development of more sophisticated thinking on the subject, aided by new research methods, this thinking has changed; the parameters of thinking on delinquency have spread to include the middle and upper classes.

Nevertheless, early research on delinquency examined differences between the classes and found evidence that lower class youth were more involved in criminality than youth of the middle and upper classes. As a result, lower class subcultural explanations were explored as one cause of delinquency (Douglas et al., 1961; Morris, 1967). Much of this research was, however, based on statistics supplied by official agents and subject to biases and various discretionary practices.

Some American versions of subcultural theories of delinquency causation have been rejected by British criminologists (Downes, 1966). It is argued

FIGURE 18.10   **British Juvenile Justice System**

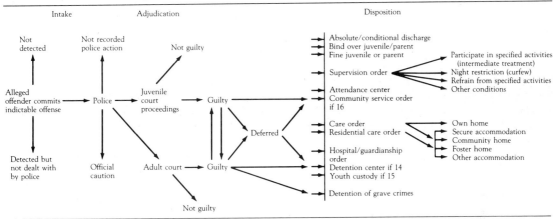

Source: Farrington, 1984; pp. 72–73.

that youth subcultures (such as postwar deviant groups like the Mods and Rockers) may represent collective solutions to problems facing working class youths at school and later at work. Some British criminologists stress that these youth cultures have been created as responses to irrelevant schooling and meaningless work, to which youths comply because they have to and not from moral endorsement. While these subcultural adaptations are based on dissociation from conventional values and on the pursuit of leisure patterns which are sources of satisfaction, they are not necessarily interpreted by British criminologists as rooted in status frustration, as many American subcultural explanations of delinquency are seen (Tanner, 1978).[14]

More contemporary explanations of British juvenile delinquency spanning the last twenty years have examined many of the same variables that American criminologists have explored. Such things as unstructured leisure time, the influence of mass communication, intergenerational conflicts, lack of education opportunities, the broken and conflict-ridden home, peer influence, and the like have been studied by sociologically oriented British criminologists (Parker and Giller, 1981; Rutter and Giller, 1984).

Psychological explanations of juvenile delinquency can also be found in Britain. Perhaps more than in the United States, considerable attention

has been devoted to pinpointing the differentiating characteristics of mentally disturbed juveniles so that their behaviors can be predicted in the future (see Gordon, 1982).

During the 1970s a number of British criminologists directed their attention to the critical or radical study of crime (see Chapter 8). From a delinquency standpoint, the critical school eschewed both a consensual and correctional perspective and instead focused on how "the legal and penal systems disproportionately (and by implication immorally) [singled] out the deprived, the poor, the minority group members and, in general, the lower class for punishment and control" (Taylor, Walton, and Young, 1975: 33). More specifically, the critical criminologists asserted that "in an inequitable society, crime is about property and that even the various offenses against the person are often committed in the pursuit of property. Property crime is [thus] better understood as a normal and conscious attempt to amass property than it is understood, for example, as the product of faulty socialization or inaccurate, and spurious, labelling" (p. 34).

Both working class and upper class crime are thought to be real features of a society involved in a struggle for wealth and property. A society that predicates itself, so the radical criminologists argue, on the unequal right to accumulate property gives rise to legal and illegal desires to accumulate these things as quickly as possible. Working class delinquents, for example, are singled out for apprehension and prosecution, thus accounting for their overrepresentation in official statistics.

Radical criminologists have offered stimulating critiques of the juvenile justice system in England, but have probably had a minimal degree of impact on the operation of the system. At least two British criminologists, Parker and Giller (1981), argue that British criminology remains social-psychological and correctional in its orientation toward delinquency, focusing on the offender and his or her environment and on how to rehabilitate the offender. Critical thinking, examining larger structural issues, has not, they argue, had a major impact on British delinquency.

British culture has been of particular interest to American scholars not only because of the common historical ties, but also because there is a similar cultural heritage, including the development of common law and a parliamentary democratic structure of government. But while there are many commonalities, there are numerous differences. For example, England has a unitary form of government instead of a federated state, which suggests a greater fusion of power in England and a greater separation of power in the United States. The role of the constable, the manner in which judges are appointed, the two types of lawyers (solicitors and barristers) are uniquely English and thus of interest to Americans. Other differences include the greater reliance in England on lay volunteers in all phases of the criminal justice system.

Even though the English are concerned about the growing problem of delinquency, their problem has not reached the proportions that we have in the United States. Greater population homogeneity, less cultural stress on materialism, the general unavailability of guns among the citizens and police force are among the reasons offered for why England's problems are less serious than ours. Yet the concerns of citizens and scholars and many of the causative theories and policy issues are very similar to those in the United States. Thus England continues to be of major interest to American criminologists and sociologists.

Delinquency in the Soviet Union

The Union of Soviet Socialist Republics (USSR) was founded upon the Russian Empire, which was overthrown in 1917. The USSR spans an area covering the northern half of Europe and the northern third of Asia. Territory added to the USSR after 1938 increased its area to about 8,600,000 square miles, making the country the largest single state on earth with a continuous territory. It occupies about 15 percent of the land surface of the globe. According to the last census, the population of the USSR makes it the third most populous country in the world after China and India. The USSR is a multinational state composed of 15 republics in which there is a rich diversity of peoples, cultures, and languages, although three-quarters of the population is made up of Slavic-speaking peoples, mostly Russians. Since the 1920s the country has undergone extensive urbanization and industrialization and ranks as a major world power today.

Soviet ideology is based on the theories of the revolutionary philosophers Karl Marx and Friedrich Engels, which were adapted to imperial Russia by V. I. Lenin, founder of the Russian Communist Party and one of the leaders of the Russian Revolution. Marxist-Leninist ideology views history and society as reflections of primarily economic relationships and calls for complete and absolute power to be vested in a small group of leaders who will direct the changes necessary in economic affairs to achieve an ideal society—Communist in nature. This small leadership group, organized into the Communist Party, operates without competition from other political parties and has full control over other institutions and organizations, including the government, the armed forces, trade unions, the press, schools, and mass organizations. For all intents and purposes the Party is the decision-making center of the Soviet state and supervises the execution of its politics and programs at all levels.

Since the 1917 revolution there have been four constitutions, the last adopted in 1977. The Soviet Constitution contains a detailed description of the Communist Party's role, as well as a detailed description of the federal state. The republic governments are concerned with the day-to-day routine administration of the republics, while the Union government retains responsibility for such matters as determining military and internal security, foreign trade, money and banking, and social policies.

Soviet law dealing with crimes against the person and property is similar in form to the law of some Western countries, especially those modeled after the Romano-Germanic legal system. However, crimes against the state (counterrevolutionary crimes) differ in at least two respects: (1) Merely speaking against the Soviet political and social system, if done with intent to weaken the Soviet power, is a crime; and (2) cases of espionage are tried by military courts.

Classification and Extent of Delinquency.   Soviet criminal law defines juveniles as those persons who have not attained the age of legal responsibility. According to the Criminal Code of the Russian Soviet Federated Socialist Republic (RSFSR), persons who have reached the age of 16 before the commission of a crime shall be subject to criminal responsibility.[15] Conditional criminal responsibility is faced by juveniles aged 14 to 16 for selected crimes: causing injury, rape, robbery, theft, malicious hooliganism, serious vandalism of public and personal property, and committing actions that can cause a train wreck.[16] Juveniles below the age of 18 who have committed minor crimes (petty hooliganism, public drunkenness) may be relieved of criminal responsibility and punishment and referred to the Commissions on Juvenile Affairs (CJAs). These commissions are predominantly composed of unpaid citizens who hear cases against juvenile lawbreakers and dispense reprimands, warnings, and sentences of confinement in rehabilitation and educational institutions.

Obtaining accurate information about any crime in the Soviet Union, especially juvenile crime, is extremely difficult. Western criminologists must rely on bits and pieces of Soviet crime data, often given in percentage form with no raw frequencies and filtered through official Soviet publications. It has been speculated that even very few Soviet criminologists are privy to official crime data. From all indications, no independent government agency is responsible for the collection of Soviet crime statistics (Juviler, 1976: 122). Also, since much delinquency is dealt with by the Commissions on Juvenile Affairs, which are basically lay organizations, inadequate records are maintained.

The Soviet approach to crime statistics may be related to the general theoretical position on crime itself. While Soviet criminologists concede that crime in Western capitalist nations, such as the United States, is a normal phenomenon, crime is not considered to be a normal phenomenon in the Soviet Union. Yet from all indicators, crime and delinquency exist in the Soviet Union. The Soviets have acknowledged concern over the increasing number of young people involved in criminal-type activities (Bannikov, 1974; Minkovsky, 1966; Neznansky, 1979). Recent Soviet statistical trends indicate that the young, the urban, the uneducated, from the working class and from broken homes, characterize the greatest proportion of the offender population (Zeldes, 1981).

Despite the lack of accurate data about crime in Soviet society, historical accounts indicate that juvenile crime was a problem in the USSR prior to and after the Soviet takeover (Bashilov, 1913). Millions of detached children, both war orphans and refugees from World War I, roamed the cities and countryside. From the beginning, the new government had to address these problems.

After the revolution, destruction, famine, devastation, and later rapid industrialization and Stalin's forced program of collectivization were believed to contribute to the growth of crimes committed by wayward children (the *besprizorniye*). Of course, what is not reported is how many of these children had done nothing criminal, but either questioned the legitimacy of the new authority or came from families perceived to be enemies of the state. What was done with these children is not known. The idea that criminal activity is rooted in a stubborn bourgeois past may suggest that many were simply made criminal by the new order and not for any traditional antisocial acts.

Originating as early as 1918, Commissions on Juvenile Affairs were created as one measure to combat juvenile crime. By the mid-1920s, juvenile crime was considered a serious problem and an estimated 6 to 7 percent of all criminal convictions involved juveniles. Thus, for the years 1923 and 1925, the total number of adolescents processed or convicted by the commissions and criminal courts increased from about 61,000 to 102,000. The greatest increase in youth crimes was for hooliganism, which increased by 70 percent between the years 1923 and 1925 (Zeldes, 1981: 85). It is quite possible, however, that these high statistics reveal the more rigid order under the rule of Joseph Stalin than real increases in youth crime.

The perceived increase in juvenile crime and the inability of the Soviets to control it led to the passage of the 1935 law, "On Measures for Combating Juvenile Delinquency." Under this law, juveniles 12 years and above could be convicted for criminal thefts and violent offenses, including murder. While estimates vary, delinquency rates during the 1930s remained high, perhaps higher than the first years of Soviet control. Some estimates suggest an increase as high as 300 percent (Zeldes, 1981: 87). After World War II there was another marked increase in crimes committed by juveniles. During these years, juvenile delinquency was linked to the direct effects of the war (loss of parents, disruption of schooling, and economic deprivation).

Both the number of delinquent children and the incidence of crime are reported to have increased in the postwar period, and all major Soviet cities added special units to their court systems for handling juvenile criminality. Solomon (1978) analyzed data on delinquency in Russia for the years 1945 through 1965 and reported dramatic fluctuations in juvenile crime rates. For example, between 1961 and 1963, the number of criminal offenses committed by juveniles increased from about 3 percent to 9 percent. The next few years revealed an increase in delinquency, probably because of increased activity on the part of Commissions on Juvenile Affairs. Initially, most cases were treated informally; very few of the cases

handled by the commissions were recorded as official delinquency.

More current studies on juvenile crime, incomplete and unreliable as they are, suggest that juvenile crime continues to grow and generally remains a serious problem for the Soviets. This is the case despite the fact that Soviet society has become increasingly stable. The proportion of offenses committed by juveniles, according to some sources, is somewhere around 10 to 20 percent (*Criminology*, 1976; Yakoviev, 1979). Juveniles are arrested most frequently for theft (often against state property) and hooliganism (60 percent), with violent offenses such as murders, rapes, and assaults comprising a smaller proportion of juvenile offenses (approximately 5 percent).

A summary of various data suggests that with respect to the age of juvenile offenders, the Commissions on Juvenile Affairs generally have heavier representations of younger juveniles (especially under age 14), while the courts tend to have a higher proportion of older juveniles. However, with the greater emphasis being placed on the informal use of commissions, these age patterns may no longer be valid. Data on the sex of juvenile offenders generally indicate that females are more widely handled by the commissions and make up less than 3 percent of juveniles processed by the courts (Connor, 1972: 87). Class distinctions for juvenile crimes, such as they are, suggest that poorly educated youth from the worker classes are disproportionately represented in delinquent and criminal activities. However, recent popular sources indicate that juvenile crime among the more affluent is on the rise.

Higher crime and delinquency rates are generally found in urban centers compared to rural areas. However, in the Soviet Union the mid-sized cities have higher rates of crime and delinquency than the largest cities (Shelley, 1981b). The Soviet internal passport system, which restricts residence mobility, and the fact that the largest cities are the Soviet showcase cities may explain this crime pattern.

The Juvenile Justice System.   The Soviets have been consistent, with few exceptions, in their efforts to promote the prevention of juvenile crime within their society. In contrast to the more punitive approach applied under the Stalin regime, today there is an all-out effort to involve all major social institutions, and to alter these institutions when necessary, so that crime will become a random and rare event (Minkovsky, 1966). Classroom teachers and teachers' councils are required to stay in contact with parents. So-called guardianship agencies in the education department of local Soviets (governing councils) place children, when necessary, in orphanages, foster homes, boarding schools, and out for adoption. They are also charged with investigating reports of bad family conditions. Both the militia and the MKVD (police) maintain "children's rooms" (similar to detention centers). These bodies arrange for various aid to children when parents for whatever reasons cannot maintain their children. Such aid may take the form of placing the minor in a boarding school, or under the guidance of public-spirited citizens (Connor, 1972: 116). Groups of unpaid auxiliary workers usually staff the children's rooms.

In the community prevention effort to curb youth crime there are several types of nonprofessional, part-time organizations. These include block and apartment house committees who work with problem youth or their parents, school organizations, workplace organizations, youth organizations such as the Komsomol (Communist Youth League), and lay judges. Any of these persons or organizations, including family members themselves, may refer a misbehaving or problem youth to Comrades' Courts or to the Commissions on Juvenile Affairs (CJAs) (see Figure 18.11).

The Commissions on Juvenile Affairs are much more vital to the Soviet juvenile justice system than Comrades' Courts. The CJAs are coordinating centers for all community organizations concerned with the upbringing of children and the prevention of juvenile lawbreaking. The CJAs are staffed by eight to twelve unpaid members who meet once or twice a month and who otherwise have other jobs and professions. They operate under two hierarchies—the local Soviets and the higher-level CJAs. Any support they receive comes from other volunteer organizations in the community.

Based on reports of the operation of the CJAs,

the powers of the commissions, limited by inadequate staffing, exceed their capacity to follow through with various dispositions concerning juveniles or their parents. The CJAs are authorized to subpoena information, to inspect conditions in the schools, labor colonies, and families. No youth may be paroled from a labor colony without CJA consent. CJAs serve as children's courts, receiving referrals form several sources for all minors under 18 who commit noncriminal violations or other socially dangerous acts or whom the judiciary has ordered to bypass criminal prosecution. In their family court capacity, CJAs may summon and sanction parents for laxity in the upbringing of the child or in extreme cases deprive parents of their parental rights and send troubled youth to special schools. Parents may be held accountable at their place of employment if they are somehow held negligent in the control of their children. As indicated in Figure 18.11, CJAs have a full range of dispositions available to them in treating juvenile offenders. Generally youths who have committed criminal acts under the influence of alcohol are treated more harshly.

The ultimate action taken against juvenile lawbreakers involves criminal prosecution. All juvenile suspects 16 or over whose cases are not dismissed or transferred to the CJAs, Comrades' Courts, or other nonjudicial agencies face criminal prosecution. For select and grave crimes such as murder and rape, juveniles 14 and 15 face automatic criminal prosecution (similar to transfer in U.S. courts). Confinement in educational labor colonies with varying degrees of severity is the usual disposition in the more extreme cases.

Beginning in the 1950s, the Soviets made advances in the use of juvenile procedures. Juveniles before a criminal court now have the right to counsel before pretrial investigation rather than after, which is the case for adults. Court personnel must do a thorough investigation of the juvenile's home life and prosecute adult confederates and instigators when possible. Procedural protections in the CJAs virtually do not exist, although youth can appeal incarceration as a disposition.

The Soviet juvenile justice system, then, is largely based on an assortment of loosely connected volunteer agencies staffed with lay citizens. Some evidence suggests that in practice these agencies

FIGURE 18.11   **The Handling of Soviet Juvenile Offenders**

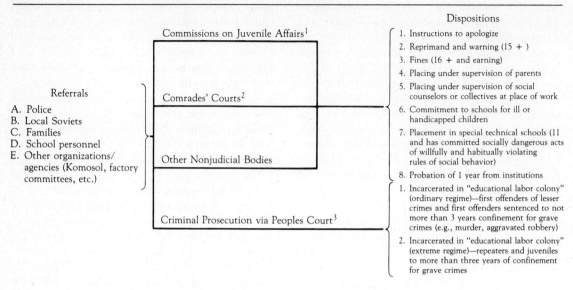

1. According to Article 10 of the Criminal Code of the RSFSR (1972), persons who, before the commission of a crime, have attained the age of 16 years, shall be subject to criminal responsibility. Persons who have committed crimes between 14–16 years shall be subject to criminal responsibility only for homicide, intentional infliction of bodily injury causing an impairment of health, rape, assault with intent to rob, theft, malicious hooliganism, damage to state or social property and others. If a court finds a person who, while under the age of 18, has committed a crime not representing a great social danger and can be reformed without application of criminal punishment, it may apply to such persons (Article 63) compulsory measures of an educational character which do not constitute a criminal punishment. The minor may be sent to a Commission on Juvenile Affairs where compulsory measures of an educational nature may be applied. The youth may be referred directly by appropriate individuals or agencies or via the Peoples Court.

2. Persons who commit any of a variety of petty offenses which, because of their insignificance or because of the character of the act committed, fall short of being crimes, may be brought before Comrades' Courts. Individual cases may be referred from the criminal court to Comrades' Courts (or vice-versa if it is determined that a criminal offense has been committed); noncriminal cases falling under the Statute on Comrades' Courts are referred directly by appropriate agencies or individuals.

3. Article 10 (RSFSR, 1972).

may be inefficient in some respects, but there is no question about their intent: to reintegrate the delinquent youth into Soviet society and to correct imperfections that caused the problem. Their less formal approach to juvenile justice, at least in theory, is what the United States has been seeking in part over the past few years (see Bassiouni, 1979; Savitsky and Shupilov, 1981; Solomon, 1978).

Causal Theories and Policies.   According to a leading Soviet criminology text, *Criminology* (1976), crime and delinquency are "survivals . . . alien to the socialist system." Soviet ideology, at variance

with some Soviet criminologists, holds that crime is a bourgeois remnant from the prerevolutionary past (Avanesov, 1981). Given that many of the remnants still exist some sixty years later, the Soviets have been hard-pressed to explain increasing delinquency and criminality in their society.

It is argued that under communism, classes will no longer exist, and one can deduce that many causes of crime will not exist—certainly, of course, those caused by the capitalist system itself. However, little is said by either Marx or Engels about the existence or nature of crime in a Communist state. Indeed, very little reference to any aspect of the future is made. Marx does suggest that communism is not to be equated with total perfection or a utopia. Under communism the individual assumes full responsibility over his or her life, barring the limitations of nature. While failure stemming from economic structural constraints will be eliminated, failure stemming from personal voracity, stupidity, and natural misfortunes will not be overcome (Karpets, 1966).

The Communist hypothesis suggests that under communism the individual assumes full blame or credit for failures or successes; the injustices are those inherent in or occurring from nature. Communism overcomes only the economic, structural, or class inequality and injustices, and not those arising from nature. But what this also suggests is that under communism, crime will not be totally eliminated either. Since there are many causes of crime, communism eradicates only some of the social, economic, and structural causes that underlie the bulk of the offenses. Marx, however, never directly addressed the question of what sorts of crime will wither away in the "development" toward communism and what will remain. He never dealt with the possibility that certain types of crimes may stem from the effects of growth, industrialization, bureaucratization, modernization, and the associated forms of alienation, which are processes common to both capitalist and socialist nations (Plamenatz, 1966; Voigt and Thornton, 1985).

In spite of the inconsistencies between Party rhetoric and the practical dynamics of crime and delinquency in Russia, and irrespective of the changes in leadership and the numerous official mood shifts, one may note a steady development of criminological thought without much deviation. From the beginning, Soviet criminology has generally rejected the biological and psychological causal models of criminal and delinquent behavior (Gertsenzon, 1968). The Russians emphasize the social structural roots of crime, arguing that the psychological and biological paradigms deal mainly with aberrant and rare events. Soviet theorists claim that the sociological variables are associated with fluctuations in the rates of crime, and therefore in order to reduce crime rates, the greatest attention must be given to the social factors (Voigt and Thornton, 1985).

Soviet criminologists make a distinction be-

tween first, second, and third order causes of crime. *First order* causes "originate in sources of crime committed mainly with contradictions of social development" (Avanesov, 1981: 97). Thus, for example, crimes involving theft of property may take place because the demand for certain consumer items has not yet been fully met (meeting the demand for goods and services is among the major economic problems in the Soviet Union). However, the government insists that such structural deficiencies will be reduced and eliminated as time goes by.

Second order causes are "causes . . . connected mainly with the world outlook of various categories of people" (p. 102). Social acceptance and reinforcement of "individualism and egoism are qualities that set the individual against society and undermine his sense of social and collective duty" (p. 103). Social and collective responsibility is not inherent in the personality, but is something learned in the family, in schools, and in a society based on collective duty and collective consciousness. Egoistic people, it is asserted, who consider their own needs and desires exclusively, are associated with the "criminal personality" (p. 103).

Third order causes of crime concentrate further on individual characteristics as an explanation for crime. Various social-psychological explanations—for example, the criminal personality who possesses "backward consciousness"—are discussed in relation to criminal pursuits (p. 110). The "backward consciousness" is social in nature, suggesting bad breeding or lack of proper upbringing. Thus, while there is no attempt to deny psychological or biological factors in the explanation of crime, these cases account largely for aberrant behavior, and their causes are considered to be mainly random, not amenable to systematic study or inclusion in causal models. Even in discussions of the "criminal personality," the emphasis is on social factors when it comes to positing causes as well as finding remedies.

Soviet criminologists have consistently placed major stress on social-structural determinants of criminal behaviors or trends. Their preference for social-structural explanations is especially relevant to their notion of the "elimination of crime." In order to control crime, and other social problems, the Soviets have attempted to manipulate and control their basic institutions (primarily the family, school, workplace, and youth organizations) to inculcate socialist principles and morality. In particular, the family has been singled out as a basic institution which can contribute to the delinquency of minors. Blame is placed on parents' inability to socialize their children to socialist standards of work, obedience, and loyalty. Lack of parental supervision, excessive drinking in the home, and the like are noted in discussions, both scholarly and popular, dealing with Soviet delinquency. Blame is also placed on the school and its inability to further inculcate motivation, expertise, loyalty, or respect and belief in the Soviet law. Various youth organizations as well as the workplace are further singled out as not adequately controlling juveniles or reinforcing work habits or furthering Communist ideals and training. In essence, all agencies that impinge on the child are held accountable for failings (Voigt and Thornton, 1985).

A range of other contributory factors can be gleaned from Soviet works, many of which sound quite familiar from our examination of American delinquency in this book. For instance, delinquent peer groups and their negative influence on Soviet youth are cited as a constant worry to the authorities and to law-abiding parents. The Soviets, however, are not just concerned about adolescent delinquent peer groups, but adult peer groups at the workplace who drink excessively and encourage youths to misbehave. Unemployment on the part of school dropouts and young unskilled workers, which the Soviets refer to as "parasitism," is also cited as contributing to delinquency.

It is interesting to note that the problem of unemployment is not treated as a government failure but as a personal failure—the unwillingness to work or to carry out one's collective duty. Unemployment or parasitism is among the characteristics included in the profile of the criminal personality. Lack of cultural and recreational facilities and the ensuing boredom and dull routines for youth in factory dormitories are frequently added as causes of delinquency. The negative influence (materialistic and narcissistic themes) of books and films and music (some of American

origin) has recently reemerged in discussions of juvenile crime (see Bordoin, 1981).

While many Western delinquency theories may not fit the Soviet situation exactly, in many ways Soviet delinquency, underneath a different veneer, is not unlike that of Western (and other industrialized) countries. The noted commonalities among socialist and capitalist nations with respect to crime patterns may raise problems with theories that relate crime to certain political and economic arrangements. In response, some radical criminologists have argued that barring the differences between systems, all industrialized nations (capitalist and socialist) are tied to a world ecosystem which may be affecting the convergence trends (similarities in the relative patterns of delinquency) (Horton and Platt, 1983). Despite some evidence of convergence between the USA and USSR, the latter does not experience the gravity or extent of American juvenile delinquency. This is the case even though the USSR surpasses the USA in population size, has greater cultural heterogeneity, has a lower standard of living, and has an extremely great amount of competition for relatively few premium positions in schools and the labor force.

SUMMARY

We have seen that certain countries around the world have wrestled with the problem of juvenile crime and the best way of handling juvenile offenders. Some countries have developed elaborate juvenile justice systems that offer a variety of dispositional options, both formal and informal. Generally, most of these countries have shifted their juvenile justice apparatus toward community-based alternatives that seek to divert less serious offenders from the juvenile court or other comparable structures. Most countries allow for serious juvenile offenders, those committing adult crime, to be tried in an adult court or to be dealt with more harshly by the appropriate juvenile courts.

Our review of cross-cultural delinquency reveals that interest in juvenile delinquency has not been limited to the United States. Reports from other nations, especially those experiencing modernization and industrialization, show that youth crime has been on the increase since the end of World War II although, as noted, we must exercise caution in positing any theories using these facts. Early studies in several nations undertaken by the United Nations in the 1950s document the post-World War II correlation between modernization, industrialization, and delinquency. Comparative surveys since that time, incomplete as they are, likewise show that juvenile crime remains a contemporary problem in many nations, including countries that did not have such a problem in the past.

The field of comparative criminology, however, has not, at least until recently, been given a priority status by criminologists in the United States and elsewhere. Current cross-cultural research on crime has been hampered by the lack of standardization of research methodologies and in many cases lack of availability of data about crime. Even when data are available, differences in legal classifications about what constitutes "juvenile delinquency" make comparisons difficult.

Several international organizations devoted to the study of crime have aided in the interchange of data regarding crime trends, control, and treatment throughout the world. These organizations have the potential of broadening the field of comparative criminology in the future so that common problems might be jointly solved. The United Nations probably remains the most active of these organizations and continues through its Crime Prevention and Criminal Justice branch to explore many parameters of youth crime throughout the world. The United Nations World Crime Survey, conducted in the mid-1970s, probably represents the most comprehensive effort to measure cross-cultural crime to date. Based on information supplied from some sixty-seven nations, it was discovered that some of the largest increases in crime rates were taking place in those countries experiencing the most rapid growth and industrialization. Juvenile crime was found to be a major problem in developing countries in Africa, Asia, and Central America.

Although our examination of juvenile delinquency in several different countries is selective and does not attempt to offer a representative sampling of countries throughout the world, we can surmise that juvenile crime is indeed a serious problem in most contemporary societies. Japan, for instance, has shown an increase in its juvenile crime since about 1973. While there is a generally low rate of personal violent juvenile crimes, property crimes are quite high—something rare in Oriental society. England and Wales have also experienced long-term increases in their juvenile crime rates, primarily property crimes, since the late 1960s. Following a similar pattern, the Soviet Union, though quite different politically, reports increases in property-related delinquent activities over the last several years.

What is interesting in our exploration of cross-cultural delinquency is that despite the cultural differences, there appears to be a high degree of similarity in causal explanations for these youth problems. It is suggested that changes in basic family structures, brought about by modernization, have lessened traditional social controls over juveniles. With some exceptions, educational institutions are criticized for not offering innovative and relevant curriculums for rapidly changing social conditions. As a result, the young in various societies often feel alienated and are at a loss to deal with expectations they feel they cannot meet. Another common finding in the explanation of delinquency revolves around the fact that often those youth who are lowest in socioeconomic status in a given society are overrepresented in official crime statistics. There is an implication here that these youth are singled out for a variety of reasons. This finding gives some validity to radical criminologists' critiques of juvenile justice systems being biased toward the deprived, the poor, and minority groups. Finally, another commonality is that youths commit their crimes in the company of companions (usually dyads and triads).

We do not doubt that the study of cross-cultural crime, especially delinquency—however it is defined—will continue to be of interest to criminologists. As more information is exchanged and compared, we may find that many of the problems which plague youth are rooted in common causes and subject to common remedies.

PROGRESS CHECK

1. Why is it difficult to make cross-national comparisons regarding juvenile delinquency? (pp. 392–396)

2. List and explain three techniques used in comparative methodology. (pp. 392–396)

3. Explain the role of the United Nations in regard to studies dealing with crime and, more specifically, delinquency cross-nationally. (p. 397)

4. What findings were obtained from the World Crime Survey? Did the survey deal with juvenile delinquency, or primarily adult criminality? (pp. 397–399)

5. Note some trends in Japanese juvenile delinquency since World War II. (pp. 399–400)

6. Under English law, who is a juvenile delinquent? (p. 405)

7. Describe the structure and the function of the Soviet Commissions on Juvenile Affairs. (pp. 414–416)

8. Give a brief history of juvenile delinquency in the Soviet Union since the 1917 revolution. (pp. 412–414)

9. Would an individual classified as a psychopath fit under first, second, or third order causes of crime, according to Soviet criminologists? (pp. 417–418)

10. The authors suggest that one particular delinquency theory appears to be espoused by Soviet criminologists. What is that theory? (p. 417)

NOTES

1. Early scholars employed the comparative method extensively: Weber's (1947) interpretive sociology, Durkheim's (1897) research on suicide, and Parsons's (1937) study of social systems. Within the field of early criminology, we could cite the works of Beccaria (1764), Garofalo (1885), Ferri (1892), Gumplowicz (1899), Lombroso (1911), and Tarde (1912) as employing the comparative method.

2. For discussions of international organizations and delinquency research, see Holyst, 1979; Pinatel, 1983; Lopez-Rey, 1973; Wickwar, 1977; Johnson, 1983; MacNamara and Stead, 1982; Mueller, 1983.

3. Algeria, Argentina, Australia, Austria, Bahamas, Bahrain, Barbados, Belgium, Canada, Chile, Colombia, Costa Rica, Cyprus, Czechoslovakia, Denmark, Ecuador, Egypt, El Salvador, Ethiopia, Finland, France, Gabon, German Democratic Republic, Federal Republic of Greece, Guatemala, Guyana, Iceland, Indonesia, Iran, Iraq, Ireland, Italy, Jamaica, Japan, Kuwait, Libyan Arab Jamahiriya, Luxembourg, Malaysia, Maldives, Mauritius, Morocco, Netherlands, New Zealand, Norway, Oman, Pakistan, Peru, Philippines, Poland, Qatar, Saudi Arabia, Seychelles, Singapore, Spain, Sweden, Syrian Arab Republic, Trinidad and Tobago, Turkey, United Kingdom of Great Britain and Northern Ireland, United States of America, and Yugoslavia. Information was also received from the following nonmember states: San Marino and Switzerland.

4. Law-breaking children under 14 years of age are below the age of criminal responsibility. They are usually handled by prefectural governors and child guidance centers and are referred to family courts when no other avenues are available.

5. This system relates only to children who are over 14 and under 20 and who have committed an offense. Other procedures apply to juveniles under 14 years of age (such as pre-offense juveniles and law-violating children). See Berezin (1982) for a comparison of the Japanese juvenile justice system with that of the United States.

6. If a juvenile is under 16 years of age or his or her offense is punishable by a fine or lesser penalty, the court cannot refer the case to the public prosecutor.

7. There are four types of schools: (1) Primary Juvenile Training Schools for juveniles with no serious mental or physical defect and who are over 14 and under 16; (2) Middle Juvenile Training Schools for juveniles with no serious mental or physical defect and who are between 16 and 20; (3) Advanced Juvenile Training Schools for juveniles with no serious mental or physical defect but more advanced in criminal tendencies and who are usually between 16 and 23; (4) Medical Juvenile Training Schools for juveniles with serious mental or physical defects and who are between 14 and 26.

8. We are not including either Scotland or Northern Ireland in our discussion. We might note that an excellent source on juvenile crime in Scotland is Parsloe (1978). Rottman (1980) offers the most comprehensive work on crime in Northern Ireland.

9. The first British Crime Survey was conducted in 1982 by the Home Office Research Planning Unit in collaboration with the Scottish Home and Health Department. It entailed a representative sample of 16,000 people over age 15 in England, Wales, and Scotland. The main aim was to estimate the extent of various crimes—whether or not reported to the police independently of statistics recorded by the police. The survey went further in collecting a wide range of additional information: factors predisposing people to victimization; the impact of crime on victims; victims' experience with the police; other contacts with the police; and nonreporting of victimization.

10. More serious offenses included in criminal statistics are violence against the person, sexual offenses, burglary, robbery.

11. As an alternative to court proceedings, the police may deal with an offender who admits to guilt by means of a formal caution. Cautioning would be considered a diversionary practice preferable to prosecution (Ditchfield, 1978). The juvenile, usually a first offender, avoids the stigma of being brought to court, thereby not receiving a criminal record (Bennett, 1979). The only formal conditions for the administration of a caution are: (1) The offender must admit to the offense; (2) the parents must agree to the child being cautioned; (3) the victim of the offense, if any, must be willing to leave the decision to the police (Landau and Nathan, 1983; Oliver, 1973). A relatively new form of cautioning is the instant caution, where a juvenile arrested for a minor offense is taken to the police station, a criminal record check is obtained, and the parents are informed. Formal cautions can include having the juvenile offender participate in some form of intermediate treatment programs (see also Mott, 1983).

12. Like America, juveniles who commit particularly grave crimes can be transferred to adult criminal courts (Crown courts).

13. The newly passed Criminal Justice Act of 1982 made several changes in the carrying out of juvenile court dispositions. While these are too detailed to enumerate here (most having been proposed in the White Paper, *Young Offenders,* 1980), one of the major changes involved the introduction of "youth custody." Youth custody centers are places where "young offenders may be detained and given training, instruction and work and prepared for their release" (Jones, 1983: 173). In lieu of Borstal training (institutions for serious juvenile offenders), if a young offender aged 15 to 20 commits an offense punishable by imprisonment for an adult and the court passes a custodial sentence of at least 4 months, the disposition shall be "youth custody." If the offender is age 14 to 20 and the court wishes to impose a custodial sentence less than 4 months, a detention center order is made. The minimum period of a detention order is 21 days (New Sentencing, 1983: 281).

14. There remains a strong interest in working class youth on the part of British criminologists. A Birmingham group of criminologists has produced a series of Marxist analyses of working class youth, examining in great detail the creation of their subcultures, life histories, and so on in relation to the British class structure (see Hall and Jefferson, 1976; Hall et al., 1978).

15. October 27, 1960, as amended March, 1972.

16. The charge of "hooliganism" is one of the most popular articles in the USSR Penal Code. It is defined as an "Action rudely violating social order and expressing obvious disrespect towards society" (Bassiouni and Savitski, 1979: 135). Hooliganistic actions usually occur under the influence of alcohol and in public places—streets, parks, public transportation. Hooliganism with the presence of alcohol, we might add, is treated more severely.

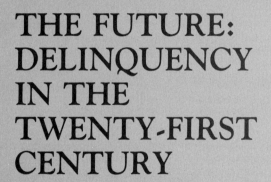

CHAPTER 19

THE FUTURE: DELINQUENCY IN THE TWENTY-FIRST CENTURY

DEMOGRAPHIC TRENDS AND PROJECTIONS

THE INFORMATION SOCIETY: IMPLICATIONS FOR YOUTH

DELINQUENCY PREVENTION AND CONTROL

JUVENILE JUSTICE POLICY

Demographic trends are dramatically changing the population distribution of the United States. They are also likely to change the scope of education and broaden the policies needed to sustain a strong and vibrant educational system. The sweep of the change is broad and deep enough to have implications for all of American society—life styles, the workplace, the link needed between education and work, the political atmosphere, and so on.

An intermingling of growth and decline among various segments of the population, regional population shifts, and a new wave of immigration prophesy a much more pluralistic society, which will require substantially more diversified policies than it has in the past.

Indeed, the demographic trends offer policy opportunities and imperatives for shaping the future of education and society:

- *Blacks and Hispanics continue to lag behind in terms of educational, economic, and political status.*
- *The emerging demographic picture augurs possible tension and conflict between generations, among racial and ethnic groups, and among regions.*
- *Policies to provide adequate education and other human services will become more difficult to devise as the nation becomes more demographically diverse.*
- *The growing minority populations represent an underdeveloped national resource that will become increasingly important to the nation's economic, political, and military strength as the majority population ages.*

Demographic data suggest the shape of America in the next several decades. It will be up to educators, civic leaders, and policy-makers to respond to these emerging realities in ways that promote equality, strengthen the economy, and sustain an adequate national defense. (Demographic Imperatives, 1983: 4)

As we approach the turn of the century, we are increasingly aware of our past, present, and future. Glimpses into the future suggest significant changes in all aspects of life: family, school, church, workplace, and government. As we have seen with the unfolding of each of the chapters in this book, delinquency does not occur in a vacuum. The changes we expect in our society have special implications for delinquency and the status of adolescence.

In this chapter we examine some of the demographics and projections; consider some of the effects of these changes on the fundamental institutions of society; and explore the future of the juvenile justice system.

Our future is already challenging our present. Our success in meeting the future is predicated on our ability to deal with the challenges now.

DEMOGRAPHIC TRENDS AND PROJECTIONS

Criminologists and sociologists believe that delinquency in the future will be influenced by the changing population or demographic structure of the United States. As a result of a high birth rate that peaked in 1947 (the baby boom era) and that continued for the next fifteen years, there has been for about twenty years a large population of adolescents in the United States. The sheer number of young people in the population has been used by researchers to account for the high rate of delinquency. When the birth rate appeared to decline in the early 1960s, many researchers assumed that as the number of young people dropped, so would delinquency rates. Unfortunately, the facts do not support this conclusion. There is evidence of a new baby boom, which is reversing the projected decline.

The Growth of a "Majority Minority" Youth Population

Profound demographic changes are currently evident in the United States. The most important of these involves population composition. At the present time, America's minority populations are growing at a much faster pace than its white majority population.

For example, the birth rate among blacks is relatively high. While the black middle and upper middle class, or professionals, have been expanding steadily, their family sizes have remained relatively small. The birth rates of blacks are characteristically highest among those in the lowest income groups. The number of poor black families, especially of single-headed female families, has been climbing at a staggering rate. Table 19.1 illustrates the high number of single-headed female families in New Orleans, which is sixth on a list of cities where blacks outnumber whites. Since the number of women of childbearing age continues to increase, there is no foreseeable decline in black births through the next several decades (*Current Population Reports*, 1984: 10–70). In the future, the "white" population will not increase more than about 40 percent as rapidly as the black population. The effect is that the proportion of the population which is black will continue to rise.

The most dramatic increase in population size, however, has been experienced by Hispanics. Because Hispanics are currently coming to their peak childbearing years, their birth rates will be greater than for other groups. If present trends hold, birth rates are expected to stay relatively high for the next twenty-five years (*Demographic Imperatives*, 1983: 7). In addition to the comparatively high birth rates, the recent wave of Hispanic immigration has contributed to the dramatic rise in population size. At the present time, the Hispanic population is concentrated in relatively few states; 80 percent reside in nine states, and

TABLE 19.1   Female-Headed Families in New Orleans*

By Race, 1984	White	%	Black	%
Total families	59,679	100%	72,290	100%
Female-headed	9,654	16	29,890	41
Female-headed with children under 18	3,743	39	21,001	70

In the New Orleans Housing Projects, 1985

Project	Percent Families Headed by Females	Percent Families Headed by Females with Children under 18
St. Bernard	82%	70%
Iberville	82	81
Florida	90	77
Desire	84	84
St. Thomas	88	84
Fischer	89	84

* The data show the high number of families headed by females in New Orleans. Note that most of the black low-income families living in housing projects are headed by single females.
Source: U.S. Bureau of the Census, Neighborhood Statistics Programs, 1986, Table P-6.

60 percent in only three. Almost all Hispanics live in urban centers. Some predict that by the year 2000 or 2030, Hispanics will comprise the largest minority group.

Another significant population trend has been the result of "the second largest wave of immigrants in history—a total of 13.9 million" (*Demographic Imperatives*, 1983: 4). Most of the second wave of immigrants who came to the United States between 1970 and 1980 were Asians.

These population data suggest that the projected decline in birth rates may be reversing due to the new baby boom. Minorities already make up the greater portion of school-aged children in twenty-three of the twenty-five largest cities in the United States. Some project that by the year 2000, minorities will constitute the majority population in fifty-three of the major cities (*Demographic Imperatives*, 1983: 4).

Age Distribution: Potential for Population Conflict

Perhaps more important than sheer numbers is the proportion of young people to older people in the population. The proportion of youths aged 14 to 24 in relation to the population aged 25 to 64 reached a high in 1970 but has shown a steady decline since that time. Unless birth rates change drastically during the 1980s and 1990s, the median age of the population—the age that half the population is over and half is under—will rise sharply from age 29 in 1977 to approximately age 37 in the year 2020 (Poplin, 1978; Samuelson, 1980). Even at the present time, the elderly (those over 65) outnumber teenagers (*Demographic Imperatives*, 1983: 4). Of great importance is the fact that the mean age of America's white population is older and that of the minority population is significantly younger. The age differential suggests that the majority of retired people will be dependent on the employability of minority youth and their tax-producing income or support of social security (*Demographic Imperatives*, 1983: 5).

What do these trends mean? The high ratio of youths to adults in the recent past has influenced delinquency rates, although the strength of this relationship is unknown. Some criminologists, for example, have suggested that the millions of youth kept out of the labor force by their sheer numbers has been directly related to several social problems, including delinquency, drug abuse, and racial unrest (Greenberg, 1977a). Also, a large proportion of young people in the population may make delinquency problems more visible and widespread than would otherwise be the case.

One might expect that as the population structure changes, employment opportunities, for instance, will be increased for younger individuals, thus eliminating one assumed cause of youth crime. However, current evidence suggests that this may not be the case. Shifts in the population pyramid may place younger individuals in direct competition with the elderly for scarce jobs (Empey, 1978). New federal legislation making it possible for adults to continue working past 65, the age of retirement established by former statutes, will undoubtedly add pressure to the employment picture in the future. Current economic figures indicate that traditional views about retirement for the elderly are no longer applicable. Working in what are supposed to be the "golden years" is an economic necessity for large numbers of the elderly.

Addressing some future policy implications, *Demographic Imperatives* lists the following points:

- Population and education trends could perpetuate the racial and ethnic division of American society.

- The recent emphasis on science and technology may increase minority underrepresentation in high-income, high-prestige jobs.

- High-technology and other economic changes also threaten the white and blue collar middle class with loss of jobs and economic status.

- Groups may be pitted against one another in the competition for scarce jobs and limited government services.

- Some projections forecast a truly high-tech future (requiring higher-order skills and paying well) for only a tiny proportion of Americans.

- Conflict also may result from the aging of the majority population and the youthfulness of the minority population.

- While the population and the economy are shifting south and west, large areas of economic and social disadvantage remain in the North and the East, especially in the large cities.

- America is becoming more diverse, not more homogeneous.

- Personal and national self-interest requires that the majority population address the needs of the minorities: for example, the retirement income of people at work today will depend on the productive employment of minority young people who are in school now, as will the future economy and military.

- The emerging demographics also suggest that national policy in education must become more diverse and flexible to serve the needs of varied regions and groups. (1983: 4)

These issues have been only marginally treated by delinquency researchers. Volumes of research, of course, imply that given these trends, the alleviation of delinquency may not be forthcoming in the near future. Young blacks and Hispanics, for instance, may be even more disproportionately represented in the crime statistics, if for no other reason than sheer numbers. The other factors, including the pressing need for change in our educational system, potential intergenerational conflict, and increasing unemployment, suggest that the relative size of various groups in the population is only one tiny aspect of a complicated phenomenon. No one questions that the changing structure of the population will have an effect on delinquency; yet no one is certain what those effects will be. We are even less certain what society's response will be.

THE INFORMATION SOCIETY: IMPLICATIONS FOR YOUTH

We are quickly entering the postindustrial era. The cybernetic revolution (computerization and telecommunications), while still in its infancy, is already suggesting massive transformations in social life (Naisbitt, 1982). Most people are now employed in jobs which create and distribute information. Information is the main product of labor. Access and control of information are now determining power and status in society. The underclasses of the future are likely to be characterized as "information poor." The character and nature of "the information society" are still unknown, and the consequences impossible to calculate, especially when we include consideration of the demographic trends discussed above. But despite the difficulties associated with forecasting the future, many speculations based on already existing reality have been offered.

At the very least, given the advent of the microcomputer industry and the advances in telecommunications, it is now technologically possible to maintain workers within their homes. Due to inflation, fuel shortages, space shortages, and the like, it may be economically too costly to bring each and every worker out of his or her home and to provide work space, parking space, insurance, and other services. If there is a substantial amount of work carried out in the home environment, we may again approach the cottage-type labor system which existed prior to industrialization. (The emergence of the "electronic cottage" has been discussed by Toffler, 1980.) The implications of this for family life and family relationships (particularly between parents and children) are far-reaching.

Moreover, there is evidence suggesting that people's attitudes toward work, family, and leisure are changing and that this may have some future consequences. For example, more and more people are opting for increased leisure time rather than increased salaries. Fewer people have just one career or one type of job throughout their lives. Indeed, in order to remain employable, many people have to retrain for new jobs. In the past and even in the present, leisure, education, and work have been concentrated during specific stages of the life cycle. Ideally, adolescents spend all their time on leisure or education; adults on work; and the elderly, when they retire, spend their time again on leisure. With recent changes in the nature of and attitudes toward work, "flexible scheduling" may become a new norm (Best, 1980). Flexible life scheduling may allow for leisure, work, and education to be interspersed throughout the

life cycle, rather than concentrating them at particular stages. At best, the development of this type of flexibility may result in less age segregation in labor, school, and recreation. One of the first signs has been that people of all ages are now attending school.

The high divorce and remarriage rates have given rise to *serial marriage* (people marrying and divorcing several times throughout their lifetimes). The extension of joint custody in this context means that youngsters are increasingly part of "family forests" rather than just a family tree. More and more youngsters are part of blended families, families emerging from the remarriages of spouses.

These emerging family structures may offer new options to parents. For example, joint custody offers more flexibility in parenting. When the burden of childcare is on one couple or one person exclusively, the options are limited. Combining parenthood with study, recreation, and work is difficult. Changes in the family may mean that children will become better integrated into the work, school, and recreational areas. Child advocacy and the children's rights movement may even lead to the lowering of the work age, the voting age, and desegregation of the young and the old. Perhaps the "computer whiz kids" can find employment in their homes on their microcomputers or even share certain jobs with their parents.

Before we become too hopeful about these trends, the reality of some potential problem areas must also be addressed: What are the effects of living in two or more homes simultaneously on the emotional stability of youth? What are the effects of the various combinations of stepparents on the young? What implications do dual home environments have for bonding the child with family and for the development of values? How will these changes in family and work affect the activities of youth?

So frequently when futurists look at the variables that are transforming society, they ignore the consequences these changes may have for individuals. For example, serial marriage, and perhaps the development of serial occupations (having several careers during a life span), may be ways in which people are adjusting to a rapidly changing information society. But we may ask how the rapidity of the changes that make self-adjustment part of an ongoing life process affects the search for self-identity which has been traditionally associated with adolescence. The adolescent search for identity is perhaps more complicated today, because it is difficult to find oneself when surrounded by adults who are themselves searching.

The social implications of the new family structures in the context of the electronic cottage and flexible life scheduling are also difficult to chart. Given the high degree of skills that presuppose such life styles, the more positive consequences associated with them may in actuality affect a relatively small proportion of young people in the future. The adult accommodation of youth, including the lowering of the work age or voting age, may not come if for no other reason than sheer racism.

Let us now take a closer look at the future of the key socializing institutions in our society. We have selected the family, the school, the church, and the media because these have played such major roles in adolescent and delinquency studies.

Family: The Rise of Family Forests

Delinquency is thought by sociologists to result at least in part from family problems. The family provides the initial learning experiences that make us human. It teaches us how to use language, how to interact with others, who we are, and perhaps most important, how to distinguish right from wrong. The home rife with conflict and discord has been alleged to be the breeding ground of juvenile delinquency. For a long time sociologists and psychologists simply held that any variation from the traditional two-parent nuclear family with mother at home caring for the children and father at work was potentially unhealthy for the raising of children. The results of the research which tested the hypothesis that delinquency was more prevalent among children from divorced homes were inconsistent and unclear, however. Part of the problem was that researchers treated the family resulting from divorce as a homogeneous

structure; they paid little attention to the many varieties of family forms.

The 1980 census disclosed the finding that the traditional family may not be an adequate measuring rod or criterion for "normal" since only 15 percent of American families technically fit the definition. The high divorce rate accompanied by high remarriage rates, growing numbers of women entering and remaining in the labor force, especially professional occupations, the acceptance of joint custody, and the increasing proportions of elderly are among the variables that have contributed to the rise of many alternative family patterns.

If the divorce rate continues at its current level, there will be a large number of single-parent families, especially among the poor. The joint custody laws and the greater extension of sole custody to fathers suggest the increasing complexities associated with factoring out the effects of single-parent family life on children. The dynamics of parent-child interactions in these families are still only dimly understood by social scientists. It is thought that the difficulty lies not so much in the absence of the mother or father, but in the "aloneness" or adaptation of the parent at home. One adaptation to this may be that grandparents and other relatives and friends are now assuming more important positions as role models to take the place of a "lost parent."

Those youngsters who will not be living in single-parent households will probably be part of blended families and extended family forests. Social scientists are only beginning to study the many varieties of family forests which are emerging and their possible effects on the behavior of youngsters, especially delinquency.

The complexity of the family forest poses unprecedented challenges for delinquency and family research. Another change in the family that will undoubtedly be of concern to those interested in delinquency involves changes in the traditional family with respect to the roles men and women occupy. As the number of married women in the labor force breaks the 50 percent mark, more and more families are operating differently than in the past. There may be more money in such families, raising their standard of living. Also, the household and childrearing functions normally associated with females may become more equalitarian, with greater male participation. All these changes may have positive impacts on children in terms of tearing down stereotypical beliefs about how males and females should think and act and making family members more sensitive to the needs of one another. However, some potential negative residues have been noted by family researchers.

More and more children from infancy on may be raised during the day in childcare centers. As children mature, they may become members of the so-called latchkey generation, in which they basically take care of themselves until their parents return at the end of the working day. Another change on the horizon is the growth of the "electronic cottage" phenomenon, where parents remain at home to work on their computers. Many questions dealing with family relationships in this context are beginning to emerge. There is already some evidence that fathers and mothers working at home on their computers interact differently with their children (see Dede and Gottlieb, 1984; Seaman, 1986). What implications the electronic family structure will have for delinquency also remains to be seen.

Obviously, our comments are just speculation at present. We expect, however, that more and more social scientists will confirm the finding that the type of family structure is not nearly as significant as the quality of family life. The American family has shown great resilience over the generations in its ability to handle change; we suspect that this will continue to be the case in the future.

School: Crisis in Learning

The school also plays an important part in the socialization of young people. Poor academic performance, negative feelings toward teachers and the school, low educational aspirations, and repeated absences from school indicate a lack of commitment to this important agent of socialization and an increased chance of involvement in delinquency (Schafer and Polk, 1967; J. Weis, 1977). Traditional thinking on the subject of school and delinquency placed almost all the blame

for academic failure on the child. Contemporary thinking, however, has tended to place the blame primarily on inadequacies within the public education system. The recent report on the nation's schools, A Nation at Risk (1983), conducted by the National Commission on Excellence in Education, documented the deplorable state American public education has fallen into over the past twenty years.

Generally, when a child fails in school, the school offers remedial education, social casework, and counseling. Although sociologists and criminologists believe these should not be stopped, they also argue that new ways of preventing school failure are needed if delinquency is to be reduced. This view is based on the premise that problems of adjustment in school, including delinquency, result from problems in the educational system.

Over the years, social scientists have recommended changes in education that they thought would reduce delinquency. The changes most frequently mentioned include these: First, local school districts must increase the chances for educational success among delinquency-prone populations. This can be accomplished in several ways: (1) training teachers to believe that all students can and should be educated; (2) expanding preschool programs, such as Head Start; (3) developing curricula and educational material relevant to the life experiences and needs of the students; (4) developing teaching methods appropriate to the student population; (5) utilizing flexible grouping and individualized curriculum, rather than **tracking** students into remedial or advanced programs; (6) reeducating teachers on a continuing basis; (7) increasing rewards for teaching in low-income schools in order to upgrade teaching staffs; and (8) creating class and racial diversity through such means as rezoning, busing, open enrollment, educational parks, and the like.

Second, social scientists argue that local school districts must strive to make school programs relevant to the current occupational market, especially for non-college-bound youth. This can be accomplished by developing programs and follow-up offices in high schools for alternative career routes and job placement and by increasing the opportunity for higher education through community and junior college expansion and greater financial aid for deserving students. The rise of programs for the nontraditional college student, taught primarily at night, has great possibilities for youth who must work during the day but desire a college degree.

Third, social scientists contend that local school districts must develop avenues for reintegrating students who are performing at unacceptable academic levels. Youth who have learning difficulties must be given attention not just in preschool and elementary programs, but throughout their school careers. However, early identification of learning problems merely for the sake of early institutional identification must be avoided. Predelinquents or potential failures are often publicly identified by school personnel, ostensibly for the purpose of providing help, when, in the experience of sociological observers, such help almost never seems to materialize.

Fourth, in our discussion of schools in Chapter 10, we advocated the use of alternative education for those youth who experienced problems in a more traditional school setting. Alternative programs embrace subject matter and teaching methodology that are not generally offered to students of the same age or grade level in traditional schools. Programs are designed to facilitate student success and are relevant to the student's educational needs and interests. In addition, these programs seek to reduce dropouts, pushouts, suspensions, expulsions, and truancy.

Fifth, according to social scientists, local school districts must try to reduce the isolation of schools from the community. School districts must make an effort to bring about closer cooperation between the school, families, and other agencies in the community. This can be accomplished in two ways: (1) establishing school-community advisory panels consisting of parents and students who are elected by their respective communities, and (2) encouraging the schools to be community places— places that local activities can center around and where continuing educational activities are made available day and night.

Sixth, social scientists argue that local school districts must be concerned with quality control in education. Decline in teacher quality has been well documented. In some states, more than 50 percent of teachers who have completed their university training cannot pass teacher competency tests. Obviously, teachers who are themselves ill-prepared in basic academic and social skills cannot logically be expected to add to the academic or life experience of adolescents.

In order to deal with both current as well as future problems of youth in our society, adequate social planning must be undertaken. One dramatic event we will be facing is the change in the social class and the ethnic or racial makeup of the school population. Because the middle and upper classes are having fewer children and the lower classes are having more, by 1990 it is projected that the majority of students will be minorities. This minority population will include blacks, Hispanics, Asian refugees, immigrants, and illegal aliens. Several potential problems will have to be dealt with as a result of these changes. In some states such as California, where English is already a second language, changes in the curriculum will have to be made. Since the percentage of poor people is increasing in urban areas, city tax bases will decline more, causing severe financial problems. Many middle class families question the quality of the education their children are receiving and resent having to pay a larger share of the taxes needed to support public education. They see insult added to injury when they send their children to private schools with high tuitions.

All in all, the future of the educational institution in America will no doubt reflect the prevailing political and economic climate. Despite that climate, however, the schools will have to be sensitive to the needs of large segments of the population in terms of both quality and relevance of school curriculums.

> Even those who cannot find lucrative, high technology jobs need an understanding of the emerging technology that touches every aspect of their lives. And the nation's military system increasingly relies on sophisticated technology. Without adequate preparation in school, young Americans will not be able to operate or maintain the technology on which both the country's economic and military strength depend. (*Demographic Imperatives*, 1983: 20–21)

Church: Religion in the Streets

The role of religion in the prevention or control of delinquency has generally been ignored by researchers. This is strange, since there are about 250 recognized denominations and sects and thousands of independent congregations in the United States. Nearly seven in ten Americans belong to some church, and of these, over half claim to be active participants. A classic study by Gerhart Lenski (*The Religious Factor*) in 1963 indicated that a person's religious affiliation can have far-reaching implications affecting such things as attitudes and behaviors toward work, politics, economics, family life, and social mobility.

The research that has examined the relationship between religion and delinquency has produced divergent results. Early research generally found no significant relationship between religious factors (church attendance) and lower rates of delinquency (Hirschi and Stark, 1969). More recent research, sparse as it is, supports the hypothesis that religiosity is negatively related to delinquency (Rhodes and Reiss, 1970; Higgins and Albrecht, 1977; Elifson, Petersen, and Hadaway, 1983). One might infer from these contemporary findings that youth who are attached to a church or who internalize certain religious principles are somehow protected from delinquency compared to youth who are not religiously active. As Emile Durkheim (1915) noted, one very important aspect of religion is its social control function. By powerfully reinforcing crucial values and norms, religion helps to maintain social control over an individual's behavior.

Although some studies indicate that American churches have become secularized to the extent that they have lost control over people (Luckman, 1967), other research indicates that this trend has changed and that there is a new consciousness and revival taking place in the churches (Bell, 1977; Berger, 1977; Bellah, 1978; Stone, 1978). As a possible reaction to organized religion stressing church doctrine, often seemingly far removed from everyday life and experience, there was a move in the 1960s and 1970s by many young people to more exotic forms of religion. Some of these religions were philosophically different from Western Christianity and included Zen Buddhism, the Unification Church, and Krishna Consciousness. They offered young people religious experiences that they could use in a very concrete way—for good or bad. There has been recent concern over the growing incidence of violence by members of various cults. But so little is known of the range of experiences and the nature of cultism in America that most existing evidence is anecdotal. The power the different cult religions have over many youth emphasizes the vulnerability of the young and their needs for relevance and guidance, and points to possible inadequacies in the way more traditional religions practice their tenets.

Many American churches have recently tried to respond to the charges that they are irrelevant and distant from the lives of their congregations, especially the young. Churches have started extending various services to their members in the form of counseling for families and individual members, organized leisure activities for children, day care centers, and a number of other innovative programs that fill important voids in the community.

A review of the history of religious institutions operating in America up to World War II indicates that many delinquency prevention and control activities were performed almost exclusively in some instances by the churches (settlement houses, youth clubs, homes for unwed mothers, and so on). It is quite possible, we believe, for American churches and synagogues to reexert their influence by attempting to deal with many of the concerns facing young people. There is much evidence to suggest that youth are not alienated from organized religion, but are simply seeking relevance, guidance, and direction from the church in some manner that makes sense to them. Theodore Caplow and his associates (1983) recently returned to Middletown (Muncie, Indiana), where the original Lynd study of American institutions and values was done in 1924. Caplow found that religion in Middletown was as important today for young people as it was some sixty years ago.

The influence of the church or synagogue on the lives of people obviously varies depending upon a number of factors. We know, for instance, that for blacks in American society, religion has served as a major social support system for individuals and families since the days of slavery. The black church has, according to many, affected the intellectual development and outlook of blacks. When blacks were denied the right to vote in the "white man's" political process, the church served as one of the only avenues available for political participation. When blacks did receive the vote, the church served as a focal point for organizing blacks behind political candidates sensitive to their plight.

Perhaps more important, the church in both rural and urban areas provided a refuge and support system for blacks in a hostile white world. It still remains a force in most communities in terms of offering real aid to families, especially in times of trouble (Frazier, 1974). The importance of church for black youth and its current role in maintaining peace, particularly in impoverished areas, have largely gone unnoticed by delinquency researchers.

Despite the many social changes, and the differential role of our religious institutions, organized religion remains strong in our society today. There is quite literally a church or synagogue on every corner. What is the congregation's role in the community and its relationship to the other institutions within the community? What is the relative impact of religion on the lives of youth? These questions are becoming increasingly important as we search for the integrative and preventive forces available in certain communities.

Media: Television and Computers

Today's youth have the opportunity of being the best informed generation ever to exist in the United States (or the world). Quite literally, every family, irrespective of social class, has access to television. Yet the mass media, especially the visual media, have not often been thought of as principally a technology for disseminating information. They have been compared to other social institutions such as the family, the school, and the church in the ability to socialize and influence children's attitudes, values, and behaviors. Available evidence indicates that the introduction of the television set into the American family has

greatly altered the way in which family members interact. It has affected such things as time spent in family communication, leisure, and recreation. Television has also affected other pursuits family members might engage in, such as going to movies, reading, listening to music, playing games, going to church, and the like.

As you may recall from Chapter 12, there is conflicting evidence among social scientists as to how much influence the media have on children. Despite this conflict, however, enough evidence does exist to indicate that children spend an inordinate amount of time watching television, and that television is a major source of information for some children, especially in the absence of other sources. Television, then, has tended to remove control over certain information entering the home from parents. Since a great deal of current television content in recent decades has been violent in nature, much of the emphasis in media research has sought to establish a causal link between exposure to media violence and some carryover into the real world. Scientific verification of a clear relationship here may never be forthcoming, given the multitude of variables that may intervene between exposure to a media event and some eventual behavioral response. Enough evidence does exist, we suggest, to merit grave concern over the amount and types of violence portrayed in television programs (and other visual media modes). Moreover, from all indicators this violent trend in content is increasing rather than decreasing.

Television is construed by some as an alternative source of social control by its reinforcement of basic American values and norms. Even violent dramatizations, it is argued, usually portray good winning over evil. While this may be true, television writers and producers often assume that American society is a homogeneous entity in which most citizens are middle class. Advertisements and commercials depict goods and products that only certain segments of the population can afford. In reality, many of these products are well beyond the means of certain individuals and may serve as a vehicle for social disharmony rather than social consensus. The "good" life of driving a new car, living in a fine house, dressing in the latest fashions, and drinking the best wine is simply not available to large segments of the population and never will be. This function of the media may be a more serious problem than portrayal of violence, but relatively little research has been done in this area.

Our comments about the mass media, primarily television, are couched in generally negative rhetoric partly out of frustration at the lack of specificity of some twenty-five years of media research, and partly out of fear of what the future holds for the media.

One innovation in mass communication that is still at the low end of the technology curve (a projected seventy-year period for maximum development of a new technology or invention) is the computer industry. The speed with which the communications industry has computerized has been astronomical. The chief source of information management and dissemination is the computer. It has thus been argued that in the future, power will no longer be associated with land or capital per se, but with the ability to control and manipulate information. In essence, then, we may have people who are information "rich" by virtue of their special skills or ability to acquire vital information and data, and those who are information "poor," without the appropriate skills or opportunities to reach vital information.

This state of possible events is quite interesting, given that the advent of the computer into American culture was hailed by some as the great equalizer. Some preliminary evidence suggests that already there may be differential exposure to computers based on social class, as measured by the type of school the child attends (Zakariya, 1984; Lipkin, 1983). Public school systems that are financially strapped may not even have microcomputers available to youngsters. If they do, the level of instruction may be less than adequate, and children may be exposed to computer skills in a reactive rather than proactive way (Thornton and Voigt, 1986). Thus, inner city ghetto youth interact with the computer in terms of "canned" or prewritten programs often routine in nature, in which they are to some extent "controlled" by the machine. Youth in well-endowed public school systems or in private schools in which there may

actually be courses in the curriculum on computer programming learn to write programs and thereby to "control" the machines. Whether this early differential interaction with computers will have any carryover in terms of later life chances is obviously speculation. There is a real potential here, we suggest, for computerization to reinforce existing social class lines rather than eliminate them.

In considering the cultural effects of computerization on society, literally every aspect of life has been touched. We have already commented on some of the implications of computers for the family. As they come into the home, we must wonder: Will computers bring families closer together, or introduce greater barriers? How will computers affect delinquency? We know computers have already given rise to new forms of crime ("computer capers").

DELINQUENCY PREVENTION AND CONTROL

Everyone agrees that delinquency should be prevented, and failing prevention, that it should be controlled. But not everyone uses the ideas of prevention and control to represent the same activities. Generally, prevention efforts are "exerted prior to the actual emergence of specifically criminal behavior," and control efforts are "exerted following or shortly prior to the actual commission of crimes" (Miller, Baum, and McNeil, 1968: 67). One criminologist, Thomas Phelps (1976), defined these concepts more specifically: "Delinquency prevention occurs when community services meet the current needs of youth; ideally, noncoercive social services are made available to the youngster not yet adjudged delinquent by the police or courts." Further, according to Phelps, "When a juvenile tangles with the law, the responses taken on his behalf by official agencies are delinquency control measures" (p. 3).

All the definitions of delinquency share the idea that prevention occurs before the actual commission of delinquent acts, and control happens when prevention was absent or when it failed. Control efforts zero in on children already accused of delinquent acts; prevention programs focus on minors not yet brought to the attention of authorities.

Delinquency prevention is often, however, thought to include more than the amelioration of social conditions contributing to delinquency and the treatment of children who have not been formally processed by the juvenile justice system. When there is intervention with predelinquents or delinquents that inhibits subsequent involvement in delinquency, prevention of delinquency has, in a sense, taken place. Using this broader concept of crime prevention, Brantingham and Faust (1976) identified three types of preventive efforts:

> *Primary* crime prevention identifies conditions of the physical and social environment that provide opportunities for or precipitate criminal acts. Here the objective of intervention is to alter those conditions so that crimes cannot occur. *Secondary* crime prevention engages in early identification of potential offenders and seeks to intervene in such a way that they never commit criminal violation. *Tertiary* crime prevention deals with actual offenders and involves intervention in their lives in such a fashion that they will not commit further offenses. (p. 290)

The second and third forms of prevention do not apparently differ from what has earlier been called delinquency control.

One of the clearest definitions of delinquency prevention and control was presented in the 1976 Report of the Task Force on Juvenile Justice and Delinquency Prevention (*National Advisory Commission on Criminal Justice Standards and Goals,* 1976b). This report defines **delinquency prevention** as efforts occurring before the police take formal action. Control, or corrections, is action limited to cases referred to the juvenile court and subject to a dispositional ruling by the court. Prevention programs strive, through modification of the social environment, to change conditions thought to be delinquency-producing. These programs are aimed primarily at two general groups:

children in general, and in particular, children identified as high risks. Control attempts include police reprimands, diversionary programs, correctional institutions, and community correctional programs; these activities are aimed at young people who have come to the attention of the police.

Trends in Prevention

Delinquency prevention is not a new goal in juvenile justice. Social conditions, especially slum life and its accompanying lack of opportunity, have long been thought to contribute to delinquency, and alleviation of these conditions has frequently been called for or attempted by individuals and groups seeking to prevent delinquency (see Miller and Ohlin, 1986).

Preventive programs usually operate at one of four levels. Programs at the first level seek to better any conditions possibly affecting children, including family life, education, religion, recreation, employment, and media. Programs at the second level, reflecting a slightly different purpose, tend to attack the "proximate causes of delinquency—[they are] concerned with the alleviation of conditions which directly contribute to delinquency, including narcotics education programs, organized group activities in high delinquency rate areas . . . [street work with gangs], surveillance of undesirable places" (Hahn, 1978: 225). Programs at the third level center on identification and treatment of predelinquent youth. Programs at the fourth level encompass what we have called corrective, or control, programs. In a way these delinquency control efforts are also preventive, since they propose to inhibit repeat offenses among already identified offenders (Brantingham and Faust, 1976; Hahn, 1978; Buckner and Chesney-Lind, 1983; Lewis, 1983). Since seven out of eight young people arrested are repeat offenders, at least to some degree, "the preventing of delinquency and the correction of the delinquent become two aspects of the same process" (Ohmart, 1976: 112).

The labors of the entire judicial and correctional system are aimed at the fourth level of prevention, reducing recidivism among apprehended offenders.

Various other types of programs have had the goals of the first, second, and third levels of prevention. Brantingham and Faust (1976) described these as including:

> . . . such diverse programs as parent education, mental health services, recreational activities, vocational education and employment counseling, drug abuse treatment services, remedial academic classes, public information programs on protection of self and property, crisis intervention telephone services, school programs on youth and the law and so forth. (p. 287)

Major efforts have been made to apply one or more of these techniques of prevention in the development of delinquency prevention projects. Some of these have been subjected to careful research on effectiveness. One of the first experimental projects was the Chicago Area Project, started in the 1920s by sociologists Clifford Shaw and Henry McKay. The goal was to change broad social conditions that cause crime. The organizers believed that, in the cities, immigration and urbanization had disrupted traditional methods of social control and that, to solve this problem, efforts should be made to reestablish community ties and informal methods of controlling deviant behavior. Local community committees sponsored recreation, community improvements, direct work with gangs, and assistance to juvenile court and parole agencies. Overall, 20 centers of community activities serving 20,000 youth were begun under the auspices of the Chicago project (Lemert, 1971; J. Weis, 1977).

Although the program appeared beneficial because it helped to organize communities and modify impersonal agency treatment of juveniles, one sociologist, Edwin Lemert (1971), concluded that subjective observations of success were not supported in more objective studies. There was no evidence, according to Lemert, that the Chicago Area Project reduced recidivism. Other sociologists, however, disagreed with Lemert's contention that the project failed to reduce delinquency (see Schlossman and Sedlak, 1983). According to Haskell and Yablonsky (1978), "In all probability delinquency was substantially reduced as a con-

sequence of the effort" (p. 459). Further, said a 1977 LEAA report, "There is support for the efficacy of indigenous leadership and community control in the reduction of delinquency rates" (J. Weis, 1977: 28).

How can we reconcile these conflicting positions on the effectiveness of the Chicago project? It appears that the more rigorous and objective studies of project success showed that delinquency was not reduced, but more subjective and less vigorous studies showed such a reduction. This lack of evaluative consistency may be the result of differing values held by the researchers. Where one may consider a small number of conforming youths to be a success, another may be interested only in statistically significant improvements, which have not yet been documented to any great degree.

Another early attempt at prevention was the Cambridge-Somerville Youth Study. The program, begun in 1939, was aimed at children considered to be at risk for delinquency. A group of 325 high-risk boys received "intensive personalized counseling" (J. Weis: 37), while a control group of 325 boys living in the area did not. Boys were selected for the project by teachers and police, and a committee was set up to determine predelinquency. In 1959 sociologists Joan and William McCord conducted an assessment of the Cambridge-Somerville Study. They concluded: "The Cambridge-Somerville Youth Study was largely a failure. Some individuals undoubtedly benefited from the program, but the group as a whole did not" (p. 96). The McCords' research was criticized, in part, for its reliance on official crime statistics. But it does appear that boys who received treatment in this program for five years did not do better in terms of recidivism than boys who received no treatment (J. Weis, 1977).

Two more recent programs had goals similar to those of the Cambridge-Somerville and Chicago projects. In the early 1960s, the New York City Youth Board, like the Cambridge-Somerville Study, planned to identify and treat predelinquents. Predictions of chances of future delinquency were based on Sheldon and Eleanor Glueck's (1960) five-factor family background scale, which included the following variables: (1) affection of mother for the boy; (2) affection of father for the boy; (3) discipline of boy by father; (4) supervision of boy by mother; and (5) family cohesiveness. The scale was given by social workers to children and their parents during home visits when the juvenile entered first grade. According to the treatment plan, boys predicted as future delinquents were sent to a clinic staffed by psychologists, psychiatrists, and social workers. The control group consisted of young people in another school who were also predicted to become delinquent but not assigned to any treatment. Emphasis in the clinic was on solving family problems (J. Weis, 1977). One criminologist who assessed the program concluded that it "failed in its objective. As in the Cambridge-Somerville Youth Study, members of the treatment group were no less likely to become delinquent than members of the control group" (Toby, 1965: 168).

A Boston program, the Midcity Youth Project, directed its attack toward delinquency prevention, but its focus was more like that of the Chicago Area Project than those of the Cambridge-Somerville or the New York efforts. The goals of the project were defined as social casework with families, organization of services to youth, and research into community need and program effectiveness. However, "The core of the project was intensive street work with seven gangs over a period of one to three years . . . [This] produced 'negligible impact' " (J. Weis, 1977: 29). Miller (1962) investigated whether the project decreased troublesome behavior by the gang youth and concluded that "with some qualifications, the answer was 'No!' " (p. 179). Miller also investigated whether there was a significant decrease in violations of statutes by gang youth in the project. Again, "the answer was, with some qualifications, 'No' " (p. 181).

A more recent delinquency prevention experiment took place in Seattle, Washington, from 1962 to 1968. In this project, social workers provided counseling services to junior high school boys entering seventh grade. However, the Seattle project, which was based on the idea that delinquency could be predicted on the basis of the opinions of school and police personnel, was apparently as unsuccessful as other such projects.

Berleman, Seaburg, and Steinburn (1972) concluded:

> Like its predecessors, the experiment did not yield evidence that the rendering of a social service to carefully selected acting-out youths and their significant others was effective in moderating these youths' acting-out behavior. This unfortunate finding is particularly convincing in this instance, for, unlike previous delinquency prevention efforts, this study achieved a level of methodological rigor. (pp. 343–344)

When Lundman, McFarlane, and Scarpitti (1976) examined the reports of twenty-five prevention programs that included research into project effectiveness, their conclusions were equally critical: "Once again, then, we find that in projects where reliable assessment of results is possible, the results reported are disappointing" (p. 306). They continued: "As a consequence, *it appears unlikely that any of these projects prevented delinquent behavior*" (p. 307). Looking for reasons for the failure of prevention programs, the authors suggest that we do not have enough data on delinquency and its causes successfully to stop or inhibit delinquency (see Morash, 1983; Frazier, 1983; Whitaker and Severy, 1984). Further, intervention strategies often do not fully implement the results of delinquency theory and research: "Inadequate funding, community sensitivities, and the like all mediate against direct translation" of delinquency theory into prevention programming (p. 308).

It quickly becomes clear that many attempts have been made to prevent delinquency. Though they have been diverse in scope and direction, these programs have been uniform in one aspect—their lack of effectiveness.

Four Approaches to Control

As this century began, there was heavy emphasis on the control of delinquency through the treatment of offenders. Delinquency was a disease, and modern scientific methods of psychology, psychiatry, and social work were felt to hold the cure. Opposed to this view was the view that the juvenile justice system mollycoddled criminals and should get tough on crime. Both views persisted to the present.

Two more recent themes were reflected in the works of the President's Commission (1967c) and the 1973 National Advisory Committee. Pointing to the inadequacies of what juvenile justice called treatment, some sociologists argued that the treatment for delinquency was worse than the so-called disease itself. This position has been called the "hands off" point of view; it has been attributed to the theoretical observations of labeling theorists. A fourth perspective has been based on the contributions of anomie and subcultural theories to the understanding of delinquency causation. This standpoint has emphasized the importance of modifying social conditions in the control of adolescent misbehavior. We will take a closer look now at each of these four approaches to delinquency control.

The Treatment Approach.   Concern for protecting children and treating delinquency forms the basis of the modern juvenile justice system in the United States (Galvin and Polk, 1983; Krisberg and Schwartz, 1983). Police and court personnel are supposed to consider what is best for the child, not just which laws have been broken. When children are involuntarily committed to institutions, placed on probation, or referred to social service agencies, the officially stated goal is not punishment or retribution, but "remedial," "curative," or "therapeutic" services (Shah, 1970). Increasingly, however, the treatment of delinquents has been termed a failure, and the range of criticism directed at treatment philosophies and programs has been extensive.

Liazos (1974) has charged that treatment is aimed only at adjusting poor children to their preordained status in the work force. According to another criminologist, Shah (1970), the therapeutic intentions of the court were "designed in large measure to avoid the constitutional prohibitions against preventive detention" (p. 3). Hakeem (1958a), zeroing in on the role of the psychiatric profession in the treatment of delinquency, has presented convincing evidence that psychiatric

diagnosis is a contemporary "tower of Babel" and that psychiatrists simply do not know how to treat delinquency. Similarly, numerous criminologists have asserted that the social sciences lack effective prescriptions for preventing recidivism among juvenile offenders. Wright and Dixon (1977), for example, have shown that when treatment programs are evaluated with a minimal degree of rigor, they have been proved unsuccessful. Wooton (1959) has called for real evidence supporting the efficacy of treatment programs: "Clear evidence of what reformative measures do in fact reform would be very welcome" (p. 335).

Toby (1965) has summarized the current state of treatment for the alleged illness of delinquency:

> Whereas medical practice aims at precise diagnosis and specific treatment, early identification and intensive treatment of delinquency usually address themselves to an unknown problem with an unproved technique. Is it any wonder that the few treatment programs that have been rigorously evaluated reveal disappointingly small effects? (p. 162)

Some of the most serious questions about treatment ideologies have been raised by legal arguments concerning the right to treatment. These arguments, proposed primarily by young lawyers and youth advocacy organizations, have made the point that juveniles appearing in juvenile court trade rights of legal protection and due process for promises for treatment. "Statutes under which juveniles . . . are civilly committed are constitutional 'only' because treatment is to be provided" (Silbert and Sussman, 1974: 611). Several cases have supported the right to treatment of juveniles committed to institutions. Yet effective treatment has not often been provided or perceived. It might even be argued that real treatment is rarely provided.

When treatment is promised by the state in return for curtailment of the offender's freedom but is not delivered, legal writers have argued that the child and his or her parents can demand the restoration of full constitutional rights. Further, "the courts have recognized a constitutional right to treatment and have required implementation of minimum standards of treatment in some cases, or in the absence of a minimally acceptable program of treatment, have declared that the child is entitled to be released" (S. M. Davis, 1974: 171).

The opposite side of the right-to-treatment coin is the juvenile's right *not* to be treated. There is growing support for the position that the child should be permitted to refuse treatment. In 1976 the Institute of Judicial Administration and the American Bar Association published a set of standards relating to juvenile justice that favored the right of the juvenile to refuse services except in three situations: "services juveniles are legally obliged to accept (i.e., school attendance), services required to prevent clear harm to physical health, and helpful services mandated by the court as a condition to a nonresidential disposition (a trade-off, to stimulate nonresidential placements by juvenile court judges)" (Standard 7.3). Although there have been court cases where the right not to be treated was upheld, both the rights to be treated and not to be treated are surrounded by a complex set of questions: "Does the inmate have the right to accept or the right to refuse all treatment? Does he [or she] have the right to choose punishment instead? Can he [or she] waive his [or her] right? Is he [or she] competent to do so? Can a guardian accept or refuse treatment in his [or her] stead?" (Simonsen and Gordon, 1979: 382).

The "Get Tough" Approach.   Although the foundations of the present juvenile justice system in the United States are deeply rooted in treatment and rehabilitative ideologies, some criminologists and politicians have advocated a return to more traditional ideas about crime and punishment. Much of the criticism of the treatment approach of the juvenile justice system has occurred in the past twenty years, but demands for harsher handling of juvenile offenders have been made since the beginning of the current system. These critics, fearing that juvenile justice processing encourages children to be increasingly outrageous and violent in lawbreaking behavior, favor a "get tough" position.

In reaction to rising rates of juvenile crime, citizens and public officials have called for an end to the mollycoddling of young offenders and a beginning of a return to harsh methods of punishment. Ohmart (1976) pointed out that public fear is generally directed toward types of crime that threaten the person of the victim and the security of the home and that these types of crime are most often committed by young males. Liazos (1974), detailing the history of public anxiety over youth crime, quoted nineteenth-century expressions of fear: "little vagrants . . . deserve our censure, and a regard for our property, and the good of society, requires that they should be stopped, reproved and punished. . . . It should be remembered that there are no dangers to the value of property, or the permanency of our institutions, so great as those from the existence of such a class of vagabond, ignorant, ungoverned children" (p. 4).

This concern over youth crime has continued and, in recent years, increased. We are now in a very conservative political period and acompanying that period are definite beliefs about retribution, incapacitation, and punishment which are already affecting juvenile policy at the local, state, and federal levels. Thus, even though delinquency rates are declining nationally, in some states juvenile incarceration rates are increasing (see Krisberg, Schwartz, Litsky, and Austin, 1986; Krisberg, Litsky, Schwartz, 1984; Krisberg and Schwartz, 1983). This increase can be attributed in part to changes in juvenile reform legislation. The latest Supreme Court ruling upholding the widespread practice of detaining juvenile delinquents before trial specifically to prevent them from committing crimes is a recent case in point. Other legislative reforms are calling for more mandatory sentencing and more determinate sentencing for juveniles, lowering of the upper age of juvenile jurisdiction, less strict requirements for waiver of a juvenile to an adult court, and greater access to juvenile records (see Ohlin, 1983: 466).

We have indicated that public anxieties and fear of crime have yielded some of the political and legislative responses to date regarding the best way to handle juvenile crime. However, many criminologists continue to argue that only a small number of juveniles commit the greatest proportion of violent offenses. Getting tough on all young offenders may therefore be a case of overkill. John Rector (1978), a former administrator of the Office of Juvenile Justice and Delinquency Prevention, commented: "[It] is vital that the lurid publicity given to a small percentage of violent youth not distract us from the reality of a system whose wide net catches predominantly nonoffenders (abandoned or neglected) and minor delinquents who are subjected to unwarranted detention and incarceration grossly disproportionate to the harm, if any, generated by their conduct" (p. i).

Regardless of the validity of public concern over juvenile crime, civic anxiety has had its effect on juvenile justice processing and reform. The State of Washington recently revamped its juvenile court system "away from traditional concerns and toward a just or 'just deserts' approach" (*More on Washington State Juvenile Justice Reform*, 1983: 1). In an effort to control juvenile crime, during the summer of 1983 Detroit Mayor Coleman Young imposed a juvenile curfew designed to clear the streets of everyone under age 18 by 10 P.M. on weeknights and 11 P.M. on weekends. Curfew violators faced misdemeanor penalties as strict as 30 days in jail or fines as high as $500 ("Mayor Imposes Juvenile Curfew," 1983).

More sweeping than changes in juvenile philosophy on a state level are those at the federal level. The National Advisory Committee for Juvenile Justice and Delinquency Prevention suggested that the federal government focus its efforts more specifically on the serious, violent, chronic delinquent and move away from programs to deinstitutionalize status offenders, separate juveniles from adult offenders, and prevent juveniles at risk from becoming delinquents ("Serious Juvenile Crime," 1984). As a result, support for community correctional programs and diversionary agencies may continue to decline. Likewise, the number of juvenile cases transferred to adult courts is increasing in some jurisdictions, and the number of juveniles held in adult jails is on the rise ("Major Issues," 1982; "Sentenced Prisoners Under 18," 1980; Bartollas and Miller, 1978; "Coming: Tougher Approach to Juvenile Violence," 1976; Rector, 1978).

The "Hands Off" Approach. Sociologists and criminologists who are opposed to the arguments of the "get tough, lock 'em up" stance are often referred to as "hands off" advocates. The punishment and "hands off" mentalities are similar because their criticisms of the juvenile justice system charge it, in different ways, with the creation, rather than the control, of delinquency. Obviously, the first of these positions holds that lack of punishment and deterrent measures results in higher rates of juvenile crime, especially serious crime. The logic of the second position, influenced by labeling theory, is considerably different: The idea that the juvenile justice system is implicated in the creation of delinquency through the labeling of young offenders is a major theme of 1967 and 1973 federal commission reports and 1968 and 1974 federal delinquency laws.

According to the President's Commission (1967c), the labeling of young offenders as "delinquents" may become an albatross around their necks, propelling juveniles into more frequent and more serious delinquency: "The evidence suggests that official response to the behavior in question may initiate processes that push the misbehaving juveniles toward further delinquent conduct, and, at least, make it more difficult for them to enter the conventional world" (p. 417). As the juvenile becomes isolated from ordinary life, his or her association with other delinquents may increase, and this increased contact with other deviants can bring about the transmission of delinquent skills and attitudes from child to child.

The labeling, or "hands off," perspective has generated several concrete recommendations for changes in the control of delinquency. Sociologists and criminologists who advocate a labeling approach think that these changes will eventually result in the reduction of recidivism among juvenile offenders. They propose that involvement of juvenile offenders in official processing should be minimal. Whenever possible, status and minor offenders should be released or referred to social service agencies. If more intervention in the child's life is absolutely necessary, the child should be sent to nonresidential, day treatment programs, foster homes, or group homes. To avoid stigmatization as a labeled delinquent and contamination by more serious offenders, institutionalization should be reserved for the most hardened offenders. Under no circumstances should status offenders find themselves committed to residential facilities (Goins, 1978; Liazos, 1974; Vorenberg and Vorenberg, 1976).

The Social Conditions Approach.   According to the social conditions approach, a juvenile's environment can virtually guarantee deviant life styles in some neighborhoods. Crime is considered to be an essential part of the early experiences of slum youth. Although the "hands off" logic can be traced to labeling theory, the social conditions position is linked to anomie, cultural disorganization, and subcultural theories.

An Office of Juvenile Justice and Delinquency Prevention report on the serious juvenile offender suggested that "[P]overty, minority status in the context of racial discrimination, the value orientations of particular youth cultures, and institutions and values surrounding youth populations are importantly related with the propensity toward violent crime" (Zimring, 1978: 26). This document does, however, point out that poverty rates have been declining over the past decade, while rates of violent delinqency have increased. Also, the "poverty breeds crime" explanation cannot account for the *lack* of delinquency among most poor youth. Lemert (1971) agreed with this observation, charging that "social conditions theories offer no explanation as to why delinquency develops in some youths exposed to poverty but not in others" (p. 72). Thus, there are some important limitations to the position that certain social situations produce delinquency.

Nevertheless, many control programs are based on the notion that poverty and slum life correlate with, and indeed cause, delinquency. If communities produce crime, it is only logical to argue that changes in communities are necessary to prevent and control crime. The President's Commission (1967c), for instance, called for broad reforms in slum conditions. A National Advisory Commission report (1967b), recommending amelioration in lower class environments, tied lack of conventional opportunity to delinquency: "The

child who views a future of deadend jobs or continuous unemployment cannot be expected to learn to respect the moral codes of society" (p. 80). For this reason, the committee proposed improvements in jobs, housing, social services, schooling, general economic conditions, and family relationships as means of increasing the lower class youth's "stake in conformity" and decreasing his or her likelihood of delinquency. Current federal efforts through the OJJDP similarly seek to strengthen basic socializing institutions such as the family and school to reduce deinquency.

JUVENILE JUSTICE POLICY

The suggestions of advocates of each of the four approaches to delinquency control are certain to influence the juvenile justice system of the future. Officials in the federal government have listened especially to the recommendations of "hands off" and social conditions theorists in formulating policies for the juvenile justice system over the past few years. This has been evidenced, for instance, by the endorsement of such policies by the Juvenile Justice Task Force of the National Advisory Commission on Criminal Justice Standards and goals (1976b) and the standards issued by the Institute of Judicial Administration and the American Bar Association (1980). It was assumed by many that these standards, or model laws, would shape juvenile justice in the 1980s and the decades beyond. The recent conservative trend taking place in the country now suggests, however, that many of the liberal views and policies regarding the handling of juveniles and the juvenile justice system may not be forthcoming.

Part of the problem regarding the shift in orientation toward the treatment of juvenile offenders, as we have indicated, originates from the public's perception of the amount of crime and fear of victimization in their lives. While much of this fear is unfounded and has no basis in fact, history reveals to us that such trends are cyclical in American society (see Kluegel, 1983; Laub, 1983). During these conservative periods, the prevailing orientation toward crime is usually "get tough." Recent recommendations from the National Advisory Committee for Juvenile Justice and Delinquency Prevention indicate that future federal efforts toward juvenile crime will be directed more toward the violent juvenile offender and not toward the status offender, as in the past. In addition to the changing political climate, it is argued by some critics that the federal government should not advocate any national juvenile justice policy, but rather should limit its activities to those crime control efforts that it can do better than the states (Olson-Raymer, 1984).

In this section we will examine the efforts of the federal government to influence and guide juvenile justice. We will also discuss the role of standards committees in setting guidelines for the operation of components of the juvenile justice system. Finally, we will discuss the future of the most important part of the juvenile justice system, the juvenile court.

The Federal Government Mandate

During the 1960s, the federal government exhibited a strong interest in juvenile delinquency. This interest began during the administration of President John F. Kennedy, an administration dedicated to improving the destiny of the nation's youth. In 1961 President Kennedy signed the Juvenile Delinquency and Youth Offenses Act, which "created the machinery for a federally coordinated program against juvenile delinquency" (Phelps, 1976: 23). The act was administered by the Office of Juvenile Delinquency and Youth Development, an agency of the U.S. Department of Health, Education, and Welfare.

In 1965 President Lyndon B. Johnson, continuing the domestic policy thrusts of the Kennedy administration, appointed the Commission on Law Enforcement and the Administration of Justice. Its purpose was to study the reasons for rising crime rates and to suggest solutions to the growing crime problem in the United States. The commission focused on four major areas relating to crime: the police, the courts, the corrections system, and an assessment of the magnitude of the crime problem. The commission also addressed the special problem area of juvenile delinquency and youth crime.

The commission made recommendations aimed at combatting rising crime rates and supporting certain changes in the processing of offenders. Within the reports published by the commission are two somewhat contradictory themes. The first was that the juvenile justice system, as well as the larger criminal justice system, was guilty of stigmatizing offenders and thus aggravating involvement in crime. The second theme was that delinquency could and should be prevented through the improvement of social conditions. More specifically, the commission advocated diversion, decarceration, and decriminalization. Diversion involves outright release of offenders or their placement in alternative programs; decarceration involves the removal of offenders from large correctional institutions; and decriminalization involves the establishment of separate programs for handling status and criminal offenders (Empey, 1978; Phelps, 1976; President's Commission, 1967c).

One major piece of legislation that resulted from the 1967 President's Commission reports was the Juvenile Delinquency Prevention and Control Act of 1968. Another was the Omnibus Crime Control and Safe Streets Act of 1968. These federal laws "were intended to help state and local communities establish new agencies or to make existing agencies more effective in dealing with youth" (Bartollas and Miller, 1978: 175). Also created by the acts were two federal agencies, the Law Enforcement Assistance Administration (LEAA) and the Office of Juvenile Delinquency and Youth Development. Funding for the LEAA greatly surpassed funding for the Office of Juvenile Delinquency (Bartollas and Miller, 1978; Juvenile Delinquency Prevention and Control Act, 1968; Omnibus Crime Control and Safe Streets Act, 1968; Phelps, 1976).

Aside from establishing new federal agencies, the two 1968 laws were intended to "encourage State and units of general local government to prepare and adopt comprehensive plans based upon their evaluation of State and local problems of law enforcement" (Omnibus Act, 1968: 1) and to "make grants to any State or local public agency to assist in preparing or revising such a plan" (Juvenile Control Act, 1968: 1). The technique by which state and local governments were to be helped in the implementation of comprehensive plans was the **block grant program**. After states, cities, and counties drafted joint plans for improvements in law enforcement and criminal justice, the states were given block grants to put the plans into action. In 1970 the Safe Streets Act was amended to require that part of the block grants be used for community correction and treatment programs. Other changes in the 1968 acts produced the Juvenile Delinquency Prevention Act of 1972. The 1972 law emphasized delinquency prevention rather than control.

Another commission was appointed to study crime and criminal justice in 1973. This commission was appointed during the administration of Richard M. Nixon and was named the National Advisory Commission on Criminal Justice Standards and Goals. "The goal of the commission was to formulate national criminal justice standards and goals for crime reduction and prevention at the state and local level; it was funded by the Law Enforcement Assistance Administration" (Phelps, 1976: 296–297). In 1973 six volumes that summarized the conclusions of the group's studies were published. The main themes of the National Advisory Commission recommendations related to justice, but a secondary point was the role of the justice system in the creation, not the prevention, of crime and delinquency. Following the lead of the 1967 commission, the 1973 commission also advocated diversion, decriminalization, and decarceration (Empey, 1978; National Advisory Commission on Criminal Justice Standards and Goals, 1973; Phelps, 1976).

To realize these aims, the Juvenile Justice and Delinquency Prevention Act of 1974 was passed by Congress. It centered on the following goals:

(1) to develop and implement effective methods of preventing and reducing juvenile delinquency; (2) to develop and conduct effective programs to prevent delinquency, to divert juveniles from the traditional juvenile justice system and to provide critically needed alternatives to institutionalization; (3) to improve the quality of juvenile justice in the United States; (4) to increase the capacity of State and local governments and public and private agencies to conduct effective juvenile justice and delinquency prevention and rehabilitation programs and to provide research, evalu-

ation, and training services in the field of juvenile delinquency prevention. (Title I, Juvenile Justice and Delinquency Prevention Act, 1974)

Responsibility for carrying out the provisions of the 1974 act was given to LEAA through the newly created Office of Juvenile Justice and Delinquency Prevention (OJJDP). Funding for state juvenile justice programs was tied to state success in separating adult and juvenile offenders, taking status offenders out of juvenile institutions, and establishing diversion, prevention, and community-based programs.

In 1978 fifty states were reported in compliance with the 1974 act and were therefore eligible to receive grant money administered by the Office of Juvenile Justice and Delinquency Prevention. According to the 1978 LEAA annual report, about $62 million in formula grants was awarded in 1978, and about $28 million, or 45 percent of the total, went to programs aimed at removing status offenders from juvenile institutions. Grant money was also used for diversion, prevention, and alternative schools, as well as advanced techniques of monitoring delinquency and programs designed to combat delinquency and handle offenders (U.S. Department of Justice, Law Enforcement Assistance Administration, 1979).

Changes in political leaders at the federal level, beginning with Jimmy Carter's presidency, led to major reorganization of federal crime control agencies. Targeted for total reform by Senator Edward Kennedy and eventually eliminated by President Carter under the Justice System Improvement Act (JSIA), LEAA was replaced in 1979 by the Office of Justice Assistance, Research and Statistics (OJARS), the National Institute of Justice (NIJ), and the Bureau of Justice Statistics. With less financial support, OJJDP became a separate entity operating under the general authority of the U.S. attorney general; the signing of the second JJDP Act in 1980 ensured the operation of OJJDP at least through 1984. However, some major modifications in its budget were made. Chief among the items cut were maintenance of effort monies earmarked for juvenile justice and delinquency prevention programs. Such a modification signaled the beginning of a new era in the federal government's orientation toward juvenile crime control.

Based on a general dissatisfaction with past efforts and programs aimed primarily at the status offender, the National Advisory Committee for Juvenile Justice and Delinquency Prevention reviewed the federal response to juvenile crime and decided that emphasis should now be on the serious, violent, chronic delinquent. In its 1984 report, *Serious Juvenile Crime—A Redirected Federal Effort,* the committee argued that although a small number of youths account for a large proportion of serious juvenile crime, the Juvenile Justice Act as it is now worded diverts most federal funds to objectives such as community-based programs that have little relation to the criminal aspects of delinquency. The committee indicated that the mandates which shaped the OJJDP were based on faulty notions about how best to prevent and control delinquency. Rather than focusing major efforts toward status offenders or juveniles at risk, future efforts should "deal directly and decisively with that small core of youth who are responsible for much of the nation's crime" (*Serious Juvenile Crime,* 1984: 1). The committee criticized the OJJDP for spending most of its funds, some \$120 million between 1975 and 1980, on discretionary "special emphasis" programs and virtually none (less than \$12,000) on the violent juvenile offender. A series of recommendations was made by the National Advisory Committee.

The first recommendation echoed the committee's views that "Any federal effort in the area of juvenile delinquency should focus primarily on the serious, violent, or chronic offender" (p. 9). The commission reasoned that the federal initiative needs to find a balance between helping youth and protecting society. Since chronic or serious delinquents are harmful to themselves and to society, the best thing that can be done is to reduce numerically the crimes they commit and decrease the probability that they will spend their adult lives in jail.

A second recommendation sets the tone for the federal government's future involvement in juvenile crime control. It was recommended that the federal government should be active in only a select number of areas in the fight against delinquency, in which it can perform better than states and localities. In particular, it should limit its activities to the following:

1. Meaningful research designed to teach us what works best, with what youth, and when;

2. Limited, specific demonstration of projects with credible evaluation components;

3. Dissemination of information;

4. Training and technical assistance.

More specifically, the committee recommended that demonstration, research, and training focus on such areas as methods for dealing with the serious offender, serious crimes in the nation's schools, victims of serious crimes, neighborhood control of delinquency, the impact of substance abuse on juvenile crime, youth gang activity, closer links between the juvenile and adult criminal justice systems, and family roles in dealing with serious juvenile crime.

As a third recommendation, the commission suggested that "The federal government should assist states, local governments, and private and public agencies in dealing with problems of delinquency, [and] not impose its latest beliefs about best practice." The rationale of previous federal policy regarding juvenile delinquency was premised on a therapeutic model of delinquency prevention and control, a model that, according to the committee, lost much of its empirical emphasis in the 1960s and early 1970s. Unsubstantiated theory governed policy and had little impact on juvenile crime. It was particularly recommended that the federal government not mandate to the states any rules for dealing with juvenile crime. Funds given to the various states and localities should not be made contingent upon compliance with complicated and often rigid standards. Such a decision, it was reasoned, would give the states a large degree of latitude to deal with juvenile crime in their own best ways.

A final recommendation stated that "The federal initiative should include all offenders identified as juveniles by state law, even if prosecuted in the adult criminal justice system" (p. 13). In their search for solutions to serious juvenile crime, so reasoned the commission, most states have enacted legislation requiring that youth who commit certain serious crimes be prosecuted in adult criminal courts. In the past, OJJDP has taken a hands-off approach toward delinquents processed in adult courts. In order to make juvenile and adult systems work together more effectively, all youth, regardless of place of prosecution, are to be included in programs.

While no one can predict what the future holds, especially when it comes to predictions about federal involvement in any types of programs, the recommendations from the members of the National Advisory Committee for Juvenile Justice and Delinquency Prevention warn us that major changes regarding national involvement in juvenile justice are on the horizon, if not already here. The basic themes in the federal government's policies about delinquency did not change much from the 1960s and 1970s. The federal government emphasized the prevention of delinquency and the reform of the juvenile justice system. The premises of the "hands off" approach to delinquency control strongly influenced the federal government to remove young offenders, especially status offenders, from the official processing of the juvenile court and the rehabilitation programs of juvenile institutions. Even though numerous critics suggested that many diversion programs simply widened the nets and drew in children who otherwise would not have contact with official agencies, by and large the rehabilitative ideal predominated in the vast majority of programs at state and local levels.

Only time will tell if the themes of the past two decades will be completely refocused toward more of a "get tough" approach in the future (see Regnery, 1986). Some people suggest that we are in a period of the "decline of the rehabilitative ideal" and that a "punishment mentality," not unlike times during our past, is upon us (Allen, 1980).

Juvenile Justice Standards

As part of its effort to direct the future of juvenile justice in the United States, the federal government, through the Law Enforcement Assistance Administration, funded the planning, drafting, and publishing of standards, or guidelines, for the juvenile justice system. In 1971 the Institute of Judicial Administration, a nonprofit organiza-

tion located at the New York University School of Law, began to plan a juvenile justice standards project. In 1973 the American Bar Association (ABA) decided to co-sponsor the program, and an IJA-ABA Joint Commission on Juvenile Justice Standards was appointed to direct the project. The IJA-ABA Joint Commission consisted of outstanding members of the legal, academic, and corrections communities. Funding was procured from LEAA and several other organizations (Nuernberger and Dvizend, 1977).

The committees drafting the standards reviewed the workings of the juvenile justice system and made recommendations concerning the rights of juveniles, societal approaches to the problems of juveniles, and methods for dealing with juveniles when society intervenes in the lives of children and their families. They wrote a twenty-three volume set of standards. In 1979 the House of Delegates of the American Bar Association reviewed the twenty-three volumes and approved seventeen of them. According to David Gillman, director of the joint commission standards project, the approved standards established the following principles:

—Right to jury trials in juvenile courts

—Open hearings

—Right to counsel at all crucial stages of the proceeding

—Elimination of *parens patriae* as the guiding philosophy of dispositions

—Severe limits on detention, treatment, or other intervention prior to adjudication

—Limitation of transfers to adult court to only the most serious offenses

—Enunciation of rights of minors vis-à-vis courts and parents

—Transformation of disposition hearings into full adversarial proceedings rather than informal fact-finding proceedings

—Elimination of prior social history as a factor in disposition

("ABA Endorses 17 Volumes of Juvenile Justice Standards; 6 Volumes Withdrawn," 1979: 1–2)

Volumes dealing with court organization, non-criminal misbehavior, juvenile probation, and delinquency sanctions were not approved (or were later modified) by the ABA House of Delegates. These volumes contained standards some legal experts thought would too drastically affect the juvenile court and "the philosophy which protects youngsters from society and society from dangerous juveniles" (p. 2). Two volumes dealing with abuse and neglect and schools and education were also withdrawn from a vote pending rewriting. The abuse and neglect volume was later revised extensively and eventually accepted.

The ABA standards, as originally conceived, sought to accomplish four goals:

1. To achieve uniformity in the law for juveniles, thus making it more uniform and predictable;

2. To develop linkages within the juvenile justice system by defining the roles of various individuals and agencies and avoiding duplication of effort and enhancing coordination;

3. To reexamine accepted concepts and premises underlying current laws in light of existing research;

4. To codify relevant case law, administrative decisions, selected statutory innovations, and fundamental principles approved in the standards in a form readily translatable into a model act or acts. (Flicker, 1982: 3)

It is difficult to evaluate the impact the ABA standards have had on juvenile justice in the various states. Since the standards are merely advisory, there is no way to ensure their acceptance. One early reference in an ABA publication, *How to Implement Criminal Justice Standards*, indicated that there were 3,664 citations of the criminal justice standards (sentencing alternatives and procedures, trial by jury, pleas of guilty, joiner and severance, criminal appeals and postconviction remedies) in appellate court decisions as of November 1975. More recent evidence of the influence of the standards is not easily available. We can surmise, however, that the standards have

been adopted in a piecemeal fashion by the states, rather than in any comprehensive or uniform manner. This policy more or less reflects the OJJDP's stance toward the standards. It failed exclusively to endorse the standards, but would "direct attention to the role of the standards [when they achieved] some of the major objectives of the JJDP Act" (Flicker, 1982: 287).

More than likely, the ABA standards will continue to be used in a model capacity for states contemplating changes in their juvenile justice systems. Generally, the standards reflect a growing trend toward making juvenile courts and procedures more similar to adult criminal courts and procedures. Given this tone, some of the standards follow the conservative philosophy prevailing today regarding the "crackdown" on serious juvenile crime.

Juvenile Court

Since the 1960s, the federal government and juvenile justice standards committees have supported several reforms in the juvenile justice system. The reforms of decarceration and diversion are related to the dispositions given to the cases of juveniles by the juvenile courts. The reforms of due process and decriminalization are related to the nature of juvenile court processing. The push to decriminalize status offenders and to extend due process of law to all court proceedings stems from contemporary dissatisfaction with the treatment philosophy of the juvenile court. In its fervor to cure delinquents, the juvenile court is thought by many criminologists and lawyers to violate basic constitutional rights and to involve status offenders unfairly in court processing.

One critic of the juvenile court has written: "Based upon the humanitarian ideology and good intentions of the child-savers, the American juvenile court system was developed: a system in which legal safeguards were considered unnecessary since the objectives were remedial and therapeutic—not punitive as in the case of the criminal law" (Shah, 1975: 7). With evidence that treatment has failed, the cries for a return to traditional concepts of due process are mounting. The U.S. Supreme Court has ruled that the juvenile court must guarantee certain rights to the juvenile—the right to counsel, the privilege against self-incrimination, the right to a full hearing when transfer to the adult criminal courts is contemplated, the right to confront and cross-examine witnesses, and the right to determination of the case based on proof beyond a reasonable doubt.

The recent Supreme Court decision in *Schall v. Martin* (1984), declaring that arrested juveniles may be placed in preventive detention if there is a serious risk that they may commit another crime before court appearance, has, according to many, eroded some of the rights juveniles obtained in the past. The Court reasoned, however, that the ruling was basically protective rather than punitive. In fact, the Supreme Court has repeatedly emphasized that past rulings regarding juvenile offenders affect only the adjudication hearing in which the juvenile court determines whether the child has committed a delinquent act. Therefore, the Justices argue that Court decisions have not altered the basic philosophy of the juvenile justice system, which embodies the concepts of rehabilitation and individualized justice (Hutzler, 1982: 29).

Public outcries concerning serious juvenile crime have prompted many states to seek ways to remove certain juveniles from the "protection" of the juvenile court and to deal with them as criminals in the adult courts. This has been accomplished in two ways: Certain offenders are excluded from the juvenile court's original jurisdiction so that they must initially be charged in criminal court, with provisions that some cases may be referred to the juvenile court (this is known as **reverse waiver**). However, in some states certain offenders are totally excluded from juvenile court jurisdiction at any point and must be prosecuted in criminal court.

From one perspective, these jurisdictional changes appear to be completely in opposition to the philosophy of the juvenile court, with its historical emphasis on rehabilitation. Certain classes of juveniles, by the commission of their crimes, are excluded from the protection of the juvenile court. However, from another perspective, for the majority of juvenile offenders—those not committing extremely serious crimes—the juvenile court continues to afford these youths individualized treatment and protection. Statutory provisions for the surrender of jurisdiction by the juvenile court over juveniles unamenable to rehabilitation are included in most state codes. Many original juvenile codes gave the juvenile court judge, based on his or her discretion, the authority to waive any offender for criminal prosecution.

From all indications, recent substantive changes in the law have not eroded the protections of juveniles. Changes in the concept of proper court functioning have obviously been influenced by the arguments of children's rights advocates, and there is every indication that this legal rights movement will continue. The standards sponsored by the IJA-ABA recommend determinate sentencing for juveniles to prevent excessive lengths of incarceration, sanctions based on the seriousness of the offenses to eradicate the arbitrariness of court decisions, and the right to counsel to limit unbridled judicial discretion. Although these modifications are proposed for the cases of juveniles judged suitable for court jurisdiction, it is also suggested that a large portion of the court clientele who commit less serious offenses or status offenses do not belong in the juvenile court at all.

Another trend in court processing is, then, the decriminalization of status offenders. Advocates of this idea contend that juveniles who commit acts that would not be criminal if they were committed by adults do not belong in the courts or in correctional institutions. The decriminalization movement has gained momentum in recent years. Some states have retained juvenile court jurisdiction over status offenders and have attempted to avoid labeling and stigmatization of noncriminal offenders through the use of such designations as PINS, MINS, CHINS, FINS, and JINS, acronyms referring to persons, minors, children, families, and juveniles in need of supervision (INS). Some critics fear that these names may create a problem, as they could come to connote the same images as the previous designation of "delinquency."

In some states, status offenders are handled in separate courts. In other states, institutionalization of status offenders is prohibited. The prohibition on institutionalization of status offenders is aimed at ending the historically harsher treatment of status offenders in terms of sentence length and also at preventing the contamination of status offenders by more experienced and hardened criminal youth. These suggestions and requirements for official processing of status offenders have received widespread support.

SUMMARY AND CONCLUSION

In the 1980s and beyond, attempts to prevent and control delinquency will almost certainly be shaped in part by the relative position of the young in the population structure of the United States. As the proportion of the population below the age of 18 declines, delinquency may become a less visible social problem for certain segments of the population. However, for other segments of the population, primarily blacks and Hispanics, who are growing at a proportionately faster rate than Caucasians, delinquency may spiral. The emergence of these "majority minority" youth, coupled with an aged white population, poses many challenges for policy-makers.

Despite the competition or inconsistency in theorizing about causes of delinquency, one area of consensus always remains constant. This involves the belief that delinquency can never be prevented or controlled unless basic socializing institutions such as the family, the school, and the church are included. Even though it may be redundant to repeat this rather time-worn assertion, we continue to emphasize that these institutions *must* be strengthened. Dramatic changes in the American family structure involving single-parent families, joint-custody families, and blended families, to mention a few, will no doubt affect children in both positive and negative ways. Much of our theorizing about the family is based on traditional conceptions of a family life that are not typical. Juvenile court judges and other practitioners must familiarize themselves with alternative family structures. Similarly, the American school system has found itself top-heavy with culturally and economically disadvantaged children who do not respond to traditional curriculums and educational goals. In order to offset the inevitable

alienation of these youth and to offer them adequate life chances, dramatic changes in our policies and philosophies of education must be forthcoming, and soon. We see little evidence of this to date. Similarly, American churches have found themselves in a position of being criticized by today's youth as not being relevant. The religious institutions in our society have tremendous resources and must make themselves more meaningful in the lives of their young constituents.

The mass media, primarily the television industry, have increasingly found themselves in the unenviable position of being accused of precipitating or at least influencing delinquency in American society. The evidence regarding these charges remains controversial and inconclusive. There is no doubt, however, that children (and adults) in our society spend an inordinate amount of time watching television, much of which is violent. Similarly, television perceptions of reality depict a middle or upper class life style that many of its viewers will probably never achieve. The impact of this discrepancy, according to some social critics, may be alienation on the part of some youth which may at least be a precursor to delinquency, if not a cause in and of itself.

Another form of alienation may come from changes regarding information dissemination in American society. Evidence suggests that more and more people will be employed in jobs which create, process, and disseminate information. The new underclass in the future may be those individuals who are characterized as the information poor. Youth who are denied education and training in the new computer technology will obviously be at a severe disadvantage.

If opportunities for education and work and healthy development are not available to all sectors of the young population, the "us against them" mentality is likely to become more pressing rather than less.

Delinquency prevention programs focus on young people who have not yet committed delinquent acts or at least have not been arrested for committing delinquent acts. Many widely divergent activities have been called preventive of delinquency, but there is little evidence that any of these programs have accomplished the goal of stopping or inhibiting delinquent behavior. Despite the difficulty associated with measuring the effectiveness of prevention programs, delinquency prevention has been a major priority of the federal government. Although the federal government continues to work in this area, it has recently refocused its policies regarding violent or serious juvenile offenders. The Office of Juvenile Justice and Delinquency Prevention, for example, has stated that as of 1985 much of its effort and finances will be directed toward programs designed to deal with that small portion of juvenile offenders who commit violent criminal acts. This shift in policy is a major departure from past preventive efforts.

Control programs or policies, on the other hand, center on the child who has already come to the attention of juvenile justice authorities. At the turn of the century, the main approach to the control of delinquency was through the treatment of offenders. Delinquency was regarded as a disease, susceptible to treatment and cure through the expertise of professionals. Opposed to this approach was the view that the juvenile justice system mollycoddles criminals and needs to get tough on crime. Another perspective on the control of delinquency focuses on the inadequacies of the official system of handling young offenders. The effects of the juvenile justice system on the delinquent are regarded as worse than the "disease" itself. Other sociologists have argued that delinquency can be controlled only through an approach that seeks to improve the social conditions which appear to produce delinquency. Each of these approaches will no doubt play a part in how we deal with juvenile delinquency in the future.

In conclusion, we stress that neither the problems of the young nor the solutions to those problems are simple; nor are they independent of more general problems such as poverty, racism, and war. The future of adolescence and our ability to cope with adolescent problems, especially delinquency, depends heavily on our capacity to come to grips with these issues. There has always been the recognition that a society which forsakes its young forsakes its future; yet apart from the relatively few "lucky" youngsters, most American youth have not derived the full benefits from

advanced knowledge and technology. Now more than ever before in history, there is a social need to reintegrate the young into society and to improve the quality of life for the young. Now more than ever, our future depends on the young.

PROGRESS CHECK

1. What are the implications of current demographic trends for the future of delinquency? In particular, how does the majority-minority fit into this picture? (pp. 423–425)

2. Explain the concept of the *information society*. How might the information-poor be the "delinquents" of tomorrow? (pp. 425–432)

3. What do the text authors mean by the term *family forests*? Relate the consequences of this to the future of delinquency in American society. (pp. 427–428)

4. Discuss and evaluate the six-point set of recommendations made by social scientists for changes in U.S. educational policy. (pp. 428–429)

5. The authors suggest that organized religion has not done enough to help youth deal with complex problems in an ever-changing society. What do you envision the role of organized religion to be with respect to juvenile delinquency? (pp. 430–431)

6. Explain the difference between delinquency prevention and delinquency control; then differentiate among primary, secondary, and tertiary types of preventive efforts. (pp. 432–435)

7. Describe and compare the following programs: (a) Chicago Area Project; (b) Cambridge-Somerville Youth Study; (c) Boston Midcity Youth Project. (pp. 434–435)

8. Which of the four approaches to delinquency control do you think is the most prevalent

today, given the existing political climate? (pp. 435–439)

9. Discuss the changing role of the federal government in juvenile delinquency. What relatively recent change has occurred regarding the funding of projects for status offenders versus violent offenders? (pp. 439–443)

10. How have recent changes in state legislatures as a reaction to the public fear of serious juvenile crime affected the operation of juvenile courts? (pp. 444–446)

References

ABA endorses 17 volumes of juvenile justice standards; 6 volumes withdrawn. *Criminal Justice Newsletter,* February 26, 1979, pp. 1–8.

Abelson, H. I., & Fishburne, P. M. Non-medical use of psychoactive substances, 1975–76. In *Nationwide study among youth and adults.* Princeton, N.J.: Response Analysis Corporation, 1976.

Abrahamsen, D. *The psychology of crime.* New York: Columbia University Press, 1960.

Achenbach, T. M. The classification of children's psychiatric symptoms: A factor analytic study. *Psychological Monographs, 80,* Whole No. 615, 1966.

Adler, A. *The practice and theory of individual psychology.* Totowa, N.J.: Littlefield, Adams, 1959.

Adler, F. *Nations not obsessed with crime.* Littleton, Colo.: Rothman, 1984.

Adler, F. *Sisters in crime.* New York: McGraw-Hill, 1975.

Adler, R. et al., *The effects of television advertising on children.* Lexington, Mass.: Lexington Books, 1980.

Ageton, S. The dynamics of female delinquency, 1976–1980. *Criminology,* 1983, *21,* 555–584.

Ageton, S. S., & Elliott, D. S. *The Incidence of Delinquent Behavior in a National Probability Sample of Adolescents.* Boulder, Colo.: Behavioral Research Institute, 1979.

Agnew, R. Goal achievement and delinquency. *Sociology and Social Research,* 1984, 68, 435–451.(a)

Agnew, R. Autonomy and delinquency. *Sociological Perspectives,* 1984, 27, 219–240.(b)

Agnew, Robert. Appearance and delinquency, *Criminology;* 1984, 22, 421–441.

Ahlstron, W. M., & R. J. Havinghurst. *Four hundred losers.* San Francisco: Jossen-Barne, 1971.

Aichhorn, A. Wayward youth (E. Bryant, J. Deming, M. Hawkins, G. Mohr, E. Mohr, H. Ross, & H. Thun, Trans.). New York: Viking Press, 1948. (Originally published, 1925.)

Akers, R. Socioeconomic status and delinquent behavior: A retest. *Journal of Research in Crime and Delinquency,* 1964, *1,* 38–46.

Akers, R. *Deviant behavior: A social learning approach.* Belmont, Calif.: Wadsworth, 1973.

Akesson, H. O., Forssman, H., & Wallin, L. Chromosomes of tall men in mental hospitals. *Lancet,* 1968, *2,* 1040.

Alcabes, A., & Jones, J. Juvenile victim assistance programs: A proposal. *Crime and Delinquency,* 1980, 202–205.

Aldridge, J. W. *In the country of the young.* New York: Harper's Press, 1970.

Alers, M. S. Transfer of jurisdiction from juvenile to criminal court. *Crime and Delinquency,* 1973, *19,* 519–527.

Alexander, F., & Staub, H. *The criminal, the judge, and the public.* New York: Free Press, 1956.

Alfaro, J. *Report on the relationship between child abuse and neglect and later socially deviant behavior.* Buffalo: New York State Assembly Committee on Child Abuse, 1978.

Allen, F. A. *The decline of the rehabilitative ideal.* New Haven: Yale University Press, 1981.

Allen, H., & Simonsen, C. *Corrections in America.* Encino, Calif.: Glencoe, 1978.

Alexander, J. F., & Parsons, R. J. Short-term behavioral intervention with delinquent families: Impact on family process and recidivism. *Journal of Abnormal Psychology,* 1973, 9, 326–333.

Alper, B. Foreward. In Y. Bakal (Ed.), *Closing correctional institutions.* Lexington, Mass.: D. C. Heath, 1973.

Alper, B., & Boren, J. *Crime: An international agenda.* Lexington, Mass.: D. C. Heath, 1972.

American Psychiatric Association. *Diagnostic and Statistical Manual—Mental Disorders (DSM I).* Washington, D.C.: American Psychiatric Association, 1952.

American Psychiatric Association. *Diagnostic and statistical manual—Mental disorders* (2nd ed.) *(DSM II).* Washington, D.C.: American Psychiatric Association, 1968.

American Psychiatric Association. *Diagnostic and statistical manual—Mental disorders* (3rd ed.) *(DSM III).* Washington, D.C.: American Psychiatric Association, 1980.

Ames, W. *Police and community in Japan.* Berkeley: University of California Press, 1981.

Amir, M., & Berman, Y. Chromosomal deviation and crime. *Federal Probation,* 1970, *34,* 55–62.

Anderson, E. A. The "chivalrous" treatment of the female offender in the arms of the criminal justice system: A review of the literature. *Social Problems,* 1976, *23,* 350–357.

Anderson, E. A., & Spanier, G. B. Treatment of delinquent youth: The influence of the juvenile probation officer's perceptions of self and work. *Criminology,* 1980, *17,* 505–514.

Andison, S. F. TV violence and viewer aggression: Accumulation of study results, 1956–1976. *Public Opinion Quarterly,* 1977, *4.*

Andry, R. G. Faulty paternal and maternal child relationships, affection and delinquency. *British Journal of Delinquency,* 1957, *8,* 34–38.

Andry, R. G. Parental affection and delinquency. In M. E. Wolfgang, L. Savitz, & N. Johnson (Eds.), *The sociology of crime and delinquency.* New York: Wiley, 1962.

Ansbacher, H. S., & Ansbacher, R. R. (Eds.) *The individual psychology of Alfred Adler.* New York: Basic Books, 1956.

Antunes, G. E., & Hurley, P. A. The representation of criminal events in Houston's two daily newspapers. *Journalism Quarterly,* 1977, *54,* 4, 756–760.

Archer, D., & Gartner, R. *Violence and crime in cross-national perspective.* New Haven: Yale University Press, 1984.

Aries, P. *Centuries of childhood.* New York: Knopf, 1962.

Ariessohn, R. M. Offense vs. offender in juvenile court. *Juvenile Justice,* 1972, *23,* 17–22.

Armstrong, G. Females under the law—protected but unequal. *Crime and Delinquency,* 1977, *23,* 109–120.

Arnold, W. R. Race and ethnicity relative to other factors in juvenile court dispositions. *American Journal of Sociology,* 1971, *77,* 211–227.

Austin, J., & Krisberg, B. Wider, stronger and different nets: The dialectics of criminal justice reform. *Journal of Research in Crime and Delinquency,* 1981, *18,* 165–196.

Austin, R. Race, father-absence, and female delinquency, *Criminology,* 1978, *15,* 487–504.

Austin, R. L. Women's liberation and increases in minor, major, and occupational offenses, *Criminology,* 1982, *20,* 207–430.

Austrin, H. R., and Boenen, D. M. Interpersonal trust and severity of developmental behavior. *Psychological Reports,* 1977, *40,* 1075–1078.

Avanesov, G. *The principle of criminology.* Moscow: Progress Publishers, 1981.

Bachmuth, R., Miller, S. M., & Rosen, L. Juvenile delinquency in the daily press. *Alpha Kappa Delta,* 1960, 47–51.

Bad child or bad diet? *Prevention,* July 1979, pp. 65–71.

Bailey, W. C. Correctional outcome: An evaluation of 100 reports. *Journal of Criminal Law, Criminology and Police Science,* 1966, *57,* 153–160.

Bakal, Y. Closing Massachusetts institutions: A case study. In Y. Bakal (Ed.), *Closing correctional institutions.* Lexington, Mass.: Lexington Books, 1973.

Baker, D. Chromosome errors and antisocial behavior. In *Critical Reviews in Clinical Laboratory Sciences,* 1972, *3(1),* 41–101.

Baker, D., Telfer, M., Richardson, C., & Clark, G. Chromosome errors in men with antisocial behavior. *Journal of the American Medical Association,* 1970, *214,* 869–878.

Baker, J. W., & Spielberg, M. J. A description personality study of delinquency-prone adolescents. *Journal of Research in Crime and Delinquency,* 1970, *7,* 11–23.

Baker, R. K., & Ball, S. J. The two worlds of violence: Television and reality. In R. K. Baker and S. J. Nall (Eds.),

Violence and the media: A staff report to the national commission on the causes and prevention of violence. Washington, D.C.: U.S. Government Printing Office, 1969.

Bakwin, H., & McLaughlin, S. M. Secular increase in height: Is the end in sight? *Lancet,* Dec. 5, 1964, 195–196.

Balch, R. W. Deferred prosecution: The juvenilization of the criminal justice system. In P. G. Boesen & S. E. Grupp (Eds.), *Community-based corrections: Theory, practice and research.* Santa Cruz, Calif.: Davis, 1976.

Ball, R. Emergent delinquency in a suburban area. In T. Ferdinand (Ed.), *Juvenile delinquency: Little brother grows up.* Beverly Hills, Calif.: Sage Publications, 1977.

Ball, R., & Lilly, R. Female delinquency in a rural county. *Criminology,* 1976, *14,* 279–281.

Ball, R. A. Development of basic norm violation: neutralization and self concept within a male cohort. *Criminology,* 1983, *21,* 75–94.

Bandura, A. *Aggression: A social learning analysis.* Englewood Cliffs, N. J.: Prentice-Hall, 1973.

Bandura, A. *Social learning theory.* Englewood Cliffs: Prentice Hall, 1977.

Bandura, A., D. Ross, & S. Ross. Imitation of film-mediated aggressive models. *Journal of Abnormal and Social Psychology,* 1963, *66,* 3–11.

Bandura, A., & Walters, R. H. Dependency conflicts in aggressive delinquents. *Journal of Social Issues,* 1958, *14,* 52–65.

Bandura, A., & Walters, R. H. *Social learning and personality development.* New York: Holt, Rinehart and Winston, 1963.

Bannikov, S. G. Sbornik postanovlonii plenuma verkhounogo suda. SSSR. (Collection of Resolutions of the Plenum of the Supreme Court of the U.S.S.R.) Moscow: *Izvestia,* 1974.

Bardwick, J. M., & Douvan, E. Ambivalence: the socialization of women. In J. Bardwick (Ed.), *Readings on the psychology of women.* New York: Harper & Row, 1972.

Baron, R., & Feeney, F. *Preventing delinquency through diversion: The Sacramento County Probation Department 601 Diversion Project—A second year report.* Davis, Calif.: Center on Administration of Criminal Justice, University of California, 1973.

Barrile, L. G. Television and attitudes about crime. Ph.D. dissertation, Dept. of Sociology, Boston College, 1980.

Bartollas, C. *Correctional treatment: Theory and practice.* Englewood Cliffs, N. J.: Prentice-Hall, 1985.

Bartollas, C. *Juvenile delinquency.* New York: Wiley, 1985.

Bartollas, C., & Miller, S. J. *The juvenile offender: Control, correction and treatment.* Boston: Allyn & Bacon, 1978.

Bartollas, C., Miller, S. J., & Dinitz, S. *Juvenile victimization: the institutional paradox.* New York: Wiley, 1976.

Barton, W. H. Discretionary decision-making in juvenile justice. *Crime and Delinquency,* 1976, *22,* 470–480.

Bashilov, B. O knuliganstve kek prestupnom yavlinii, ne predusmotrennyn zakonom. (Hooliganism as a criminal phonomenon not envisioned by the law) *Journal of the Ministry of Justice, 2,* 1913.

Bassiouni, C. Terrorism, law enforcement and the mass media: Perspectives, problems, prospects. *The Journal of Criminal Law and Criminology*, 1981, *72*.

Bassiouni, M. C., & Savitski, V. M. *The criminal justice systems of the U.S.S.R.* Springfield, Ill.: Chas. Thomas, 1979.

Batchford, R. *Not guilty—A defense of the bottom dog.* New York: A. and C. Boni, 1913.

Bealer, R., Willits, F. and Maida, P. *Rural youth in crisis: Facts, myths, and social change.* Washington, D.C.: United States Department of Health, Education and Welfare, 1965.

Beasley, R. W., & Antunes, G. The ecology of urban crime: An ecological analysis. *Criminology*, 1974, *11*, 439–461.

Beattie, R. Criminal statistics in the United States—1960. *Journal of Criminal Law, Criminology and Police Science*, 1960, *51*, 49–65.

Beccaria, C. *Of crime and punishment* (Translated in 1764 by H. Paolucci). London: Alnon, 1963.

Becker, H. *Outsiders: Studies in the sociology of deviance.* New York: Free Press, 1963.

Behar, D., and Steward, M. A. Aggressive conduct disorders of children. *Acta Psychiatrica Scandinavia*, 1982, *65*, 210–20.

Beirne, P. Empiricism and the critique of Marxism on law and crime. *Social Problems*, 1979, *26*, 373–385.

Bell, D. The return of the sacred? The argument on the future of religion. *British Journal of Sociology*, 1977, *28*, 419–449.

Bell, R. Q. Stimulus control of parent or caretaker behavior by offspring. *Developmental Psychology*, 1971, *4*, 63–72.

Bell, S. M., & Answorth, M. Infant crying and maternal responsiveness. *Child Development*, 1972, *43*, 1171–1190.

Bellah, R. N. Religion and legitimation in American republic. *Society*, 1978, 16–23.

Belson, W. *Television violence and the adolescent boy.* Westmead, England: Saxon House, 1978.

Belson, W. A. *The development of a procedure for eliciting information from boys about the nature and extent of their stealing.* London: London School of Economics and Political Science, Survey Research Center, 1970.

Benedict, R. *Patterns of culture.* Boston: Houghton Mifflin, 1934.

Benedict, R. Continuities and discontinuities in cultural conditioning. *Psychiatry*, 1938, *1* 161–167.

Beng, D., & Shichor, D. Methodological and theoretical issues in juvenile diversion: Implications for evaluations. In D. H. Kelly (Ed.), *Deviant behavior: Readings in the sociology of deviance.* New York: St. Martin's, 1979.

Bennett, T. The social distribution of criminal labels. *British Journal of Criminology*, 1979, *19*.

Berezin, E. P. Comparative analysis of the U.S. and Japanese juvenile justice system. *Juvenile and Family Court Journal.* 1982, *33*, 4.

Berger, P. L. 'A great revival' coming for America's churches. *U.S. News and World Report*, April 11, 1977, pp. 70–72.

Berger, P., & Luckman, T. *The social construction of reality.* Garden City, N. Y.: Anchor Books, 1967.

Berkowitz, L. Violence in the mass media. In L. Berkowitz (Ed.), *Aggression: A psychological analysis.* New York: McGraw-Hill, 1962.

Berman, L. *New creations in human beings.* New York: Doubleday, 1938.

Berman, S. Antisocial character disorder. In R. S. Cavan (Ed.), *Readings in juvenile delinquency.* Philadelphia: Lippincott, 1964.

Bernard, T. The distinction between conflict and radical criminology. *The Journal of Criminal Law and Criminology*, 1981, *72*, 362–379.

Bernard, T. J. Control criticisms of strain theories: An assessment of theoretical and empirical adequacy. *Journal of Research in Crime and Delinquency*, 1984, *21*, 353–372.

Berne, E. *Transactional analysis in psychotherapy.* New York: Grove Press, 1961.

Bernstein, B. *Class codes and controls: Theoretical studies towards a sociology of language.* New York: Schocken, 1975.

Bernstein, S. *Youth on the streets: Work with alienated youth groups.* New York: Associated Press, 1964.

Berry, B. J. L., & Kasarda, J. D. *Contemporary urban ecology.* New York: Macmillan, 1977.

Berscheid, E., Walster, E., & Bohrnstedt, G. The happy American body: A survey report. *Psychology Today*, 1973, *7*, 119–131.

Berzensky, M. D. Formal reasoning in adolescence: An alternative view. *Adolescence*, 1978, *13*, 279–290.

Beschner, G. M., & Friedman, A. S. (Eds.). *Youth drug abuse.* Lexington, Mass.: Lexington Books, 1979.

Best, F. *Flexible Life Scheduling: Breaking the education-work-retirement lockstep.* New York: Praeger, 1980.

Bettelheim, B. *The children of the dream.* New York: Macmillan, 1969.

Biderman, A. D., Johnson, L. A., McIntyre, J., & Weir, A. *Report of the District of Columbia on victimization and attitudes toward law enforcement.* (Field Surveys I, President's Commission on Law Enforcement and the Administration of Justice). Washington, D.C.: U.S. Government Printing Office, 1967.

Biderman, A. D., & Reiss, A. J., Jr. On exploring the dark figure of crime. *Annals of the American Academy of Political and Social Science*, 1967, *374*, 369–374.

Billingsley, A. *Black families in white America.* Englewood Cliffs, N. J.: Prentice-Hall, 1968.

Binder, A., & Geis, G. A popular argumentation in criminology: Juvenile diversion as rhetoric. *Crime and Delinquency*, 1984, *30*, 309–333.

Birns, B. Individual differences in human neonates' responses to stimulation. *Child Development*, 1965, *36*, 249–256.

Biron, L., & LeBlanc, M. Family components and home-based delinquency. *British Journal of Criminology*, 1977, *17*, 157–168.

Bittner, E. *The functions of the police in modern society: A review of background factors, current practices and possible role models.* (U.S. Department of Health, Education and Welfare, National Institute of Mental Health, Center for Studies of Crime and Delinquency). Washington, D.C.: U.S. Government Printing Office, 1970.

Bittner, E. The police on skid row: A study of peace keeping. *American Sociological Review*, 1967, *32*, 699–715.

Black, D. J. The production of crime rates. *American Sociological Review*, 1970, *35*, 733–748.

Black D. J. & Reiss, A. J., Jr. Police control of juveniles, *American Sociological Review*, 1970, *35*, 63–77.

Blackburn, R. Dimensions of hostility and aggression in abnormal offenders. *Journal of Consulting and Clinical Psychology*, 1972, *38*, 20–26.

Blacker, E., Demone, H., & Freeman, H. Drinking behavior of delinquent boys. *Quarterly Journal of Studies on Alcohol*, 1965, *26*, 223–237.

Blackmore, J. The Relationship between self reported delinquency and official convictions among older boys. *British Journal of Criminology*, 1974, *14*.

Black's Law Dictionary. St. Paul, Minn.: West Publishing, 1979.

Blane, H. T., & Hewitt, T. Alcohol and youth and analysis of the literature: Final report of NIAAA, DHEW, 1977.

Bloch, H. A., & Niederhoffer, A. *The gang: A study in adolescent behavior*, New York: Philosophical Library, 1958.

Blomberg, T. G. Diversion and accelerated social control. *Journal of Criminal Law and Criminology*, 1977, 68, 274–282.

Blomberg, T. G. *Where to go from here with juvenile diversion.* Paper presented at The Tenth World Congress of Sociology, Mexico City, 1982.

Blomberg, J. G. Widening the net: An anomaly in the evaluation of diversion programs. In M. W. Klien & K. S. Teilmann (Eds.), *Handbook of criminal justice evaluation.* Beverly Hills, Calif.: Sage, 1980.

Blumer, H., & Hauser, P. *Movies, delinquency and crime.* New York: Macmillan, 1933.

Blumer, H. *Symbolic interactionism.* Englewood Cliffs, N.J.: Prentice-Hall, 1969.

Boesen, P., & Grupp, S. (Eds.). *Community based corrections: Theory, practice and research.* Santa Cruz, Calif.: Davis, 1976.

Bogen, D. Beating the rap in juvenile court. *Juvenile and Family Court Journal*, 1980, *31*, 19–22.

Bohm, R. M. Radical criminology: An explication. *Criminology*, 1982, 19, 4, 565–589.(a)

Bohm, R. M. Reflexivity and critical criminology. In G. F. Jensen (Ed.) *Sociology of delinquency: Current issues.* Beverly Hills, Calif.: Sage, 1982.(b)

Boldyrev, N. I. The study and prevention of juvenile delinquency. *The Soviet Review*, May 1961 (translated from *Sovetskoe gosudarstvo i provo*, #2, 1960).

Bolton, F. G., Reich, J. W., & Gutieries, S. E. Delinquency patterns in maltreated children and siblings. *Victimology*, 1977, *2*, 349–357.

Bonger, W. *An introduction to criminology*, London: Methuen, 1936.

Bonomo, T. A., & Wenger, M. G. *A critique of radical criminology on surplus population: An examination of Quinney's thesis.* Paper presented at the annual meetings of the American Society of Criminology, Dallas, Texas, 1978.

Bookin, H., Weiner, N., and Horowitz, R. The end of youth gangs: Fad or fact? *Criminology*, 1983, *21*, 4, 585–602.

Bordua, D. J. Juvenile delinquency and "anomie": An attempt at replication. *Social Problems*, 1958, 6, 230–238.

Bouma, D. *Kids and cops: A study in mutual hostility.* Grand Rapids, Mich.: Eerdman, 1969.

Bowker, L., & Klein, M. W. Female participation in delinquent gang motivation. *Adolescence, 1980, 15.*

Bowker, L. H. *Women, crime and the criminal justice system.* Lexington, Mass.: Lexington Books, 1972.

Bowlby, J. *Forty-four juvenile thieves.* London: Bailliere, Tindall, 1946.

Braithwaite, J. The myth of social class and criminality reconsidered. *American Sociological Review*, 1981, 46, 36–57.

Brakel, S. J., & Rock, R. S. *The mentally disabled and the law.* Chicago: University of Chicago Press, 1971.

Brantingham, P. J., & Faust, F. L. A conceptual model of crime prevention. *Crime and Delinquency*, 1976, *22*, 284–296.

Breckinridge, S. P., & Abbott, E. *The delinquent child and the home.* New York: Arno Press, 1970.

Breed, A. F., & Voss, P. H. Procedural due process in the discipline of incarcerated juveniles. *Pepperdine Law Review*, 1978, *5*, 641–671.

Bremner, R. H. *Children and youth in America: A documentary history* (Vol. 1: 1600–1865; Vol. 2: 1866–1932). Cambridge, Mass.: Harvard University Press, 1971.

Brennan, T., Elliott, D. S., & Knowles, B. A. *Patterns of multiple drug use: A descriptive analysis of static types and change pattern, 1976–1978.* Boulder, Colo.: Behavioral Research Institute, April, 1981.

Bromberg, W. *The mold of murder: A psychiatric study of homicide.* New York: Grune & Straton, 1961.

Bromberg, W. *Crime and the mind.* Philadelphia: Lippincott, 1965.

Brown, C. *Manchild in the promised land.* New York: New American Library, 1965.

Brown, E. J., Flanagan, J., & McLeod, M. (Eds.) *Sourcebook of criminal justice statistics, 1983.* U.S. Department of Justice, Bureau of Justice Statistics. Washington, D.C.: U.S. Government Printing Office, 1984.

Brown, J. K. Adolescent initiation rites among preliterate peoples. In Robert Ginder (Ed.), *Studies in adolescence*, 2nd ed. London: MacMillan, 1969.

Brown, S. E. Social class, child maltreatment, and delinquent behavior. *Criminology*, 1984, *22*, 259–278.

Brown, W. K. Black female gangs as family extensions. *International Journal of Offender Therapy and Comparative Criminology*, 1978, *22*, 39–45.

Brown, W. M. C. Males with an XYY chromosome complement. *Journal of Medical Genetics*, 1968, *5*, 341–359.

Browning, C. J. Differential impact of family disorganization on male adolescents. *Social Problems*, 1960, 8, 37–44.

Bruce, A. A. One hundred years of criminological development in Illinois. *Journal of Criminal Law and Criminology*, 1933, 24, 11–49.

Buckner, J. C. and Chesney-Lind, M. Dramatic cures for juvenile crime: An evaluation of a prisoner-run delinquency prevention program. *Criminal Justice and Behavior*, 1983, 10, 227–247.

Buikhuisen, W. et al. Ongeregistreerde criminaliteitstest onder studenten. *Nederlands Tijdschrift voor Criminologie* (jun), 1976.

Bullington, B., Sprowls, J., Katkin, D., & Phillips, M. A critique of diversionary juvenile justice. *Crime and Delinquency*, 1978, 24, 59–71.

Burgdorff, K. *The national study of the incidence and severity of child abuse and neglect.* Washington, D.C.: National Center on Child Abuse and Neglect, 1981.

Burgess, R. L., & Akers, R. L. Differential association-reinforcement theory of criminal behavior. *Social Problems*, 1968, 14, 128–147.

Bursik, R. J. The dynamics of specialization in juvenile offenses. *Social Forces*, 1980, 58, 851–864.

Bursik, R. J. Delinquency Rates as Ecological Change. In J. Byrne and R. Sampson (Eds.) *The Social Ecology of Crime.* Beverly Hills, Calif.: Sage, 1984. (a)

Bursik, R. J. Urban dynamics and ecological studies of delinquency. *Social Forces*, 1984, 63, 393–413. (b)

Bursik, R. J. and Webb, J. Community change and patterns of delinquency. *American Journal of Sociology*, 1982, 88, 24–43.

Burt, C. *The young delinquent* (2nd ed.). New York: Appleton, 1929.

Buss, A. H. and Plomin, R. *A Temperamental Theory of Personality Development.* New York: Wiley, 1975.

Bynum, T. S. and Green, J. R. How wide the net? Probing the boundaries of the juvenile court. In S. H. Decker (Ed.), *Juvenile justice policy: Analyzing trends and outcomes.* Beverly Hills, Calif.: Sage, 1984.

Byrne, J. and Sampson, R. *The Social Ecology of Crime.* Beverly Hills, Calif.: Sage, 1984.

Caditz, S. Effect of a training school experience on the personality of delinquent boys. *Journal of Consulting Psychology*, 1959, 23, 501–509.

Caldwell, C. *Elements of phrenology.* Lexington, Ky.: A. G. Meriwether, 1824.

Caldwell, R. G. The juvenile court: Its development and some major problems. In R. Giallombardo (Ed.), *Juvenile delinquency: A book of readings.* New York: Wiley, 1972.

Canon, B. C., & Kolson, K. Rural compliance with Gault: Kentucky, a case study. *Journal of Family Law*, 1971, 10, 300–326.

Canter, R. J. Sex differences in self-report delinquency. *Criminology*, 1982, 20, 373–393. (a)

Canter, R. J. Family correlates of male and female delinquency. *Criminology*, 1982, 20, 149–167. (b)

Cantwell, D. P., Mattison, R., Russell, A. T., & Will, L. A comparison of DSM II and DSM III in the diagnosis of childhood disorders. *Archives of General Psychiatry*, 1979, 36, 1227–28.

Caplan, N. S. Intellectual functioning. In H. C. Quay (Ed.), *Juvenile delinquency.* Princeton, N.J.: Van Nostrand, 1965.

Caplow, T., Bahr, H. M., & Chadwick, B. A. *All faithful people: Change and continuity in Middletown's religion.* Minneapolis: University of Minnesota Press, 1983.

Caplow, T., & Bahr, H. M. Half a century of change in adolescent attitudes: Replication of a Middletown survey by the Lynds. *Public Opinion Quarterly* 1979, 43, 1–17.

Caplow, T. R., Bahr, H., Chadwick, B., Reuben Hill, R., & Williamson, M. H. *Middletown families: Fifty years of change and continuity.* Minneapolis: University of Minnesota Press, 1982.

Caputo, D. V., & Mandell, W. Consequences of low birth weight. *Developmental Psychology*, 1970, 3, 363–83.

Carey, J. T., Goldfarb, J., Rowe, M., & Lowman, J. *The handling of juveniles from offense to disposition* (U.S. Department of Health, Education and Welfare). Washington, D.C.: U.S. Government Printing Office, 1967.

Carr, L. J. Most courts have to be substandard. *Federal Probation*, 1949, 13, 29–33.

Carter, R. M., & Klein, M. (Eds.). *Back on the street: The diversion of juvenile offenders.* Englewood Cliffs, N.J.: Prentice-Hall, 1976.

Carter, T. J. Juvenile court dispositions: A comparison of status and non-status offenders. *Criminology*, 1979, 17, 341–359.

Carter, T. J., & Clelland, D. *A critical model of juvenile corrections.* Paper presented at the meetings of the Southern Sociological Society, Atlanta, Georgia, 1977.

Carter, T. J., & Clelland, D. A neo-Marxian critique, formulation and test of juvenile dispositions as a function of social class. *Social Problems*, 1979, 27, 96–108.

Cartwright, D. S., Tomson, B., & Schwartz, H. *Gang delinquency.* Monterey, Calif.: Brooks/Cole Publishers, 1975.

Cavan, R. S. The concepts of tolerance and contraculture as applied to delinquency. *Sociological Quartery*, 1961, 2, 243–258.

Cavan, R., & Cavan, J. *Delinquency and crime: Cross cultural perspectives.* Philadelphia: Lippincott, 1968.

Cavan, R. S., & Ferdinand, T. N. *Juvenile delinquency* (3rd ed.). Philadelphia: Lippincott, 1975.

Cavanagh, J. R. The comics war. *Journal of Criminal Law and Criminology*, 1949, 40, 28–35.

Cavenagh, W. E. England and Wales. In V. Lorne Stewart (Ed.) *Justice and troubled children around the world* (Vol. 2). New York: New York University Press, 1981.

Cavior, N., & Howard, C. Facial attractiveness and juvenile delinquency among black and white offenders. *Journal of Abnormal Child Psychology*, 1973, 1, 203–213.

Cayton, C. E. Relationship of the probation officer and the defense attorney after Gault. In R. Giallombardo (Ed.), *Juvenile delinquency: A book of readings.* New York: Wiley, 1972.

Center for Studies of Crime and Delinquency. *Community based correctional programs: Models and practices* (Public Health Service Publication No. 2130). Washington, D.C.: U.S. Government Printing Office, n.d.

Cernkovich, S. A. Evaluating two models of delinquency causation: Structural theory and control theory. *Criminology,* 1978, *16,* 335–352.

Cernkovich, S. A., & Giordano, P. C. Delinquency, opportunity and gender. *Journal of Criminal Law and Criminology,* 1978, *70,* 145–151.

Census of Prisoners in State Correctional Facilities 1973. *National prisoner statistics, special report.* U.S. Department of Justice, LEAA, National Criminal Justice Information and Statistics Service, December 1976.

Chaffee, S. H., & J. M. McLeod. Adolescent television use in the family context. In G. S. Comstock and E. A. Rubinstein (Eds.), *Television and social behavior* (Vol. 3), pp. 149–172, 1972.

Chalidze, V. *Criminal Russia: Essays on crime in the Soviet Union.* New York: Random House, 1977.

Chambliss, W. J. A sociological analysis of the law of vagrancy. *Social Problems,* 1964, *12,* 67–77.

Chambliss, W. J. *Crime and the legal process.* New York: McGraw-Hill, 1969.

Chambliss, W. J. The saints and the roughnecks. *Society,* 1973, *2,* 24–31.

Chambliss, W. J. *Criminal law in action* (2nd ed.). New York: John Wiley and Sons, 1984.

Chambliss, W., & Mankoff, M. *Whose law, what order?* New York: John Wiley, 1976.

Chambliss, W. J., & Nagasawa, R. On the validity of official statistics: A comparative study of white, black and Japanese high school boys. *Journal of Research in Crime and Delinquency,* 1969, *6,* 71–77.

Chandler, M. J. Egocentrism and antisocial behavior: The assessment and training of social perspective-taking skills. *Developmental Psychology,* 1973, *9,* 326–333.

Charney, F. L. Inpatient treatment programs. In W. H. Reid (Ed.), *The psychopath: A comprehensive study of antisocial disorders and behaviors.* New York: Brunner/Mazel, 1979.

Chen, H., & Rossi, P. H. The multigoal, theory-driven approach to evaluation: A model linking basic and applied social services. *Social Forces,* 1980, *39,* 106–120.

Chesney-Lind, M. Judicial enforcement of the female sex role: The family court and the female delinquency. *Issues in Criminology,* 1973, *8,* 51–71.

Chesney-Lind, M. Judicial paternalism and the female status offender: Training women to know their place. *Crime and Delinquency,* 1977, *23,* 121–130.

Chesney-Lind, M. Juvenile delinquency: The sexualization of female crime. *Psychology Today,* July 1974, pp. 43–46.

Chesney-Lind, M. Young women in the arms of the law. In L. H. Bowker (Ed.), *Women, crime and the criminal justice system.* Lexington, Mass.: Lexington Books, 1978.

Chess, S. et al. Characteristics of the individual child's behavioral responses to the environment. *American Journal of Orthopsychiatry* 1959, *29,* 791–802.

Child abuse, incest connected to murder, split personalities. *The Times-Picayune,* November 4, 1984, A-30.

Children and the law. *Newsweek,* September 8, 1975, pp. 66–72.

Children in custody. See U.S. Department of Justice, Law Enforcement Assistance Administration, National Criminal Justice Information and Statistics Service, *Children in custody* entries.

Children in adult jails, Children's Defense Fund or the Washington Research Project, Inc., Washington, D.C., December, 1976.

Chilton, R. J. Continuities in delinquency area research: A comparison of studies for Baltimore, Detroit, and Indianapolis. *American Sociological Review,* 1964, *29,* 71–83.

Chilton, R. J. Criminal statistics in the United States. *Journal of Criminal Law and Criminology,* 1980, *71,* 56–67.

Chilton, R., & Marble, G. Family disruption, delinquent conduct, and the effect of sub-classification. *American Sociological Review,* 1972, *37.*

Chilton, R. J., & Spielberger, A. Is delinquency increasing? Age structure and the crime rate. *Social Forces,* 1971, *49,* 487–493.

Christiansen, K. O. A preliminary study of criminality among twins. In S. Mednick & K. O. Christiansen (Eds.), *Biosocial basis of criminal behavior.* New York: Gardner, 1977, pp. 89–108. (a)

Christiansen, K. O. A review of studies of criminality among twins. In S. Mednick and K. O. Christiansen (Eds.), *Biosocial basis of criminal behavior.* New York: Gardner, 1977, pp. 45–88. (b)

Christiansen, K. O. Threshold of tolerance in various population groups illustrated by results from Danish criminological twins study. In A. B. DeReuck and R. Porter (Eds.), *Ciba foundation symposium on the mentally abnormal offender.* London: Churchill Ltd., 1968, 107–116.

Christie, N. A study of self reported crime. In K. O. Christiansen (Ed.), *Scandinavian studies in criminology,* Volume 1. London: Tavistock, 1965.

Christie, N., Andenaes, J., & Skerbaekk, S. A study of self-reported crime. In K. O. Christiansen (Ed.), *Scandinavian studies in criminology* (Vol. 1). London: Tavistock, 1965.

Chute, C. L. The juvenile court in retrospect. *Federal Probation,* 1949, *13,* 3–8.

Cicourel, A. V. *The social organization of juvenile justice.* New York: Wiley, 1968.

Cicourel, A. V., & Kitsuse, J. I. The social organization of the high school and deviant adolescent career. In E. Rubington & M. S. Weinberg (Eds.), *Deviance: The interactionist perspective.* New York: Macmillan, 1968.

Clark, D. G., and Blankenburg, W. B. Trends in violent content in selected mass media. In G. A. Comstock and E. A. Rubinstein (Eds.), *Television and Social Behavior* (Vol. 1). Washington, D.C.: U.S. Government Printing Office, 1972.

Clark, J. P., & Haurek, E. Age and sex roles of adolescents and their involvement in misconduct. *Sociology and Social Research*, 1966, 50, 495–508.

Clark, J. P., & Tifft, L. Polygraph and inverview validation of self-reported deviant behavior. *American Sociological Review*, 1966, 31, 516–523.

Clark, J. P., & Wenninger, E. Socio-economic class and area as correlates of illegal behavior among juveniles. *American Sociological Review*, 1962, 27, 826–836.

Clarke, S. H. Getting 'em out of circulation: Does incarceration of juvenile offenders reduce crime? *Journal of Criminal Law and Criminology*, 1975, 65, 528–535.

Clayton, R. R., and Tuchfeld, B. S. The drug-crime debate: Obstacles to understanding and relationship. *Journal of Drug Issues*, 1982, 12, 153–166.

Cleckley, H. M. *The Mask of Sanity*. St. Louis: C. V. Mosby, 1955; 1964, (4th ed.).

Clemmer, D. Observations on imprisonment as a source of criminality. *Journal of Criminal Law, Criminology and Police Science*, 1951, 41, 311–319.

Clemmer, D. *The prison community*. Boston: Christopher, 1940.

Clifford, W. *Crime control in Japan*. Lexington, Mass.: Lexington Books, 1976.

Clinard, M. B. The process of urbanization and criminal behavior. *American Journal of Sociology*, 1942, 48, 202–213.

Clinard, M. B. Rural criminal offenders. *American Journal of Sociology*, 1944, 50, 38–45.

Clinard, M. B. *Sociology of deviant behavior* (4th ed.). New York: Holt, Rinehart and Winston, 1974 (a); 1968 (3rd ed.).

Clinard, M. B. Some implications of "the new criminology." *International Journal of Criminology and Penology*, 1974, 2, 85–91. (b)

Clinard, M. B. and Abbot, D. *Crime in developing countries: A comparative perspective*. New York: Wiley, 1973.

Clinard, M. B., & Meier, R. *Sociology of deviant behavior* (5th ed.). New York: Holt Rinehart and Winston, 1979.

Cline, V. B., Croft, R. G., & Courrier, S. Desensitization of children to television violence. *Journal of Personality and Social Psychology*, 1973, 27, 360–365.

Cloninger, C. R. & Guze, S. B. Female criminals: Their personal, familial and social backgrounds. *Archives of General Psychiatry*, 1970, 23, 554–558.

Cloward, R., & Ohlin, L. *Delinquency and opportunity: A theory of delinquent gangs*. New York: Free Press, 1960.

Coates, R. B., Miller, A. D. Neutralization of community resistance to group homes. In Y. Bakal (Ed.), *Closing correctional institutions*. Cambridge, Mass.: Ballinger Publishing, 1973.

Coates, R. B., Miller, A. D. & Ohlin, L. E. *Diversion in a youth correctional system*. Cambridge, Mass.: Ballinger, 1978.

Coffey, A. R. *Juvenile justice as a system*. Englewood Cliffs, N.J.: Prentice-Hall, 1974.

Cohen, A. C. *Delinquent boys: The culture of the gang*. Glencoe, Ill.: Free Press, 1955.

Cohen, A. K. *Deviance and control*. Englewood Cliffs, N.J.: Prentice-Hall, 1966.

Cohen, A. K. Middle class delinquency and the social structure. In E. W. Vaz (Ed.), *Middle class juvenile delinquency*. New York: Harper & Row, 1967.

Cohen, A. Y., & Santo, Y. Youth drug abuse and education: Empirical and theoretical considerations. In G. M. Beschner & A. S. Friedman (Eds.), *Youth drug abuse*. Lexington, Mass.: Lexington Books, 1979.

Cohen, L. E. *Pre-adjudicatory detention in three juvenile courts* (U.S. Department of Justice, Law Enforcement Assistance Administration). Washington, D.C.: U.S. Government Printing Office, 1975.

Cohen, L. E., & Kleugel, J. R. Determinants of juvenile court dispositions: Ascriptive and achieved factors in two metropolitan courts. *American Sociological Review*, 1978, 43, 162–176.

Cohen, L. E. & Kleugel, J. R. The detention decision: A study of the impact of social characteristics and legal factors in two metropolitan juvenile courts. *Social Forces*, 1979, 58, 146–161. (a)

Cohen, L. E. & Kleugel, J. R. Selecting delinquents for adjudication: An analysis of intake screening decisions in two metropolitan courts. *Journal of Research in Crime and Delinquency*, 1979, 16, 143–163. (b)

Cohen, S. *The drug dilemma*. New York: McGraw-Hill, 1976.

Coleman, J. *The adolescent society*. New York: Free Press, 1961.

Coleman, J. *Intimate relationship marriage and family*. Indianapolis: Bobbs Merrill, 1984.

Coleman, J. C., Butcher, J. N., & Carson, R. C. *Abnormal psychology and modern life*. Glenview, Ill.: Scott, Foresman, 1984; 1980.

Columbia Broadcasting System. *The Gerbner violence profile*. New York: CBS, 1977.

Columbia Broadcasting System. *Network violence tabulations for 1978–1979 season*. New York: CBS, 1980.

Columbia Broadcasting System, Inc. Office of Social Research. *Network prime-time violence tabulations for the 1976–77 season and instructions to coders*, 1977.

Colvin, M. & Pauly, J. A critique of criminology: toward an integrated structural Marxist theory of delinquency production. *American Journal of Sociology*. 1983, 89, 513–551.

Coming: Tougher approach to juvenile violence. *U.S. News & World Report*, June 7, 1976, pp. 65–67.

Comparative survey of juvenile delinquency: Part I: North American (1958); Part II: Europe (1952); Part III: Latin America (1950, 1965); Part IV: Asia and the Far East (1958); Part V: Middle East United Nations (1953, 1965). New York.

Comstock, G. Violence in television content: An overview. In J. Murray, E. Rubinstein, & G. A. Comstock (Eds.), *Television and Behavior*, (Vol. 2), 1982.

Comstock, G. et al. *Television and human behavior.* New York: Columbia University Press, 1978.

Comstock, G. A. & Rubinstein, E. A. *Television and social behavior.* Technical Reports to the Surgeon General's Scientific Advisory Committee on Television and Social Behavior (Vols. 1–5). Washington, D.C.: U.S. Government Printing Office, 1972.

Comte, A. *The positive philosophy of Auguste Comte.* London: J. Chapman, 1873.

Comte, A. *The positive philosophy.* New York: AMS Press Inc. 1974. (Originally published, 1855).

Conger, J. J., & Miller, W. C. *Personality, social class and delinquency.* New York: Wiley, 1966.

Conger, R. D. The child as victim: An emerging issue of child abuse. *Journal of Crime and Justice,* 1980, *3,* 35–63.

Connor, W. D. *Deviance in Soviet society: Crime, delinquency and alcoholism.* New York: Columbia University Press, 1972.

Conway, A., & Brogdan, C. Sexual delinquency: The persistence of a double standard. *Crime and Delinquency,* 1977, *23,* 131–135.

Cooley, C. H. *Human nature and the social order.* New York: Schocken, 1964. (Originally published, 1909).

Cortes, J. B., & Gatti, F. *Delinquency and crime: A biopsychological approach.* New York: Seminar Press, 1972.

Coser, L. A. *The functions of social conflict.* New York: Free Press, 1956.

Court-Brown, W. M., & Smith, P. G. Human population cytogenetics. *British Medical Bulletin,* 1969, *25,* 74–80.

Covington, J. Insulation from labeling: Deviant defenses in treatment. *Criminology,* 1984, *22,* 612–613.

Cowden, J., & Monson, L. An analysis of some relationships between personality adjustment, placement and post release adjustment of delinquent boys. *Journal of Research in Crime and Delinquency,* 1969, *6,* 63–70.

Coxe, S. Lawyers in juvenile court. *Crime and Delinquency,* 1967, *13,* 448–493.

Cressey, D. R. Application and verification of the differential association theory. *Journal of Criminal Law, Criminology and Police Science,* 1952, *43,* 43–52.

Cressey, D. R. The differential association theory and compulsive crimes. *Journal of Criminal Law, Criminology and Police Science,* 1954, *45,* 29–40.

Cressey, D. R. The state of criminal statistics. *National Probation and Parole Association Journal,* 1957, *3,* 230–241.

Cressey, D. R. The theory of differential association: An introduction. *Social Problems,* 1960, *8,* 2–6.

Cressey, P. G., & Thrasher, F. M. *Boys, movies, and city streets.* New York: Macmillan, 1933.

Crime and disruption in the schools: A selected bibliography. U.S. Department of Justice. Washington, D.C.: LEAA, U.S. Government Printing Office, Jan. 1979.

Criminal personality (*Lichnost' prestupnika*). Moscow, 1971.

Criminal victimization in urban schools. U.S. Department of Justice. Washington, D.C.: LEAA, U.S. Government Printing Office, 1979.

Criminology. Juriditcheskaya Literatura. Moscow: Publishing House, 1976.

Croll, P. The deviant image. Paper presented at British Sociological Association of Mass Communications Study Groups, March, 1974.

Cross, H., & Tracy, J. Personality factors in delinquent boys: Differences between blacks and whites. *Journal of Research in Crime and Delinquency,* 1970, *7,* 10–22.

Culbertson, R. G. The effects of institutionalization on the delinquent inmate's self concept. *Journal of Research in Crime and Delinquency,* 1975, *66,* 88–93.

Cullen, F. T., Golden, K. M., & Cullen, J. B. Sex and delinquency: A partial test of the masculinity hypothesis. *Crimnology,* 1979, *17,* 301–310.

Culver, J. Y., & Knight, K. L. Evaluating TV impressions of law enforcement roles. In R. Baker and F. A. Meyer (Eds.) *Evaluating Alternative Law-Enforcement Policies.* Lexington, Mass.: Lexington Books, 1979.

Cumberbatch, G., & Beadsworth, A. Criminals, victims and mass communications. In E. Viano (Ed.) *Victims and society.* Washington, D.C.: Visage Press, 1976.

Cumberbatch, G., & Howitt, D. Identification with aggressive television characters and children's moral judgements. In W. W. Hartup and J. DeWit (Eds.), *Determinants and origins of aggressive behavior.* The Hague: Mouton, 1974.(a)

Cumberbatch, G., & Howitt, D. Social communication and war: The mass media. In *La communication sociale et la guerre.* Bruxelles: Editions Bruylant, 1974.(b)

Cumberbatch, G., & Howitt, D. *Public anxiety: The mass media and war.* Paper presented at the First International Conference on Psychological Stress and Adjustments in Time of War and Peace. Tel Aviv, January, 1975.

Current population reports. Projections of the population of the United States, by age, sex and race: 1983 to 2080. U.S. Department of Commerce, May, 1984.

Dade County Public Safety Department. *Florida law enforcement handbook, 1977.* Miami: Board of County Commissioners, 1977.

Dahrendorf, R. *Class and conflict in industrial society.* Stanford, Calif.: Stanford University Press, 1959.

Daley, S. Youth gangs and fans after show. *New York Times,* July 24, 1982.

Dalgard, O. S., and Krinklon, E. Criminal behavior in twins. In L. D. Savitz and N. Johnston (Eds.), *Crime in society.* New York: Wiley, 1979.

Dalton, E. G. *The premenstrual syndrome.* Springfield, Ill.: Charles C. Thomas, 1964.

Dalton, E. G. Menstruation and crime. *British Medical Journals,* 1961, *2,* 1752–1753.

Dannefer, D., & Schutt, R. K. Race and juvenile justice processing in court and police agencies. *American Journal of Sociology,* 1982, *87,* 113–1132.

Danser, K. R., & Laub, J. H. Analysis of national crime victimization survey data to study serious delinquent behavior. Monograph Four. *Juvenile criminal behavior and its relation to economic conditions.* U.S. Department of Justice, LEAA, NIJJDP, May, 1981.

Darrow, C. *Crime, its causes and treatment.* Montclair, N.J.: Patterson Smith, 1972.

Darwin, C. *Origin of Species.* London: John Murray, 1859.

Darwin, C. *The descent of man and selection in relation to sex.* New York: Appleton, 1897. (The first edition was published in two volumes, 1871.)

Dasen, J. P. Cross-cultural Piagetian research: A summary. *Journal of Cross-Cultural Psychology,* 1972, *3,* 23–29.

Datesman, E., Scarpitti, F., & Stephenson, R. M. Female delinquency: An application of self and opportunity theories. *Journal of Research in Crime and Delinquency,* 1975, *12,* 107–123.

Davis, F. J. Crime news in Colorado newspapers. *American Journal of Sociology,* 1952, *57* (June), 325–330.

Davis, K. C. *Police discretion.* St. Paul, Minn.: West Publishing, 1975.

Davis, N. J. Labeling theory in deviance research: A critique and reconsideration. *Sociological Quarterly,* 1972, *13,* 447–474.

Davis, N. J. *Sociological construction of deviance.* Dubuque, Iowa: W. M. Brown, 1975.

Davis, S. M. *Rights of juveniles: The juvenile justice system.* New York: Clark Boardman, 1974, 1980, 1984.

Dean, C. W., & Reppucci, N. D. Juvenile correctional institutions. In D. Glaser (Ed.), *Handbook of criminology.* Chicago: Rand McNally, 1974.

Debs, E. V. *Walls and bars.* New York: Socialist Party of the U.S.A., 1927.

DeFleur, L. B. Biasing influences on drug arrest records: Implications for deviance research. *American Sociological Review,* 1975, *40,* 88–103.

DeFleur, M. L. *Social problems in American society.* Boston: Houghton Mifflin, 1983.

DeFleur, M. L. *Theories of mass communication* (2nd ed.). New York: David McKay, 1970.

DeFleur, M., & Ball-Rokeach, S. *Theories of mass communication.* New York: David McKay, 1975.

DeFleur, M., & Ball-Rokeach, S. *Theories of mass communication.* New York: Longman, 1982.

Deming, R. *Women: The new criminals.* Nashville: Thomas Nelson, 1977.

Demographic imperatives: Implications for educational policy. Report of the June, 1983 forum on "The Demographics of Changing Ethnic Populations and Their Implications for Elementary, Secondary, and Post-Secondary Educational Policy." American Council on Education, 1983.

Dentler, R. A., & Monroe, L. J. Social correlates of early adolescent theft. *American Sociological Review,* 1961, *26,* 733–743.

Department of Justice, Office of Juvenile Justice and Delinquency Prevention. *Fiscal year 1984 program plan,* n.d.

Department of Justice, Office of Juvenile Justice and Delinquency Prevention. *Fiscal year 1985 Program Plan,* n.d.

De Santis, C. An investigation of English convicts and criminal anthropology. *Journal of Criminal Law, Criminology and Police Science,* 1914–15, *5,* 228–240.

Deutschmann, P. J. *News-page content of twelve metropolitan dailies.* Cincinnati: Scripps-Howard Research Center, 1959.

DiChiara, A., & Galliher, J. F. Thirty years of deterrence research: Characteristics, causes, and consequences. *Contemporary Crises,* 1984, *8,* 243–263.

Dickson, D. Bureaucracy and morality: An organizational perspective on a moral crusade. *Social Problems,* 1968, *16,* 143–156.

Dinitz, S., & Pfau-Vincent, B. Self concept and juvenile delinquency. *Youth and Society,* 1982, *14, 2,* 133–158.

Ditchfield, J. A. *Police cautioning in England and Wales.* Home Office Research Study No. 37. London: HMSO, 1978.

Dobkin de Rios, M., & Smith, D. The function of drug rituals in human society: Continuities and changes. *Journal of Psychedelic Drugs,* 1977, *9,* 269–274.

Dod, S., Platt, T., Schwendinger, H., Shrank, G., & Takagi, P. The politics of street crime. *Crime and Social Justice,* 1976, *5,* 1–4.

Doering, C. H., et al. A cycle of plasma testosterone in the human male. *Journal of Clinical Endocrinology and Metabolism.* 1975, *40.*

Doerner, W. G., & Meade, A. On replication and the implications of findings of nonlinearity in crime research. In E. E. Flynn and J. P. Conrad (Eds.), *The new and the old criminology.* New York: Praeger, 1978.

Dohrenwent, B. P., Dohrenwent, B. S., Gould, M. S., Link, B., Neugebauer, R., & Wunsch-Hitzig, R. *Mental illness in the United States: Epidemiological estimate.* New York: Praeger, 1980.

Doleschal, E. Crime—Some popular beliefs. *Crime and Delinquency,* 1979, *25,* 1–8.

Doleschal, E., & Wilkins, L. *Criminal statistics* (U.S. Department of Health, Education and Welfare, National Institute of Mental Health, Center for Studies of Crime and Delinquency). Washington, D.C.: U.S. Government Printing Office, 1972.

Dominick, J. R., & Greenberg, B. S. Attitudes toward violence: The interaction of television exposure, family attitudes and social class. In G. A. Comstock and E. A. Rubinstein (Eds.), *Television and social behavior* (Vol. 3), pp. 314–335, 1972.

Dominick, J. R. Crime and law enforcement in the mass media. In C. Winick (Ed.), *Deviance and mass media.* Beverly Hills, Calif.: Sage, 1978.

Dominick, J. R. Crime and law enforcement on prime-time television. *Public Opinion Quarterly,* 1973, *37* (2), 241–250.

Douglas, J. (Ed.). *Deviance and respectability: The social construction of moral meanings.* New York: Basic Books, 1970.

Douglas, J. *Research on deviance.* New York: Random House, 1972.

Douglas, J. *Investigative social research.* Beverly Hills, Calif.: Sage, 1976.

Douglas, J. W., Ross, J., Hammon, J., & Milligan, D. G. Delinquency and social class. *British Journal of Criminology*, 1961.

Downes, P. *The delinquency solution.* London: Routledge & Kegan Paul, 1966.

Drabman, R. S., & Thomas, M. H. Does media violence increase children's toleration of real life aggression? *Personality and Social Psychology Bulletin*, 1974, *1*, 198–199.

Drapin, I., & Viano, E. *Victimology: A new focus.* Lexington, Mass.: D. C. Heath, 1974.

Dreger, R. M., Lewis, P. M., Rich, T. A., Miller, K. S., Reid, M. P., Overlade, D. C., Taffel, C., & Flemming, E. I. Behavioral classification project. *Journal of Consulting Psychology*, *28*, 1964, 1–13.

Drug abuse. Philadelphia: Smith, Klein and French Labs, 1968.

Dubin, R. Deviant behavior and social structure: Continuities in social theory. *American Sociological Review*, 1959, *24*, 147–164.

Duffee, D., & Fitch, F. *An introduction to corrections: A policy and systems approach.* Santa Monica, Calif.: Goodyear, 1976.

Dugdale, R. L. *The Jukes: A study in crime, pauperism, disease and heredity.* New York: Putnam, 1877.

Dulit, E. Adolescent thinking à la Piaget: The formal stage. *Journal of Youth and Adolescence*, 1972, *l*, 281–301.

Dunbar, R. Comparative analysis of psychological theories of delinquency. In U.S. Department of Justice, Law Enforcement Assistance Administration, National Institute for Juvenile Justice and Delinquency Prevention, *Preventing delinquency* (Vol. 1). Washington, D.C.: U.S. Government Printing Office, 1977.

Dunford, F. W., Osgood, D. F. and Weichselbaum, H. F. *National evaluation of youth service systems.* Boulder, Colo.: Behavioral Research Institute, 1981.

Dunham, H. W. The juvenile court: Contradictory orientations in processing offenders. In R. Giallombardo (Ed.), *Juvenile delinquency: A book of readings.* New York: Wiley, 1972.

Durkheim, E. *Elementary forms of the religious life.* New York: Macmillan, 1915.

Durkheim, E. *The division of labor in society* (G. Simpson, Trans.). New York: Free Press, 1933. (Originally published, 1893).

Durkheim, E. *The rules of sociological method* (G. E. Catlin, Ed., and S. A. Solovay & J. H. Mueller, Trans.). New York: Free Press, 1938. (Originally published, 1904.)

Durkheim, E. *Suicide* (J. A. Spaulding & G. Simpson, Trans.). New York: Free Press, 1951. (Originally published, 1897.)

Dussuyer, I. *Crime news: A study of 40 Ontario newspapers.* Toronto, Canada: Centre of Criminology, University of Toronto, 1979.

Duxbury, E. Violence by youth: Violence against youth. *American Behavioral Scientist*, 1980, *23*, 667–680.

Edwards, D. Specific objectives for the institutional treatment of juveniles. *Federal Probation*, 1971, *35*, 26–29.

Eigen, J. P. Punishing youth homicide offenders in Philadelphia. *Journal of Criminal Law and Criminology*, 1981, *72*, 1072–1093.

Eisner, V. Delinquency labeling. In D. H. Kelly (Ed.), *Delinquent behavior: Interactional and motivational aspects.* Belmont, Calif.: Dickenson, 1978.

Eldefonso, E. *Law enforcement and the youthful offender: Juvenile procedures.* New York: Wiley, 1967.

Elifson, K. W., Petersen, D., & Hadaway, K. Religiosity and delinquency: A contextual analysis. *Criminology*, 1983, *21*, 429–527.

Elkin, D. & Westly, W. The myth of adolescent culture. *American Sociological Review*. 1955, *20*, 680–684.

Elkind, D., & Weiner, I. *Development of the child.* New York: Wiley, 1978.

Elkind, D. *All grown up and no place to go: Teen-agers in crisis.* Reading, Mass.: Addison Wesley, 1984.

Elkind, D. Conceptual orientation shifts in childhood and adolescence. *Child Development*, 1966, *37*, 493–498.

Elkind, D. Egocentrism in adolescence. *Child Development*, 1967, *38*, 1025–1034.

Elkind, D., & Bowen, R. Imaginary audience behavior in children and adolescents. *Developmental Psychology*, 1979, *15* (1), 38–44.

Elkind, D. *A sympathetic understanding of the child six to sixteen.* Boston: Allyn and Bacon, 1971.

Elkind, D. *The hurried child.* Boston: Addison Wesley, 1981.

Elliott, D. S. Delinquency, school attendance and dropout. *Social Problems*, 1966, *13*, 307–314.

Elliott, D. S., & Ageton, S. Reconciling race and class differences in self reported and official estimates of delinquency. *American Sociological Review*, 1980, *45*.

Elliott, D. S., & Ageton, S. The relationship between drug use and crime among adolescents. Appendix to *Drug use and crime report of the panel on drug use and criminal behavior*, NIDA, 1976.

Elliott, D. S., Ageton, S., Huizinga, D., Knowles, B., & Canter, R. *The prevalence and incidence of delinquent behavior: 1976–1980.* Behavioral Research Institute. Boulder, Colo.: 1983.

Elliott, D. S., & Huizinga, D. Social class and delinquent behavior in a national youth panel: 1976–1980. *Criminology*, 1983, *21*, 149–177.

Elliott, D. S., & Voss, H. *Delinquency and dropout.* Lexington, Mass.: Lexington Books, 1974.

Ellis, L. Genetics and criminal behavior: evidence through the end of the 1970s. *Criminology*, 1982, *20*, 43–46.

Elmhorn, K. Study in self reported delinquency among school children in Stockholm. In K. O. Christiansen (Ed.), *Scandinavian Studies in Criminology* (Vol. 1). London: Tavistock, 1965.

Emerson, R. M. *Judging delinquents: Context and process in juvenile court.* Chicago: Aldine, 1969.

Empey, LaMar T. *American delinquency.* Homewood, Ill.: The Dorsey Press, 1978, 1982.

Empey, L. T. Juvenile justice reform: Diversion, due process and deinstitutionalization. In L. E. Ohlin (Ed.), *Prisoners in America*. Englewood Cliffs, N.J.: Prentice-Hall, 1973.

Empey, L. T., & Erickson, M. L. Hidden delinquency and social status. *Social Forces*, 1966, *44*, 546–554.

Empey, L. T., & Erickson, M. L. *The Provo experiment*. Lexington, Mass.: Lexington Books, 1972.

Empey, L. T., & Lubeck, S. G. *Explaining delinquency*. Lexington, Mass.: Lexington Books, 1971. (a)

Empey, L. T., & Lubeck, S. G. *The Silverlake experiment: Testing delinquency theory and community interaction*. Chicago: Aldine, 1971. (b)

Endell, R. V. Bioenvironmental criminology: Political and policy implications for crime prevention strategies. *Juvenile and Family Court Journal*, 1983, 41–62.

Ennis, P. *Criminal victimization in the United States: A report of a national survey* (Field Surveys 2, President's Commission on Law Enforcement and the Administration of Justice). Washington, D.C.: U.S. Government Printing Office, 1967.

Erickson, M. L. The group context of delinquent behavior. *Social Problems*, 1971, *19*, 114–129.

Erickson, M. L. The changing relationship between official and self-reported measures of delinquency: An exploratory-predictive study. *Journal of Criminal Law, Criminology and Police Science*, 1972, *63*, 388–395.

Erickson, M. L. Group violations and official delinquency: The group hazard hypothesis. *Criminology*, 1973, *11*, 127–160. (a)

Erickson, M. L. Group violations, socioeconomic status and official delinquency. *Social Forces*, 1973, *52*, 41–52. (b)

Erickson, M. L. Delinquency in a birth cohort: A new direction in criminological research. *Journal of Criminal Law and Criminology*, 1973, *64*, 362–367. (c)

Erickson, M. L., & Empey, L. T. Court records, undetected delinquency and decision making. *Journal of Criminal Law, Criminology and Police Science*, 1963, *54*, 456–469.

Erickson, M. L., & Empey, L. T. Class position, peers and delinquency. *Sociology and Social Research*, 1965, *49*, 268–282.

Erickson, M. L., & Jensen, G. Delinquency is still group behavior: Toward revitalizing the group premise in the sociology of deviance. *Journal of Criminal Law and Criminology*, 1977, *68*, 262–273.

Erikson, E. *Childhood and society*. New York: W. W. Norton, 1963.

Erikson, E. H. *Identity: youth and crisis*. New York: Norton, 1968.

Erikson, K. T. Notes on the sociology of deviance. *Social Problems*, 1962, *9*, 307–314.

Erikson, K. T. *Wayward puritans: A study in the sociology of deviance*. New York: Wiley, 1966.

Erikson, R., & Baranck, P. *The ordering of justice*. Toronto: University of Toronto Press, 1982.

Esbensen, Finn-Aage. Net widening? Yes and no: Diversion impact assessed through a systems processing rate analysis.

In Scott H. Decker (Ed.), *Juvenile justice policy: Analyzing trends and outcomes*. Beverly Hills, Calif:. Sage, 1984.

Essex-Cater, A. Boys in remand: A study of 367 cases. *British Journal of Criminology*, 1961, *2*, 132–148.

Evans, S., & Scott, J. The seriousness of crime cross culturally: The impact of religiosity. *Criminology*, 1984, *22*.

Eynon, T., Allen, H., & Reckless, W. C. Measuring impact of a juvenile correctional institution by perceptions of inmates and staff. *Journal of Research in Crime and Delinquency*, 1971, *18*, 93–101.

Eysenck, H. J. *Crime and personality*. Boston: Houghton Mifflin, 1964.

Eysenck, H. J. *Crime and Personality* (3rd ed.). London: Routledge and Kegan Paul, 1977.

Eysenck, H. J., & Eysenck, S. B. G. Psychopathy, personality and genetics. In P. O. Hare and D. Schalling (Eds.), *Psychopathic behavior*. New York: Wiley, 1978.

Eysenck, H. J., & Nias, D. K. B. *Sex, violence and the media*. New York: Harper & Row, 1978.

Eysenck, S. B. G., & Eysenck, H. J. Crime and personality: Item analysis of questionnaire responses. *British Journal of Criminology*, 1971, *11*, 49–62.

Fadely, J., & Hosler, V. *Confrontation in adolescence*, St. Louis, Mo.: C. V. Mosby, 1979.

Farrington, D. England and Wales. In M. W. Klein (Ed.), *Western system of juvenile justice*. Beverly Hills, Calif.: Sage, 1984.

Farrington, D. Self-reports of deviant behavior: Predictive and stable? *Journal of Criminal Law and Criminology*, 1973, *64*, 99–110.

Farrington, D. & Bennett, T. Police cautioning of juveniles. *British Journal of Criminology*, 1981, *21*, *2*.

Faulkner, W. *As I lay dying*. New York: Random House, 1930.

Federal Bureau of Investigation (FBI). *Uniform crime reports—1970*. Washington, D.C.: U.S. Government Printing Office, 1971.

Federal Bureau of Investigation (FBI). *Uniform crime reports—1976*. Washington, D.C.: U.S. Government Printing Office, 1977.

Federal Bureau of Investigation (FBI). *Uniform crime reports—1977*. Washington, D.C.: U.S. Government Printing Office, 1978.

Federal Bureau of Investigation (FBI). *Uniform crime reports—1978*. Washington, D.C.: U.S. Government Printing Office, 1979.

Federal Bureau of Investigation (FBI). *Uniform crime reports—1979*. Washington, D.C.: U.S. Government Printing Office, 1980.

Federal Bureau of Investigation (FBI). *Uniform crime reports—1982*. Washington, D.C.: U.S. Government Printing Office, 1983.

Federal Bureau of Investigation (FBI). *Uniform crime reports—1983*. Washington, D.C.: U.S. Government Printing Office, 1984.

Federal Bureau of Investigation (FBI). *Uniform crime reports—1984.* Washington, D.C.: U.S. Government Printing Office, 1985.

Feeney, F. The PINS problem—A "no fault" approach. In L. Teitelbaum & A. Goufh (Eds.), *Beyond control: Status offenders in juvenile court.* Cambridge, Mass.: Ballinger, 1977.

Feld, D. C. Delinquency careers and criminal policy: Just deserts and the waiver occasion. *Criminology,* 1983, *21,* 195–212.

Feld, D. C. Legislative policies toward the serious juvenile offender: On the virtues of automatic adulthood. *Crime and Delinquency,* 1981, *27,* 497–521.

Feldman, H. W. Ideological supports to becoming and remaining a heroin addict. *Journal of Health and Social Behavior,* 1968, *9,* 131–139.

Feldman, P. *Criminal behavior: A psychological analysis.* New York: Wiley, 1977.

Fenwick, C. R. *The criminal justice system of Japan. Curriculum and course development project: International criminal justice systems,* ACJS, 1984–85.

Fenwick, C. R. Juvenile court intake decision making: The importance of family affection. *Journal of Criminal Justice,* 1982, *10.*

Ferdinand, T. *Typologies of delinquency.* New York: Random House, 1966.

Ferdinand, T., & Luchterhand, E. G. Inner-city youth, the police, the juvenile court and justice. *Social Problems,* 1979, *17,* 519–527.

Ferguson, A. B., & Douglas, A. C. A study of juvenile waiver of rights. *San Diego Law Review,* 1970, *7,* 39–54.

Ferguson, T. *The young delinquent in his social setting.* London: Oxford University Press, 1952.

Ferri, E. The present movement in criminal anthropology apropos of a biological investigation in the English prisons (R. Ferrari, Trans.). *Journal of Criminal Law, Criminology and Police Science,* 1914–15, *5,* 224–227.

Ferri, E. *Criminal sociology* (J. Kelly & J. Lisle, Trans.). Boston: Little, Brown, 1917. (Originally published, 1892.)

Fersch, Jr., E. A. *Psychology and psychiatry in courts and corrections.* New York: Wiley, 1980.

Feuer, L.S. *The conflict of generations.* New York: Basic Books, 1969.

Feyerherm, W. The group hazard hypothesis: A reexamination. *Journal of Research in Crime and Delinquency,* 1980, *17,* 58–68.

Figlio, R. The biological bases of delinquent behavior. In U.S. Department of Justice, Law Enforcement Assistance Administration, National Institute for Juvenile Justice and Delinquency Prevention, *Preventing delinquency* (Vol. 1). Washington, D.C.: U.S. Government Printing Office, 1977.

Finckenauer, J. O. Scared crooked. *Psychology Today,* 1979, *12,* 6–11.

Fink, A. *The causes of crime: Biological theories in the United States 1800–1915.* Philadelphia: University of Pennsylvania Press, 1938.

Fishburne, P. M., Abelson, H. I., & Cisin, I. *National survey on drug abuse: Main findings (1980)* (U.S. Department of Health and Human Services, National Institute on Drug Abuse). Washington, D.C.: U.S. Government Printing Office, 1981.

Fisher, B. The juvenile court: Purpose, problems and promise. *Social Service Review,* 1960, *34,* 75–82.

Fisher, C. J., & Mawby, R. I. Juvenile delinquency and police discretion in an inner city area. *British Journal of Criminology,* 1982, *22,* 1.

Fixsen, D. L., Phillips, E. L., & Wolf, M. M. The teaching family model of group home treatment. In Y. Bakal (Ed.), *Closing correctional institutions.* Lexington, Mass.: D. C. Heath, 1973.

Flicker, B. D. *Standards for juvenile justice: A summary and analysis.* Cambridge, Mass.: Ballinger, 1982.

Florida Bureau of Criminal Justice Assistance. *Florida criminal justice system.* Tallahassee, Fla.: Author, n.d.

Florida Department of Health and Rehabilitative Services. *Analysis of the penetration of children into the adult criminal justice system in Florida.* Tallahassee: Youth Services Program Office, 1980.

Florida Department of Law Enforcement. *Crime in Florida—1975.* Tallahassee: Florida Department of Law Enforcement.

Florida Department of Law Enforcement. *Crime in Florida—1983.* Tallahassee: Florida Department of Law Enforcement.

Florida Statutes, Chapters 39.02; 39.03 (6)(a); 39.03 (6)(b); 812.021 (5)(g); 901.151. (1979).

Florida Statutes, Chapter 39, 1984.

Florida Statutes, Chapters 316.193; 396.

Ford, C. A. Homosexual practices of institutionalized females. *Journal of Abnormal and Social Psychology,* 1929, *23,* 442–448.

Foster, J. D., Dinitz, S., & Reckless, W. C. Perceptions of stigma following public intervention for delinquent behavior. *Social Problems,* 1972, *20,* 202–209.

Foucault, M. *Discipline and punishment: The birth of the prison* (Alan Sheridan, Trans.). New York: Vintage Books, 1979.

Fox, R. G. The XYY offender: A modern myth. *Journal of Criminal Law, Criminology and Police Science,* 1971, *62,* 59–73.

Fox, S. J. Juvenile justice reform: An historical perspective. *Stanford Law Review,* 1970, *22,* 1187–1239.

Fox, S. J. *Juvenile courts in a nutshell.* St. Paul, Minn.: West Publishing, 1977.

Frazier, C. Evaluation of youth services programs: Problems and prospects from a case study. *Youth and Society,* 1983, *14,* 335–362.

Frazier, F. F. *The negro church in America.* New York: Schocken, 1974.

Frease, D. E. Delinquency, social class and the schools. *Sociology and Social Research,* 1973, *57,* 443–459. (a)

Frease, D. E. Schools and delinquency: Some interesting processes. *Pacific Sociological Review,* 1973, *16,* 426–449. (b)

Freeman, J. S. England. In G. Cole, S. Frankowski, and M.

Gertz (Eds.), *Major criminal justice systems.* Beverly Hills, Calif.: Sage, 1981.

Freeman, D. *Margaret Mead and Samoa and the unmaking of an anthropological myth.* Cambridge, Mass.: Harvard University Press, 1983.

French, P. Violence in the cinema. In O. Larson (Ed.), *Violence and the mass media.* New York: Harper & Row, 1968.

Freud, A. *Ego and the mechanism of defense.* New York: International Universities Press, 1946.

Freud, A. *Psychoanalytic study of the child.* New York: International Universities Press, 1958.

Freud, S. *A general introduction to psychoanalysis* (S. Hall, Trans.). New York: Boni and Liveright, 1920.

Freud, S. *Civilization and its discontents* (J. Strachey, Trans.). New York: Norton, 1930/1961.

Freud, S. *A general introduction to psychoanalysis* (J. Riviere, Trans.). New York: Perma Books, 1953. (a) (Originally published, 1920)

Freud, S. *Three essays on the theory of sexuality.* London: Hogarth Press, 1953. (b) (Originally published, 1905)

Friday, P. International organizations: An introduction. In E. Johnson (Ed.), *International handbook of contemporary developments in criminology: General issues and the Americas.* Westport, Conn.: Greenwood Press, 1983.

Friday, P. Problems in comparative criminology: Comments on the feasibility and implication of research. *International Journal of Criminology and Penology,* 1971, *1.*

Friday, P. C., & Stewart, V. *Youth crime and juvenile justice: International perspectives.* New York: Praeger, 1977.

Friday, P., & Hage, J. Youth crime in postindustrial societies. *Criminology,* 1976, *14.*

Friedan, B. *The feminine mystique.* New York: Dell, 1963.

Friedenberg, E. *Coming of Age in America.* New York: Random House, 1965.

Friedenberg, E., & Becker, H. (Ed.). Adolescence as a social problem. In *Social Problems.* New York: Wiley, 1967.

Friedlander, K. *The psychoanalytic approach to juvenile delinquency.* London: Routledge & Kegan Paul, 1947.

Fromm, E. *Marx's concept of man.* New York: Frederick Ungar, 1970.

Furstenberg, F. K., & Nord, C. W. *The life course of children of divorce: Marital disruption and parental contrast.* Paper presented at the annual meeting of the Population Association of America, San Diego, 1982.

Garbarino, J. *Adolescent development: An ecological perspective.* Columbus, Ohio: Charles Merrill, 1985.

Gallagher, J. M., & Moppe, I. C. Cognitive development and learning. In J. F. Adams (Ed.), *Understanding Adolescence* (3rd ed.). Boston: Allyn and Bacon, 1976.

Galliher, J. F., & Walker, A. Bureau of Narcotics as moral entrepreneurs. *Crime and Social Justice,* 1978, *10,* 29–33.

Galvin, J., & Karacki, L. *Manpower and training in correctional institutions* (Staff Report of the Joint Commission on Correction and Manpower and Training). Washington, D.C.: U.S. Government Printing Office, December 1969.

Galvin, J., & Polk, K. Juvenile justice: Time for a new direction. *Crime and Delinquency,* 1983, *29,* 325–332.

Gandessy, R. P., Williams, J. K., Cohen, J., & Harwood, H. F. *Drugs and crime: A survey and analysis of the literature.* Washington, D.C.: U.S. Government Printing Office, May, 1980.

Gans, H. J. *The Levittowners: Ways of life and politics in a new suburban community.* New York: Pantheon, 1967.

Garfinkel, H. *Studies in ethnomethodology.* Englewood Cliffs, N.J.: Prentice-Hall, 1967.

Garmezy, N. DSM III: Never mind the psychologists; is it good for the children? *The Clinical Psychologist,* 1978, *31,* 1–6.

Garofalo, J. Radical criminology and criminal justice: Points of divergence and contact. *Crime and Social Justice,* 1978, *10,* 17–27.

Garofalo, J. Crime and the mass media: A selective review of research. *Journal of Research in Crime and Delinquency,* 1981, *18, 2.*

Garofalo, J., & Hindelang, M. J. *An introduction to the National Crime Survey* (Analytic Report Sd-UAD-4, U.S. Department of Justice, Law Enforcement Assistance Administration). Washington, D.C.: U.S. Government Printing Office, 1977.

Garofalo, R. Criminology (R. Wyness, Trans.). Boston: Little, Brown, 1914. (Originally published, 1885.)

Garret, M. *The policeman and his delinquent: Critical factors in police-juvenile encounters.* Unpublished doctoral dissertation, Washington State University, 1972.

Garret, M., & Short, Jr., J. F. Social class and delinquency: Predictions and outcomes of police-juvenile encounters. In P. Wickman and P. Whitten (Eds.), *Readings in criminology.* Lexington, Mass.: D. C. Heath, 1978.

Garrison, K. C. Physiological Development. In J. F. Adams (Ed.), *Understanding adolescence.* Boston: Allyn and Bacon, 1976.

Gastil, R. D. Homicide and a regional culture of violence. *American Sociological Review,* 1971, *36,* 412–427.

Gaze, S. B. *Criminality and psychiatric disorders.* New York: Oxford University Press, 1976.

Gazzaniga, M. S. *Fundamentals of psychology.* New York: Academic Press, 1973.

Geary, D. P. Nutrition, chemicals and criminal behavior: Some physiological aspects of anti-social conduct. *Juvenile and Family Court Journal,* 1983, 9–13.

Geis, G. Statistics concerning race and crime. *Crime and Delinquency,* 1965, *11,* 142–150.

Geller, A., & Boas, M. *The drug beat.* New York: McGraw-Hill, 1969.

Gelles, R. J. *Family violence.* Beverly Hills, Calif.: Sage, 1979.

Gendreau, P., & Ross, R. Correctional treatment: Some reconsiderations for effective intervention. *Juvenile and Family Court Journal,* 1983–84, 31–39.

Gerald, E. *News of crime: Courts and press in conflict.* Westport, Conn.: Greenwood Press, 1984.

Gerbner, G. Comments on measuring violence on television: The Gerbner Index. Bruce M. Owen. (Staff Research Paper, Office of Telecommunications Policy.) Annenberg School of Communications, University of Pennsylvania, 1972. (a)

Gerbner, G. Violence in television drama: Trends and symbolic functions. In G. A. Comstock and E. A. Rubinstein (Eds.), *Television and social behavior,* Vol. 1, pp. 28–187, 1972. (b)

Gerbner, G., & Gross, L., *Violence profile no. 6: Trends in network television drama and viewer conceptions of social reality: 1967–1973.* Unpublished manuscript. Annenberg School of Communications, University of Pennsylvania, 1974.

Gerbner, G., & Gross, L. Living with television: The violence profile. *Journal of Communication,* 1976, 26.

Gerbner, G., Gross, L., Eleey, M., Jackson-Beeck, M., Jeffries-Fox, S. and Signorielli, N. The Gerbner violence profile—An analysis of the CBS report. *Journal of Broadcasting,* 1977, 21, 280–286. (a)

Gerbner, G., Gross, L., Eleey, M., Jackson-Beeck, M., Jeffries-Fox, S., & Signorielli, N. One more time: An analysis of the CBS "Final comments on the violence profile." *Journal of Broadcasting,* 1977, 21, 297–303. (b)

Gerbner, G., Gross, L., M. F., Jackson-Beeck, M., Jeffries-Fox, S., & Signorielli, N. Violence profile no. 8: Trends in network television drama and viewer conceptions of social reality, 1967–1976. Philadelphia: Annenberg School of Communications, University of Pennsylvania, 1977. (c)

Gerbner, G., Gross, L., Morgan, M., & Signorielli, N. The "mainstreaming" of America: Violence profile no. 11. *Journal of Communication,* 1980, 30(3), 10–29. (a)

Gerbner, G., Gross, L., Morgan, M., & Signorielli, N. Some additional comments on cultivation analysis. *Public Opinion Quarterly,* 1980, 44, 408–411. (b)

Gerbner, G., Gross, L., Signorielli, N., & Morgan, M. Aging with television: Images on television drama and conceptions of social reality. *Journal of Communication,* 1980, 30(1), 37–47. (c)

Gerbner, G., Gross, L., Signorielli, J., Morgan, M., & Jackson-Beeck, M. Violence profile no. 10: Trends in network television drama and viewer conceptions of social reality. Philadephia: Annenberg School of Communications, University of Pennsylvania, 1979.

Gerbner, G., et al. *Violence Profile No. 9.* Philadelphia: Annenberg School of Communications, University of Pennsylvania, 1978.

Giallombardo, R. *The social world of imprisoned girls: A comparative study of institutions for juvenile delinquents.* New York: Wiley, 1974.

Giallombardo, R. *Society of women: A study of a women's prison.* New York: Wiley, 1966.

Gibbons, D. C. *Changing the lawbreaker: The treatment of delinquents and criminals.* Englewood Cliffs, N.J.: Prentice-Hall, 1965.

Gibbons, D. C. *Society, crime and criminal careers.* Englewood Cliffs, N.J.: Prentice–Hall, 1968.

Gibbons, D. C. *Delinquent behavior* (3rd ed.). Englewood Cliffs, N.J.: Prentice-Hall, 1981.

Gibbons, D. C., & Garabedian, P. Conservative, liberal and radical criminology. In C. Reasons (Ed.), *The criminologist: Crime and the criminal.* Pacific Palisades, Calif.: Goodyear, 1974.

Gibbs, J. P., & Martin, W. T. Toward a theoretical system of human ecology. *Pacific Sociological Review,* 1959, 2, 29–36.

Gibson, H. B. The factorial structure of juvenile delinquency: A study of self reported rates. *British Journal of Social Clinical Psychology,* 1971, 10.

Gillen, J. *The Wisconsin Prisoner: Studies in Crimogonsis.* Madison: University of Wisconsin, 1946.

Gillham, J. R., & Bersani, C. A. People or paperwork: An analysis of influences upon juvenile court personnel. *Criminology,* 1976, 13, 521–534.

Gilligan, C. *In a different voice.* Cambridge: Harvard University Press, 1983.

Gillis, J. K. *Youth and history.* New York: Academic Press, 1981.

Giordano, P. C. Girls, guys and gangs: The changing social context of female delinquency. *Journal of Criminal Law and Criminology,* 1978, 69, 126–132.

Giordano, P. C., & Cernkovich, S. A. On complicating the relationship between liberation and delinquency. *Social Problems,* 1979, 26, 467–481.

Giordano, P. C. The sense of injustice: An analysis of juvenile reactions to the justice system. *Criminology,* 1976, 14, 95–112.

Giovannoni, J. M. and Becerra, R. M. *Defining Child Abuse.* New York: Free Press, 1979.

Glaser, D. Criminality theories and behavioral images. *American Journal of Sociology,* 1955, 61, 433–444.

Glasser, W. *Reality of therapy.* New York: Harper & Row, 1965.

Glassner, B., Ksander, M., Berg, B., & Johnson, B. D. A note on the deterrent effect of juvenile vs. adult jurisdiction. *Social Problems,* 1983, 31, 219–221.

Glenn, N. D. *Cohort analysis.* Beverly Hills, Calif.: Sage, 1977.

Globetti, G. A comparative study of white and Negro teenage drinking in two Mississippi communities. *Phylon,* 1967, 28, 131–138.

Glow, R. A. Treatment alternatives for hyperactive children—A comment on 'problem children' and stimulant drug therapy. *Australian Journal of Psychiatry,* 1981, 15(2), 123–128.

Glueck, S., & Glueck, E. T. Delinquency prediction method reported highly accurate. *Roche Reports,* 1969, 6(15), 3.

Glueck, S., & Glueck, E. *Of delinquency and crimes: A panorama of years of search and research,* Springfield, Ill.: Charles C. Thomas, 1974.

Glueck, S., & Glueck, E. *Unraveling juvenile delinquency.* Cambridge, Mass.: Harvard University Press (for the Commonwealth Fund), 1950.

Glueck, S., & Glueck, E. *Physique and delinquency.* New York: Harper & Row, 1956.

Goddard, H. H. *The Kallikak family.* New York: Macmillan, 1912. (Reprinted by Arno Press, 1973.)

Goddard, H. H. *Feeblemindedness: Its causes and consequences.* New York: Macmillan, 1914.

Goddard, H. H. *Juvenile delinquency.* New York: Dodd, Mead, 1921.

Goffman, E. *Asylums: Essays on the social situation of mental patients and other inmates.* New York: Doubleday, 1961.

Gokhale, S. D., & Sohoni, N. K. The juvenile justice system in India. In *Juvenile justice: An international survey.* Publication #12, U.N. Social Defense Research Institute, Via Giulia 52, Rome, 1976.

Goins, S. The serious or violent juvenile offender: Is there a treatment response? In *The serious juvenile offender: Proceedings of a national symposium.* Washington, D.C.: U.S. Government Printing Office, 1978.

Gold, M. *Delinquent behavior in an American city.* Belmont, Calif.: Brooks/Cole, 1970.

Gold, M. Scholastic experiences, self-esteem and delinquent behavior: A theory for alternative schools. *Crime and Delinquency,* 1978, *24,* 3.

Gold, M. Undetected delinquent behavior. *Journal of Research in Crime and Delinquency,* 1966, *13,* 27–46.

Gold, M., & Mann, D. Delinquency as defense. *American Journal of Orthopsychiatry,* 1972, *42,* 463–477.

Gold, M., & Reimer, D. J. Changing patterns of delinquent behavior among Americans 13 through 16 years old: 1967–72. *Crime and Delinquency Literature,* 1975, *7,* 483–517.

Godfried, M. R. Feelings of inferiority and the depreciation of others: A research review and theoretical reformation. *Journal of Individual Psychology,* 1963, *19,* 27–48.

Goldman, N. *The differential selection of juvenile offenders for court appearance.* New York: National Research and Information Center, National Council on Crime and Delinquency, 1963.

Goldstein, Abraham. *The insanity defense.* New Haven: Yale University Press, 1970.

Goldstein, J. Police discretion not to invoke the criminal process: Low visibility decisions in the administration of justice. *Yale Law Journal,* 1960, 69, 543–594.

Goode, E. *Drugs in American society* (2nd ed.). New York: Knopf, 1984.

Goodman, P. *Growing up absurd: Problems of youth in the organized society.* New York: Vintage, 1960.

Gordon, D. M. Class and the economics of crime. In W. J. Chambliss and M. Mankoff (Eds.), *Whose law, what order?* New York: Wiley, 1976.

Gordon, L. *Sociology and American social issues.* Boston: Houghton Mifflin, 1978.

Gordon, R. A. Prevention, sentencing and the dangerous offender. *British Journal of Criminology,* 1982, *#3, 22.*

Goring, C. *The English convict: A statistical study.* London: His Majesty's Stationery Office, 1913.

Gottfredson, M. R., Chandler, M. A., & Cohen, L. Legal aim, discretion and social control: A case study of the federal youth corrections act. *Criminology,* 1983, *21,* 187–202.

Gough, A. Beyond control: Youth in the juvenile court—the climate for change. In L. Teitelbaum and A. Gough (Eds.), *Beyond control: Status offenders in juvenile court.* Cambridge, Mass.: Ballinger, 1977.

Gough, H. C. *Systematic validation of a test for delinquency.* Paper read at the annual meeting of the American Psychological Association, September 1945. Cited in M. L. Erickson, The changing relationship between official and self-reported measures of delinquency: An exploratory-predictive study. *Journal of Criminal Law, Criminology and Police Science,* 1972, 63, 388–395.

Gough, H. G. The assessment of wayward impulses by means of the personnel reaction blank. *Personnel Psychology,* 1971, *29,* 669–667.

Gould, L. C. Who defines delinquency? A comparison of self-reported and officially reported indices of delinquency for three racial groups. *Social Problems,* 1969, *16,* 325–336.

Gould, L. C., Walker, A., Crane, L., & Liz, C. *Connections: Notes from the heroin world.* New Haven: Yale University Press, 1974.

Gould, M., & Kern-Daniels, R. Toward a sociological theory of gender and sex. *The American Sociologist,* 1977, *12,* 162–189.

Graber, D. *Crime news and the public.* New York: Praeger, 1980.

Green, E. Race, social status, and criminal arrest. *American Sociological Review,* 1970, *35,* 476–490.

Green, J. Overview of adolescent drug use. In G. M. Beschner & A. S. Friedman (Eds.), *Youth drug abuse.* Lexington, Mass.: Lexington Books, 1979.

Green, R. G., & Bynum, T. S. T.V. crooks: Implications of latent role models for theories of delinquency. *Journal of Criminal Justice,* 1982, *10,* 177–190.

Green, R. G., & O'Neal, C. C. Activation of cue-elicited aggression by general arousal. *Journal of Personality and Social Psychology,* 1969, *11,* 289–292.

Greenberg, B. S. The content and context of violence in the mass media. In R. K. Baker & S. J. Ball (Eds.), *Mass media and violence,* 1969.

Greenberg, D. F. Problems in community corrections. *Issues in Criminology,* 1975, *10,* 1–33.

Greenberg, D. F. The correctional effects of corrections: A survey of evaluations. In D. F. Greenberg (Ed.), *corrections and punishment.* Beverly Hills, Calif.: Sage, 1977. (c)

Greenberg, D. F. Delinquency and the age structure of society. *Contemporary Crisis,* 1977, *1,* 189–224. (a)

Greenberg, D. F. Socioeconomic status and criminal sentences: Is there an association? *American Sociological Review,* 1977, *42,* 174–175. (b)

Greenberg, D. F. *Crime and capitalism.* Palo Alto, Calif.: Mayfield, 1981.

Greenwald, H. Eighth amendment—Minors and the death penalty: Decision and avoidance. *The Journal of Criminal Law and Criminology,* 1983, *73,* 1525–1552.

Griest, D. I., & Wells, K. C. Behavioral family therapy with conduct disorders in children. *Behavioral Therapy,* 1983, *14,* 37–53.

Griffin, B. S., & Griffin, C. T. *Juvenile delinquency in perspective.* New York: Harper & Row, 1978.

Grisso, T. *Juveniles' waiver of rights: Legal and psychological competence.* New York: Plenum Press, 1981.

Gross, R. T., & Duke, P. The effect of early versus late physical maturation on adolescent behavior. In a symposium on adolescent medicine, I. Litt (Ed.). *The Pediatric Clinics of North America,* 1980, *27 910,* 71–78.

Grossman, A. Working mothers and their children. In U. S. Department of Labor, Bureau of Labor Statistics, *Monthly labor review* 1981, *104,* 49–54.

Groth, A. N. Sexual trauma in the life histories of rapists and child molesters. *Victimology,* 1979, *4,* 10–16.

Grupp, S. *The positive school of criminology.* Pittsburgh: University of Pittsburgh Press, 1968.

Grygier, T., Chesley, J., & Tuters, E. W. Parental deprivation: A study of delinquent children. *British Journal of Criminology,* 1969, *9,* 209–253.

Gulevich, G., & Bourne, P. Mental illness and violence. In D. Daniels, M. Gilula, & F. Ochberg (Eds.), *Violence and the struggle for existence.* Boston: Little, Brown, 1970.

Gumplowicz, L. *The outlines of sociology.* Philadelphia: American Academy of Political and Social Science, 1899.

Guttmacher, M. *The mind of the murderer.* New York: Farrar, Straus, and Cudahy, 1960.

Habermas, J. *Legitimation crisis.* Boston: Beacon Press, 1975.

Hackler, J. The new criminology: Ideology or explanation. *Canadian Journal of Criminology and Corrections,* 1977, *19,* 192–195.

Hagan, J. The legislation of crime and delinquency: A review of theory, method, and research. *Law and Society Review,* 1980, *14,* 601–628.

Hahn, P. H. *The juvenile offender and the law* (2nd ed.). Cincinnati: Anderson, 1978.

Haislip, G. A. *Drug abuse and the law.* Speech before the Governor's Conference on Drug and Alcohol Abuse, Miami Beach, 1970.

Hakeem, M. A critique of the psychiatric approach. In J. S. Roucek (Ed.), *Juvenile delinquency.* New York: Philosophical Library, 1958. (a)

Hakeem, M. A critique of the psychiatric approach to crime and corrections. *Law and Contemporary Problems,* 1958, *23,* 650–682. (b)

Hall, G. S. *Adolescence: Its psychology and its relationship to physiology, anthropology, sociology, sex, crime, religion and education.* New York: D. Appleton, 1905.

Hall, J. *Theft, law and society.* Indianapolis: Bobbs-Merrill, 1952.

Hall, P. M. Identification with the delinquency subculture and level of self evaluation. *Sociometry,* 1966, *29,* 146–158.

Hall, S., & Jefferson, T. *Resistance through rituals.* London: Hutchinson, 1976.

Hall, S. et al. *Policing the city.* London: MacMillan, 1978.

Halleck, S. L. *Psychiatry and the dilemmas of crime: A study of causes, punishment, and treatment.* New York: Harper & Row, 1967.

Hamparian, D. M., Estep, L. K., Muntean, S. M., Priestino, R. R., Swisher, R. G., Wallace, P. L., & White, J. L. *Youth in adult courts: Between two worlds.* Columbus, Ohio: Academy for Contemporary Problems, 1982.

Handler, J. F. The juvenile court and the adversary system: Problems of function and form. *Wisconsin Law Review,* 1965, 7–51.

Hardman, D. Small town gangs. *Journal of Criminal Law, Criminology and Police Science,* 1969, *60,* 173–181.

Hardt, R., & Hardt, S. P. On determining the quality of the delinquency self-report method. *Journal of Research in Crime and Delinquency,* 1977, *14,* 247–261.

Hare, R. D., & D. Schalling (Eds.). *Psychopathic behavior.* New York: Wiley, 1978.

Hargreaves, D. H. *Social relations in a secondary school.* New York: Humanities Press, 1967.

Harries, K. *The geography of crime and justice.* New York: McGraw-Hill, 1974.

Harring, S., & McMullin, L. The Buffalo police, 1872–1900: Labor unrest, political power, and the creation of the police institution. *Crime and Social Justice,* 1975, *4,* 5–14.

Harris, C. D., & Ullman, E. L. The nature of cities. *Annals of the American Academy of Political and Social Science,* 1945, *242,* 7–17.

Harris, F. *Presentation of crime in newspapers.* Minneapolis, Minn.: Minneapolis Sociological Press, 1932.

Harris, P. The interpersonal maturity of delinquents and nondelinquents. In William S. Laufer and James M. Day, *Personality theory, moral development and criminal behavior.* Lexington, Mass.: D. C. Heath, 1983.

Hartl, E. M., Monnelly, E. P., and Elderkind, R. D. *Physique and delinquent behavior.* New York: Academic Press, 1982.

Harstone, E., & Hansen, K. V. *The violent offender: An empirical portrait.* In Robert A. Mathias (Ed.), *Violent juvenile offenders: An anthology.* San Francisco: National Council on Crime and Delinquency, 1984.

Hartjen, C. A., & Priyadarsini, S. *Delinquency in India.* New Brunswick, N.J.: Rutgers University Press, 1984.

Haskell, M. R. *An introduction to socioanalysis.* Long Beach, Calif.: California Institute of Scoioanalysis, 1967.

Haskell, M. R., & Yablonsky, L. *Juvenile delinquency* (2nd ed.). Chicago: Rand McNally, 1978.

Hathaway, S., & McKinley, J. *Minnesota multiphasic personality inventory manual.* New York: The Psychological Corporation, 1970.

Hathaway, S., & Monachesi, E. The MMPI in the study of juvenile delinquents. *American Sociological Review,* 1952, *17,* 704–709.

Hathaway, S., & Monachesi, E. (Eds.) *Analyzing and predicting juvenile delinquency with the Minnesota Multiphasic Personality Inventory.* Minneapolis: University of Minnesota Press, 1953.

Hathaway, S., & Monachesi, E. *Adolescent personality and behavior: MMPI patterns of normal, delinquent, dropout and other outcomes.* Minneapolis: University of Minnesota Press, 1963.

Hauge, R. Crime and the press. In N. Christie (Ed.), *Scandinavian studies in criminology* (Vol. I). London: Tavistock, 1965.

Havighurst, R. J., Bowman, P. H., Liddle, G. P., Matthews, C. V., & Pierce, J. V. *Growing up in River City.* New York: Wiley, 1962.

Havihurst, R. J. *Developmental Tasks and Education.* New York: Longmans Green, 1951.

Hawkes, J. J. *Children in urban society.* New York: Oxford University Press, 1971.

Hawley, A. H. *Human ecology.* New York: Ronald Press, 1950.

Hayeslip, Jr., D. W. The impact of defense attorney presence on juvenile court dispositions. *Juvenile and Family Court Journal,* 1979, *39,* 9–15.

Head, S. W. Content analysis of television drama programs. *Quarterly of Film, Radio and Television,* 1954, *9,* 175–194.

Healy, W. *The individual delinquent.* Boston: Little, Brown, 1915.

Healy, W. Thoughts about juvenile courts. *Federal Probation,* 1949, *13,* 16–19.

Healy, W., & Bronner, A. *New light on delinquency and its treatment.* New Haven: Yale University Press, 1936.

Help! Teacher can't teach. *Time,* June 16, 1980.

Henderson, M., & Hollin, O. A critical review of social skills training with young offenders. *Criminal Justice and Behavior,* 1983, *10,* 316–341.

Hennesey, M., Richards, P. J., & Berk, R. A. Broken homes and middle class delinquency. *Criminology,* 1978, *15,* 505–528.

Henslin, J. M., Henslin, L. K., & Keiser, S. D. Schooling for social stability: Education in the corporate society. In J. M. Henslin & L. T. Reynolds, *Social problems in American society.* Boston: Allyn & Bacon, 1976.

Hepburn, J. R. The role of the audience in deviant behavior and deviant identity. *Sociology and Social Research,* 1975, *59,* 387–405.

Hepburn, J. R. Testing alternative models of delinquency causation. *Journal of Criminal Law and Criminology,* 1977, *67,* 450–460. (a)

Hepburn, J. R. Total institutions and inmate self-esteem. *British Journal of Criminology,* 1977, *17,* 237–249. (b)

Hepburn, J. R. Race and the decision to arrest: An analysis of warrants issued. *Journal of Research in Crime and Delinquency,* 1978, *15,* 54–73.

Heussenstamm, F. K. Bumper stickers and cops. *Trans-Action,* 1971, *8,* 32–33.

Hewitt, L. E., & Jenkins, R. I. *Fundamental patterns of maladjustment: The dynamics of origins. A statistical analysis based on five hundred case records of children examined at the Michigan Child Guidance Institute.* Springfield: State of Illinois, 1947.

Higgins, P. C., & Albrecht, G. Cars and kids: A self reported study of juvenile auto theft and traffic violations. *Sociology and Social Research,* 1981, *66,* 29–41.

Higgins, P. C., Albrecht, G., & Albrecht, M. Black-white adolescent drinking: The myth and the reality. *Social Problems,* 1977, *25,* 214–224.

Higgins, P. C., & Albrecht, G. L. Hellfire and delinquency revisited. *Social Forces,* 1977, *55,* 952–58.

Highfield, R. D. The effects of news of crime and scandal upon public opinion. *Journal of Criminal Law and Criminology,* 1926–27.

Hindelang, M. J. Age, sex and the versatility of delinquent involvement. *Social Problems,* 1971, *18,* 527–535.

Hindelang, M. J. Causes of delinquency: A partial replication and extension. *Social Problems,* 1973, *20,* 470–487.

Hindelang, M. J. The relationship of self reported delinquency to scales of the CPI and MMPI. *Journal of Criminal Law, Criminology and Police Science,* 1972, *63,* 75–81.

Hindelang, M. J. Race and involvement in common law personal crimes. *American Sociological Review,* 1978, *43,* 93–109.

Hindelang, M. J. Sex differences in criminal activity. *Social Problems,* 1979, *27,* 143–156.

Hindelang, M. J. The *Uniform Crime Reports* revisited. *Journal of Criminal Justice,* 1974, *2,* 1–17.

Hindelang, M. J. With a little help from their friends: Group participation in reported delinquent behaviors. *British Journal of Criminology,* 1976, *16,* 109–125.

Hindelang, M. J., Hirschi, T., & Weis, J. G. Correlates of delinquency. *American Sociological Review,* 1979, *44,* 995–1014.

Hindelang, M. J., Hirschi, T., & Weis, J. G. *Measuring Delinquency.* Beverly Hills, Calif.: Sage, 1981.

Hindelang, M. J., & McDermott, M. Analysis of national crime victimization survey data to study serious delinquent behavior. Monograph Two. *Juvenile criminal behavior: An analysis of rates and victim characteristics.* U.S. Department of Justice, LEAA, NIJJP, January, 1981.

Hindelang, J. J., Gottfredson, M. R., & Flanagan, T. J. *Sourcebook of criminal justice statistics—1980* (U.S. Department of Justice, Bureau of Justice Statistics). Washington, D.C.: U.S. Government Printing Office, 1981.

Hinton, J. W. *Dangerousness: Problems of assessment and prediction.* London: George Allen and Unwin, 1983.

Hippchen, L. (Ed.). *Ecologic-biochemical approaches to treatment of delinquents and criminals.* New York: Van Nostrand Reinhold, 1978.

Hirschi, T. *Causes of delinquency.* Berkeley: University of California Press, 1969.

Hirschi, T., & Gottfredson, M. Age and the explanation of crime. *American Journal of Sociology,* 1983, 89, 552–584.

Hirschi, T., & Hindelang, M. J. Intelligence and delinquency: A revisionist review. *American Sociological Review,* 1977, 47, 571–587.

Hirschi, T., & Selvin, H. C. *Principles of survey analysis.* New York: Free Press, 1967.

Hirschi, T., & Stark, R. Hellfire and delinquency. *Social Problems,* 1969, 17, 202–213.

Hirst, P. W. Marx and Engels on law, crime and morality. In I. Taylor, P. Walton, & J. Young (Eds.), *Critical criminology.* London: Routledge & Kegan Paul, 1975.

Hochstedler, E. Dimensions of police types: A study of perspective and passion. *Criminal Justice and Behavior,* 1981, 8, 303–323. (b)

Hochstedler, E. Testing types: A review and test of police types. *Journal of Criminal Justice,* 1981, 9, 451–466. (a)

Hoffer, A. Some theoretical principles basic to orthomolecular psychiatric treatment. In Leonard J. Hippchen (Ed.), 1978, 31–56.

Hoffer, A. The relation of crime to nutrition. *Humanist in Canada,* 1975, 8, 3–9.

Hogan, R., & Jones, W. H. A role-theoretical model of criminal conduct. In W. S. Laufer & J. M. Day, *Personality theory, moral development, and criminal behavior.* Lexington, Mass.: Lexington Books, 1983.

Hohenstein, W. F. Factors influencing the police disposition of juvenile offenders. In T. Sellin & M. Wolfgang (Eds.), *Delinquency: Selected studies.* New York: Wiley, 1969.

Hollingshead, A. B. *Elmstown youth.* New York: Wiley, 1949.

Hollingshead, A. B., & Redlich, F. *Social class and mental illness.* New York: Wiley, 1958.

Holmes, J. C. Crime and the press. *Journal of Criminal Law and Criminology,* 1929–1930, 20.

Holyst, B. *Comparative criminology.* Lexington, Mass.: Lexington Books, 1979.

Hood, R. B. Research in the effectiveness of punishments and treatments. In *Collected studies in criminological research* (Vol. 1). Strasbourg, France: Council of Europe, 1967.

Hooten, E. *Crime and man.* Cambridge, Mass.: Harvard University Press, 1931.

Horney, K. *The neurotic personality of our time.* New York: W. W. Norton, 1937.

Horton, J. Order and conflict theories of social problems as competing ideologies. In R. S. Denisoff & C. McCaghy (Eds.), *Deviance, conflict and criminality.* Chicago: Rand McNally, 1973.

Horton, J., & Platt, T. *Crime and criminal justice under capitalism and socialism: Towards a world-system perspective.* San Francisco: Institute for the Study of Labor and Economic Crisis, 1983.

Hoult, T. F. Comic books and juvenile delinquency. *Sociology and Social Research,* 1949, 33, 279–284.

Howlett, F. Is the YSB all it's cracked up to be? *Crime and Delinquency,* 1973, 19, 485–492.

Hoyt, J. Effect of media violence justification on aggression. *Journal of Broadcasting,* 1970, 4, xiv.

Hubbard, J. C., DeFleur, M., & DeFleur, L. B. Mass media influences on public conceptions of social problems. *Social Problems.* 1975, 1, 23.

Hudson, J. R. Police-citizen encounters that lead to citizen complaints. *Social Problems.* 1970, 1, 18 .

Huesmann, L. R. Television violence and aggressive behavior. In *Television and Behavior,* 1982, 2, 126–137.

Huizinga, D. H. *Description of the national youth sample.* Boulder, Colo.: Behavioral Research Institute, 1978.

Huizinga, D. H., & Elliott, D. S. *A longitudinal study of drug use and delinquency in a national sample of youth: An assessment of causal order.* Boulder, Colo.: Behavioral Research Institute, 1981.

Hunner, P. J., & Walker, Y. E. *Exploring the relationship between child abuse and delinquency.* Montclair, N.J.: Allerheld, Osmun, 1981.

Hunt, J. Rapists have big ears: Genetic screening in Massachusetts. *The Real Paper,* July 4, 1973, p. 4.

Hutzler, J. L. Cannon to the left, Cannon to the right: Can the juvenile court survive? *Today's delinquent,* Pittsburgh, PA.: National Center for Juvenile Justice, 1982, 25–38.

Ilfeld, F. W. Environmental theories of violence. In D. Daniels, M. Gilula, & F. Öchberg (Eds.), *Violence and the struggle for existence.* Boston: Little, Brown, 1970.

Illinois Institute for Juvenile Research. *Juvenile delinquency in Illinois.* Chicago: Illinois Department of Mental Health, 1972.

Inciardi, J. A. Youth, drugs and street crime. In F. Z. Scarpetti & S. K. Dalesman (Eds.). *Drugs and the youth culture.* Beverly Hills, Calif.: Sage, 1980.

Inciardi, J. A. From the editor's desk. *Criminology,* 1979, 16, 443–444.

Inciardi, J. A. *Radical criminology: The coming crisis.* Beverly Hills, Calif.: Sage, 1980.

Inciardi, J. A. (Ed.). *The drugs-crime connection.* Beverly Hills, Calif.: Sage, 1981.

Inglis, B. *A history of medicine.* Cleveland: World, 1965.

Inhelder, B., & Piaget, J. *The growth of logical thinking from childhood to adolescence* (Anne Parsons and Stanley Milgram Trans.). New York: Basic Books, 1958.

Institute of Judicial Administration and American Bar Association. *Standards relating to corrections administration.* Cambridge, Mass.: Ballinger, 1976.

Irwin, J., & Cressey, U. Thieves, convicts and the inmate culture. *Social Problems,* 1962, 10, 142–155.

Isaacs, N. E. The crime of crime reporting. *Crime and Delinquency*, 1961, *7* (3), 312–320.

Jackson, D. J., & Borgotta, E. F. Selecting a data analysis model for factorial ecological research. In D. J. Jackson & E. F. Borgotta (Eds.), *Factor analysis and measurement in sociological research*. Beverly Hills, Calif.: Sage, 1981.

Jackson, K., & Clark, S. Thefts among college students. *Personnel and Guidance Journal*, 1958, *36*, 557–562.

Jacobs, P. A., Brunton, M., & Melville, M. M. Aggressive behavior, mental abnormality and the XYY male. *Nature*, 1965, *208*, 1351.

Jacobs, P. A., Price, W. H., Court-Brown, W. M., Brittain, R. P., & Whatmore, P.B. Chromosome studies on men in a maximum security hospital. *Annals of Human Genetics*, 1968, *31*, 339–347.

Jacoby, R. The repression of psychoanalysis: The lost Freudian left. *Nation*, October 15, 1983, pp. 341–344.

Jacoby, R. *The repression of psychoanalysis: Otto Fenichel and the political Freudians*. New York: Basic Books, 1983.

Jacquith, S. M. Adolescent marijuana and alcohol use: An empirical test of differential association theory. *Criminology*, 1981, *19*, 271–280.

Jaffe, E. D. Family anomie and delinquency: Development of the concept and some empirical findings. *British Journal of Criminology*, 1969, *9*, 376–388.

James, J. & Thornton, W. Women's liberation and the female delinquent. *Journal of Research in Crime and Delinquency*, 1980, *17*, 230–244.

James, J., & Thornton, W. *Youth service bureaus: New variations on old themes*. Paper presented at the Mid-South Sociological Meetings, Jackson, Mississippi, 1978.

Japan Times (Tokyo), May 25, 1975, p. 12.

Jarvik, L. S., Klodin, V., & Matsuyama, S. S. Human aggression and the extra Y chromosome: Fact or fantasy. In I. Jacks & S. G. Cos (Eds.), *Psychological approaches to crime and its correction: Theory, research, practice*. Chicago: Nelson-Hall, 1984.

Jarvis, D. C. *Institutional treatment of the offender*. New York: McGraw-Hill, 1978.

JCS. *See* National Council of Juvenile and Family Court Judges.

Jeffery, C. R. An integrated theory of crime and criminal behavior. *Journal of Criminal Law, Criminology and Police Science*, 1959, *49*, 533–552.

Jeffery, C. R. Criminology as an interdisciplinary science. *Criminology*, 1978, *16*, 149–170.

Jeffery, C. R. *Biology and crime*. Beverly Hills, Calif.: Sage, 1979.

Jenkins, P. The radicals and the rehabilitative ideal, 1890–1930. *Criminology*, 1982, *20*, 347–372.

Jenkins, R. L. The varieties of adolescent's behavioral problems and family dynamics. *American Journal of Psychiatry*, 1968, *124*, 1440–1445.

Jennings, W., Kilkenny, R., & Kohlberg, L. Moral development theory and practice for youthful and adult offenders. In William Laufer and James Day (Eds.), *Personality theory, moral development and criminal behavior*. Lexington, Mass.: D. C. Heath, 1983.

Jennings, M. K., & Niemi, R. A. Continuity and change in political orientations: A longitudinal study of two generations. *American Political Science Review*, 1975, *69*, 1316–1335.

Jensen, G. F. Inner containment and delinquency. *Criminology*. 1973, *64*, 464–470.

Jensen, G. F. Parents, peers, and delinquent action: A test of the differential association perspective. *American Journal of Sociology*, 1972, *78*, 562–575.

Jensen, G. F., & Eve, R. Sex differences in delinquency: An examination of popular sociological explanations. *Criminology*, 1976, *12*, 427–448.

Jersild, A. T. *In search of self*. New York: Columbia University Press, 1952.

Jesness, C. *Sequential I-level classification manual*. Sacramento, Calif.: American Justice Institute, 1974.

Jesness, K. F. *The Fricot Ranch study: Outcomes with small vs. large living groups in the rehabilitation of delinquents* (Research Report No. 47). Sacramento, Calif.: California Youth Authority, October 1965.

Jesness, K. F. The impact of behavior modification and transactional analysis on institution social climate. *Journal of Research in Crime and Delinquency*, 1975, *12*, 79–91.

Jessor, R., & Jesser, S. L. *Problem behavior and psychosocial development*. New York: Academic Press, 1977.

Johnson, E. *International handbook of contemporary developments in criminology: General issues and the Americas*. Westport, Conn.: Greenwood Press, 1983.

Johnson, R. E. *Juvenile delinquency and its origins*. New York: Cambridge University Press, 1979.

Johnston, L. D., Bachman, J. G., and O'Malley, P. M. *Highlights from student drug use in America, 1975–80* (U. S. Department of Health and Human Services, National Institute on Drug Abuse). Washington, D.C.: U.S. Government Printing Office, 1981.

Johnston, L. D., O'Malley, P. M., & Bachman, J. G. *Drugs and American high school students, 1975–1983*. National Institute on Drug Abuse, 1984.

Johnston, L., O'Malley, P., & Eveland, L. Nonaddictive drug use and delinquency: A longitudinal analysis. *Drug use and crime: Report of the panel on drug use and criminal behavior*. Springfield, Va.: National Technical Information Service, 1976.

Johnston, L., O'Malley, P., & Eveland, L. Drugs and delinquency: A search for causal connections. In D. Kandel (Ed.), *Longitudinal research on drug use*. New York: Wiley, 1978.

Johnstone, J. W. C. Delinquency and the changing American Family. In D. Shichor and D. H. Kelly (Eds.), *Control issues in juvenile delinquency*. Lexington, Mass.: D. C. Heath, 1981.

Johnstone, J. W. Social class, social areas and delinquency. *Sociology and Social Research*, 1978, *63*, 49–72.

Johnstone, T. Recruitment to a youth gang. *Youth and Society,* 1983, *14,* 3.

Joint Committee on New York Drug Law Evaluation. *The nation's toughest drug law: Evaluating the New York experience.* Washington, D.C.: U.S. Government Printing Office, 1978.

Jones, E. E., Kanouse, D. E., Kelly, H. H., Nisbett, R. R., Walins, S., & Weiner, B. *Attribution: Perceiving the causes of behavior.* Morristown, N.J.: General Learning Press, 1971.

Jones, E. T. Needs of negro youth. In D. Winter & E. M. Nuss (Eds.), *The young adult: Identity and awareness.* Glenville, Ill.: Scott, Foresman, 1969.

Jones, S. The Criminal Justice Act of 1982. *British Journal of Criminology,* 1983.

Jonsson, G. Delinquent boys, their parents and grandparents, *Acts Psychiatric Scandinavia* (Supplement), 1967, *43,* 195–210.

Jung, C. G. *The integration of personality.* London: Routledge & Kegan Paul, 1940.

Junger-Tass, J. Hidden delinquency and judicial selection in Belgium. In Paul Friday & V. L. Stewart (Eds.), *Youth crime and juvenile justice: International perspectives.* New York: Praeger, 1977.

Junger-Tass, J. et al. Jeugddelinquentie WODC. Ministerie van Justice, 1983.

Justice, B., & Justice, R. *The abusing family.* New York: Human Sciences Press, 1976.

Juvenile confessions: Whether state procedures ensure constitutionally permissible confessions. *Journal of Criminal Law and Criminology,* 1976, *67,* 195–208.

Juvenile Court Statistics. See National Council of Juvenile and Family Court Judges; U.S. Department of Health, Education and Welfare, Office of Youth Development; and U.S. Department of Justice, Law Enforcement Assistance Administration, National Institute for Juvenile Justice and Delinquency Prevention, Office of Juvenile Justice and Delinquency Prevention.

Juvenile Delinquency Prevention and Control Act of 1968 (Public Law 90-445), Title I.

Juvenile Delinquency Prevention and Control Act of 1974 (Public Law 93-415), Title I.

Juvenile delinquency. (From Summary of the White Paper on Crime). Japan Ministry of Justice Research and Training Institute, Toyko, Japan, 1981.

Juvenile justice: An international survey. U.N. Social Defense Research Institute, Rome, 1976.

Juvenile offenders in Duluth literally come before a jury of their peers—other kids. *People,* June 9, 1980, pp. 83–84.

Juvenile violence and gang related crime. San Diego Association of Government, San Diego, Calif., June, 1932.

Juviler, P. E. *Revolutionary law and order.* New York: The Free Press, 1976.

Kahn, R, and Bowers, W. The social context of the rank and file student activist: A test of four hypotheses. *Sociology of Education,* 1970, *43,* 38–55.

Kamerman, S. B., & Kahn, A. J. *Family policy: Government and families in fourteen countries.* New York: Columbia University Press, 1976.

Kandel, D. B. *Longitudinal research on drug use: Empirical findings and methodological issues.* New York: Wiley, 1978.

Kaplan, H. *Deviant behavior in defense of self.* New York: Academic Press, 1980.

Kaplan, L. *Adolescence, the farewell to childhood.* N.Y.: Simon & Schuster, 1984.

Karacki, L., & Toby, J. The uncommitted adolescent: Candidate for gang socialization. *Sociological Inquiry,* 1962, *2,* 203–215.

Karpets, I. I. The nature and causes of crime in the U.S.S.R. *Sovetskoe gosudarstvo i pravo,* 1966, *4.*

Kassebaum, G., Ward, D., & Welner, D. *Prison treatment and its outcome.* New York: Wiley, 1971.

Katkin, D., Hyman, D., & Kramer, J. *Delinquency and the juvenile justice system.* North Scituate, Mass.: Duxbury Press, 1976.

Katz, J., & Abel, C. F. The medicalization of repression: Eugenics and crime. *Contemporary Crisis,* 1984, *8,* 227–241.

Keller, R. L. *A sociological analysis of the conflict and critical criminologist.* Ph.D. Dissertation, University of Montana, 1976.

Kelley, T. Status offenders can be different: A comparative study of delinquent careers. *Crime and Delinquency,* 1983, *29,* 365–380.

Kelly, D. H. School failure, academic self-evaluation, school avoidance and deviant behavior. *Youth and Society,* 1971, *2,* 489–509.

Kelly, D. H., & Balch, R. Social origins and school failure: A re-examination of Cohen's theory of working class delinquency. *Pacific Sociological Review,* 1971, *14,* 413–430.

Kelly, Henry E. Biosociology and crime. In Jeffrey, C. R. (Ed.), *Biology and crime.* Beverly Hills, Calif.: Sage, 1979.

Kephart, W. M. *The family, society, and the individual* (4th ed.). Boston: Houghton Mifflin, 1977.

Kessen, W. *The child.* New York: Wiley, 1965.

Kessler, S., & Moos, R. H. The XYY karyotype and criminality: A review. *Journal of Psychiatric Research,* 1970, *7,* 153–170.

Khlief, B. B. Teachers as predictors of juvenile delinquency and psychiatric disturbance. *Social Problems,* 1964, *12,* 270–282.

Kiester, Jr., E. Explosive youngsters: What to do about them. *Today's Health,* 1974, *52* (1), 49–53; 64–65.

King, J. L. *A comparative analysis of juvenile codes.* Urbana: Champaign University of Illinois Community Research Forum, 1980.

Kitsuse, J. I., & Cicourel, A. A note on the use of official statistics. *Social Problems,* 1963, *11,* 131–139.

Kitsuse, J. I., and Dietrick, D. C. Delinquent boys: A critique. *American Sociological Review,* 1959, *24,* 208–215.

Kittel, H. G. Juvenile justice philosophy in Minnesota. *Juvenile and Family Court Journal,* 1983, *34,* 93–102.

Kittrie, N. N. *The right to be different: Deviance and enforced therapy.* Baltimore, Md.: Johns Hopkins Press, 1971.

Klapmuts, N. Children's rights: The legal rights of minors in conflict with law or custom. *Crime and Delinquency Literature,* 1972, *4,* 449–477.

Klein, M. W. *Evaluation in an imported gang homicide deterrence program.* Narrative from proposal for WIJ Grant, June, 1981.

Klein, M. W. *Western systems of criminal justice.* Beverly Hills, Calif.: Sage, 1984.

Klein, M. W. Violence in American juvenile gangs. In D. Mulvihill & M. Tumin (Eds.), *Crimes of violence* (National Commission on the Causes and Prevention of Violence). Washington, D.C.: U.S. Government Printing Office, 1969.

Klein, M. W., & Teilmann, K. S. *Pivotal ingredients of police diversion programs* (U.S. Department of Justice, Law Enforcement Assistance Administration, National Institute on Juvenile Justice and Delinquency Prevention). Washington, D.C.: U.S. Government Printing Office, May 1976.

Klockars, C. B. The contemporary crisis of Marxist criminology. *Criminology,* 1979, *16,* 477–515.

Kluegel, J. R. Contemporary juvenile justice: Responding to public mandates for change. In James R. Kluegel (Ed.), *Evaluating juvenile justice.* Beverly Hills, Calif.: Sage, 1983.

Knell, B. E. F. Capital punishment: Its administration in relation to juvenile offenders in the nineteenth century and its possible administration in the eighteenth. *British Journal of Criminology,* 1965, *5,* 198–207.

Kobetz, R. W. *The police role and juvenile delinquency.* Gaithersburg, Md.: International Association of Chiefs of Police, 1971.

Kobrin, S. The Chicago Area Project—A 25-year assessment. *Annals of the American Academy of Political and Social Science,* 1959, *322,* 20–29.

Kobrin, S., & Klein, M. W. *Community treatment of juvenile offenders: The DSO experiments.* Beverly Hills, Calif.: Sage, 1983.

Kohlberg, L., & Gilligan, C. The adolescent as a philosopher: The discovery of the self in a post conventional world. *Daedalus,* Fall, 1971, 1051–1086.

Kohlberg, L. The development of moral character and moral ideology. In M. Hoffman & L. Hoffman (Eds.), *Review of child development Research,* (Vol. 1). New York: Russell Sage, 1964.

Kohlberg, L. Moral development and identification. *Child psychology: Yearbook of the national society for the study of education.* Chicago: University of Chicago Press, 1963.

Kohlberg, L. Stage and sequence: The cognitive-developmental approach to socialization. In D. Goslin (Ed.), *Handbook of socialization: Theory and research.* Chicago: Rand McNally, 1969.

Kohn, M. *Class and conformity.* Chicago: University of Chicago Press, 1977.

Korner, A. F. Mother-child interaction: One or two-way street. *Social Work,* 1965, *10,* 47–51.

Kovel, J. *The age of desire: Reflections of a radical psychiatrist.* New York: Pantheon, 1981.

Kraepelin, E. *Compendium der psychiatrie.* Leipzig: Abel, 1883.

Krajick, K. The work ethic approach to punishment. *Corrections Magazine,* Oct. 1982, 6–19.

Kranz, H. *Lebenschicksale krimineller zwillinge,* Berlin: Springer-Verlag OHG, 1936.

Kratcoski, P. L. Differential treatment of delinquent boys and girls in juvenile court. *Child Welfare,* 1974, *53,* 16–22.

Kretschmer, E. *Physique and character.* London: Kegan Paul, 1925.

Krisberg, B. *Crime and privilege.* Englewood Cliffs, N.J.: Prentice-Hall, 1975.

Krisberg, B., & Austin, J. (Eds.). *The children of Ishmael: Critical perspectives on juvenile justice.* Palo Alto, Calif.: Mayfield, 1978.

Krisberg, B., & Schwartz, I. Rethinking juvenile justice. *Crime and Delinquency,* 1983, *29,* 333–364.

Krisberg, B., Litsky, P., & Schwartz, I. Youth in confinement: Justice by geography. *Journal of Research in Crime and Delinquency,* 1984, *21,* 153–181.

Krisberg, B., Schwartz, I. M., Litsky, P., & Austin, J. The watershed of juvenile justice reform. *Crime and Delinquency,* 1986, *32,* 5–38.

Krohn, M., & Mancy, J. Social control and delinquent behavior. *The Sociological Quarterly,* 1980, *21.*

Krohn, M., Waldo, G., & Chiricos, T. Self-reported delinquency: A comparison of structured interviews and self-administered checklists. *Journal of Criminal Law and Criminology,* 1975, *65,* 545–553.

Kuhn, T. *The structure of scientific revolutions.* Chicago: University of Chicago Press, 1973.

Kulkarni, A. India. In V. L. Stewart (Ed.), *Justice and children around the world* (Vol. 1). New York: New York University Press, 1981.

Kurtines, W., & Hogan, R. Sources of conformity in unsocialized college students. *Journal of Abnormal Psychology,* 1972, *80,* 49–51.

Kuykendell, J. L. Styles of community policing. *Criminology,* 1974, *12,* 229–240.

Kvaraceus, W. C. *Juvenile delinquency and the school.* New York: World, 1945.

Lab, S. P. *The identification of juveniles for non-intervention.* Tallahassee: Florida State University, unpublished dissertation, 1982.

Lacassagne, A. Les suicides à Lyn. *Archives D'Anthropologie Criminelle de Medicine Legale* (Vol. II). (Originally published, 1896.) Parts reproduced in S. Schafer & R. Knudten (Eds.), *Criminological theory.* Lexington, Mass.: Lexington Books, 1977.

LaFave, W. R. *Arrest: The decision to take a suspect into custody.* Boston: Little, Brown, 1965.

Lalli, M., & Savitz, L. *Delinquency and city life.* Washington, D.C.: U.S. Government Printing Office, 1972.

Landau, S. F. Future time perspectives of delinquents and non-delinquents: The effect of institutionalization. *Criminal Justice and Behavior*, 1975, *2*, 22–36.

Landau, S., & Nathan, G. Selecting delinquents for cautioning in the London metropolitan area. *British Journal of Criminology*, 1983, *23*, 2.

Lander, B. *Towards an understanding of juvenile delinquency.* New York: Columbia University Press, 1954.

Langner, T. S., Gersten, J. C., Greene, E. I., Eisenberg, J. G., Herson, J. H., & McCarthy, E. D. Treatment of psychological disorders among urban children. *Journal of Consulting and Clinical Psychology*, 1974, *42*, 2, 70–79.

Larsen, O. *Violence and the mass media.* New York: Harper & Row, 1968.

Larson, J. Rural female delinquents' adaptation to institutional life. *Juvenile and Family Court Journal*, February, 1983, 83–92.

Latessa, E. J., Travis, L. F., & Wilson, G. T. Juvenile diversion: Factors related to decision making and outcome. In S. H. Decker (Ed.), *Juvenile Justice Policy.* Beverly Hills, Calif.: Sage, 1984.

Laub, J. H. Trends in serious juvenile crime. *Criminal Justice and Behavior*, 1983, *10*, 485–506.

Laub, J. H., & Hindelang, M. J. Analysis of national crime victimization survey data to study serious delinquent behavior. Monograph Three. *Juvenile criminal behavior in urban, surburban and rural areas.* U.S. Department of Justice, LEAA, NIJJDP, February, 1981.

Law Enforcement Assistance Administration. *See* U.S. Department of Justice, Law Enforcement Assistance Administration.

LeBlanc, M., & Biron, L. Status offenses: A legal term without meaning. *Journal of Research in Crime and Delinquency*, 1980, *17*, 114–125.

Lee, R., & Haynes, N. M. Project CREST and the dual-treatment approach to delinquency: Methods and research summarized. In R. R. Ross and P. Gendreau (Eds.), *Effective correctional treatment.* Toronto: Butterworth, 1980.

Lefcourt, R. *Law against the people.* New York: Vintage, 1971.

Lefkowitz, M. M., Eron, I. D., Walder, L. O., & Huesmann, L. R. *Growing up to be violent: A longitudinal study of the development of aggression.* New York: Pergamon Press, 1977.

Lefstein, M., Stapleton, V., & Teitelbaum, L. In search of juvenile justice: Gault and its implementation. *Law and Society Review*, 1969, *3*, 491–502.

Lemert, E. M. *Social pathology: A systematic approach to the theory of sociopathic behavior.* New York: McGraw-Hill, 1951.

Lemert, E. M. *The juvenile court—Quest and realities.* In President's Commission on Law Enforcement and the Administration of Justice, *Task force report: Juvenile delinquency and youth crime.* Washington, D.C.: U.S. Government Printing Office, 1967.

Lemert, E. M. *Instead of court: Diversion in juvenile justice.* Washington, D.C.: U.S. Government Printing Office, 1971.

Lemert, E. M. *Human deviance, social problems and social control* (2nd ed.). Englewood Cliffs, N.J.: Prentice-Hall, 1972.

Lennard, H., Epstein, L., Berstein, A., & Ransom, D. Hazards implicit in prescribing psychoactive drugs. *Science*, 1970, *169*, 438–441.

Lenski, G. *The religious factor.* Garden City, N.Y.: Doubleday, 1963.

Lerman, P. Gangs, networks, and subcultural delinquency. *American Journal of Sociology*, 1967, *73*, 63–71.

Lerman, P. Evaluative studies of institutions for delinquents: Implications for research and social policy. *Social Work*, 1968, *13*, 55–64.

Lerman, P. Child convicts. In P. Wickman & P. Whitten (Eds.), *Readings in criminology.* Lexington, Mass.: D. C. Heath, 1978.

Leslie, G. R. *The family in social context* (4th ed.). New York: Oxford University Press, 1979.

Leukefeld, C., & Clayton, R. Drug abuse and delinquency: A study of youths in treatment. In G. M. Beschner & A. S. Friedman (Eds.), *Youth drug abuse.* Lexington, Mass.: Lexington Books, 1979.

Levin, M., & Sarri, R. *Juvenile delinquency: A study of juvenile codes in the U.S.* (National Assessment of Juvenile Corrections). Ann Arbor: University of Michigan, 1974.

Levinson, A. The rebellion of blue collar youth. *Annual editions: Readings in social problems '73/'74.* Guilford, Conn.: Dushkin, 1973.

Lewin, K. Channels of group life. *Human Relations*, 1947, *1*, 143–153.

Lewis, D., Balla, D., Shanak, S., & Snell, L. Delinquency, parental psychopathology and parental criminality: Clinical and epidemological findings. *Journal of the American Academy of Child Psychiatry*, 1976, *15*, 665–678.

Lewis, H. *Deprived children.* London: Oxford University Press, 1952.

Lewis, M., & Rosenblum, L. A. (Eds.). *The effect of the infant on its caregiver.* New York: Wiley, 1974.

Lewis, Roy V. Scared straight—California style: Evaluation of the San Quentin Squires Program. *Criminal Justice and Behavior*, 1983, *10*, 2, 209–226.

Liazos, A. Class oppression: The function of juvenile justice. *Insurgent Sociologist*, 1974, *1*, 2–24.

Liazos, A. The poverty of the sociology of deviance: Nuts, sluts, and preverts. *Social Problems*, 1972, *20*, 103–120.

Liebert, R. M., Neale, J. M., & Davidson, E. S. *The early window: Effects of television on children and youth.* New York: Pergamon, 1973.

Lindesmith, A. R. *Addiction and opiates.* Chicago: Aldine, 1968,

Lindesmith, A. R., & Levin, Y. The Lombrosian myth in criminology. *American Journal of Sociology*, 1937, *42*, 663–671.

Lipkin, J. P. Equity in computer education. *Educational Leadership*, 1983, *41*, 26.

Lipset, S. Youth and politics. In R. Martin & R. Nisbet (Eds.), *Contemporary social problems* (3rd Ed.). New York: Harcourt, 1972.

Lipton, D., Martinson, R., & Wilks, J. *The effectiveness of correctional treatment.* New York: Praeger, 1975.

Locke, J. *Some thoughts concerning education* (4th ed.). London: A. and J. Churchill, 1699. (Originally published, 1693.)

Loevinger, G. The court and the child. *Focus,* 1949, *28,* 65–69.

Lombroso, C. *Crime: Its causes and remedies* (H. P. Horton, Trans.). Boston: Little, Brown, 1911. (Originally published, 1876.)

Lombroso, C. *The female offender.* New York: Wisdom Library, 1952. (Originally published, 1899.)

Lombroso-Ferrero. *Lombroso's criminal man.* Montclair, N.J.: Pattersen Smith, 1972. (Originally published, 1876.)

Lombroso-Ferrero, G. Charles Goring's "The English Convict": A symposium. *Journal of Criminal Law, Criminology and Police Science,* 1914–15, *5,* 207–223.

Looft, W. R. Egocentrism and social interaction across the lifespan. *Psychological Bulletin,* 1972, *2,* 73–92.

Lopez-Rey, M. The role of the United Nations Congress in the prevention of crime and the treatment of offenders. *Federal Probation,* 1973.

Loth, D. *Crime in the suburbs.* New York: William Morrow, 1967.

Lou, H. H. *Juvenile courts in the United States.* Chapel Hill: University of North Carolina Press, 1927.

Lovibond, S. H. The effects of media stressing crime and violence upon children's attitudes. *Social Problems,* 1967, *15.*

Luckman, T. *The invisible religion.* New York: Macmillan, 1967.

Lundman, R. J. Routine arrest practices: A commonwealth perspective. *Social Problems,* 1974, *22,* 127–141.

Lundman, R. J. Will diversion reduce recidivism? *Crime and Delinquency,* 1976, *22,* 428–437.

Lundman, R. J., McFarlane, P., & Scarpitti, F. Delinquency prevention: A description and assessment of projects reported in the professional literature. *Crime and Delinquency,* 1976, *22,* 297–308.

Lundman, R. J., Sykes, R. E., & Clark, J. P. Police control of juveniles: A replication. *Journal of Research in Crime and Delinquency,* 1978, *15,* 74–91.

Lynch, M. A. Annotation: The prognosis of child abuse. *Journal of Child Psychology and Psychiatry,* 1978, *19,* 175–180.

Lynd, R. S., & Lynd, H. *Middletown,* New York: Harcourt, Brace and World, 1929.

Lynn, D. B. *Parental and sex role identification.* Berkeley, Calif.: McCutchan, 1969.

Maccoby, E. Children and working mothers. *Child,* 1958, *5,* 83–89.

MacNamara, D. E., & Stead, P. J. *New dimensions in transnational crime.* New York: John Jay Press, 1982.

McAdoo, H. D. *Black families.* Beverly Hills, Calif.: Sage, 1981.

McAnany, P. D. Gault attorneys in the second decade: Some normative reflections. *Juvenile and Family Court Journal,* 1978, *29,* 37–45.

McAuliffe, T. M., & Handal, P. J. PIC delinquency scale: Validity in relation to self-reported delinquent acts. *Criminal Justice and Behavior,* 1984, *11,* 35–46.

McCaghy, C. H. *Deviant behavior: Crime, conflict, and interest groups.* New York: Macmillan, 1976.

McCaghy, C. H. *Crime in American society.* New York: Macmillan, 1980.

McCandless, B. R. *Adolescents: behavior and development.* Hinsdale, Ill.: Dryden Press, 1970.

McCandless, B. R., Persons, W., & Roberts, A. Perceived opportunity, delinquency, race and body build among delinquent youth. *Journal of Consulting Psychology,* 1972, *38,* 281–287.

McCord, J., & McCord, W. A follow-up report on the Cambridge-Somerville Youth Study. *Annals of the American Academy of Political and Social Science,* 1959, *322,* 88–96.

McCord, J., McCord, W., & Thurber, E. Some effects of paternal absence on male children. *Journal of Abnormal and Social Psychology,* 1962, *64,* 361–369.

McCord, W., & McCord, J. *Psychopathy and delinquency.* New York: Grune and Stratton, 1956.

McCord, W., & McCord, J. The effects of parental role model on criminality. *Journal of Social Issues,* 1958, *14,* 66–75.

McCord, W., McCord, J., & Gudeman, J. *Origins of alcoholism.* Palo Alto, Calif.: Stanford University Press, 1960.

McCord, W., McCord, J., & Zola, I. K. *Origins of Crime.* New York: Columbia University Press, 1959.

McDermott, J. Crime in the school and in the community: Offenders, victims and fearful youths. *Crime and Delinquency,* 1983, 270–282.

McDermott, M., & Hindelang, M. J. Analysis of national crime victimization data survey to study serious delinquent behavior. Monograph One. *Juvenile Criminal Behavior in the United States: Its Trends and Patterns,* U.S. Department of Justice, LEAA, NIJJDP, January, 1981.

McDonald, L. *Social class and delinquency.* London: Faber, 1969.

McDonough, J. F. On the usefulness of Merton's anomie theory: Academic failure and deviance among high school students. *Youth and Society,* 1983, *14,* 259–279.

McEachern, A. W., & Bauzer, R. Factors related to disposition in juvenile police contacts. In M. W. Klein (Ed.), *Juvenile gangs in context: Theory, research and action.* Englewood Cliffs, N.J.: Prentice-Hall, 1967.

McHugh, P. A common-sense conception of deviance. In J. Douglas (Ed.), *Deviance and respectability: The social construction of moral meanings.* New York: Basic Books, 1970.

McIntyre, J. J., Teevan, J. J., & Hartnagel, T. Television violence and deviant behavior. In G. A. Comstock & E. A. Rubinstein (Eds.), *Television and Social Behavior*, 1972, 3, 383–435.

McKinney, F., Miller, D. J., Beier, L., & Bohannon, S. R. Self-concept and positive peer culture. *Criminology*, 1978, 15, 529–536.

McKinney, J. P., & Moore, D. Attitudes and values during adolescence. In B. B. Wolman (Ed.), *Handbook of developmental psychology*. Englewood Cliffs, N.J.: Prentice-Hall, 1982.

McLeod, J. M., Atkin, C. K., & Chaffee, S. H. Adolescents, parents, and television use: Adolescent self report measures from Maryland and Wisconsin Samples. In G. A. Comstock & S. A. Rubinstein (Eds.), *Television and Social Behavior*. 1972, 3, 173–238. (a)

McLeod, J. M., Atkin, L. K., & Chaffee, S. H. Adolescents, parents and television use: Self report and other measures for the Wisconsin sample. In G. A. Comstock & E. A. Rubinstein (Eds.), *Television and Social Behavior*, 1972, 4, 239–314. (b)

McLeod, J. M., Atkin, C. K., & Eswara, H. S. *Family communications patterns and communication research*. Paper presented at the meeting of the Association for Education in Journalism, Iowa City, Iowa, Aut., 1966.

McPherson, S. J., McDonald, J. D., & Ryer, C. W. Intensive counseling with families of juvenile offenders, *Juvenile and Family Court Journal*, 1983, 27–33.

McPartland, J. M., & McDill, E. *Violence in Schools: Perspectives, Programs, and Positions*. Lexington, Mass.: D. C. Heath, 1976.

Maden, M. F., & Wrench, D. F. Significant findings in child abuse research. *Victimology*, 1977, 2, 196–224.

Major issues in juvenile justice information and training: Youth in adult courts: Between two worlds. *Academy for Contemporary Problems*, 1982.

Malinowski, B. *Crime and custom in savage society*. Totowa, N.J.: Littlefield, Adams, 1982.

Malinowski, B. *The dynamics of culture change*. New Haven: Yale University Press, 1945.

Malinowski, B. *Sex and repression in primitive society*. London: Routledge & Kegan Paul, 1953.

Mankoff, M. Societal reaction and career deviance: A critical analysis. *Sociological Quarterly*, 1971, 12, 204–218.

Mann, C. *Female crime and delinquency*. University Station, Ala.: University of Alabama Press, 1984.

Manneheim, H. *Comparative criminology* (Vols. 1 and 2). London: Routledge and Kegan Paul, 1965.

Mannheim, H. *Pioneers in criminology*. Montclair, N.J.: Patterson Smith, 1972.

Mannheim, K. *Ideology and utopia*. New York: Harcourt, Brace, 1936.

Manning, P. K. Observing the police: Deviants, respectables and the law. In J. Douglas (Ed.), *Research on deviance*. New York: Random House, 1972.

Marcuse, H. *Eros and civilization: A philosophical inquiry into Freud*. Boston: Beacon Press, 1974.

Margolick, D. Ruling on juvenile detention: Praise and criticism. *New York Times*, June 5, 1984.

Marijuana: A signal of misunderstanding. Washington, D.C.: U.S. Government Printing Office, 1972.

Marinello, M. J., Berkson, R. A., Edwards, J. A., & Bannerman, R. H. A study of the XYY syndrome in tall men and juvenile delinquents. *Journal of the American Medical Association*, 1969, 208, 321–325.

Marion, A. The juvenile diversion system in action: Some recommendations for change. *Crime and Delinquency*, 1976, 22, 461–469.

Mark, V., & Erwin, F. *Violence and the brain*. New York: Harper & Row, 1970.

Marshall, C., Marshall, I. H., & Thomas, C. The implementation of formal procedures in juvenile court processing of status offenders. *Journal of Criminal Justice*, 1983, 11, 195–211.

Martin, R. G., & Conger, R. A comparison of delinquency trends: Japan and the United States. *Criminology*, 1980, 18, 1.

Martinson, R. What works? Questions and answers about prison reforms. In J. Leger & J. Stratton (Eds.), *The sociology of corrections*. New York: Wiley, 1977.

Marvit, R. C. Guilty but mentally ill—an old approach to an old problem. *The Clinical Psychologist*, 34 (4), 1981, 22–23.

Marx, K. *Contributions to a critique of political economy*. Chicago: Charles Kerr, 1904. (Originally published, 1859.)

Marx, K. Theories of surplus value. In T. B. Bottomore and M. Rubel (Eds.), *Karl Marx: Selected writings in sociology and social philosophy*. New York: McGraw Hill, 1964.

Marx, K., & Engels, F. *Capital: A critique of political economy* (E. Aveling, Trans.). Chicago: Charles Kerr, 1906. (Originally published, 1867–1894.)

Marx, K., & Engels, F. *The communist manifesto* (S. Moore, Trans.). New York: Washington Square Press, 1964. (Originally published, 1848.)

Marx, K., & Engels, F. *The German ideology*. New York: International Library, 1970.

Maslow, A. *Motivation and personality*. New York: Harper & Row, 1954.

Matsuda, R. L. Testing control theory and differential association: A causal modeling approach. *American Sociological Review*, 1982, 47, 489–504.

Matteson, D. *Adolescence today: Sex roles and the search for identity*. Homewood, Ill.: Dorsey, 1975.

Matza, D. *Delinquency and drift*. Englewood Cliffs, N.J.: Prentice-Hall, 1964.

Matza, D. *Becoming deviant*. Englewood Cliffs, N.J.: Prentice-Hall, 1969.

Mawby, R. The victimization of juveniles: A comparative study of three areas of publicly owned housing in Sheffield. *Journal of Research in Crime and Delinquency*, 1979, 16, 98–113.

Maxim, P. S. Cohort, size and juvenile delinquency: A test of the Easterlin hypothesis. *Social Forces*, 1985, 63, 661–681.

Mayer, K. Kinds of aggression and their physiological basis. *Communications in Behavioral Biology*, 1968, 2, 65–87.

Mayhew, P., & Hough, M. The British crime survey. *British Journal of Criminology*, 1983, 23, 1.

Mayor imposes juvenile curfew: Hot summer in Detroit. *Criminal Justice Newsletter*, August 1, 1983, p. 7.

Mazur, A. Bomb threats and the mass media. *American Sociological Review*, 1982, 47.

Mazur, A., & Robertson, L. *Biology and social behavior*. New York: Free Press, 1972.

McCaghy, C. H. *Deviant behavior*. New York: Macmillan, 1976.

Mead, G. H. *Mind, self and society*. Chicago: University of Chicago Press, 1934.

Mead, M. *Coming of age*. New York: New American Library, 1950.

Mead, M. *Growing up in New Guinea*. New York: New American Library, 1953.

Meade, A. C. The labeling approach to delinquency: State of the theory as a function of method. *Social Forces*, 1974, 53, 83–91.

Mednick, S. A., & Christiansen, K. O. *Biosocial bases of criminal behavior*. New York: Gardner Press, 1977.

Mednick, S. A., & Hutchings, B. Genetic psychophysiological factors in asocial behavior, *Journal of the American Academy of Child Psychiatry*, 1978, 17, 209–223.

Megargee, E. E., & Bohn, M. J. *Classifying criminal offenders: A new system based on the MMPI*. Beverly Hills, Calif., 1979.

Meier, R. F. The new criminology: Continuity in criminological theory. *The Journal of Criminal Law and Criminology*, 1976, 67, 461–469.

Melnuk, J., Derencsenvi, A., Vanacek, F., Rucci, A. J., & Thompson, J. XYY survey in an institution for sex offenders and the mentally ill. *Nature*, 1969, 224, 369–370.

Mennel, R. M. *Thorns and thistles: Juvenile delinquents in the United States, 1825–1949*. Hanover, N.H.: University Press of New England, 1973.

Merton, R. K. Social structure and anomie. *American Sociological Review*, 1983, 3, 672–682.

Michalowski, R. J., & Bohlander, E. W. Repression and criminal justice in capitalist America. *Sociological Inquiry*, 1976, 46, 95–106.

Miers, D. Victim compensation as a labelling process. *Victimology: An International Journal*, 1980, 5, 3–16.

Milavsky, R. J., et al. *Television and Aggression: A Case Study*. New York: Academic Press, 1982. (a)

Milavsky, R. J., et al. Television and aggression: results of a panel study. In E. A. Rubinstein and G. A. Comstock (Eds.), *Television and Behavior*, 1982, 2, 138–157. (b)

Milgram, S., & Shotland, R. L. *Television and antisocial behavior*. New York: Academic Press, 1973.

Miller, A. *The drama of the gifted child* (Ruth Ward, Trans.). New York: Basic Books, 1981.

Miller, A. D., & Ohlin, L. B. *Delinquency and community*. Beverly Hills, Calif.: Sage, 1986.

Miller, J. D. *National survey on drug abuse: Main findings, 1982*. Rockville, Md.: National Institute on Drug Abuse, 1983.

Miller, J. P. Piaget, Kohlberg and Erikson: Developmental implications for secondary education. *Adolescence*, 13 (Summer, 1978), 237–250.

Miller, W. B. Lower class culture as a generating milieu of gang delinquency. *Journal of Social Issues*, 1958, 15, 5–19.

Miller, W. B. *Violence by youth gangs and youth groups as a crime problem in major American cities* (U.S. Department of Justice, Law Enforcement Assistance Administration, National Institute for Juvenile Justice and Delinquency Prevention). Washington, D.C.: U.S. Government Printing Office, 1975.

Miller, W. B., Baum, R. C., & McNeil, R. Delinquency prevention and organizational relations. In S. Wheeler (Ed.), *Controlling delinquency*. New York: Wiley, 1968.

Mills, C. W. The professional ideology of social pathologists. *American Journal of Sociology*, 1943, 49, 165–180.

Ministry of Justice. *The trends of juvenile delinquency and procedures for handling delinquents in Japan*, 1970.

Minkovsky, G. M. Some causes of juvenile delinquency in the U.S.S.R. and measures to prevent it. *Sovetskoye gosudarstvo in provo*, May 1966 (*The Current Digest of the Soviet Press*, Aug. 1966).

Minora, Y. Delinquency control programs in the community in Japan. *International Journal of Comparative and Applied Criminal Justice*, 1981, 5, 169–78.

Mischel, W. *Personality and assessment*. New York: Wiley, 1968.

Mitchell, J. D., & Cochrum, D. L. Positive peer culture and a legal system: A comparison in an adolescent treatment facility. *Criminal Justice and Behavior*, 1980, 7, 399–406.

Moffit, T. E., Gabrielli, W. F., Mednick, S. A., & Schulsinger, F. Socioeconomic status, I.Q. and delinquency. *Journal of Abnormal Psychology*, 1980. 90 (2), 152–56.

Monahan, T. P. Broken homes by age of delinquent children. *Journal of Social Psychology*, 1960, 51, 387–397.

Monahan, T. P. Family status and the delinquent child: A reappraisal and some new findings. *Social Forces*, 1957, 35, 250–258.

Monahan, T. P. Police dispositions of juvenile offenders: The problems of measurement and a study of Philadelphia data. *Phylon*, 1970, 21, 129–141.

Monroe, R. R. *Brain dysfunction in aggressive criminals*. Lexington, Mass.: Lexington Books, 1978.

Montague, A. The biologist looks at crime. *Annals of the American Academy of Political and Social Science*, 1941, 217, 46–57.

Montague, A. Chromosomes and crime. *Psychology Today*, October 1968, pp. 42–49.

Moore, J. *Homeboys: Gangs, drugs, and prison in the barrios of Los Angeles.* Philadelphia: Temple University Press, 1978.

Moran, R. Biomedical research and the politics of crime control: A historical perspective. *Contemporary Crises,* 1978, *2,* 335–357.

Morash, M. The application of social impact assessment to the study of criminal and juvenile justice programs: A case study. *Journal of Criminal Justice,* 1983, *11,* 229–240.

Morash, M. Establishment of a juvenile police record: The influence of individual peer group characterization. *Criminology,* 1984, *12,* 1.

More, T. *Utopia* (Notes and introduction by E. Surtz.) New Haven: Yale University Press, 1964.

More on Washington State juvenile justice reform. *Criminal Justice Newsletter,* September 26, 1983, pp. 1–3.

Morris, T. *The criminal area.* London: Routledge & Kegan Paul, 1967.

Morton, J. H., Addison, R. G., Addison, L., Hunt, L., & Sullivan, J. J. A clinical study of premenstrual tension. *American Journal of Obstetrics and Gynecology,* 1953, *65,* 1182–1191.

Mott, J. Police decisions for dealing with juvenile offenders. *British Journal of Criminology,* 1983, *23,* #3.

Mouzakitis, C. M. Characteristics of abused adolescents and guidelines for intervention. *Child Welfare,* 1984, *63,* 149–157.

Mouzakitis, C. M. An inquiry into the problem of child abuse and juvenile delinquency. In R. J. Bunner & Y. E. Walker (Eds.), *Exploring the relationship between child abuse and delinquency.* Montclair, N.J.: Allanheld, Osmun, 1981.

Muehlbauer, G., & Dodder, L. *The losers: Gang delinquency in an American suburb.* New York: Praeger, 1983.

Mueller, G. O. The United Nations and criminology. In E. Johnson (Ed.), *International handbook of contemporary developments in criminology: General issues and the Americas.* Westport, Conn.: Greenwood, 1983.

Muir, Jr., W. K. *Police: Streetcorner politicians.* Chicago: University of Chicago Press, 1977.

Muller, G. O., Gage, M., & Kupperstein, L. R. *The legal norms of delinquency: A comparative study.* New York: New York University School of Law, 1969.

Mulvihill, D., Tumin, M., & Curtis, L. *A staff report submitted to the National Commission on the Causes and Prevention of Violence* (Vol. 2). Washington, D.C.: U.S. Government Printing Office, 1968.

Murdock, G. *Social structure.* New York: Macmillan, 1949.

Murray, C. *The link between learning disabilities and juvenile delinquency: Current theory and knowledge.* Washington, D.C.: U.S. Government Printing Office, 1976.

Murray, C., & Cox, L. *Beyond probation: Juvenile corrections and the chronic delinquent.* Beverly Hills, Calif.: Sage, 1979.

Murray, J. A. (Ed.). *The new English dictionary on historical principles* (Vol. I). Oxford: Clarenden Press, 1888.

Murray, J. P. *Status offenders: A sourcebook.* Boys Town, Neb.: The Boys Town Center, 1983.

Murray, J. P. *Television and youth: 25 years of research and controversy.* Stanford, Wash.: Boy's Town Center for the Study of Youth Development, 1980.

Muuss, R. E. Adolescent development and the secular trend. *Adolescence,* 1970, *5,* 109–129.

Muuss, R. E. *Theories of adolescence* (3rd ed.). New York: Random House, 1975.

Myerhoff, H., & Myerhoff, B. Field observations of middle class gangs. In E. Vaz (Ed.), *Middle class juvenile delinquency.* New York: Harper & Row, 1967.

Naisbitt, J. *Mega trends: Ten new directions transforming our lives.* New York: Warner Books, 1982.

Nagle, B. K. Juvenile delinquent in society. *Indian Journal of Criminology,* 1979, *9,* 1.

Nakayama, K. Japan. In G. Cole, S. Frankowski, & M. Gertz (Eds.), *Major Criminal Justice Systems.* Beverly Hills, Calif.: Sage, 1981.

A nation at risk. See U.S. Department of Education, 1983.

National Advisory Commission on Criminal Justice Standards and Goals. *A national strategy to reduce crime.* Washington, D.C.: U.S. Government Printing Office, 1974.

National Advisory Commission on Criminal Justice Standards and Goals. Diversion from the criminal justice system. In P. Boesen & S. Grupp (Eds.), *Community based corrections: Theory, practice and research.* Santa Cruz, Calif.: Davis, 1976. (a)

National Advisory Commission on Criminal Justice Standards and Goals. *Juvenile justice and delinquency prevention: A report of the task force on juvenile justice and delinquency prevention.* Washington, D.C.: U.S. Government Printing Office, 1976. (b)

National Commission on Marijuana and Drug Abuse. *Drug use in America: Problem in perspective.* Washington, D.C.: U.S. Government Printing Office, 1973.

The National Center on Institutions and Alternatives. *Sentenced prisoners under 18 years of age in adult correctional facilities: A national survey.* Washington, D.C., March, 1980.

National Conference of Superintendents of Training and Reformatories. *Institutional rehabilitation of delinquent youth: Manual for training school personnel.* Albany, N.Y.: Delman, 1962.

National Council of Juvenile and Family Court Judges. *Juvenile court statistics, 1975.* Pittsburgh: National Center for Juvenile Justice, Oct. 1979.

National Council of Juvenile and Family Court Judges. *Juvenile court statistics, 1976–78.* Pittsburgh: National Center for Juvenile Justice, Oct. 1981.

National Council of Juvenile and Family Court Judges. *Juvenile court statistics, 1981.* Pittsburgh: National Center for Juvenile Justice, Oct. 1983.

National Council of Juvenile and Family Court Judges. *Juvenile court statistics, 1982.* Pittsburgh: National Center for Juvenile Justice, 1984.

National Institute of Mental Health. *See* U.S. Department of Health, Education and Welfare, National Institute of Mental Health.

National Institute of Drug Abuse. *See* U.S. Department of Health, Education and Welfare, National Institute on Drug Abuse.

National jail census, 1970, U.S. Department of Justice, LEAA. National Criminal Justice Information and Statistics Service. Washington, D.C., February, 1971.

National Task Force to Develop Standards and Goals for Juvenile Justice and Delinquency Prevention. *Preventing delinquency* (Vol. 1). (U.S. Department of Justice.) Washington, D.C.: U.S. Government Printing Office, 1977.

Needle, J. A., & Stapleton, V. *Police handling of youth gangs. Reports of the National Juvenile Assessment Center,* OJJDP, September, 1983.

Needleman, C. Discrepant assumptions in empirical research: The case of juvenile court screening. *Social Problems,* 1981, *28,* 247–262.

Nejelski, P. Diversion: The promise and the danger. *Crime and Delinquency,* 1976, *22,* 393–410.

Nettler, G. Cruelty, dignity and determinism. *American Sociological Review,* 1959, *24,* 375–384.

Nettler, G. *Explaining crime.* New York: McGraw-Hill, 1978; 1984.

New forms of juvenile delinquency: Their origin, prevention, and treatment. A report prepared by the Secretariat, Second United Nations Congress on the Prevention of Crime and the Treatment of Offenders, London, August, 1960.

New law extends OJJDP, grants authority for missing children. *Criminal Justice Newsletter,* November, 1984.

New sentencing powers under the criminal justice act, 1982. *The Criminal Law Review,* May, 1983, 281–283.

Newbolt, H. L., Philpot, W., & Mandell, M. *Psychiatric syndromes produced by allergies: Ecologic mental illness.* Paper presented at the annual meeting of Orthomolecular Psychiatry, Dallas, 1972.

Newman, G. *Crime and deviance: A comparative perspective.* Beverly Hills, Calif.: Sage, 1980.

Neznansky, F. Soviet crime statistics: Reading the political message. *Freedom at Issue,* Nov./Dec., 1979.

Niederhoffer, A. *Behind the shield: The police in urban society.* New York: Anchor Books, 1969.

Nielsen, J., Tsuboi, T., Sturup, G., & Romano, D. XYY chromosomal constitution in criminal psychopaths. *Lancet,* 1968, *2,* 576.

Noel, B., Quack, B., Durand, Y., & Rethore, M. D. Les hommes, 47, XYY, *Annales de Genetique,* 1969, *12,* 223–235.

Norland, S., & Shover, N. Gender roles and female criminality: Some critical comments. *Criminology,* 1977, *15,* 87–104.

Norland, S., Shover, N., Thornton, W., & James, J. Intrafamily conflict and delinquency. Paper read at the annual meeting of the Society for the Study of Social Problems, San Francisco, 1978. The published version of the paper,

containing a more detailed analysis, appears in *Pacific Sociological Review,* 1979, *2,* 223–240.

Normandeau, A. The measurement of delinquency in Montreal. *Journal of Criminal Law, Criminology and Police Science,* 1966, *57,* 172–177.

Nuernberger, W. W., & Dvizend, R. Development of standards for juvenile justice: An overview. *Juvenile Justice,* 1977, *28,* 3–6.

Numberg, H. Problems in the structure of juvenile court. *Journal of Criminal Law, Criminology and Police Science,* 1958, *48,* 500–517.

Nye, F. I. *Family relationships and delinquent behavior.* New York: Wiley, 1958.

Nye, F. I., & Short, J. F., Jr. Scaling delinquent behavior. *American Sociological Review,* 1957, *22,* 326–331.

Nye, F. I., Short, J. F., Jr., & Olsen, V. J. Socioeconomic status and delinquent behavior. *American Journal of Sociology,* 1958, *53,* 381–389.

O'Donnell, J. A. The rise and fall of a subculture. *Social Problems,* 1966, *14,* 73–84.

O'Donnell, J. A., Voss, H. L., Clayton, R. R., Slaton, G. T., & Room, R. *Young men and drugs—A nationwide survey* (NIDA Research Monograph 5). Rockville, Md.: National Institute on Drug Abuse, 1976.

Ogden, T. Japan. In D. H. Chang, *Criminology: A cross cultural perspective* (Vol. 2). New Delhi: Vikas, 1976.

Ohlin, L. The future of juvenile justice policy and research. *Crime and Delinquency,* 1983, *29,* 463–489.

Ohmart, H. The community and the juvenile. In P. G. Boesen & S. E. Grupps (Eds.), *Community-based corrections: Theory, practice and research.* Santa Cruz, Calif.: Davis, 1976.

OJJDP puts out for comment Program Plan for Fiscal '84. *Criminal Justice Newsletter,* March 15, 1984, 5–6.

Okun, M. A., & Sasfy, S. H. Adolescence, the self concept, and formal operations. *Adolescence,* 1977, *12,* 373–379.

Olson-Raymer, G. National juvenile justice policy: Myth or reality? In S. H. Decker (Ed.), *Juvenile justice policy: Analyzing trends and outcomes.* Beverly Hills, Calif.: Sage, 1984.

Olson-Raymer, G. The role of the federal government in juvenile delinquency prevention: Historical and contemporary perspective. *The Journal of Criminal Law and Criminology,* 1983, *74,* 578–600.

Oltman, J., McGarry, J., & Friedman, S. Parental deprivation and the "broken home" in dementia praecox and other mental disorders. *American Journal of Orthopsychiatry,* 1952, *108,* 685–694.

Omnibus Crime Control and Safe Streets Act of 1968 (Public Law 90-351), Title I.

Osbun, L. A., & Rode, P. Prosecuting juveniles as adults: The quest for objective decision. *Criminology,* 1984, *22,* 187–202.

Osgood, W., & Weichselbaum, H. F. Juvenile diversion: When practice matches theory. *Journal of Research in Crime and Delinquency,* 1984, *21,* 33–56.

Otis, M. A. A perversion not commonly noted. *Journal of Abnormal Psychology*, 1913, 8, 113–116.

Otto, H. Sex and violence on the American newstand. *Journalism Quarterly*, 1963, 40, 19–26.

Packard, V. *Our endangered children: Growing up in a changing world.* Boston: Little, Brown, 1983.

Palmer, S. *The psychology of murder.* New York: Thomas Crowell, 1962.

Palmer, T. California's community treatment project and delinquency, 1971, 8, 74–92.

Palmer, T. *Correctional intervention and research.* Lexington, Mass.: Lexington Books, 1978.

Palmer, T. *Differential placement of delinquents in group homes: Final report.* Sacramento: California Youth Authority and National Institute of Mental Health, 1972.

Palmer, T. *Personality characteristics and professional orientations of five groups of community project workers.* A preliminary report on differences among treaters. Community Treatment Project Report Series, 1967, No. 1.

Palmer, T. The Youth Authority Community Treatment Project, *Federal Probation*, 1974, 38, 3–14.

Pandiani, J. A. Crime time TV: If all we knew is what we see . . . *Contemporary Crises*, 1978, 2 (4): 437–458.

Papageannis, G., Bickel, R., & Fuller, R. The social creation of school dropouts: Accomplishing the reproduction of an underclass. *Youth and Society*, 1983, 14, 3.

Park, R. E., Burgess, E. W., & McKenzie, R. D. *The city.* Chicago: University of Chicago Press, 1925.

Parker, H., & Giller, H. More or less the same: British delinquency research since the sixties, *British Journal of Criminology*, 1981, 21, 3.

Parnell, R. W. *Behavior and physique: Applied somatometry.* London: Arnold, 1958.

Parsloe, D. *Juvenile justice in Britain and the United States: The balance of needs and rights.* London: Routledge & Kegan Paul, 1978.

Parsons, T. The school class as a social system: Some of its functions in American society. *Harvard Educational Review*, 1959, 29, 297–318.

Parsons, T. *The structure of social action.* New York: McGraw-Hill, 1937.

Paulsen, M. G., & Whitebread, C. H. *Juvenile law and procedure.* Reno, Nev.: National Council of Juvenile Court Judges, 1974.

Pawlak, E. J. Differential selection of juveniles for detention. *Journal of Research in Crime and Delinquency*, 1977, 14, 1–12.

Pawlak, V. *Megavitamin therapy and the drug wipeout syndrome.* Phoenix, Ariz.: Do It Now Foundation, 1972.

Pearson, G. *The deviant imagination: Psychiatry, social work and social change.* New York: Holmes and Meier, 1975.

Pelfrey, W. V. *The evolution of criminology.* Cincinnati: Anderson, 1980.

Pemberton, D. A., & Benady, D. R. Consciously rejected children. *British Journal of Psychiatry*, 1973, 123, 575–78.

Pena, E. H. Introduction to the role of the juvenile court—Social or legal institution? *Pepperdine Law Review*, 1978, 5, 633–649.

Pepinsky, H. Police patrolmen's offense reporting behavior. *Journal of Research in Crime and Delinquency*, 1976, 13, 33–47.

Persons, R. W. Psychological and behavioral change in delinquents following psychotherapy. *Journal of Clinical Psychology*, 1966, 22, 337–400.

Peterson, D. R. Behavior problems of middle childhood. *Journal of Counseling Psychology*, 1961, 25, 205–9.

Peterson, D. R., & Becker, W. C. Family interaction and delinquency. In H. C. Quay (Ed.), *Juvenile delinquency: Research and theory.* Princeton, N.J.: D. Van Nostrand, 1965.

Peterson, R. D., & Hagan, J. Changing conceptions of race: Towards an account of anomalous finding of sentencing research. *American Sociological Review*, 1984, 49, 56–70.

Pfohl, S. Deciding dangerousness: Prediction of violence as social control. *Crime and Social Justice*, 1979.

Pfuhl, E. H. The relationship of comic and horror comics to juvenile delinquency. *Research Studies of the State College of Washington*, 1956, 24, 170–77.

Pfuhl, Jr., E. H. Mass media and reported delinquent behavior: A negative case. In M. E. Wolfgang, L. Savitz, & N. Johnson (Eds.), *The sociology of crime and delinquency*, 2nd ed. New York: Wiley, 1970.

Phelps, T. R. *Juvenile delinquency: A contemporary view.* Santa Monica, Calif.: Goodyear, 1976.

Phillips, D. The impact of mass media violence on U.S. homicides. *American Sociological Review*, 1983, 48.

Phillips, E. L., Phillips, R. A., Fixen, D. L., & Wolf, M. W. Behavior shaping works for delinquency. *Psychology Today*, 1973, 6, 75–79.

Phillipson, C. M. Juvenile delinquency and the schools. In W. G. Carson & P. Wiles (Eds.), *Crime and delinquency in Britain.* London: Martin Robertson, 1971.

Phillipson, C. M. Critical theorizing and the new criminology. *British Journal of Criminology*, 1973, 13, 398–400.

Philpott, W. H. Ecological aspects of antisocial behavior. In L. Hippchen (Ed.), *Ecologic-biochemical approaches to treatment of delinquents and criminals.* New York: Van Nostrand Reinhold, 1978.

Piaget, J. Intellectual evolution from adolescence to adulthood. *Human Development*, 1972, 15, 1012.

Piaget, J. The theory of stages in cognitive development. In D. Green (Ed.), *Measurement and Piaget.* New York: McGraw-Hill, 1971.

Piaget, J., & Inhelder, B. *The psychology of the child.* New York: Basic Books, 1969.

Piliavin, I., & Briar, S. Police encounters with juveniles. *American Journal of Sociology*, 1964, 70, 206–214.

Pinatel, J. International Society for Criminology. In E. Johnson (Ed.), *International handbook of contemporary developments in criminology: General issues and the Americas.* Westport, Conn.: Greenwood, 1983.

Pittman, D. J. Drugs, addiction and crime. In D. Glaser (Ed.), *Handbook of criminology.* Chicago: Rand McNally, 1974.

Plamenatz, J. *Man and society* (Vol. II). London: Longmans, Green, 1966.

Platt, A. M. *The child savers: The invention of delinquency.* Chicago: University of Chicago Press, 1969.

Platt, A. M. The triumph of benevolence: The origins of the juvenile justice system in the U.S. In R. Quinney (Ed.), *Criminal justice in America: A critical understanding.* Boston: Little, Brown, 1974.

Platt, A. M. Prospects for a radical criminology in the U.S. In I. Taylor, P. Walton, & J. Young (Eds.), *Critical criminology.* London: Routledge & Kegan Paul, 1975.

Platt, A. M., Schechter, H., and Tiffany, P. In defense of youth: A case study of the public defender in juvenile court. In B. Krisberg & J. Austin (Eds.), *The children of Ishmael: Critical perspectives on juvenile justice.* Palo Alto, Calif.: Mayfield, 1978.

Platt, A. M., & Takagi, P. Biosocial criminology: A critique. *Crime and Social Justice: Issues in Criminology,* 1979, *17,* 5–13.

Platt, T. Crime and punishment in the United States: Immediate and long term reforms from a Marxist perspective. *Crime and Social Justice,* 1982, *18,* 38–46.

Platt, T., & Takagi, P. Meeting the challenge of the 1980s. *Crime and Social Justice,* 1982.

Playing games: Data banks become kid's stuff. *Time,* August, 1983, p. 14.

Police white paper. Tokyo, Japan, 1976.

Polk, K. *A note on the relationship between broken homes, disposition, and juvenile delinquency.* Unpublished manuscript, 1958. Cited in E. H. Sutherland, & D. Cressey, *Criminology* (10th ed.). Philadelphia: Lippincott, 1978.

Polk, K., Frease, D., & Richmond, L. Social class, school experience, and delinquency. *Criminology,* 1974, *12,* 84–96.

Polk, K., & Halferty, D. School cultures, adolescent commitments, and delinquency. In K. Polk, & W. Schafer (Eds.), *Schools and delinquency.* Englewood Cliffs, N.J.: Prentice-Hall, 1972.

Polk, K., & Pink, W. School pressures toward deviance: A cross-cultural comparison. In K. Polk & W. Schafer (Eds.), *Schools and delinquency.* Englewood Cliffs, N.J.: Prentice-Hall, 1972.

Polk, K., & Richmond, F. L. Those who fail. In K. Polk & W. Schafer (Eds.). *Schools and delinquency.* Englewood Cliffs, N.J.: Prentice-Hall, 1972.

Polk, K., and Schafer, W. *Schools and delinquency.* Englewood Cliffs, New Jersey: Prentice-Hall, 1972.

Pollak, O. *The criminality of women.* Philadelphia: University of Pennsylvania Press, 1950.

Polsky, H. W. *Cottage six: The social system of delinquent boys in residential treatment.* New York: Krieger, 1962.

Poole, E. D., & Regoli, R. M. Violence in juvenile institutions: A comparative study. *Criminology,* 1983, *21,* 213–232.

Pope, C. Race and crime revisited. *Crime and Delinquency,* 1979, *25,* 347–357.

Poplin, D. E. *Social problems.* Glenview, Ill.: Scott, Foresman, 1978.

Porteous, M. A. High school personality questionnaire: Results from a sample of delinquent boys. *Community School Gazette,* 1973, *67,* 424–426.

Porter, B. California prison gangs. *Corrections Magazine,* December, 1982.

Porterfield, A. C. *Youth in trouble.* Fort Worth, Tex.: Leo Potishman Foundation, 1946.

Poston, R. M. *The gang and the establishment.* New York: Harper & Row, 1971.

Poulin, J., Levitt, J., Young, T., & Pappenfort, D. *Juveniles in detention centers and jails: An analysis of state variations during the mid-1970's.* Washington, D.C.: National Institute for Juvenile Justice and Delinquency Prevention.

Poveda, T. The fear of crime in a small town. *Crime and Delinquency,* 1972, *18,* 147–153.

Power, M. J., Benn, R. T., & Morris, J. N. Neighbourhood, school and juveniles before the courts. *British Journal of Criminology,* 1972, *12,* 111–132.

Prentice, N. M., & Kelly, F. J. Intelligence and delinquency: A reconsideration. *Journal of Social Psychology,* 1963, *60,* 327–337.

President's Commission on Law Enforcement and the Administration of Justice. *The challenge of crime in a free society.* Washington, D.C.: U.S. Government Printing Office, 1967. (a)

Presdient's Commission on Law Enforcement and the Administration of Justice. *Task force report: Corrections.* Washington, D.C.: U.S. Government Printing Office, 1967. (b)

President's Commission on Law Enforcement and the Administration of Justice. *Task force report: Juvenile delinquency and youth crime.* Washington, D.C.: U.S. Government Printing Office, 1967. (c)

President's Commission on Law Enforcement and the Administration of Justice. *Task force report: Narcotics and drug abuse.* Washington, D.C.: U.S. Government Printing Office, 1967. (d)

President's Commission on Obscenity and Pornography. *The report of the commission on obscenity and pornography.* New York: Bantam Books, 1970.

Preston, M. Children's reactions to movie horrors and radio crime. *Journal of Pediatrics,* 1941, *19,* 147–168

Prevention of delinquency through alternative education. U.S. Department of Justice, OJJDP, Feb., 1980.

Price, W. H., Whatmore, P. B., & McClemont, W. Criminal patients with XYY sex-chromosome complement. *Lancet,* 1966, *1,* 565–566.

Propper, A. M. Lesbianism in female and coed correctional institutions. *Journal of Homosexuality,* 1978, *3,* 265–274.

Propper, A. M. Make-believe families and homosexuality among imprisoned girls. *Criminology,* 1982, *20,* 127–138.

Quay, H. C. Classifications. In H. C. Quay & J. S. Wherry (Eds.), *Psychopathological disorders of childhood.* New York: Wiley, 1979.

Quay, H. C. Personality dimensions in delinquent males as inferred from the factor analysis of behavior ratings. *Journal of Research in Crime and Delinquency,* 1964, *1,* 73–96.

Quay, H. C. Psychopathic personality as pathological stimulation seeking. *American Journal of Psychiatry,* 1965, *122,* 180–183.

Quicker, J. C. The effect of goal discrepancy on delinquency. *Social Problems,* 1974, *22,* 76–86.

Quicker, J. C. *The Los Angeles war on youth gangs: Will justice be administered?* Paper read at Academy of Criminal Justice Sciences, Louisville, Ky.: March, 1982. (a)

Quicker, J. C. *Seven Decades of Gangs: The California Commission on Crime Control and Violence Prevention,* State of California, 1982. (b)

Quicker, J. C. *Home girls: Characterizing Chicana gangs.* San Pedro, Calif.: International University Press, 1983.

Quinney, R. A. *The social reality of crime.* Boston: Little, Brown, 1970.

Quinney, R. A. *Critique of legal order: Crime control in capitalist society.* Boston: Little, Brown, 1974.

Quinney, R. A. *Criminology: An analysis and critique of crime in America.* Boston: Little, Brown, 1975. (a)

Quinney, R. A. Who is the victim? In J. Hudson & B. Galawzy (Eds.) *Considering the victim.* Springfield, Ill: Charles Thomas, 1975. (b)

Quinney, R. A. *Class, state, and crime.* New York: David McKay, 1977.

Quinney, R. A. The production of criminology, *Criminology,* 1979, *16,* 445–457.

Radzinowicz, L., & King, J. *The growth of crime.* New York: Basic Books, 1977.

Randolph, K. D. Dialectical correlates of juvenile delinquency. Ph.D. dissertation, Texas Tech University, 1973.

Rank, O. *Will therapy and truth and reality.* New York: Knopf, 1936.

Rankin, J. H. The family context of delinquency. *Social Problems,* 1983, *30,* 466–479.

Rankin, J. School factors and delinquency. *Sociology and Social Research,* 1980, *64,* 470–434.

Rasche, G. E. The female offender as an object of criminological research. *Criminal Justice and Behavior,* 1974, *1,* 307–314.

Rathus, S., & Seigel, L. Crime and personality revisited: Effects of MMPI response sets in self-report studies. *Criminology,* 1980, *18,* 245–251.

Rausch, S. Court processing versus diversion of status offender: A test of deterrence and labeling theories. *Journal of Research in Crime and Delinquency,* 1983, *20.*

Rausch, S. P. Diversion from juvenile court: Panacea or Pandora's box. In J. R. Kluegel (Ed.), *Evaluating juvenile justice.* Beverly Hills, Calif.: Sage, 1983.

Ray, O. *Drugs, society and human behavior.* St. Louis, Mo.: C. V. Mosby, 1978.

Reasons, C. F. Gault: Procedural change and substantive effect. *Crime and Delinquency,* 1970, *16,* 163–171.

Reckless, W. C. A new theory of delinquency and crime. *Federal Probation,* 1961, *25,* 42–46. (a)

Reckless, W. C. *The crime problem* (3rd ed.). Englewood Cliffs, N.J.: Appleton-Century-Crofts, 1961. (b)

Reckless, W. C. *The Crime Problem* (5th ed.). Englewood Cliffs, N.J.: Prentice-Hall, 1973.

Reckless, W. C., & Dinitz, S. *The prevention of juvenile delinquency.* Columbus, Ohio: Ohio State University Press, 1972.

Reckless, W. C., Dinitz, S., & Murray, E. Self-concept as an insulator against delinquency. *American Sociological Review,* 1956, *21,* 744–746.

Reckless, W. C., Dinitz, S., & Murray, E. The 'good boy' in a high delinquency area. *Journal of Criminal Law, Criminology and Police Science,* 1957, *48,* 18–25.

Rector, J. M. Preface. In *The serious juvenile offender: Proceedings of a national symposium.* Washington, D.C.: U.S. Government Printing Office, 1978.

Redo, L. M. The new criminology: The problem of etiology of crime. *Acta Universitatis Nicolar Copernici,* 1979, *18,* 109–112.

Regnery says juvenile grants follow Regan blueprint. *Criminal Justice Newsletter,* October 1, 1984.

Rehnquist, W. From the Opinion. *New York Times,* June 5, 1984.

Reich, C. *The greening of America.* New York: Random House, 1970.

Reichel, P., & Seyfrity, C. A peer jury in the juvenile court. *Crime and Delinquency,* 1984, *30,* 423–438.

Reid, S. T. *Crime and Criminology,* (2nd ed.). New York: Holt, Rinehart and Winston, 1979.

Reidy, T. J. The aggressive characteristics of abused and neglected children. *Journal of Clinical Psychology,* 1977, *33,* 1140–1145.

Reiman, J. *The rich get richer and the poor get prison.* New York: Wiley, 1979.

Reiss, A. J., Jr. Delinquency as the failure of personal and social controls. *American Sociological Review,* 1951, *16,* 196–207.

Reiss, A. J., Jr. *Studies in crime and law enforcement in major metropolitan areas* (Field Surveys 3, President's Commission on Law Enforcement and the Administration of Justice, Vol. 1). Washington, D.C.: U.S. Government Printing Office, 1967. (a)

Reiss, A. J., Jr. Studies of crime and law enforcement in major metropolitan areas, section 2. In *Career orientations, job satisfaction and the assessment of law enforcement problems by police officers* (U.S. Department of Justice, Law Enforcement Assistance Administration). Washington, D.C.: U.S. Government Printing Office, 1967. (b)

Reiss, A. J., Jr. *The police and the public.* New Haven: Yale University Press, 1972.

Reiss, A. J., Jr., & Rhodes, A. L. The distribution of juvenile delinquency in the social class structure. *American Sociological Review,* 1961, 26, 730–732.

The report of the commission on obscenity and pornography. Superintendent of Documents, U.S. Government Printing Office, 1970.

Report on youth gang violence in California. Attorney General's Youth Gang Task Force, Sacramento, Calif.: June, 1981.

Rennie, Y. *The search for criminal man.* Lexington, Mass.: D. C. Heath, 1978.

Reppetto, T. A. The influence of police organizational style on crime control effectiveness. *Journal of Police Science and Administration,* 1975, 3, 274–279.

Rhodes, A. L., & Reiss, A. J., Jr. Apathy, truancy and delinquency as adaptations to school failure. *Social Forces,* 1969, 48, 12–22.

Rhodes, A., & Reiss, A. The religious factor and delinquency behavior. *Journal of Research in Crime and Delinquency,* 1970, 7, 83–98.

Rice, F. *The adolescent: Developments, relationships and culture* (3rd ed.). Boston: Allyn & Bacon, 1978; 1981.

Rivers, W. C. The press as a communication system. *Handbook of communication.* Chicago: Rand McNally, 1973.

Roberts, J. L. Factors associated with truancy. *Personnel and Guidance Journal,* 1956, 34, 431–436.

Roberts, L. M. Actiological implications of childhood histories relating to antisocial personality. In R. D. Hare and D. Schalling (Eds.), *Psychopathic behavior: Approaches to research.* New York: Wiley, 1978.

Robins, L. N. *Deviant children grown up.* Baltimore, Md.: Williams and Wilkins, 1966.

Robinson, J. P., & Bachman, J. G. Television viewing habits and aggression. In G. A. Comstock and E. A. Rubinstein (Eds.), *Television and Social Behavior,* 1972, 3, 372–382.

Robison, J., & Smith, G. The effectiveness of correctional programs. *Crime and Delinquency,* 1971, 27, 67–80.

Roblin, R. *The Boston XYY case* (Hastings Center Report). Hastings on Hudson, N.Y.: Institution of Society, Ethics, and the Life Sciences, 1975.

Roebuck, J. B. *Criminal typology: The legalistic, physical-constitutional-hereditary, psychological-psychiatric and sociological approaches.* Springfield, Ill.: Charles C. Thomas, 1967.

Rogers, C. *Client-centered therapy.* Boston: Houghton-Mifflin, 1951.

Rogers, Y. B. The involuntary drugging of juveniles in state institutions. *Clearinghouse Review,* 1977, 2, 623–629.

Rojek, D. G., & Erickson, H. L. Delinquent careers: A test of the career escalation model. *Criminology,* 1982, 20, 5–20.

Rosanoff, A. J., Handy, L. M., & Plesset, R. Criminality and delinquency in twins. *Journal of Criminal Law and Criminology,* 1934, 24, 923–934.

Rosen, G. *Madness in society.* Chicago: University of Chicago Press, 1968.

Rosen, L. The broken home and male delinquency. In M. Wolfgang, L. Savitz and N. Johnston (Eds.), *The sociology of crime and delinquency.* New York: Wiley, 1970.

Rosen, L., Lalli, M., & Savitz, L. *City life and delinquency: The family and delinquency.* Report submitted to the National Institute for Juvenile Justice and Delinquency Prevention, LEAA, 1975.

Rosenbaum, M. B. The changing body-image of the adolescent girl. In M. Sugar (Ed.), *Female adolescent development.* New York: Brunner/Mazel, 1979.

Rosenberg, M. Conceptual and methodological notes on affective and cognitive role taking (sympathy and empathy): An illustrated example of delinquent and non-delinquent boys. *Journal of Genetic Psychology,* 1974, 125, 177–185.

Rosenberg, J., Kasl, S., & Berberian, R. Sex differences in adolescent drug use: Recent trends. *Addictive Diseases,* 1974, 1, 73–96.

Rosenblatt, J. Prescription drug abuse. *Editorial Research Review,* June 11, 1982, 431–443.

Rosenheim, M. K. Perennial problems in the juvenile court. In M. K. Rosenheim (Ed.), *Justice for the child.* New York: Free Press, 1962.

Rosenthal, D. Heredity in criminality. In I. Jacks & S. G. Cos, (Eds.), *Psychological approaches to crime and the correction: Theory, research, practice.* Chicago: Nelson-Hall, 1984.

Rosenthal, R., & Jacobson, L. *Pygmalion in the classroom.* New York: Holt, Rinehart and Winston, 1968.

Roshier, R. Crime and the press. *New Society,* 1971, 46.

Ross, A., & Pelhan, W. E. Child psychopathology. In *Annual Review of Psychology,* 1981, 32, 243–78.

Ross, R., & Gendreau, P. *Effective correctional treatment.* Toronto: Butterworth, 1980.

Ross, R., & McKay, H. B. A study of institutional treatment programs. *International Journal of Offender Therapy and Comparative Criminology,* 1976, 20, 165–173.

Roszak, T. *The making of a counter culture.* Garden City, N.Y.: Doubleday, 1968.

Rothman, D. J. *The discovery of the asylum: Social order and disorder in the new republic.* Boston: Little, Brown, 1971.

Rottman, D. *Crime in the Republic of Ireland: Statistical trends and their interpretation.* Dublin: The Economic and Social Research Institute, 1980.

Rousseau, J. J. *Emile* (Barbara Foxley, Trans.). New York: Everyman's Library, 1977. (Originally published, 1762).

Rowe, D. C. Biomedical genetic models of self-reported delinquent behavior: A twin study. *Behavior Genetics,* 1983, 13, 473–489.

Rowe, D. C., & Osgood, W. Heredity and sociological theories of delinquency. *American Sociological Review*, 1984, 49, 526–540.

Rowland, H. Radio crime dramas. *Educational Research Bulletin*, 1944, 210–217.

Rubin, S. *Law of juvenile justice*. Dobbs Ferry, N.Y.: Oceana, 1976.

Rubin, S. *Crime and delinquency—A rational approach to penal problems* (2nd ed.). Dobbs Ferry, N.Y.: Oceana Publications, 1961.

Rubin, T. The emerging prosecutor dominance of the juvenile court intake process. *Crime and Delinquency*, 1980, 26, 299–318.

Rubin, T. *Behind the black robes: Juvenile court judges and the court*. Beverly Hills, Calif.: Sage, 1985.

Rutherford, A. Young offenders: Comments on the White Paper on young adult and juvenile offenders. *British Journal of Criminology*, 1981, 21, 1.

Rutter, M., & Giller, H. *Juvenile delinquency: Trends and perspectives*. New York: Guilford, 1984.

Sagatun, U. J., & Edwards, L. P. The role of the district attorney in juvenile court: Is the juvenile court becoming just like adult court? *Juvenile and Family Court Journal*, 1979, 30, 17–23.

Sager, M. A. *A content analysis of juvenile delinquency and juvenile crime issues as reported in the Arizona Republic newspaper*. Unpublished paper, Center for the Study of Justice, Arizona State University, 1983.

Sagi, A., & Eisikovits, Z. Juvenile delinquency and moral development. *Criminal Justice and Behavior*, 1981, 8, 73–93.

Sahlins, M. *The use and abuse of biology*. Ann Arbor: University of Michigan Press, 1979.

Samuelson, R. J. Aging America–Who will shoulder the growing burden. In H. Cox (Ed.), *Aging*. Guilford, Conn.: Dushkin, 1980.

Sarri, R. C. *Under lock and key: Juveniles in jails and detention*. Ann Arbor, Mich.: National Assessment of Juvenile Corrections, 1974.

Sarri, R. C., & Vinter, R. D. Justice for whom? Varieties of juvenile correctional approaches. In M. Klein (Ed.), *The juvenile justice system*. Beverly Hills, Calif.: Sage, 1976.

Sarri, R. C., & Vinter, R. D. Juvenile justice and injustice. *Resolution*, 1977, Winter, 43–54.

Saul, J. A., & Davidson, W. S. Implementation of juvenile diversion programs: Cast your net on the other side of the boat. In J. R. Kluegel (Ed.), *Evaluating Juvenile Justice*. Beverly Hills, Calif.: Sage, 1983.

Savitsky, V. M., & Shupilov, V. P. Union of Soviet Socialist Republics. In G. Cole, S. Frankowski, and M. Gertz (Eds.), *Major criminal justice systems*. Beverly Hills, Calif.: Sage, 1981.

Savitz, L., Lalli, M., & Rosen, L. *City life and delinquency—Victimization, fear of crime and gang membership*. U.S. Department of Justice, LEAA, National Institute for Juvenile Justice and Delinquency Prevention. Washington, D.C.: U.S. Government Printing Office, April, 1977.

Savitz, L. D., Turner, S., & Dickman, T. The origin of scientific criminology: Franz Joseph Gall as the first criminologist. In R. F. Meir (Ed.), *Theory in criminology*. Beverly Hills, Calif.: Sage, 1977.

Savitz, L., Rosen, L., & Lalli, M. Delinquency and gang membership as related to victimization. *Victimology: An International Journal*, 1982.

Scanlon, J. R., & Harville, V. L. *Profile of recidivism*. Atlanta: Georgia Family and Children Services Department, 1966.

Scared straight: The myth that roared. *Institutions, Etc.*, 1979, 2, 1–20.

Schafer, S. *Victimology: The victim and his criminal*. Reston, Va.: Reston, 1977.

Schafer, S., & Knudten, R. *Juvenile delinquency: An introduction*. New York: Random House, 1970.

Schafer, W. E., Olexa, C., & Polk, K. Programmed for social class: Tracking in high school. In K. Polk & W. E. Schafer (Eds.), *Schools and delinquency*. Englewood Cliffs, N.J.: Prentice-Hall, 1972.

Schafer, W. E., & Polk, K. Delinquency and the schools. In President's Commission on Law Enforcement and the Administration of Justice, *Task force report: Juvenile delinquency and youth crime*. Washington, D.C.: U.S. Government Printing Office, 1967.

Scharfman, M., & Clark, R. W. Delinquent adolescent girls: Residential treatment in a municipal hospital setting. *Archives of General Psychiatry*, 1967, 17, 441–47.

Schauss, A. *Diet, crime and delinquency* (rev. ed.). Berkeley, Calif.: Parker House, 1981.

Schichor, D. Socialization: The political aspects of a delinquency explanation. *Sociological Spectrum*, 1983, 85–100.

Schilder, P. The cure of criminals and prevention of crime. *Journal of Criminal Psychopathology*, 1940, 2, 149–161.

Schlapp, M. G., & Smith, E. H. *The new criminology*. New York: Boni and Liveright, 1928.

Schlossman, S., & Sedlak, M. The Chicago Area Project revisited. *Crime and Delinquency*, 1983, 29, 398–462.

Schonfeld, W. A. The body and the body image in adolescence. In G. Caplan & S. Lebovici (Eds.), *Adolescence: Psychosocial perspectives*. New York: Basic Books, 1961.

School crime: The problems and some attempted solutions. U.S. Department of Justice, LEAA, 1979.

Schrag, C. Some functions for a theory of corrections. In D. R. Cressey (ed.), *The prison: Studies in institutional organization and change*. New York: Holt, Rinehart and Winston, 1961.

Schramm, G. Philosophy of the juvenile court. *Annals of the American Academy of Political and Social Science*, 1949, 261, 101–108.

Schroeder, R. *The politics of drugs*. Washington, D.C.: Congressional Quarterly, 1975.

Schuessler, K. F., & Cressey, D. R. Personality characteristics of criminals. *American Journal of Sociology*, 1950, 55, 476–484.

Schultz, J. L. The cycle of juvenile court history. In *The Aldine Crime and justice annual, 1973*. Chicago: Aldine, 1974.

Schumacker, K. E., & Anderson, D. G. An attitude factor in juvenile court decision-making. *Juvenile and Family Court Journal*, 1979, *32*, 31–35.

Schur, E. M. *Our criminal society*. Englewood Cliffs, N.J.: Prentice-Hall, 1969.

Schur, E. M. *Labeling deviant behavior: Its sociological implications*. New York: Harper & Row, 1971.

Schur, E. M. *Radical non-intervention: Rethinking the delinquency problem*. Englewood Cliffs, N.J.: Prentice-Hall, 1973.

Schwartz, M., & Stryker, S. *Deviance, selves and others*. Washington, D.C.: American Sociological Association, 1970.

Schwendinger, H., & Schwendinger, J. Defenders of order or guardians of human rights? *Issues in Criminology*, 1970, *5*, 123–157.

Schwendinger, H., & Schwendinger, J. *Sociologists of the chair*. New York: Basic Books, 1974.

Schwendinger, H., & Schwendinger, J. Delinquency and the collective varieties of youth. *Crime and Social Justice*, 1976, *5*, 7–25. (a)

Schwendinger, H., & Schwendinger, J. Marginal youth and social policy. *Social Problems*, 1976, *24*, 184–191. (b)

Schwendinger, H., & Schwendinger, J. Social class and the definition of crime. *Crime and Social Justice*, 1977, *9*, 4–13.

Schwendinger, H., & Schwendinger, J. The paradigmatic crisis in delinquency theory. *Crime and Social Justice*, 1982, *18*, 70–79.

Schwendinger, H., & Schwendinger, J. *Adolescent subcultures and delinquency*. New York: Praeger, 1985.

Scott, R., & Douglas, J. (Eds.). *Theoretical perspectives on deviance*. New York: Basic Books, 1972.

Scranton Report, Presidential Commission on Campus Unrest. Washington, D.C.: U.S. Government Printing Office, 1970.

Scull, A. T. *Decarceration: Community treatment and the deviant—A radical view*. Englewood Cliffs, N.J.: Prentice-Hall, 1977.

Seaman, J. *Home computers and family interaction patterns*. Paper presented at Society for the Study of Social Problems, Washington, D.C., 1985.

Sebald, H. *Adolescence: A social psychological analysis* (2nd ed.). Englewood Cliffs, N.J.: Prentice-Hall, 1977.

Siegel, D. Personality development in adolescence. In B. B. Wolman (ed.), *Handbook of developmental psychology*. Englewood Cliffs, N.J.: Prentice-Hall, 1982.

Seckel, J. M. *Experiments in group counseling at two youth authority institutions* (Research Report No. 46). Sacramento, Calif.: California Youth Authority, 1965.

Segrave, J. O., & Hastad, D. N. Evaluating structural and control models of delinquency causation: A replication and extension. *Youth and Society*, 1983, *14*, 437–456.

Seidenberg, R. Advertising and drug acculturation. In R. H. Coombs, L. Fry, & P. Lewis (Eds.), *Socialization in drug abuse*. Cambridge, Mass.: Schenkman, 1976.

Sellin, T. *Culture conflict and crime*. New York: Social Science Research Council, 1938.

Sellin, T., & Wolfgang, M. E. *The measurement of delinquency*. New York: Wiley, 1964.

Sellin, T., & Wolfgang, M. E. The legal basis of juvenile delinquency. In R. Giallombardo (Ed.), *Juvenile delinquency: A book of readings*. New York: Wiley, 1972.

Selling, L. S. The pseudo-family. *American Journal of Sociology*, 1981, *37*, 247–253.

Sentenced prisoners under 18 years of age in adult correctional facilities: A national survey. The National Center on Institutions and Alternatives, Washington, D.C. 1980.

Serious juvenile crime: A redirected federal effort. Report of the National Advisory Committee for Juvenile Justice and Delinquency Prevention, U.S. Department of Justice, March, 1984.

Serrill, M. S. Washington's new juvenile code. *Corrections Magazine*, 1980, *6*, 36–41.

Sexton, P. *Education and income*. New York: Viking Press, 1961.

Shah, S. A. Community mental health and the criminal justice system: Some issues and problems. *Mental Hygiene*, 1970, *54*, 1–12.

Shah, S. A. Recent developments in human genetics and their implications for problems of social deviance. *Advances in Human Genetics and Their Impact on Society*, 1972, 8(4), 42–82.

Shah, S. A. Juvenile delinquency: A national perspective. In J. Khanna (Ed.), *New treatment approaches to juvenile delinquency*. Springfield, Ill.: Charles C. Thomas, 1975.

Shah, S. A., & Roth, L. H. Biological and psychophysiological factors in criminality. In D. Glaser (Ed.), *Handbook of criminology*. Chicago: Rand McNally, 1974.

Shakespeare, W. *As you like it*. New York: Penguin Books, 1970.

Shanas, E. *Recreation and delinquency*. Chicago: Clarke-McElroy, 1942.

Shannon, L. *Assessing the relationship of adult criminal careers to juvenile careers*. U.S. Department of Justice, OJJDP, June 1982.

Shannon, L. W. A longitudinal study of delinquency and crime. In C. Wellford (Ed.), *Quantitative studies in criminology*, Beverly Hills, Calif.: Sage, 1978.

Shapland, J. Self reported delinquency in boys aged 11 to 14. *British Journal of Criminology*, 1978, *18*, 3.

Shapland, J. M., & Campbell, A. C. Deprivation by neglect of children aged 15 to 16. In A. Franklin, *The Challenge of Child Abuse*. London: Academic Press, 1977.

Shaw, C. R. *Delinquency areas*. Chicago: University of Chicago Press, 1929.

Shaw, C. R. *Brothers in crime*. Chicago: University of Chicago Press, 1936.

Shaw, C. R. *The jackroller: A delinquent boy's own story* (6th impression). Chicago: University of Chicago Press, 1968. (Originally published, 1930.)

Shaw, C. R., & McKay, H. D. *Social factors in juvenile delinquency* (Report of the National Commission on Law Observance and Enforcement—Wickersham Commission—No. 13, Vol. 2). Washington, D.C.: U.S. Government Printing Office, 1931.

Shaw, C. R., & McKay, H. D. Are broken homes a causative factor in juvenile delinquency? *Social Forces*, 1932, *10*, 514–524.

Shaw, C. R., & McKay, H. D. *Juvenile delinquency and urban areas* (rev. ed.). Chicago: University of Chicago Press, 1942.

Shaw, C. R., & McKay, H. D. *Juvenile delinquency and urban areas*. Chicago: University of Chicago Press, 1969.

Shaw, C. R., & McKay, H. D. Cultural transmission. In M. Wolfgang, L. Savitz, & N. Johnston (Eds.) *The sociology of crime and delinquency*. New York: Wiley, 1970.

Shaw, C. R., Zorbaugh, E. M., McKay, H. D., & Cottrell, L. S. *Delinquency areas*. Chicago: University of Chicago Press, 1929.

Shaw, G. B. *The crime of imprisonment*. New York: Modern Library, 1946.

Sheldon, W. H. *The varieties of human physique*. New York: Harper & Row, 1940.

Sheldon, W. H. *Varieties of delinquent youth: An introduction to constitutional psychiatry*. New York: Harper & Bros., 1949.

Shelley, L. *Crime and modernization: The impact of industrialization and urbanization on crime*. Carbondale: Southern Illinois University Press, 1981. (b)

Shelley, L. *Readings in comparative criminology*. Carbondale: Southern Illinois University Press, 1981. (a)

Shepard, G. H. The juvenile specialist in community relations. In D. Pursuit, J. Gerlette, N. Brown, & S. Ward (Eds.), *Police programs for preventing crime and delinquency*. Springfield, Ill: Charles C. Thomas, 1972.

Sherizen, S. Social creations of crime news: All the news fitted to print. In C. Winick (Ed.), *Deviance and mass media*. Beverly Hills, Calif.: Sage, 1978.

Sherman, L. Causes of police behavior: The current state of quantitative research. *Journal of Research in Crime and Delinquency*, 1980, *17*, 69–100.

Shichor, D. Socialization: The political aspects of a delinquency explanation. *Sociological Spectrum*, 1983, 85–100.

Shichor, D., Decker, D., & O'Brien, R. Population density and criminal victimization. *Criminology*, 1979, *17*, 184–193.

Shikita, M., & Tsuchiya, S. The juvenile justice system in Japan. In *Juvenile Justice: An International Survey*, Publication #12, U.N. Social Defence Research Institute, Via Giulia 52, Rome, 1976.

Shoemaker, Donald. *Theories of delinquency*. New York: Oxford University Press, 1984.

Short, J. F., Jr. Differential association as a hypothesis: Problems of empirical testing. *Social Problems*, 1960, *8*, 14–25.

Short, J. F., Jr. Gang delinquency and anomie. In M. B. Clinard (Ed.), *Anomie and deviant behavior*. New York: Free Press, 1964.

Short, J. F., Jr. *The study of juvenile delinquency by reported behavior: An experiment in method and preliminary findings*. Paper read at the annual meeting of the American Sociological Society, Washington, D.C., September 1955. (Cited in M. E. Erickson. The changing relationship between official and self-reported measures of delinquency: An exploratory-predictive study. *Journal of Criminal Law, Criminology and Police Science*, 1958, 49, 296–302.)

Short, J. F., Jr., & Nye, Z. Extent of unrecorded delinquency: Tentative conclusions. *Journal of Criminal Law, Criminology and Police Science*, 1958, 49, 296–302.

Short, J. F., Jr., Tennyson, R., & Howard, K. Behavior dimensions of gang delinquency. *American Sociological Review*, 1963, *28*, 411–428.

Shotland, R., Hayward, S., Young, C., Signorella, M., Mindingall, K., Kennedy, J., Robine, M., & Danowitz, E. Fear of crime in a residential community. *Criminology*, 1979, *17*, 34–45.

Shover, N. *A sociology of American corrections*. Homewood, Ill.: Dorsey Press, 1979.

Shover, N., Norland, S., James, J., & Thornton, W. E. Gender roles and delinquency. *Social Forces*, 1979, *58*, 162–175.

Shulman, H. M. Intelligence and delinquency. *Journal of Criminal Law and Criminology*, 1951, *41*, 763–781.

Shulman, H. M. The family and juvenile delinquency. In S. Glueck (Ed.) *The problem of delinquency*. New York: Houghton Mifflin, 1959.

Silberman, C. *Crisis in the classroom: The remaking of American education*. New York: Vintage, 1970.

Silbert, J. D., & Sussman, A. N. The rights of juveniles confined in training schools and the experience of a training school ombudsman. *Brooklyn Law Review*, 1974, *40*, 605–634.

Siler, Jr., E. The need for defense counsel in juvenile court. *Crime and Delinquency*, 1965, *11*, 45–58.

Simmel, G. *Conflict* (Kurt H. Wolf, Trans.). Glencoe, Ill.: The Free Press, 1955.

Simon, R. J. *Women and crime*. Lexington, Mass.: Lexington Books, 1975.

Simon, W., & Gagnon, J. Children of the drug age. *Saturday Review*, September 21, 1968, pp. 60–63; 75–78.

Simmons, R. G. and Rosenberg, F. Sex, sex roles, and self-image. *Journal of Youth and Adolescence*, 1975, *4*, 225–258.

Simons, R. L., Miller, H. G., & Aigner, S. M. Contemporary theories of deviance and female delinquency: An empirical test. *Journal of Research in Crime and Delinquency*, 1980, *17*, 42–57.

Simonsen, C. E., & Gordon, M. *Juvenile justice in America*. Encino, Calif.: Glencoe, 1979.

Simpson, G. E., and Yinger, J. M. *Racial and cultural minorities*. New York: Harper & Row, 1972.

Sinclair, C. A radical Marxist interpretation of juvenile justice in the United States. *Federal Probation*, 1983, 20–28.

Singer, S. L. Homogeneous victim offender populations: A review and some research implications. *The Journal of Criminal Law and Criminology*, 1981, *72*, 779–788.

Skinner, B. F. *Beyond freedom and dignity*. New York: Bantam Books, 1971.

Skolnick, A. The Family and Its Discontents. *Society*, 1981, *10*, 42–49.

Slaikeu, K. A. Evaluation studies of group treatment of juvenile and adult offenders in correctional institutions: A review of the literature. *Journal of Research in Crime and Delinquency*, 1973, *10*, 87–100.

Slater, P. *The pursuit of loneliness*. Boston: Beacon Press, 1970.

Slocum, W. L., & Stone, C. L. Family culture patterns and delinquent-type behavior. *Marriage and Family Living*, 1963, *25*, 202–208.

Smart, R. G., Fejer, D., & White, J. *The extent of drug use in Metropolitan Toronto schools: A study of changes from 1968 to 1970*. Toronto, Canada: Addiction Research Foundation, 1970.

Smith, C., Berkman, D., Fraser, W., & Sutton, J. *A preliminary national assessment of the status offender and the juvenile justice system: Role conflicts, constraints, and information gaps* (Reports of the National Juvenile Justice Assessment Centers, U.S. Department of Justice, Law Enforcement Assistance Administration, Office of Juvenile Justice and Delinquency Prevention). Washington, D.C.: U.S. Government Printing Office, April 1980.

Smith, D. A. The organizational context of legal control. *Criminology*, 1984, *22*, 19–38.

Smith, D. E., Finnegan, T., & Snyder, H. *Delinquency 1977: United States estimates of cases processed by courts with juvenile jurisdictions*. Pittsburgh: National Center for Juvenile Justice, April, 1980.

Smith, D. E., & Gay, G. R. (Eds.). *It's so good, don't even try it once*. Englewood Cliffs, N.J.: Prentice-Hall, 1972.

Smith, D. E., Levy, S. J., & Striar, E. Treatment services for youthful drug users. In G. M. Beschner & A. S. Friedman (Eds.), *Youth drug abuse*. Lexington, Mass.: Lexington Books, 1979.

Smith, K. C. A profile of juvenile court judges in the United States. *Juvenile Justice*, 1974, *25*, 27–38.

Smith, P. M. Broken homes and juvenile and delinquency. *Sociology and Social Research*, 1955, *39*, 307–311.

Smith, P. S. Turning point for juvenile justice: Are jury trials really essential? *Journal of Juvenile Law*, 1978, *2*, 1–28.

Smith, R. C. A profile of juvenile court judges in the United States. *Juvenile Justice*, 1974, *26*, 27–39.

Smith, S. Victimization in the inner city: A British case study. *British Journal of Criminology*, 1982, *22*, 2.

Snyder, H., Finnegan, T., & Hutzler, J. L. *Delinquency in the United States*. Pittsburgh: National Center for Juvenile Justice, 1985.

Society for the Reformation of Juvenile Delinquents. *Annual report*. New York: Author, 1835. (Cited in R. M. Mennel.

Thorns and thistles: Juvenile delinquents in the United States, 1825–1949. Hanover, N.H.: University Press of New England, 1973.)

Solomon, G. Psychodynamic aspects of aggression, hostility and violence. In D. Daniels, M. Gilula, & F. Ochberg (Eds.), *Violence and the struggle for existence*. Boston: Little, Brown, 1970.

Solomon, H. M. *Community corrections*. Boston: Holbrook Press, 1976.

Solomon, J. Why gamble? A psychological profile of pathology, *The Sciences*, *12* (5), 1972, 20–21.

Solomon, P. H. *Soviet criminologists and criminal policy: Specialists in policy making*. New York: Columbia University Press, 1978.

Sommerville, C. J. *The rise and fall of childhood*. Beverly Hills, Calif.: Sage, 1982.

Sorokin, P. *Social and cultural dynamics*. New York: Harper & Row, 1941.

Sorrells, J. M. Kids who kill. *Crime and Delinquency*, 1977, *23*, 312–320.

Sparks, R. Britain. In E. Johnson (Ed.), *International handbook of contemporary developments in criminology: Europe, Africa, the Middle East and Asia*. Westport, Conn.: Greenwood, 1983.

Sparks, R. F., Genn, H., & Dodd, D. J. *Surveying victims*. London: Wiley, 1977.

Spencer, J. W. Accounts, attitudes and solutions: Probation officer—Defendant negotiations of subjective orientations. *Social Problems*, 1983, *30*, 370–531.

Spergel, I. A. Interactions between community structure, delinquency and social policy in the inner city. In M. Klein (Ed.), *The juvenile justice system*. Beverly Hills, Calif.: Sage, 1976.

Spitzer, S. Toward a Marxian theory of deviance. *Social Problems*, 1975, *22*, 638–651.

Sprowls, J. T. *Discretion and lawlessness: compliance in the juvenile courts*. Lexington, Mass.: Lexington Books, 1980.

Spurzheim, J. C. *Outlines of phrenology*. Boston: Marsh, Capen and Lyon, 1832.

Stanford, R. M. Implementing the multigoal evaluation techniques in diversion programs. In Scott Decker (Ed.), *Juvenile justice policy: Analyzing trends and outcomes*. Beverly Hills, Calif.: Sage, 1984.

Stapleton, V., Aday, D. P. Jr., & Ito, J. A. An empirical typology of American metropolitan juvenile courts. *American Journal of Sociology*, 1982, *88*, 549–564.

Stapleton, V., & Teitelbaum, L. *In defense of youth: A study of the role of counsel in American juvenile courts*. New York: Russell Sage Foundation, 1973.

Statistics of the criminal justice system: England and Wales. 1963–1978. London: Her Majesty's Stationery Office, 1979.

Statsky, W. *Family law*. St. Paul, Minn.: West, 1984.

Steele, B. Violence within the family. In R. Helfer, & C. Kempe, *Child abuse and neglect: The family and the community*. Cambridge, Mass.: Ballinger, 1976.

Steffensmeier, D. J. Crime and the contemporary woman: An analysis of changing levels of female property crime: 1960–75. *Social Forces*, 1978, *57*, 566–584.

Steffensmeier, D. J. Sex differences in patterns of adult crime, 1965–77: A review and assessment. *Social Forces*, 1980, 1080–1108.

Steffensmeier, D. J., & Steffensmeier, R. N. Trends in female delinquency: An examination of arrest, juvenile court, self-report, and field data. *Criminology*, 1980, *18*, 62–85.

Stein, K. B., Gough, H., and Sarbin, T. R. The dimensionality of the CPI socialization scale and an empirically derived typology among delinquent and nondelinquent boys. *Multivariate Behavior Research*, 1966, *1*, 197–208.

Stein, K. B., & Sarbin, T. R. Future time perspective: Its relation to the socialization process and the delinquent role. *Journal of Consulting and Clinical Psychology*, 1968, *32*, 257–268.

Sterling, C. H., & Haight, T. R. (Eds.). *The mass media: Aspen Guide to communications industry trends.* New York: Praeger, 1978.

Stewart, M. A., Deblois, C. S., Meardon, J., Cummings, C. Aggressive conduct disorders of children: The clinical picture. *Journal of Nervous Mental Disorders*, 1980, *68*, 604–610.

Stone, D. The human potential movement. *Society*, 1978, *15*, 66–71.

Strasburg, P. A. *Violent delinquents.* New York: Monarch, 1978.

Street, D., Vinter, R. D., & Perrow, C. *Organization for treatment: A comparative study of institutions for delinquents.* New York: Free Press, 1966.

Streib, V. L. The juvenile justice system and children's law: Should juvenile defense lawyers be replaced as children's lawyers? *Juvenile and Family Court Journal*, 1980, *31*, 53–59.

Strong, B., DeVoult, C., Said, M., & Reynolds, N. *The marriage and family experience*, St. Paul, Minn.: West, 1983.

Sullivan, C. E., Grant, M. Q., & Grant, J. D. The development of interpersonal maturity: Applications to delinquency. *Psychiatry*, 1957, *20*, 272–283.

Summer, C. Marxism and deviance theory. In P. Wiles (Ed.), *The sociology of crime and delinquency: The new criminologists.* New York: Barnes & Noble, 1977.

Sumpter, G. R. The youthful offender: A description analysis. *Canadian Journal of Criminology and Corrections*, 1972, *14*, 282–296.

Sundean, R. A. The community connection: Locally based juvenile justice programs and their settings. *Juvenile and Family Court Journal*, Feb. 1983, 15–21.

Sussman, A. Practitioner's guide to changes in juvenile law and procedure. *Criminal Law Bulletin*, 1978, *14*, 311–342.

Sussman, F. B. *Law of juvenile delinquency.* Dobbs Ferry, N.Y.: Oceana, 1950.

Sutherland, E. H. Mental deficiency and crime. In K. Young (Ed.), *Social attitudes.* New York: Henry Holt, 1939.

Sutherland, E. H. Critique of Sheldon's varieties of delinquent youth. *American Sociological Review*, 1951, *16*, 10–14.

Sutherland, E. H., & Cressey, D. R. *Principles of Criminology* (6th ed.). New York: Lippincott, 1960.

Sutherland, E. H., & Cressey, D. R. *Criminology* (10th ed.). Philadelphia: Lippincott, 1978.

Suttles, G. D. *The social order of the slum: Ethnicity and territory in the inner city.* Chicago: University of Chicago Press, 1968.

Suzuki, Y. Corrections in Japan. In Robert J. Wicks & H. H. A. Cooper, *International corrections.* Lexington, Mass.: D. C. Heath, 1979.

Suzuki, Y. Japan. In V. L. Stewart (Ed.), *Justice and troubled children around the world* (Vol. 3). New York: New York University Press, 1981.

Swanger, H. Juvenile institutional litigation, *Clearinghouse Review*, 1977, *11*, 219–221.

Swanson, C. E. What they read in 130 daily newspapers. *Journalism Quarterly*, 1955, *32* (4), 411–421.

Sykes, G. M. The rise of critical criminology. *Journal of Criminal Law and Criminology*, 1974, *65*, 206–213.

Sykes, G. M. *The society of captives: A study of a maximum security prison.* Princeton, N.J.: Princeton University Press, 1958.

Sykes, G. M., & Matza, D. Techniques of neutralization: A theory of delinquency. *American Sociological Review*, 1957, *22*, 664–670.

Szasz, T. *The myth of mental illness.* New York: Harper & Row, 1967.

Szasz, T. *Ideology and insanity.* New York: Doubleday, 1970.(a)

Szasz, T. *The manufacture of madness.* New York: Harper & Row, 1970.(b)

Takagi, P. Review of *Whose law? What order?* by W. J. Chambliss and M. Mankoff. *Journal of Criminal Law and Criminology*, 1976, *67*, 256–257.

Takagi, P., & Platt, A. Behind the gilded ghetto: An analysis of race, class and crime in Chinatown. *Crime and Social Justice*, 1978, *9*, 2–25.

Talarico, S. M., & Swanson, C. R., Jr. Policing styles: Notes on an empirical synthesis of Wilson and Muir. *Journal of Criminal Justice*, 1980, *8*, 327–334.

Tancredi, L. R., Lieb, J., Slaby, A. E. *Legal issues in psychiatric care.* New York: Harper & Row, 1975.

Tanay, E. Psychiatric study of homicide. *American Journal of Psychiatry*, 1969, *125*, 1252–1258.

Tannenbaum, F. *Crime and the community.* New York: Columbia University Press, 1938.

Tanner, J. M. Earlier maturation in man, *Scientific American*, 1968, *218*, 21–27.

Tanner, J. M. *Fetus into man: Physical growth from conception to maturity.* Cambridge, Mass.: Harvard University Press, 1978.

Tanner, J. M. New directions. In *Subcultural theory: An analysis of British working class youth culture. Youth and Society*, 1978, *9*, 4.

Tappan, F. The nature of juvenile delinquency. In R. Giallombardo (Ed.), *Juvenile delinquency: A book of readings.* New York: Wiley, 1976.

Tarde, G. *Penal philosophy.* Boston: Little Brown, 1912.

Taylor, I., Walton, P., & Young, J. *Critical criminology.* Boston: Routledge & Kegan Paul, 1975.

Taylor, I., Walton, P. Radical deviancy theory and Marxism: A repy to Paul Q. Hirst's "Marx and Engels on law, crime and morality." In I. Taylor, P. Walton, & J. Young (Eds.), *Critical criminology.* London: Routledge & Kegan Paul, 1975.

Taylor, I., Walton, P., & Young, J. *The new criminology.* New York: Harper & Row, 1973.

Teaching about drug abuse. *Today's Education,* March 1969, pp. 35–50. (Reprinted from U.S. Department of Health, Education and Welfare, National Institute of Mental Health. *Students and drug abuse.* Washington, D.C.: U.S. Government Printing Office, 1969.)

Teele, J. E. *Juvenile delinquency: A reader.* Itasca, Ill.: F. E. Peacock, 1970.

Teilmann, K. S., & Landry, P. H., Jr. Gender bias in juvenile justice. *Journal of Research in Crime and Delinquency,* 1981, *18,* 47–79.

Television and behavior: Ten years of scientific progress and implications for the eighties (Vol. 1). Summary Report, NIMH, 1982.

Television and behavior: Ten years of scientific progress and implications for the eighties (Vol. 2). Summary Report, NIMH, 1982.

Television and social behavior (1972). A Technical Report to the Surgeon General's Scientific Advisory Committee (5 Volumes). Washington, D.C.: U.S. Government Printing Office, 1972.

Tennenbaum, D. J. Personality and criminality: A summary and implications of the literature. *Journal of Criminal Justice,* 1977, *5,* 225–235.

Terrill, R. J. *World criminal justice systems.* Cincinnati, Ohio: Anderson, 1984.

Terror from the tube. *Times-Picayune,* June 16, 1982, p. 1.

Terry, R. Discrimination in the handling of juvenile offenders by social control agencies. *Journal of Research in Crime and Delinquency,* 1967, *4,* 218–230. (a)

Terry, R. The screening of juvenile offenders. *Journal of Criminal Law, Criminology and Police Science,* 1967, *58,* 173–181. (b)

Thio, A. Class bias in the sociology of deviance. *American Sociologist,* 1973, *8,* 1–12.

Thio, A. The phenomenological perspective of deviance: Another case of class bias. *American Sociologist,* 1974, *9,* 146–149.

Thio, A. *Deviant behavior.* Boston: Houghton Mifflin, 1978.

Thomas, C., Hyman, J., & Winfree, L. T. The impact of confinement on juveniles. *Youth and Society,* 1983, *14,* 301–319.

Thomas, C. W. Prisonization or resocialization? a study of external factors associated with the impact of imprisonment. *Journal of Research in Crime and Delinquency,* 1973, *19,* 13–21.

Thomas, C. W., & Fitch, A. W. *An inquiry into the association between respondents' personal characteristics and juvenile court dispositions.* Williamsburg, Va.: Metropolitan Criminal Justice Center, College of William and Mary, 1975.

Thomas, C. W., & Foster, C. The importation model perspective on inmate social roles: An empirical test. *Sociological Quarterly,* 1973, *16,* 226–234.

Thomas, C. W., & Sieverdes, C. H. An analysis of discretionary decision-making. *Criminology,* 1975, *12,* 413–432.

Thomas, M. H., Horton, R. W., Lippincott, E. C., & Durham, R. S. Desensitization to portrayals of real life aggression as a function of exposure to television violence. *Journal of Personality and Social Psychology,* 1977, *35.*

Thomas, M. H., & Drabman, R. S. Toleration of real life aggression as a function of exposure to television violence and age of subject. *Mennol-Palmer Quarterly,* 1975, *21.*

Thomas, R. *Comparing theories of child development.* Belmont, Calif.: Wadsworth, 1979.

Thomas, W. I. The relation of research to the social process. In *Essays on research in the social sciences.* Washington, D.C.: The Brookings Institution, 1931.

Thomas, W. I. *The child in America. Problems and programs.* New York: Knopf, 1928.

Thomas, W. I. *The Polish peasant in Europe and America.* Chicago: University of Chicago Press, 1918–1920.

Thornberry, T. P. Race, socioeconomic status and sentencing in the juvenile justice system. *Journal of Criminal Law and Criminology,* 1973, *64,* 90–96.

Thornberry, T. P., & Christenson, R. L. Juvenile justice decision-making as a longitudinal process. *Social Forces,* 1984, *63,* 433–444.

Thornberry, T., & Christenson, R. L. Unemployment and criminal involvement. *American Sociological Review,* 1984, *49,* 291–411.

Thornton, E. M. *The Freudian fallacy.* New York: Doubleday, 1984.

Thornton, W. E. *A study in social problem process: Child abuse legislation in the sixties.* Paper presented at the North Central Association meetings, Cincinnati, May 1978.

Thornton, W. E. Gender traits and delinquency involvement of boys and girls. *Adolescence,* 1982, *21,* 749–760.

Thornton, W. E. Marijuana use and delinquency: A reexamination. *Youth and Society,* 1981, *13,* 23–37.

Thornton, W. E., & James, J. Unpublished data from Wisconsin Youth Survey, 1977.

Thornton, W., & James J. Masculinity and delinquency revisited. *British Journal of Criminology,* 1979, *19,* pp. 225–241.

Thornton, W. E., & Voigt, L. *Computer literacy: A new social class determinant.* Unpublished manuscript, 1986.

Thornton, W., & Voigt, L. Television and delinquency: A neglected dimension of social control. *Youth and Society,* 1984, *15,* 445–463.

Thorsell, B., & Klemke, L. The labeling process: Reinforcement and deterrent. In R. M. Carter & M. Klein (Eds.), *Back on the street: The diversion of juvenile offenders.* Englewood Cliffs, N.J.: Prentice-Hall, 1976.

Thrasher, F. M. *The gang: A study of 1,313 gangs in Chicago* (2nd abridged ed.). Chicago: University of Chicago Press, 1966. (Originally published, 1927.)

Tittle, C., Villemez, W. & Smith, D. The myth of social class and criminality: An empirical assessment of the empirical evidence. *American Sociological Review,* 1978, *43,* 643–656.

Tobias, J. The affluent suburban male delinquent. *Crime and Delinquency,* 1970, *16,* 273–279.

Toby, J. Affluence and adolescent crime. In L. Shelley, *Readings to comparative criminology.* Carbondale, Ill.: Southern Illinois, 1981.

Toby, J. The differential impact of family disorganization. *American Sociological Review.* 1957, *22,* 505–212.

Toby, J. An evaluation of early identification and intensive treatment programs for predelinquents. *Social Problems,* 1965, *16,* 160–175.

Toby, J. Crime in America's public schools. *Public Interest,* 1980, *58,* 18–42. (a)

Toby, J. The new criminology is the old baloney. In J. A. Inciardi (Ed.), *Radical Criminology: The coming crisis.* Beverly Hills, Calif.: Sage, 1980. (b)

Toby, J. The new criminology is the old sentimentality. *Criminology,* 1979, *16,* 516–526.

Toby, J. Violence in school. In M. Tonry & N. Morris, *Crime and justice: An annual review* (Vol. 4). Chicago: University of Chicago Press, 1983.

Toennies, F. Community and society (C. P. Loomis, Ed. and trans.). East Lansing: Michigan State University Press, 1957. (Originally published, 1887.)

Toffler, A. *The third wave.* New York: William Morrow, 1980.

Tokoro, K. Japan. In E. Johnson (Ed), *International handbook of contemporary developments in criminology: Europe, Africa, the Middle East and Asia* (Vol. 1). Westport, Conn.: Greenwood, 1983.

Traitel, R. B. *Dispositional alternatives in juvenile justice: A goal-oriented approach.* Reno, Nev.: National Council of Juvenile Court Judges, 1974.

Trasler, G. *The explanation of criminality.* London: Routledge & Kegan Paul, 1962.

Treating sex offenders in New Jersey. *Corrections Magazine,* 1974, November-December, 12–24.

Tucker, R. C. (Ed.). *The Marx-Engels reader.* New York: W. W. Norton, 1978.

Turk, A. T. Conflict and criminality. *American Sociological Review,* 1966, *31,* 338–352.

Turk, A. T. *Criminality and the legal order.* Chicago: Rand McNally, 1969.

Turk, A. T. Radical criminology. *Crime and Social Justice,* 1975, *4,* 42.

Turk, A. T. Class, conflict and criminalization. *Sociological Focus,* 1977, *10,* 209–220.

Turk, A. T. Analyzing official deviance: For nonpartisan conflict analyses. *Criminology,* 1979, *16,* 459–476.

Tutt, N., & Giller, H. Police cautioning of juveniles: The practice of diversity. *Criminal Law Review,* 1983.

Ulmar, G. Adolescent girls who steal. *Psychiatric Diagnoses,* 1971, *32,* 27–28.

Ulmar, G., & Haddox, V. *Drug abuse and the law: Cases and text materials* (2nd Ed.). New York: Clark Boardman, 1983.

United Nations General Assembly, Crime Prevention and Control: Report of the Secretary General, Sept. 1977.

United Nations General Assembly, Seventh Congress on the Prevention of Crime and the Treatment of Offenders, April 14, 1983.

United Nations General Assembly, Sixth Congress on the Prevention of Crime and the Treatment of Offenders. *Juvenile justice before and after the onset of delinquency.* Caracas, Venezuela, Sept. 1980.

The publications of the various departments of the U.S. government are arranged in order of the department name, followed by the bureau or institute name, and any other subdivisions. Thus, all the entries for a department that show no subdivisions will appear before the entries with subdivisions.

U.S. Department of Commerce, Bureau of the Census. *1970 census users' guide* (Part 1). Washington, D.C.: U.S. Government Printing Office, 1970.

U.S. Department of Commerce, Bureau of the Census. *Current population reports* (Series P-25, No. 643). Washington, D.C.: U.S. Government Printing Office, 1977.

U.S. Department of Commerce, Bureau of the Census. Projections of the population of the United States by age, sex, and race: 1983 to 2080. *Current population reports.* Washington, D.C.: U.S. Government Printing Office, May, 1984.

U.S. Department of Education. *A nation at risk: The imperative for educational reform.* Washington, D.C.: The National Commission on Excellence in Education, April, 1983.

U.S. Department of Health, Education and Welfare. *The challenge of youth service bureaus.* Washington, D.C.: U.S. Government Printing Office, 1973.

U.S. Department of Health, Education and Welfare. *Marijuana and health: Fifth annual report to the U.S. Congress.* Washington, D.C.: U.S. Government Printing Office, 1977.

U.S. Department of Health, Education and Welfare. *Marijuana and health: Sixth annual report to the U.S. Congress.* Washington, D.C.: U.S. Government Printing Office, 1979.

U.S. Department of Health, Education and Welfare. *The special report to the U.S. Congress on alcohol and health.* Washington, D.C.: U.S. Government Printing Office, 1978.

U.S. Department of Health, Education and Welfare. *Marijuana and health: Eighth annual report to the U.S. Congress.* Washington, D.C.: U.S. Government Printing Office, 1980.

U.S. Department of Health, Education and Welfare, National Center for Social Statistics. *Statistics on public institutions for delinquency children.* Washington, D.C.: U.S. Government Printing Office, 1969.

U.S. Department of Health, Education and Welfare, National Institute of Mental Health. *Report on the XYY chromosomal abnormality.* Washington, D.C.: U.S. Government Printing Office, 1970.

U.S. Department of Health, Education and Welfare, National Institute on Drug Abuse. *Drug abuse among American high school students, 1975–1977.* Washington, D.C.: U.S. Government Printing Office, 1977.

U.S. Department of Health, Education and Welfare. *Violent schools–Safe schools: The safe school study report* (Vol. 1). Washington, D.C.: National Institute of Education, U.S. Government Printing Office, 1978.

U.S. Department of Health, Education and Welfare, Office of Youth Development. *Juvenile court statistics, 1968.* Washington, D.C.: U.S. Government Printing Office, 1970.

U.S. Department of Health, Education and Welfare, Office of Education. Delinquency and the schools. In President's Commission on Law Enforcement and the Administration of Justice, *Task force report: Juvenile delinquency and youth crime.* Washington, D.C.: U.S. Government Printing Office, 1967.

U.S. Department of Justice, Law Enforcement Assistance Administration, National Institute for Juvenile Justice and Delinquency Prevention. *Juvenile court statistics, 1974.* Washington, D.C.: U.S. Government Printing Office, 1975.

U.S. Department of Justice, Law Enforcement Assistance Administration, National Institute for Juvenile Justice and Delinquency Prevention. Office of Juvenile Justice and Delinquency Prevention. *Abuse and neglect: A comparative analysis of standards and state practices* (Vol. 6 of Abuse). Washington D.C.: U.S. Government Printing Office, 1977. (a)

U.S. Department of Justice, Law Enforcement Assistance Administration, National Institute for Juvenile Justice and Delinquency Prevention, Office of Juvenile Justice and Delinquency prevention. *Police juvenile operations: A comparative analysis of standards and state practices.* Washington, D.C.: U.S. Government Printing Office, 1977. (b)

U.S. Department of Justice. *Criminal victimization in the United States, 1979.* Bureau of Justice Statistics, September, 1981.

U.S. Department of Justice. *Criminal victimization in the United States, 1981.* Bureau of Justice Statistics, November, 1983.

U.S. Department of Justice. *Criminal victimization in the United States, 1982.* Bureau of Justice Statistics, August, 1984.

U.S. Department of Justice. *Criminal victimization in the United States, 1983,* Bureau of Justice, 1985.

U.S. Department of Justice, Drug Enforcement Administration. *Drugs of abuse* (3rd ed.). Washington D.C.: U.S. Government Printing Office, 1976.

U.S. Department of Justice, Law Enforcement Assistance Administration. *National jail census, 1970: A report on the nation's local jails and type of inmates.* Washington, D.C.: U.S. Government Printing Office, 1971.

U.S. Department of Justice, Law Enforcement Assistance Administration. *Juvenile court statistics, 1974.* Washington, D.C.: U.S. Government Printing Office, 1975.

U.S. Department of Justice, Law Enforcement Assistance Administration. *Pre-adjudicatory detention in three juvenile courts: An empirical analysis of the factors related to detention decision outcomes.* Albany, N.Y.: Criminal Justice Research Center, 1975.

U.S. Department of Justice, Law Enforcement Assistance Administration. *Children in custody: Advance report on the juvenile detention and correctional facility census of 1975.* Washington, D.C.: U.S. Government Printing Office, 1977.

U.S. Department of Justice, Law Enforcement Assistance Administration. *Criminal victimization in the United States, 1975* (A National Crime Survey Report). Washington, D.C.: U.S. Government Printing Office, December, 1977.

U.S. Department of Justice, Law Enforcement Assistance Administration. *Children in custody: Advance report on the 1977 census of private juvenile facilities.* Washington, D.C.: U.S. Government Printing Office, 1979. (a)

U.S. Department of Justice, Law Enforcement Assistance Administration. *Children in custody: Advance report on the 1977 census of public juvenile facilities.* Washington, D.C.: U.S. Government Printing Office, 1979. (b)

U.S. Department of Justice, Law Enforcement Assistance Administration. *Criminal victimization in the United States, 1977* (A National Crime Survey Report). Washington, D.C.: U.S. Government Printing Office, 1980.

U.S. Department of Justice, Office of Juvenile Justice and Delinquency Prevention. National Criminal Justice Information and Statistics Service. *Children in custody: Advance report on the 1982 census of private juvenile facilities, including comparisons with public facilities.* Washington, D.C.: U.S. Government Printing Office, March, 1984.

U.S. Department of Justice, Office of Juvenile Justice and Delinquency Prevention. National Criminal Justice Information and Statistics Service. *Children in custody: Advance report on the 1982 census of public juvenile facilities.* Washington, D.C.: U.S. Government Printing Office, December, 1983.

Van Dijk, J. J. M. The extent of public information and the nature of public attitudes towards crime. In *Public opinion on crime and criminal justice.* Strasbourg, France: Council of Europe, 1979.

Van Gennep, A. *The rites of passage.* Chicago: University of Chicago Press, 1960. (Originally published, 1908.)

Van Hentig, Hans. *The criminal and his victim: Studies in the sociobiology of crime.* New York: Schocken Books, 1948/ 1979.

Vaz, E. (Ed.). *Middle class delinquency.* New York: Harper & Row, 1967.

Vedder, C. B. *Juvenile offenders*. Springfield, Ill.: Charles C. Thomas, 1963.

Vedder, C. B., Somerville, D. *The delinquency girl*. Springfield, Ill.: Charles C. Thomas, 1970.

Velman, G. E., & Haddox, U. *Drug abuse and the law*. New York: Clark, Boardman, 1984.

Venezia, P. Delinquency prediction: A critique and suggestion. *Journal of Research in Crime and Delinquency*, 1971, 8, 108–117.

Vinter, R. D., Downs, G., & Hall, J. *Juvenile corrections in the states: Residential programs and deinstitutionalization—A preliminary report*. Ann Arbor: National Assessment of Juvenile Corrections, Institution of Continuing Legal Education, School of Social Work, University of Michigan, 1976.

Vinter, R. D., & Sarri, R. *Time out: A national study of juvenile correctional programs*. Ann Arbor: National Assessment of Juvenile Corrections, Institute of Continuing Legal Education, School of Social Work, University of Michigan, June, 1976.

Violence in school. National Institute of Justice. U.S. Department of Justice, December, 1983.

Violent schools–Safe schools: Overview. In B. Galway, & J. Hudson, *Perspectives on crime victims*. St. Louis: C. V. Mosby, 1981.

Visher, C. A. Gender, police arrest decisions, and notions of chivalry. *Criminology*, 1983, 21, 5–28.

Vitiello, M. Constitutional safeguards for juvenile transfer procedure: Ten years since Kent v. United States. *DePaul Law Review*, 1976, 26, 23–53.

Voigt, L., & Thornton, W. *The delinquent as victim*. Paper presented at Southern Sociological Society, Memphis, Tenn., 1982.

Voigt, L., & Thornton, W. The rhetoric and politics of Soviet delinquency. In Richard Tomasso (Ed.), *Comparative social research*. Greenwich, Conn.: Jai Press, 1985.

Vold, G. B. *Theoretical criminology* (2nd ed.). New York: Oxford University Press, 1979. (Originally published, 1958.)

Volkman, A. A matched group personality comparison of delinquent and non-delinquent juveniles. *Social Problems*, 1958–1959, 6, 238–245.

Vorenberg, E. W., & Vorenberg, J. Early diversion from the criminal justice system: Practice in search of a theory. In P. G. Boesen & S. E. Grupp (Eds.), *Community-based corrections: Theory, practice, and research*. Santa Cruz, Calif.: Davis, 1976.

Vorrath, H. H., & Brendtro, L. *Positive peer culture*. Chicago: Aldine, 1974.

Voss, H. L. Ethnic differentials in delinquency in Honolulu. *Journal of Criminal Law, Criminology and Police Science*, 1963, 54, 322–327.

Voss, H. L. Differential association and containment theory: A theoritical convergence. *Social Forces*, 1969, 47, 381–391.

Voss, H. L. Socio-economic status and reported delinquent behavior. *Social Problems*, 1966, 13, 314–324.

Voss, H. L., & Petersen, D. (Eds.). *Ecology, crime and delinquency*. New York: Appleton-Century-Crofts, 1971.

Wahler, R. G. The insular mother: Her problems in parent-child treatment, *Journal of Applied Behavioral Analysis, 13*, 1980, 207–219.

Wahler, R. G., Hughey, J. B., & Gordon, H. S. Chronic patterns of mother-child cohesion: Some differences between insular and noninsular families. *Analysis and Intervention in Developmental Disorders*, 1981, 1, 145–156.

Walberg, H. J. Urban schooling and delinquency: Toward an integrative theory. *American Educatioal Research Journal*, 1972, 9, 285–300.

Wald, P. Making sense out of the rights of youth. *Child Welfare*, 1976, 55, 379–393.

Waldo, G. P., & Chiricos, T. G. Perceived penal sanctions and self-reported criminality: A neglected approach to deterrence research. *Social Problems*, 1972, 19, 522–540.

Waldo, G. P., & Dinitz, S. Personality attributes of the criminal: An analysis of research studies, 1950–65. *Journal of Research in Crime and Delinquency*, 1967, 4, 185–201.

Wallace, A. F. C. *Religion: An anthropological view*. New York: Random House, 1966.

Walker, D. *Rights in conflict*. New York: New American Library, 1968.

Wallerstein, J. A., & Wyle, J. C. Our law-abiding law-breakers. *Probation*, 1947, 25, 107–112.

Walter, J. D., & Ostrander, S. A. An observational study of a juvenile court. *Juvenile and Family Court Journal*, 1982, 33, 53–69.

Walter, T. L., & Mills, C. M. A behavioral-employment intervention program for reducing juvenile delinquency. In J. S. Stumhauzer (Ed.), *Progress in behavior therapy with delinquents*. Springfield, Ill.: Thomas, 1979.

Walther, R. M., & McCune, S. C. Juvenile court judges in the United States, part II: Working styles and characteristics. *Crime and Delinquency*, 1965, 11, 334–393.

Walzer, S., Breau, G., & Gerald, P. S. A chromosome survey of 2,500 normal newborn infants, *Journal of Pediatrics*, 1969, 74, 433–448.

Ward, D. A., & Kasselbaum, G. G. *Women's prison: Sex and social structure*. Chicago: Aldine, 1965.

Warr, M. The accuracy of public beliefs about crime. *Criminology*, 1982, 20, 185–204.

Warren, M. Q. Intervention with juvenile delinquents. In M. Rosenheim (Ed.), *Pursuing justice for the child*. Chicago: University of Chicago Press, 1976.

Warren, M. Q. Applications of interpersonal-maturity theory to offender populations. In W. S. Laufer & J. M. Day (Eds.), *Personality theory, moral development and criminal behavior*. Lexington, Mass.: Lexington Books, 1983.

Warren, M. Q., & the Community Treatment Staff. Interpersonal maturity level classification: Juvenile: Diagnosis of low, middle and high maturity delinquents. Sacramento: California Youth Authority, 1976.

Warren, M. Q., & Hindelang, M. Differential explanations of offender behavior. In H. Toch, Ed., *Psychology and criminal justice*. New York: Holt, Rinehart and Winston, 1979.

Warren, R. *The community in America*. Chicago: Rand McNally, 1978.

Wattenberg, W. W. *Boy repeaters*. Detroit: Wayne State University Press, 1947.

Wattenberg, W. W., & Balistrieri, J. Gang membership and juvenile delinquency. *American Sociological Review*, 1950, *15*, 744–752.

Waugh, I. Labeling theory. In U.S. Department of Justice, Law Enforcement Assistance Administration, National Institute for Juvenile Justice and Delinquency Prevention, *Preventing delinquency* (Vol. 1). Washington, D.C.: U.S. Government Printing Office, 1977.

Wayson, W. *Correctional myths and economic realities*. Proceedings of the Second National Workshop on Correctional and Parole Administration. College Park, Md.: American Correctional Association, 1974.

Webb, J. What can we learn from Japan's prisons? *Parade*, Jan. 15, 1984, pp. 6–8.

Weber, J. B. *The theory of social and economic organization*. New York: The Free Press, 1947.

Weeks, H. A. Male and female broken home rates by types of delinquency. *American Sociological Review*, 1940, *5*, 601–609.

Weimann, G. The two step flow of communication. *American Sociological Review*, 1982, *47*, 764–773.

Weinberg, K. *Society and personality disorders*. Englewood Cliffs, N.J.: Prentice-Hall, 1952.

Weiner, N. L. The teenage shoplifter: A microcosmic view of middle class delinquency. In J. Douglas (Ed.), *Observations of deviance*. New York: Random House, 1970.

Weiner, N. L., & Willie, C. V. Decisions by juvenile officers. *American Journal of Sociology*, 1971, *77*, 199–210.

Weis, J. Comparative analysis of social control theories of delinquency. In U.S. Department of Justice, Law Enforcement Assistance Administration, National Institute for Juvenile Justice and Delinquency Prevention. *Preventing delinquency* (Vol. 1). Washington, D.C.: U.S. Government Printing Office, 1977.

Weissman, J. C. Understanding the drugs and crime connection. *Journal of Psychedelic Drugs*, 1979.

Weissman, J. C. *Drug abuse: The law and treatment alternatives*. Cincinnati: Anderson, 1978.

Weissman, J. C., & DuPont, R. L. *Criminal justice and drugs: The unresolved connection*. Port Washington, N.Y.: Kennikat Press, 1982.

Wellford, C. Labelling theory and criminology: An assessment. *Social Problems*, 1975, *22*, 332–345.

Wellford, C. Factors associated with the adoption of the inmate code: A study of normative assimilation. *Journal of Criminal Law, Criminology and Police Science*, 1967, *56*, 197–203.

Wenk, E. A., Robison, J. O., & Smith, G. W. Can violence be predicted? In I. Jacks & S. G. Cox (Eds.), *Physiological approaches to crime and its corrections: Theory, research and practice*. Chicago: Nelson-Hall, 1984.

Werkentin, F., Hofferbert, M., & Bauerman, M. Criminology as police science or How old is the new criminology? *Crime and Social Justice*, 1974, *2*, 24–41.

Werthman, F. The comics . . . very funny. *Saturday Review of Literature*, May 29, 1948, 6–7.

Wertham, F. *Seduction of the innocent*. New York: Rinehart, 1954.

Wertham, F. What parents don't know about comic books. *Ladies Home Journal*, November, 1953.

Wertham, C., & Piliavin, I. Gang members and the police. In D. Bordua (Ed.), *The police: Six sociological essays*. New York: Wiley, 1967.

West, D. J. Prevention and treatment can reduce delinquency. *LEAA Newsletter*, December 1979-January 1980, pp. 1–18.

West, D. J., & D. P. Farrington. *The delinquent way of life*. New York: Crane Russak, 1973.

West, D. J. *Young offenders*. HMSO, October, 1980.

Westley, W. *Violence and the police: A sociological study of law, custom, and morality*. Cambridge, Mass.: MIT Press, 1970.

Wheeler, S. Criminal statistics: A reformulation of the problem. *Journal of Criminal Law, Criminology and Police Science*, 1967, *58*, 317–324.

Whitaker, J. M., & Severy, L. J. Service accountability and recidivism for diverted youth: A client and service comparison analysis. *Criminal Justice and Behavior*, 1984, *11*, 47–74.

White House Conference on Children. *Emergence of identity*. Washington, D.C.: U.S. Government Printing Office, 1970.

Why you do what you do: Sociobiology—A new theory of behavior. *Time*, August 1, 1977, pp. 54–63.

Whyte, W. F. *Street corner society*. Chicago: University of Chicago Press, 1943.

Wiatrowski, M. D., Griswold, D. B., & Roberts, M. M. Social control theory and delinquency. *American Sociological Review*. 1984, *46*, 525–541.

Wick, D. Child abuse as causation of juvenile delinquency in central Texas. In R. J. Eunner & Y. E. Walker (Eds.), *Exploring the relationship between child abuse and delinquency*. Montclair, N.J.: Allanhel, Osmun, 1981.

Wicks, R. J. & Cooper, H. *International corrections*. Lexington, Mass.: Lexington Books, 1976.

Wickwar, H. *The place of criminal justice in development planning* (Vol. I). Monographs of the United States Crime Prevention and Criminal Justice Section. New York: New York University Press, 1977.

Widom, C. S., Katkin, F. S., Stewart, A. J., & Fondacaro, M. Multivariate analysis of personality and motivation in female delinquents. *Journal of Research in Crime and Delinquency*, 1983, *20*, 277–290.

Wilde, O. (Quoted in M. V. Waters, The juvenile court from the child's viewpoint: A glimpse into the future. In J. Addams [Ed.], *The child, the clinic and the court.* New York: New Republic, 1925).

Wiles, P. *The sociology of crime and delinquency: The new criminologies.* New York: Barnes & Noble, 1977.

Wilkinson, K. The broken home and delinquent behavior: an alternative interpretation of contradicting findings. In T. Hirschi & M. Gottfredson (Eds.), *Understanding crime: Current theory and research,* Beverly Hills, Calif.: Sage, 1980.

Wilkinson, K. The broken home and juvenile delinquency: Scientific explanation or ideology. *Social Problems,* 1974.

Wilkinson, K., Stitt, G., & Erickson, M. Siblings and delinquent behavior: An exploratory study of a neglected family variable. *Criminology,* 1982, 20.

Wilks, J. A. Ecological correlates of crime and delinquency. In President's Commission on Law Enforcement and the Administration of Justice, *Task force report: Crime and its impact—An assessment.* Washington, D.C.: U.S. Government Printing Office, 1967.

Williams, E. Reality therapy in a correctional institution. *Corrective and Social Psychiatry and Journal of Behavior Technology Methods and Therapy,* 1976, 22, 6–111.

Williams, J., & Gold, M. From delinquent behavior to official delinquency. *Social Problems, 1972, 20, 209–229.*

Wilson, E. O. *Sociobiology: The new synthesis.* Cambridge, Mass.: Harvard University Press, 1975.

Wilson, J. Q. The police and the delinquent in two cities. In P. G. Garabedian & D. C. Gibbons (Eds.), *Becoming delinquent.* Chicago: Aldine, 1970.

Wilson, J. Q. *Varieties of police behavior: The management of law and order in eight communities.* Cambridge, Mass.: Harvard University Press, 1973.

Wilson, J. Q., & Herrnstein, R. *Crime and human nature.* New York: Simon & Schuster, 1985.

Wilson, R. Juvenile inmates: The long-term trend is down. *Corrections Magazine,* 1978, 4, 3–11. (a)

Wilson, R. Massachusetts: The legacy of Jerome Miller. *Corrections Magazine,* 1978, 4, 12–18. (b)

Wilson, R. Recidivism: Disappointing numbers. *Corrections Magazine,* 1978, 4, 14–16. (c)

Wink, E. A., & Moos, R. Social climates in prison: An attempt to conceptualize and measure environmental factors in total institutions. *Journal of Research in Crime and Delinquency,* 1972, 1, 134–149.

Wirth, L. Urbanism as a way of life. *American Journal of Sociology,* 1938, 44, 1–24.

Wise, N. Juvenile delinquency among middle class girls. In E. Vaz (Ed.), *Middle class delinquency.* New York: Harper & Row, 1967.

Wolberg, L. R. *The techniques of psychotherapy.* New York: Grune & Stratton, 1967.

Wolfe, K., & Fishe, M. The children talk about comics. In P. Lazarsfeld, et al., *Communications research.* New York: Harper & Row, 1948.

Wolfe, L. D., O'Malley, P.M., & Bachman, T. L. Drugs and American High School Students 1975–1983. Rockville, Md.: U.S. Department of Health and Human Service NIDA, 1984.

Wolfgang, M. E. International crime statistics: A proposal. *Journal of Civil Law and Criminology,* 1967, 59.

Wolfgang, M. E., & Cohen, B. *Crime and race: Conceptions and misconceptions.* New York: Institute of Human Relations Press, 1970.

Wolfgang, M. E., & Ferracuti, F. *The subculture of violence: Toward an integrated theory of criminology.* London: Tavistock, 1967.

Wolfgang, M. E., Figlio, R. M., & Sellin, T. *Delinquency in a Birth Cohort.* Chicago: University of Chicago Press, 1972.

Wollan, L. A. After labelling and conflict. *Criminology,* 1979, 16, 545–560.

Wooden, K. *Weeping in the playtime of others: America's incarcerated children.* New York: McGraw-Hill, 1976.

Woodward, M. The role of low intelligence in delinquency. *British Journal of Delinquency,* 1955, 5, 281–303.

Wooton, B. *Social science and social pathology. London:* Allen and Union, 1959.

Wright, E. O. *The politics of punishment.* New York: Harper & Row, 1973.

Wright, W. E., & Dixon, M. C. Community prevention and treatment of juvenile delinquency: A review of evaluation studies. *Journal of Research in Crime and Delinquency,* 1977, 14, 35–67.

Yablonsky, L. The delinquent gang as a near group. *Social Problems,* 1959, 7, 108–117.

Yablonsky, L. *The Hippie Trip.* Baltimore, Md.: Penguin Books, 1973.

Yablonsky, L. *The violent gang.* New York: Macmillan, 1962.

Yakoviev, A. M. Criminological foundation of the criminal progress. In M. C. Bassioni & V. M. Savistski, *The criminal justice system of the U.S.S.R.* Springfield, Ill.: Charles Thomas, 1979.

Yanagimoto, M. The juvenile delinquent in Japan. *British Journal of Criminology,* 1973, 13, 2.

Yankelovich, D. *The new morality: A profile of American youth in the 70's.* New York: McGraw-Hill, 1974.

Yarrow, M. R., et al. Child effects on adult behavior, *Developmental Psychology,* 1971, 5, 300–311.

Yaryura-Tobias, J. A. Biological research on violent behavior. In L. J. Hippchen (Ed.), *Ecologic-biomedical approaches to treatment of delinquents and criminals.* New York: Van Nostrand Reinhold, 1978.

Yinger, M. Contraculture and subculture. *American Sociological Review.* 1960, 25, 625–635.

Yochelson, S., & Samenow, S. E. *The criminal personality* (Vol. I, II). New York: Aronsen, 1979.

Yokoyama, M. Delinquency control programs in the community in Japan. *International Journal of Comparative and Applied Criminal Justice,* 1981, 5, 169–178.

Yoshimasu, S. Criminal life curves of monozygotic twin-pairs, *Acta Criminologiae et Medicines Legalis Japanica*, 1965, *31*, 9–20.

Yoshimasu, S. The criminological significance of the family in the light of the studies of criminal twins, *Acts Criminologiae et Medicines Legalis Japanica*, 1961, *27*, 117–141.

Young, F. W. *Initiation ceremonies: A cross-cultural study of status dramatization*. Indianapolis, Ind.: Bobbs-Merrill, 1965.

Young, J. Forward. In F. Pearce, *Crimes of the powerful*. London: Pluto, 1976.

Young, J. Working class criminology. In I. Taylor, P. Walton & J. Young (Eds.), *Critical criminology*. Boston: Routledge & Kegan Paul, 1975.

Youniss, J., & Dean, A. Judgment and imagining aspects of operations: A Piagetian study with Korean and Costa Rican children. *Child Development*, 1974, *45*, 1020–1031.

Zakariya, S. B. In school (as elsewhere), the rich get computers: The poor get poorer. *American School Board Journal*, 1984, *71*, 29–32.

Zald, M. N. The correctional institution for juvenile offenders: An analysis of organizational character. *Social Problems*, 1960, *8*, 57–67.

Zanden, V. J. *Sociology: A systematic approach*. New York: Ronald Press, 1970.

Zeisel, H. *The future of law enforcement statistics: A summary view of federal statistics* (Report of the President's Commission on Law Enforcement and the Administration of Justice, Vol. 2). Washington, D.C.: U.S. Government Printing Office, 1971.

Zeldes, I. *The problem of crime in the U.S.S.R.* Springfield, Ill.: Charles Thomas, 1981.

Zillmann, D. Excitation transfer in communication mediated aggressive behavior. *Journal of Experimental and Social Psychology*, 1971, *7*, 419–434.

Zimring, F. E. The serious juvenile offender: Notes on an unknown quantity. In *The serious offender: Proceedings of a national symposium*. Washington, D.C.: U.S. Government Printing Office, 1978.

Zimring, F. E. Kids, groups and crimes: Some implications of a well kept secret. *Journal of Criminal Law and Criminology*, 1981, *72*, 3.

Zimring, F. E. *The changing legal world of adolescence*. New York: Free Press, 1982.

Appendix

Abstracts of Leading Cases

Escobedo v. Illinois, 364 U.S. 478 (1964)

Escobedo was held as a homicide suspect, questioned for fourteen hours, released, and later picked up for a second interrogation. When brought in for the second interrogation session, Escobedo asked to see his attorney, but his request was denied. While his attorney waited more than four hours at the police station, officers told Escobedo that his lawyer was not at the police station and did not wish to see him. When an alleged accomplice was produced, Escobedo claimed that the accomplice, whom he admitted hiring, was the one who pulled the trigger. Under state law, Escobedo was equally guilty and was sentenced to twenty years' imprisonment. The United States Supreme Court overturned the conviction on the grounds that Escobedo was denied due process and should have been granted access to his attorney since this interrogation represented a critical stage and Escobedo was the main suspect in the case.

Gideon v. Wainwright, 372 U.S. 335 (1963)

Gideon, an indigent, requested a court-appointed attorney while standing trial for burglary and larceny charges. The request was denied, since state law at that time allowed appointment of a lawyer only in capital cases. Gideon appealed his own case from prison and was granted a review. The United States Supreme Court ruled that an accused person cannot conduct an adequate defense on his or her own behalf without the benefit of counsel. Although this ruling was originally interpreted as applicable only in felony and other serious cases where the defendant faced a possible lengthy sentence, the right to counsel has been extended to all criminal cases.

Gilbert v. California, 332 U.S. 263 (1967)

Gilbert was convicted of the armed robbery of a bank and the murder of a police officer. Prior to trial, Gilbert was forced, without benefit of counsel, to participate in a lineup. Based on his identification there, Gilbert was later convicted and sentenced to death. In conjunction with his identification, samples of Gilbert's handwriting were compared with the holdup note given to a bank teller in the initial robbery. Gilbert contended that the lineup identification and the handwriting sample violated his Sixth Amendment right to counsel and his Fifth Amendment right against self-incrimination.

Basing itself on the unanimous Wade opinion, the United States Supreme Court ruled that Gilbert did have a right to counsel at the postindictment lineup. However, the Court stated that if the person who identified Gilbert at the lineup could also identify him at trial, then the failure to provide counsel was a harmless error, making the in-court identification admissible.

The Court further stated that taking fingerprints and writing samples are not of such critical importance that the presence of counsel is required and that an individual's privilege against self-incrimination is not violated by the use of handwriting samples or fingerprints because the Fifth Amendment protects only "testimonial" incrimination, not physical evidence.

In re Gault, 387 U.S. 1, 70 (1967)

Gerald Gault, a juvenile, received a five-year sentence for making a lewd phone call. Under state law, an adult charged with the same offense could receive a maximum sentence of $50 or sixty days in jail. Appeals to the Superior Court and the Arizona Supreme Court were denied because state law in juvenile court cases did not allow for appeals. The United States Supreme Court overturned the lower courts and ruled that Gault's constitutional right to due process was violated. As a result of this case, juveniles possess the right to notice of charges, the right to counsel, the right to confront and to cross-examine witnesses, the right against self-incrimination, the right to a transcript of proceedings, and the right to appeal.

In re Winship, 397 U.S. 358 (1970)

Samuel Winship, a juvenile, was found delinquent after committing a larceny and was sentenced to a maximum of six years. The presiding judge followed state law and found Winship guilty based upon a "preponderance of evidence." The argument presented during appeals was that the judge should have applied the more stringent "proof beyond a reasonable doubt" criterion. The U.S. Supreme Court overturned the earlier decisions and ruled that the "proof beyond a reasonable doubt" criterion was necessary to protect due process.

Kent v. U.S., 383 U.S. 541 (1966)

Kent, a juvenile, broke into a woman's apartment, raped her, and stole her wallet. If tried as an adult, Kent faced a maximum sentence of capital punishment, compared to a five-year commitment from the juvenile court. The juvenile court waived Kent to the adult court without holding a waiver hearing and without informing Kent or his attorney of the waiver proceedings. The United States Supreme Court overturned the case. All waiver procedures now require a full hearing, the right to counsel at the waiver hearing, access to all records and reports used in the waiver hearing, and a statement issued by the judge outlining the reasons for permitting a waiver.

Mapp v. Ohio, 367 U.S. 645 (1961)

Mapp was convicted for possession of obscene materials after police conducted a search of her residence without a search warrant. Mapp appealed her conviction on the ground that the evidence had been seized during an illegal search and seizure. The United States Supreme Court overturned the conviction and affirmed the exclusionary rule. The exclusionary rule holds that evidence seized during an illegal search—that is, one conducted without a search warrant or without the consent of the person being searched prior to arrest—cannot form the basis of a conviction.

McKeiver v. Pennsylvania, 403 U.S. 528 (1971)

McKeiver, a juvenile, requested a trial by jury after being charged with robbery, larceny, and receiving stolen property. The United States Supreme Court ruled that juveniles did not have a constitutional right to a trial by jury. This decision reaffirmed the *parens patriae* doctrine of the juvenile court.

Miranda v. Arizona, 384 U.S. 436 (1966)

Miranda was arrested on charges of rape and kidnapping and was not advised of his right to counsel before being interrogated by police for two hours. At the end of the interrogation, Miranda signed a written confession and a statement saying that the confession was voluntary. An attempt to suppress the confession failed, and Miranda was found guilty and eventually received a forty- to fifty-five-year sentence. The United States Supreme Court ruled that Miranda should have been advised of his right to counsel and the privilege against self-incrimination. As a result of this ruling, an arrested person must be advised of his or her rights prior to a custodial interrogation. The *Miranda* warning does not apply to volunteered statements, such as in situations in which a person blurts out a confession prior to advisement and interrogation.

Robinson v. California, 370 U.S. 660 (1962)

A California court convicted Robinson for being a narcotics addict and sentenced him to a minimum of ninety days' imprisonment. The conviction was based on a statute which made being addicted to the use of narcotics without being under the supervision of a person licensed to administer narcotics a criminal offense. Upon appeal, the U.S. Supreme Court overturned the lower court and ruled that drug addiction is an illness, not a crime. Therefore, receiving a penal sentence for being ill was cruel and unusual punishment.

Terry v. Ohio, 392 U.S. 1 (1968)

A police officer observed three men acting suspiciously in front of several stores. The officer concluded that the men were about to commit a robbery, stopped them, conducted a pat-down, and found two guns. The men were charged with carrying concealed weapons and were convicted. During the appeal, the United States Supreme Court ruled that the officer was justified in conducting a pat-down search of the outer clothing in order to ensure his own safety. This case, then, forms the basis for stop-and-frisk practices.

United States v. Wade, 388 U.S. 218 (1967)

Wade was indicted by a grand jury for the robbery of a bank. After arrest and indictment, Wade was shown in a lineup to some bank employees, two of whom identified him as the robber. Wade's attorney was not informed of the lineup and was not present at it. Based on his identification by the two bank employees, Wade was convicted and sent to jail. Wade's counsel argued that, under the Sixth Amendment, Wade was entitled to counsel at the postindictment lineup. The Supreme Court agreed with this argument in a 9–0 opinion.

The Court stated that simply being forced to stand in a lineup is not a violation of an individual's Fifth Amendment privilege against self-incrimination. However, when a person has been formally charged and then forced to stand in a lineup without counsel, his or her Sixth Amendment rights have been violated. Lineup identification, therefore, cannot be used as evidence in a later trial.

The Court further stated that counsel needs to be present at a postindictment lineup because identification lineups are often "suggestive" (for example, all persons in the lineup except the suspect are known to the identifying witness) and because accused persons may not be able later at trial to give their views of what happened at the lineup.

Wong Sun v. U.S., 371 U.S. 471 (1963)

Federal narcotics officers arrested Hom Way and found narcotics in his possession. Upon questioning, Hom Way claimed that he had bought the heroin from a "Blackie Toy." At 6:00 A.M. that day, federal officers went to a laundry operated by a man named James Toy. When Toy answered the door, one officer identified himself, and Toy slammed the door and ran to his living quarters behind the laundry. The agents broke into the living quarters and arrested Toy in his bedroom. Toy told the agents that he knew that a person he identified as Johnny Yee was selling heroin. The agents went to Yee's house and found him in the bedroom. Yee

surrendered the heroin to the police and claimed to have gotten the heroin from Wong Sun. The officers went to Wong Sun's house, were granted entrance by Sun's wife, and arrested Wong Sun while he was sleeping. No narcotics were found during the search. Several days later Wong Sun made an oral confession during interrogation. During the appeal, the United States Supreme Court ruled that Toy's arrest was illegal, as was the subsequent search of his bedroom. In addition, Toy's verbal statements were ruled excludable as fruits of an illegal search. The Court further ruled that the narcotics taken from Yee were also the product of an illegal search and therefore inadmissible. However, the Court denied Wong Sun's claim that his arrest resulted from tainted evidence. Although Wong Sun's arrest was made without probable cause, the inadmissibility of the narcotics against Toy did not mean automatic inadmissibility against Sun. The Court did, however, set aside Wong Sun's conviction on other grounds.

Schall v. Martin, 104 S.Ct. 2403 (1984)

Appellee Gregory Martin was arrested on December 13, 1977, and charged with first degree robbery, second degree assault, and criminal possession of a weapon based on an incident in which he, with two others, allegedly hit a youth on the head with a loaded gun and stole his jacket and sneakers. Martin had possession of the gun when he was arrested. He was 14 years old at the time and therefore came within the jurisdiction of New York's Family Court. The incident occurred at 11:30 at night, and Martin lied to the police about where and with whom he lived. He was consequently detained overnight. A petition of delinquency was filed after Martin made his initial appearance in Family Court on December 14. Based on the facts of his case, Martin was detained and a probable cause hearing was held five days later. A juvenile court judge ordered Martin confined not to ensure his appearance at trial, but because he was regarded as a serious risk to commit new crimes while awaiting trial. At the fact-finding hearing held on December 27–29, Martin was found guilty on the robbery and criminal possession, charges. He was adjudicated a delinquent and placed on two years' probation. On December 21, 1977, while still in preventive detention pending his fact-finding hearing, Gregory Martin instituted a habeas corpus class action on behalf of all children in preventive detention in New York State, and won in two federal courts. The

United States Supreme Court overturned those decisions and ruled that preventive detention was constitutionally valid for juveniles. The decision has national import because every state has provision for preventive custody of accused young delinquents.

Other Important Cases

Lollis v. N.Y. State Dept. of Social Services, 322 F. Supp. 473 (S.D.N.Y. 1970).

Morales v. Turman, 326 F. Supp. 677 (E. D. Tex. 1971).

Robin R. v. Wyman, Civ. No. 70–1402 (S.D.N.Y. May 26, 1971).

Rouse v. Cameron, 373 F. 2d 451 (D.C. Cir. 1966).

U.S. ex rel. Stewart v. Coughlin, No. C. 1793 (N.D. Ill., Nov. 22, 1971).

White v. Reid, 125 F. Supp. 647 (D.D.C.) 1954

Brewer v. Williams, 430 U.S. 387 (1977)

Edwards v. Arizona, 451 U.S. 477 (1981)

Glossary

addiction: the periodic or chronic abuse of a drug; characterized by physical dependence, psychological dependence, and tolerance. (p. 266)

adjudicated: to have been settled or passed on judicially; to have been judged by a court of proper jurisdiction. (p. 15)

adjudication: that stage in the juvenile justice system that involves a court hearing either before a judge or a hearing officer. The presiding officer reviews the case and enters a finding of either delinquent or nondelinquent. (p. 22)

adjudicatory hearing: in juvenile proceedings, the factfinding process wherein the juvenile court determines whether there is sufficient evidence to sustain the allegations of a petition. (p. 327)

adolescence: refers to the period between childhood and adulthood, a period of rapid growth. (p. 4)

age effects: changes that can be attributed solely to developmental or maturational processes. (p. 76)

aggravated assault: an unlawful attack by one person upon another with the intent to kill or do bodily harm. (p. 36)

altruistic suicide: suicide that occurs when an individual is tightly bound to the norms of his or her culture; comes from Durkheim's *Suicide.* (p. 144)

anal stage: Freud's second stage of psychosexual development, in which behavior is presumed to focus on anal pleasure and activities. (p. 112)

anomic suicide: suicide that results when the individual is cut off from the social control of marriage and a family; from Durkheim's *Suicide.* (p. 141)

anomie: condition of normative confusion in which the person has few socially validated guides to behavior. (p. 126)

appellate review: the review by a higher court of a lower court's decision. (p. 314)

arbitration: the submission of an offender's case to one or more persons who make a nonjudicial decision on the case. The decision is binding on the offender. (p. 464)

arson: the willful or malicious burning or attempt to burn a house or other structure. (p. 36)

attachment time: refers to whether the juvenile court receives jurisdiction at the time an offense is committed or at the time the suspect is apprehended. (p. 19)

bail: to set at liberty a person arrested or imprisoned, on written security taken for his or her appearance on a day and at a place named. (p. 11)

bailiff: an officer of a court who executes the arrest process. (p. 368)

biological determinism: the belief that qualities biological in nature cause behavior and that environmental influences on the individual are minimal at most. (p. 87)

birth cohort: all persons born in the same year in a particular geographical area. (p. 73)

blended or reconstituted families: families that emerge from the remarriages of spouses. (p. 211)

block grant program: federal funding to states to improve the criminal justice system and to aid crime control and prevention programs. (p. 441)

bourgeoisie: from Marx, the owners of the means of production; the ruling class in capitalist societies. (p. 174)

bracketing: *see* **phenomenological reduction.**

burglary: breaking and entering a structure to commit a felony, usually theft. (p. 36)

census tract: an area smaller than a zone; composed of several city blocks. (p. 128)

Chicago school: refers to a group of sociologists working out of the University of Chicago from the 1920s through the 1940s who studied several social problems, especially crime and delinquency. The Chicago school sociologists hypothesized that residents of transitional inner city slum areas culturally transmit attitudes and behaviors from one generation to the next. (p. 233)

children's rights movement: the efforts of reformers during the 1960s and 1970s to extend the legal and social rights of adults to children and to protect children from physical and emotional abuse by parents and other adults. (p. 364)

chromosomes: the parts of cells that contain genes, the biological structures responsible for the transmission, development, and determination of hereditary characteristics. (p. 93)

citation: a summons to appear in court. (p. 360)

civil case: action which has for its object the protection of private or civil rights or compensation for their infraction. (p. 314)

cohort: a group of individuals who share the same event during some common point in time. (p. 73)

cohort analysis: longitudinal study of a cohort's deviant behavior over time. (p. 73)

cohort effects: generational differences among particular groups. (p. 76)

complaint: the charge made before a proper officer that an offense has been committed by a person named or described therein. (p. 323)

community corrections: refers to "any activity in the community directly addressed to the offender and aimed at helping him [or her] to become a law-abiding citizen." (p. 376)

concentric zone model: theory that portrays the city as composed of a series of circular rings representing various areas of the city. (p. 127)

concordance rate: refers to the similarity of behavioral outcome among pairs of individuals. (p. 92)

conditioning: a learning process in which one stimulus is substituted for another. (p. 120)

conformity: a type of adaptation by which people accept cultural goals and pursue legitimate cultural means. (p. 134)

consensual model: a perspective that sees deviance as dysfunctional, not contributing to the maintenance of the total society. (p. 168)

conspiracy: an unlawful combination or agreement among two or more persons to carry into effect a purpose hurtful to some individual or class or to the public at large. (p. 314)

continuing jurisdiction: the power by which a court that has once acquired jurisdiction continues to possess it. (p. 19)

conventional others: *see* **significant others.**

criminal case: a case involving a violation of criminal law; an offense against a state or the United States. (p. 314)

criminal homicide: includes murder and manslaughter; the willful (nonnegligent) killing of one human being by another. (p. 36)

cross examination: the questioning of a witness by the party opposed to the party which called the witness for direct examination. (p. 352)

cruel and unusual punishment: provided in the Eighth Amendment to the United States Constitution, a guarantee of freedom from cruel and unusual punishment. The term's definition has rested with the courts. In recent years, the U.S. Supreme Court has revised various sentences as unconstitutional and has set certain standards for these sentence lengths and conditions. (p. 311)

cultural axioms: ideal beliefs thought to promote success. (p. 133)

cultural goals: legitimate objectives, such as success or monetary wealth. (p. 133)

cultural means: certain legitimate or socially acceptable ways of achieving legitimate objectives; some examples are education and work. (p. 133)

curvilinear relationship: a relationship in which there is an increase in values up to a certain point and then a decrease after that point. (p. 128)

custody: in the juvenile justice system, that stage when the juvenile is arrested (taken into custody), transported to the juvenile hall, and processed. (p. 322)

decarceration: *see* **deinstitutionalization.**

deinstitutionalization: the movement to put juvenile offenders in community-based programs rather than in traditional institutions. (p. 369)

delinquency: refers to youthful misbehavior; legal definitions vary with respect to upper and lower age limits, types of misbehaviors, and geographic location. (p. 4)

delinquency petition: a request that a juvenile court hear the case of a juvenile and determine whether the juvenile should be adjudicated delinquent. (p. 324)

delinquency prevention: social programs that focus on young people who have either not yet committed delinquent acts or not been arrested for committing delinquent acts. (p. 433)

delinquent: a misbehaving youth or a youth who has been adjudicated delinquent by the court. (p. 20)

dependency: legal term describing the status of children whose parents are unable to provide properly for them. (p. 17)

dependent variable: the effect that a researcher seeks to explain. (p. 130)

detention: the holding of a juvenile in a juvenile detention facility deemed appropriate by the juvenile court. (p. 293)

detention hearing: in juvenile proceedings, a hearing by a judicial officer of a juvenile court to determine whether a juvenile is to be detained (or is to continue to be detained) or released while juvenile proceedings are pending in his or her case. (p. 327)

differential association theory: theory indicating that delinquency is the product of social interaction. (p. 131)

discordance rate: refers to the dissimilarity of behavioral outcome among pairs of individuals. (p. 92)

disposition: that stage in the juvenile justice system where the juvenile court judge reviews the adjudicated delinquent's case and pronounces a sentence. (p. 322)

disposition detention: detention that occurs when the court has sentenced the youth to detention for a special or indeterminate period of time, either in a juvenile correctional institution or a foster home. (p. 293)

disposition hearing: a hearing in juvenile court, conducted after an adjudicatory hearing, to determine the most appropriate handling of a juvenile who has been adjudicated a delinquent, a status offender, or a dependent. (p. 327)

diversion: the avoidance of formal juvenile court processing through direct release of youth or referrals to youth service bureaus, intensive counseling, and other such programs. (p. 369)

division of labor: the specialization of the labor of members of a society that makes members dependent upon one another via exchange and consumption. (p. 126)

docket: an agenda for the proceedings of a court. (p. 330)

double jeopardy: a defense to a prosecution for crime, raising the claim that the defendant is being placed on trial for a second time for the same offense for which he or she has previously been tried. According to the Fifth Amendment to the United States Constitution, no person may be subject to twice being put in jeopardy of life or limb for the same offense. (p. 316)

drug: a chemical substance with qualifying dimensions such as medical utility, psychological activity, or recreational use. (p. 266)

drug abuse: excessive use of a drug, regardless of whether an individual has reached the point of physical dependence. (p. 266)

drug dependency: the tendency to rely overly on drugs (dependency can be psychological or physiological). (p. 266)

due process: a flexible term for the compliance with the fundamental rules for fair and orderly legal proceedings. (p. 13)

ecological fallacy: the assignment of group characteristics to individual members. (p.75)

ego: in Freud's theory, that part of the personality which mediates between the id and the superego and keeps the person in touch with reality. (p. 112)

egoistic suicide: suicide that results from relatively weak group integration; from Durkheim's *Suicide*. (p. 144)

Electra complex: assumed sexual desire of a young girl for her father; the mother is allegedly seen as a competitor for the father's attention; adjunctive in Freud to the Oedipus complex. (p. 113)

endocrine glands: regulate body activities such as growth, the shape of the body, and the way in which the body uses food. (p. 96)

epilepsy: a chronic disease of the nervous system; characterized by convulsions, unconsciousness, and other manifestations. (p. 96)

equity: justice that is administered to the aim of fairness rather than the rigid principles of the common law. Relief under this system was sought in the equity courts rather than in the common law courts in England. (p. 7)

extinction: in learning theory, the gradual disappearance of a conditioned response when it is no longer reinforced. (p. 120)

factor analysis: a statistical technique that identifies clusters of variables that cling together. (p. 128)

felonies: crimes of graver or more serious natures than those designated as misdemeanors. Felonies are punishable by at least one year in prison. (p. 36)

field investigation: a firsthand examination of the alleged crime and its location, the questioning of witnesses, and related activities done by officers upon taking a youth into custody. (p. 323)

focal concerns: value orientations of trouble, toughness, smartness, excitement, fate, and autonomy; attributed by some sociologists to lower class males. (p. 137)

forcible rape: the having of unlawful carnal knowledge by a man of a woman forcibly without her consent. (p. 36)

Gemeinschaft society: a society built around primary relationships. (p. 126)

gender: a social definition; based upon the human construction of what is masculine and what is feminine. (p. 150)

Gesellschaft society: a society operating through secondary relationships. (p. 126)

grand jury: a body of persons, not less than twelve, nor more than twenty-four, whose duty it is, on hearing the evidence for the prosecution in each proposed bill of indictment, to decide whether a sufficient case is made out on which to hold the accused for trial. (p. 316)

habituation: another term for psychological dependence on drugs, frequently used in connection with drug addiction or drug addicts (p. 266)

human ecology: the study of how humans adapt to the surrounding environment. (p. 125)

hyperactivity: a syndrome that causes overactivity, distractability, and aggressiveness in young children. (p. 98)

id: Freud's term, in psychoanalytic theory, for the reservoir of instinctual drives; the most inaccessible and primitive part of the mind. (p. 112)

independent variable: causal or explanatory aspects of a study; cause altered behavior of dependent variables. (p. 130)

in loco parentis: in place of the parents (Latin); a guardian or an agency given the rights, duties, and responsibilities of a parent. (p. 343)

inmate subculture: ways of feeling, thinking, and acting that develop among inmates in a correctional (or other) institutional setting. (p. 279)

inner containment: self-controls originating from socialization (for example, self-concept). (p. 146)

innovation: a form of adaptation where people accept cultural goals but embrace nonstandard means for attaining them. (p. 134)

instinct: an inborn tendency to behave in a way characteristic of a species. (p. 252)

intake: that stage in the juvenile justice system during which it is determined whether the child falls within the juvenile court's jurisdiction and, if so, what course of action ought to be pursued. (p. 322)

intelligence: in general experience, the demonstrated ability to learn what the school teachers and what intelligence tests measure. (p. 218)

joint custody or divided custody: refers to an agreement (legal or informal) following a divorce in which both parents share responsibilities for upbringing the child or children. (p. 211)

jurisdiction: the types of cases a court is empowered to hear. (p. 17)

jury: a body of citizens selected and sworn to deliver a true verdict upon evidence submitted to it in a judicial proceeding. (p. 354)

jury trial: a legal proceeding where a jury delivers a verdict in a case. (p. 354)

juvenile delinquent: *see* **delinquent.**

juvenile court disposition: the decision of a juvenile court concluding a disposition hearing. The disposition may be that a juvenile be committed to a correctional facility, placed in a care or treatment program, required to meet certain standards of conduct, or released. (p. 366)

larceny-theft: the unlawful taking, carrying, leading, or riding away of property from the possession or constructive possession of another. (p. 36)

law enforcement situations: situations in which emphasis is not just on maintaining order, but on enforcing the law. Officers are afforded less discretionary power in these situations. (p. 299)

learning disabilities: disorders in one or more of the basic psychological or physiological processes involved in understanding or using spoken or written language. (p. 219)

learning or reinforcement theories: the part of psychology that sees behaviors, deviant and nondeviant, as resulting from past learning experiences. Reinforcement and punishment are two types of stimuli involved in the learning process. (p. 104)

legalistic style of policing: type of policing that emphasizes interpretations of situations in law enforcement terms exclusively. (p. 299)

long-term facility: a physically restricting facility, such as a juvenile correctional institution, that holds adjudicated delinquents for a long period of time. Also used to describe other institutions; for example, nursing homes. (p. 348)

mala in se: comprises those acts (crimes) which are immoral or wrong in themselves (Latin), such as murder, rape, arson, and burglary. (p. 147)

mala prohibita: applied to acts made criminal or illegal by legislation. (p. 147)

masculinity hypothesis: an explanation for female delinquency which maintains that rates of female-committed crime and delinquency have increased because females display more traditionally ascribed masculine personality traits. (p. 269)

maturity: the age, state, or condition of life at which a person is considered fully developed physically, emotionally, socially, intellectually, and spiritually. (p. 27)

medical model: a way of viewing such social problems as crime and delinquency as symptomatic of disease and thus susceptible to treatment. (p. 106)

mental illness: a large category of mental disorders, ranging from psychoneuroses to psychoses. (p. 106)

middle-range theory: a theory that focuses on a relatively specific area and codifies research results from that area into overall theoretical forms. (p. 238)

Miranda rights: legal rights stemming from 1966 United States Supreme Court ruling that arrested suspects must be advised of their rights before interrogation. These rights include the right to remain silent, the right to consult with an attorney, and the right to court-appointed counsel if the suspect cannot afford private counsel. (p. 291)

misdemeanor: any crime or offense not amounting to a felony. (p. 291)

modeling: learning new behaviors vicariously through watching other people engage in certain activities. (p. 120)

moral entrepreneurs: individuals or groups of individuals that transform general values into specific rules or specific legislation. These rules may or may not reflect the views of a majority of citizens. (p. 158)

motor vehicle theft: the theft or attempted theft of a motor vehicle. (p. 36)

neglect: the willful failure of parents to provide properly for their children. (p. 17)

neurosis: *see* **psychoneurosis.**

norms: rules about proper behavior; may be written or not. (p. 6)

Oedipus complex: in Freud, the assumed desire on the part of a child for sexual relations with the parent of opposite sex; specifically, that of a boy for his mother. (p. 113)

operant conditioning: a type of learning in which a given response is reinforced (rewarded) so that it becomes more likely to occur. (p. 132)

operational: activities (called operations) carried out in the measurement of a concept. (p. 81)

oral stage: in Freud, the first stage of psychosexual development, in which mouth (oral) activities are the primary source of gratification. (p. 112)

order maintenance: police function, geared toward "keeping the peace" rather than making arrests. (p. 298)

original jurisdiction: jurisdiction in the first instance; term used in courts, often in appeals cases. (p. 23)

outer containment: social controls or constraints on an individual's behavior that encourage conformity to group or community norms. (p. 146)

pains of imprisonment: the acute loss of freedoms and luxuries experienced by inmates in correctional institutions. (p. 361)

paradigm: a collection of major assumptions, concepts, and propositions in a substantive area. (p. 87)

paranoia: a psychosis; sometimes characterized by a systematized delusional system. (p. 107)

parens patriae: literally, the parent of the country (Latin); the protective power of the equity court and the King's Chancellor over children and other legal incompetents in England; this protective power over children was adopted by courts in the United States. (p. 7)

period effects: changes that reflect the life experiences of a particular group. (p. 76)

personality trait theories: that branch of psychology which seeks to identify and measure various personality traits or characteristics presumed to be indicative of antisocial behaviors. (p. 104)

phallic stage: in Freud, that stage of psychosexual development during which genital exploration and manipulation occurs. (p. 112)

phenomenological bracketing: *see* **phenomenological reduction.**

phenomenological reduction: technique utilized by phenomenologists to repress their own beliefs and ideas about a situation. (p. 162)

physical dependence: an altered physiological state caused by repeated consumption of a drug with the result that the drug has become needed to maintain normalcy. (p. 266)

PINS: Persons In Need of Supervision. (p. 370)

pluralistic model: a perspective that sees crime and delinquency as products of conflict between diverse groups. Under the model, laws may come to reflect the interests of a powerful group rather than the interests of the majority. (p. 408)

population: the aggregate of all the cases that conform to some designated set of specifications. (p. 73)

predisposition detention: detention that occurs when a minor is held in custody before a decision is made on his or her case. (p. 293)

primary deviance: the original commission of a deviant, antisocial, or criminal act. (p. 155)

primary relationship: a relationship in which the individuals know each other very well and interact on a close, friendly basis in everyday life. (p. 126)

probable cause: means there is "a reasonable ground or suspicion supported by circumstances sufficiently strong in themselves to warrant a cautious person in believing the accused to be guilty." (p. 322)

probation: allowing a juvenile who has either been adjudicated delinquent or is under control of the court to remain in the community under supervised control. (p. 379)

proletariat: in Marxist philosophy, the working class in capitalist society. (p. 174)

psychiatry: the study and treatment of various forms of maladaptive behavior. (p. 104)

psychoanalytic perspective: that branch of psychology that sees behaviors, especially deviant behaviors, as largely the product of certain drives or instincts, of which the individual is largely unconscious, or cognitively unaware. (p. 111)

psychological dependence: type of drug dependence in which the drug user experiences a strong craving for the drug, but does not suffer withdrawal effects when the drug is withheld. (p. 266)

psychoneurosis: any of a number of emotional disorders sometimes thought to derive from excessive anxiety or the inability to endure anxiety. This type of disorder is, generally speaking, less serious in nature than psychosis. (p. 94)

psychopathic personality: refers to outwardly normal but inwardly egocentric individual, insensitive to others and prone to hostility. (p. 108)

psychosexual stages: in Freud, the view of development involving a succession of stages, each characterized by a dominant mode of achieving libidinal pleasure. (p. 112)

psychosis: as opposed to neurosis or psychoneurosis, a psychosis is a mental disorder thought to involve more severe and complete personality disruptions. Organic psychoses are physiological in origin, resulting from brain damage, tumors, some substance abuse, and so on. Functional psychoses are thought to be psychological in origin. (p. 107)

puberty: means that the individual is able to reproduce. (p. 27)

pubescence: a period of rapid physical growth lasting two years including the development of reproductive sex organs and other sex characteristics. (p. 27)

punishment: in learning theory, the application of aversive stimulation in response to behavior considered undesirable; a type of negative reinforcement, opposite to reward. In juvenile justice history, a goal of institutions prior to the house-of-refuge movement. (p. 105)

rate: the number of events during a specified time, measured against some population base. (p. 50)

reaction formation: an ego-defense mechanism in which an individual's conscious attitudes and overt behavior are opposite to repressed unconscious desires. (p. 134)

reasonable grounds: *see* **reasonable suspicion.**

reasonable suspicion: circumstances reasonably indicating to police officers that a person has committed, is committing, or is about to commit a violation of any law; may apply to more than one individual at a time. (p. 359)

rebellion: a type of adaptation in which a person rejects both the prevalent cultural means and cultural goals and attempts to substitute a new order. (p. 134)

recidivism: the reconfinement of juveniles in an institution or correctional facility after release. (p. 127)

reinforcement: in learning theory, the strenghtening of a new response by its repeated association with an unconditioned stimulus. Reinforcement may be either positive or negative. (p. 104)

replication: the repetition of one research study or design, usually with a different sample, to determine whether similar results can be obtained. (p. 121)

representative sample: a group of people chosen as a cross section of an entire population. (p. 70)

restitution: the act of restoring or making good; giving equivalent value for any loss, damage, or injury inflicted. Some juvenile court judges utilize this technique by giving juvenile offenders a chance to "make good" the harm caused by their deeds rather than receive a more traditional disposition. (p. 279)

retreatism: a type of adaptation involving the rejection of both the cultural goals and cultural means. (p. 134)

reverse waiver: sending a juvenile from the adult criminal court which had the original jurisdiction to the juvenile court. (p. 445)

reward: *see* **operant conditioning.**

Ritalin: a stimulant. Sometimes used for paradoxical calming effect with hyperactive children. *See also* **stimulants.** (p. 293)

ritualism: an adaptation that involves abandonment of the cultural goal of success but strict adherence to the cultural means. (p. 134)

robbery: taking or attempting to take any object of value by force or threat of force. (p. 36)

role responsibility: the capacity to live up to others' expectations of the behavior appropriate to roles. (p. 217)

sample: the selection of some subset from a prespecified population. (p. 73)

schizophrenia: a psychosis characterized by the breakdown of integrated personality functioning, withdrawal from reality, emotional blunting and distortion, and disturbances in thought and behavior. (p. 107)

search and seizure: a police practice whereby a person or place is searched and evidence useful in the investigation and prosecution of a crime is seized. (p. 311)

secondary deviance: nonconforming behavior due to societal labeling; the labeling theory that societal reaction to initial misbehavior transforms a "normal" individual into a deviant. (p. 155)

secondary relationship: a relationship in which people interact with each other on the basis of social roles; secondary relationships are goal oriented. (p. 126)

self-fulfilling prophecy: the proposition that people behave in a manner that brings about the results that they or others have expected of themselves or others. (p. 40)

service style of policing: type of policing; stresses alternatives to formal processing in the form of referral to social service agencies, traffic education programs, and drug education programs. (p. 299)

sex: a biological concept based on chromosomal differences. (p. 150)

sex role socialization: the process through which humans learn masculine or feminine traits. Masculinity and femininity are cultural designations and vary from culture to culture. (p. 150)

short-term facility: a facility that provides temporary care for juveniles in custody pending court adjudication. These may be physically restricting environments, as in the case of detention centers, or nonrestricting environments, as in the case of shelters. Also used to describe other care facilities, such as safe homes for runaways. (p. 345)

shotgun approach: research in which variables are not theoretically derived but sorted mathematically and then theoretically oriented. (p. 130)

significant others: those other persons who are most important in determining an individual's behavior; most ordinarily, parents, friends, close relatives. (p. 40)

social class: a category of people who have been grouped together on the basis of one or more common characteristics. These characteristics commonly include income, education, and occupation. (p. 59)

social disorganization: normative conflict in a community; due to lack of social pressures for conformity on the individual. (p. 126)

socialization: the process whereby a child learns the rules and beliefs of the society. (p. 198)

sociopathic personality: *see* **psychopathic personality.**

status deprivation: feelings of frustration and insecurity that develop when the individual does not achieve success in social terms. (p. 221)

status offense: an offense illegal for juveniles but not for adults; for example, running away. (p. 16)

stop and frisk: the procedure through which an officer with reasonable suspicion may temporarily detain a subject in order to find out who the person is and what that person is doing at the present location. (p. 322)

subculture: a particular group or subsegment of society that has somewhat distinctive patterns of norms, beliefs, attitudes, values, and other cultural elements. (p. 278)

sublimation: a Freudian concept which refers to the act of expressing natural drives (aggression, sex) in more socially acceptable forms of behavior (sports, art, work, etc.). (p. 34)

superego: in psychoanalytic theory, that part of the personality, often referred to as the conscience, that represents the individual's regulation of his or her own conduct. (p. 112)

suspended sentence: a court decision in which the court pronounces a fine or a prison sentence and then orders that, upon certain conditions, the payment of the fine and the prison term, or either of them, need not be met. (p. 366)

symbolic interactionism: theory in social psychology; stresses the process of interaction among human beings conducted at the symbolic level (for example, through language). This school of thought places much importance on the process of socialization in the development of normally functioning individuals. (p. 151)

taking into custody: the process of formally detaining a juvenile thought to have committed a delinquent act; the arresting of a juvenile for some offense. (p. 290)

tautology: circular logic; for example, the notion that delinquent behavior is caused by delinquent children. (p. 129)

techniques of neutralization: rationalizations occurring prior to releases from moral constraint which enable individuals to break the moral bind of law. (p. 147)

theoretical stance: *see* **phenomenological reduction.**

theory: a speculation, usually stated in some logical framework, about why and how certain behaviors or events occur. (p. 81)

tolerance: an effect of certain drugs whereby the drug must be taken in progressively larger doses in order to achieve the desired result. (p. 266)

total institution: any facility, such as a traditional correctional or mental institution, that has complete control over the individual on a daily basis. (p. 341)

tracking: the assignment of students to academic groups based on the school's assessment of the child's ability and potential for the future. (p. 227)

transcript of proceedings: an official record of a court proceeding. (p. 353)

verified complaint: a complaint supported by accurate information about the nature of the youth's alleged offense or alleged need for supervision and care.

volume: refers to the absolute number of events committed in a particular locale during a specified period of time. (p. 50)

waiver: the process whereby the juvenile court judge can transfer a juvenile case to the adult criminal justice system so that the juvenile must stand trial as an adult. (p. 17)

watchman style: policing style which emphasizes the maintainance of order. (p. 299)

withdrawal syndrome: physical symptoms of a dependent drug user that occur when the drug is withdrawn; may include irritability, diarrhea, stomach cramps, and other reactions varying in severity and danger. (p. 266)

XYY chromosome: a relatively rare chromosomal abnormality in which the male sex gene has an extra Y chromosome. The abnormality is associated with certain physical and mental characteristics (extreme height and retardation). (p. 94)

youth service bureau: an agency that provides counseling to children viewed as problems by the police, parents, school personnel, or themselves. Youth service bureaus may be funded either privately or through local, state, or federal funding sources. (p. 370)

Acknowledgments

Chapter 1

Specified excerpts from *Juvenile Delinquency*, Third Edition by Ruth Shonle Cavan & Theodore N. Ferdinand. Copyright © 1975, 1969, 1962 by J.B. Lippincott Company. Reprinted by Harper & Row, Publishers, Inc.

Chapter 3

Table 3.1 from *Juvenile Court Statistics, 1982.* National Council of Juvenile and Family Court Judges. Pittsburgh: National Center for Juvenile Justice, December 1984.

Tables 3.7 & 3.8 from D.S. Elliott and D. Huizinga, "Social Class and Delinquent Behavior in a National Youth Panel." *Criminology*, 1983, Vol. 21, 2, 156–157; 166–167.

Chapter 4

Table 4.1 from J.B. Cortes and F. Gatti, *Delinquency and Crime: A Bio-Social Approach.* New York: Academic Press, 1972. Reprinted by permission of the publisher and the authors.

Chapter 6

(Headings) "Developmental Explanations of Criminal Behavior" (pp. 80–82) in *Criminology*, Tenth Edition by Edwin H. Sutherland and Donald R. Cressey. Copyright © 1978 by J.B. Lippincott Company. Reprinted by permission of Harper & Row, Publishers, Inc.

Robert K. Merton, "Social Structure and Anomie," *ASR*, Vol. 3, 1958, p. 676.

Chapter 7

From *Outsiders: Studies in the Sociology of Deviance* by Howard S. Becker. Copyright © 1963 by The Free Press of Glencoe,

A Division of Macmillan Publishing Company, Inc. Reprinted by permission.

From "The Labeling Process: Reinforcement and Deterrent" by Bernard A. Thorsell and Lloyd W. Klemke, *Law & Society Review*, Vol. 6, No. 3, 1972, pp. 393–403. *Law & Society Review* is the official publication of the Law and Society Association. Copyright © 1972 Law and Society Association. Reprinted by permission.

Chapter 8

Adapted from Richard Quinney, *The Social Reality of Crime.* Boston: Little, Brown and Company, 1970. Copyright © Richard Quinney. Reprinted by permission of the author.

Excerpts from *Selected Writings in Sociology and Social Philosophy* by Karl Marx. Translated by T.B. Bottomore. Copyright © 1956 C.A. Watts and Company, Ltd. London. First McGraw-Hill edition, 1964. Reprinted by permission of the McGraw-Hill Book Company.

Chapter 10

Excerpt from "Deviance in the Public School: An Interactional View," from Walter E. Schafer in *Behavioral Science for Social Workers* by Edwin J. Thomas. Copyright © 1967 by The Free Press, a Division of Macmillan Publishing Co., Inc. Reprinted by permission.

Chapter 11

From *The Gang* by Frederic M. Thrasher, in summary, from the 1963 abridged version with new introduction by James Short. Copyright © 1963 by University of Chicago Press. Reprinted by permission.

From Desmond S. Cartwright, "The Nature of Gangs," *Gang Delinquency*, pp. 1–22. Copyright © 1975 by Wadsworth Publishing Company, Inc.

From Joanna M. Shapland, "Self-Reported Delinquency in Boys Aged 11–14," *The British Journal of Criminology*—Delinquency and Deviant Social Behaviour, Vol. 18 No. 3, pp. 263.

Chapter 17

"The Teaching-Family Model of Group Home Treatment" by Dean L. Fixsen, Elery R. Phillips and Montrose M. Wolf from *Closing Correctional Institutions* edited by Yitzhak Bakal (Lexington, Mass.: Lexington Books, D.C. Heath and Company, © 1973). Reprinted by permission of the publisher.

Chapter 18

Tables 18.1 and 18.2 reprinted by permission of New York University Press from *Justice and Troubled Children Around the World*, Volume III, edited by V. Lorne Stewart. Copyright © 1981 by New York University.

Figure 18.10 from David T. Farrington, "England and Wales," pp. 72–73 in *Western Systems of Juvenile Justice*, Malcolm W. Klein (ed.). Copyright © Sage Publications, Inc. Reprinted by permission of Sage Publications, Inc.

Chapter-opening photos: Chapter 1: Photograph by Jacob A. Riis. Jacob A. Riis Collection, Museum of the City of New York. Chapter 2: Ellis Herwig/Stock, Boston. Chapter 3: Roberta Hershenson/PhotoResearchers. Chapter 4: Peter Menzel. Chapter 5: Michael Weisbrot & Family/Stock, Boston. Chapter 6: Katrina Thomas/Photo Researchers. Chapter 7: Fredrik D. Bodin/Stock, Boston. Chapter 8: Jeffrey D. Smith/Woodfin Camp & Associates. Chapter 9: Frank Siteman/The Picture Cube. Chapter 10: George W. Gardner/Stock, Boston. Chapter 11: Ed Lettau/Photo Researchers. Chapter 12: Mark Antman/The Image Works. Chapter 13: Margaret Thompson/The Picture Cube. Chapter 14: Glynne Robinson Betts/Photo Researchers. Chapter 15: Mary Ellen Mark/Archive. Chapter 16: Richard Hutchings/Photo Researcherrs. Chapter 17: Mark Antman/The Image Works. Chapter 18: Peter Menzel/Stock, Boston. Chapter 19: Susan Lapides/Design Conceptions.

Index

About the Authors

William E. Thornton, Jr., is an associate professor of sociology and the Director of Criminal Justice at Loyola University—New Orleans. He has been interested in all areas of research dealing with juvenile delinquency and the juvenile justice system, especially juvenile corrections. His more recent published works examine the interaction of mass media and social control variables on delinquent behavior. Dr. Thornton is also an applied criminologist and has a consulting practice specializing in crime analysis. He is currently serving on the District Attorney's Commission to study the impact of casino gambling on the criminal justice system in the city of New Orleans.

Lydia Voigt is associate professor and chairperson of the sociology department at Loyola University—New Orleans. Her publications include *The Limits of Justice: A Sociological Analysis* (1984), which examines the inherent dilemma in applying the concept of justice to social problems such as the application of correctional punishment. Dr. Voigt is especially interested in the problems of youth from a cross cultural perspective, and has been concentrating on the study of delinquency in the Soviet Union. In addition to her academic pursuits, she maintains a family counseling practice which specializes in adolescent adaptation to joint custody and blended family relationships.

William G. Doerner is an associate professor in the School of Criminology at Florida State University. He is also a reserve police officer with the Tallahassee Police Department. Areas of research interest include homicide, victimology, and law enforcement. Dr. Doerner has had articles published in *Criminology*, *Victimology*, and other journals.